I Belong to the L

Eric Arthur Blair – better known as George Orwell – was born on 25 June 1903 in Bengal. He was educated at Eton and then served with the Indian Imperial Police in Burma. He lived in Paris for two years, and then returned to England where he worked as a private tutor, schoolteacher and bookshop assistant. He fought on the Republican side in the Spanish Civil War and was wounded in the throat. During the Second World War he served as Talks Producer for the Indian Service of the BBC and then joined *Tribune* as its literary editor. He died in London in January 1950.

Dr. Peter Davison is Professor of English and Media at De Montfort University, Leicester. He has written and edited fifteen books as well as the Facsimile Edition of the Manuscript of *Nineteen Eighty-Four* and the twenty volumes of Orwell's *Complete Works*. From 1992 to 1994 he was President of the Bibliographical Society, whose journal he edited for twelve years. From 1961 Ian Angus was Deputy Librarian and Keeper of the Orwell Archive at University College, London, and from 1975 Librarian of King's College, London. With Sonia Orwell he co-edited the *Collected Essays, Journalism and Letters of George Orwell* (4 vols., 1986). Since early retirement in 1982 he has divided his time equally between assisting in the editing of this edition and growing olives in Italy.

Sheila Davison was a teacher until she retired, for some time teaching the deaf. She checked and proofread all twenty volumes of the complete edition and assisted with the research and indexing.

Down and Out in Paris and London
Burmese Days
A Clergyman's Daughter
Keep the Aspidistra Flying
The Road to Wigan Pier
Homage to Catalonia
Coming Up for Air
Animal Farm
Nineteen Eighty-Four
A Kind of Compulsion (1903-36)
Facing Unpleasant Facts (1937-39)
A Patriot After All (1940-41)
All Propaganda is Lies (1941-42)
Keeping Our Little Corner Clean (1942-43)
Two Wasted Years (1943)
I Have Tried to Tell the Truth (1943-44)
I Belong to the Left (1945)
Smothered Under Journalism (1946)
It is What I Think (1947-48)
Our Job is to Make Life Worth Living (1949-50)

Also by Peter Davison

Books: *Songs of the British Music Hall: A Critical Study; Popular Appeal in English Drama to 1850; Contemporary Drama and the Popular Dramatic Tradition; Hamlet: Text and Performance; Henry V: Masterguide; Othello: The Critical Debate; Orwell: A Literary Life*

Editions: Anonymous: *The Fair Maid of the Exchange* (with Arthur Brown); Shakespeare: *Richard II*; Shakespeare: *The Merchant of Venice*; Shakespeare: *1 Henry IV*; Shakespeare: *2 Henry IV*; Shakespeare: *The First Quarto of King Richard III*; Marston: *The Dutch Courtesan; Facsimile of the Manuscript of Nineteen Eighty-Four*; Sheridan: *A Casebook; The Book Encompassed: Studies in Twentieth-Century Bibliography*

Series: *Theatrum Redivivum* 17 Volumes (with James Binns); *Literary Taste, Culture, and Mass Communication* 14 Volumes (with Edward Shils and Rolf Meyersohn)

Academic Journals: *ALTA: University of Birmingham Review*, 1966-70; *The Library: Transactions of the Bibliographical Society*, 1971-82

Publication of *The Complete Works of George Orwell* is a unique bibliographic event as well as a major step in Orwell scholarship. Meticulous textual research by Dr Peter Davison has revealed that all the current editions of Orwell have been mutilated to a greater or lesser extent. This authoritative edition incorporates in Volumes 10-20 all Orwell's known essays, poems, plays, letters, journalism, broadcasts, and diaries, and also letters by his wife, Eileen, and members of his family. In addition there are very many of the letters in newspapers and magazines of readers' reactions to Orwell's articles and reviews. Where the hands of others have intervened, Orwell's original intentions have been restored.

I Belong to the Left

1945

GEORGE ORWELL

Edited by Peter Davison
Assisted by Ian Angus and Sheila Davison

SECKER & WARBURG

———

LONDON

Revised and updated edition published by Secker & Warburg 2001

2 4 6 8 10 9 7 5 3 1

First published in Great Britain in 1998 by
Secker & Warburg
Random House, 20 Vauxhall Bridge Road,
London SW1V 2SA

Random House Australia (Pty) Limited
20 Alfred Street, Milsons Point, Sydney,
New South Wales 2061, Australia

Random House New Zealand Limited
18 Poland Road, Glenfield,
Auckland 10, New Zealand

Random House South Africa (Pty) Limited
Endulini, 5A Jubilee Road, Parktown 2193, South Africa

The Random House Group Limited Reg. No. 954009
www.randomhouse.co.uk

A CIP catalogue record for this book
is available from the British Library

ISBN 0 436 20554 8

Papers used by Random House are natural,
recyclable products made from wood grown in sustainable forests;
the manufacturing processes conform to the environmental
regulations of the country of origin

Typeset in Monophoto Bembo by
Deltatype Limited, Birkenhead, Merseyside
Printed and bound in Great Britain by
Mackays of Chatham PLC

CONTENTS

Titles may be modified and shortened.
Topics discussed in Orwell's column, 'As I Please', are listed in the
Cumulative Index in Volume XX.
Correspondence following Orwell's articles and reviews is not usually listed.

Contents

Contents

Contents

Contents

INTRODUCTION to VOLUME XVII

1945: *I Belong to the Left*

The year 1945 was doubly marked for Orwell. On 29 March Eileen died, aged 39, whilst an anaesthetic was being administered. Her last, long, very moving letters to her husband are printed here uncut for the first time. It is not difficult to see through his often brief letters how deeply he felt her death. Less than five months later, on 17 August 1945, the novel that she might be said to have nurtured and which gave Orwell world-wide fame, *Animal Farm*, was published (see editorial note preceding its proposed preface, 'The Freedom of the Press,' *2721*). *Animal Farm* was then, and has continued to be, misunderstood (as has *Nineteen Eighty-Four*). The Duchess of Atholl, seeking to enlist Orwell's support for the League for European Freedom, a body which, he wrote, had 'nothing to say about British imperialism', was told on 15 November 1945: 'I belong to the Left and must work inside it, much as I hate Russian totalitarianism' (p. 385). See also Orwell's letter to Dwight Macdonald, 5 December 1946, with its cryptic reference to Kronstadt (*3128*, especially *n. 4*).

For a little over three months Orwell worked as a War Correspondent for *The Observer* and the *Manchester Evening News*, writing eighteen despatches about conditions in France, Germany, and Austria. These are now reprinted for the first time. The topics include the effect of the German Occupation on the outlook of the French (*2631*); the political aims of the French Resistance (*2632*); de Gaulle's intention to hold on to Indo-China (*2636*); chaos in Cologne (*2641*); the future for a ruined Germany (*2654*); the food crisis in Germany (*2657* and *2662*); the effect of French women being allowed to vote for the first time (*2658*); and the uncertain fate of displaced persons (*2675*). What he saw of hunger in Germany and the desperate situation of the displaced would motivate his action and writing in the months ahead, for example, 'The Politics of Starvation' and its ensuing correspondence (*2866*, XVIII, 42–48).

It was another year in which Orwell was very active in essay-writing and reviewing. As well as 74 books specifically reviewed, many others were discussed briefly in essays and 'As I Please' (of which he wrote another seven contributions before laying this task aside until November 1946). Among the essays was one that is still among his most important: 'Politics and the English Language' (*2815*). Although this was rejected by George Weidenfeld for his new magazine, *Contact*, it was published by *Horizon* and immediately reprinted for journalists of *The Observer* and *News of the World* as a guide to good writing (a purpose it still serves). With it here are reproduced Orwell's preliminary notes for the essay. (Other important essays in this volume include 'Anti-Semitism in Britain' (*2626*); 'Poetry and the Microphone'

(*2629*); 'Notes on Nationalism' (*2668*); 'You and the Atom Bomb' (*2770*); 'What is Science?' (*2771*); 'Catastrophic Gradualism' (*2778*); 'Revenge is Sour (*2786*, and see Orwell's despatch from Stuttgart, *2661*); and 'The Prevention of Literature' (*2792*). His defence of P. G. Wodehouse was written at a time when Wodehouse was still under a cloud and, as the correspondence shows, Orwell gave him practical encouragement when he took Wodehouse and his wife out to dinner in Paris when they were badly in need of a good meal. Wodehouse at the time expressed his admiration for Orwell's insight into his work but later, after Orwell's death (as is recounted in the annotations), he castigated Orwell for what he had written (see *2624* and *2625*).

The texts of three broadcasts, two on Samuel Butler and one on Jack London, are printed, as are the essays and articles he wrote for *The Observer*, *Manchester Evening News* and *Evening Standard*, one of which, 'In Defence of English Cooking' may have led to the commission from the British Council to write a booklet on British cookery, now published for the first time in Volume 18. The essay was one of a number written for the *Evening Standard* and reprinted in the newspaper produced for servicemen in the Far East (see p. 421). Correspondence shows Orwell working in defence of those whose freedom was threatened and that he had written 'the first twelve pages of his new novel' – *Nineteen Eighty-Four* (see afterword to *2677*).

Orwell kept a careful record of what he was paid to assist in the preparation of his income tax return. The only surviving section covers the period 12 July 1943 to 31 December 1945. This is printed, fully annotated, as an appendix and the dates given are used to assist in identifying articles and placing them in chronological order. Eileen's will (*2643*) and Orwell's first notes for his literary executor (*2648*, and a list of 'possibly reprintable fragments' (*2649*), are also reproduced.

A full General Introduction will be found in the preliminaries to Volume X

ACKNOWLEDGEMENTS and PROVENANCES

specific to Volume XVII

The editor wishes to express his gratitude to the following institutions and libraries, their trustees, curators, and staffs for their co-operation and valuable help, for making copies of Orwell material available, and for allowing it to be reproduced: BBC Written Archives Centre, Caversham; Henry W. and Albert A. Berg Collection and the Rare Books and Manuscripts Division, New York Public Library, Astor, Lenox and Tilden Foundations; Hamish Hamilton Archive, Bristol University Library; British Library, Department of Manuscripts (for the Orwell papers, Add. Mss 49384 and 73083); Elisaveta Fen (Lydia Jackson) papers, Leeds Russian Archive, Brotherton Library, University of Leeds; Lilly Library, Indiana University, Bloomington, Indiana; Secker & Warburg Archive, Reading University Library; Royal Literary Fund; Harry Ransom Humanities Research Center, University of Texas at Austin; Dwight Macdonald papers, Manuscripts and Archives, Yale University Library; and the Library of University College London for material in the Orwell Archive.

Gratitude is expressed to George Allen & Unwin Ltd, Hamish Hamilton Ltd and Martin Secker & Warburg Ltd for making their Orwell material available and to Sotheby's for their help.

Thanks are due to the editors of *Commentary* and Rosemary Davidson for making available letters by Orwell in their possession and to the anonymous person who has made available Orwell's letter to Jack Hilton. I am also deeply indebted to those whose letters by Orwell or members of his family are available because they have donated them or presented copies of them to the Orwell Archive: G. H. Bantock, Frank Barber, Gerry Byrne, Lettice Cooper, Humphrey Dakin, Maurice Hussey, Lydia Jackson, Dwight Macdonald, Sally McEwan, Michael Meyer, Anthony Powell, Kathleen Raine, Roger Senhouse, W. J. Strachan, Gleb Struve, Edward R. Ward and George Woodcock.

I would like to thank the following publications for permission to reproduce material which first appeared in their pages: *Commentary*, *The Evening Standard*, *Freedom*, *The Manchester Evening News*, *The Observer*, *Partisan Review* and *Tribune*.

I would like to thank the following for granting me permission to use material whose copyright they own: Lady Warner, the Literary Executor of the Duchess of Atholl, to publish a letter by the Duchess of Atholl to *Tribune* and another by her to Orwell; Alex Comfort to reprint a letter by him to *Tribune*; The Provost and Scholars of King's College, Cambridge to quote from two letters by E. M. Forster to Orwell; Polly Bird, the Literary Executor of Douglas Goldring, to reprint a letter by Douglas Goldring to

Tribune; Yale University Library to quote from a letter by Dwight Macdonald to Orwell; Shivaun O'Casey to publish a letter by Sean O'Casey to *The Observer*; David Higham Associates Ltd to publish a letter by Herbert Read to Orwell and to quote from another by him to Orwell; Lady Spender to reprint a letter by Stephen Spender to *Tribune*; Mary Struve to publish a letter by Gleb Struve; Peters, Fraser and Dunlop Group Ltd to quote from a letter by Evelyn Waugh to Orwell; and A. P. Watt Ltd on behalf of the Trustees of the Wodehouse Estate to quote from four letters by P. G. Wodehouse.

My thanks are due to Clive Fleay, Peter Tucker and Lord Weidenfeld for help and valuable information.

A number of individual acknowledgements are made in foot and headnotes to those who have provided information in books or verbally that I have quoted or referred to.

The editor and publishers have made every effort to trace copyright holders of the material published in this volume, but in some cases this has not proved possible. The publishers therefore wish to apologise to the authors or copyright holders of any material which has been reproduced without permission and due acknowledgement.

PROVENANCES

The locations of letters and documents printed in this volume are indicated against their item numbers in the list given below. Where there are letters or documents at an item which come from more than one source, this is indicated, e.g. 2686 Bristol, Texas.

However, letters and documents which are not listed below should be taken as being available for consultation in the Orwell Archive, University College London, either as originals or in the form of copies. Sonia Orwell gave all the Orwell papers then in her possession to the Orwell Archive at its foundation in 1960. Many friends, relations and associates of Orwell have given their Orwell letters or copies of them to the Orwell Archive. There were in Orwell's pamphlet collection that Sonia Orwell gave to the British Museum in 1950 some Orwell papers (now in the British Library. Department of Manuscripts, Add. Mss. 49384 and 73083) and copies of these, at her request, were given by the Director and Principal Librarian of the British Museum to the Orwell Archive in 1965. For simplicity's sake, the British Library Orwell papers are not indicated as such in the location list, but are regarded as being available for consultation in the form of copies in the Orwell Archive.

KEY TO LOCATIONS

A & U	George Allen & Unwin Ltd
Anon	Anonymous
BBC	BBC Written Archives Centre, Caversham
Berg	Henry W. and Albert A. Berg Collection, The New York Public Library, Astor, Lenox and Tilden Foundations
Bristol	Hamish Hamilton Archive, Bristol University Library
Commentary	*Commentary*
Danielson	Richard Ely Danielson papers, Rare Books and Manuscripts Division, The New York Public Library, Astor, Lenox and Tilden Foundations
Davidson	Rosemary Davidson
Leeds	Elisaveta Fen (Lydia Jackson) papers, Leeds Russian Archive, Brotherton Library, University of Leeds
Lilly	Lilly Library, Indiana University, Bloomington, Indiana
OA	Orwell Archive, University College London Library
Reading	Secker & Warburg Archive, Reading University Library
RLF	Royal Literary Fund
Sotheby's	Sotheby's Catalogue
Texas	Harry Ransom Humanities Research Center, University of Texas at Austin
Yale	Dwight Macdonald papers, Manuscript and Archives, Yale University Library

2600 BBC
2605A Leeds
2607 Berg
2617 BBC
2618 Texas
2619 Berg
2620 RLF
2630 Berg
2639 Berg
2644 BBC
2646 Berg
2650 Davidson
2651 Lilly
2652 Yale
2674 BBC
2679 BBC
2680 BBC
2682 Berg
2686 Bristol, Texas

2689 BBC
2694 Berg
2696 Anon
2703 Reading
2715 BBC
2716 Lilly
2718 Sotheby's
2722 BBC
2724 Lilly
2727 Lilly
2730 Lilly
2731 Lilly
2733 BBC
2736 Lilly
2740A *Commentary*
2747 Lilly
2750 BBC
2753 Berg
2754 Texas

2756 Berg
2759 Berg
2761 BBC
2762 Berg
2776 Sotheby's
2787 Berg
2788 BBC
2791 Danielson
2792 Danielson
2793 Berg
2797 Berg
2804 BBC
2806 Berg
2810 Berg
2815 OA, A & U
2826 Reading

Editorial Note

THE CONTENTS are, in the main, arranged in chronological order of Orwell's writing. Letters arising from his articles or reviews are usually grouped immediately after that item and Orwell's replies to those letters follow thereon. If there is a long delay between when it is known an article or essay was completed and its publication, it is printed at the date of completion. If items are printed much earlier in the chronological sequence than their date of publication, a cross-reference is given at the date of publication. All entries, whether written by Orwell or anyone else, including lengthy notes and cross-references, are given an item number. Because the printing of the edition has taken place over seven years, some letters came to light after the initial editing and the numbering of items had been completed. These items (or those that had in consequence to be repositioned) are given a letter after the number: e.g., *335A*. Some items included after printing and page-proofing had been completed are given in a final appendix to Volume XX and two (received by the editor in mid January 1997) in the Introduction to Volume XV. Numbers preceding item titles are in roman; when referred to in notes they are italicised.

The provenance of items is given in the preliminaries to each volume. Every item that requires explanation about its source or date, or about textual problems it may pose, is provided with such an explanation. Some articles and broadcasts exist in more than one version. The basis upon which they have been edited is explained and lists of variant readings provided. No Procrustean bed has been devised into which such items must be constrained; individual circumstances have been taken into account and editorial practice explained.

Although this is not what is called a 'diplomatic edition'—that is, one that represents the original precisely even in all its deformities to the point of reproducing a letter set upside down—the fundamental approach in presenting these texts has been to interfere with them as little as possible consistent with the removal of deformities and typographic errors. Orwell took great pains over the writing of his books: the facsimile edition of *Nineteen Eighty-Four*[1] shows that, but in order to meet the demands of broadcasting and publication schedules he often wrote fast and under great pressure. The speed with which he sometimes wrote meant that what he produced was not always what he would have wished to have published had he had time to revise. And, of course, as with any printing, errors can be introduced by those setting the type. It would be easy in places to surmise what Orwell would have done but I have only made changes where there would otherwise have been confusion. Obvious spelling mistakes, which could well be the compositor's or typist's (and the typist might be Orwell), have been corrected silently, but if there is any doubt, a footnote has drawn attention to the problem.

In brief, therefore, I have tried to present what Orwell wrote in his manuscripts and typescripts, not what I thought he should have written; and what he was represented as having written and not what I think should have been typed or printed on his behalf. This is not a 'warts and all' approach because gross errors are amended, significant changes noted, and textual complexities are discussed in preliminary notes. The aim is to bring Orwell, not the editor's version of Orwell, to the fore. Although textual issues are given due weight, an attempt has been made to produce an attractive, readable text.

The setting of this edition has been directly from xeroxes of original letters (if typed), typed copies of manuscript (prepared by one or other of the editors), surviving scripts for broadcasts, and xeroxes of essays, articles, and reviews as originally published (unless a headnote states otherwise). For *The Collected Essays, Journalism and Letters of George Orwell* a 1968 house style was adopted but for this edition, no attempt has been made to impose a late twentieth-century house style on the very different styles used by journals and editors of fifty to eighty years ago. Texts are therefore reproduced in the style given them in the journals from which they are reprinted. To 'correct' might well cause even more confusion as to what was and was not Orwell's: see below regarding paragraphing. Nevertheless, although it is not possible *to know*, one may sometimes hazard a guess at what underlies a printed text. Thus, I believe that most often when 'address' and 'aggression' are printed, Orwell typed or wrote 'adress' (especially until about the outbreak of World War II) and 'agression.' Although American spellings (such as 'Labor') have been retained in articles published in the United States, on very rare occasions, if I could be certain that a form of a word had been printed that Orwell would not have used—such as the American 'accommodations'—I have changed it to the form he would have used: 'accommodation'. Some variations, especially of proper names, have been accepted even if they look incongruous; so, 'Chiang Kai-Shek' as part of a book title but 'Chiang Kai-shek' throughout the text that follows.

Hyphenation presents tricky problems, especially when the first part of a word appears at the end of a line. Examples can be found in the originals of, for example, 'the middle-class,' 'the middle class', and 'the middleclass.' What should one do when a line ends with 'middle-'? Is it 'fore-deck' or 'foredeck'? If 'fore-' appears at the end of a line of the copy being reproduced, should the word be hyphenated or not? *OED* 1991 still hyphenates; Chambers in 1972 spelt it as one word. Where it would help (and it does not include every problem word), the ninth edition of F. Howard Collins, *Authors' & Printers' Dictionary*, Oxford University Press, 1946 (an edition appropriate to the mature Orwell) has been drawn upon. But Collins does not include fore-deck/foredeck. On a number of occasions Orwell's letters, or the text itself, is either obscure or wrong. In order to avoid the irritating repetition of *sic*, a small degree sign has been placed above the line at the doubtful point (°). It is hoped that this will be clear but inconspicuous. It is not usually repeated to mark a repetition of that characteristic in the same item. Orwell was sparing in his use of the question-mark in his letters; his practice has in the main been followed.

Paragraphing presents intractable problems. Orwell tended to write in long paragraphs. Indeed, it is possible to show from the use of many short paragraphs that News Review scripts so written are not by Orwell. The key example is News Review, 30, 11 July 1942 (*1267*), for which there is also external evidence that this is not by Orwell. This has twenty-one paragraphs as compared to eight in the script for the following week. It so happens that we know that Orwell was not at the BBC for two weeks before the 11 July nor on that day: he was on holiday, fishing at Callow End, Worcestershire (and on that day caught a single dace). But though paragraph length is helpful in such instances in identifying Orwell's work, that is not always so. It is of no use when considering his articles published in Paris in 1928–29 nor those he wrote for the *Manchester Evening News*. These tend to have extremely short paragraphs—sometimes paragraphs of only a line or two, splitting the sense illogically. A good example is the series of reviews published on 2 November 1944 (*2572*) where a two-line paragraph about Trollope's *The Small House at Allington* should clearly be part of the preceding four-line paragraph, both relating the books discussed to Barchester; see also *2463*, n. *2* and *2608*, n. *4*. There is no question but that this is the work of sub-editors. It would often be possible to make a reasonable stab at paragraphing more intelligently, but, as with verbal clarification, the result might be the more confusing as to what really was Orwell's work and what this editor's. It has been thought better to leave the house-styles as they are, even if it is plain that it is not Orwell's style, rather than pass off changes as if the edited concoction represented Orwell's work.

Usually it is fairly certain that titles of essays are Orwell's but it is not always possible to know whether titles of articles are his. Reviews were also frequently given titles. Orwell's own typescript for his review of Harold Laski's *Faith, Reason and Civilisation* (*2309*), which survived because rejected by the *Manchester Evening News*, has neither heading (other than the name of the author and title of the book being reviewed), nor sub-headings. That would seem to be his style. In nearly every case titles of reviews and groups of letters, and cross-heads inserted by sub-editors, have been cut out. Occasionally such a title is kept if it is an aid to clarity but it is never placed within quotation marks. Other than for his BBC broadcasts (where Orwell's authorship is clear unless stated otherwise), titles are placed within single quotation marks if it is fairly certain that they are Orwell's.

Telegrams and cables are printed in small capitals. Quite often articles and reviews have passages in capitals. These look unsightly and, in the main, they have been reduced to small capitals. The exceptions are where the typography makes a point, as in the sound of an explosion: BOOM! Orwell sometimes abbreviated words. He always wrote an ampersand for 'and' and there are various abbreviated forms for such words as 'about'. It is not always plain just what letters make up abbreviations (and this sometimes applies to his signatures) and these have regularly been spelt out with the exception of the ampersand for 'and'. This serves as a reminder that the original is handwritten. Orwell often shortened some words and abbreviations in his own way, e.g., Gov.t, Sup.ts (Superintendents), NB. and N.W (each with a single stop), and ie.; these forms have been retained. In order that the diaries should readily be apparent for what they are, they have been set in sloped roman (rather than italic, long passages of which can be tiring to the eye), with roman for textual variations. Square and half square brackets are used to differentiate sources for the diaries (see, for example, the headnote to War-Time Diary II, *1025*) and for what was written and actually broadcast (see, for example, Orwell's adaptation of Ignazio Silone's *The Fox*, *2270*). Particular usages are explained in headnotes to broadcasts etc., and before the first entries of diaries and notebooks.

Orwell usually dated his letters but there are exceptions and sometimes he (and Eileen) give only the day of the week. Where a date has to be guessed it is placed within square brackets and a justification for the dating is given. If Orwell simply signs a letter, the name he used is given without comment. If he signs over a typed version of his name, or initials a copy of a letter, what he signed or initialled is given over the typed version. There has been some slight regularisation of his initialling of letters. If he omitted the final stop after 'E. A. B', no stop is added (and, as here, editorial punctuation *follows* the final quotation mark instead of being inside it). Sometimes Orwell placed the stops midway up the letters: 'E·A·B'; this has been regularised to 'E. A. B'.

Wherever changes are made in a text that can be deemed to be even slightly significant the alteration is either placed within square brackets (for example, an obviously missing word) or the alteration is footnoted. Attention should be drawn to one particular category of change. Orwell had a remarkably good memory. He quoted not only poetry but prose from memory. Mulk Raj Anand has said that, at the BBC, Orwell could, and would, quote lengthy passages from the Book of Common Prayer.[2] As so often with people with this gift, the quotation is not always exact. If what Orwell argues depends precisely upon what he is quoting, the quotation is not corrected if it is inaccurate but a footnote gives the correct reading. If his argument does not depend upon the words actually quoted, the quotation is corrected and a footnote records that.

So far as possible, I have endeavoured to footnote everything that might puzzle a reader at the risk of annoying some readers by seeming to annotate too readily and too frequently what is known to them. I have, therefore, tried to identify all references to people, events, books, and institutions. However, I have not been so presumptuous as to attempt to rewrite the history of this century and, in the main, have relied upon a small number of easily accessible histories. Thus, for the Spanish Civil War I have referred in the main to *The Spanish Civil War* by Hugh Thomas; and for the Second World War, to Winston Churchill's and Liddell Hart's histories. The former has useful and conveniently available documents, and the latter was by a historian with whom Orwell corresponded. They were both his contemporaries and he reviewed the work of both men. These have been checked for factual information from more recent sources, one by Continental historians deliberately chosen as an aid to objectivity in an edition that will have world-wide circulation. It is assumed that readers with a particular interest in World War II will draw on their own knowledge and sources and the annotation is relatively light in providing such background information. Similarly, biographical details are, paradoxically, relatively modest for people as well known as T. S. Eliot and E. M. Forster, but far fuller for those who are significant to Orwell but less well known and about whom information is harder to track down, for example, George(s) Kopp, Joseph Czapski, and Victor Serge. It is tricky judging how often biographical and explicatory information should be reproduced. I have assumed most people will not want more than one volume at a time before them and so have repeated myself (often in shortened form with cross-references to fuller notes) more, perhaps, than is strictly necessary. Whilst I would claim that I have made every attempt not to mislead, it is important that historical and biographical information be checked if a detail is significant to a scholar's argument. History, as Orwell was quick to show, is not a matter of simple, indisputable fact. In annotating I have tried not to be contentious nor to direct the reader unfairly, but annotation cannot be wholly impartial.[3]

Each opening is dated. These dates, though drawn from the printed matter, are not necessarily those of the text reproduced on the page on which a date appears. The dates, known or calculated of letters, articles, broadcasts, diaries, etc., will correspond with the running-head date, but, for example, when correspondence (which may have run on for several weeks) springs from an article and follows directly on that article, the date of the article is continued *within square brackets*. Sometimes an item is printed out of chronological order (the reason for which is always given) and the running-head date will again be set within square brackets. Wherever practicable, the running-head date is that of the first item of the opening; if an opening has no date, the last date of a preceding opening is carried forward. Articles published in journals dated by month are considered for the purpose to be published on the first of the month. Inevitably some dates are more specific than is wholly justified, e.g., that for 'British Cookery' (*2954*). However, it is hoped that if readers always treat dates within square brackets with circumspection, the dates will give a clear indication of 'where they are' in Orwell's life.

Great efforts have been made to ensure the accuracy of these volumes. The three editors and Roberta Leighton (in New York) have read and re-read them a total of six times but it is obvious that errors will, as it used to be put so charmingly in the sixteenth century, have 'escaped in the printing.' I offer one plea for understanding. Much of the copy-preparation and proof-reading has been of type set during and after the war when newsprint was in short supply and mere literary articles would be set in microscopic-sized type. Many of the BBC scripts were blown up from microfilm and extremely difficult to puzzle out. When one proof-reads against xeroxes of dim printing on creased paper, the possibilities for error are increased and the eyes so run with tears that vision is impaired. We hope we have corrected most errors, but we know we shall not have caught them all.

P.D.

A slightly fuller version of this note is printed in the preliminaries to Volume X.

1. George Orwell, *Nineteen Eighty-Four: The Facsimile of the Extant Manuscript*, edited by Peter Davison, London, New York, and Weston, Mass., 1984.
2. Information from W. J. West, 22 July 1994.
3. The problems of presenting acceptable history even for the professional historian are well outlined by Norman Davies in *Europe: A History*, Oxford University Press, Oxford and New York, 1996, 2–7. I am obviously attempting nothing so grand, yet even 'simple' historical explication is not always quite so simple.

REFERENCES

References to Orwell's books are to the editions in Vols I to IX of the *Complete Works* (edited P. Davison, published by Secker & Warburg, 1986–87). The pagination is almost always identical with that in the Penguin Twentieth-Century Classics edition, 1989–90. The volumes are numbered in chronological order and references are by volume number (in roman), page, and, if necessary (after a diagonal) line, so: II.37/5 means line five of page 37 of *Burmese Days*. Secker editions have Textual Notes and apparatus. Penguin editions have A Note on the Text; these are not identical with the Secker Textual Notes and Penguin editions do not list variants. There is a 32-page introduction to the Secker *Down and Out in Paris and London*. Items in Volumes X to XX are numbered individually; they (and their notes) are referred to by italicised numerals, e.g. *2736* and *2736 n. 3*.

REFERENCE WORKS: These are the principal reference works frequently consulted:

The Oxford English Dictionary, second edition (Compact Version, Oxford 1991): (*OED*).
The Dictionary of National Biography (Oxford 1885–1900, with supplements and *The Twentieth-Century*, 1901–): (*DNB*).
Dictionary of American Biography (New York, 1946, with supplements).
Dictionnaire biographique du mouvement ouvrier français, publié sous la direction de Jean Maitron, 4ᵉ ptie 1914–1939: De la Première à la Seconde Guerre mondiale (t. 16–43, Paris, Les Éditions Ouvrières, 1981–93).
Who's Who; Who Was Who; Who's Who in the Theatre; Who Was Who in Literature 1906–1934 (2 vols., Detroit, 1979); *Who Was Who Among English and European Authors 1931–1949* (3 vols., Detroit 1978); *Contemporary Authors* and its *Cumulative Index* (Detroit, 1993); *Who's Who In Filmland*, edited and compiled by Langford Reed and Hetty Spiers (1928); Roy Busby, *British Music Hall: An Illustrated Who's Who from 1850 to the Present Day* (London and New Hampshire, USA, 1976).
The Feminist Companion to Literature in English, edited by Virginia Blain, Patricia Clements, and Isobel Grundy, Batsford 1990.
The New Cambridge Bibliography of English Literature, edited by George Watson and Ian Willison, 4 vols., Cambridge, 1974–79.
Martin Seymour-Smith, *Guide to Modern World Literature*, 3rd revised edition, Macmillan 1985.
The War Papers, co-ordinating editor, Richard Widdows, 75 Parts, Marshall Cavendish, 1976–78.

The following are referred to by abbreviations:

CEJL: *The Collected Essays, Journalism and Letters of George Orwell*, ed. Sonia Orwell

References

and Ian Angus, 4 volumes, Secker & Warburg 1968; Penguin Books, 1970; references are by volume and page number of the more conveniently available Penguin edition.

Crick: Bernard Crick, *George Orwell: A Life*, 1980; 3rd edition, Penguin Books, Harmondsworth, 1992 edition. References are to the 1992 edition.

Eric & Us: Jacintha Buddicom, *Eric and Us: A Remembrance of George Orwell*, Leslie Frewin, 1974.

Lewis: Peter Lewis, *George Orwell: The Road to 1984*, Heinemann, 1981.

Liddell Hart: B. H. Liddell Hart, *History of the Second World War*, Cassell, 1970; 8th Printing, Pan, 1983.

Orwell Remembered: Audrey Coppard and Bernard Crick, eds., *Orwell Remembered*, Ariel Books, BBC, 1984.

Remembering Orwell: Stephen Wadhams, *Remembering Orwell*, Penguin Books Canada, Markham, Ontario; Penguin Books, Harmondsworth, 1984.

Shelden: Michael Shelden, *Orwell: The Authorised Biography*, Heinemann, London; Harper Collins, New York; 1991. The American pagination differs from that of the English edition; both are given in references, the English first.

Stansky and Abrahams I: Peter Stansky and William Abrahams, *The Unknown Orwell*, Constable 1972; edition referred to here, Granada, St Albans, 1981.

Stansky and Abrahams II: Peter Stansky and William Abrahams, *The Transformation*, Constable 1979; edition referred to here, Granada, St Albans, 1981.

Thomas: Hugh Thomas, *The Spanish Civil War*, 3rd edition; Hamish Hamilton and Penguin Books, Harmondsworth, 1977.

Thompson: John Thompson, *Orwell's London*, Fourth Estate 1984.

West: *Broadcasts*: W. J. West, *Orwell: The War Broadcasts*, Duckworth/BBC 1985.

West: *Commentaries*: W. J. West, *Orwell: The War Commentaries*, Duckworth/BBC, 1985.

Willison: I. R. Willison, 'George Orwell: Some Materials for a Bibliography,' Librarianship Diploma Thesis, University College London, 1953. A copy is held by the Orwell Archive, UCL.

2194 Days of War: *2194 Days of War*, compiled by Cesare Salmaggi and Alfredo Pallavisini, translated by Hugh Young, Arnoldo Mondadori, Milan 1977; rev. edn Galley Press, Leicester 1988.

A Bibliography of works, books, memoirs and essays found helpful in preparing Volumes X to XX of *The Complete Works of George Orwell* will be found in the preliminaries to Volume X.

CHRONOLOGY

In the main, Orwell's publications, except books, are not listed

25 June 1903 Eric Arthur Blair born in Motihari, Bengal, India.

---

15 February–end Mar 1945 War correspondent for *The Observer* and *The Manchester Evening News* in France and Germany.

29 March 1945 Eileen Blair dies.

31 March 1945 Signs first of his instructions for his literary executor.

8 May 1945 VE-Day: end of war in Europe.

8 April–24 May 1945 Returns as war correspondent to France, Germany and Austria.

7 June 1945 Continued writing regularly for *The Observer* and *Manchester Evening News*.

25 June 1945 Warburg reports that Orwell 'has written the first twelve pages of his new novel' [*Nineteen Eighty-Four*]
  Orwell told that the head of Harper Brothers and of the OWI's Paris Office, was 'greatly impressed' by Orwell's *Observer* articles from the Continent.

3 July 1945 Agrees to write four long articles for *Polemic*.

Summer 1945–Dec 1948 Works on *Nineteen Eighty-Four*

August 1945 Elected Vice-Chairman of the Freedom Defence Committee.

15 August 1945 VJ-Day: end of war with Japan.

17 Aug 1945 After many rejections, *Animal Farm* published by Secker & Warburg. Published by Harcourt, Brace, New York, 1946, and made American Book-of-the-Month Club choice. By the time Orwell died, *Animal Farm* had been published in Portuguese, Swedish, Norwegian, German, Polish, Persian, Dutch, French, Italian, Gujarati, Ukrainian (with Orwell's Introduction, November 1947), Danish, Estonian, Spanish, Korean, Japanese, Telugu, Indonesian, Icelandic, Papiamento, and Russian editions.

10–22 Sep 45 Stays in fisherman's cottage, Jura.

12 October 1945 Continued writing for *Tribune*.

---

21 January 1950 Orwell dies of pulmonary tuberculosis, aged 46.

THE COMPLETE WORKS OF
GEORGE ORWELL · SEVENTEEN

I BELONG TO THE LEFT

1945

2597. Review of *Der Führer* by Conrad Heiden

Manchester Evening News, 4 January 1945

About eight years ago, from the same publishing house as has just produced "Der Führer,"[1] there appeared another fat and imposing book about Hitler, entitled, significantly, "Hitler, the Pawn." Its thesis, then a widely accepted one, was that Hitler was a nonentity, a mere puppet of German big business.

Later events have made that incredible, and Mr. Heiden's long detailed but very readable book is an attempt to disentangle the extremely complex causes—causes which are intellectual and religious as well as economic and political—that have allowed a semi-lunatic to gain control of a great nation and cause the death of some tens of millions of human beings.

Mr. Heiden ends his story with the June purge of 1934—which, as he points out, is not altogether an arbitrary stopping-point, because with that atrocious deed there began a new historical phase which has not yet ended.

The story starts some time before Hitler's birth. It starts, to be precise, in 1864, with an illegal and now forgotten pamphlet attacking Napoleon III.

Somewhat later the Czarist secret police were to get hold of this pamphlet and concoct out of it that celebrated forgery, "The Protocols of the Elders of Zion."[2] Their object was to frighten the Czar with tales of a Jewish conspiracy and thus provoke him into violent measures against the Russian Revolutionaries.

Rosenberg, the racial theorist,[3] a Baltic Russian, and at the time of the revolution a student in Moscow, brought a copy of the protocols with him when he fled to Germany: and it was from this source that Hitler derived the anti-Semitism that was to be both a cherished delusion and a cunning political device.

Mr. Heiden follows up Hitler's early history with great minuteness, plugging the gaps in "Mein Kampf" with the statements of a painter named Hanisch, who shared Hitler's poverty for several years in Vienna.

It appears from Mr. Heiden's researches that the autobiographical part of "Mein Kampf" is reasonably truthful. Even on his own showing, Hitler was a complete failure, even a ne'er-do-well, until the outbreak of war in 1914. His main characteristics were laziness, an inability to make friends, a hatred of the society which had failed to give him a decent livelihood, and a vague leaning towards painting.

(Many dictators, it is worth noticing, are failed artists—Henry VIII and Frederick the Great both wrote bad verse, and Napoleon and Mussolini wrote plays which nobody would produce.)

The war was Hitler's great opportunity. He loved every moment of it, and it appears to be true, though it has often been denied, that he served with distinction and was decorated for bravery. He says himself that he wept when the war stopped, and from then onwards to restore the atmosphere of war was his main aim.

In the chaotic Germany of 1918 it was natural for a man of Hitler's temperament to plunge into conspiratorial politics. He joined the German Workers' party—later to become the National Socialist party—which at that date consisted of six members and had as its entire equipment a single briefcase and a cigar-box which was used as a cash-box.

The disbanded Reichswehr officers, who were already planning to rebuild the German Army in defiance of the Versailles Treaty, were on the look-out for a political party which could act as a cover for their aims, and the German Workers' party, with its sham-Socialist programme, seemed to them to have possibilities.

Hitler, therefore, had a measure of support almost from the start, but it was not until some time later, when he was already a political force to be counted with, that the industrialists began to finance him in a big way.

As a politician he had three great assets. One was his complete lack of pity, affection, or human ties of any kind. Another was his bottomless belief in himself and contempt for everybody else. And the third was his powerful and impressive voice, which within a few minutes could make any audience forget his Charlie Chaplin-like appearance.

Within a few years he had talked a formidable movement into existence, pouring out on platform after platform a message—anti-Jewish, anti-Capitalist, anti-Bolshevik, and anti-French—which appealed equally to the unemployed workers, the ruined middle-class, and the officers who were pining for another war.

However, to win supreme power was another matter, and for years the history of the National Socialist party was one of ups and downs. Broadly speaking, when things went badly, Hitler's star rose; when they went well, it sank. In the prosperous period of the middle twenties, the period of the Dawes Plan,[4] the economic recovery in Britain and the U.S.A. and the N.E.P.[5] in Russia the National Socialist party seemed likely to disappear.

Then came the great depression, and Hitler rose again like a rocket. We shall never know whether even at that late date he might have been defeated, but at any rate it is a fact that his only real enemies inside Germany, the Communists and the Social Democrats, persisted in fighting one another instead of combining against the common enemy.

Having made use of their dissensions, Hitler destroyed both of them, and finally made quite sure of his position by massacring the Left Wing of his own party. The rest of the story is only too well known.

This book gives useful background information about others besides Hitler—in particular, Hess, Goering, Roehm,[6] and Houston Chamberlain[7] the strange renegade Englishman who was one of the founders of the Pan-German Movement. It is a valuable book because it neither underrates Hitler nor overrates him. It does not, that is to say, explain him away in narrow economic terms, nor does it pretend that the major problems of the world will be solved by his disappearance. To quote Mr. Heiden's own words—

"Hitler was able to enslave his own people because he was able to give them something that even the traditional religions could no longer provide—the belief in a meaning to existence beyond the narrowest self-interest. The real degradation began when people realised that they were in league with the devil, but felt that even the devil was preferable to the emptiness of an existence which lacked a larger significance.

"The problem to-day is to give that larger significance and dignity to a life that has been dwarfed by the world of material things. Until that problem is solved, the annihilation of Nazism will be no more than the removal of one symptom of the world's unrest."

[Fee: £8.0.0; 3.1.45]

1. Victor Gollancz, Ltd.
2. For a brief account of this forgery, see *2416, n. 2.*
3. Alfred Rosenberg (1893–1946), born in Estonia; his *Der Mythus des 20 Jahrhunderts* (The Myth of the Twentieth Century) (1930), served as a quasi-scientific basis for Hitler's racial policy. He was hanged following conviction at Nuremberg as a war criminal.
4. The Dawes Plan was devised in 1924 by a commission headed by Charles Gates Dawes (1865–1961), American lawyer, financier, statesman, who was the first director of the U.S. Bureau of the Budget, 1921. The plan sought to reduce the amount of reparations payable by Germany following her defeat in World War I and attempted to stabilize the country's finances. Dawes, later, was U.S. Vice-President, 1925–29, Ambassador to Great Britain, 1929–32, and co-recipient, with Sir Austen Chamberlain, of the Nobel Peace Prize, 1925.
5. The New Economic Policy introduced by Lenin in March 1921 following the Tenth Congress of the Bolshevik Party. It was designed to restore levels of production by allowing some private business to develop. Though opposed by hard-line Communists, it proved effective, and by 1927 production in the Soviet Union had reached the level achieved in 1913. The policy came to an end under Stalin in 1929.
6. Ernst Roehm (1887–1934), leader of the Nazi 'Brownshirts' (SA), was executed, along with more than eighty others, by Himmler's 'Blackshirts' (SS) during the weekend 29 June–2 July 1934 ('The Night of the Long Knives').
7. Houston Stewart Chamberlain (1855–1927), British political philosopher and racial ideologist, exemplified by his *Foundations of the Nineteenth Century* (1899). In the summer of 1923—before Hitler's attempted *putsch* in Munich, November 1923—Hitler visited Wahnfried, the home of the Wagner family in Bayreuth. Alan Bullock writes of this occasion that Hitler 'impressed Winnifried Wagner and captivated the aged Houston Stewart Chamberlain, who had married one of Wagner's daughters and who wrote to him afterwards: "My faith in the Germans had never wavered for a moment, but my hope, I must own, had sunk to a low ebb. At one stroke you have transformed the state of my soul" ' (*Hitler: A Study in Tyranny*, revised edition, 1962); the passage quoted by Bullock is from Konrad Heiden, *Der Führer* (1944, 198).

2598. 'Books and the People: A New Year Message'

Tribune, 5 January 1945

For some months past we have intended to make some kind of explanatory statement about *Tribune's* literary policy, present and future, and the first week of the new year seems a suitable time to do it.

Regular readers of *Tribune* will have noted that during recent months we have printed short stories only intermittently, we have printed less verse than we used to do, and we have altered our system of reviewing, giving a full-length review each week to only one book, and 200-word "shorts" to all the others. The new system of reviewing seems to be giving general satisfaction. By means of it we can cover—including the books in Daniel George's[1] column—anything up to fifteen books a week, and thus can keep more or less abreast of the current output, which was quite impossible before. We can also in this way make some mention of cheap reprints and even a certain number of pamphlets and periodicals. From time to time we are charged by our readers with concentrating on books which the average person cannot afford to buy, but anyone who chooses to look back through our columns, will see that Penguins and other very cheap publications have had their fair share of notice.

The gradual dropping of short stories is deliberate. In future we shall probably abandon short stories almost completely, though we shall not refuse a *good* short story when we happen to get one. We shall also from time to time, as we have done once or twice already, print detachable excerpts from old books. This seems to us a useful thing to do at a time like the present, when so many standard books are unobtainable.

It was only unwillingly that we decided on the dropping of short stories, but the quality of the stories sent in to me makes them, in much more than nine cases out of ten, simply not worth ink and paper. For long past there had been a volume of justified complaints from readers that *Tribune's* stories were "always so gloomy." The trouble, as anyone who had my job would quickly appreciate, is that one almost never nowadays sees a story with any serious literary pretensions that is *not* gloomy. The reasons for this are many and complex, but I think literary fashion is one of them. A "happy ending," or indeed any admission that anything is right with the world anywhere, seems to be as out of date as Dundreary whiskers, and it hardly seems worth diffusing gloom from the final pages of the paper unless exceptional literary distinction goes with it. Many readers have told me, in writing and by word of mouth, how tired they are of the kind of story that begins *Marjorie's husband was to be hanged on Tuesday, and the children were starving,* or *For seven years no ray of sunlight had penetrated the dusty room where William Grocock, a retired insurance agent, lay dying of cancer;* but I don't fancy they are more tired of them than myself, who have to work my way through round about twenty such stories every week.

By printing less stories we shall have more room for essays and articles on literary or general (i.e., not directly political) subjects. But upon all those readers who complain that we do not have enough articles on music, or painting, or the drama, or radio, or modern educational methods, or psycho-analysis, or what-not, I urge one important consideration: that we have very little space. In most weeks we have well under five pages at our disposal, and we have already been driven into smaller print for the short reviews. It is principally lack of space that has prevented us from undertaking any notes on radio, gramophone records and music generally. We could not do it regularly, and therefore should not be able to keep sufficiently up to date. Nor can we notice concerts, exhibitions, etc., because these occur only in one place, usually London, and *Tribune's* readers are spread all over the country.

So far I have been dealing with details. But a more general defence, or at least explanation, of our literary policy is needed, because there are certain criticisms of an adverse kind that come up in varying forms over and over again. Our critics are divisible into two main schools. It would be manifestly impossible to satisfy both, and in practice, I should say, impossible to satisfy either.

The first school accuses us of being lowbrow, vulgar, ignorant, obsessed with politics, hostile to the arts, dominated by back-scratching cliques and anxious to prevent talented young writers from getting a hearing. The other school accuses us of being highbrow, arty, bourgeois, indifferent to politics and constantly wasting space on material that can be of no interest to a working man and of no direct use to the Socialist movement. Both points need meeting, because between them they express a difficulty that is inherent in running any paper that is not a pure propaganda sheet.

Against the first school, we point out that *Tribune* reaches a large, heterogeneous Left-Wing audience and cannot be turned into a sort of trade paper for young poets, or a tilting-ground on which rival gangs of Surrealists, Apocalyptics and what-not can fight out their battles. We can assume that our public is intelligent, but not that its primary interests are literary or artistic, and still less that all of our readers have been educated in the same way and will know the same jokes and recognise the same allusions. The smaller literary magazines tend to develop a sort of family atmosphere— almost, indeed, a private language unintelligible to outsiders—and, at the risk of offending a contributor now and then, we have made efforts to prevent that kind of thing from being imported into *Tribune*. We never, for instance, review books written in foreign languages, and we try to cut out avoidable foreign quotations and obscure literary allusions. Nor will we print anything that is verbally unintelligible. I have had several angry letters because of this, but I refuse to be responsible for printing anything that I do not understand. If I can't understand it, the chances are that many of our readers will not be able to either. As to the charge that we are dominated by cliques (contributions sometimes arrive with a sarcastic enquiry as to whether "someone outside the clique" may put a word in), a quick glance through our back numbers would easily disprove it. The number of our contributors is much larger than is usual in a paper of these dimensions, and many of them are people whose work has hardly appeared elsewhere.

The other school of critics presents a more serious difficulty. Any Socialist paper which has a literary section is attacked from time to time by the person who says: "What is the use of all this literary stuff? Does it bring Socialism any nearer? If not, drop it. Surely our task should be to work for Socialism and not waste our time on bourgeois literature?" There are various quick answers to this person (he is easily quelled, for instance, by pointing out that Marx wrote some excellent criticism of Shakespeare), but nevertheless he has a case. Here it is, put in an extreme form by a correspondent in last week's issue:

"May I ask if the Book Reviews in your paper contribute largely (if at all) to its upkeep? If not, why is so much precious space taken up each week with descriptions of books which (I guess) few of your readers buy?

"As a Socialist, my aim in life is to destroy Toryism.

"For this purpose I require all the ammunition I can get, and I look to *Tribune* as the main source of supply.

"You may reply that some of the books would be useful for that purpose, but I think it would be a very small percentage, and in any case I have neither the money to buy nor the time to read them."

This correspondent, by the way, like many others who write in the same vein, is under the misconception that in order to read books you have to buy them. Actually you could read most of the books mentioned in *Tribune* without ever buying a book from one year's end to the other. What else are libraries for—not merely Boots, Smith's,[2] etc., but the public libraries at which anyone who numbers a householder among his acquaintances can get three tickets without any charge whatever? But our correspondent also assumes (a) that a Socialist needs no recreations, and (b) that books are of no use to the Socialist movement unless they consist of direct propaganda. It is this viewpoint that we tacitly challenge when, for instance, we use up a whole column on a poem, or print a popularisation of some little-known dead writer, or give a good review to a book written by a Conservative.

Even the most unpolitical book, even an outright reactionary book, can be of use to the Socialist movement if it provides reliable information or forces people to think. But we also assume that books are not to be regarded simply as propaganda, that literature exists in its own right—as a form of recreation, to put it no higher—and that a large number of our readers are interested in it. This involves, unavoidably, a slight divergence between the political and the literary sections of the paper, Obviously we cannot print contributions that grossly violate *Tribune's* policy. Even in the name of free speech a Socialist paper cannot, for instance, throw open its columns to anti-semitic propaganda. But it is only in this negative sense that any pressure is put upon contributors to the literary end of the paper. Looking through the list of our contributors, I find among them Catholics, Communists, Trotskyists, Anarchists, Pacifists, Left-Wing Conservatives, and Labour Party supporters of all colours. All of them knew, of course, what kind of paper they were writing for and what topics were best left alone, but I think it is true to say that none of them has ever been asked to modify what he had written on the ground that it was "not policy."

This is particularly important in the case of book reviews, in which it is often difficult for the reviewer to avoid indicating his own opinion. To my knowledge, some periodicals coerce their reviewers into following the political line of the paper, even when they have to falsify their own opinions to do so. *Tribune* has never done this. We hold that the reviewer's job is to say what he thinks of the book he is dealing with, and not what we think our readers ought to think. And if, as a result, unorthodox opinions are expressed from time to time—even, on occasion, opinions that contradict some editorial statement at the other end of the paper—we believe that our readers are tough enough to stand a certain amount of diversity. We hold that the most perverse human being is more interesting than the most orthodox gramophone record. And though, in this section of the paper, our main aim is to talk about books as books, we believe that anyone who upholds the freedom of the intellect, in this age of lies and regimentation, is not serving the cause of Socialism so badly either.

The correspondent to whom Orwell referred was Mrs. O. Grant. Her letter was taken up by two correspondents in this same issue of *Tribune*. A. Reid supported Mrs. Grant. Adelaide R. Poole pleaded for book and film reviews to be retained; *Tribune*'s reviewers were to be trusted. Mrs. Grant responded on 12 January. She had been, she wrote, a 'greedy reader' all her life and had derived not only pleasure but a lively social conscience, and 'a desire to leave the world a little better than I found it. This last not by setting the example of a cultured and broadminded old lady, but (forgive me, Mr. Orwell, I must have a one-track mind) by kicking Tories. When one reaches 60 the path is not only straight and narrow—it is also short.'

A second letter published on 12 January, from Stephen Spender (see *411, n. 2*), strongly supported the inclusion in *Tribune* of reviews and cultural features:

. . . The fundamental mistake your correspondents make is to separate the "Left-Wing struggle" from all other aims in life and to insist that politics are conducted for the sake of politics and not for the sake of a life which includes writing and reading books and cultivating gardens. The fallacy of thinking and acting entirely in terms of politics is one of the greatest evils of our times, and it is particularly dangerous to the Left, because if Socialism has any meaning at all it should be Socialism-for-the-sake-of-life and not Socialism-for-the-sake-of-Socialism. We have already seen all over the world that Socialism-for-the-sake-of-Socialism soon becomes Socialism-for-the-sake-of-Socialist-politicians, that is to say, for the sake of those excellent Socialist agitators, Mussolini, Laval, Doriot,[3] etc. . . .

No one can hope to keep straight in politics whose ideas are purely political: the only honest politicians are those whose politics are attached to a whole view of life. Directly people are told by their political leaders that there is no time now for a whole view of life and that everything must be converted into "political ammunition," they are well on their way to that kind of opportunism, propagandist lying and cynicism which makes it so difficult to distinguish between the various totalitarian policies which now dominate the greater part of the world.

Spender's argument was supported by John Atkins (Orwell's predecessor as literary editor of *Tribune*; see *1340, n. 1*), in *Tribune*, 2 February 1945. He maintained that the 'activity we call politics' had 'been moving away from the orbit of common people's lives' and that this was due to the attempt 'to breed a specialised politician.' He concluded:

Without a knowledge of the noblest achievements of mankind, it is impossible to realise fully how sordid our society is. Because of this the most damning indictment of it has not been made by Socialists, but by two Royalist Catholics, Chesterton and Belloc. This is in spite of their royalism, and because of their spiritual orientation. There is one other example I would like to give. Most political literature today is uninspired and uninspiring. The two men who can still rouse the reader with their political analyses are neither professional politicians nor political journalists, but artists and men of wide cultural experience: J. Middleton Murry and Sean O'Faolain, writing in *Adelphi* and *The Bell* respectively.

In its issue for 13 April 1945, *Tribune* published an appreciative letter about book reviews, and Orwell's column in particular, from M. E. Farmer, serving in the RAF in South-East Asia:

As a regular reader of your paper for the past year, I would like to say how much I appreciate the amount of space devoted to book reviews. They have proved to be of great value to me when choosing something to read.

I would also like to thank George Orwell for the splendid work he puts into his column; keep it up!

Your correspondent, A. Reid, in your issue of January 5, seems to be of the opinion that everything available should be converted into "political ammunition." There are, no doubt, a number of people who—politically minded and eager for the success of Socialism—still find time to enjoy a good book.

So I ask you, don't cut out your reviews from this interesting weekly.

1. For Daniel George, see *2561, n. 1*.
2. Boots the Chemists, and W. H. Smith, newspaper and magazine retailers and stationers. Both then ran large-scale subscription lending libraries.
3. Jacques Doriot (1898–1945) was originally a Communist but, having been expelled from the party in 1934 as a Trotskyist, drifted to the extreme right. He founded the Parti Populaire Français and collaborated with the German occupying powers during World War II. He was killed in Germany when his car was strafed by a plane. See also *662, n. 4*.

2599. 'As I Please,' 53

Tribune, 5 January 1945

I have just been looking through a bound volume of the *Quarterly Review* for the year 1810, which was, I think, the second year of the *Quarterly Review's* existence.[1]

1810 was not quite the blackest period, from the British point of view, of the Napoleonic war, but it was nearly the blackest. It perhaps corresponded to 1941 in the present war. Britain was completely isolated, its commerce barred from every European port by the Berlin decrees. Italy, Spain, Prussia, Denmark, Switzerland and the Low Countries had all been subjugated. Austria was in alliance with France. Russia was also in an uneasy agreement with France, but it was known that Napoleon intended to invade Russia shortly. The United States, though not yet in the war, was openly hostile to Britain. There was no visible cause for hope, except the revolt in Spain, which had once again given Britain a foothold on the Continent and opened the South American countries to British trade. It is therefore interesting to observe the tone of voice in which the *Quarterly Review*—a Conservative paper which emphatically supported the war—speaks about France and about Napoleon at this desperate moment.

Here is the *Quarterly* on the alleged war-making propensities of the French people. It is reviewing a pamphlet by a Mr. Walsh, an American who had just returned from France.

"We doubt the continued action of those military propensities which Mr. Walsh ascribes to the French people. Without at all questioning the lively picture which he has drawn of the exultation excited amongst the squalid and famished inhabitants of Paris at the intelligence of every fresh triumph of their armies, we may venture to observe that such exultation is, everywhere, the usual concomitant of such events; that the gratification of national vanity is something, and that the festivities which victory brings with it may afford a pleasing dissipation to wretches who are perfectly free from any feelings of ambition. Our belief indeed is, that those feelings are, at present, nearly confined to the breast of the great conqueror; and that amongst his subjects, we may almost say among his officers and armies, the universal wish is for PEACE."

Compare this with the utterances of Lord Vansittart, or, indeed, of the greater part of the Press. The same article contains several tributes to the military genius of Napoleon. But the thing I find most impressive is that this year's issue of the *Quarterly* contains numerous reviews of recently-published French books—and they are careful, serious reviews, not different in tone from the rest of its articles. There is, for instance, an article of about 9,000 words on the publication of the French scientific body known as the Société d'Arcueil. The French scientists, Gay-Lussac, Laplace and the rest of them, are treated with the utmost respect, and given their "Monsieur" every time. From reading this article it would be impossible to discover that there was a war on.

Can you imagine current German books being reviewed in the British Press during the present war? No, I don't think you can. I do not, indeed, remember hearing the name of a single book published in Germany throughout the war. And if a contemporary German book did get mentioned in the Press, it would almost certainly be misrepresented in some way. Looking through the reviews of French books in the *Quarterly*, I note that only when they are on directly political subjects does any propaganda creep in, and even then it is extremely mild by our standards. As for art, literature and science, their international character is taken for granted. And yet, I suppose, Britain was fighting for existence in the Napoleonic war just as surely as in this one, and relative to the populations involved the war was not much less bloody or exhausting. . . .[2]

When Burma comes into the centre of the news again, somebody could do a useful job by evolving a sensible method of spelling Burmese place names. What is the average newspaper-reader to make of names like Taungdwingyi, Myaungmya and Nyaungbinzeik?

When the Japs invaded Burma at the beginning of 1942, efforts were made to get correct pronunciation of Burmese names on the radio.[3] The B.B.C.

announcers took no notice and went merrily ahead, mispronouncing every name that could be mispronounced. Since then the newspapers have made matters a little worse by supplying their own pronunciations, which are generally wrong.

At present, Burmese names are spelt by transliterating the Burmese characters as nearly as possible. This is a very bad system unless one knows the Burmese alphabet. How is the average person to know that in a Burmese name e spells ay, ai spells eye, gy spells j, ky spells ch, and so on? It should be quite easy to evolve a better system, and the British public, which can now make quite a good stab at pronouncing Dniepropetrovsk, could also learn to pronounce Kyaukse and Kungyangon if it were taught how.

I have been re-reading with some interest *The Fairchild Family*, which was written in 1813 and was for fifty years or more a standard book for children. Unfortunately I only possess the first volume,[4] but even that, in its unexpurgated state—for various pretty-pretty versions, with all the real meat cut out, have been issued in recent years—is enough of a curiosity.

The tone of the book is sufficiently indicated by the sentence: "Papa," said Lucy (Lucy was aged nine, by the way), "may we say some verses about mankind having bad hearts?" And, of course, Papa is only too willing, and out come the verses, all correctly memorised. Or here is Mrs. Fairchild, telling the children how when she herself was a child she disobeyed orders by picking cherries in company with the servant girl:

"Nanny was given up to her mother to be flogged; and I was shut up in the dark room, where I was to be kept several days upon bread and water. At the end of three days my aunts sent for me, and talked to me for a long time.

" 'You broke the Fourth Commandment,' said my Aunt Penelope, 'which is, *Remember the Sabbath day to keep it holy:* and you broke the Fifth, which is, *Honour your parents.* . . . You broke the Eighth too, which is, *Thou shalt not steal.* Besides,' said my Aunt Grace, 'the shame and disgrace of climbing trees in such low company, after all the care and pains we have taken with you, and the delicate manner in which we have reared you.' "

The whole book is in this vein, with a long prayer at the end of every chapter, and innumerable hymns and verses from the Bible interspersed through the text. But its chief feature is the fearful visitations from Heaven which fall upon the children whenever they misbehave themselves. If they swing in the swing without leave, they fall out and break several teeth; if they forget to say their prayers they fall into the trough of pig-swill; the theft of a few damsons is punished by an attack of pneumonia and a narrow escape from death. On one occasion Mr. Fairchild catches his children quarrelling. After the usual flogging, he takes them for a long walk to see the rotting body of a murderer hanging on a gibbet—the result, as he points out, of a quarrel between two brothers.

A curious and interesting feature of the book is that the Fairchild children, reared upon these stern principles, seem to be rather exceptionally untrustworthy. As soon as their parents' backs are turned they invariably misbehave themselves, which suggests that flogging and bread and water are not a very satisfactory treatment after all. It is worth recording, by the way, that the author, Mrs. Sherwood, brought up several children, and at any rate they did not actually die under her ministrations.

1. Publication of the *Quarterly Review* began with the February 1809 issue.
2. The marks representing an ellipsis are in the original; nothing has been cut from this reprinting.
3. For Orwell's effort in attempting to have Burmese words pronounced correctly at the BBC, see his letter to M. Myat Tun, 10 April 1942, *1097*, which has a list of names with suggested pronunciations.
4. *The History of the Fairchild Family: or The Child's Manual, being a collection of stories calculated to show the importance and effects of a religious education*, Mrs. Mary Sherwood (1775–1851), (3 vols., 1818–47). She also wrote *The History of Henry Milner* (4 vols., 1822–37), and *Little Henry and His Bearer Boosy* (1832) for children, as well as many other books. Orwell asked Brenda Salkeld whether she had read *The Fairchild Family* when recommending books to her in his letter of Sunday, [September 1932]; see *142*.

2600. To Miss Sunday Wilshin

10 January 1945   Typewritten

On 2 January 1945, Sunday Wilshin,[1] who had replaced Orwell in the BBC's Indian Section, wrote to ask him if he would contribute a talk on the poet Housman in a series entitled 'Book of Verse,' which was linked with the syllabuses 'of the Indian University'—a series of programmes with which Orwell had been deeply associated. She enclosed a script to indicate the general lines of what was being offered (and also sent Orwell's wife, Eileen, her kindest regards). Orwell replied:

Tribune

Dear Miss Wilshin,
I am very sorry, but I am afraid I cannot possibly do any talks at present. I have to write three articles a week apart from other work, and I cannot take on anything extra.

Yours sincerely,
[Signed] Geo. Orwell
Literary Editor

1. Sunday Wilshin (so named because she was born on a Sunday—26 February 1905) made her stage debut at ten, and from then on had a continuous stage and film career; she first appeared on the New York stage in 1926. She joined the BBC, as an actress, in 1938, and later worked as a producer. W. Macqueen-Pope, discussing *Charlot's Show of 1926*, in which she appeared, described her as 'one of the beauties of the period' (*The Footlights Flickered*, 1959, 162). In *Remembering Orwell*, she describes her meetings with him at the BBC. He had, she said, 'many ideas for programmes, and he could write scripts, but when it came to actually being in the studio, he needed someone to guide his hand.' He had, for example, no understanding of the use of effects (125–26).

2601. Review of *Authorship* (Careers Books No. 2) by L. A. G. Strong

Manchester Evening News, 11 January 1945

It is said to be the practice of the sterner religious orders to discourage proselytes, and Mr. L. A. G. Strong goes on rather the same principle in his advice to aspiring authors. Himself a highly successful writer of novels, short stories and radio scripts and with experience as a teacher in a school of journalism, he makes it clear from the outset that this profession is not an easy one. It has to be learned like any other, it entails endless work, and you are unlikely ever to make very much money out of it.

Indeed, Mr. Strong records that he himself was writing for fifteen years before literature became his main source of livelihood, and of the first forty manuscripts he sent out thirty-nine came back.

Most of the books (and they are numberless) on "How To Become An Author" are quite worthless. They are worthless because they are written by people who regard writing simply as a way of making money. Everything is wrong in this approach.

To begin with, writing is not a lucrative profession (a novelist who made as much as the average country doctor would be doing very well indeed), and even on its lowest levels it has to be practised for its own sake.

And secondly most of the self-styled teachers of journalism are the worst possible guides, even from a commercial point of view, because they are unable to put their own precepts into practice. If they really knew how to make money out of journalism they would be doing it, instead of selling their secret to others.

However Mr. Strong is a very exceptional man, and his advice is well worth listening to. He is a successful writer, but he happens to be such a fast worker that he has time to run journalistic courses as a side-line.

He knows that literature is a trade as well as an art, but, unlike the vast majority of teachers, he also understands the nature of creation and realises that even hack journalism needs sincerity as well as competence. Over and over again he says in different ways, "don't falsify. Even from a financial point of view it doesn't pay."

In his early days one of those kind friends who take it upon them to advise young writers said to him, "Write what they want first. Then, when you have made a name, write what you want."

Mr. Strong adds, "I repudiated the advice as damnable, and I repudiate it even more passionately to-day . . . my own experience is all on the side of honesty. Once, for a short time, when I was very hard up, I tried desperately to write what I thought the public wanted.

"The result was a disastrous failure. I never sold a line of it . . . insincerity is no substitute for talent.

"The sincere writer, however small his gift, has a better chance of success than the faker."

In these and other similar passages, Mr. Strong is not referring merely to æsthetic faking. There is also the political pressure that is put so strongly upon many journalists to-day. Some topics are practically unmentionable, and the cult of the "happy ending" is mixed up with the desire to present society in the rosiest possible light.

The correspondence tutors employed by schools of journalism frequently warn their pupils that anything "unpleasant" or "controversial" is difficult to sell. Mr. Strong's comment on all such false counsellors is "tell them to go where they belong."

But this is not to say that he despises or ignores the business side of the writing profession.

To begin with, every writer, however unusual his gifts may be, must learn to be readable. He must learn, by practice and apprenticeship, how to arrange his material and make his meaning unmistakably clear.

Mr Strong insists, and perhaps over-insists, that in a short article or story it is better to "concentrate on one point only and never attempt to make more."

Again, a writer must be ready to fall in with the wishes of editors and publishers on any question where his intellectual honesty is not involved. He must submit to having his articles cut when they are too long, and he must realise that one cannot write in the same style for a daily paper, a weekly review, and a technical magazine.

And he must study his market and not, for instance, "send a women's magazine an article about Rugby football, or a yachting magazine an article on white mice."

Submissions quite as silly as this are made every day, and many a promising novel has found its way to the dustbin because its author sent it to the wrong kind of publisher and then gave up hope when it came back to him.

Mr Strong gives some useful technical notes on the novel, the article, and the short story, and advises the budding writer not to despise that thankless and ill-paid job, lecturing.

He does, however, discourage the beginner from attempting the play or the film. There is, he considers, not one chance in ten thousand that a play written by a beginner will be produced.

Whereas a publisher risks a few hundred pounds on a book, a theatrical manager has to risk tens of thousands, and naturally he prefers to deal with writers who have already made a name for themselves in some other way.

The films are even more inaccessible. Indeed, the biggest film companies, it seems, make a practice of returning all unsolicited manuscripts unopened.

The radio is a much more promising field for the beginner. Its special technique, different from that of ordinary writing, has to be learned, but the demand for scripts is so large that there is comparatively little prejudice against newcomers.

Mr Strong ends with some notes on literary agents (useful to the writer of books, but less so to the free-lance journalist), schools of journalism, publishers, honest and otherwise, and contracts.

This is a useful little book. No book can teach you to write if you have not the initial gift, but at least you can learn how to use language simply, how to avoid unnecessary technical errors, how to market your writings, and how to dodge the innumerable crooks who haunt the fringes of the literary profession.

Mr. Strong never loses sight of the need to make a living but his advice carries all the more weight because he knows that the desire for money is not the ultimate motive of any writer worth reading.[1]

[Fee: £8.0.0; 10.1.45]

1. Reprinted, unabridged, in *Synopsis*, vol. 6, no. 1, Spring 1945.

2602. Home Guard Old Comrades Association

On 11 January, the Chairman of the Committee of Old Comrades Association, 5th County of London Battalion, Home Guard, 'C' Company Branch (Frank Samuel), sent prospective members, including Orwell (addressed as 'Dear Blair'), a circular inviting them to join the Association. The annual subscription was to be 2s 6d and the first meeting was to be held on 24 January 1945 at the Allitsen Road Canteen, at which a presentation was to be made to the Company Sergeant Major. Orwell did not complete the application for membership attached to the circular.

2603. 'As I Please,' 54

Tribune, 12 January 1945

Some time back a correspondent wrote to ask whether I had seen the exhibition of waxworks, showing German atrocities, which has been on show in London for a year or more. It is advertised outside with such captions as: HORRORS OF THE CONCENTRATION CAMP. COME INSIDE AND SEE REAL NAZI TORTURES. FLOGGING, CRUCIFIXION, GAS CHAMBERS, ETC. CHILDREN'S AMUSEMENT SECTION NO EXTRA CHARGE.

I did go and see this exhibition a long time ago, and I would like to warn prospective visitors that it is most disappointing. To begin with many of the figures are not life-size, and I suspect that some of them are not even real waxworks, but merely dressmakers' dummies with new heads attached. And secondly, the tortures are not nearly so fearful as you are led to expect by the posters outside. The whole exhibition is grubby, unlifelike and depressing. But the exhibitors are, I suppose, doing their best, and the captions are interesting in the complete frankness of their appeal to sadism and masochism. Before the war, if you were a devotee of all-in wrestling, or wrote letters to your M.P. to protest against the abolition of flogging, or haunted secondhand bookshops in search of such books as *The Pleasures of the Torture Chamber*,[1] you laid yourself open to very unpleasant suspicions. Moreover, you were probably aware of your own motives and somewhat ashamed of them. Now, however, you can wallow in the most disgusting descriptions of torture and massacre, not only without any sensation of guilt, but with the feeling that you are performing a praiseworthy political action.

I am not suggesting that the stories about Nazi atrocities are untrue. To a great extent I think they are true. These horrors certainly happened in German concentration camps before the war, and there is no reason why they should have stopped since. But they are played up largely because they give the newspapers a pretext for pornography. This morning's papers are splashing the official British Army Report on Nazi atrocities. They are careful to inform you that naked women were flogged, sometimes spotlighting this detail by means of a headline. The journalists responsible know very well what they are doing. They know that innumerable people get a sadistic kick out of thinking about torture, especially the torture of women, and they are cashing in on this widespread neurosis. No qualms need be felt, because these deeds are committed by the enemy, and the enjoyment that one gets out of them can be disguised as disapproval. And one can get a very similar kick out of barbarous actions committed by one's own side so long as they are thought of as the just punishment of evil-doers.

We have not actually got to the point of Roman gladiatorial shows yet, but we could do so if the necessary pretext were supplied. If, for instance, it were announced that the leading war criminals were to be eaten by lions or trampled to death by elephants in the Wembley Stadium, I fancy that the spectacle would be quite well attended.

I invite attention to an article entitled "The Truth about Mihailovich?" (the author of it also writes for *Tribune*, by the way) in the current *World Review*. It deals with the campaign in the British Press and the B.B.C. to brand Mihailovich as a German agent.[2]

Jugoslav politics are very complicated and I make no pretence of being an expert on them. For all I know it was entirely right on the part of Britain as well as the U.S.S.R. to drop Mihailovich and support Tito. But what interests me is the readiness, once this decision had been taken, of reputable British newspapers to connive at what amounted to forgery in order to discredit the man whom they had been backing a few months earlier. There is no doubt that this happened. The author of the article gives details of one out of a number of instances in which material facts were suppressed in the most impudent way. Presented with very strong evidence to show that Mihailovich was *not* a German agent, the majority of our newspapers simply refused to print it, while repeating the charges of treachery just as before.

Very similar things happened during the Spanish civil war. Then, Anarchists, Trotskyists and others who opposed Franco, but also opposed the official political line of the Spanish Republican Government, were accused of being traitors in Fascist pay. Various British newspapers sympathetic to the Republic took up this charge and repeated it with picturesque exaggerations of their own, at the same time refusing to print any kind of reply, even in letter form. They had the excuse that the Spanish Republic was fighting for its life and that to discuss its internecine troubles too frankly was to give a handle to the pro-Fascist Press in this country. Still, they did confuse the issues and make entirely unfounded accusations against innocent people. And, then as now, if you protested you got the answer, first, that the charges were true, and secondly, that perhaps they weren't true but that these people were politically undesirable and deserved what they got.

I recognise the force of this argument. In fighting against Fascism you cannot always be bound by the Marquess of Queensberry rules, and sometimes a lie is almost unavoidable. There are always unscrupulous opponents on the look-out for damaging admissions, and on some questions the truth is so complex that a plain statement of the facts simply misleads the general public. Still, I think it could be shown from the history of the past twenty years that totalitarian methods of controversy—falsification of history, personal libel, refusal of a fair hearing to opponents, and so forth—have on the whole worked against the interests of the Left.

A lie is a boomerang, and sometimes it comes back surprisingly soon. During the Spanish civil war one Left-wing paper employed a certain journalist[3] to "write up" the charges against the Spanish Trotskyists, which he did with considerable unscrupulousness. It was impossible to answer him, at any rate in the columns of this particular paper. Less than three years later this man was being hired by another paper to do the worst kind of "anti-Red" propaganda during the Russian war against Finland. And I suppose that the anti-Russian lies which he told in 1940 carried all the more weight because the pro-Russian lies which he was telling in 1937 had not been exposed.

In the same number of *World Review* I note that Mr. Edward Hulton[4] remarks rather disapprovingly that "the small city of Athens possesses far more daily newspapers than London." All I can say is, good luck to Athens! It is only when there are large numbers of newspapers, expressing all tendencies, that there is some chance of getting at the truth. Counting evenings, London has only twelve daily papers, and they cover the whole of the South of England and penetrate as far north as Glasgow. When they all decide to tell the same lie, there is no minority Press to act as a check. In pre-war France the Press was largely venal and scurrilous, but you could dig more news out of it than out of the British Press, because every political fraction had its paper and every viewpoint got a hearing. I shall be surprised if Athens keeps its multiplicity of newspapers under the kind of government that we apparently intend to impose.

1. By John Swain, first published in 1931 and often reprinted.
2. For Mihailović, see *1579*, *n. 2* and *2721*, *n. 1*.
3. Not positively identified, but Orwell may have in mind John Langdon Davies (sometimes hyphenated; 1897–1971; MBE), a journalist who earned Orwell's contempt for his reporting of the Barcelona uprising in 1937, in particular his reports to the *News Chronicle* that this was 'A Trotskyist Revolt' by the POUM; see *519, News Chronicle*, May 10, and *n. 16*. He published *Behind the Spanish Barricades* (1937) and in 1940 reported on the Soviet attack on Finland and wrote *Finland: The First Total War* (1940; in U.S. as *Invasion in the Snow*, Boston, 1941). He was Commandant of the South-Eastern Army Fieldcraft School, 1941–44, and in that time wrote several books on Home Guard training.
4. Edward Hulton (1906–88; Kt., 1957), lawyer and magazine editor of liberal views; see *2852*, *n. 1*.

2604. Review of *The Unquiet Grave: A Word Cycle* by
Palinurus[1]

The Observer, 14 January 1945

"Palinurus" is the easily penetrable pseudonym of a well-known literary
critic, but even without knowing his identity one could infer that the writer
of this book is about 40, is inclined to stoutness, has lived much in
Continental Europe, and has never done any real work. His book is a kind of
diary, or rather journal, interspersed with quotations from Pascal, Lao-Tze,
La Rochefoucauld, and others, and having as its dominant note a refined,
rather pessimistic, hedonism. In his previous incarnations, the author says,
he was "a melon, a lobster, a lemur, a bottle of wine, Aristippus," [2] and the
periods in which he lived were the Augustan age in Rome and "then in Paris
and London from 1660 to 1740, and lastly from 1770 to 1850. . . . Afternoons at Holland House, dinners chez Magny."

With his background of classical culture, religious scepticism, travel,
leisure, country houses, and civilised meals, "Palinurus" naturally contem-
plates the modern world without enthusiasm and even, at moments, with
sheer aristocratic disdain: but also—and this is the peculiar mark of our age—
with self-accusation and the consciousness of being an end-product, a mere
ghost, like the cultivated pagans of A.D. 400. On almost every page this book
exhibits that queer product of capitalist democracy, an inferiority complex
resulting from a private income. The author wants his comforts and
privileges, and is ashamed of wanting them: he feels that he has a right to
them, and yet feels certain that they are doomed to disappear. Before very
long the mob will rise and destroy its exploiters, but in doing so it will also
destroy civilisation:

> The English masses are lovable: they are kind, decent, tolerant,
> practical, and not stupid. The tragedy is that there are too many of them,
> and that they are aimless, having outgrown the servile functions for which
> they were encouraged to multiply. One day these huge crowds will have to
> seize power because there will be nothing else for them to do, and yet they
> neither demand power nor are ready to make use of it: they will only learn
> to be bored in a new way. Sooner or later the population of England will
> turn Communist, and then it will take over. Some form of Communism is
> the only effective religion for the working class; its coming is therefore as
> inevitable as was that of Christianity. The Liberal Die-hard then comes to
> occupy historically the same position as the "good pagan": he is doomed to
> extinction.

Throughout the book this is repeated over and over again, in varying
forms. The Beehive State is upon us,[3] the individual will be stamped out of
existence, the future is with the holiday camp, the doodle-bug,[4] and the
secret police. "Palinurus," however, differs from most of his similarly placed
contemporaries in not acquiescing in the process. He refuses to desert the
sinking ship of individualism. To the statement that man "will find
fulfilment only through participation in the communal life of an organised

21

group", he answers "No" seven times over. Yet he sees no escape from the Beehive future. He sees or thinks he sees, ways in which order and liberty, reason and myth, might be combined, but he does not believe that is the turn civilisation will take. Finally, he has no resource except a sort of lonely defiance, as of the last mammoth, or, like Faustus, trying to forget damnation in the embraces of Helen.

This outlook, product of totalitarianism and the perversion of science, is probably gaining ground, and if only for that reason this rather fragmentary book is a valuable document. It is a cry of despair from the rentier who feels that he has no right to exist, but also feels that he is a finer animal than the proletarian. Its error lies in assuming that a collectivist society would destroy human individuality. The ordinary English Communist or "fellow-traveller" makes the same assumption, and yields up his intellectual integrity in a frenzy of masochism. "Palinurus" refuses to yield, but just as blindly as the other he takes "Communism" at its own valuation.

The mechanism is the same in both cases. They are *told* that the aim of Socialism or Communism is to make men resemble insects: they are conscious that they are privileged people, and that if they resist Socialism their motives must be doubtful: therefore, they look no deeper. It does not occur to them that the so-called collectivist systems now existing only try to wipe out the individual because they are *not* really collectivist and certainly not egalitarian—because, in fact, they are a sham covering a new form of class privilege. If one can see this, one can defy the insect-men with a good conscience. But certainly it is a lot harder to see it, or at any rate to say it aloud, if one is carrying the burden of an unearned income.

[Fee: £10.0.0; 11.1.45]

1. Palinurus was the pilot of Aeneas's ship in the *Aeneid* (Books V and VI), and his name was taken by Cyril Connolly as his *nom de plume*.
2. Aristippus, a pupil of Socrates, regarded pleasure as the only absolute good in life, but because some pleasures caused pain, it was essential to be selective in pursuing pleasure.
3. 'It is usual to speak of the Fascist objective as the "beehive state", which does a grave injustice to bees,' *The Road to Wigan Pier*, *CW*, V, 200 (and see 194).
4. Properly the V-1 (see *2501*, *n. 1*), but possibly used loosely by Orwell for the V-2; see *2553*, *headnote* and also, for example, *2608*, paragraph 3.

2605. 'As I Please,' 55

Tribune, 19 January 1945

Last week Henri Béraud, the French journalist, was sentenced to death—later commuted to life imprisonment—for collaboration with the Germans. Béraud used to contribute to the Fascist weekly paper *Gringoire*, which in its later years had become the most disgusting rag it is possible to imagine. I have seldom been so angered by anything in the Press as by its cartoon when the wretched Spanish refugees streamed into France with Italian aeroplanes machine-gunning them all the way. The Spaniards were pictured as a procession of villainous-looking men, each pushing a handcart piled with jewellery and bags of gold. *Gringoire* kept up an almost continuous outcry for the suppression of the French Communist Party, but it was equally fierce against even the mildest politicians of the Left. One can get an idea of the moral level at which it conducted political controversy from the fact that it once published a cartoon showing Léon Blum in bed with his own sister. Its advertisement columns were full of ads. for clairvoyants and books of pornography. This piece of rubbish was said to have a circulation of 500,000.

At the time of the Abyssinian war Béraud wrote a violent pro-Italian article in which he proclaimed "I hate England," and gave his reasons for doing so. It is significant that it was mostly people of this type, who had made no secret of their Fascist sympathies for years beforehand, that the Germans had to make use of for Press propaganda in France. A year or two ago Mr. Raymond Mortimer published an article on the activity of French writers during the war, and there have been several similar articles in American magazines. When one pieces these together, it becomes clear that the French literary intelligentsia has behaved extremely well under the German occupation. I wish I could feel certain that the English literary intelligentsia as a whole would have behaved equally well if we had had the Nazis here. But it is true that if Britain had also been overrun, the situation would have been hopeless and the temptation to accept the New Order very much stronger.

I think I owe a small apology to the twentieth century. Apropos of my remarks about the *Quarterly Review* for 1810—in which I pointed out that French books could get favourable reviews in England at the height of the war with France—two correspondents have written to tell me that during the present war German scientific publications have had fair treatment in the scientific Press in this country. So perhaps we aren't such barbarians after all.

But I still feel that our ancestors were better at remaining sane in war time° than we are. If you ever have to walk from Fleet Street to the Embankment, it is worth going into the office of the *Observer* and having a look at something that is preserved in the waiting-room. It is a framed page from the *Observer* (which is one of our oldest newspapers) for a certain day in June, 1815. In appearance it is very like a modern newspaper, though slightly worse printed, and with only five columns on the page. The largest letters used are not much more than a quarter of an inch high. The first column is given up to "Court and Society," then follow several columns of advertisements, mostly of rooms to let. Halfway down the last column is a headline SANGUINARY BATTLE IN FLANDERS. COMPLETE DEFEAT OF THE CORSICAN USURPER. This is the first news of Waterloo!

"To-day there are only eighty people in the United Kingdom with net incomes of over six thousand pounds a year." (Mr. Quintin Hogg, M.P., in his pamphlet *The Times We Live In*.)

There are also about eighty ways in the English and American languages of expressing incredulity—for example, *garn, come off it, you bet, sez you, oh yeah, not half, I don't think, less of it* or *and the pudding!* But I think *and then you wake up* is the exactly suitable answer to a remark like the one quoted above.

Recently I read the biography of Edgar Wallace which was written by Margaret Lane some years ago. It is a real "log cabin to White House" story, and by implication a frightful commentary on our age. Starting off with every possible disadvantage—an illegitimate child, brought up by very poor foster parents in a slum street—Wallace worked his way up by sheer ability, enterprise and hard work. His output was enormous. In his later years he was turning out eight books a year, besides plays, radio scripts and much journalism. He thought nothing of composing a full-length book in less than a week. He took no exercise, worked behind a glass screen in a super-heated room, smoked incessantly and drank vast quantities of sweetened tea. He died of diabetes at the age of 57.

It is clear from some of his more ambitious books that Wallace did in some sense take his work seriously, but his main aim was to make money, and he made it. Towards the end of his life he was earning round about £50,000 a year. But it was all fairy gold. Besides losing money by financing theatres and keeping strings of racehorses which seldom won, Wallace spent fantastic sums on his various houses, where he kept a staff of twenty servants. When he died very suddenly in Hollywood, it was found that his debts amounted to £140,000, while his liquid assets were practically nil. However, the sales of his books were so vast that his royalties amounted to £26,000 in the two years following his death.

The curious thing is that this utterly wasted life—a life of sitting almost continuously in a stuffy room and covering acres of paper with slightly pernicious nonsense—is what is called, or would have been called a few years ago, "an inspiring story." Wallace did what all the "get on or get out" books, from Smiles's Self Help[1] onwards, have told you to do. And the world gave him the kind of rewards he would have asked for, after his death as well as in life. When his body was brought home—

"He was carried on board the Berengaria . . . They laid a Union Jack over him, and covered him with flowers. He lay alone in the empty saloon under his burden of wreaths, and no journey that he had ever taken had been made in such quiet dignity and state. When the ship crept into Southampton Water her flag was flying at half-mast, and the flags of Southampton slipped gently down to salute him. The bells of Fleet Street tolled, and Wyndham's was dark."[2]

All that and £50,000 a year as well! They also gave Wallace a plaque on the wall at Ludgate Circus. It is queer to think that London could commemorate Wallace in Fleet Street and Barrie in Kensington Gardens, but has never yet got round to giving Blake a monument in Lambeth.

On 2 February 1945, Tribune published a letter from Quintin Hogg (1907–), Conservative M.P. and later Lord Chancellor; see 512, n. 3. He wrote that it was 'curious that your commentator did not attribute the statement to its correct source,' which, he said, was an official statement made by the Chancellor of the Exchequer (Sir Kingsley Wood) in the House of Commons on 30 September 1942. He considered it even more curious that the figures had not been challenged by any of the editors of *Tribune*, 'who are almost all Members of the House.' (Aneurin Bevan, editor and one of the two directors of *Tribune*, was an M.P.; the other director, George Strauss, was also an M.P.; both represented the Labour Party). He asked whether Orwell had overlooked the source of the information, 'and that information, in spite of his rude noises, is true?' Orwell's response was printed below Hogg's letter:

The statement was made in Mr. Quintin Hogg's pamphlet without any reference to its source, but the fact that it originally emanated from Mr.° Kingsley Wood does not necessarily increase its credibility. It is obvious, from the kind of life that is still being lived in expensive hotels, in large country houses, etc., that there are very many people in England whose net expenditure is more than £6,000 a year. By what method they evade taxation is a separate question. The point is that Mr. Hogg's statement, if taken at its face value, would be highly misleading.

Sir (not Mr) Kingsley Wood (1881–1943; see *1107, n. 2*) had been Minister of Air at the outbreak of war. He served in the War Cabinet as Chancellor of the Exchequer under Churchill. He died after a Cabinet meeting, just before he was to make a statement in the House of Commons explaining the principles of Pay As You Earn taxation, which was to be introduced. In praising his achievements, Churchill wrote that he had managed to raise half the cost of the war by taxation and the rest by borrowing at only two per cent.

1. *Self-Help* by Samuel Smiles (1812–1904) was published in 1859 and was given subtitles such as 'with illustrations of character and conduct' and 'with illustrations of conduct and perseverance,' perseverance being a word dear to Smiles's heart and suggested to him by the engineer George Stephenson (whose life he wrote). Smiles himself thought the title 'unfortunate.' In a preface to the 1866 edition he said he wished to make it plain that he did not aim to promote selfishness: 'the duty of helping one's self in the highest sense involves the helping of one's neighbours.' The book was enormously successful (and often misrepresented). By 1953 it had gone through seventy-one impressions, and in 1958 Asa Briggs wrote a long introduction to a centenary edition.
2. Edgar Wallace (1875–1932) had been manager of Wyndham's Theatre, Charing Cross Road, London; his *The Ringer* was presented there in 1926.

2605A. To Lydia Jackson

23 January 1945   Typewritten

Tribune

On 11 January 1945, Lydia Jackson sent Orwell a story of some 1,200 words, 'The Patient', by Mikhail Zoshchenko[1] for publication in *Tribune*.

Dear Lydia,
I don't think we can use this. We are practically discontinuing stories – there are just one or two I have to work off, and probably after that we shan't take any more. But in any case, I can't take any at present. Sorry!

Yours,
[Signed] George[2]

1. Mikhail Zoshchenko (1895–1958) was a popular Soviet satirical writer. Martin Seymour-Smith compares him to Swift (*Guide to Modern World Literature*, 1061) and it might have been this characteristic that Lydia Jackson thought would appeal to Orwell. She, presumably, had translated the story from Russian. The story was not published in *Tribune*.
2. The letter is annotated (in Lydia Jackson's hand), '@ Tribune, Monday, Tuesday & Friday.' There is no further correspondence between Orwell and Lydia Jackson concerning *Tribune*.

2606. To Gleb Struve

23 January 1945   Typewritten

The Tribune,
222, Strand,
London, W.C.2.

Dear Mr. Struve,
We would be delighted to have you do some reviewing for us, especially of books dealing with literary developments. When something important comes along, I'd like you to do the leading review of it. (If you have seen "Tribune" lately, you will have seen that we now divide the reviews into one 1500-word one and a lot of 200-word shorts).

At present we don't seem to have a single book dealing with the U.S.S.R. in hand. We have a couple dealing with Poland (on mainly political lines). Do you know anything about Poland?

Yours sincerely,
Geo. Orwell

2607. To Leonard Moore

23 January 1945   Handwritten

[No salutation]
Herewith the MS. of the book of essays[1] to send to the USA. I am giving Warburg the other copy. This hasn't any address on it so should have a label attached. I'll be sending the signed contract in a day or two.

Eric Blair

1. This volume of essays was first mentioned by Orwell in correspondence on 9 January 1944; see *2403*. It was published as *Critical Essays* by Secker & Warburg on 14 February 1946 and as *Dickens, Dali & Others: Studies in Popular Culture* by Reynal & Hitchcock, New York, on 29 April 1946. Orwell noted in his Payments Book for 1 February 1945, 'S. & Warburg   Book (45,000)*' with no sum recorded in payment and the asterisk explained by 'Not to be published till autumn 1945 or spring 1946.'

2608. Review of *The Natural Order: Essays on the Return to Husbandry*, edited by H. J. Massingham

Manchester Evening News, 25 January 1945

One does not have to be a mediævalist to feel that the modern world has something seriously wrong with it. One glance out of the nearest window, at any rate in any big town, would convince the most cheery optimist that scientific progress has not been an unmixed blessing.

However, most observers are satisfied that the cause of our present ills lies in an outworn economic system which makes it impossible to consume all the goods that are produced and leads inevitably to struggles for markets and hence to Imperialist wars.

Few thoughtful people would agree that machine civilisation is itself the enemy. Use the machine properly, most people would say, and it can set us free from brute labour instead of, as at present, merely fouling our countryside with smoke and wrecking our towns with doodle-bugs.

Ever since the early days of the Industrial Revolution, however, there has been an opposite school of thought—it included such thinkers as Cobbett, Ruskin, Chesterton—which refused to admit that the machine could be the friend of humanity if its products were distributed more evenly. According to this school creative labour is psychologically necessary to the human being.

No one has ever advocated the complete scrapping of mechanical progress, but it is argued that a truly human life—and, consequently, private happiness and international peace—is only possible on a basis of hand labour and wide distribution of property.

The present book is a forcible restatement of this view by a varied collection of writers, some of whom are working agriculturists.

Mr. H. J. Massingham defines the word "husbandry" at considerable length in his introduction, and finds it to mean more than mere cultivation of the soil.

"If we look well into the word 'husbandry' we can risk a definition of it, namely, loving management. It means man the head of Nature, but acting towards Nature in a family spirit. Nothing could be farther from its meaning than the modern and scientific 'conquest of Nature,' which is not only contrary to the natural law but an absurdity.

"Modern secularism debases man by making him purely the creature[1] of earth with no destiny beyond it. At the same time it elevates this reduced animal beyond his station by making him the conqueror of Nature—an altogether childish conception—but loving management exactly defines man's place in Nature, and so honours the natural law, which regards man as chief of the creatures of earth, but subject, like them, to their Creator."

Mr. Massingham also contributes an essay on the qualitative approach to work and the difficulty, or impossibility, of combining it with mass production.

Mr. L. F. Easterbrook,[2] farming correspondent of the "News Chronicle," Mr. Philip Mairet, editor of the "New English Weekly," Mr. Philip Oyler,

Mr. C. Howard Jones, and others write of the importance of a well-balanced agriculture and of the need, even from the point of view of self-preservation, to make Britain self-supporting in food.

Lord Northbourne traces the connection between sound farming methods and national health. Mr. Rolf Gardiner contributes a stimulating essay, highly critical of the methods now being adopted in this country, on reafforestation.

Mr. J. E. Hosking writes on the mechanisation of agriculture, its possibilities and its limitations. There is a number of other essays on kindred subjects, and a useful bibliography.

No thinking person would deny that Mr. Massingham and his associates have a strong case.

In England farming can only flourish when the fact of being at war forces us to economise our shipping. What happens is that home agriculture is depressed in order to make way for imported food from Canada, Australia, Argentina, etc., these imports being the return for British exports of manufactured goods, or of capital, and both here and abroad powerful influences are at work to prevent British agriculture from reviving.

Meanwhile, in England the population is more and more driven off the land, while in the primary producing countries huge areas of the earth are converted into dust-bowls by means of "monoculture."

And the various authors of this book are quite right in insisting that machine civilisation raises deeper problems than that of mere economic security. It is a commonplace that to work in one's own time and after one's own fashion at something that needs skill and can be a source of pride is better than to stand eight hours a day beside a conveyor belt, tightening up the same nut over and over again.

As Mr. Massingham points out, the argument usually put forward in defence of machine civilisation—that mechanical work need only occupy a few hours a day and the resulting leisure can be used for creative activities—is probably a fallacy. Man is a working animal, his work is and must be the central factor in his life, and those whose work is soul-destroying tend to seek mechanical, mass-produced amusements (the film and the radio) in their spare time.

This point has never been satisfactorily met by the defenders either of Socialism or of large-scale Capitalism, and the writers of this book are quite right to raise it.

Nevertheless, they do not face up to the fact that, so far as we can see, the machine and the machine civilisation are here and cannot be got rid of.

None of these writers clearly admits that the vast majority of modern men prefer the machine civilisation. So far from wanting to get back to the village, they want to get away from it—a fact which is even more obvious in genuinely agricultural countries such as India than it is in England.

Secondly, the machine culture is inescapable because, in the modern world, any country which remains unindustrialised is helpless in a military sense. A peasant country is inevitably dominated, and usually exploited, by some more highly industrialised country.

And since nationalism[3] is immensely powerful one must assume that any country which is in a position to do so will strive to maintain its independence and will be ready to pay the necessary price in ships, guns, aeroplanes, and the complex industrial machinery that those imply.

These are facts, seemingly inescapable at present, working against the world view that Mr. Massingham and his colleagues put forward. What they advocate may be desirable, but it is not going to happen, at any rate not yet. But that is not to say that such books as this are not needed.

On the contrary, they are a useful corrective to the optimism which still flourishes, even amid the bombs. And even those who are contemptuous of the past and refuse to believe in the superiority of the village over the industrial town need to be reminded that such major disasters as soil erosion and de-afforestation are happening all the time.

The book is pleasantly illustrated by Thomas Hennell.[4]

[Fee: £8.0.0.; 24.1.45]

1. creature] creative *in Manchester Evening News*
2. L. F. Easterbrook broadcast under Orwell's aegis at the BBC; see *1241, n. 1.*
3. nationalism] nationalisation *in Manchester Evening News*
4. The very short paragraphs of this review and of some others published by the *Manchester Evening News* (e.g. *2615* and *2632*) are not typical of Orwell; they may be a sub-editor's work. See Orwell's remark that very short paragraphs 'insult the reader', *2463.*

2609. 'As I Please,' 56

Tribune, 26 January 1945

The other night I attended a mass meeting of an organisation called the League for European Freedom. Although officially an all-party organisation—there was one Labour M.P. on the platform—it is, I think it is safe to say, dominated by the anti-Russian wing of the Tory Party.

I am all in favour of European freedom, but I feel happier when it is coupled with freedom elsewhere—in India, for example. The people on the platform were concerned with the Russian actions in Poland, the Baltic countries, etc., and the scrapping of the principles of the Atlantic Charter that those actions imply. More than half of what they said was justified, but curiously enough they were almost as anxious to defend our own coercion of Greece as to condemn the Russian coercion of Poland.[1] Victor Raikes,[2] the Tory M.P., who is an able and outspoken reactionary, made a speech which I should have considered a good one if it had referred only to Poland and Yugoslavia. But after dealing with those two countries he went on to speak about Greece, and then suddenly black became white, and white black. There was no booing, no interjections from the quite large audience—no one there, apparently, who could see that the forcing of quisling governments upon unwilling peoples is equally undesirable whoever does it.

It is very hard to believe that people like this are really interested in political liberty as such. They are merely concerned because Britain did not get a big enough cut in the sordid bargain that appears to have been driven at Teheran.[3] After the meeting I talked with a journalist whose contacts among influential people are much more extensive than mine. He said he thought it probable that British policy will shortly take a violent anti-Russian swing, and that it would be quite easy to manipulate public opinion in that direction if necessary. For a number of reasons I don't believe he was right, but if he does turn out to be right, then ultimately it is *our* fault and not that of our adversaries.

No one expects the Tory Party and its press to spread enlightenment. The trouble is that for years past it has been impossible to extract a grown-up picture of foreign politics from the Left-wing press either. When it comes to such issues as Poland, the Baltic countries, Yugoslavia or Greece, what difference is there between the Russophile press and the extreme Tory press? The one is simply the other standing on its head. The *News Chronicle* gives the big headlines to the fighting in Greece but tucks away the news that "force has had to be used" against the Polish Home Army in small print at the bottom of a column. The *Daily Worker* disapproves of dictatorship in Athens, the *Catholic Herald* disapproves of dictatorship in Belgrade. There is no one who is able to say—at least, no one who has the chance to say in a newspaper of big circulation—that this whole dirty game of spheres of influence, quislings, purges, deportations, one-party elections and hundred per cent. plebiscites is morally the same whether it is done by ourselves, the Russians or the Nazis. Even in the case of such frank returns to barbarism as the use of hostages, disapproval is only felt when it happens to be the enemy and not ourselves who is doing it.

And with what result? Well, one result is that it becomes much easier to mislead public opinion. The Tories are able to precipitate scandals when they want to, partly because on certain subjects the Left refuses to talk in a grown-up manner. An example was the Russo-Finnish war of 1940. I do not defend the Russian action in Finland, but it was not especially wicked. It was merely the same kind of thing as we ourselves did when we seized Madagascar. The public could be shocked by it, and indeed worked up into a dangerous fury about it, because for years they had been falsely taught that Russian foreign policy was morally different from that of other countries. And it struck me as I listened to Mr. Raikes the other night that if the Tories do choose to start spilling the beans about the Lublin Committee,[4] Marshal Tito and kindred subjects, there will be—thanks to prolonged self-censorship on the Left— plenty of beans for them to spill.

But political dishonesty has its comic side. Presiding over that meeting of the League for European Freedom was no less a person than the Duchess of Atholl.[5] It is only about seven years since the Duchess—"the red duchess" as she was affectionately nicknamed—was the pet of the *Daily Worker* and lent the considerable weight of her authority to every lie that the Communists happened to be uttering at the moment. Now she is fighting against the monster that she helped to create. I am sure that neither she nor her Communist ex-friends see any moral in this.

I want to correct an error that I made in this column last week. It seems that there *is* a plaque to William Blake, and that it is somewhere near St. George's church in Lambeth. I had looked for one in that area and had failed to find it. My apologies to the L.C.C.

If one cares about the preservation of the English language, a point one often has to decide is whether it is worth putting up a struggle when a word changes its meaning.

Some words are beyond redemption. One could not, I imagine, restore "impertinent" to its original meaning, or "journal," or "decimate." But how about the use of "infer" for "imply" ("He didn't actually say I was a liar, but he inferred it"), which has been gaining ground for some years? [6] Ought one to protest against it? And ought one to acquiesce when certain words have their meanings arbitrarily narrowed? Examples are "immoral" (nearly always taken as meaning sexually immoral), and "criticise" (always taken as meaning criticise unfavourably). It is astonishing what numbers of words have come to have a purely sexual significance, partly owing to the need of the newspapers for euphemisms. Constant use of such phrases as "intimacy took place twice" has practically killed the original meaning of "intimacy," and quite a dozen other words have been perverted in the same way.

Obviously this kind of thing ought to be prevented if possible, but it is uncertain whether one can achieve anything by struggling against the current usage. The coming and going of words is a mysterious process whose rules we do not understand. In 1940 the word "wallop," meaning mild beer, suddenly became current all over London. I had never heard it until that date, but it seems that it was not a new word, but had been peculiar to one quarter of London. Then it suddenly spread all over the place, and now it appears to have died out again. Words can also revive, for no very clear reason, after lying dormant for hundreds of years: for example the word "car," which had never had any currency in England except in high-flown classical poetry, but was resurrected about 1900 to describe the newly invented automobile.

Possibly, therefore, the degradation which is certainly happening to our language is a process which one cannot arrest by conscious action. But I would like to see the attempt made. And as a start I would like to see a few dozen journalists declare war on some obviously bad usage—for example, the disgusting verb "to contact," [7] or the American habit of tying an unnecessary preposition on to every verb—and see whether they could kill it by their concerted efforts.

Tribune for 9 February published three letters in response to this column. 'Fabian' gave a further example of what he called Orwell's 'justly condemnatory remarks regarding dishonest propaganda,' a passage from *Principles of Prosperity* by F. W. Hirst, 'the well-known Cobdenite-Liberal.' This, he claimed, gave readers a false impression of the aims of the Fabian Society and Socialist leaders. Hirst alleged that, under them, all great industrial enterprises and the banks would be confiscated; state debts repudiated; and 'all important journals and printing presses' would be monopolised by the working class.

The Duchess of Atholl, Interim Chairman of the British League for European

Freedom (who later asked Orwell to address the League; see his response, 15 November 1945; *2795*), wrote:

> I observe that in your issue of January 26 you lament the fact that no one has had the chance to say in a newspaper of big circulation that "quislings, purges, deportations, one-party elections and 100 per cent. plebiscites are morally the same whether they are done by ourselves, the Russians or the Nazis." I do not know the circulation of your paper, but whatever its extent, I shall be grateful if you will find space for me to make clear that this has always been my view and is precisely the reason why I opposed an unconstitutional dictatorship in Spain that mainly owed its seizure of power to the Nazi dictatorship in Germany, and today equally oppose an unconstitutional "Government" in Poland that, even more than in the Spanish case, owes its position to another foreign Government.
>
> And may I conclude this by saying that the British League for European Freedom has been formed just to combat the above-mentioned evils, and how glad I am to know that the *Tribune* is protesting so emphatically against the threatened extermination of the brothers-in-arms of the heroes of the Warsaw rising?

Douglas Goldring[8] discussed issues affecting Poland, East Prussia, and Czechoslovakia, referred to by Orwell in 'As I Please', 56 (*2609*) and 57 (*2613*) (and by others), Goldring's opening quotatation not being from anything Orwell wrote:

> "The Lublin Committee is a creature of Russia's and from all the evidence it had no popular basis among the Poles." Which Poles? The landlords? Or those Poles who had to go down on their knees to kiss the hem of their masters' garments before addressing them? According to "evidence," which has never been contradicted, the Lublin Committee, even before the Russian advance, had begun to break up the big estates and had settled 900,000 peasants on their own land.
>
> The wholesale evacuation of East Prussia, which Mr. Orwell deplores, appears to have been undertaken largely on their own volition by the East Prussians. In any case, it forms a minor part of those enormous migrations and uprootings which have been going on throughout Europe for over five years, and for which not Stalin, but Hitler, is responsible. The assertion that an exchange of populations, if well organised and humanely carried out, necessarily breeds future wars is disproved by the only pre-war example of such a racial resettlement. The transference of the Greek population of Asia Minor to Metropolitan Greece, though it occasioned much temporary suffering, proved a complete success in the long run and led to the establishment of friendly relations between two peoples who had been enemies for centuries.
>
> What Czechoslovakia "should" or should not do in regard to the problem of the Sudeten Germans, at some future date, is surely a matter for the Czechoslovakians to decide. When British Socialists have set an example to the world by insisting on some sort of decency in our relations with India, Burma, Italy, Greece, not to mention Belgium and France, they will be in a position to lecture their Allies but not before.

1. For a later comment by Orwell on the Russian/Polish and the British/Greek relationships, see his unpublished letter to *Tribune*, 26[?] June 1945, *2685*.
2. H. Victor Raikes (1901–1986); Kt., 1953), barrister, first elected to Parliament in 1931, served in the RAF during the war and was elected for Wavertree, Liverpool in 1945, and, when that constituency disappeared under redistribution, for Garston, 1950–57. By 1957 he had become an Independent Conservative.
3. The Teheran Conference, 28 Nov–1 Dec 1943, was attended by Churchill, Roosevelt, and Stalin in order to co-ordinate the Allied landings in France and a renewed Soviet offensive against Germany. It failed to agree on the post-war government of Poland.
4. On 18 January 1945, a Soviet-backed puppet government of Poland was installed in Lublin under President Boleslaw Bierut. Its first actions were to demand the rounding-up of what it called irresponsible members of the Home Army and those following the London Polish government in exile. It condemned General Bor-Komorowski, who had led the Warsaw uprising, and maintained that that rising was 'provocative' and the surrender of those who had fought the Germans against desperate odds had actually aided the Germans. The purge of all non-Communists followed.
5. Katharine Stewart-Murray, Duchess of Atholl (1874–1960), devoted her life to public service, becoming the second woman, and first Conservative, to hold ministerial office. Orwell reviewed her *Searchlight on Spain* (1938) twice; see *466* and *469*. For fuller biographical details, see *466, n. 1*. See also *2795*.
6. The idea that 'infer' used to mean 'imply' (rather than to reason one thing from another) attracts this comment in the Revised *OED*: 'This use is widely considered to be incorrect, esp. with a person as the subject,' but it goes on to cite examples of such usage, with a person as subject, from the seventeenth century.
7. Note Orwell's use of 'contact' in his letter to Roger Senhouse, 28 February 1945, *2628*.
8. Douglas Goldring, novelist, critic, and travel writer; see *2412, n. 4*; *2541, n. 4* and *3732* where he is included in Orwell's list of crypto-Communists and fellow-travellers.

2610. Review of *Visions and Memories* by H. W. Nevinson

The Observer, 28 January 1945

In his introduction to this book—it is a collection of occasional essays written over a period of about 30 years—Professor Gilbert Murray suggests that H. W. Nevinson was an outstanding journalist partly because he did not possess the qualities that usually make for success in that profession. "He was too gentle, too passionately revolted by scenes of violence and cruelty, to be mixed up in such things as wars or great oppressions; yet in whatever part of the world such things occurred there was always a cry for Nevinson." He adds that Nevinson was "a sensitive scholar" and a champion of lost causes: and indeed these two qualities, together with that other one of always happening to be there when the guns are firing, are apparent in nearly every essay in this book.

Most of them are on literary subjects, but it is interesting to see how even in his most violent adventures Nevinson preserves the outlook of a civilised man. In 1897 we find him volunteering to fight for the Greeks against the Turks and suffering fearful hardships in the passes of the Pindus Mountains, but observing his comrades, the Greek irregulars, with a disillusioned eye, and never forgetting the classical associations of the land he is crossing. When, after a three-days march, he staggers to the top of the pass and looks down towards the sea, he thinks promptly of the Battle of Actium and the

33

Empress Theodora. Three years later we find him riding into Pretoria with Roberts's victorious army, which he had followed from Bloemfontein to Johannesburg "guided by the stench of dead horses and the flights of vultures." In Pretoria he watches the Union Jack being hoisted and the troops marching past the Commander-in-Chief, and then he notes that in a house nearby "someone of the defeated race was playing Beethoven." He reflects that the music will be remembered when the victory and the defeat are both forgotten. In Central Africa—

> A wild native shot one of my few carriers with a cube of copper through the hand, and the other carriers called on me to execute the criminal. I object to capital punishment, but I set the man in the middle of the circle, and raised my rifle, aiming at his heart, while his black face turned a kind of green with terror. Suddenly three of the carriers rushed upon me, knocked up the rifle, and implored me not to shoot. I was immensely relieved, all the more because I knew the rifle was hopelessly jammed and would rather fly than fire.

Nevinson likes to put in little touches, like that of the jammed rifle, which make him appear a slightly ineffectual person. But it was the combination of "objecting to capital punishment," and yet habitually getting into the kind of situation where it is sometimes necessary to kill people, that lifted him above the ordinary run of journalists.

Nevinson's thoughts were never absent very long from classical antiquity, and the two modern writers who meant most to him seem to have been Goethe and Matthew Arnold. The best thing in this book is the description of an encounter, presumably imaginary, between Marcus Aurelius and a Christian saint. But he also had some rather unexpected enthusiasms. The book contains an excellent reminiscence of W. B. Yeats, and a violent defence of Blake's paintings, which, at the date when it was written (1913), must have been founded on a genuinely independent judgment. A year later, however, Nevinson is writing an equally vigorous defence of Marinetti, the Futurist poet, afterwards to become the official poet of the Fascist regime.[1] In this essay Nevinson even borrows for a few pages Marinetti's vulgar iconoclasm and glorification of bloodshed, and these passages bring out the strain of perversity that undoubtedly existed in Nevinson's own nature. He was in favour of any cause that was unpopular—his championship of women's suffrage no doubt was partly explained by this—and Marinetti was certainly not popular in 1914. As Professor Murray says: "He was a fiery partisan with an extraordinary power of understanding the other side," and when one of his lost causes happened to win after all, he tended to lose interest in it.

Nevinson died towards the end of 1941 at the age of 85. Both Professor Murray and Miss Evelyn Sharp, the editor of the book, remark that it was unbearable to him to have to look on, aged and helpless, at a bigger war, and a war for a clearer purpose, than any he had experienced in his youth. He seems to have kept his mental vigour to the last, however; the last essay is dated only a month before his death. Even if one had never heard of him before, this book would be enough to reveal him as an unusual man. He was at once courageous, civilised, and intellectually honest—a combination that grows rarer and rarer as we move further from the nineteenth century. The book contains a couple of good photographs, and is better bound and printed than is usual in these days.

[Fee: £10.0.0; 25.1.45]

1. Filippo Tommaso Marinetti (1876–1944), Italian poet, dramatist, and author of 'The Futurist Manifesto,' published in Paris, 20 February 1909, and, in 1912, of 'The Technical Manifesto of Futurist Literature.' He advocated scientific modernity, technology and the machine, and was an early supporter of Mussolini (see his *Futurismo e Fascismo*, 1924). He supported fascism until his death.

2611. *Animal Farm* Page Proofs

On 31 January 1945, two sets of page proofs of *Animal Farm* were sent by Secker & Warburg to Orwell at the offices of *Tribune* with the original typescript. He was asked to return the marked set.

2612. Review of *Shanghai Harvest* by Rhodes Farmer; *Fountains in the Sand* by Norman Douglas

Manchester Evening News, 2 February 1945

Mr. Rhodes Farmer ends his book—it is an account of his experiences as a war correspondent in China between July, 1937, and the end of 1939—with an epilogue written in 1944. Its final words are: "China's refusal to surrender to Japan was as decisive in world history as Britain's refusal to surrender to Germany in 1940." He gives reasons for this statement, pointing out that if China had not stood firm and kept great Japanese armies engaged for five years, the Japanese might have been able to conquer not only Australia but also India; they might even have been able to join hands with the Germans somewhere in the neighbourhood of Egypt, with disastrous consequences for both Britain and the U.S.S.R.

His epilogue is a powerful plea, very badly needed at this moment, for remembrance of China's important part in the war, both present and future, and her fearful sufferings. The main body of the book illustrates and reinforces his message.

It is a hurriedly written book, and, no doubt, full of minor inaccuracies, but it is lively in every page. In 1937 Mr. Farmer, an Australian newspaper-man, was on his way to Shanghai for a holiday. He was not especially anti-Japanese in sentiment—indeed, he chose to make his journey as the sole passenger in a small Japanese cargo boat, and was on excellent terms with the officers. But as soon as he arrived at Shanghai things started happening.

The "China Incident," as the Japanese liked to call it, suddenly flamed up into total war, and the bombs rained down on the unprotected inhabitants of the Chinese suburbs all round the International Settlement. Mr. Farmer had a ringside view of the fighting, and accepted a post on the staff of the "North China Daily News." Later he became editorial adviser in the Chinese Ministry of Information, in which he handled most of Generalissimo Chiang Kai-shek's war messages, and edited and superintended the publication of Madame Chiang's first book.

After the Chinese forces were driven out of Shanghai, the Chinese defences almost collapsed for some months, and Nanking, the capital, was swiftly captured. It became the scene of one of the most frightful massacres in modern history. Observers on the spot considered that the Japanese put to death about 20,000 military prisoners and 30,000 civilians, many of whom were either burned alive or used for bayonet practice.

Mr. Farmer prints a photograph showing Japanese soldiers bayoneting manacled Chinese prisoners. This photograph is of some historical interest. It was printed in "Picture Post" about the end of 1941, and was then suspected by many people as a forgery. However, Mr. Farmer explains how it, and others like it, came into his possession. These photographs, showing tortures, decapitations, and so forth, were taken by Japanese soldiers, who sometimes sent their films to be developed in the International Settlement at Shanghai. Thence, through the agency of alert Chinese on the spot, copies of them reached the Chinese Ministry of Information.

Mr. Farmer had some of them published in American magazines as early as 1938, and, as he says, they "would really have shocked the world had the victims been Westerners instead of humble Chinese."

Mr. Farmer travelled over great areas of unoccupied China, and in spite of the confusion, the backwardness, the lack of industrial resources, the displacement of population owing to the bombing of defenceless cities, and the poor equipment of the Chinese armies,[1] the main impression left upon him was of China's invincibility. But he insists that her present plight, since the fresh Japanese offensive of last year, is much more serious than is generally recognised in the West, and that the loss of the South China airfields will make the final conquest of Japan a longer business than it need have been.

It might have been better, he hints, to send to China some of the arms and other materials that were actually sent to the U.S.S.R. or the European resistance movements. In effect China was starved of supplies from 1940 onwards, and "the declaration that more supplies are being flown into China to-day than ever bumped over the Burma Road is a factual misrepresentation." (So, incidentally, is the current statement that the Burma Road has been "reopened": it is not effectively open until Rangoon is recaptured.)

"China," Mr. Farmer concludes, "has been tragedy corner of the Big Four alliance, in which only Stalin, Churchill, and Roosevelt have the cards to deal."

Mr. Farmer has an unbounded admiration for both Chiang Kai-shek and Madame Chiang, and his tributes to them should be valuable at the present moment when mysterious political disagreements have caused what amounts to a campaign against the Generalissimo in parts of the Press. The book has numerous photographs, some of which are of documentary value.

"Fountains in the Sand" also comes under the heading of travel literature, but it might almost have been written as a corrective to Mr. Farmer's tale of the miseries of war-torn China.

In 1911, or thereabouts, Mr. Norman Douglas was knocking about in Southern Tunisia, and fetched up for some weeks at the ancient town of Gafsa, much frequented by the Romans for the sake of its medicinal springs, and thousands of years earlier than that by palæolithic men who have left their stone implements behind them in unusual profusion.

Later he visited the oases farther south, and the "Chotts," the great depressions in the Sahara Desert, which are thought to be the beds of vanished lakes. With the peculiar leisurely charm that belongs to all his travel books, Mr. Douglas discourses on the Arabs, the colonial French, the flint implements, the Roman remains, the date palms, the mineral deposits, the Arab drug known as kiff, the snakes, the scorpions, and other features of Tunisia.

Those who have read "Old Calabria" and "Siren Land" will know Mr. Douglas for one of the most engaging travel writers we have ever produced. It was a useful service on the part of the Penguin Library to reprint the present book which is less known than the other two and has been long out of print.

[Fee: £8.8.0; 31.1.45]

1. Orwell's article was illustrated by a photograph of a Chinese soldier captioned, 'No longer ragged, badly armed, and no match for the Japanese, the 1945 Chinese soldier, like this warrior, has automatic weapons, first-class training and a fighting man's equipment'.

2613. 'As I Please,' 57

Tribune, 2 February 1945

I have just been re-reading, with great interest, an old favourite of my boyhood, *The Green Curve*, by "Ole Luk-Oie." "Ole Luk-Oie" was the pseudonym of Major Swinton (afterwards General Swinton),[1] who was, I believe, one of the rather numerous people credited with the invention of the tank. The stories in this book, written about 1908, are the forecasts of an intelligent professional soldier who had learned the lessons of the Boer War and the Russo-Japanese War, and it is interesting to compare them with what actually happened a few years later.

One story, written as early as 1907 (at which date no aeroplane had actually risen off the ground for more than a few seconds), describes an air raid. The aeroplanes carry eight-pounder bombs! Another story, written in the same year, deals with a German invasion of England, and I was particularly interested to notice that in this story the Germans are already nicknamed "Huns." I had been inclined to attribute the use of the word "Hun," for German, to Kipling, who certainly used it in the poem that he published during the first week of the last war.[2]

In spite of the efforts of several newspapers, "Hun" has never caught on in this war, but we have plenty of other offensive nicknames. Someone could write a valuable monograph on the use of question-begging names and epithets, and their effect in obscuring political controversies. It would bring out the curious fact that if you simply accept and apply to yourself a name intended as an insult, it may end by losing its insulting character. This appears to be happening to "Trotskyist," which is already dangerously close to being a compliment. So also with "Conchy" during the last war. Another example is "Britisher." This word was used for years as a term of opprobrium in the Anglophobe American Press. Later on, Northcliffe and others, looking round for some substitute for "Englishman" which should have an Imperialistic and jingoistic flavour, found "Britisher" ready to hand, and took it over. Since then the word has had an aura of gutter patriotism, and the kind of person who tells you that "what these natives need is a firm hand," also tells you that he is "proud to be a Britisher"—which is about equivalent to a Chinese Nationalist describing himself as a "Chink."

A leaflet recently received from the Friends' Peace Committee states that if the current scheme to remove all Poles from the areas to be taken over by the U.S.S.R., and, in compensation, all Germans from the portions of Germany to be taken over by Poland, is put into operation, "this will involve the transfer of not less than seven million people."

Some estimates, I believe, put it higher than this, but let us assume it to be seven millions. This is equivalent to uprooting and transplanting the entire population of Australia, or the combined populations of Scotland and Ireland. I am no expert on transport or housing, and I would like to hear from somebody better qualified a rough estimate (a) of how many wagons and locomotives, running for how long, would be involved in transporting those seven million people, plus their livestock, farm machinery and household goods; or, alternatively, (b) of how many of them are going to die of starvation and exposure if they are simply shipped off without their livestock, etc.

I fancy the answer to (a) would show that this enormous crime cannot actually be carried through, though it might be started, with confusion, suffering and the sowing of irreconcilable hatreds as the result. Meanwhile, the British people should be made to understand, with as much concrete detail as possible, what kind of policies their statesman are committing them to.

A not-too-distant explosion shakes the house, the windows rattle in their sockets, and in the next room the 1964 class[3] wakes up and lets out a yell or two. Each time this happens I find myself thinking, "Is it possible that human beings can continue with this lunacy very much longer?" You know the answer, of course. Indeed, the difficulty nowadays is to find anyone who thinks that there will *not* be another war in the fairly near future.

Germany, I suppose, will be defeated this year, and when Germany is out of the way Japan will not be able to stand up to the combined power of Britain and the U.S.A. Then there will be a peace of exhaustion, with only minor and unofficial wars raging all over the place, and perhaps this so-called peace may last for decades. But after that, by the way the world is actually shaping, it may well be that war will *become permanent*. Already, quite visibly and more or less with the acquiescence of all of us, the world is splitting up into the two or three huge super-states forecast in James Burnham's *Managerial Revolution*. One cannot draw their exact boundaries as yet, but one can see more or less what areas they will comprise. And if the world does settle down into this pattern, it is likely that these vast states will be permanently at war with one another, though it will not necessarily be a very intensive or bloody kind of war. Their problems, both economic and psychological, will be a lot simpler if the doodle-bugs are more or less constantly whizzing to and fro.

If these two or three super-states do establish themselves, not only will each of them be too big to be conquered, but they will be under no necessity to trade with one another, and in a position to prevent all contact between their nationals. Already, for a dozen years or so, large areas of the earth have been cut off from one another, although technically at peace.

Some months ago, in this column, I pointed out that modern scientific inventions have tended to prevent rather than increase international communication. This brought me several angry letters from readers, but none of them were able to show that what I had said was false. They merely retorted that if we had Socialism, the aeroplane, the radio, etc., would not be perverted to wrong uses. Very true, but then we haven't Socialism. As it is, the aeroplane is primarily a thing for dropping bombs and the radio primarily a thing for whipping up nationalism. Even before the war there was enormously less contact between the peoples of the earth than there had been thirty years earlier, and education was perverted, history rewritten and freedom of thought suppressed to an extent undreamed of in earlier ages. And there is no sign whatever of these tendencies being reversed.

Maybe I am pessimistic. But, at any rate those are the thoughts that cross my mind (and a lot of other people's too, I believe) every time the explosion of a V bomb booms through the mist.[4]

A little story I came upon in a book.

Someone receives an invitation to go out lion hunting. "But," he exclaims, "I haven't lost any lions!"

1. Major-General Sir Ernest Dunlop Swinton (1868–1951), Professor of Military History, Fellow of All Souls College, Oxford. In addition to his stories, he wrote and translated a number of military histories. As Ole (Old) Luk-Oie he published *The Green Curve* (1909) and *The Great Tab Dope* (1915).
2. Ironically, the twentieth-century use of 'Hun' derives from a speech by Kaiser Wilhelm II to German troops sailing for China in 1900. Kipling is cited by the OED as referring to the 'shameless Hun' in *The Times*, 22 December 1902. Kipling's poem, 'For all we have and are' (1914), has as its fourth line, 'The Hun is at the gate!'
3. '1964 class' is presumably a reference to Richard, Orwell's adopted son, then nine months old, who would be twenty in 1964, the age of a graduating class.
4. This section includes several ideas developed in *Nineteen Eighty-Four*.

2614. On Orwell's behalf to W. J. Strachan

7 February 1945   Typewritten

Tribune

Dear Mr. Strachan,
I am keeping the Dunkirk poem and shall try to use it round about the anniversary.[1]

Yours truly,
[Signed] E. Stafford
p.p. George Orwell

1. The poem was printed, and on 1 August, Strachan wrote to ask why he had not been paid. John Peck, literary editor, replied on 3 August to apologise: 'I am afraid it was the departure of George Orwell that was responsible for your not having had a cheque for your poem. Not that it was his fault—I simply did not know what arrangement he had made with you for payment and whether any third person entered into this.' He arranged to send Strachan one guinea (£1.1.0). For Strachan, see *2456, n. 1.*

2615. Review of *Independent People* by Halldor° Laxness, translated from the Icelandic by Anderson Thompson

Manchester Evening News, 8 Feburary 1945

When one reads a book translated from a foreign language the hardest thing to be sure about is its level of probability. Fine shades of meaning are lost in the translation, and one is constantly in danger of mistaking a joke for a serious statement or a wild burlesque for a realistic description of everyday life.

Dickens, for instance, is regarded in some European countries not primarily as a humorist but as a serious social historian.

"Uncle Tom's Cabin" has a surprisingly high reputation in France, its powerful story being justly admired, while the faint atmosphere of absurdity which an English-speaking reader can perceive in it goes unnoticed.

One ought to keep this consideration in mind when approaching this Icelandic novel, "Independent People." There is no question that it is an outstanding book. Indeed, it is a great treat to encounter such a book after the things calling themselves novels that we have had to put up with during the past few years.

But is it actually a novel—or is it a sort of pastoral romance with touches of satire? It is a story about Icelandic peasants, the poorest class of peasants, who live by sheep-farming, are in debt from the cradle to the grave, and frequently die of starvation in the winter—but just how realistic it is intended to be is a difficult question to decide.

It is the story of Bjartur of Summerhouses (as in the Highlands of Scotland, these peasants are called by the names of their farms), a crofter, who, after 18 years of servitude on a big estate, has contrived to set up an establishment of his own.

The abandoned croft which he takes over has the disadvantage of being haunted by a demon, a relic of the ancient Viking days, and Bjartur's life is a long history of calamities, ending with bankruptcy, and including the deaths of several wives and numerous children.

Bjartur, however, is an unusual man and not easily daunted. He will not even make the customary sacrifice to the local demon, which is probably the root cause of his misfortunes, and to be caught 20 miles from anywhere in a mid-winter blizzard, or to swim across an ice-filled river on the back of a wild reindeer, is all in the day's work to him.

Bjartur has two interests in life—sheep and poetry. All the Icelandic peasants, it seems, are either poets themselves or at least appreciative of poetry; and their taste is not, as one might perhaps expect, for simple songs and ballads, but for a highly elaborate and artificial type of verse, with complex rhyme schemes. Bjartur himself throws off verses of this kind almost continuously.

But sheep are an even more absorbing interest. There is no occasion, either a wedding, a funeral, a christening, or a meeting of the local council, when the conversation does not swiftly revert to sheep and, above all, the various kinds of worms to which sheep are subject.

When Bjartur's first wife is within a day or two of child-bed he sets out into the mountains in search of a lost lamb which his half-starved wife has, in fact, secretly eaten. When he returns it is to find his wife dead, and a new-born child being kept warm by the sheep-dog. Bjartur goes to seek help at a neighbouring house, but, even so, there is a long conversation about sheep, and the recitation of one or two poems before he gets round to announcing the news.

The newly-born child is not really his own, and it is on his complex relations with this child, a girl, that the book largely turns.

For an English reader its most interesting feature is its revelation of the terrible poverty, made worse by ignorance and superstition, in which the peasants live. Everything depends on keeping the sheep alive through the winter—a late spring, a failure to get enough hay in during the short northern summer, can mean swift ruin, and even starvation. Bjartur for many years does not even possess a cow. One child after another dies for lack of milk, but fodder for the cow would mean less fodder for the all-important sheep.

In the tiny turf-walled huts all ages and sexes sleep huddled together: salt fish is the principal food: ragged clothes and body vermin are taken for granted.

The book takes its title from Bjartur's wish to be his own master, to owe nothing to anybody. For years he will not even join the peasants' co-operative, which seems to him to infringe upon his independence.

In the background one can dimly discern the pattern of Icelandic politics—the basis of which is the bondage of the inland farmers to the commercial interests of the seaport towns—and the half-understood effects of world events.

After years of struggling, not completely without success, against hardship and low prices, Bjartur and thousands of others like him are finally ruined by the false prosperity induced by the war of 1914–18. Suddenly the warring nations are in need of fish, wool, oil, and salted mutton, and the peasants find themselves selling their products at unheard-of prices, and even beginning to pay off their debts.

Not grasping that these conditions will not last, they launch out into unwise expenditure, and the after-war slump finds Iceland less prosperous than ever. Finally, the Government is obliged to sell off the island's only real wealth, its fishing grounds.

Bjartur is ruined because he rashly decides to build a real house, with concrete walls, a tin roof, and glass windows, in place of his turf hut. The house turns out to be cold and uncomfortable and the cost of building it eats up his capital.

On the last page he is setting forth, at the age of about 60, to start all over again on a ruined croft which is the property of his mother-in-law.

This is an unusual book. Perhaps the life of the sheep-farming Icelandic peasants is not precisely as it is here described. Perhaps they are less primitive, less poetic, more like ourselves; perhaps the scenes pictured here only bear the same relation to the real thing as Thomas Hardy's novels do to contemporary rural England.

But certainly this book "creates a world of its own," as the saying goes, and no one who reads it is likely to forget it.

It is one more illustration of the lamentable fact that when one does come across a good novel these days it is almost always a translation.[1]

[Fee: £8.8.0; 7.2.45]

1. Halldór Laxness (pseudonym of Halldór Kiljan Gudjónsson; 1902–) was awarded the Nobel Prize for Literature in 1955. *Independent People* was published in Icelandic in 1934–35 and in an English translation in 1945.

2616. 'As I Please,' 58

Tribune, 9 February 1945

Every time I wash up a batch of crockery I marvel at the unimaginativeness of human beings who can travel under the sea and fly through the clouds, and yet have not known how to eliminate this sordid time-wasting drudgery from their daily lives. If you go into the Bronze Age room in the British Museum (when it is open again) you will notice that some of our domestic appliances have barely altered in three thousand years. A saucepan, say, or a comb, is very much the same thing as it was when the Greeks were besieging Troy. In the same period we have advanced from the leaky galley to the 50,000 ton liner, and from the ox cart to the aeroplane.

It is true that in the modern labour-saving house in which a tiny percentage of human beings live, a job like washing-up takes rather less time than it used to. With soap-flakes, abundant hot water, plate racks, a well-lighted kitchen, and—what very few houses in England have—an easy method of rubbish-disposal, you can make it more tolerable than it used to be when copper dishes had to be scoured with sand in porous stone sinks by the light of a candle. But certain jobs (for instance, cleaning out a frying-pan which has had fish in it) are inherently disgusting, and this whole business of messing about with dish mops and basins of hot water is incredibly primitive. At this moment the block of flats I live in is partly uninhabitable: not because of enemy action, but because accumulations of snow have caused water to pour through the roof and bring down the plaster from the ceilings. It is taken for granted that this calamity will happen every time there is an exceptionally heavy fall of snow. For three days there was no water in the taps because the pipes were frozen: that, too, is a normal, almost yearly, experience. And the newspapers have just announced that the number of burst pipes is so enormous that the job of repairing them will not be completed till the end of 1945—when, I suppose, there will be another big frost and they will all burst again. If our methods of making war had kept pace with our methods of keeping house, we should be just about on the verge of discovering gunpowder.

To come back to washing-up. Like sweeping, scrubbing and dusting, it is of its nature an uncreative and life-wasting job. You cannot make an art out of it as you can out of cooking or gardening. What, then, is to be done about it? Well, this whole problem of housework has three possible solutions. One is to simplify our way of living very greatly; another is to assume as our ancestors did, that life on earth is inherently miserable, and that it is entirely natural for the average woman to be a broken-down drudge at the age of thirty; and the other is to devote as much intelligence to rationalising the interiors of our houses as we have devoted to transport and communications.

I fancy we shall choose the third alternative. If one thinks simply in terms of saving trouble and plans one's home as ruthlessly as one would plan a machine, it is possible to imagine houses and flats which would be comfortable and would entail very little work. Central heating, rubbish chutes, proper consumption of smoke, cornerless rooms, electrically-warmed beds and elimination of carpets would make a lot of difference. But as for washing-up, I see no solution except to do it communally, like laundry. Every morning the municipal van will stop at your door and carry off a box of dirty crocks, handing you a box of clean ones (marked with your initial, of course) in return. This would be hardly more difficult to organise than the daily diaper service which was operating before the war. And though it would mean that some people would have to be full-time washers-up, as some people are now full-time laundry-workers, the all-over saving in labour and fuel would be enormous. The alternatives are to continue fumbling about with greasy dish mops, or to eat out of paper containers.

A sidelight on the habits of book reviewers.

Some time ago I was commissioned to write an essay for an annual scrapbook which shall be nameless. At the very last minute (and when I had

had the money, I am glad to say) the publishers decided that my essay must be suppressed.[1] By this time the book was actually in process of being bound. The essay was cut out of every copy, but for technical reasons it was impossible to remove my name from the list of contributors on the title page.

Since then I have received a number of press cuttings referring to this book. In each case I am mentioned as being "among the contributors," and not one reviewer has yet spotted that the contribution attributed to me is not actually there.

Now that "explore every avenue" and "leave no stone unturned" have been more or less laughed out of existence, I think it is time to start a campaign against some more of the worn-out and useless metaphors with which our language is littered.[2]

Three that we could well do without are "cross swords with," "ring the changes on," and "take up the cudgels for." How lifeless these and similar expressions have become you can see from the fact that in many cases people do not even remember their original meaning. What is meant by "ringing the changes," for instance? Probably it once had something to do with church bells, but one could not be sure without consulting a dictionary. "Take up the cudgels for" possibly derives from the almost obsolete game of singlestick. When an expression has moved as far from its original meaning as this, its value as a metaphor—that is, its power of providing a concrete illustration—has vanished. There is no sense whatever in writing "X took up the cudgels for Y." One should either say "X defended Y" or think of a new metaphor which genuinely makes one's meaning more vivid.

In some cases these overworked expressions have actually been severed from their original meaning by means of a mis-spelling. An example is "plain sailing" (plane sailing). And the expression "toe the line" is now coming to be spelled quite frequently "tow the line." People who are capable of this kind of thing evidently don't attach any definite meaning to the words they use.

I wonder whether people read Bret Harte nowadays. I do not know why, but for an hour past some stanzas from *The Society upon the Stanislaus* have been running in my head. It describes a meeting of an archæological society which ended in disorder:

> Then Abner Dean of Angel's raised a point of order, when
> A chunk of old red sandstone took him in the abdomen:
> And he smiled a kind of sickly smile, and curled up on the floor,
> And the subsequent proceedings interested him no more.

It has perhaps been unfortunate for Bret Harte's modern reputation that of his two funniest poems, one turns on colour prejudice and the other on class snobbery. But there are a number that are worth re-reading, including one or two serious ones: especially *Dickens in Camp*, the now almost forgotten poem which Bret Harte wrote after Dickens's death and which was about the finest tribute Dickens ever had.

On 16 February, *Tribune* published a letter from Betty Miller stoutly contradicting Orwell on the subject of washing up—especially because his remarks were those of a mere amateur. 'Of all human occupations (literature not discounted),' she wrote, 'dish-washing stands highest in my estimation as the activity most capable of pleasing the senses and gratifying the spirit of the being engaged upon it.' To rationalise our homes, as Orwell suggested, was 'a cunning method of self-sabotage.' Home life, she claimed, was a last resort of self-expression: 'let the planners beware female energy denied its natural as its practical outlet; let them beware the women thwarted by the machine; beware the housewife "liberated" by Mr. Orwell and the Handy-Gadget Association . . . the empty sink is as dangerous to the stability of national life as the empty cradle.' Mrs. Miller's argument, though seriously put forward, was presented with a light and humorous touch.

1. 'Benefit of Clergy: Some Notes on Salvador Dali' was intended for *The Saturday Book*, No. 5; see *2481, headnote*.
2. All these worn-out metaphors except 'cross swords with' and the alternative spelling 'plain/ plane' in the next paragraph but one appear on the first page of Orwell's notes for 'Politics and the English Language,' see *2816*. For 'creates a world of its own' see the penultimate paragraph of *2615*.

2617. BBC Talks on Samuel Butler

On 14 February 1945, Mrs. M. P. ('Becky') Cocking initiated a BBC talks booking form for Orwell to give two talks in the BBC Schools' Programme 'Talks for Sixth Forms.' He was booked to discuss Samuel Butler's *Erewhon* on 8 June 1945 (see *2674*) and his *The Way of All Flesh* on 15 June 1945 (see *2679*). The fee for each twenty-minute talk was £12.12s. Mrs. Cocking's letter cannot now be traced. On 16 February, Ronald Boswell, Talks Booking Manager (with whom Orwell had been associated in his BBC days), wrote, referring to Mrs. Cocking's letter and sending a formal contract. The contract was based on the assumption that Orwell would not only write the talks but also take part in them. Should he not be able to participate, Boswell said the fees could be adjusted later. See Eileen's letter to Mrs. Cocking, 25 March 1945, *2644*.

2618. To Kay Dick

15 February 1945   Typewritten

27B Canonbury Square   Islington   London N 1

Dear Kay,[1]

I am sorry I have not been able to see you, but have been snowed under with work. I am just leaving for France and expect to be away quite two months. If the proof of the Wodehouse article[2] needs correcting, could you be kind enough to send it to my wife? Her address is

> Mrs Eric Blair
> Greystone
> Carlton
> Stockton-on-Tees   Co. Durham.

If you do send it to her it might be better to send the MS with it. She has full powers to act for me if any difficulty should arise. I hope I'll see you when I get back.

> Yours
> [Signed] Geo. Orwell
> George Orwell

1. Kay Dick (1915–) wrote under the names Edward Lane (see *n. 2* below) and Jeremy Scott. Under the former, *By the Lake* (1949) and *The Uncertain Element: An Anthology of Fantastic Conceptions* (1950) were published; under the latter, *The Mandrake Root: An Anthology of Fantastic Tales* (1946).
2. 'In Defence of P. G. Wodehouse,' published in *The Windmill*, No. 2, [July] 1945; see *2624*. *The Windmill* was edited by Reginald Moore and Edward Lane (Kay Dick). Twelve numbers were published, 1944–48.

2619. To Leonard Moore

15 February 1945   Typewritten

Dear Mr Moore,
I am sending back these contracts after some delay as I have been very busy.

I have signed the one relating to Animal Farm, but not the other, and I have struck out references to the second one where they occur in the first. I have spoken to Warburg about this. I have not written any novel and do not know when I shall again, and I don't quite see what the necessity for this second contract was. But in any case I am still under contract to give Gollancz[1] first refusal of two more novels *of standard length*. When this came up before I asked you to let me know what "standard length" meant, as I was determined that my next two, when written, should be *less* than that length so that I need not submit them to Gollancz. It seems to me that the contract which I have signed sufficiently covers my dealings with Warburg.

I am just going to France for two months or more,[2] so I suppose I shall be away when Animal Farm comes out. I am sending Warburg a list of the people to send complimentary copies and special review copies to. I wonder if you could be kind enough to send my press cuttings and any other communications direct to my wife

> Mrs Eric Blair
> Greystone
> Carlton
> Stockton-on-Tees   Co. Durham.

She has full powers to make decisions for me on any question that may come up.

If the Dial people[3] or any other American publishers make an offer for the book of essays, perhaps you could deal with that for me. Warburg has the other copy. He wants me to add to it an essay to appear in the "Windmill" and not yet published. If he asks about this, would you tell him I couldn't get another copy typed and suggest that he procure a copy of the "Windmill" (it is a quarterly published by Heinemann's) when it appears. I suppose no new contract will be needed for that book, but it might be well if possible to fix with Warburg a date for its appearance—say, not later than early 1946.

Yours sincerely
Eric Blair

1. Victor Gollancz (1893–1967; Kt., 1965) had published seven of Orwell's books, including his first, between 1933 and 1940. See *132, n. 1*. He rejected *Homage to Catalonia* and *Animal Farm* on political grounds.
2. As war correspondent for *The Observer* and the *Manchester Evening News*.
3. Publishers of the literary magazine, *The Dial*, 1840–1944. Contributors in its later years included T. S. Eliot, Pablo Picasso, Ezra Pound, and William Carlos Williams.

2620. To The Royal Literary Fund

15 February 1945   Typewritten

c/o The Observer,
Tudor Street, E.C.4

Dear Sirs,
I would like to add my recommendation to Mr. Paul Potts'[1] application for a grant to enable him to be free to finish his first prose book, which Nicholson & Watson are publishing as soon as he gets it ready.

Mr. Potts is a Canadian poet, who has lived for some years in England. Before the War he published broadsheets and one pamphlet of his poems. He has been discharged from a Commando for reasons of health and has no private means whatsoever.

I hope you will look with favour on his application as judging by his first book of poems, which he will submit with his application, it is obvious that he must be considered to be someone who is trying to be a serious writer.

Yours sincerely,
Geo. Orwell

P.S. I am leaving almost immediately for Paris, but any communication in regard to this matter will reach me if addressed to the OBSERVER's London office.

1. For Paul Potts (1911–1990), see *1971, n. 1*. The British Library Catalogue does not record any prose book by Paul Potts published in Orwell's lifetime. His *Instead of a Sonnet* (8 + 45 pages) was published in 1944 by Editions Poetry as Ballad Book No. 2.

2621. To Roger Senhouse

15 February 1945   Typewritten

27B Canonbury Square   Islington   N 1

Dear Roger,
Herewith the list of people for review copies etc.[1] I hope there will be enough to manage all these.

I am leaving today and expect to be away at least two months. If any difficulty arises, would you refer it to my wife, who has full powers to act for me? Her address is

> Greystone
> Carlton
> Stockton-on-Tees   Co. Durham.

I hope Fred[2] is going on well.

Yours
George

1. Of *Animal Farm*.
2. Fredric Warburg, of Secker & Warburg, was then ill.

2622. War Correspondent for *The Observer* and the Manchester Evening News

15 February–24 May 1945

On 15 February, Orwell went to Paris to begin three months' service as war correspondent for *The Observer* and the *Manchester Evening News*. He stayed, as did many journalists, at the Hotel Scribe.

The *Manchester Evening News* for 22 February announced at the foot of the feature 'Life, People and Books,' that their critic, Mr. George Orwell, had 'gone to France, and during the next few weeks he will write about the life, people and occasionally about the literature which he knows so well. During his absence Mr. Orwell's Thursday feature will be written by the well known critic Mr. Daniel George'; see *2561, n. 2*. Orwell's first contribution from Paris to the *Manchester Evening News* appeared on 28 February. His first contribution for the *The Observer* was published on 25 February (see XX, Appendix 15)

Tribune announced on 23 February, 'George Orwell has gone to France where he will stay for approximately two months.' 'As I Please' was taken over by Jennie Lee. It was not until 8 November 1946 that Orwell again contributed this column.

Jennie Lee (1904–1988; Baroness Lee of Ashridge, 1970), a miner's daughter from Fife, Scotland, was brought up under the influence of the ILP (particularly as a result of her friendship with James Maxton), but she broke from the party in 1942 over its stand on pacifism. A lawyer, she was elected to Parliament in 1929 and served until 1931 and also in 1945–70. She married Aneurin Bevan in 1934, and later was the first Minister for the Arts.

2623. 'As I Please,' 59

Tribune, 16 February 1945

Last week I received a copy of a statement on the future of Burma, issued by the Burma Association, an organisation which includes most of the Burmese resident in this country. How representative this organisation is I am not certain, but probably it voices the wishes of a majority of politically-conscious Burmese. For reasons I shall try to make clear presently, the statement just issued is an important document. Summarised as shortly as possible, it makes the following demands:—

(i) An amnesty for Burmese who have collaborated with the Japs during the occupation. (ii) Statement by the British Government of a definite date at which Burma shall attain Dominion status. The period, if possible, to be less than six years. The Burmese people to summon a Constituent Assembly in the meantime. (iii) No interim of "direct rule." (iv) The Burmese people to have a greater share in the economic development of their own country. (v) The British Government to make an immediate unequivocal statement of its intentions towards Burma.

The striking thing about these demands is how moderate they are. No political party with any tinge of nationalism, or any hope of getting a mass following, could possibly ask for less. But why do these people pitch their claims so low? Well, I think one can guess at two reasons. To begin with, the experience of Japanese occupation has probably made Dominion status seem a more tempting goal than it seemed three years ago. But—much more important—if they demand so little it is probably because they expect to be offered even less. And I should guess that they expect right. Indeed, of the very modest suggestions listed above, only the first is likely to be carried out.

The Government has never made any clear statement about the future of Burma, but there have been persistent rumours that when the Japs are driven out there is to be a return to "direct rule," which is a polite name for military dictatorship. And what is happening, politically, in Burma at this moment? We simply don't know: nowhere have I seen in any newspaper one word about the way in which the reconquered territories are being administered. To grasp the significance of this one has to look at the map of Burma. A year ago Burma proper was in Japanese hands and the Allies were fighting in wild territories thinly populated by rather primitive tribes who have never been much interfered with and are traditionally pro-British. Now they are penetrating into the heart of Burma, and some fairly important towns, centres of administration, have fallen into their hands. Several million Burmese must be once again under the British flag. Yet we are told nothing whatever about the form of administration that is being set up. Is it surprising if every thinking Burmese fears the worst?

It is vitally important to interest the British public in this matter, if possible. Our eyes are fixed on Europe, we forget that at the other end of the world there is a whole string of countries awaiting liberation and in nearly every case hoping for something better than a mere change of conquerors. Burma will probably be the first British territory to be reconquered, and it will be a test case: a more important test than Greece or Belgium, not only because more people are involved, but because it will be almost wholly a British responsibility. It will be a fearful disaster if through apathy and ignorance we let Churchill, Amery[1] and Co. put across some reactionary settlement which will lose us the friendship of the Burmese people for good.

For a year or two after the Japanese have gone, Burma will be in a receptive mood and more pro-British than it has been for a dozen years past. Then is the moment to make a generous gesture. I don't know whether Dominion status is the best possible solution. But if the politically conscious section of the Burmese ask for Dominion status, it would be monstrous to let the Tories refuse it in a hopeless effort to bring back the past. And there must be a date attached to it, a not too distant date. Whether these people remain inside the British Commonwealth or outside it, what matters in the long run is that we should have their friendship—and we *can* have it if we do not play them false at the moment of crisis. When the moment comes for Burma's future to be settled, thinking Burmese will not turn their eyes towards Churchill. They will be looking at *us*, the Labour movement, to see whether our talk about democracy, self-determination, racial equality and what-not has any truth in it. I do not know whether it will be in our power to force a decent settlement upon the Government; but I do know that we shall harm ourselves irreparably if we do not make at least as much row about it as we did in the case of Greece.

When asked, "Which is the wisest of the animals?" a Japanese sage replied, "The one that man has not yet discovered."

I have just seen in a book the statement that the grey seals, the kind that are found round the coasts of Britain, number only ten thousand. Presumably there are so few of them because they have been killed off, like many another over-trustful animal. Seals are quite tame, and appear to be very inquisitive. They will follow a boat for miles, and sometimes they will even follow you when you are walking round the shore. There is no good reason for killing them. Their coats are no use for fur, and except for eating a certain amount of fish they do no harm.

They breed mostly on uninhabited islands. Let us hope that some of the islands remain uninhabited, so that these unfortunate brutes may escape being exterminated entirely. However, we are not quite such persistent slaughterers of rare animals as we used to be. Two species of birds, the bittern and the spoonbill, extinct for many years, have recently succeeded in re-establishing themselves in Britain. They have even been encouraged to breed in some places. Thirty years ago, any bittern that dared to show its beak in this country would have been shot and stuffed immediately.

The Gestapo is said to have teams of literary critics whose job is to determine, by means of stylistic comparison, the authorship of anonymous pamphlets. I have always thought that, if only it were in a better cause, this is exactly the job I would like to have.

To any of our readers whose tastes lie in the same direction, I present this problem: Who is now writing "Beachcomber's" column in the *Daily*

Express? It is certainly not Mr. J. B. Morton, who was "Beachcomber" until recently. I have heard that it is Mr. Osbert Lancaster, the cartoonist, but that was merely a piece of gossip, and I have not made any careful examination.[2] But I would bet five shillings that the present "Beachcomber," unlike Mr. Morton, is not a Catholic.

1. L. S. (Leo) Amery (1875–1955), Conservative Party politician, was particularly associated in office with British colonies and dominions: Colonial Secretary, 1924–29; Dominions Secretary, 1925–29; Secretary of State for India and for Burma, 1940–45. He had supported Italy in its attack on Abyssinia, 1935, and denounced the League of Nations. After the failure of the Norwegian campaign in 1940, he was among those who opposed Chamberlain, concluding a speech against him with Cromwell's words addressed to the Rump of the Long Parliament in April 1653: 'Depart, I say, and let us have done with you. In the name of God, go!'
2. Richard Boston's *Picture of Osbert Lancaster* (1989) does not have an index entry for Beachcomber and there seems to be no reference in the text. Boston records that Lancaster returned to England in 1946 after spending eighteen months in Greece, so it is unlikely that the gossip Orwell had heard was correct.

2624. 'In Defence of P. G. Wodehouse'

Recorded in Payments Book 20 February 1945
The Windmill, No. 2, [July] 1945

Orwell records in his Payments Book the date this essay was completed, 20 February 1945, and that his fee was £10.00. This entry and that for 26 February ('Anti-Semitism in Britain,' for *Contemporary Jewish Record*; see *2626*) are entered in reverse chronological order. Orwell went to France on 15 February and made no entries in his Payments Book for March, April, and the first half of May 1945. It is probable, especially as the ink is like that for the May entries, that these entries were made in May after Orwell resumed his practice of entering payments. Since the essay was not printed for several months, it is placed here when it was recorded in Orwell's Payments Book, which is about the time Orwell met Wodehouse in Paris. The essay was reprinted in *Critical Essays* (1946) and *Dickens, Dali & Others* (1946). The text reproduced here is from *CrE*, which (with *DD*) has a few sentences not included in *The Windmill*. The notes indicate substantive changes, and the one variant in *DD*.

When the Germans made their rapid advance through Belgium in the early summer of 1940, they captured, among other things,[1] Mr. P. G. Wodehouse,[2] who had been living throughout the early part of the war in his villa at Le Touquet, and seems not to have realised until the last moment that he was in any danger. As he was led away into captivity, he is said to have remarked, "Perhaps after this I shall write a serious book." He was placed for the time being under house arrest, and from his subsequent statements it appears that he was treated in a fairly friendly way, German officers in the neighbourhood frequently "dropping in for a bath or a party".[3]

Over a year later, on 25th June 1941, the news came that Wodehouse had been released from internment and was living at the Adlon Hotel in Berlin. On the following day the public was astonished to learn that he had agreed to

51

do some broadcasts of a "non-political" nature over the German radio. The full texts of these broadcasts are not easy to obtain at this date, but Wodehouse seems to have done five of them between 26th June and 2nd July,[4] when the Germans took him off the air again. The first broadcast, on 26th June, was not made on the Nazi radio but took the form of an interview with Harry Flannery, the representative of the Columbia Broadcasting System, which still had its correspondents in Berlin. Wodehouse also published in the *Saturday Evening Post* an article which he had written while still in the internment camp.

The article and the broadcasts dealt mainly with Wodehouse's experiences in internment, but they did include a very few comments on the war. The following are fair samples:

"I never was interested in politics. I'm quite unable to work up any kind of belligerent feeling. Just as I'm about to feel belligerent about some country I meet a decent sort of chap. We go out together and lose any fighting thoughts or feelings."

"A short time ago they had a look at me on parade and got the right idea; at least they sent us to the local lunatic asylum. And I have been there forty-two weeks. There is a good deal to be said for internment. It keeps you out of the saloon and helps you to keep up with your reading. The chief trouble is that it means you are away from home for a long time. When I join my wife I had better take along a letter of introduction to be on the safe side."

"In the days before the war I had always been modestly proud of being an Englishman, but now that I have been some months resident in this bin or repository of Englishmen I am not so sure. . . . The only concession I want from Germany is that she gives me a loaf of bread, tells the gentlemen with muskets at the main gate to look the other way, and leaves the rest to me. In return I am prepared to hand over India, an autographed set of my books, and to reveal the secret process of cooking sliced potatoes on a radiator. This offer holds good till Wednesday week."

The first extract quoted above caused great offence. Wodehouse was also censured for using (in the interview with Flannery) the phrase "whether Britain wins the war or not", and he did not make things better by describing in another broadcast the filthy habits of some Belgian prisoners among whom he was interned. The Germans recorded this broadcast and repeated it a number of times. They seem to have supervised his talks very lightly, and they allowed him not only to be funny about the discomforts of internment but to remark that "the internees at Trost camp all fervently believe that Britain will eventually win". The general upshot of the talks, however, was that he had not been ill treated and bore no malice.

These broadcasts caused an immediate uproar in England. There were questions in Parliament, angry editorial comments in the press, and a stream of letters from fellow-authors, nearly all of them disapproving, though one or two suggested that it would be better to suspend judgment, and several pleaded that Wodehouse probably did not realise what he was doing. On 15th

July, the Home Service of the B.B.C. carried an extremely violent Postscript by "Cassandra" of the *Daily Mirror*, accusing Wodehouse of "selling his country". This postscript made free use of such expressions as "Quisling" and "worshipping the Führer".[5] The main charge was that Wodehouse had agreed to do German propaganda as a way of buying himself out of the internment camp.

"Cassandra's" Postscript caused a certain amount of protest, but on the whole it seems to have intensified popular feeling against Wodehouse. One result of it was that numerous lending libraries withdrew Wodehouse's books from circulation. Here is a typical news item:

"Within twenty-four hours of listening to the broadcast of Cassandra, the *Daily Mirror* columnist, Portadown (North Ireland) Urban District Council banned P. G. Wodehouse's books from their public library. Mr. Edward McCann said that Cassandra's broadcast had clinched the matter. Wodehouse was funny no longer." (*Daily Mirror*.)

In addition the B.B.C. banned Wodehouse's lyrics from the air and was still doing so a couple of years later. As late as December 1944 there were demands in Parliament that Wodehouse should be put on trial as a traitor.[6]

There is an old saying that if you throw enough mud some of it will stick, and the mud has stuck to Wodehouse in a rather peculiar way. An impression has been left behind that Wodehouse's talks (not that anyone remembers what he said in them) showed him up not merely as a traitor but as an ideological sympathiser with Fascism. Even at the time several letters to the press claimed that "Fascist tendencies" could be detected in his books, and the charge has been repeated since. I shall try to analyse the mental atmosphere of those books in a moment, but it is important to realise that the events of 1941 do not convict Wodehouse of anything worse than stupidity. The really interesting question is how and why he could be so stupid. When Flannery met Wodehouse (released, but still under guard) at the Adlon Hotel in June 1941, he saw at once that he was dealing with a political innocent, and when preparing him for their broadcast interview he had to warn him against making some exceedingly unfortunate remarks, one of which was by implication slightly anti-Russian. As it was, the phrase "whether England wins or not" did get through.[7] Soon after the interview Wodehouse told him that he was also going to broadcast on the Nazi radio, apparently not realising that this action had any special significance. Flannery comments:*

"By this time the Wodehouse plot was evident. It was one of the best Nazi publicity stunts of the war, the first with a human angle. . . . Plack (Goebbels's assistant) had gone to the camp near Gleiwitz to see Wodehouse, found that the author was completely without political sense, and had an idea. He suggested to Wodehouse that in return for being released from the prison camp he write a series of broadcasts about his experiences; there would be no censorship and he would put them on the air himself. In making that proposal Plack showed that he knew his man.

* *Assignment to Berlin*, by Harry W. Flannery. (Michael Joseph, 1942) [Orwell's footnote].

He knew that Wodehouse made fun of the English in all his stories and that he seldom wrote in any other way, that he was still living in the period about which he wrote and had no conception of Nazism and all it meant. Wodehouse was his own Bertie Wooster."

The striking of an actual bargain between Wodehouse and Plack seems to be merely Flannery's own interpretation. The arrangement may have been of a much less definite kind, and to judge from the broadcasts themselves, Wodehouse's main idea in making them was to keep in touch with his public and—the comedian's ruling passion—to get a laugh. Obviously they are not the utterances of a Quisling of the type of Ezra Pound or John Amery,[8] nor, probably, of a person capable of understanding the nature of Quislingism. Flannery seems to have warned Wodehouse that it would be unwise to broadcast, but not very forcibly. He adds that Wodehouse (though in one broadcast he refers to himself as an Englishman) seemed to regard himself as an American citizen. He had contemplated naturalisation, but had never filled in the necessary papers. He even used, to Flannery, the phrase, "We're not at war with Germany".

I have before me a bibliography of P. G. Wodehouse's works. It names round about fifty books, but is certainly incomplete. It is as well to be honest, and I ought to start by admitting that there are many books by Wodehouse—perhaps a quarter or a third of the total—which I have not read. It is not, indeed, easy to read the whole output of a popular writer who is normally published in cheap editions. But I have followed his work fairly closely since 1911, when I was eight years old, and am well acquainted with its peculiar mental atmosphere—an atmosphere which has not, of course, remained completely unchanged, but shows little alteration since about 1925. In the passage from Flannery's book which I quoted above there are two remarks which would immediately strike any attentive reader of Wodehouse. One is to the effect that Wodehouse "was still living in the period about which he wrote", and the other that the Nazi Propaganda Ministry made use of him because he "made fun of the English". The second statement is based on a misconception to which I will return presently. But Flannery's other comment is quite true and contains in it part of the clue to Wodehouse's behaviour.

A thing that people often forget about P. G. Wodehouse's novels is how long ago the better-known of them were written. We think of him as in some sense typifying the silliness of the nineteen-twenties and nineteen-thirties, but in fact the scenes and characters by which he is best remembered had all made their appearance before 1925. Psmith first appeared in 1909, having been foreshadowed by other characters in earlier school-stories. Blandings Castle, with Baxter and the Earl of Emsworth both in residence, was introduced in 1915. The Jeeves-Wooster cycle began in 1919, both Jeeves and Wooster having made brief appearances earlier. Ukridge appeared in 1924. When one looks through the list of Wodehouse's books from 1902 onwards, one can observe three fairly well-marked periods. The first is the school-story period. It includes such books as *The Gold Bat*, *The Pothunters*, etc., and has its high-spot in *Mike* (1909). *Psmith in the City*, published in the following year, belongs in this category, though it is not directly concerned with school life. The next is the American period. Wodehouse seems to have lived in the United States from about 1913 to 1920, and for a while showed signs of becoming Americanised in idiom and outlook. Some of the stories in *The Man with Two Left Feet* (1917) appear to have been influenced by O. Henry, and other books written about this time contain Americanisms (*e.g.* "highball" for "whisky and soda") which an Englishman would not normally use *in propria persona*. Nevertheless, almost all the books of this period—*Psmith, Journalist*; *The Little Nugget*; *The Indiscretions of Archie*; *Piccadilly Jim* and various others—depend for their effect on the *contrast* between English and American manners. English characters appear in an American setting, or *vice versa*: there is a certain number of purely English stories, but hardly any purely American ones. The third period might fitly be called the country-house period. By the early nineteen-twenties Wodehouse must have been making a very large income, and the social status of his characters moved upwards accordingly, though the Ukridge stories form a partial exception. The typical setting is now a country mansion, a luxurious bachelor flat or an expensive golf club. The schoolboy athleticism of the earlier books fades out, cricket and football giving way to golf, and the element of farce and burlesque becomes more marked. No doubt many of the later books, such as *Summer Lightning*, are light comedy rather than pure farce, but the occasional attempts at moral earnestness which can be found in *Psmith, Journalist*; *The Little Nugget*; *The Coming of Bill*; *The Man with Two Left Feet* and some of the school stories, no longer appear. Mike Jackson has turned into Bertie Wooster. That, however, is not a very startling metamorphosis, and one of the most noticeable things about Wodehouse is his *lack* of development. Books like *The Gold Bat* and *Tales of St. Austin's*, written in the opening years of this century, already have the familiar atmosphere. How much of a formula the writing of his later books had become one can see from the fact that he continued to write stories of English life although throughout the sixteen years before his internment he was living at Hollywood and Le Touquet.

Mike, which is now a difficult book to obtain in an unabridged form, must be one of the best "light" school stories in English. But though its incidents are largely farcical, it is by no means a satire on the public-school system, and *The Gold Bat*, *The Pothunters*, etc., are even less so. Wodehouse was educated at Dulwich, and then worked in a bank and graduated into novel-writing by way of very cheap journalism. It is clear that for many years he remained "fixated" on his old school and loathed the unromantic job and the lower-middle-class surroundings in which he found himself. In the early stories the "glamour" of public-school life (house matches, fagging, teas round the study fire, etc.) is laid on fairly thick, and the "play the game" code of morals is accepted with not many reservations. Wrykyn, Wodehouse's imaginary public school, is a school of a more fashionable type than Dulwich, and one gets the impression that between *The Gold Bat* (1904) and *Mike* (1909) Wrykyn itself has become more expensive and moved farther[9] from London.

Psychologically the most revealing book of Wodehouse's early period is *Psmith in the City*. Mike Jackson's father has suddenly lost his money, and Mike, like Wodehouse himself, is thrust at the age of about eighteen into an ill-paid subordinate job in a bank. Psmith is similarly employed, though not from financial necessity. Both this book and *Psmith, Journalist* (1915) are unusual in that they display a certain amount of political consciousness. Psmith at this stage chooses to call himself a Socialist—in his mind, and no doubt in Wodehouse's, this means no more than ignoring class distinctions—and on one occasion the two boys attend an open-air meeting on Clapham Common and go home to tea with an elderly Socialist orator, whose shabby-genteel home is described with some accuracy. But the most striking feature of the book is Mike's inability to wean himself from the atmosphere of school. He enters upon his job without any pretence of enthusiasm, and his main desire is not, as one might expect, to find a more interesting and useful job, but simply to be playing cricket. When he has to find himself lodgings he chooses to settle at Dulwich, because there he will be near a school and will be able to hear the agreeable sound of the ball striking against the bat. The climax of the book comes when Mike gets the chance to play in a county match and simply walks out of his job in order to do so. The point is that Wodehouse here sympathises with Mike: indeed he identifies himself with him, for it is clear enough that Mike bears the same relation to Wodehouse as Julien Sorel to Stendhal. But he created many other heroes essentially similar. Through the books of this and the next period there passes a whole series of young men to whom playing games and "keeping fit" are a sufficient life-work. Wodehouse is almost incapable of imagining a desirable job. The great thing is to have money of your own, or, failing that, to find a sinecure. The hero of *Something Fresh* (1915) escapes from low-class journalism by becoming physical-training instructor to a dyspeptic millionaire: this is regarded as a step up, morally as well as financially.[10]

In the books of the third period there is no narcissism and no serious interludes, but the implied moral and social background has changed much less than might appear at first sight. If one compares Bertie Wooster with Mike, or even with the rugger-playing prefects of the earliest school stories, one sees that the only real difference between them is that Bertie is richer and lazier. His ideals would be almost the same as theirs, but he fails to live up to them. Archie Moffam, in *The Indiscretions of Archie* (1921), is a type intermediate between Bertie and the earlier heroes: he is an ass, but he is also honest, kind-hearted, athletic and courageous. From first to last Wodehouse takes the public-school code of behaviour for granted, with the difference that in his later, more sophisticated period he prefers to show his characters violating it or living up to it against their will:

"Bertie! You wouldn't let down a pal?"

"Yes, I would."

"But we were at school together, Bertie."

"I don't care."

"The old school, Bertie, the old school!"

"Oh, well—dash it!"

Bertie, a sluggish Don Quixote, has no wish to tilt at windmills, but he would hardly think of refusing to do so when honour calls. Most of the people whom Wodehouse intends as sympathetic characters are parasites, and some of them are plain imbeciles, but very few of them could be described as immoral. Even Ukridge is a visionary rather than a plain crook. The most immoral, or rather un-moral, of Wodehouse's characters is Jeeves, who acts as a foil to Bertie Wooster's comparative high-mindedness and perhaps symbolises the widespread English belief that intelligence and unscrupulousness are much the same thing. How closely Wodehouse sticks to conventional morality can be seen from the fact that nowhere in his books is there anything in the nature of a sex joke. This is an enormous sacrifice for a farcical writer to make. Not only are there no dirty jokes, but there are hardly any compromising situations: the horns-on-the-forehead motif is almost completely avoided. Most of the full-length books, of course, contain a "love interest", but it is always at the light-comedy level: the love affair, with its complications and its idyllic scenes, goes on and on, but, as the saying goes, "nothing happens". It is significant that Wodehouse, by nature a writer of farces, was able to collaborate more than once with Ian Hay,[11] a serio-comic writer and an exponent (vide *Pip*, etc.) of the "clean-living Englishman" tradition at its silliest.

In *Something Fresh* Wodehouse had discovered the comic possibilities of the English aristocracy, and a succession of ridiculous but, save in a very few instances, not actually contemptible barons, earls and what-not followed accordingly. This had the rather curious effect of causing Wodehouse to be regarded, outside England, as a penetrating satirist of English society. Hence Flannery's statement that Wodehouse "made fun of the English", which is the impression he would probably make on a German or even an American reader. Some time after the broadcasts from Berlin I was discussing them with a young Indian Nationalist who defended Wodehouse warmly. He took it for granted that Wodehouse *had* gone over to the enemy, which from his own point of view was the right thing to do. But what interested me was to find that he regarded Wodehouse as an anti-British writer who had done useful work by showing up the British aristocracy in their true colours. This is a mistake that it would be very difficult for an English person to make, and is a good instance of the way in which books, especially humorous books, lose their finer nuances when they reach a foreign audience. For it is clear enough that Wodehouse is *not* anti-British, and not anti-upper class either. On the contrary, a harmless old-fashioned snobbishness is perceptible all through his work. Just as an intelligent Catholic is able to see that the blasphemies of Baudelaire or James Joyce are not seriously damaging to the Catholic faith, so an English reader can see that in creating such characters as Hildebrand Spencer Poyns de Burgh John Hanneyside Coombe-Crombie, 12th Earl of Dreever, Wodehouse is not really attacking the social hierarchy. Indeed, no one who genuinely despised titles would write of them so much. Wodehouse's attitude towards the English social system is the same as his attitude towards the public-school moral code—a mild facetiousness covering an unthinking acceptance. The Earl of Emsworth is funny because an earl ought to have more dignity, and Bertie Wooster's helpless dependence on Jeeves is funny partly because the servant ought not to be superior to the master. An American reader can mistake these two, and others like them, for hostile caricatures, because he is inclined to be Anglophobe already and they correspond to his preconceived ideas about a decadent aristocracy. Bertie Wooster, with his spats and his cane, is the traditional stage Englishman. But, as any English reader would see, Wodehouse intends him as a sympathetic figure, and Wodehouse's real sin has been to present the English upper classes as much nicer people than they are. All through his books certain problems are consistently[12] avoided. Almost without exception his moneyed young men are unassuming, good mixers, not avaricious: their tone is set for them by Psmith, who retains his own upper-class exterior but bridges the social gap by addressing everyone as "Comrade".

But there is another important point about Bertie Wooster: his out-of-dateness. Conceived in 1917 or thereabouts, Bertie really belongs to an epoch earlier than that. He is the "knut" of the pre-1914 period, celebrated in such songs as "Gilbert the Filbert" or "Reckless Reggie of the Regent's Palace". The kind of life that Wodehouse writes about by preference, the life of the "clubman" or "man about town", the elegant young man who lounges all the morning in Piccadilly with a cane under his arm and a carnation in his buttonhole, barely survived into the nineteen-twenties. It is significant that Wodehouse could publish in 1936 a book entitled *Young Men in Spats*. For who was wearing spats at that date? They had gone out of fashion quite ten years earlier. But the traditional "knut", the "Piccadilly Johnny", *ought* to wear spats, just as the pantomime Chinese ought to wear a pigtail. A humorous writer is not obliged to keep up to date, and having struck one or two good veins, Wodehouse continued to exploit them with a regularity that was no doubt all the easier because he did not set foot in England during the sixteen years that preceded his internment. His picture of English society had been formed before 1914, and it was a naïve, traditional and, at bottom, admiring picture. Nor did he ever become genuinely Americanised. As I have pointed out, spontaneous Americanisms do occur in the books of the middle period, but Wodehouse remained English enough to find American slang an amusing and slightly shocking novelty. He loves to thrust a slang phrase or a crude fact in among Wardour Street English ("With a hollow groan Ukridge borrowed five shillings from me and went out into the night"), and expressions like "a piece of cheese" or "bust him on the noggin" lend themselves to this purpose. But the trick had been developed before he made any American contacts, and his use of garbled quotations is a common device of English writers running back to Fielding. As Mr. John Hayward has pointed out,* Wodehouse owes a good deal to his knowledge of English literature and especially of Shakespeare. His books are aimed, not, obviously, at a highbrow audience, but at an audience educated along traditional lines. When, for instance, he describes somebody as heaving "the kind of sigh that

---

* *P. G. Wodehouse*, by John Hayward. (*The Saturday Book*, 1942.) I believe this is the only full-length critical essay on Wodehouse [Orwell's footnote].

Prometheus might have heaved when the vulture dropped in for its lunch", he is assuming that his readers will know something of Greek mythology. In his early days the writers he admired were probably Barry Pain, Jerome K. Jerome, W. W. Jacobs, Kipling and F. Anstey, and he has remained closer to them than to the quick-moving American comic writers such as Ring Lardner or Damon Runyon. In his radio interview with Flannery, Wodehouse wondered whether "the kind of people and the kind of England I write about will live after the war", not realising that they were ghosts already. "He was still living in the period about which he wrote," says Flannery, meaning, probably, the nineteen-twenties. But the period was really the Edwardian age, and Bertie Wooster, if he ever existed, was killed round about 1915.

If my analysis of Wodehouse's mentality is accepted, the idea that in 1941 he consciously aided the Nazi propaganda machine becomes untenable and even ridiculous. He *may* have been induced to broadcast by the promise of an earlier release (he was due for release a few months later, on reaching his sixtieth birthday), but he cannot have realised that what he did would be damaging to British interests. As I have tried to show, his moral outlook has remained that of a public-school boy, and according to the public-school code, treachery in time of war is the most unforgivable of all the sins. But how could he fail to grasp that what he did would be a big propaganda score for the Germans and would bring down a torrent of disapproval on his own head? To answer this one must take two things into consideration. First, Wodehouse's complete lack—so far as one can judge from his printed works—of political awareness. It is nonsense to talk of "Fascist tendencies" in his books. There are no post-1918 tendencies at all. Throughout his work there is a certain uneasy awareness of the problem of class distinctions, and scattered through it at various dates there are ignorant though not unfriendly references to Socialism. In *The Heart of a Goof* (1926) there is a rather silly story about a Russian novelist, which seems to have been inspired by the factional struggle then raging in the U.S.S.R. But the references in it to the Soviet system are entirely frivolous and, considering the date, not markedly hostile. That is about the extent of Wodehouse's political consciousness, so far as it is discoverable from his writings. Nowhere, so far as I know, does he so much as use the word "Fascism" or "Nazism". In left-wing circles, indeed in "enlightened" circles of any kind, to broadcast on the Nazi radio, to have any truck with the Nazis whatever, would have seemed just as shocking an action before the war as during it. But that is a habit of mind that had been developed during nearly a decade of ideological struggle against Fascism. The bulk of the British people, one ought to remember, remained anæsthetic to that struggle until late into 1940. Abyssinia, Spain, China, Austria, Czechoslovakia—the long series of crimes and aggressions had simply slid past their consciousness or were dimly noted as quarrels occurring among foreigners and "not our business". One can gauge the general ignorance from the fact that the ordinary Englishman thought of "Fascism" as an exclusively Italian thing and was bewildered when the same word was applied to Germany. And there is nothing in Wodehouse's writings to suggest that he was better informed, or more interested in politics, than the general run of his readers.

The other thing one must remember is that Wodehouse happened to be taken prisoner at just the moment when the war reached its desperate phase. We forget these things now, but until that time feelings about the war had been noticeably tepid. There was hardly any fighting, the Chamberlain government was unpopular, eminent publicists like Lloyd George and Bernard Shaw[13] were hinting that we should make a compromise peace as quickly as possible, trade union and Labour Party branches all over the country were passing anti-war resolutions.[14] Afterwards, of course, things changed. The Army was with difficulty extricated from Dunkirk, France collapsed, Britain was alone, the bombs rained on London, Goebbels announced that Britain was to be "reduced to degradation and poverty". By the middle of 1941 the British people knew what they were up against and feelings against the enemy were far fiercer than before. But Wodehouse had spent the intervening year in internment, and his captors seem to have treated him reasonably well. He had missed the turning-point of the war, and in 1941 he was still reacting in terms of 1939. He was not alone in this. On several occasions about this time the Germans brought captured British soldiers to the microphone, and some of them made remarks at least as tactless as Wodehouse's. They attracted no attention, however. And even an outright Quisling like John Amery was afterwards to arouse much less indignation than Wodehouse had done.[15]

But why? Why should a few rather silly but harmless remarks by an elderly novelist have provoked such an outcry? One has to look for the probable answer amid the dirty requirements of propaganda warfare.

There is one point about the Wodehouse broadcasts that is almost certainly significant—the date. Wodehouse was released two or three days before the invasion of the U.S.S.R., and at a time when the higher ranks of the Nazi party must have known that the invasion was imminent. It was vitally necessary to keep America out of the war as long as possible, and in fact, about this time, the German attitude towards the U.S.A. did become more conciliatory than it had been before. The Germans could hardly hope to defeat Russia, Britain and the U.S.A. in combination, but if they could polish off Russia quickly—and presumably they expected to do so—the Americans might never intervene. The release of Wodehouse was only a minor move, but it was not a bad sop to throw to the American isolationists. He was well known in the United States, and he was—or so the Germans calculated—popular with the Anglophobe public as a caricaturist who made fun of the silly-ass Englishman with his spats and his monocle. At the microphone he could be trusted to damage British prestige in one way or another, while his release would demonstrate that the Germans were good fellows and knew how to treat their enemies chivalrously. That presumably was the calculation, though the fact that Wodehouse was only broadcasting for about a week suggests that he did not come up to expectations.

But on the British side similar though opposite calculations were at work. For the two years following Dunkirk, British morale depended largely upon the feeling that this was not only a war for democracy but a war which the common people had to win by their own efforts. The upper classes were discredited by their appeasement policy and by the disasters of 1940, and a social levelling process appeared to be taking place. Patriotism and left-wing sentiments were associated in the popular mind, and numerous able journalists were at work to tie the association tighter. Priestley's 1940 broadcasts, and "Cassandra's" articles in the *Daily Mirror*, were good examples of the demagogic propaganda flourishing at that time.[16] In this atmosphere, Wodehouse made an ideal whipping-boy. For it was generally felt that the rich were treacherous, and Wodehouse—as "Cassandra" vigorously pointed out in his broadcast—was a rich man. But he was the kind of rich man who could be attacked with impunity and without risking any damage to the structure of society. To denounce Wodehouse was not like denouncing, say, Beaverbrook. A mere novelist, however large his earnings may happen to be, is not *of* the possessing class. Even if his income touches £50,000 a year he has only the outward semblance of a millionaire. He is a lucky outsider who has fluked into a fortune—usually a very temporary fortune—like the winner of the Calcutta Derby Sweep. Consequently, Wodehouse's indiscretion gave a good propaganda opening. It was a chance to "expose" a wealthy parasite without drawing attention to any of the parasites who really mattered.

In the desperate circumstances of the time, it was excusable to be angry at what Wodehouse did, but to go on denouncing him three or four years later—and more, to let an impression remain that he acted with conscious treachery—is not excusable.[17] Few things in this war have been more morally disgusting than the present hunt after traitors and Quislings. At best it is largely the punishment of the guilty by the guilty. In France, all kinds of petty rats—police officials, penny-a-lining journalists, women who have slept with German soldiers—are hunted down while almost without exception the big rats escape. In England the fiercest tirades against Quislings are uttered by Conservatives who were practising appeasement in 1938 and Communists who were advocating it in 1940. I have striven to show how the wretched Wodehouse—just because success and expatriation had allowed him to remain mentally in the Edwardian age—became the *corpus vile* in a propaganda experiment, and I suggest that it is now time to regard the incident as closed. If Ezra Pound is caught and shot by the American authorities, it will have the effect of establishing his reputation as a poet for hundreds of years; and even in the case of Wodehouse, if we drive him to retire to the United States and renounce his British citizenship, we shall end by being horribly ashamed of ourselves. Meanwhile, if we really want to punish the people who weakened national morale at critical moments, there are other culprits who are nearer home and better worth chasing.[18]

1. they captured . . . things,] one of their captures was *W*
2. P. G. Wodehouse (1881–1975), author, dramatist, and lyricist. Although best remembered for his outstanding series of humorous novels (of which those featuring Jeeves are probably the best examples of his fantasy, language, wit, and story construction), he also had considerable success in the theatre on both sides of the Atlantic, collaborating with, among

others, Jerome Kern and Ira and George Gershwin, and wrote scripts for some two dozen films. Oxford University awarded him a D. Litt. in 1939. A year later, when France was overrun by the Germans, he was interned. In the summer of 1941 he gave an interview in Berlin for the CBS network to be broadcast to the United States (then neutral), and recorded five talks which were broadcast to the United States and to Britain (see *n. 4* below). He was immediately vilified in Britain as a traitor. As Iain Sproat explains in *Wodehouse at War* (1981), the campaign was led by the Ministry of Information under Duff Cooper against the advice of the Governors of the BBC. Duff Cooper overruled them and insisted that a vitriolic attack be broadcast by the popular journalist William Connor, 'Cassandra' of the *Daily Mirror* (105). It is now remarkable that the *content* of these broadcasts should have caused such anger, though, given the circumstances in which Britain was then placed, it is not surprising that Wodehouse's motives were suspect. A full analysis, with the MI5 (secret service) report of 28 September 1944, which 'found no acceptable evidence of Wodehouse's guilt,' is given in *Wodehouse at War* (12). When Orwell wrote his essay, he did not have access to the MI5 report. The texts of the broadcasts were published by *Encounter*, reprinted in *Performing Flea: A Self-Portrait in Letters* (Penguin Books, 1961), which also includes details of his time as an internee, ironically titled, 'Wodehouse in Wonderland,' and by Sproat. After the war Wodehouse lived in virtual self-exile in the United States, but his work remained very popular, even during the war (Sproat, 28). In 1975, six weeks before he died, he was knighted. For Wodehouse's immediate and later reactions to Orwell's defence, see *2625*.

3. Wodehouse denied this; see Sproat, 42–43.

4. The BBC provided Major E. J. P. Cussen, the MI5 officer who interrogated Wodehouse, with the details known to them of the broadcasts. The interview with Flannery was broadcast to the United States from Berlin on 27 June 1941, and it was in June that Wodehouse recorded his five talks. The first was broadcast to America on 28 June, repeated to the Far East on 1 July and again to America the next day. Talks two to five were broadcast from 9 July to 6 August 1941. The five talks were broadcast to Britain from 9 to 14 August 1941 (Sproat, 160). Orwell's uncertainty here is indicative of the general lack of knowledge of precisely what had happened.

5. This postscript . . . the Führer''.] *not in W*

6. In addition . . . trial as a traitor] *not in W*

7. In an interview with a British journalist, Hubert Cole (*Illustrated*, 7 December 1946), Wodehouse maintained that this statement, which appeared in his interview, was written by Flannery: 'He wrote the whole script, including the words you mention, and I read them without realising their intention. I did not even notice them at the time' (Sproat, 58).

8. John Amery (1912–1945), right-wing politician and son of Leo Amery, who was a Conservative and patriotic M.P. and Secretary of State for India 1940–45. John Amery, an ardent admirer of Hitler, broadcast from Germany during the war urging British subjects in captivity to fight for Germany against England and Russia, and made public speeches throughout occupied Europe on behalf of the German regime. He was executed for treason in December 1945.

9. farther] further   *W*

10. a step up, morally as well as financially.] a step up.   *W*

11. Ian Hay (John Hay Beith, 1876–1952), novelist and dramatist; see *2552, n.2*. Wodehouse and Hay collaborated on the plays *A Damsel in Distress* (1928) and *Baa, Baa, Black Sheep* (1929).

12. consistently] constantly   *DD*

13. like Lloyd George and Bernard Shaw | *set in page proof, 1945, but marked for omission (from a passage not found in* Windmill*; see no. 14). The excision was probably due to in-house censorship, for fear of libel. Lloyd George, World War I Prime Minister, died in 1945, but George Bernard Shaw did not die until 1950, and until his death a libel action could have been launched. It seems likely that Orwell intended these words to be included, and so they have been restored.*

14. eminent publicists . . . antiwar resolutions] *not in W (and see no. 13)*

15. And even an outright Quisling . . . had done.] *not in W. Examples of interviews with Allied soldiers captured in April 1941 after the failure of the campaign in Greece, with their photographs, can be found in* Signal *(1940–45), the German propaganda magazine circulated outside Germany. See* Hitler's Wartime Picture Magazine, *edited by S. L. Mayer (1976), for examples; and also 'The Road to Dunkerque: On the Structure of English Society', by Dr Ernst Lewalter, illustrated with drawings appropriate to a Wodehouse story. (Its pages are not numbered.)*

16. Priestley's 1940 broadcasts . . . at that time.] *not in W*

17 For thirty-five years, successive British governments kept Wodehouse's file under seal as an 'official secret.' This included the M15 interrogation report. The suspicion of Wodehouse's treachery was allowed to stand unanswered authoritatively (Sproat, 104). The papers were released in October 1999; see Iain Sproat, 'In all innocence', *TLS*, 29 October 1999, pp. 14–15.

18 When Evelyn Waugh reviewed *Critical Essays*, he referred to Wodehouse's 'pacifist strain.' This prompted Orwell to look up 'a rare early book,' *The Gold Bat* (1904), where he found passages suggesting that 'Wodehouse had had some kind of connection with the Liberal Party, about 1908, when it was the anti-militarist party.' (Orwell has slightly mistaken the date.) He told Waugh in his letter to him of 16 May 1948 (see *3401*),, 'I will add a footnote to this effect if I ever reprint the essays.' Orwell died before the essays were reprinted, so this reference has been added here.

2625. P. G. Wodehouse to Orwell

Among Orwell's papers were two letters P. G. Wodehouse wrote to him, on 25 July and 1 August 1945, from his flat at 78 Ave Paul Doumer, Paris XVI. He thanked Orwell very warmly for writing about him in the way he had in 'In Defence of P. G. Wodehouse' (*2624*).

In the first of these letters he wrote: 'I don't think I have ever read a better bit of criticism. You were absolutely right in everything you said about my work. It was uncanny.'

In the second letter, he said: 'I want to thank you again for that article. It was extraordinarily kind of you to write like that when you did not know me, and I shall never forget it. . . . I have been re-reading the article a number of times and am more than ever struck by the excellence of its criticism. It was a masterly bit of work and I agree with every word of it.'

Orwell had evidently taken the Wodehouses for a meal in a restaurant near Les Halles when he was in Paris for *The Observer*. He had, presumably, wished to follow up the writing of his article with a small, direct, gesture of kindness. The Wodehouses had not been to a restaurant since, but P. G. Wodehouse was anxious to reciprocate if Orwell returned to Paris, for he felt he owed him 'a Grade A lunch.'

It seems that Orwell replied to Wodehouse's letter of 25 July and told Wodehouse of Eileen's death, for in his letter of 1 August Wodehouse wrote with warm sympathy of Orwell's loss: 'I am afraid there is nothing much one can say at a time like this that will be any good, but my wife and I are feeling for you with all our hearts, the more so as a year ago we lost our daughter and so can understand what it must be for you.'

In a letter to his friend William Townend, of 29 April 1945, he said that Orwell's 'criticism of my stuff was masterly' and he praised Orwell for writing such an article 'at a time when it was taking a very unpopular view. He really is a good chap.' This seems to indicate that Orwell had sent Wodehouse an advance copy of his article, in typescript or proof. After Orwell's death, Wodehouse wrote to Denis Mackail (biographer of J. M. Barrie) on 11 August 1951 in rather different terms. He described the essay as 'practically one long roast of your correspondent. Don't you hate the way these critics falsify the facts in order to make a point?' His complaint was directed particularly at what Orwell had described as Wodehouse's out-of-touchness. This, Wodehouse claimed, was caused by his living in America where he couldn't write American stories and 'the only English characters the American public would read about were exaggerated dudes.' These two letters were published in a special feature 'Yours, Plum,' *Sunday Telegraph Review*, 19 August 1990.

2625A. Paris Puts a Gay Face on her Miseries, *The Observer*, 25

February 1945: see Vol. XX, Appendix 15

2626. 'Anti-Semitism in Britain'

Contemporary Jewish Record, April 1945[1]

There are about 400,000 known Jews in Britain, and in addition some thousands or, at most, scores of thousands of Jewish refugees who have entered the country from 1934 onwards. The Jewish population is almost entirely concentrated in half a dozen big towns and is mostly employed in the food, clothing and furniture trades. A few of the big monopolies, such as the I.C.I., one or two leading newspapers and at least one big chain of department stores are Jewish-owned or partly Jewish-owned, but it would be very far from the truth to say that British business life is dominated by Jews. The Jews seem, on the contrary, to have failed to keep up with the modern tendency towards big amalgamations and to have remained fixed in those trades which are necessarily carried out on a small scale and by old-fashioned methods.

I start off with these background facts, which are already known to any well-informed person, in order to emphasize that there is no real Jewish "problem" in England. The Jews are not numerous or powerful enough, and it is only in what are loosely called "intellectual circles" that they have any noticeable influence. Yet it is generally admitted that anti-Semitism is on the increase, that it has been greatly exacerbated by the war, and that humane and enlightened people are not immune to it. It does not take violent forms (English people are almost invariably gentle and law-abiding), but it is ill-natured enough, and in favorable circumstances it could have political results. Here are some samples of anti-Semitic remarks that have been made to me during the past year or two:

Middle-aged office employee: "I generally come to work by bus. It takes longer, but I don't care about using the Underground from Golders Green nowadays. There's too many of the Chosen Race travelling on that line."

Tobacconist (woman): "No, I've got no matches for you. I should try the lady down the street. *She's* always got matches. One of the Chosen Race, you see."

Young intellectual, Communist or near-Communist: "No, I do *not* like Jews. I've never made any secret of that. I can't stick them. Mind you, I'm not anti-Semitic, of course."

Middle-class woman: "Well, no one could call me anti-Semitic, but I do think the way these Jews behave is too absolutely stinking. The way they push their way to the head of queues, and so on. They're so abominably selfish. I think they're responsible for a lot of what happens to them."

Milk roundsman: "A Jew don't do no work, not the same as what an Englishman does. 'E's too clever. We work with this 'ere" (flexes his bicep). "They work with that there" (taps his forehead).

Chartered accountant, intelligent, left-wing in an undirected way: "These bloody Yids are all pro-German. They'd change sides tomorrow if the Nazis got here. I see a lot of them in my business. They admire Hitler at the bottom of their hearts. They'll always suck up to anyone who kicks them."

Intelligent woman, on being offered a book dealing with anti-Semitism and German atrocities: 'Don't show it me, *please* don't show it to me. It'll only make me hate the Jews more than ever."

I could fill pages with similar remarks, but these will do to go on with. Two facts emerge from them. One—which is very important and which I must return to in a moment—is that above a certain intellectual level people are ashamed of being anti-Semitic and are careful to draw a distinction between "anti-Semitism" and "disliking Jews." The other is that anti-Semitism is an irrational thing. The Jews are accused of specific offenses (for instance, bad behavior in food queues) which the person speaking feels strongly about, but it is obvious that these accusations merely rationalize some deep-rooted prejudice. To attempt to counter them with facts and statistics is useless, and may sometimes be worse than useless. As the last of the above-quoted remarks shows, people can remain anti-Semitic, or at least anti-Jewish, while being fully aware that their outlook is indefensible. If you dislike somebody, you dislike him and there is an end of it: your feelings are not made any better by a recital of his virtues.

It so happens that the war has encouraged the growth of anti-Semitism and even, in the eyes of many ordinary people, given some justification for it. To begin with, the Jews are one people of whom it can be said with complete certainty that they will benefit by an Allied victory. Consequently the theory that "this is a Jewish war" has a certain plausibility, all the more so because the Jewish war effort seldom gets its fair share of recognition. The British Empire is a huge heterogeneous organization held together largely by mutual consent, and it is often necessary to flatter the less reliable elements at the expense of the more loyal ones. To publicize the exploits of Jewish soldiers, or even to admit the existence of a considerable Jewish army in the Middle East, rouses hostility in South Africa, the Arab countries and elsewhere: it is easier to ignore the whole subject and allow the man in the street to go on thinking that Jews are exceptionally clever at dodging military service. Then again, Jews are to be found in exactly those trades which are bound to incur unpopularity with the civilian public in war time. Jews are mostly concerned with selling food, clothes, furniture and tobacco—exactly the commodities of which there is a chronic shortage, with consequent overcharging, black-marketing and favoritism. And again, the common charge that Jews behave in an exceptionally cowardly way during air raids was given a certain amount of color by the big raids of 1940. As it happened, the Jewish quarter of Whitechapel was one of the first areas to be heavily blitzed, with the natural result that swarms of Jewish refugees distributed themselves all over London. If one judged merely from these war-time phenomena, it would be easy to imagine that anti-Semitism is a quasi-rational thing, founded on mistaken premises. And naturally the anti-Semite thinks of himself as a reasonable being. Whenever I have touched on this subject in a newspaper article, I have always had a considerable "come-back," and invariably some of the letters are from well-balanced, middling people—doctors, for example—with no apparent economic grievance. These people always say (as Hitler says in *Mein Kampf*) that they started out with no anti-Jewish prejudice but were driven into their present position by mere observation of the facts. Yet one of the marks of anti-Semitism is an ability to believe stories that could not possibly be true. One could see a good example of this in the strange accident that occurred in London in 1942, when a crowd, frightened by a bomb-burst nearby, fled into the mouth of an Underground station, with the result that something over a hundred people were crushed to death. The very same day it was repeated all over London that "the Jews were responsible."[2] Clearly, if people will believe this kind of thing, one will not get much further by arguing with them. The only useful approach is to discover *why* they can swallow absurdities on one particular subject while remaining sane on others.

But now let me come back to that point I mentioned earlier—that there is widespread awareness of the prevalence of anti-Semitic feeling, and unwillingness to admit sharing it. Among educated people, anti-Semitism is held to be an unforgivable sin and in a quite different category from other kinds of racial prejudice. People will go to remarkable lengths to demonstrate that they are *not* anti-Semitic. Thus, in 1943 an intercession service on behalf of the Polish Jews was held in a synagogue in St. John's Wood. The local authorities declared themselves anxious to participate in it, and the service was attended by the mayor of the borough in his robes and chain, by representatives of all the churches, and by detachments of RAF, Home Guards, nurses, Boy Scouts and what-not. On the surface it was a touching demonstration of solidarity with the suffering Jews. But it was essentially a *conscious* effort to behave decently by people whose subjective feelings must in many cases have been very different. That quarter of London is partly Jewish, anti-Semitism is rife there, and, as I well knew, some of the men sitting round me in the synagogue were tinged by it. Indeed, the commander of my own platoon of Home Guards, who had been especially keen beforehand that we should "make a good show" at the intercession service, was an ex-member of Mosley's Blackshirts. While this division of feeling exists, tolerance of mass violence against Jews, or, what is more important, anti-Semitic legislation, are not possible in England. It is not at present possible, indeed, that anti-Semitism should *become respectable*. But this is less of an advantage than it might appear.

One effect of the persecutions in Germany has been to prevent anti-Semitism from being seriously studied. In England a brief inadequate survey was made by Mass Observation a year or two ago, but if there has been any other investigation of the subject, then its findings have been kept strictly secret. At the same time there has been conscious suppression, by all thoughtful people, of anything likely to wound Jewish susceptibilities. After 1934 the "Jew joke" disappeared as though by magic from postcards, periodicals and the music-hall stage, and to put an unsympathetic Jewish character into a novel or short story came to be regarded as anti-Semitism.

On the Palestine issue, too, it was *de rigueur* among enlightened people to accept the Jewish case as proved and avoid examining the claims of the Arabs—a decision which might be correct on its own merits, but which was adopted primarily because the Jews were in trouble and it was felt that one must not criticize them. Thanks to Hitler, therefore, you had a situation in which the press was in effect censored in favor of the Jews while in private anti-Semitism was on the up-grade, even, to some extent, among sensitive and intelligent people. This was particularly noticeable in 1940 at the time of the internment of the refugees. Naturally, every thinking person felt that it was his duty to protest against the wholesale locking-up of unfortunate foreigners who for the most part were only in England because they were opponents of Hitler. Privately, however, one heard very different sentiments expressed. A minority of the refugees behaved in an exceedingly tactless way, and the feeling against them necessarily had an anti-Semitic under-current, since they were largely Jews. A very eminent figure in the Labor Party—I won't name him, but he is one of the most respected people in England—said to me quite violently: "We never asked these people to come to this country. If they choose to come here, let them take the consequences." Yet this man would as a matter of course have associated himself with any kind of petition or manifesto against the internment of aliens. This feeling that anti-Semitism is something sinful and disgraceful, something that a civilized person does not suffer from, is unfavorable to a scientific approach, and indeed many people will admit that they are frightened of probing too deeply into the subject. They are frightened, that is to say, of discovering not only that anti-Semitism is spreading, but that they themselves are infected by it.

To see this in perspective one must look back a few decades, to the days when Hitler was an out-of-work house-painter whom nobody had heard of. One would then find that though anti-Semitism is sufficiently in evidence now, it is probably *less* prevalent in England than it was thirty years ago. It is true that anti-Semitism as a fully thought-out racial or religious doctrine has never flourished in England. There has never been much feeling against intermarriage, or against Jews taking a prominent part in public life. Nevertheless, thirty years ago it was accepted more or less as a law of nature that a Jew was a figure of fun and—though superior in intelligence—slightly deficient in "character." In theory a Jew suffered from no legal disabilities, but in effect he was debarred from certain professions. He would probably not have been accepted as an officer in the Navy, for instance, nor in what is called a "smart" regiment in the Army. A Jewish boy at a public school almost invariably had a bad time. He could, of course, live down his Jewishness if he was exceptionally charming or athletic, but it was an initial disability comparable to a stammer or a birthmark. Wealthy Jews tended to disguise themselves under aristocratic English or Scottish names, and to the average person it seemed quite natural that they should do this, just as it seems natural for a criminal to change his identity if possible. About twenty years ago, in Rangoon, I was getting into a taxi with a friend when a small ragged boy of fair complexion rushed up to us and began a complicated story about having arrived from Colombo on a ship and wanting money to get back. His manner and appearance were difficult to "place," and I said to him: "You speak very good English. What nationality are you?"

He answered eagerly in his chi-chi accent: "I am a *Joo*, sir!"

And I remember turning to my companion and saying, only partly in joke, "He admits it openly." All the Jews I had known till then were people who were ashamed of being Jews, or at any rate preferred not to talk about their ancestry, and if forced to do so tended to use the word "Hebrew."

The working-class attitude was no better. The Jew who grew up in Whitechapel took it for granted that he would be assaulted, or at least hooted at, if he ventured into one of the Christian slums nearby, and the "Jew joke" of the music halls and the comic papers was almost consistently ill-natured.* There was also literary Jew-baiting, which in the hands of Belloc, Chesterton and their followers reached almost a Continental level of scurrility. Non-Catholic writers were sometimes guilty of the same thing in a milder form. There has been a perceptible anti-Semitic strain in English literature from Chaucer onwards, and without even getting up from this table to consult a book I can think of passages which *if written now* would be stigmatized as anti-Semitism, in the works of Shakespeare, Smollett, Thackeray, Bernard Shaw, H. G. Wells, T. S. Eliot, Aldous Huxley and various others. Offhand, the only English writers I can think of who, before the days of Hitler, made a definite effort to stick up for Jews are Dickens and Charles Reade. And however little the average intellectual may have agreed with the opinions of Belloc and Chesterton, he did not acutely disapprove of them. Chesterton's endless tirades against Jews, which he thrust into stories and essays upon the flimsiest pretexts, never got him into trouble—indeed Chesterton was one of the most generally respected figures in English literary life. Anyone who wrote in that strain *now* would bring down a storm of abuse upon himself, or more probably would find it impossible to get his writings published.

If, as I suggest, prejudice against Jews has always been pretty widespread in England, there is no reason to think that Hitler has genuinely diminished it. He has merely caused a sharp division between the politically conscious person who realizes that this is not a time to throw stones at the Jews, and the unconscious person whose native anti-Semitism is increased by the nervous strain of the war. One can assume, therefore, that many people who would perish rather than admit to anti-Semitic feelings are secretly prone to them. I have already indicated that I believe anti-Semitism to be essentially a neurosis, but of course it has its rationalizations, which are sincerely believed in and are partly true. The rationalization put forward by the common man is

---

* It is interesting to compare the "Jew joke" with that other standby of the music halls, the "Scotch joke," which superficially it resembles. Occasionally a story is told (e.g., the Jew and the Scotsman who went into a pub together, and both died of thirst) which puts both races on an equality, but in general the Jew is credited *merely* with cunning and avarice while the Scotsman is credited with physical hardihood as well. This is seen, for example, in the story of the Jew and the Scotsman who go together to a meeting which has been advertised as free. Unexpectedly there is a collection, and to avoid this the Jew faints and the Scotsman carries him out. Here the Scotsman performs the athletic feat of carrying the other. It would seem vaguely wrong if it were the other way about [Orwell's footnote].

that the Jew is an exploiter. The partial justification for this is that the Jew, in England, is generally a small business man—that is to say a person whose depredations are more obvious and intelligible than those of, say, a bank or an insurance company. Higher up the intellectual scale, anti-Semitism is rationalized by saying that the Jew is a person who spreads disaffection and weakens national morale. Again there is some superficial justification for this. During the past twenty-five years the activities of what are called "intellectuals" have been largely mischievous. I do not think it an exaggeration to say that if the "intellectuals" had done their work a little more thoroughly, Britain would have surrendered in 1940. But the disaffected intelligentsia inevitably included a large number of Jews. With some plausibility it can be said that the Jews are the enemies of our native culture and our national morale. Carefully examined, the claim is seen to be nonsense, but there are always a few prominent individuals who can be cited in support of it. During the past few years there has been what amounts to a counterattack against the rather shallow Leftism which was fashionable in the previous decade and which was exemplified by such organizations as the Left Book Club. This counterattack (see for instance such books as Arnold Lunn's *The Good Gorilla* or Evelyn Waugh's *Put Out More Flags*) has an anti-Semitic strain, and it would probably be more marked if the subject were not so obviously dangerous. It so happens that for some decades past Britain has had no nationalist intelligentsia worth bothering about. But British nationalism i.e. nationalism of an intellectual kind, may revive, and probably will revive if Britain comes out of the present war greatly weakened. The young intellectuals of 1950 may be as naively patriotic as those of 1914. In that case the kind of anti-Semitism which flourished among the anti-Dreyfusards in France, and which Chesterton and Belloc tried to import into this country, might get a foothold.

I have no hard-and-fast theory about the origins of anti-Semitism. The two current explanations that it is due to economic causes, or on the other hand that it is a legacy from the Middle Ages—seem to me unsatisfactory, though I admit that if one combines them they can be made to cover the facts. All I would say with confidence is that anti-Semitism is part of the larger problem of nationalism, which has not yet been seriously examined, and that the Jew is evidently a scapegoat, though *for what* he is a scapegoat we do not yet know. In this essay I have relied almost entirely on my own limited experience, and perhaps every one of my conclusions would be negatived by other observers. The fact is that there are almost no data on this subject. But for what they are worth I will summarize my opinions. Boiled down, they amount to this:

There is more anti-Semitism in England than we care to admit, and the war has accentuated it, but it is not certain that it is on the increase if one thinks in terms of decades rather than years.

It does not at present lead to open persecution, but it has the effect of making people callous to the sufferings of Jews in other countries.

It is at bottom quite irrational and will not yield to argument.

The persecutions in Germany have caused much concealment of anti-Semitic feeling and thus obscured the whole picture.

The subject needs serious investigation.

Only the last point is worth expanding. To study any subject scientifically one needs a detached attitude, which is obviously harder when one's own interests or emotions are involved. Plenty of people who are quite capable of being objective about sea urchins, say, or the square root of 2, become schizophrenic if they have to think about the sources of their own income. What vitiates nearly all that is written about anti-Semitism is the assumption in the writer's mind that *he himself* is immune to it. "Since I know that anti-Semitism is irrational," he argues, "it follows that I do not share it." He thus fails to start his investigation in the one place where he could get hold of some reliable evidence—that is, in his own mind.

It seems to me a safe assumption that the disease loosely called nationalism is now almost universal. Anti-Semitism is only one manifestation nationalism, and not everyone will have the disease in that particular form. A Jew, for example, would not be anti-Semitic: but then many Zionist Jews seem to me to be merely anti-Semites turned upside-down, just as many Indians and Negroes display the normal color prejudices in an inverted form. The point is that something, some psychological vitamin, is lacking in modern civilization, and as a result we are all more or less subject to this lunacy of believing that whole races or nations are mysteriously good or mysteriously evil. I defy any modern intellectual to look closely and honestly into his own mind without coming upon nationalistic loyalties and hatreds of one kind or another. It is the fact that he can feel the emotional tug of such things, and yet see them dispassionately for what they are, that gives him his status as an intellectual. It will be seen, therefore, that the starting point for any investigation of anti-Semitism should not be, "Why does this obviously irrational belief appeal to other people?" but "Why does anti-Semitism appeal to *me*? What is there about it that I feel to be true?" If one asks this question one at least discovers one's own rationalizations, and it may be possible to find out what lies beneath them. Anti-Semitism should be investigated—I will not say by anti-Semites, but at any rate by people who know that they are not immune to that kind of emotion. When Hitler has disappeared a real inquiry into this subject will be possible, and it would probably be best to start not by debunking anti-Semitism, but by marshalling all the justifications for it that can be found, in one's own mind or anybody else's. In that way one might get some clues that would lead to its psychological roots. But that anti-Semitism will be definitively *cured*, without curing the larger disease of nationalism, I do not believe.[3]

1. Orwell's Payments Book lists this essay as completed on 26 February 1945 and his fee as £30.00. Although published quite shortly afterwards, and so not meriting placement here on the grounds of a delay between completion and publication, it does merit this juxtaposition with the essay in defence of P. G. Wodehouse in that both are concerned with prejudice and 'unpopular causes.'
2. At Bethnal Green underground station on 3 March 1943, a woman with a small child tripped at the first of a flight of twenty steps as an air-raid siren sounded. Her baby and 177 others were killed in the ensuing crush. The mother survived. No bombs had fallen by then. There was no 'Jewish dimension' to this sad accident.
3. See Tosco Fyvel, *George Orwell: A Personal Memoir* (1982), 63, 178–82 (and see *2653, n. 1*); and David Walton, 'George Orwell and Antisemitism,' *Patterns of Prejudice*, 16 (1982), 19–34.

2627. Inside the Pages in Paris

Manchester Evening News, 28 February 1945

Orwell went to France as a war correspondent for *The Observer* on 15 February 1945. During his time in Paris he stayed at the Hotel Scribe (as did many correspondents). In place of his book reviews for the *Manchester Evening News* he contributed articles, and was described as that paper's 'Correspondent in Paris' on 28 February, 7 and 20 March, and as ' "Manchester Evening News" War Correspondent in Germany' on 4 May. For the five articles in this series there are no entries in the Payments Book. The titles given to the articles published in both newspapers may not be Orwell's. *L'Humanité* was printed without the accent supplied here. Where they are missing, accents have been silently supplied. If articles are dated, this is stated.

There are not quite so many newspapers in Paris as there were before the war, but the number is still large by English standards. To be exact, there are 23 daily and evening papers, and another half-dozen will be appearing shortly. Out of this total only four were in existence before the war. The majority were started clandestinely during the occupation.

Several have quite considerable circulations. The Communist "L'Humanité," with a circulation of 400,000, is well ahead of the rest, but several others have reached 200,000 or thereabouts. Meanwhile, new weeklies and monthlies, some of them of a very high intellectual standard, are popping up like mushrooms.

In spite of all this activity the French Press shows at this moment some discouraging symptoms. A newcomer, trying to find his bearings among the enormous array of newspapers and periodicals spread out in the kiosks, notices two things, one good and the other bad.

The first is that the Paris Press has lost its one-time venality and scurrility. Every kind of paper is sober in tone and reasonably enlightened in outlook. The pre-war Press, especially in Paris, killed itself off by collaborating with the Germans, and the new papers that arose during the occupation are largely run by ardent young Socialists in their early twenties.

Moreover, these papers can be run at very low cost. Nearly all of them consist only of a single sheet, a quarter of which is taken up by advertisements, and their rents and other overheads are not high. They can, therefore, live off their circulations, and the subsidies and straight forward° bribery by which much of the French Press used to support itself are no longer necessary.

The other thing that a newcomer notices is how alike all these papers are. At first sight they seem only to differ in their names, and even those overlap in a bewildering way. Of course, the tiny size of the present-day newspapers does not make for variety, but the basic cause of similarity is censorship, both official and voluntary.

The Government's censorship is strict, and the French Press sometimes finds itself in the humiliating position of being unable to print items of news which appear in the Paris editions of English and American papers.

The Government is also able to exercise indirect pressure through the reallotment of paper supplies, which takes place at short intervals. But the self-censorship resulting from the general desire for national unity, and for the re-establishment of France as a Great Power, is partly responsible for the timidity of the daily Press in discussing major problems.

It is already being said that the golden age of the French Press was the period when it was illegal. Extraordinary boldness and ingenuity were shown in printing and distributing newspapers under the noses of the Germans. One weekly paper was clandestinely printed in the same building and on the same machines as the German occupation daily, the "Pariser Zeitung."

Other illegal papers were distributed through the post, the postal charges being avoided by the simple expedient of printing forged stamps. There are countless similar stories, and the files of these illegal papers, starting off as miserable cyclostyled sheets and ending as quite presentable and well-informed newspapers—even illustrated, in some cases—are a fascinating study.

But the underground Press was also in an intellectual and political sense more adventurous than most of the Press is now able to be. It was in opposition to the existing regime, and oppositions are not afraid to discuss large issues. Now, however, the entire Press is substantially in agreement with the status quo, and the level of criticism suffers accordingly.

The weeklies have more freedom of action, but certain subjects seem to be almost barred from the daily Press. No paper will express anything that could be described as opposition to General de Gaulle. No paper will utter any really searching criticism of present-day French foreign policy.* No paper will be overtly anti-British or anti-American, and still less will any paper be anti-Russian.

Necessarily this leads to a certain sameness throughout the Press, and on the other hand to a hullabaloo about secondary matters which actually conceal larger political issues.

Two such questions are food distribution and the "purge" of collaborationists. In each case the problem, seemingly administrative, is really political. But the casual reader, skimming through a score of papers, could be forgiven for imagining that there are now no serious disagreements in France.

He would notice, however, that there is a marked difference in the priority given to news. And if he followed up this clue he would find that the papers which are in fact, though not on the surface, hostile to Britain and the U.S.A., show it in the only way they can by keeping the news from the western front out of the big headlines.

When one looks more closely four main tendencies can be discerned in the Press. First there are the papers that preach unquestioning loyalty to de Gaulle. These include several papers of vaguely conservative colour which have appeared since the liberation and have gained a certain amount of

* Since Mr. Orwell's dispatch was sent "Combat" has declared that "after so many disillusioning experiences it is up to France to achieve that organisation of liberty which other nations, too, are expecting—and which some expect from us." [Footnote printed in Manchester Evening News.]

ground against the ex-illegal papers. Then there are the Communist papers, which also follow de Gaulle unswervingly but put their main emphasis on the U.S.S.R.

Then there are various Catholic papers, some of them with syndicalist leanings. And finally there are the Left-wing Socialist papers, which do criticise as boldly as they are able and are sometimes in trouble with the censorship. Much the most interesting and courageous daily papers now running in Paris are the group "Combat," "Franc Tireur," "France Soir," with the weekly paper "Libertés."

"Combat," with a circulation of 180,000, is definitely one of the leading Paris papers. And though it does not belong to this group, mention should also be made of Léon Blum's paper "Le Populaire," one of the few papers that have survived from pre-war days. Blum,[1] immured in some German concentration camp, is still named on its front page as editor-in chief. "Le Populaire," like the "Combat" group, is relatively outspoken and not afraid to discuss delicate subjects such as Franco-American relations.

It is hard to be sure about the future development of the Paris Press. When the paper shortage ends and freedom of speech becomes easier, several of the tiny sheets now existing are capable of developing into newspapers of the very first rank. But the same conditions might favour the reappearance of heavily capitalised commerical papers of the old type, with which the amateurs who learned their journalism in the cellars of the resistance might not be able to compete.

Rumours are already floating round that one or two of the more recently arrived papers are being financed by foreign Governments, or that some of the discredited papers of pre-war days are going to be revived under new names.

But the experience of the occupation has produced in large numbers a new type of journalist—very young, idealistic and yet hardened by illegality, and completely non-commercial in outlook—and these men are bound to make their influence felt in the post-war Press.

The public, also, has been educated by suffering, and French opinion as a whole has moved decisively to the Left. If any freedom of the Press survives it is difficult to believe that the French people will again tolerate newspapers so stupid, scurrilous, and dishonest as the bulk of those they possessed before 1940.

1. León Blum (1872–1950). Socialist politician, was Prime Minister, 1936–37, 1938, and 1946–47. For a succinct recent account of Blum, especially his not seeing what he did not want to see, and his disinclination to take difficult decisions, see Eugen Weber, *The Hollow Years: France in the 1930s* (1995), 161–63.

2628. To Roger Senhouse

28 February 1945   Typewritten

Hotel Scribe[1]
Rue Scribe
Paris 9e

Dear Roger,

When I sent you that list for review copies etc. of ANIMAL FARM, I forgot to say, would you send a copy to Edmund Wilson at the New Yorker. I dare say he would give it a mention and on a long-term view that might be helpful.

Also, have you got a copy of HOMAGE TO CATALONIA left? If so, could you send it to me at the above address? I want a copy to give to André Malraux when I can contact him.[2]

I hope all goes well and that Fred is getting better. This town is horribly depressing compared with what it used to be.[3]

Yours
George

1. The Hotel Scribe, from which this letter was sent, was used to house war correspondents.
2. The letter is date-stamped as being received by Secker & Warburg on 7 March 1945. An annotation indicates that a copy of *Homage to Catalonia* was sent that same day 'per Min. of Inf[ormation].' Malraux had been suggested as an appropriate person to write an introduction to the French edition of *Homage to Catalonia* (see *CW*, VII, 251–52). See also Orwell's correspondence with Yvonne Davet, 13 January and 7 April 1947, *3151* and *3209*. In the event, Orwell did not give the copy to Malraux; see *2635*. Note the use of 'contact' and compare Orwell's strictures against this verb in 'As I Please,' 56; see *2609*.
3. Roger Senhouse acknowledged Orwell's letter on 8 March. He said Edmund Wilson's name had been added to the free list; that a copy of *Homage to Catalonia* was being sent via the Ministry of Information; that Warburg was improving and would be back at the end of March; and that he wanted to see Orwell in Paris for a couple of days. There is also a description of a reading by Louis Aragon of three of his poems at Cyril Connolly's rooms: 'It was a moving experience, especially to see that old eagle, T. S. Eliot, blinking and occasionally closing his eyes for long periods, and to hear the resonance of a gifted French declamation.' He found the rhythms more exciting than the content but 'it was enough to see him in person and to realise through his voice, more closely than before, something of what the Occupation means to the great majority of his countrymen. . . .'

2629. 'Poetry and the Microphone'

Written Summer 1943?; *The New Saxon Pamphlet*, No. 3, March 1945

It is probable that this essay was written a year and a half to two years before it was published. It is not listed in Orwell's Payments Book, July 1943 to December 1945. The opening words, 'About a year ago,' refer to the 'Voice' broadcasts which Orwell organised and which were concluded in December 1942, which indicates that he was writing no later than December 1943. Later in the essay (paragraph nine), he writes, 'yet after three years of war,' which suggests autumn 1942 to summer 1943—thus the probability that the essay was written in the summer of 1943. Orwell may have intended it for *Horizon* (which published three reviews but no essays of his between February 1942 and October 1944), but it was not accepted—hence it does not appear in his Payments Book for this period.

The New Saxon Pamphlets, Nos. 1–3 and *The New Saxon Review*, Nos. 4 and 5, March 1944–47, were edited by John Atkins (1916–), literary editor of *Tribune* before Orwell. He read Treece's poems in the latter's absence in 'Voice,' 1, broadcast 11 August 1942; see *1373*. Atkins's introductory note to this *Pamphlet* refers to *Troisième Front et Pièces Detachées* by E. L. T. Mesens with 'English translations by Roland Penrose and the author opposite,' that is, Orwell, whose article begins on the opposite page. However, Orwell had no part in that book; the second translator was Mesens himself.

About a year ago I and a number of others were engaged in broadcasting literary programmes to India, and among other things we broadcast a good deal of verse by contemporary and near-contemporary English writers—for example, Eliot, Herbert Read, Auden, Spender, Dylan Thomas, Henry Treece, Alex Comfort, Robert Bridges, Edmund Blunden, D. H. Lawrence. Whenever it was possible we had poems broadcast by the people who wrote them. Just why these particular programmes (a small and remote outflanking movement in the radio war) were instituted there is no need to explain here, but I should add that the fact we were broadcasting to an Indian audience dictated our technique to some extent. The essential point was that our literary broadcasts were aimed at the Indian university students, a small and hostile audience, unapproachable by anything that could be described as British propaganda. It was known in advance that we could not hope for more than a few thousand listeners at the most, and this gave us an excuse to be more "highbrow" than is generally possible on the air.

If you are broadcasting poetry to people who know your language but don't share your cultural background, a certain amount of comment and explanation is unavoidable, and the formula we usually followed was to broadcast what purported to be a monthly literary magazine. The editorial staff were supposedly sitting in their office, discussing what to put into the next number. Somebody suggested one poem, someone else suggested another, there was a short discussion and then came the poem itself, read in a different voice, preferably the author's own. This poem naturally called up another, and so the programme continued, usually with at least half a minute of discussion between any two items. For a half-hour programme, six voices seemed to be the best number. A programme of this sort was necessarily somewhat shapeless, but it could be given a certain appearance of unity by making it revolve round a single central theme. For example, one number of our imaginary magazine was devoted to the subject of war. It included two poems by Edmund Blunden, Auden's *September, 1941*,° extracts from a long poem by G. S. Fraser (*A Letter to Anne Ridler*), Byron's *Isles of Greece* and an extract from T. E. Lawrence's *Revolt in the Desert*. These half-dozen items, with the arguments that preceded and followed them, covered reasonably well the possible attitudes towards war. The poems and the prose extract took about twenty minutes to broadcast, the arguments about eight minutes.

This formula may seem slightly ridiculous and also rather patronising, but its advantage is that the element of mere instruction, the textbook motif, which is quite unavoidable if one is going to broadcast serious and sometimes "difficult" verse, becomes a lot less forbidding when it appears as an informal discussion. The various speakers can ostensibly say to one another what they are in reality saying to the audience. Also, by such an approach you at least give a poem a context, which is just what poetry lacks from the average man's point of view. But of course there are other methods. One which we frequently used was to set a poem in music. It is announced that in a few minutes' time such and such a poem will be broadcast; then the music plays for perhaps a minute, then fades out into the poem, which follows without any title or announcement, then the music is faded [in] again and plays up for another minute or two—the whole thing taking perhaps five minutes. It is necessary to choose appropriate music, but needless to say, the real purpose of the music is to insulate the poem from the rest of the programme. By this method you can have, say, a Shakespeare sonnet within three minutes of a news bulletin without, at any rate to my ear, any gross incongruity.

These programmes that I have been speaking of were of no great value in themselves, but I have mentioned them because of the ideas they aroused in myself and some others about the possibilities of the radio as a means of popularising poetry. I was early struck by the fact that the broadcasting of a poem by the person who wrote it does not merely produce an effect upon the audience, if any, but also on the poet himself. One must remember that extremely little in the way of broadcasting poetry has been done in England, and that many people who write verse have never even considered the idea of reading it aloud. By being set down at a microphone, especially if this happens at all regularly, the poet is brought into a new relationship with his work, not otherwise attainable in our time and country. It is a commonplace that in modern times—the last two hundred years, say—poetry has come to have less and less connection either with music or with the spoken word. It needs print in order to exist at all, and it is no more expected that a poet, as such, will know how to sing or even to declaim than it is expected that an architect will know how to plaster a ceiling. Lyrical and rhetorical poetry have almost ceased to be written, and a hostility towards poetry on the part of the common man has come to be taken for granted in any country where everyone can read. And where such a breach exists it is always inclined to widen, because the concept of poetry as primarily something printed, and something intelligible only to a minority, encourages obscurity and "cleverness." How many people do not feel quasi-instinctively that there must be something wrong with any poem whose meaning can be taken in at a single glance? It seems unlikely that these tendencies will be checked unless it again becomes normal to read verse aloud, and it is difficult to see how this can be brought about except by using the radio as a medium. But the special advantage of the radio, its power to select the right audience, and to do away with stage-fright and embarrassment, ought here to be noticed.

In broadcasting your audience is conjectural, but it is an audience of *one*. Millions may be listening, but each is listening alone, or as a member of a small group, and each has (or ought to have) the feeling that you are speaking to him individually. More than this it is reasonable to assume that your audience is sympathetic, or at least interested, for anyone who is bored can promptly switch you off by turning a knob. But though presumably sympathetic, the audience *has no power over you.* It is just here that a broadcast differs from a speech or a lecture. On the platform, as anyone used to public speaking knows, it is almost impossible not to take your tone from the audience. It is always obvious within a few minutes what they will respond to and what they will not, and in practice you are almost compelled to speak for the benefit of what you estimate as the stupidest person present, and also to ingratiate yourself by means of the balleyhoo known as "personality." If you don't do so, the result is always an atmosphere of frigid embarrassment. That grisly thing, a "poetry reading," is what it is because there will always be some among the audience who are bored or all-but frankly hostile and who can't remove themselves by the simple act of turning a knob. And it is at bottom the same difficulty—the fact that a theatre audience is not a selected one—that makes it impossible to get a decent performance of Shakespeare in England. On the air these conditions do not exist. The poet *feels* that he is addressing people to whom poetry means something, and it is a fact that poets who are used to broadcasting can read into the microphone with a virtuosity they would not equal if they had a visible audience in front of them. The element of make-believe that enters here does not greatly matter. The point is that in the only way now possible the poet has been brought into a situation in which reading verse aloud seems a natural unembarrassing thing, a normal exchange between man and man: also he has been led to think of his work as *sound* rather than as a pattern on paper. By that much the reconciliation between poetry and the common man is nearer. It already exists at the poet's end of the aether-waves, whatever may be happening at the other end.

However, what is happening at the other end cannot be disregarded. It will be seen that I have been speaking as though the whole subject of poetry were embarrassing, almost indecent, as though popularising poetry were essentially a strategic manoeuvre, like getting a dose of medicine down a child's throat or establishing tolerance for a persecuted sect. But unfortunately that or something like it is the case. There can be no doubt that in our civilization poetry is by far the most discredited of the arts, the ony art, indeed, in which the average man refuses to discern *any* value. Arnold Bennett was hardly exaggerating when he said that in the English-speaking countries the word "poetry" would disperse a crowd quicker than a fire hose. And as I have pointed out, a breach of this kind tends to widen simply because of its existence, the common man becoming more and more anti-poetry, the poet more and more arrogant and unintelligible, until the divorce between poetry and popular culture is accepted as a sort of law of nature, although in fact it belongs only to our own time and to a comparatively small area of the earth. We live in an age in which the average human being in the highly-civilized countries is aesthetically inferior to the lowest savage. This state of affairs is generally looked upon as being incurable by any *conscious* act, and on the other hand is expected to right itself of its own accord as soon as society takes a comelier shape. With slight variations the Marxist, the anarchist and the religious believer will all tell you this, and in broad terms it is undoubtedly true. The ugliness amid which we live has spiritual and economic causes and is not to be explained by the mere going-astray of tradition at some point or other. But it does not follow that no improvement is possible within our present framework, nor that an aesthetic improvement is not a necessary part of the general redemption of society. It is worth stopping to wonder, therefore, whether it would not be possible even now to rescue poetry from its special position as the most-hated of the arts and win for it at least the same degree of toleration as exists for music. But one has to start by asking, in what way and to what extent is poetry unpopular?

On the face of it, the unpopularity of poetry is as complete as it could be. But on second thoughts, this has to be qualified in a rather peculiar way. To begin with, there is still an appreciable amount of folk poetry (nursery rhymes, etc.) which is universally known and quoted and forms part of the background of everyone's mind. There is also a handful of ancient songs and ballads which have never gone out of favour. In addition there is the popularity, or at least the toleration, of "good bad" poetry, generally of a patriotic or sentimental kind. This might seem beside the point if it were not that "good bad" poetry has all the characteristics which, ostensibly, make the average man dislike true poetry. It is in verse, it rhymes, it deals in lofty sentiments and unusual language—all this to a very marked degree, for it is almost axiomatic that bad poetry is more "poetical" than good poetry. Yet if not actively liked it is at least tolerated. For example, just before writing this I have been listening to a couple of B.B.C. comedians doing their usual turn before the 9 o'clock news. In the last three minutes one of the two comedians suddenly announces that he "wants to be serious for a moment" and proceeds to recite a piece of patriotic balderdash entitled *A Fine Old English Gentleman*, in praise of His Majesty the King. Now, what is the reaction of the audience to the sudden lapse into the worst sort of rhyming heroics? It cannot be very violently negative, or there would be a sufficient volume of indignant letters to stop the B.B.C. doing this kind of thing. One must conclude that though the big public is hostile to *poetry*, it is not strongly hostile to *verse*. After all, if rhyme and metre were disliked for their own sakes, neither songs nor dirty limericks could be popular. Poetry is disliked because it is associated with untelligibility, intellectual pretentiousness and a general feeling of Sunday-on-a-weekday. Its name creates in advance the same sort of bad impression as the word "God," or a parson's dog-collar. To a certain extent, popularising poetry is a question of breaking down an acquired inhibition. It is a question of getting people to listen instead of uttering a mechanical raspberry. If true poetry could be introduced to the big public in such a way as to make it seem *normal*, as that piece of rubbish I have just listened to presumably seemed normal, then part of the prejudice against it might be overcome.

It is difficult to believe that poetry can ever be popularised again without some deliberate effort at the education of public taste, involving strategy and perhaps even subterfuge. T. S. Eliot once suggested that poetry, particularly dramatic poetry, might be brought back into the consciousness of ordinary people through the medium of the music hall; he might have added the pantomine, whose vast possibilities do not seem ever to have been completely explored. *Sweeney Agonistes* was perhaps written with some such idea in mind, and it would in fact be conceivable as a music-hall turn, or at least as a scene in a revue. I have suggested the radio as a more hopeful medium, and I have pointed out its technical advantages, particularly from the point of view of the poet. The reason why such a suggestion sounds hopeless at first hearing is that few people are able to imagine the radio being used for the dissemination of anything except tripe. People listen to the stuff that does actually dribble from the loudspeakers of the world, and conclude that it is for that and nothing else that the wireless exists. Indeed the very word "wireless" calls up a picture either of roaring dictators or of genteel throaty voices announcing that three of our aircraft have failed to return. Poetry on the air sounds like the Muses in striped trousers. Nevertheless one ought not to confuse the capabilities of an instrument with the use it is actually put to. Broadcasting is what it is, not because there is something inherently vulgar, silly and dishonest about the whole apparatus of microphone and transmitter, but because all the broadcasting that now happens all over the world is under the control of governments or great monopoly companies which are actively interested in maintaining the status quo and therefore in preventing the common man from becoming too intelligent. Something of the same kind has happened to the cinema, which, like the radio, made its appearance during the monopoly stage of capitalism and is fantastically expensive to operate. In all the arts the tendency is similar. More and more the channels of production are under the control of bureaucrats, whose aim is to destroy the artist or at least to castrate him. This would be a bleak outlook if it were not that the totalitarianisation which is now going on, and must undoubtedly continue to go on, in every country of the world, is mitigated by another process which it was not easy to foresee even as short a time as five years ago.

This is, that the huge bureaucratic machines of which we are all part are beginning to work creakily because of their mere size and their constant growth. The tendency of the modern state is to wipe out the freedom of the intellect, and yet at the same time every state, especially under the pressure of war, finds itself more and more in need of an intelligentsia to do its publicity for it. The modern state needs, for example, pamphlet-writers, poster artists, illustrators, broadcasters, lecturers, film producers, actors, song-composers, even painters and sculptors, not to mention psychologists, sociologists, biochemists, mathematicians and what-not. The British government started the present war with the more or less openly declared intention of keeping the literary intelligentsia out of it; yet after three years of war almost every writer, however undesirable his political history or opinions, has been sucked into the various Ministries or the B.B.C., and even those who enter the armed forces tend to find themselves after a while in Public Relations or some other essentially literary job. The Government has absorbed these people, unwillingly enough, because it found itself unable to get on without them. The ideal, from the official point of view, would have been to put all publicity into the hands of "safe" people like A. P. Herbert or Ian Hay: but since not enough of these were available, the existing intelligentsia had to be utilised, and the tone and even to some extent the content of official propaganda have been modified accordingly. No one acquainted with the Government pamphlets, A.B.C.A. lectures,[1] documentary films and broadcasts to occupied countries which have been issued during the past two years imagines that our rulers would sponsor this kind of thing if they could help it. Only, the bigger the machine of government becomes, the more loose ends and forgotten corners there are in it. This is perhaps a small consolation, but it is not a despicable one. It means that in countries where there is already a strong liberal tradition, bureaucratic tyranny can perhaps never be complete. The striped-trousered ones will rule, but so long as they are forced to maintain an intelligentsia, the intelligentsia will have a certain amount of autonomy. If the Government needs, for example, documentary films, it must employ people specially interested in the technique of the film, and it must allow them the necessary minimum of freedom; consequently, films that are all wrong from the bureaucratic point of view will always have a tendency to appear. So also with painting, photography, script-writing, reportage, lecturing and all the other arts and half-arts of which a complex modern state has need.

The application of this to the radio is obvious. At present the loudspeaker is the enemy of the creative writer, but this may not necessarily remain true when the volume and scope of broadcasting increase. As things are, although the B.B.C. does keep up a feeble show of interest in contemporary literature, it is harder to capture five minutes on the air in which to broadcast a poem than twelve hours in which to disseminate lying propaganda, tinned music, stale jokes, faked "discussions" or what-have-you. But that state of affairs may alter in the way I have indicated, and when that time comes serious experiment in the broadcasting of verse, with complete disregard for the various hostile influences which prevent any such thing at present, would become possible. I don't claim it as certain that such an experiment would have very great results. The radio was bureaucratised so early in its career that the relationship between broadcasting and literature has never been thought out. It is not certain that the microphone is the instrument by which poetry could be brought back to the common people and it is not even certain that poetry would gain by being more of a spoken and less of a written thing. But I do urge that these possibilities exist, and that those who care for literature might turn their minds more often to this much-despised medium, whose powers for good have perhaps been obscured by the voices of Professor Joad and Doctor Goebbels.

1. The Army Bureau of Current Affairs organised lectures for servicemen on topical issues, for example, the Welfare State, the Atom Bomb.

2630. Eileen Blair to Leonard Moore

2 March 1945   Typewritten

> Greystone,
> Carlton,
> Near Stockton-on-Tees,
> Co. Durham.[1]

Dear Mr. Moore,

Thank you very much for your letter and various press cuttings. I am sorry to have been so dilatory but I had to go to London to complete the adoption of the son that Eric may have told you about and was held up there by illness while my mail waited for me here.

I am afraid I can't sign the letter on his behalf. If I had been in London while he was getting ready to go I should probably have a power of attorney as before, but as it is I have only the most informal authority. So I have sent the letter on to him and I suppose it will be back in about three weeks. I have had one letter and that took eleven days. I have also written to Warburg about the letter—I know Eric spoke to Frederick° Warburg about it and I imagine there will be no trouble about it, though I quite see that from your point of view these loose ends are very unsatisfactory.

I have no real news from Eric. He wrote the day after arriving in Paris and had seen little except his hotel which seems to be full of war correspondents and quite comfortable—with central heating on. I expect the next letter will be more informative, though it will mostly concern this son we have adopted in whom Eric is passionately interested. The baby is now nine months old and according to his new father very highly gifted—"a very thoughtful little boy" as well as very beautiful. He really is a very nice baby. You must see him sometime. His name is Richard Horatio.

> Yours sincerely,
> Eileen Blair

1. Greystone was the house Eileen's sister-in-law, Gwen O'Shaughnessy, had taken when her children were evacuated from London when the flying-bomb raids began. It was the O'Shaughnessy family home. Eileen, who was in very poor health, had gone to stay there. Richard (born 14 May 1944), went there when the Blairs were bombed out of their flat at 10A Mortimer Crescent in Maida Vale on 28 June 1944. He was looked after by the O'Shaughnessys' nanny, Joyce Pritchard. Horatio was a Blair family name. The letters written by Orwell to Eileen whilst he was abroad have not been traced.

2631. Occupation's Effect on French Outlook: Different Political Thinking

The Observer, 4 March 1945

Paris, March 3

The visit of M. Bidault, French Foreign Minister, to London continues to be keenly discussed, and beneath the warm expressions of Franco-British friendship one can discern in part of the Press a faint uneasiness about the probable Brittsh attitude on the subject of the Rhine frontier.

Nevertheless, so far as one can gather from random conversations, the French are still somewhat in the dark about certain aspects of public opinion in Britain. The two peoples have had a totally different political development over five years, and their future relationship will probably be happier if the points of disagreement are brought into the open as early as possible.

One of the first things that strike a newcomer is that almost any Frenchman has a far tougher attitude towards Germany than almost any Englishman. I have been impressed by this in private conversations even more than in reading the newspapers, and it applies not merely to Communists and 100 per cent. Gaullists, but to Socialists and members of the Left-wing Resistance groups.

There are, of course, individual variations, but there seems hardly to be such a thing as a Frenchman who does not assume that dismemberment of Germany, the dismantling of German war industries, heavy reparations, forced labour and military occupation over a long period are the minimum needs for French security.

The real situation in France would be hard to assess even if internal communications were better. Some of the main forces are not operating on the surface. Irreconcilable enemies are observing a temporary truce, the Press is timid, and great numbers of people are made apathetic by privation.

But so far as the articulate minorities go, the effect of the occupation seems to have been a harshening of political thought and the disappearance of various trends once looked upon as progressive. Pacifism, for instance, seems to have disappeared completely. Not only did some of the leading Pacifists discredit themselves by collaborating, but the desire to see France reappear as soon as possible as a great military power, with a large mechanised army, seems universal.

The ultra Left sects, which were not absolutely negligible in pre-war France, seem also to have vanished. Some groups of Trotskyists do manage to exist and publish an illegal paper, but they evidently have little influence. The nexus of ideas, Army-Fatherland-Glory, seems to have re-established itself to an extent that is surprising when one remembers that it is only a decade or so since French Left-Wingers thought it proper to denounce the Versailles Treaty as an iniquity and to cover such figures as Foch and Clemenceau with abuse.

Anti-imperialist propaganda has faded out of the picture. De Gaulle's statement that Indo-China, once liberated, would be integrated more closely into the French Empire, without interference from outside powers, was received without comment.

Another phenomenon, not strictly political but symptomatic of the change in the mental climate, is the widespread anxiety about the state of the French birth-rate. Left-Wing newspapers and reviews carry articles discussing the best way to encourage maternity and deploring the practice of deliberate limitation of families—an attitude which is well justified but which would have been considered reactionary only a few years ago.

Since, in the long run, the enforcement of policy depends on the common people, the present divergence of French and British political thought has its dangers. In a way, France is politically to the Left of Britain. The ruling class is largely discredited, and, on the other hand, there is comparatively little overt opposition to such projects as the nationalisation of major industries.

But the internationalist and humanitarian ideas once thought inseparable from Socialism have receded, and respect for democracy has probably been weakened. This has not happened to the same extent in England, and the fact ought to be made clear to the French people. In particular, it ought to be made clear that the British public is very unlikely for any length of time to support a peace settlement that appears vindictive, and certainly will not support any policy that entails a permanent army of occupation.

On the other hand, we ourselves ought to make a better effort to understand the French point of view.

No matter to whom you talk in this country, you are soon brought up against the same fact—that Britain has not known what it is like to be occupied.

It is impossible to discuss the "purge," for instance, without being reminded of this.

The people who would like to see the "purge" in full swing—and some of them say freely that they believe several thousand executions to be necessary—are not reactionaries and not necessarily Communists: they may be thoughtful, sensitive people whose antecedents are Liberal, Socialist, or non-political.[1]

Your objections always get much the same answer: "It's different for you in England. You can do things peacefully because there is no real division within the nation. Here we have to deal with actual traitors. It's not safe to let them remain alive." So also with the attitude towards Germany. A highly intelligent Frenchman, brushing aside my suggestion that a Democratic Germany might arise when Hitler is gone, said to me:

"It's not a question of wanting revenge. It's merely that after having had them here for four years, I have great difficulty in believing that the Germans are the same kind of people as ourselves."

Some observers think that the present rather Chauvinist cast of French thought is a superficial symptom, and that quite other tendencies will show themselves when the war is safely won.

Meanwhile, whatever divergencies there may be either in high policy or in public opinion, there appears to be no anti-British feeling in France.

If one may judge by Paris, France has never been more Anglophile, and one is paid quite embarrassing compliments on the subject of Britain's lonely struggle in 1940 and on the "très correct" bearing of the comparatively few British soldiers who are to be seen in the streets.

1. The taking of revenge by French men and women on their own people after the Occupation was particularly savage. David Pryce-Jones in his *Paris in the Third Reich: A History of the German Occupation, 1940–1944* (1981) quotes Robert Aron's conservative estimate that after the liberation there were between 30,000 and 40,000 summary executions; but Adrien Tixier, the post-war Minister of Justice, stated that there were 105,000 such executions between June

1944 and February 1945 throughout France; the journal *Historia* (No. 41) records apparently one million arrests, of which 100,000 were in the Paris area, between 21 August and 1 October 1944 (Pryce-Jones, 206). The Germans deported 75,721 Jews from France, though this must be taken as 'the minimum number'; about one-third were French nationals; about 3,000 survived (144). Pryce-Jones concludes: 'the number of Frenchmen killed by other Frenchmen, whether through summary execution or rigged tribunals akin to lynch mobs or court-martials° and High Court trials, equaled° or even exceeded the number of those sent to their death by the Germans as hostages, deportees, and slave laborers' (207). These figures exaggerate and underestimate. Officially, some 10,000 people were 'executed,' although Professor M. R. D. Foot has suggested to the editor that that number should be about 20,000. The Mémorial des Martyrs et de la Déportation in Paris commemorates 200,000 French men, women, and children deported to their deaths in Germany.

2632. The Political Aims of the French Resistance

Manchester Evening News, 7 March 1945

This article is illustrated by a cartoon showing General de Gaulle contemplating a 'Welcome' mat outside a doorway marked 'France.' This leads to a conference room labelled 'San Francisco,' the meeting place where forty-six nations conferred on 25 April to plan the United Nations. De Gaulle, on stilts, is too tall to make his entrance. The caption reads: 'A Question of Altitude.' In the event, when the World Security Charter was signed on 26 June, France was elected a permanent member of the Security Council.

Sharp personal criticism of General de Gaulle is impossible in France at this moment, but the French Left is becoming more and more disappointed with his internal policies.

Competent observers consider that there are now five real political forces in France.

First, there are the Conservatives ranging from old-style Nationalists to outright supporters of Pétain.

Secondly, there is the large, well-organised Communist party.

Thirdly, there is General de Gaulle, who is sufficiently powerful and popular to be considered a political force in himself.

Fourthly, there are the old "moderate" parties, including the Socialist party, which are now rapidly reviving and which represent all the middling people who are neither revolutionaries nor Vichyites.

Finally there are the resistance groups, which include in them most of the elements that could be called revolutionary but reject the aims and methods of the Communists.

The aims of the Resistance Movement boil down to democratic Socialism. Their immediate demands are far-reaching measures of nationalisation, and (what is closely bound up with the former) a ruthless purge of collaborators. The Communists are also anxious to continue the purge, and more intermittently have campaigned for nationalisation, but they stand for a regimented and hierarchical form of Socialism which great numbers of Frenchmen are unable to accept.

The great fear of the resistance groups, which they express as openly as they are able, is that the economic and social reforms which were expected to follow the liberation will fail to materialise and that the big trusts and the "Two Hundred Families" will be able to re-establish their power.

At this moment that is the direction in which events are actually moving. The demand for harsher measures against war criminals is not simply a demand for vengeance.

By and large the people who collaborated with the Germans are the people who control the economic life of France and whose power will have to be broken if France becomes a Socialist country.

It is widely felt that the punishment of a few really prominent collaborators (so far, with very few exceptions, the purge has only struck at secondary figures such as journalists and minor officials) would be a sign that radical changes in the social structure are intended.

On the other hand the continued immunity of known war criminals, and the rather vague references that General de Gaulle has made to Government control of industry, are taken as heralding some kind of State capitalism in which the big trusts would still be in control.

Almost all people of "Left" views in France are united in wanting an intensification of the purge.

From our side of the Channel this attitude may appear somewhat distasteful, but one has to remember not only the bitterness resulting from the occupation but the fact that a real political division, amounting almost to latent civil war, has existed in France for decades past.

In the moment of crisis there was open, conscious treachery on a scale that would have been impossible in a well-united country like Britain, and it is probably true that France's future cannot be safeguarded unless some thousands of people are killed or driven into exile, or in some way rendered harmless.

The veiled struggle that is going on between the forces of the Left and of the Right was already happening during the occupation.

The resistance groups not only had to battle against Vichy, but found themselves to some extent in opposition to the Free French authorities in London, and later Algiers, who viewed them with suspicion and were unwilling to supply them with arms in very large quantities. But the struggle was also developing between the Communists and the rest of the resistance groups, who could collaborate in fighting the Germans but whose ultimate aims were irreconcilable.

The basic difference was on the question of political democracy and the preservation of freedom of speech. This showed itself even in the structure of the various underground military formations, and it now shows itself in endless controversies in the Press.

The writers in the Resistance Press always attack the Communists from the angle of democratic Socialism. The minor Marxist sects, which are lumped together under the name of "Trotskyism," seem almost to have disappeared for the time being.

It is not yet certain whether the resistance groups will harden into a regular political party; but at any rate they constitute a well-defined political tendency, extremist and yet democratic, and containing some of the more gifted and idealistic people in France.

France's political future is still very uncertain. The reviving forces of Conservatism and de Gaulle's powerful personality may stave off any real revolution, or on the other hand the Communists may come to power, legally or otherwise.

Recent statements by the Communist leaders, however, have made it clear that they themselves realise that they could not remain in power without the support of other Left parties. In such circumstances the resistance groups might play an important part, and their steady insistence, after all the bloodshed and illegality of the last five years, on democracy and freedom of speech is an encouraging symptom.

2633. Clerical Party May Re-emerge in France: Educational Controversy

The Observer, 11 March 1945

Paris, March 10

During this week Paris has been discussing a yellow poster which appeared all over the city last Tuesday and which bore a title roughly translatable as "Secularism versus National Unity."

It was unsigned but obviously emanated from the Catholic Press, and it called for a public demonstration against anti-Clerical intolerance.

The reference was clearly to some remarks made by a Communist speaker in the Assembly on the question of State subsidies to Catholic Schools. The amount of private comment, as well as some guarded but acrimonious remarks in the Press, shows how important the issue is felt to be.

So far as it refers to education, the controversy between Clericals and anti-Clericals is very similar to the one that recently occurred in Britain. Under the Third Republic, education was secularised. Religious instruction in the State schools was voluntary, and though "private" schools (meaning, in the great majority of cases, Catholic schools) were allowed to exist, they received no aid from the State.

The Pétain Government introduced compulsory religious instruction and subsidised the private schools to the extent of 500,000,000 francs a year.[1] It now appears, or at least it is generally believed, that the Provisional Government intends to continue with this arrangement. There has been no official statement to this effect, but at any rate the Communist speaker in the Assembly who referred to the continuance of the subsidy was not contradicted.

The Catholics put forward the same argument as their co-religionists in Britain, i.e., that they pay taxes which help to support the State schools, and consequently that State aid for Catholic schools is an elementary act of justice. However, the issue is not merely educational. The Catholics now have a large and fairly vigorous Press, both daily and weekly, and some observers expect the re-emergence in the near future of Clericalism as a political force.

The special importance of this at the present moment is that women have now been given the vote. The Church has far more women than men among its followers, and the appearance of any party which could be identified as the Church Party would be a serious development from the Left-Wing point of view.

Sectarian intolerance has always been fiercer in France than in Britain, even when no obvious political issue was involved. One reason, clearly, is that in France the Reformation failed. Not only did Protestantism cease long ago to be a political force, but there never developed the innumerable gradations of belief which exist in Britain, and which make for tolerance and allow the established Church to survive. In France one had to be Catholic or nothing, and though at this moment bishops, generals, Communists, and Socialists are uneasily collaborating, no one imagines that there is real friendliness between them.

For long past great numbers of people in France have been wholly outside the orbit of the Church—many people prefer to be buried without any religious rite. For instance, some of the legislation of the Third Republic was provocatively anti-clerical. In the Left Wing political parties religious disbelief was almost obligatory, and such figures as, for instance, the late Archbishop of Canterbury or the late George Lansbury[2] would have been hard to fit into the French political scene.

The occupation temporarily blurred the picture, because the distinction between resisters and collaborators was partly a distinction of character and cut across political divisions. It was true that the Pétain regime drew much of its support from the Church, and some of the hierarchy made themselves apologists of the Germans, but it could not be said that a Catholic as such was a collaborator or a pro-Fascist.

Individual Catholics everywhere took part in the Resistance Movement, and De Gaulle, the living symbol of France's will to fight, was himself a Catholic. Nor did the Catholic Press, in the early days of the liberation, strike out any independent line of its own. Now however, it begins to appear as though the old battle between clericals and anti-clericals may reopen.

It was possibly significant that the first protest against the continuation of the subsidy came from a Communist member of the Assembly.

Although it has never succeeded in overcoming the suspicions of the Church, the Communist Party has for the greater part of the last decade been the least anti-Clerical of the Left Wing parties. When the danger presented by Nazi Germany became obvious, the Communists saw that they must come to terms with the Catholics if possible, and they tried hard to do so.

It was in 1936 that Maurice Thorez[3] coined the phrase "We hold out our hand to our Catholic comrades," and the same phrase is repeated—this time with a slightly menacing air—in Communist newspapers of the current week. During much of the intervening time the hand has remained held out, but the expected handshake has never quite happened.

Other topics much discussed in recent weeks have been the attempt of the deputies who voted for Pétain to get themselves reinstated; the campaign of the Parti Social Français (La Rocque's[4] semi-Fascist party) for recognition as a legal party; the appearance of several new newspapers of noticeably Conservative tendency; and various scandals, which do not always get into print, connected with the purge.

These usually tell of the appointment of some notorious collaborator to some important post. From such odds and ends one has to make up one's picture, but all seem to point in the same direction: that is, to the wearing off of the unreal unity of the liberation period and the re-emergence of several of the political forces which dominated France before the war.

1. In 1945, 500,000,000 francs was about £2,500,000 or $10,000,000 (there were then approximately four dollars to the pound sterling).
2. William Temple (1881–1944), Archbishop of Canterbury, 1942–44. George Lansbury (1859–1940), leader of the Labour Party, 1931–35. He was a pacifist and resigned the leadership on that issue.
3. Maurice Thorez (1900–1964), leader of the French Communist Party; see 2579, n. 3.
4. Colonel François de la Rocque, a leading figure of the extreme right in France who led the Croix de Feu, an anti-Marxist and anti-capitalist group before the war. It was banned but reconstituted as the Parti Social Français. See Orwell's Morocco Diary, 511, 10.12.38, and his Diary of Events Leading Up to the War, 562, 6.8.39, Party Politics, 4.

2634. To Mrs. Sally McEwan

12 March 1945   Typewritten

Room 329
Hotel Scribe
Rue Scribe
Paris 9e

Dear Sally,[1]

I hope you are getting on O.K. I won't say without me but in my absence. I haven't had a copy of Tribune yet, thanks to the condition of the posts I suppose. I expect you also got via the Observer some frantic S.O.Ss for tobacco, but at the moment the situation isn't so bad because I got a friend who was coming across to bring me some. None has arrived by post, needless to say. Our Paris opposite number, Libertés, with whom I want Tribune to arrange a regular exchange, are never able to get the paper commercially but see copies at the Bibliotheque Nationale and frequently translate extracts. I went to a semi-public meeting of their readers and also to the paper's weekly meeting which was very like Tribune's Friday meeting but on a higher intellectual level I thought. I don't know whether Louis Levy[2] came and saw Bevan and Strauss about his idea of a continental edition of T., but if that can't be arranged it would certainly be a good idea if they could manage to send a few copies over here weekly, even say 50. A lot of British and American papers are sold regularly here, and there is a considerable public which would be glad to get hold of T.

I am trying to arrange to go to Cologne for a few days, or, if not Cologne, at any rate some where in occupied territory. After that I fancy I shall go to Toulouse and Lyons, then return to Paris and come back to England towards the end of April. By the time the posts seem to take, I don't think it would be worth forwarding any letters after about the 10th of April. Otherwise they are liable to arrive here after I have left and then will probably be lost for good. But it's all right forwarding letters while I am out of Paris because I should come back here to pick up my stuff in any case. I wonder whether you could be kind enough to do one thing for me. I only rather hurriedly saw, before leaving, Stefan Schimanski[3] who had had a war diary of mine from which he thought he might like to use extracts in some book or other. I wonder if you could ring him up (I think he is at Lindsay Drummonds[°]) and impress upon him that if he does want to use such extracts, he must in no case do so without my seeing them beforehand.

I dare say you heard that the court case went off all right and little Richard is now legally mine. I hear that he has 5 teeth and is beginning to move about a bit. I saw the other day a knitted suit in a shop that I thought would be nice for him, so I went in and asked the price and it was Frs. 2500, ie. about £12–10.[4] That is what prices are like here. If you take two people out to lunch it costs at least Frs 1000 for the three. However it isn't me that is paying. I am glad I managed to bring a lot of soap and coffee across with me because you can produce a terrific effect by distributing small quantities of either, also English cigarettes. Luckily it isn't at all cold. I've taken to wearing a beret, you'll be glad to hear. Please give everyone my love and impress on them again not to expect any silk stockings because there just aren't such things here. The Americans bought them all up long ago.

Yours
George

P.S. Before being able to send this off, ie. before getting hold of some envelopes which aren't too plentiful here, I got your letter of March 6th and 2 Tribunes, 2nd and 9th March. It was nice to see Tribune again, and it seems so fat and heavy compared with French papers.

1. Sally McEwan was working on *Tribune*; when Orwell was literary editor, she was his secretary. The opening line of the letter suggests a close relationship.
2. Louis Levy was editor of *Libertés*.
3. Stefan Schimanski (d. 1950), journalist and editor (for example, of the annual *Transformation*, with Henry Treece, 1943–47). He and Treece edited *Leaves in the Storm: A Book of Diaries* (published by Lindsay Drummond, 1947). Orwell's diaries were not included. In an editorial to *World Review* (which Schimanski assisted its owner, Edward Hulton, to produce), new series, no. 16, June 1950, in which he published extracts from two of Orwell's diaries in an issue devoted to Orwell, Schimanski said they had been omitted in 1947 because the time was not propitious. Schimanski was killed when the plane in which he was travelling on an assignment to Korea for *Picture Post* to cover the war, exploded. See Tom Hopkinson, *Of This Our Time* (1982), 278–81.
4. This amount (in today's currency, £12.50) might conveniently be compared with a case reported in the *Manchester Evening News* alongside Orwell's review of *Independent People* by Halldór Laxness on 8 February 1945; see 2615. The article concerned the rights of those who had been called into the armed forces or civil defence units to get their jobs back on demobilisation. An employer had offered a man 35 shillings per week after five years of

military service—that being his pay on leaving his firm for war service. An official Reinstatement Committee decided the man must be employed at £4 per week. The knitted suit was equivalent to three weeks' pay at that rate.

2635. To Roger Senhouse

17 March 1945   Typewritten

Room 329
Hotel Scribe
Rue Scribe
Paris 9e

Dear Roger,

Thanks so much for your letter, and for sending the copy of "Homage to Catalonia." I didn't after all give it to André Malraux, who is not in Paris, but to, of all people, Jose Rovira, who was the commander of my division in Spain and whom I met at a friend's house here.

I don't know whether "Animal Farm" has definitely gone to press. If it has not actually been printed yet, there is one further alteration of one word that I would like to make. In Chapter VIII (I think it is VIII), when the windmill is blown up, I wrote "all the animals including Napoleon flung themselves on their faces." I would like to alter it to "all the animals except Napoleon." If the book has been printed it's not worth bothering about, but I just thought the alteration would be fair to J.S., as he did stay in Moscow during the German advance.[1]

I hope Fred will have a good long rest. I know how long it takes to get one's strength back. I am trying to arrange to go to Cologne for a few days, but there keep being delays. I shall be back in England at the end of April.

Yours
George

1. In the margin there is an annotation: 'p 73 l 5.' See *CW*, VIII, 69 l. 22 and Textual Note on 20.2. Orwell's letter was received at Secker & Warburg on 3 April 1945. The source of this change is almost certainly Orwell's meeting in Paris with Joseph Czapski, a survivor of Starobielsk, and of the series of massacres of Polish prisoners carried out by the Russians and associated especially with that at Katyn. See Orwell's letter to Arthur Koestler, 5 March 1946, *2919*, in connection with their attempt to publish an English version of his pamphlet describing his experiences at the hands of the Soviets.

2636. De Gaulle Intends to Keep Indo-China: But French Apathetic on Empire

The Observer, 18 March 1945

Paris, March 17

General de Gaulle's recent broadcast on the fighting in Indo-China aroused much discussion, and the newspapers printed it in full with big headlines, though in many cases without commenting on it.

His earlier statement on Indo-China a few weeks ago had passed almost unnoticed, but the present crisis has set many people talking anew about the half-forgotten problem of the French colonies.

The broadcast included a warm tribute to the courageous fight put up by the French and Indo-Chinese troops, and also included the usual implied criticism of Britain and America, but its main object was evidently to emphasise the importance of France's part in the Pacific end of the war. De Gaulle is too good a soldier not to realise, better than the majority of his countrymen, that the position of France's remoter colonies will be precarious, even after Japan is defeated, and doubtless it seems to him good policy to stake out as large a claim as possible in the forthcoming Pacific victory.

Some of what he said was exaggerated and misleading, and he has been able to make similar statements before, precisely because the average Frenchman is only intermittently interested in imperial policy.

This has been especially true since the liberation. Except when something violent happens, the French overseas territories hardly find their way into the French Press. It is only by dipping into quite obscure periodicals that one can learn, for instance, that in Algeria and Morocco the Vichy apparatus is still largely functioning and the local Socialist and Communist Press is fighting for its life against heavily subsidised newspapers of reactionary tendency.

But, even when home affairs were less pressing, the word "Empire" has never aroused the same powerful emotions, for or against, in France as it does in England.

In England the anti-Imperialist tradition of the Labour Party, inherited from the old Liberal Party, is no doubt partly hypocritical, but it exists, and to some extent it influences policy.

In France, even before the disaster of 1940, it was always noticeable that the Left-Wing parties had much less to say on this subject. No doubt this was partly because Frenchmen, as well as foreigners, tended to generalise too freely from the admirable lack of colour prejudice in France itself.

But one has also got to consider the psychological effects of the defeat, which have left so deep a mark on French political thought, even in extreme-Left circles.

It is curious that there is very little awareness here of the strategic dependence of the French Empire on other Powers. Large portions of it would be quite indefensible without American or British help, and Indo-China, in particular, is very unlikely to remain in French possession without the agreement of China as well.

Yet one does not see admissions of this kind made in print or in public speeches, though thoughtful Frenchmen may make them in private. It is apparently more painful to have to admit in France that Madagascar lies within the British orbit, than to admit in England that Jamaica lies in the American orbit.

The shock of the defeat naturally induced in almost everyone a desire to feel strong, and one can see the result in the unrealistic way in which strategic questions are often discussed.

One can see it again in the general tendency to attribute the defeat of 1940 primarily, though not wholly, to deliberate treachery. It is significant that Pétain is often referred to in the Press as Pétain-Bazaine, thus being linked with the other great scapegoat of French history.[1]

It would probably have made no difference to the outcome of the war of 1870 if the wretched Bazaine had held out in Metz for six weeks longer, but an identifiable traitor on whom to put the blame was no doubt helpful in the recovery of national pride. The recrudescence of the nationalistic outlook, product of defeat, is very marked in France at present, and the equivocal attitude even of Communists and Socialists towards imperialism is one symptom of it.

De Gaulle has not yet made any very comprehensive statement on imperial policy. From what he has said hitherto, his ideas seem to lie towards vigorous economic development, and the raising of the standard of living of the colonial populations, rather than towards an extension of self-government.

One newspaper, reporting Wednesday's broadcast, stated hopefully that de Gaulle had promised "a new status" to Indo-China, but the text of the broadcast does not seem to bear this out. Indeed, if his various pronouncements on this subject mean anything, they mean that he intends to keep Indo-China inside the French Empire and on as nearly as possible the same footing as before.

His speech aroused great interest, but, as usual, received no genuine criticism in the Press. It is an index of the state of the French Press that not a single paper pointed out that this was a matter on which China might have something to say.

Indeed, when such topics do get any discussion, it is usually not in the daily Press but in little struggling weeklies, whose pages are all too often chequered by blank spaces bearing nothing but the dismal word, Censure.

1. Achille-François Bazaine (1811–1888), Marshal of France, capitulated with his army of 140,000 men at Metz, 27 October 1870, during the Franco-Prussian War. For this he was tried for treason in 1873 and sentenced to degradation and death. The sentence was commuted to twenty years' imprisonment by the President of France, Marshal MacMahon, who, ironically, had suffered severe defeat at Sedan on 1 September whilst attempting to relieve Metz. Bazaine escaped abroad and died in poverty in Madrid.

2637. The French Believe We Have Had a Revolution
Manchester Evening News, 20 March 1945

So far as one can judge from casual conversations and from the Press, Britain's reputation has never stood higher in France than it does now. The attitude of the average man is not only friendlier than General de Gaulle's speeches would lead one to suppose but it is also far friendlier than one would infer from what might be called the mechanics of the situation.

For four years France was subjected to a barrage of anti-British propaganda, some of it extremely skilful, and at the same time Britain was driven by military necessity to bomb French cities, sink French ships, and commit other acts of war which the average man could hardly be blamed for resenting at the time when they happened. But on top of this, the invasion and the subsequent campaigns have seriously disrupted the economic life of the country. It is generally agreed that in the later period of the occupation France was better off in a physical sense than she is now, in spite of the huge-scale looting practised by the Germans.

The transport system has not yet recovered from the invasion, and the heaviest fighting took place in some of the best agricultural areas, upsetting first the hay harvest, then the grain harvest, and resulting in enormous losses of livestock. One gets some idea of what this means when one sees butter, almost unobtainable in any legal way, being black-marketed at something over £2 a pound. It is the same with many other foodstuffs, and thanks to the lack of locomotives the fuel situation in the big towns is catastrophic. Paris shivered through the winter of 1940, under the Germans, and shivered again through the winter of 1944, under the Anglo-Americans. Moreover it is realised that the food crisis has been accentuated in recent months by the diversion of Allied shipping to the Pacific.

Yet there seems to be remarkably little resentment. No doubt the forces that supported Vichy are still there, under the surface, but the only body of expressed opinion that could be possibly called anti-British is that of the Communists. The Communists are to some extent politically hostile to Britain because they see in Britain the likeliest leader of the "western bloc" which it is the object of Soviet policy to prevent. The ordinary man is pro-British both personally and politically, and if asked why, he gives two reasons, one rather trivial, the other more serious and possibly containing in it the seeds of future misunderstanding.

The first reason is that the British troops have on the whole been better ambassadors for their country than the Americans. The comparison is not really a fair one, because the British are here in comparatively small numbers. The bulk of the British forces are in Belgium, and the vast majority of the soldiers who throng the streets of Paris are Americans. Most of them have come from several months in the unbearable conditions of the front line, and they have a large accumulation of pay in their pockets and only a few hours in which to spend it. But the other reason for the present friendly attitude of the French towards Britain is a flattering but somewhat exaggerated estimate of British political achievement during the war.

Frenchmen are much impressed not only by the obstinacy with which Britain continued the struggle in 1940 but by the national unity she displayed. They say with truth that in the moment of crisis Britain had no fifth column and not even any great bitterness of feeling between classes. But to a surprising extent they are inclined to mistake the surface changes of war-time Britain for an actual social revolution, accomplished by common consent. The word "revolution" is used again and again in connection with Britain's present-day development, both in conversation and in print.

Frenchmen who might be expected to take a more cynical view are to be heard saying that class privilege is no longer rampant in England, that large incomes have been taxed out of existence, and that private capitalism has in effect given way to a centralised economy. And they remark with admiration that all this has been achieved without bloodshed, almost without friction, in the middle of a struggle for existence.

To anyone who knows how little real structural change has taken place in Britain during the war, these eulogies are rather disconcerting. Curiously enough they are repeated by Frenchmen who have visited war-time Britain, and perhaps spent several years there. The mistake made, in many cases, seems to be to confuse patriotism with social enlightenment. Without a doubt the general *behaviour* in Britain during the war has been good. All classes have been willing to sacrifice either their lives or their comfort, rationing has been equitable and efficient, profiteering and black-marketing have never been a major problem, industrial production has soared in spite of every kind of difficulty, and women have flung themselves into the war effort to an unprecedented extent. Frenchmen compare these phenomena with the much more discouraging things that have happened in their own country, and are apt not to realise that the essential social structure of Britain has remained almost unchanged and may reassert itself when the danger has passed.

There are other current misconceptions—in particular, the failure of nearly all Frenchmen to grasp the British attitude towards Germany and the peace settlement. Few Frenchmen realise how unwilling the British people will be to maintain a permanent army of occupation in Germany, or to support any settlement that would make such an army necessary. Not many Frenchmen understand the extent to which Britain's policy is conditioned by her close association with the U.S.A., and hardly any realise that Britain can never act internationally without considering the Dominions.

The present relations between France and Britain are good, but the possible sources of discord are many, and they could do with more illumination than they are getting at present.

France looks hopefully towards Britain as the land of true democracy, the country that has been able to recover from its past mistakes without civil disturbance, without dictatorship, and without infringing intellectual liberty. This picture is not altogether false, but it could be the cause of serious disappointment, and it would be well if more Frenchmen were able to distinguish between the real social changes that have taken place in Britain and the temporary expedients that have been forced upon a country fighting for its life.

2638. Eileen Blair to her husband

Wednesday 21 March 1945   Typed and handwritten

Greystone,[1]
Carlton,
Stockton-on-Tees.

Dearest your letter came this morning—the one written on the 7th after you got my first one. I was rather worried because there had been an interval of nearly a fortnight, but this one took 14 days whereas the last one came in 10 so probably that explains it. Or one may have gone astray.

I am typing in the garden. Isn't that wonderful? I've only got a rug for myself and typewriter and the wind keeps blowing the paper down over the machine which is not so good for the typing but very good for me. The wind is quite cold but the sun is hot. Richard is sitting up in his pram talking to a doll. He has the top half of a pram suit on but he took off the rest some time ago and has nothing between himself and the sky below his nappies. I want him to get aired before the sun gets strong so that he'll brown nicely. That's my idea anyway. And he is enjoying the preliminaries anyway. I bought him a high chair—the only kind I could get. It sort of breaks in half and turns up its tail like a beetle if you want it to, and then you have a low chair attached to a little table, the whole on wheels. As a high chair it has no wheels and the usual tray effect in front of the chair. He loves it dearly and stretches out his hands to it—partly I'm afraid because what normally happens in the chair is eating. When it is being a low chair Laurence[2] takes him for rides round the nursery and down the passage— indeed Laurence wheeled the whole contraption home from the station and I found it very useful myself on the way up as a luggage trolley. I came by night in the end so that George Kopp[3] could see me off at King's X which was very nice, but there were no porters at all at Thornaby or Stockton— and only one at Darlington but I got him. There is no real news about Richard. He is just very well. I was sorry to be away from him for a week because he always stops feeding himself when I don't act as waiter, but today he did pick up the spoon himself from the dish and put it in his mouth—upside down of course, but he was eating rather adhesive pudding so he got his food all right. I bought him a truck too for an appalling sum of money. I had to forget the price quickly but I think it's important he should have one.

We're no longer in the garden now. In fact Richard is in bed and has been for some time. Blackburn[4] came and told me all about his other jobs and how Mr. Wilson fished and Sir John once had to go to his office on August 12th but the car went with him full of guns and sandwiches and they got to the moors by 1.30. And Blackburn's predecessor here shot himself. I think perhaps the general shooting standard was rather lower than at Sir John's, because this man shot a wood pigeon and tried to pull it out of the bush into which it had fallen with his gun (this might be better expressed but you can guess it). Naturally the bush pulled the trigger and there was another shot in the other barrel and the ass was actually holding the barrel to his belly, so he might as well have been an air raid casualty. This convinced me not that Richard must never have a gun but that he must have one very young so that he couldn't forget how to handle it.

Gwen rang up Harvey Evers[5] and they want me to go in for this operation at once. This is all a bit difficult. It is going to cost a terrible lot of money. A bed in a kind of ward costs seven guineas a week and Harvey Evers's operation fee is forty guineas. In London I would have to pay about five guineas a week in a hospital but Gwen says the surgeon's fee would be higher. The absurd thing is that we are too well off for really cheap rates—you'd have to make less than £500 a year. It comes as a shock to me in a way because while you were being ill I got used to paying doctors nothing. But of course it was only because Eric[6] was making the arrangements. I suppose your bronchoscopy would have cost about forty guineas too—and I must say it would have been cheap at the price, but what worries me is that I really don't think I'm worth the money. On the other hand of course this thing will take a longish time to kill me if left alone and it will be costing some money the whole time. The only thing is, I think perhaps it might be possible to sell the Harefield house[7] if we found out how to do it. I do hope too that I can make some money when I am well—I could of course do a job but I mean really make some money from home as it were. Anyway I don't know what I can do except go ahead and get the thing done quickly. The idea is that I should go in next week and I gather he means to operate quickly—he thinks the indications are urgent enough to offset the disadvantages of operating on a bloodless patient; indeed he is quite clear that no treatment at all can prevent me from becoming considerably more bloodless every month. So I suppose they'll just do a blood transfusion and operate more or less at once.

While I was in London I arranged to take Evelyn's[8] manuscript in to Tribune. I set off with it all right, broke the journey to go to the bank and was taken with a pain just like the one I had the day before coming North, only rather worse. I tried to have a drink in Selfridges' but couldn't and all sorts of extraordinary things then happened but after a bit I got myself into the Ministry. I simply could not do any more travelling, so Miss Sparrow[9] rang up Evelyn for me and they arranged between them about the transfer of the manuscript. People from Tribune then rang up in the *most* friendly way, offering to come and look after me, to bring me things and to *get you home*. I was horrified. But yesterday I had a phase of thinking that it was really outrageous to spend all your money on an operation of which I know you disapprove, so Gwen rang Tribune to know whether they had means of communicating with you quickly and could get your ruling. They hadn't but suggested she should ring the Observer, which she did and talked to Ivor Brown. He said you were in Cologne now he thought and that letters would reach you very slowly if at all. He suggested that they would send you a message about me by cable and wireless, like their own. Gwen says he couldn't have been nicer. But I'm not having this done. It's quite impossible to give you the facts in this way and the whole thing is bound to sound urgent and even critical. I have arranged with Gwen however that when the thing is over she'll ask the Observer to send you a message to that effect. One very good thing is that by the time you get home I'll be convalescent, really convalescent at last and you won't have the hospital nightmare you would so much dislike. You'd more or less have to visit me and visiting someone in a ward really is a nightmare even to me with my fancy for hospitals—particularly if they're badly ill as I shall be at first of course. I only wish I could have had your approval as it were, but I think it's just hysterical. Obviously I can't just go on having a tumour or rather several rapidly growing tumours. I *have* got an uneasy feeling that after all the job might have been more cheaply done somewhere else but if you remember Miss Kenny's fee for a cautery, which is a small job, was fifteen guineas so she'd certainly charge at least fifty for this. Gwen's man might have done cheaper work for old sake's sake, but he's so very bad at the work and apparently he would have wanted me in hospital for weeks beforehand—and I'm morally sure I'd be there for weeks afterwards. Harvey Evers has a very high reputation, and George Mason[10] thinks very well of him and says Eric did the same, and I am sure that he will finish me off as quickly as anyone in England as well as doing the job properly—so he may well come cheaper in the end. I rather wish I'd talked it over with you before you went. I knew I had a "growth". But I wanted you to go away peacefully anyway, and I did *not* want to see Harvey Evers before the adoption was through in case it was cancer. I thought it just possible that the judge might make some enquiry about our health as we're old for parenthood and anyway it would have been an uneasy sort of thing to be producing oneself as an ideal parent a fortnight after being told that one couldn't live more than six months or something.

You may never get this letter but of course it's urgent about the house in the country. Inez[11] thinks we might do something together with her cottage near Andover. It's quite big (6 rooms and kitchen) but it has disadvantages. The 25/- a week rent which she considers nominal I think big considering there is no sanitation whatever and only one tap, no electricity or gas, and expensive travelling to London. She and Hugh[12] (incidentally they are more or less parting company at present but they might join up again I think) hire furniture for another 25/- a week which wouldn't be necessary if we were there, and it might be possible a) to get a long lease for a lower rent and b) to have modern conveniences installed. I am now so confident of being strong in a few months that I'm not actually frightened as I should have been of living a primitive life again (after all when you were ill soon after we were married I did clean out the whole of Wallington's sanitation and that was worse than emptying a bucket) but it does waste a lot of time. So we can consider that. Then George Kopp has a clever idea. Apparently people constantly advertise in the Times wanting to exchange a house in the country for a flat in London. Most of these, probably all, would want something grander than N.1, but we might advertise ourselves—asking for correspondingly humble country accommodation. In the next few months people who have been living in the country for the war will be wanting somewhere in London and we might do well like that. Meanwhile there is a letter from the Ardlussa factor enclosing the contractor's estimate for repairing Barnhill—which is £200. I found to my distress that George was not forwarding letters to you, although I gave him the address by telephone the day I got it, because he had not heard from you. I opened one from the Borough and found it was to say that the electricity supply would be cut off as soon as the man could get in to do it. I paid that bill and decided I'd better look at the rest of the mail. There was nothing else quite so urgent except perhaps a letter from the BBC Schools about your two broadcasts for them. They want the scripts as soon as possible! There's also a contract. I didn't send anything on at once because I thought you might be moving and in view of Ivor Brown's news of you I'm not sending them now, but I've written to say that you are abroad but expected home next month. The broadcasts aren't till June after all. If you don't come next month I'll have to think again, but there may be a firmer address to write to. I can do nothing with this except send it to the Hotel Scribe and hope they'll forward it. To get back to Barnhill. I'm going to write to the factor to say that you're away and I'm ill and will he wait till you get back. He's very apologetic about having kept us waiting and I'm sure they won't let the house to anyone else. I think this £200 can be very much reduced, but the house is quite grand—5 bedrooms, bathroom, W.C., H & c° and all, large sitting room, kitchen, various pantries, dairies etc. and a whole village of "buildings"—in fact just what we want to live in twelve months of the year. But we needn't have all this papered and painted. I put my hopes on Mrs. Fletcher.[13] The only thing that bothers me is that if it's thought worth while to spend £200 on repairs the kind of rent they have in mind must be much higher than our £25–£30, let alone David's £5.[14] Incidentally I had a letter from David who just missed you in Paris.

It's odd—we have had nothing to discuss for months but the moment you leave the country there are dozens of things. But they can all be settled, or at least settled down, if you take this week's leave when you get back. I don't know about Garrigill.[15] It depends when you come. But at worst you could come here couldn't you? If you were here we should stay mainly in my room, indeed I suppose I'll be there for some time after I get back in any case, and Richard will be available. Mary[16] and Laurence both spend a lot of time with me now but they could be disposed of. Laurence by the way has improved out of recognition. He has three passions: farms, fairy tales, Richard. Not in that order—Richard probably comes first. So you ought to get on nicely. He has begun to invent fairy tales now, with magic cats and things in them, which is really a great advance. The pity is that the country isn't better but almost any country is good round about May and if I'm still at the picturesque stage of convalescence you could go out with Blackburn who knows every inch of the countryside or perhaps amuse yourself with Mr. Swinbank the farmer who would enjoy it I think. Or you could go over to Garrigill for a weekend's fishing on your own.

I liked hearing about Wodehouse.[17] And I'm *very* glad you're going to

Cologne. Perhaps you may get East of the Rhine before you come home. I have innumerable questions.

I think it's quite essential that you should write some book again. As you know, I thought Tribune better than the BBC and I still do. Indeed I should think a municipal dustman's work more dignified and better for your future as a writer. But as I said before I left London, I think you ought to stop the editing soon, as soon as possible, whether or not you think it worth while to stay on the editorial board or whatever it's called. And of course you must do much less reviewing and nothing but specialised reviewing if any. From my point of view I would infinitely rather live in the country on £200 than in London on any money at all. I don't think you understand what a nightmare the London life is to me. I know it is to you, but you often talk as though I *liked* it. I don't like even the things that you do. I can't stand having people all over the place, every meal makes me feel sick because every food has been handled by twenty dirty hands and I practically can't bear to eat anything that hasn't been boiled to clean it. I can't breathe the air, I can't think any more clearly that° one would expect to in the moment of being smothered, everything that bores me happens all the time in London and the things that interest me most don't happen at all and I can't read poetry. I never could. When I lived in London before I was married I used to go away certainly once a month with a suitcase full of poetry and that consoled me until the next time—or I used to go up to Oxford and read in the Bodleian and take a punt up the Cher if it was summer or walk in Port Meadow or to Godstow if it was winter. But all these years I have felt as though I were in a mild kind of concentration camp. The place has its points of course and I could enjoy it for a week. I like going to theatres for instance. But the fact of living in London destroys any pleasure I might have in its amenities and in fact as you know I never go to a theatre. As for eating in restaurants, it's the most barbarous habit and only tolerable very occasionally when one drinks enough to enjoy barbarity. And I can't drink enough beer. (George Mason took me out to dinner the night after I got to London and gave me to drink just what I would have drunk in peacetime—four glasses of sherry, half a bottle of claret and some brandy—and it did cheer me up I admit.) I like the Canonbury flat but I am suicidal every time I walk as far as the bread shop, and it would be very bad for Richard once he is mobile. Indeed if the worst comes to the worst I think he'd better go to Wallington for the summer, but it would be better to find somewhere with more space because you and Richard would be too much for the cottage very soon and I don't know where his sister could go. And I think the cottage makes you ill—it's the damp and the smoke I think.

While this has been in progress I have read several stories to Laurence, dealt with Richard who woke up (he has just stopped his 10 o'clock feed), dealt with Mary who always cries in the evening, had my supper and listened to Mrs. Blackburn's distresses about Raymond[18] who has just got a motor bike. That's why it's so long. And partly why it's so involved. But I should like to see you stop living a literary life and start writing again and it would be much better for Richard too, so you need have no conflicts about it. Richard sends you this message. He has no conflicts. If he gets a black eye he cries while it hurts but with the tears wet on his cheeks he laughs heartily at a new blue cat who says miaow to him and embraces it with loving words. Faced with any new situation he is sure that it will be an exciting and desirable situation for him, and he knows so well that everyone in the world is his good friend that even if someone hurts him he understands that it was by accident and loses none of his confidence. He will fight for his rights (he actually drove Mary off the blue cat today, brandishing a stick at her and shouting) but without malice. Whether he can keep his certainties over the difficult second year I don't know of course but he's much more likely to if he has the country and you have the kind of life that satisfies you—and me. I think Richard really has a natural tendency to be sort of satisfied, balanced in fact. He demands but he demands something specific, he knows what he wants and if he gets it or some reasonable substitute he is satisfied; he isn't just *demanding* like Mary. I'm not protecting him. That is, he takes the troubles I think proper to his age. He gets no sympathy when his face is washed and very little when he topples over and knocks his head and I expect him to take in good part the slight sort of bumps he gets when the children play with him. But he can be tough only if he knows that it's all right really.

Now I'm going to bed. Before you get this you'll probably have the message about this operation and you may well be in England again if you keep what Ivor Brown calls on the move. What a waste that would be.

All my love, and Richard's.

E.

Mary calls Richard Which or Whicher or Which-Which. I suppose he'll call himself something like that too. Whicher I find rather attractive. She is better with him now and I must say I am proud to see that she is more apt to be frightened of him than he of her, sad though it is. I actually heard her say to him yesterday "No no Whicher, no hurt Mamie." She takes things from him but she runs away from him, relying on her mobility; once he can move himself I don't believe she'll dare to—she never stays within his reach once she has the thing in her hand. She tries to gain confidence for herself by saying *Baby wet* all the time—generally with truth because he has now got to the stage of rejecting his pot (this is the usual preliminary to being "trained" and I hope we'll reach that stage soon though at present I see not the slightest indication of it), but when she dirtied her pants for the second time today I heard this conversation with Nurse: "No cross with Mamie Nurse?" "Yes I *am* cross this time." "Iodine no cross?" "Yes, Iodine's cross too." "Whicher cross?" "Whicher says he'll have to lend you some nappies." "No. . . . Baby's." And she began to cry—so she's not sure of her superiority even in this. She isn't so superior either. This has been a bad day, but she never gets through one with dry pants poor little wretch.

Dearest thank you very much for the books—Psmith in the City[19] has been making me laugh aloud. By the way, he arrived yesterday and the other three this afternoon although according to your letter you posted the three first. The oranges came too, and the fats.[20] I think you're being too generous but as the oranges *have* come I'm going to eat them. Blackburn got some the other day and I gave all mine and most of Richard's to the children so they're all right for the moment. Richard has the juice of half an orange every other day and Mary has his other half and Laurence a whole one.

This is being typed under difficulties as Mary is on my knee and trying to contribute.

Tomorrow I'm going to Newcastle, primarily to see the man in charge of Welfare Foods for the North of England. So far as I can see I can't get Richard's back orange juice as Stockton Food Office has stolen the coupons, but I hope to arrange that they won't bring off the same coup again. I now have some reason to think that they take orange juice out of stock on these extra coupons and sell it but of course I'm not proposing to mention this theory to Watkins. I'm also going to three food meetings and two infant welfare clinics with Nell.[21] If I stay the course. It will be very interesting and I hope profitable because I ought to lay hold of some Ostermilk[22] somewhere.

Don't bother about blankets. I've bought two from Binns' in Sunderland—they cost 22/- each and are more like rugs than blankets but they'll do quite well. I hope to make one into a frock for myself. They're dark grey which isn't I think the colour of choice for blankets but they'll come in useful one way or another and they're certainly cheap. I hope you have enough at home and are not economising by leaving out the underblanket because without that you'll be cold if you have a dozen on top of you.

The playpen has come and all the children are entranced by it. Richard laughed heartily as soon as he was put in and then the others joined him and there was a riot. I don't know how he'll take to it when he is left alone but I think he'll be OK. I have made him some strings of beads which he passionately loves and he will now play by himself quite happily for as long as you like. He's had more trouble with his teeth but no more are through. He might have another couple by the 21st though. As for his appetite, he ate for his lunch the same food as Mary and very nearly the same quantity, but he didn't want his milk. I'd just announced that I was going to replace the midday milk by water so this came very aptly. But I've had to replace the cereal after his evening bath. I gave him Farex[23] for a couple of nights and the last two he has had MOF again made much thinner. When he had just milk he was restless at night and screaming for his late feed by nine o'clock. So I'm just going to risk his getting overweight—he's still below the average for his age and length I'm sure. He's beginning to drink cows' milk instead of Ostermilk but I can't go ahead with this as fast as I might because I'm terrified that he'll turn against the Ostermilk and we'll be dependent on that when we're in London. The other thing that doesn't progress well is his drinking. He's much worse at it since he had the° teeth.

But I think part of the trouble is that he can't manage the mug which he's supposed to use now. I'll try to buy one or two cups or mugs in Newcastle (I'm staying the night there and coming back on Friday to fit all these things in).

I've been dressed every day since you went away but I've done very little else except give Richard most of his food and have him for his social between five and six and play with Mary for half an hour or so after feeding Richard because she's so jealous of him, quite naturally. This morning [Handwritten] At this point typing became impossible—I am now in the train but I got your wire last night (Wed). I hope you'll be able to do the Court[24] but of course you mustn't mess up the French trip.

Could you ring me up on Friday or Saturday evening? It's quite easy—Stillington, Co. Durham, 29. A trunk call of course—you dial TRU & ask for the number. Then we can talk about the plans. Unless of course you're coming up this weekend which would be nice. I'll be home at Greystone on Friday afternoon.

Eileen[25]

1. Greystone was the O'Shaughnessy family home. Joyce Pritchard, the O'Shaughnessys' nanny, told Ian Angus in a letter of 27 September 1967 that Eileen visited Greystone frequently between July 1944 (when the children were taken there) and March 1945.
2. Laurence (born 13 November 1938) was the son of Gwen and Laurence O'Shaughnessy, both doctors. Eileen was the sister of the elder Laurence, who was familiarly called Eric, derived from his second name, Frederick. He was killed at Dunkirk; see *632, n. 1*. Joyce Pritchard (in a letter to Ian Angus, 27 September 1967) said that Eileen typed out a story Laurence dictated to her, dated 2 March 1945, a copy of which she still had.
3. George Kopp, Orwell's commander in Spain, married Gwen O'Shaughnessy's half-sister Doreen Hunton, see *359, n. 2* and *1395, n. 1*. See Shelden, 298–301 (U. S.: 272–74), for his suppositions regarding Eileen's relationship with Kopp, and 413–14 (U. S.: 378) for Kopp's taking Eileen to Kings Cross station. He and Doreen lived a few doors away from the Orwells' in Canonbury Square (see *2640*), so he had not got far to go to collect the mail, which he failed to forward (see below).
4. Raymond Blackburn was gardener and odd-job man at Greystone.
5. Harry Evers was Eileen's surgeon.
6. Gwen O'Shaughnessy's husband; see *n. 2*.
7. Eileen owned a house, Ravensden, at Harefield, Middlesex; this was let. See her letter of 25 March 1945, *2642*, and for a reference to its disposal, 11 January 1946, *2856*.
8. Evelyn Anderson, foreign editor of *Tribune*. She came to England as a refugee, having studied at Frankfurt. Orwell had 'volunteered Eileen's help . . . in correcting her English for a book' (Crick, 446). This was *Hammer or Anvil: The Story of the German Working-Class Movement* (Gollancz, 1945), reviewed by Orwell in the *Manchester Evening News*, 30 August 1945; see *2734*.
9. Presumably Miss Sparrow was a secretary at the Ministry of Food, where Eileen had worked until June 1944.
10. George Mason was a surgeon and one-time colleague of Laurence O'Shaughnessy.
11. For Inez Holden (1904–1974), author and journalist, see *1326, n. 1*. She was at the time working on the Continent as a reporter. 'Behind the Barbed Wire,' a report on conditions in which German prisoners-of-war were held by the British, *Manchester Evening News*, 9 April 1945, by 'A Special Correspondent,' was probably by Inez Holden.
12. Hugh (Humphrey) Slater (1906–1958) founded *Polemic* (which published Orwell) in 1945; see *2314, n. 1*. Crick states, 'He became an intimate friend of Inez Holden,' making another of several links with Orwell (footnote on 398).

13. Margaret Fletcher (1917–; later Mrs. Nelson) went to Jura with her husband, Robin, when he inherited the Ardlussa Estate, on which stood Barnhill. See Crick, 465–66; and *Orwell Remembered* for a transcript of an interview she gave the BBC (225–29).
14. See *2543, n. 1* for how Orwell came to be interested in Jura.
15. Garrigill is a village near Alston, Cumbria, about midway between Penrith and Hexham.
16. Catherine Mary, Gwen O'Shaughnessy's adopted daughter, who was known as Mary until her cousin, Mary Kopp was born, when she took Catherine as her first name. She was also known as 'Mamie.'
17. Orwell had taken P. G. Wodehouse and his wife to a small restaurant near Les Halles in Paris.
18. Raymond Blackburn, son of Mrs. Blackburn, the housekeeper.
19. *Psmith in the City*, a novel by P. G. Wodehouse (1910) is discussed in 'In Defence of P. G. Wodehouse'; see *2624*.
20. Oranges were unobtainable for most of the war and fats were severely rationed. A special allowance of concentrated orange juice was made available to children as a Welfare Food.
21. Not identified with certainty, but probably Nell Heaton, a friend of Eileen's. They met when they worked together at the Ministry of Food. In 1947 Nell Heaton published *The Complete Cook*, the foreword of which states: 'I owe a debt of gratitude . . . to George Orwell and Emily Blair, to whose sympathy and encouragement I owe so much.' Eileen was known as Emily at the Ministry of Food (Lettice Cooper [see *2640, n. 3*] in *Remembering Orwell*, 130).
22. Ostermilk is a proprietary brand of milk powder for babies.
23. Farex is a proprietary brand of food for newly weaned babies.
24. This may possibly mean attend Court in connection with the final formalities for Richard's adoption, although Eileen, in her letter to Lettice Cooper, says 'Richard's adoption was through'; see *2640*. An alternative possibility is the kind of Court Orwell refers to later in *2641*.
25. The signature is an indecipherable scrawl.

2639. Eileen Blair to Leonard Moore

22 March 1945   Typewritten

Greystone,
Carlton,
Stockton-on-Tees,
Co. Durham.

Dear Mr. Moore,

I have been hoping to establish some reasonable means of communication with my husband, but the opposite has happened. I hear from the Observer that he is now on the move—at this moment he is probably in Cologne. But I can only go on writing to him at the Hotel Scribe in Paris. Letters take a fortnight to get to Paris and I have just had an acknowledgement from him of my first letter. He may possibly have got the Warburg letter before he left Paris but if not it can well follow him round until he gets back to England. I hope the publication of the book won't be held up, but I suppose there is not much danger of that. Frederick° Warburg really knows quite well what Eric was prepared to sign and that he will sign it. In any case once the book is ready for distribution I expect they will distribute it.

There is another complication now in that I have to go in to hospital next week for an operation. I have been ill for a long time and shall be happy to get it over, but I suppose I shall be out of all running for a week or so as it's rather a big job. If anything urgent turns up, my sister-in-law will know whether I can be communicated with and she will also know when Eric is expected home—if any of us know. He went for a minimum period of two months, as I expect you know. That will finish on April 16 or so, but he may of course stay longer, particularly if events move. My sister-in-law is Dr. Gwen O'Shaughnessy, 24 Crooms Hill, Greenwich, S.E.10—GRE 0896.

Yours sincerely,
Eileen Blair

2640. Eileen Blair to Lettice Cooper

23 March 1945 'or thereabouts'[1]   Typed and handwritten[2]

Greystone,
Carlton,
Near Stockton-on-Tees,
Co. Durham.

Dear Lettice,[3]

I'm sorry about the paper and the typewriter but Mary[4] got at both. You practically can't buy paper here so I can't waste that and although I could do something about the machine I am bored with it after about twenty minutes spent in collecting the ribbon and more or less replacing it. A typewriter ribbon is the longest thing in the world. It will go round every chair leg in a good sized house. So I've just discovered.

Richard was delighted with his coat and it will see him through the summer. He was just getting very short of jackets because he is so large. Mary's cast-offs will hardly go on, knitted things anyway. He took over her nightgowns the day after she inherited some pyjamas of Laurence's and even those aren't at all too big. He's still backward but has great charm which will be a lot more useful to him than talent. And he is not so stupid as Mogador[5] because he found out about pulling trucks by their strings before he was ten months old and is now investigating the principles of using one object to drag nearer or to pick up another. He's a hard worker.

I really would have written sooner but I came up to London about a fortnight ago to see my dentist so I thought I'd ring you up. Then I got ill and rang no one up and finished with all kinds of dramas at the Ministry. On the way up I went to see a Newcastle surgeon because as Richard's adoption was through I thought I might now deal with the grwoth° (no one could object to a grwoth°) I knew I had. He found it or rather them without any difficulty and I'm going into his nursing home next week for the removal. I think the question about the hysterectomy is answered because there is hardly any chance that the tumours can come out without more or less everything else removable. So that on the whole is a very good thing. It was worth coming to the north country because there is to be none of the fattening up in hospital before the operation that I was to have in London. London surgeons love preparing their patients as an insurance against unknown consequences. I think they're all terrified of their knives really—probably they have a subconscious hope that the patient will die before getting as far as the theatre and then they can't possibly be blamed. In London they said I couldn't have any kind of operation without a preparatory month of blood transfusions etc.; here I'm going in next Wednesday to be done on Thursday. Apart from its other advantages this will save money, a lot of money. And that's as well. By the way, if you could write a letter that would be nice. Theoretically I don't want any visitors, particularly as I can't get a private room; in practice I'll probably be furious that no one comes—and no one can because such friends as I have in Newcastle will be away for the school holidays. So if you have time write a letter to Fernwood House, Clayton Road, Newcastle. It's a mercy George is away—in Cologne at the moment. George visiting the sick is a sight infinitely sadder than any disease-ridden wretch in the world.

[Handwritten] I hate to think that you are no longer at the Ministry & that this will be the last extract from Miss Tomkins' conversation. I clearly remember the sweetly pretty painting of snowdrops.

Tell me whether the flat materialises. It sounds perfect. Incidentally if you want somewhere to work or to live for that matter, use our flat which is rotting in solitude. Doreen Kopp, who lives at 14A Cannonbury° Square, has the key. Ours is 27B Cannonbury Square. And her telephone number is CAN 4901. She has a son, very large, with the hair and hands of a talented musician. I expected to be jealous but find that I didn't prefer him to Richard, preferable though he is. To return to the flat, Doreen can tell you whatever you don't know about its amenities, which don't include sheets. The last lot have disappeared since I came North. But you could have a peat fire which is a nice thing.

Raymond Blackburn[6] is going to Stockton & he must carry this in his hand. It has taken about a week to write . . .[7] But all this time we have been thanking you for Richard's present, he & I.

Lots of love
Emily[8]

1. The date is given as '23.3.45 or thereabouts.'
2. Crick refers to this letter (476), as does Shelden (413–14; U.S.: 378–79).
3. Lettice Cooper (1897–1994), novelist and biographer, worked during the war at the Ministry of Food with Eileen and had just resigned her post there. See 2528A, n. 3.
4. Catherine Mary O'Shaughnessy; see 2638, n. 16.
5. Unidentified, but possibly a grand form of 'Moggie' and therefore the blue cat Eileen refers to in her letter of 21 March 1945; see 2638.
6. For Raymond Blackburn, see 2638, ns. 4 and 18.
7. As in the original; nothing has been omitted.
8. 'Emily' was the name by which Eileen was known at the Ministry of Food.

2641. Creating Order Out of Cologne Chaos: Water Supplied from Carts

The Observer, 25 March 1945

Cologne, March 24

There are still a hundred thousand Germans living among the ruins of Cologne. Most of them, however, are living in the suburbs, where habitable houses are comparatively common.

The whole central part of the city, once famous for its romanesque churches and its museums, is simply a chaos of jagged walls, overturned trams, shattered statues, and enormous piles of rubble out of which iron girders thrust themselves like sticks of rhubarb.

When the Americans first entered, many of the streets were quite impassable until the bulldozers had swept them clear. The town has no piped water, no gas, no transport, and only enough electrical power for certain vital jobs such as keeping the electric ovens of a few bakeries working. However, the Germans appear still to have fairly good stocks of food, and the Military Government—in this area a purely American concern—is tackling the job of reorganisation with praiseworthy energy.

It has arranged a primitive water supply in horse-drawn carts, it has set up a health service, it is issuing a weekly paper in German, and it is about half-way through the considerable labour of re-registering and finger-printing the entire population. This is a necessary preliminary to the issue of new ration books, and it also helps a little in the important task of sifting Nazis from non-Nazis.

In the first day or two of the occupation there was civilian looting on a large scale, and it was obviously necessary to enrol some civil police. Under the control of an experienced American police officer a scratch force of about 150 Germans, unarmed and not in uniform, is already in being. With these and all other employees of the Military Government, the principle followed is never to employ a known Nazi in any capacity whatever.

The new chief of police, for instance, is a Jew, who held the same post until 1933, when the Nazis evicted him. Three separate courts have been set up to try offences ranging from espionage to infringement of traffic regulations. I attended the first sitting of the intermediary court, which deals with comparatively serious offences and has powers of imprisonment up to ten years. A young Nazi of rather unappetising appearance, who had been the local secretary of the Hitler Jugend, was on trial, not for having belonged to this organisation—the Military Government has declared that belonging to the Nazi organisation is not an offence in itself—but for concealing the fact and attempting to withhold the list of members from the American authorities. He was sentenced to seven years' imprisonment and a fine of 10,000 marks, with an extra day's imprisonment for every mark that remained unpaid.

This would have seemed tolerably severe if such sentences were ever served in full, but he was obviously guilty, and the fairness of the whole procedure was so impressive that even the German lawyer who defended him remarked on it. All in all the American Military Government seems to have made a very good start, though one may guess that difficulties will arise later when people have got over the bombing and the food situation becomes more acute.

After years of war it is an intensely strange feeling to be at last standing on German soil. The Herrenvolk are all round you, threading their way on their bicycles between the piles of rubble or rushing out with jugs and buckets to meet the water cart.

It is queer to think that these are the people who once ruled Europe from the Channel to the Caspian Sea, and might have conquered our own island if they had known how weak we were. Propaganda, and especially their own propaganda, has taught us to think of them as tall, blond, and arrogant. What you actually see, in Cologne, is smallish, dark-haired people, obviously of the same racial stock as the Belgians across the border, and in no way extraordinary. They are better clothed and, by the look of them, better fed than the people in France and Belgium, and they have newer bicycles and more silk stockings than we have in England: really there is no more to remark.

The servility on which several observers have already commented did not particularly strike me. It is true that some of the inhabitants try to curry favour, hang round the offices of the Military Government at all hours, and, when spoken to, doff their hats with a rather horrifying readiness, but the majority seem aloof and perhaps slightly hostile.

In some of the eyes that met mine I caught a sort of beaten defiance which, if it meant anything, seemed to me to mean that these people are horribly ashamed of having lost the war.

It is not true that all of them deny having ever been Nazis. Some of them admit when making their registration that they have been party members, though they always claim that they were forced to join the party against their will.

Orwell was taken ill in Cologne after filing this report and admitted to hospital. See Crick (473) and Shelden (416; U.S.: 380).

2642. Eileen Blair to her husband

25 March 1945   Handwritten

> Greystone,
> Carlton,
> Stockton-on-Tees.

Dearest   I'm trying to get forward with my correspondence because I go into the nursing home on Wednesday (this is Sunday) & of course I shan't be ready. It's impossible to write or do anything else while the children are up. I finish reading to Laurence about a quarter to eight (tonight it was five to eight), we have supper at 8 or 8.15, the 9 o'clock news now must be listened to & lasts till at least 9.30 (the war reports the last two nights have been brilliant[1]) & then it's time to fill hotwater bottles etc. because we come to bed early. So I write in bed & don't type. Incidentally I did while explaining the poaching laws as I understand them to Laurence make my will[2]—in handwriting because handwritten wills are nearly always valid. It is signed & witnessed. Nothing is less likely than that it will be used but I mention it because I have done an odd thing. I haven't left anything to Richard. You are the sole legatee if you survive me (your inheritance would be the Harefield house which ought to be worth a few hundreds, that insurance policy, & furniture). If you don't, the estate would be larger & I have left it to Gwen absolutely with a note that I hope she will use it for Richard's benefit but without any legal obligation. The note is to convince Richard that I was not disinheriting him. But I've done it that way because I don't know how to devise the money to Richard himself. For one thing, there has been no communication from the Registrar General so I suppose Richard's name is still Robertson. For another thing he must have trustees & I don't know who you want & they'd have to be asked. For another, if he is to inherit in childhood it's important that his trustees should be able to use his money during his minority so that he may have as good an education as possible. We must get all this straightened out properly when you come home but I thought I must cover the possibility that you might be killed within the next few days & I might die on the table on Thursday. If you're killed after I die that'll be just too bad but still my little testament will indicate what I wanted done. Gwen's results in child-rearing have not been encouraging so far but after the war she will have a proper house in the country containing both the children & herself, she loves Richard & Laurie adores him. And all the retainers love him dearly. I'm sure he would be happier in that household than with Marjorie though I think Marjorie would take him on. Avril I think & hope would not take him on anyway. That I couldn't bear.[3] Norah & Quartus[4] would have him & bring him up beautifully but you've never seen either of them. Quartus is in India & I can't arrange it. So in all the circumstances I thought you would agree that this would be the best emergency measure.

RICHARD HAS SIX TEETH. Also he got hold of the playpen rail when I was putting him in & stood hanging on to it without other support. But he doesn't really know at all how to pull himself up so don't expect too much. Yesterday Nurse & I took all three to the doctor for whooping cough injections. He lives about $2\frac{1}{2}$–3 miles away, partly across fields. We got lost & had to cross ploughland. The pram wouldn't perambulate & neither would Mary. She sat in a furrow & bellowed until carried. Laurence cried to be carried too . . .[5] Laurence however didn't cry when the needle went in but Mary did *and* made an enormous pool on the surgery floor. Richard was done last. He played with a matchbox on my knee, looked at the doctor in some surprise when his arm was gripped & then turned to me in astonishment as though to say "Why is this apparently nice man sticking needles into me? Can it be right?" On being told it was he looked up at the doctor again rather gravely—& then smiled. He didn't make a sound & he was perfectly good all day too, though his arm is sort of bruised. The other two unfortunately remembered that they'd been injected & screamed in agony if either arm was touched. It was a happy day.

But Richard did a *terrible* thing. He will *not* use his pot, nearly always goes into a tantrum when put on it & if he does sit on it does nothing more. The tooth upset his inside a bit too. After lunch I sent the other two to bed & left Richard in his playpen while I helped wash up. Then there were cries of agony. He had done what Mary calls tick-tocks for the third time, got his hands in it & *put his hands in his mouth*. I tried to wash his mouth out, hoping he'd be sick. But no. He seemed to swallow most of the water I poured in, so it was worse than useless. In the end I scoured his mouth with cotton wool, gave him some boiled water & hoped for the best. And he is very well. Poor little boy. And I was sorry for myself too. I *was* sick. Blackburn however says a lot of children do this every day – – – – – [5]

I haven't had a copy of Windmill[6] & I haven't had a proof. Surely you said they were sending a proof. And I failed to get the Observer one week which must have been the relevant one. I've also failed to get today's but shall get it I hope.

Your letter with the Animal Farm document came yesterday & I've sent the enclosure on to Moore. He will be pleased. This is much the quickest exchange we've had.

I suppose I'd better go to sleep. By the way the six teeth are 3 top & 3 bottom which gives rather an odd appearance, but I hope the fourth top one will be through soon.

All my love & Richard's

E.

1. On 23 March, Operation Plunder, the offensive across the Rhine, began; it may be reports of this that Eileen means.
2. For Eileen's will, see 2643.
3. After Orwell had also died, it was Avril who took care of Richard, and he was very happy with her. Eileen's fears proved completely unfounded.
4. Neither has been identified.
5. Nothing has been deleted at either of these points: the stops and dashes are Eileen's.
6. The journal *Windmill*, in which 'In Defence of P. G. Wodehouse' was to appear; see 2624.

2643. Eileen Blair's Will

25 March 1945   Handwritten

This is the last Will & Testament of me Eileen Maud Blair of Greystone, Carlton, Stockton-on-Tees in the County of Durham.

(i) I leave everything of which I may die possessed & any monies or goods that may accrue to my estate after my death to my husband Eric Arthur Blair absolutely.

(ii) In the event of my husband predeceasing me I leave everything of which I may die possessed & any monies or goods of which° may accrue to my estate after my death to my sister-in-law Gwendolen Mary O'Shaughnessy.

I desire that my sister-in-law the said Gwendolen Mary O'Shaughnessy shall apply such monies as she may inherit from me for the benefit of my adopted son Richard Horatio Blair at her own discretion and not being legally accountable either to my aforesaid adopted son or to any other person whatsoever.

Dated this 25th day of March 1945 & signed by me
Eileen Blair

In the presence of [signed] Joyce Pritchard.
and [signed] Gladys M. Blackburn.[1]

1. The witnesses were the O'Shaughnessy nanny and housekeeper; see *2638*, *ns. 1* and *4*. In the margin of the first of the two pages of the will are Orwell's signature (as E. A. Blair) and John Bunden's, a Commissioner for Oaths, made during the application for probate.

2644. Eileen Blair to Mrs. M. P. Cocking

25 March 1945   Handwritten

Greystone,
Carlton,
Near Stockton-on-Tees
Co. Durham.

Dear Mrs. Cocking,

On February 14 you wrote to my husband, George Orwell, about his two talks for Schools. I have been up here for months hovering about hospitals, so he arranged for his mail to be forwarded direct from London,[1] but when I was up there a few days ago I found that the arrangements had broken down completely & most of the mail was still there—it included your letter & the contract for Ronald Boswell. I am so sorry but there is nothing constructive I can do. George is now moving about & may never get mail that's sent to him so I haven't forwarded anything. I have written to him *about* some of the letters, including yours, on the chance that my letter may reach him. Unfortunately I haven't a Power of Attorney so I can't sign the contract. And still less can I write the scripts. George however is due home in the latter half of next month & he is a curiously reliable man.[2]

Yours sincerely
Eileen Blair

1. By George Kopp; see Shelden, 412–13; U.S.: 377. He lived at 14A Canonbury Square; the Orwells, at 27A.
2. Becky Cocking replied on 27 March. She was sorry that Eileen had been worried, hoped she would have frequent news from her husband, and said that as long as she heard from him before May was out, she would be content.

2645. Eileen Blair to Cyril Connolly
25 March 1945   Handwritten

> Greystone,
> Carlton,
> Stockton-on-Tees
> Co. Durham.

Dear Cyril,

As I have been up here for months in a ridiculous attempt to avoid an operation, George arranged with a man in London to forward his mail. (I'm assuming you know George himself is in France or Germany, reporting for the Observer.) But he picked a good business man° who thought he should not forward anything until he had the address in writing from George. George of course has never written to him at all & I thought myself pretty admirable because I gave him the address by telephone as soon as I had it. But I've just been to London & discovered the whole lot, waiting. I opened one from the Borough which said that the electricity would be cut off as soon as the man succeeded in getting in. The Gas Company's letter was much the same. So then I opened some more & found a passionate appeal from the BBC who want a contract signed for 2 talks, & the scripts; an extract from some kind of Who's Who in which George is described as having married me before I was born & some years before he went to Eaton°; & your questionnaire.[1] I'm not sure whether I could have helped all this, but you'll see I can't now.

I'm so sorry you & Lys (?)[2] never saw Richard. I was in bed more than half the time before coming North & never arranged anything without cancelling the arrangement. However I'm going to have my dear operation next week & hope to be back again exceedingly healthy in a month or two. Then perhaps you'll come to the christening. The adoption is through at last.

> Yours,
> Eileen Blair.

1. Concerning 'The Cost of Letters'; Orwell's response was published in *Horizon*, September 1946; see *3057*.
2. Lys Lubbock, 'the handsome young wife of a struggling actor and schoolteacher' (Michael Shelden, *Friends of Promise*, 69). Her marriage was breaking up, and she and Connolly fell in love. She was then twenty-two and Connolly thirty-seven. She lived with him from 1941 until mid-1950, not always on the best of terms. Connolly then married Barbara Skelton his second wife. Lys Lubbock settled in New York, working as an assistant editor for Doubleday. In 1955 she married Sigmund Koch, a psychologist who became a professor at Duke University, in North Carolina (*Friends of Promise*, especially 222–28). A photograph of her with Sonia Brownell in the *Horizon* office is reproduced by Crick (plate 27) and Shelden.

2646. Eileen Blair to Leonard Moore

25 March 1945   Handwritten

> Greystone,
> Carlton,
> Near Stockton-on-Tees
> Co. Durham.

Dear Mr Moore,

Most surprisingly, this letter[1] has come back from Eric. The posts are very erratic; this exchange was much quicker than usual. He says that he will pick up mail occasionally in Paris but doesn't want anything important sent. If on these terms you do want to write to him the address is simply Hotel SCRIBE, rue Scribe, Paris. George Orwell is probably better than Eric Blair for the envelope.

> Yours sincerely
> Eileen Blair

1. Presumably 'the Animal Farm document' (a contract?) to which Eileen refers in her letter to her husband of this same day; see *2642*.

2647. Eileen Blair to her husband

29 March 1945   Handwritten

> Fernwood House
> Clayton Road
> Newcastle-on-Tyne.

Dearest I'm just going to have the operation, already enema'd, injected (with morphia in the *right* arm which is a nuisance), cleaned & packed up like a precious image in cotton wool & bandages. When its' ° over I'll add a note to this & it can get off quickly. Judging by my fellow patients it will be a *short* note. They've all had their operations. Annoying—I shall never have a chance to feel superior.

I haven't seen Harvey Evers since arrival & apparently Gwen didn't communicate with him & no one knows what operation I am having! They don't believe that Harvey Evers really left it to me to decide—he always 'does what he thinks best'! He will of course. But I must say I feel irritated though I am being a *model* patient. They think I'm wonderful, so placid & happy they say. As indeed I am once I can hand myself over to someone else to deal with.

This is a nice room—ground floor so one can see the garden. Not much in it except daffodils & I think arabis but a nice little lawn. My bed isn't next the window but it faces the right way. I also see the fire & the clock.

. . . . .

The letter ends here. No note was added. Eileen suffered a heart attack and died under the anaesthetic. She was thirty-nine. Orwell was in Paris when he received the news that Eileen had died—but see *2651, n. 1*; he got to Greystone on Saturday, 31 March. Eileen was buried in St Andrew's and Jesmond Cemetery, Newcastle upon Tyne (see Shelden, 418; U.S.: 382). The grave is number 145 in Section B. Orwell took Richard back with him to London, and Doreen Kopp took care of the child when Orwell returned to France; see *2650*.

2648. Notes for My Literary Executor

Signed 31 March 1945   Typewritten

These notes were probably drafted before Orwell went to France on 15 February 1945, doubtless in case he should be killed whilst in Europe. He should have signed the document before leaving, but did so only on his return for Eileen's funeral. The date of the signing might at first suggest that it was prepared then, but there was little time (40–48 hours) between Eileen's death late on 29 March and the signing of this document, too little time for its preparation even supposing Orwell could concentrate on this task as well as make the funeral arrangements. According to Orwell's letter to Moore of 1 April 1945 (see *2651*), he arrived at Greystone only on Saturday, 31 March.

The typewriter faces of Eileen's last letter (which has a badly blocked 'a,' though that could have been cleaned) and of this document do not seem identical. Crick suggests that Orwell posted the document to Eileen from the Continent (473).

The witnesses were the O'Shaughnessys' nanny (Joyce Pritchard) and Winifred Hunton, who has not been certainly identified. Hunton was Gwen O'Shaughnessy's family name. Her father married twice; Winifred might have been the name of his second wife or of one of their children, or she might have been the wife of Gwen's brother, Arthur Hunton.

In the notes, Orwell refers to the reprinting of 'bits' of his 'As I Please' columns as well as other periodical pieces. There is a manuscript list in Orwell's hand (see *2649*) suggesting what might be reprintable. It cannot be dated, but the latest date noted is 2 February 1945; there are, however, passages in Biro, which must have been written later.

On at least one and more probably two later occasions Orwell listed and annotated his work. There is a three-page handwritten list, with some facing-page notes, which refers to no work published after the first part of 1947; and there is a detailed typed schedule which includes work published in 1949. The first of these two lists will be found in *3323*; the second in *3728*.

NOTES FOR MY LITERARY EXECUTOR

1. UNPUBLISHED MSS. I don't think there is anything at the time of writing except a diary kept in London between May 1940 and November 1942 intermittently. This would be of historical interest by say 1950. Also somewhere among my papers there is an MS "How the Poor Die" which was rejected by "Horizon" and which I did not try elsewhere.[1] This contains a truthful account of some experiences in the Hopital Cochin in

Paris in 1929 and the bit marked between brackets is worth printing. If I should die suddenly, my agents Christy & Moore should be consulted, as there is always the possibility of some MS being with them.

2. REPRINTS OF BOOKS. Roger Senhouse told me Secker & Warburg wished to issue a uniform edition of my books after the war. I told them I did not wish two novels, A CLERGYMAN'S DAUGHTER and KEEP THE ASPIDISTRA FLYING, to be reprinted.[2] These are silly potboilers which I ought not to have published in the first place, and I have already refused to let the second of them to appear as a Penguin. Nor do I think THE LION AND THE UNICORN is worth reprinting (though there have been suggestions of this) and still less a little propaganda book I did for the "Britain in Pictures" series, THE ENGLISH PEOPLE. Of course, after I am dead I do not object to cheap editions of any book which may bring in a few pounds for my heirs, but I told S. & W. that of my books which have appeared up to the present, the only ones I thought worth putting into a uniform edition are:—

DOWN AND OUT IN PARIS AND LONDON

BURMESE DAYS (this should be from the original American edition, published in 1934 by Harper's and followed in the Penguin edition, NOT the Gollancz version.)

THE ROAD TO WIGAN PIER

HOMAGE TO CATALONIA

COMING UP FOR AIR

ANIMAL FARM (to appear April 1945)

CRITICAL ESSAYS (to appear autumn 1945).

The above list does not include INSIDE THE WHALE because two out of the three essays in that are in the collection of CRITICAL ESSAYS. However the name-essay of the book, which has not been reprinted in England, would be worth reprinting at some time or other—possibly in combination with some longish piece which I may do later.

COMING UP FOR AIR was to have been reprinted by the Albatross Library in Paris[3] but this fell through owing to the war. There are some passages early in the book which I think make it worth reprinting. But the one I'm most anxious about is HOMAGE TO CATALONIA, as this book has some historical value. If it ever re-appears, one or two slips about names etc. should be corrected, and it would be well if the book had a preface by someone who knows the Spanish background better than I do.

3. REPRINTS OF PERIODICAL PIECES. Bits of my "As I Please" column in "Tribune" are worth reprinting in some context or other. I think I have a full collection of these, and in any case back numbers can be obtained from the paper.

There are also the "London Letters" which I have done quarterly in the "Partisan Review" (New York) from the beginning of 1941 onwards. I think possibly these could be combined in some kind or book with the diary mentioned above.

Also just conceivably some of the many short critical essays I have done in "Tribune", the "Observer" the "Manchester Evening News" and elsewhere—though as a rule I don't think anythi[n]g less than 1000 words is worth reprinting.

Among my papers is a long satyrical poem published in "Tribune" in 1943 by "Obadiah Hornbooke" (Alex Comfort) and a reply in the same vein by myself. Each is 150 lines long, and the two together would be worth reprinting as a pamphlet if Comfort agreed (which he would.)

4. PAMPHLETS AND MISCELLANEOUS PAPERS. I have been collecting pamphlets since 1935 and must have at least 1000. They are only very roughly classified and some are unclassified. One or two of them, especially foreign ones (eg. a little Trotskyist pamphlet published in Paris in 1937 or 1938 about the fate of Kurt Landau[4]), must be great rarities. My executor must decide whether to give the whole lot to the B.M.[5] (who I imagine would be willing to take them, as they don't get pamphlets as regularly as books) or to put them aside in some damp-proof place for the next few decades. Ditto with many leaflets etc. which will be found among my papers, roughly classified. These things are valueless and mostly uninteresting *now*, but they might not be so in 1970.

At need I will add to these notes at some future time.

Signed	Eric Blair 31 $\frac{3}{45}$
Witness	Winifred Hunton
Witness	Joyce Pritchard

1. 'How the Poor Die' was published in *Now*, November 1946; see *3104*.
2. Orwell's reluctance to have these two novels reprinted may be explained in part by his recognition of their weaknesses, but may stem much more from their troubled publishing histories, in particular the degree of in-house censorship they suffered. To Orwell, both would seem 'garbled,' to use his word for an author's text which had suffered from editorial interference (see *Nineteen Eighty-Four*, *CW*, IX, 44–45). See Textual Notes to these novels in the *Complete Works* series and also the Note on the Text to each volume in the Penguin Twentieth-Century Classics series, 1989 and 1990 respectively.
3. For the attempt to publish *Coming Up for Air* in the Albatross Library, see correspondence with Leonard Moore from 4 August 1939, *561*; for the Albatross Library, *561*, *n. 1*. For Orwell's contract, see *566*.
4. Kurt Landau is described by Hugh Thomas in *The Spanish Civil War* as a German Trotskyist (1081) and as an Austrian socialist who, like other international sympathisers of the POUM. died in mysterious circumstances in the months following the murder of Andrés Nin in June 1937 (705–06). In Orwell's pamphlet collection (now in the British Library) is *Le Stalinisme en Espagne* by Katia Landau (1937). Orwell refers to Landau in *Homage to Catalonia*, VI/161.
5. Orwell's pamphlet collection was given to the British Museum, with certain other papers; it is now held in the British Library at 1899 ss 1–21, 23–47; there is an index, dated c. 1950 by the British Library at 1899 ss 48. However, the index probably dates from 1946. There is no Box 22. For an earlier, classified, list of 335 pamphlets, made by Orwell, see *3733*.

2649. 'Possibly reprintable fragments'

[1945–49]   Handwritten

This list, written on two loose sheets of paper, irregularly torn from a book or pad, measuring approximately 22.5 × 17 cm, was almost certainly composed on more than one occasion. 'Winter (1ˢᵗ) 1945' refers to a London Letter written in the autumn of 1944 (see *2553 headnote*), so the latest specific date is 2 February 1945. It would seem that the list was prepared before Orwell went to France on 15 February 1945, in connection with his Notes for My Literary Executor (see *2648*), although that was not signed until 31 March 1945. The list was prepared hastily. 'Summer 1944' appears twice and six of the twenty-five dates for issues of 'As I Please' are incorrect. If it were argued that 'Summer 1944' should be 'Summer 1945,' that might mean the list was not prepared until after that letter was written (5 June 1945), but even if Orwell intended 1945, he might well have assumed he would write to *Partisan Review* following his experiences in Europe. The section devoted to *Partisan Review* is written in lead pencil, except for two underlines to 'PR' which are in blue pencil. The 'As I Please' section is written in blue pencil except for the ticks; these are in blue ink.

At some later stage, probably mid-1949, Orwell annotated the list in blue Biro, a kind of pen he seems first to have acquired about February 1946 (see *2904* and his letter to Julian Symons requesting a Biro, 26 December 1947, *3318*). The heading 'Possibly reprintable fragments,' 'See also 1945,' 'O.P.,' and the section devoted to poems are written in Biro. 'O.P.' was much used by Orwell when writing *Nineteen Eighty-Four*; it means 'Over the Page.' Details of the poems are written on the verso of the second leaf. These details were later typed up by Orwell in his 1949 notes on his books and essays; see *3728*. Those notes have a section, 'Reprintable Essays Etc.' and against the sub-head 'London Letters.' Orwell states that fragments from *Partisan Review*, 1940–46, and 'As I Please,' 1943–47, would be reprintable, and he concludes: 'See list of possibly usable fragments.' This could refer to the list reproduced here, but it is likely that this list served as the basis for an up-dated list which has not survived. The blue-ink ticks against all but three of the 'As I Please' references may indicate those transferred to such an up-dated list.

These two leaves were not found with the 1945 notes for Orwell's literary executor, but with those prepared in 1949. It is probable, then, that the two lists of articles were written out in February–March 1945 and used to prepare an up-dated list in 1949, which has not survived except for the details of the poems that might be reprinted.

Because the bulk of the information reveals what Orwell thought was worth reprinting from these two series of prose contributions when he made these notes early in 1945, the lists have been reproduced here; it should simply be borne in mind that the list of poems was not added until mid-1949.

Lists and instructions for his literary executor prepared, probably, in 1947 or early 1948, and in mid-1949 are reproduced as appendixes to 1947 and 1949; see *3323* and *3728*.

Possibly reprintable fragments

PR	March April 1941	Diary Extract + earlier on air raids. (marked).[1]
,,	March April 1942	Passage marked.
,,	March April 1943	ditto
,,	Spring 1944	,,
,,	Summer 1944	,,
,,	Fall 1944	,,
,,	Winter (1st) 1945[2]	,,

,,	Summer 1944[3]	,,
	See also 1945	
<u>AS I PLEASE</u>	3.12.43[4]	Marked passage (2)
	24.12.43	,,
	31.12.43	,,
	7.1.44	,,
	4.2.44	,,
	28.2.44[5]	,,
	10.3.44	,,
	17.3.44	,, (whole)
	24.3.44	passage marked (all)[6]
	31.3.44	,,
	21.4.44	,, (2)
	28.4.44	,,
	12.5.44	,,
	19.5.44	,,
	9.6.44	,,
	7.7.44	,,
	1.8.44[7]	,, (whole)
	15.8.44[8]	,,
	6.9.44[9]	,,
	20.9.44[10]	,,
	27.9.44[11]	
	17.11.44	,, (2)
	1.12.44	,,
	12.1.45	
	2.2.45	
	O.P.[12]	

Also a few poems: One beginning "A dressed man and a naked man" (Adelphi 1931). Another beginning "Not the pursuit of knowledge" (Tribune 1943 or 1944). Another beginning, "A happy vicar I might have been" (Adelphi 1936).[13]

1. 'Diary' is an expansion of what looks very like 'Dig.' Orwell's first London Letter to *Partisan Review* concluded with 'a few extracts' from his diary and this was preceded by comment on air-raids comprising about a paragraph and a half of the whole Letter; see *740*. This was, indeed, 'a fragment.' What Orwell marked up here and elsewhere is not known. A question mark follows 'Diary Extract' but Orwell crossed it out.
2. '1945' refers to the winter at the end of 1944 and beginning of 1945; see *2553*.
3. Possibly intended as 1945, but see headnote.
4. All 'As I Please' dates are preceded by a tick in blue ink except 4.2.44, 1.8.44, and 12.1.45. For the possible significance of these ticks, see headnote.
5. Incorrectly dated; should be 25.2.44.
6. The second leaf begins with this item, hence repetition of 'passage marked.'
7. Incorrectly dated; should be 1.9.44.
8. Incorrectly dated; should be 15.9.44.
9. Incorrectly dated; should be 6.10.44.
10. Incorrectly dated; should be 20.10.44.

11. Incorrectly dated; should be 27.10.44. There are no ditto marks here, nor for the last two items.
12. Over the Page; see headnote.
13. 'A dressed man and a naked man' was published by *The Adelphi* in October 1933; see *182*. 'Not the pursuit of knowledge' was published by *Tribune*, 21 January 1944, as 'Memories of the Blitz'; see *2409*. 'A happy vicar I might have been' was published in *The Adelphi*, December 1936; see *335*.

2650. To Lydia Jackson

1 April 1945   Typewritten

at Greystone
Carlton
Stockton-on-Tees
Co. Durham

Dear Lydia,[1]
I do not know whether you will have heard from anyone else the very bad news. Eileen is dead. As you know she had been ill for some time past and it was finally diagnosed that she had a growth which must be removed. The operation was not supposed to be a very serious one, but she seems to have died as soon as she was given the anaesthetic, and, apparently, as a result of the anaesthetic. This was last Thursday. I was in Paris and didn't even know she was to have the operation till two days before. It was a dreadful shock and a very cruel thing to happen, because she had become so devoted to Richard and was looking forward to living a normal life in the country again as soon as the war was over. The only consolation is that I don't think she suffered, because she went to the operation, apparently, not expecting anything to go wrong, and never recovered consciousness. It is perhaps as well that Richard wasn't a bit older, because I don't think he actually misses her, at any rate he seems in very good spirits as well as health. I am going to bring him back to London when I come, and for the time being he is going to stay with Doreen who lives in the same square and has a baby a month old herself.[2] I think we shall be able to find a nurse whom we can share, and when the war stops I can probably get him a nurse of his own and make a proper home for him in the country. It is a shame Eileen should have died just when he is becoming so charming, however she did enjoy very much being with him during her last months of life. Please give my love to Pat. I don't know about my plans, but I think that if the Observer want me to I shall go back to France for a month or two when I have settled Richard.

Yours
George

1. Lydia Jackson (1899–1983), psychologist, writer and translator (using the pen-name Elisaveta Fen), was born in Russia and came to England in 1925. She met Eileen in 1934 at University College London, and they remained friends. Lydia Jackson was sharing Orwell's cottage at Wallington with a friend, Patricia Donahue. See 534A.
2. Doreen Kopp lived at 14A Canonbury Square; see Eileen's letter to Lettice Cooper, 2640. Her baby was a boy, called Quentin.

2651. To Leonard Moore

1 April 1945   Typewritten

As from 27 B Canonbury Square   Islington   N 1

Dear Mr Moore,

I am very sorry to have to tell you that my wife is dead. She died under the anaesthetic during an operation which should not in itself have been very serious. It happened on Thursday. I was in Paris at the time[1] and could not get here till Saturday morning. This has been a great shock to me, and I think that if the Observer agree I shall go back to France as soon as I have settled everything and do some more reporting for them, as I do not feel that I could settle to any ordinary work at present. I will let you know my movements later, but letters sent to the above address should be forwarded to me.[2]

I do not know whether my wife had had to transact any business with you during my absence. You refer in your letter to a payment of £23–3–5.[3] Could you pay this, and any other sums which may come in while I am abroad, into my bank, which is Barclay's, Highbury Branch, Highbury Corner, N 5.°

Warburg I think is still ill and I haven't heard from him or Senhouse recently. I don't know exactly when ANIMAL FARM is coming out, but as I corrected the proofs a long time ago it should be fairly soon, and perhaps you could get a date from them. I would also like to hear whether any American publisher bit at the book of essays. In the English edition of this Senhouse wanted to reprint the essay on P. G. Wodehouse, published after I had sent them the MS of the book. I hadn't a copy to send them, but in case Senhouse still hasn't got one you might tell him the essay is in the last number of the WINDMILL (quarterly) published by Heinemann's.[4]

Yours sincerely
[Signed] Eric Blair

1. The impression is usually given that Orwell was in Cologne when he heard that Eileen had died. He had certainly been in hospital there at about the time she was admitted to hospital in Newcastle. See Crick, 473, and Shelden, 416; U.S.: 380.
2. Orwell's letter is annotated to indicate that Moore wrote privately to Orwell on 4 April 1945.
3. There is no record of this payment in Orwell's Payments Book.
4. The page proofs of the first impression of *Critical Essays* do not include 'In Defence of P. G. Wodehouse' in the list of Contents nor in the note on the verso on sources of the essays. The details are added to the proof in what looks like Senhouse's hand. See *Critical Essays*, 14 February 1946, *2898*.

2652. To Dwight Macdonald

4 April 1945   Typewritten; handwritten postscript

27 B Canonbury Square
Islington
London N 1

Dear Macdonald,

Many thanks for your letter of February 27th which has only just got here. I had already had a talk with Roger Senhouse and I think also with Warburg about Victor Serge's memoirs[1] and told them it was the kind of book they should get hold of. On political grounds they might be rather funky but I fancy could be prodded into doing it. The big difficulty is likely to be paper. The paper situation as you know is ghastly and S. and W. as small publishers don't get a big allottment.° So in all probability they wouldn't bring the book out before 1946. I know they are chartering books for as late as 1947, and many other publishers are doing likewise. I think one can take it as certain they *would* do it but with a long delay. I should in any case speak to Read[2] about it. Read of course would be politically in sympathy but he has to consider Routledge's interests and I doubt whether they would risk anything overtly Trotskyist. The other possible people are Faber's and I will also speak to Eliot about the book or write to him, but the trouble with Eliot is that though of course anti-Stalinist he is at heart simply a conservative and doesn't like fighting against public opinion for the sake of some left fraction[3] he feels no sympathy for. When I tried to get Faber's to do my little anti-Stalin book which S. and W. are doing and which I had such trouble with, he wrote me a rambling sort of letter of which the upshot was that one only ought to publish that kind of thing if politically in sympathy with it, which he was not. (I asked Warburg to send you a copy of that book when it appears by the way.) I look forward to seeing the MS of Serge's book. If it arrives when I'm in France again I'll see that it's sent straight to S. and W. and I'll remind Roger Senhouse beforehand. There would be no difficulty about arranging a translation.

The wad of comic strips you sent (at least you said some time back you were sending them) never arrived—stopped by the censorship perhaps. I'll do you another article some time but I can't start anything now and I think I'm going back to France or rather occupied Germany for another month or two. I was over there for five weeks till last week. I don't want to bore you with my private affairs, but my wife has just died very suddenly and in particularly distressing circumstances, and it has upset me so that I cannot settle to anything for the time being. As soon as I have fixed up a temporary home for my little boy I want to go back and do some more reporting, and perhaps after a few weeks of bumping about in jeeps etc. I shall feel better.

Yours

[Signed] Geo. Orwell

P.S. Since writing this I've seen Senhouse again. He's interested. S. & W. published one of Serge's books before.

1. Victor Serge (1889–1947), writer and journalist, Russian by parentage, French by adoption, settled in 1941 in Mexico. For a fuller account, see *1046, n. 7*.
2. Herbert Read (1893–1968), poet, critic, and a director of Routledge's, broadcast to India under Orwell's aegis; see *1006*.
3. 'fraction' may be intended; see *2441, n. 4*.

2653. Fredric Warburg to Orwell

6 April 1945   Typewritten; carbon copy

My dear George,
I heard the terrible news from Tosco[1] yesterday and I write immediately to say how sorry I am. This must be a frightful blow to you and I wish I had been able to see you yesterday when you came to the office. There is so little that can be said on these occasions but anyone who has himself suffered losses of a similar kind will know how you must be feeling.

I do not think there is anything worth writing you about while you are in France, since it can all await your return. There is a hitch in the signature of our agreement with you which, however, we shall not allow to hold up the production of ANIMAL FARM. There are certain other matters which Roger may well have discussed with you.

I look forward to seeing you again when you finally get back from Europe.

Yours as ever,
[Initialled] FW

1. Tosco Fyvel (1907–1985), writer, editor, journalist, and broadcaster, first met Orwell in January 1940 (see *660, n. 1*) and they became good friends. They jointly edited the Searchlight Series, of which Orwell's *The Lion and the Unicorn* (1941) was the first to be issued. He was literary editor of *Tribune* and later of the *Jewish Chronicle*—he lived in Palestine in the late twenties and developed expert knowledge of Jewish-Arab affairs—and was one of those involved in the founding of *Encounter*. In 1982 he published *George Orwell: A Personal Memoir*, an affectionate and percipient study. As his obituary in *The Times* (25 July 1985) put it, 'Probably, aside from family, Fyvel knew and understood Orwell better than anyone else.' In his memoir Fyvel says 'that Eileen's death was a blow to [Orwell] from which in his personal life he never fully recovered' (134). See also *3325, n. 4*.

2654. Future of a Ruined Germany: Rural Slum Cannot Help Europe

The Observer, 8 April 1945

As the advance into Germany continues and more and more of the devastation wrought by the Allied bombing planes is laid bare, there are three comments that almost every observer finds himself making.

The first is, "The people at home have no conception of this." The second is, "It's a miracle that they've gone on fighting." And the third is, "Just think of the work of building this all up again!"

It is quite true that the scale of the Allied blitzing of Germany is even now not realised in this country, and its share in the breaking-down of German resistance is probably much underrated. It is difficult to give actuality to newspaper or radio reports of air warfare, and the man in the street can be forgiven if he imagines that what we have done to Germany over the past four years is merely the same kind of thing as they did to us in 1940.

But this error, which must be even commoner in the United States, has in it a potential danger, and the many protests against indiscriminate bombing which have been uttered by pacifists and humanitarians have merely confused the issue.

Bombing is not especially inhumane. War itself is inhumane, and the bombing plane, which is used to paralyse industry and transport rather than to kill human beings, is a relatively civilised weapon. "Normal" or "legitimate" warfare is just as destructive of inanimate objects, and enormously more so of human lives.

Moreover, a bomb kills a casual cross-section of the population, whereas the men killed in battle are exactly the ones that the community can least afford to lose. The people of Britain have never felt easy about the bombing of civilians, and no doubt they will be ready enough to pity the Germans as soon as they have definitely defeated them; but what they have still not grasped—thanks to their own comparative immunity—is the frightful destructiveness of modern war and the long period of impoverishment that now lies ahead of the world as a whole.

To walk through the ruined cities of Germany is to feel an actual doubt about the continuity of civilisation. For one has to remember that it is not only Germany that has been blitzed. The same desolation extends, at any rate in considerable patches, all the way from Brussels to Stalingrad. And where there has been ground fighting, the destruction is even more thorough than where there has merely been bombing. In the 300 miles or so between the Marne and the Rhine there is not, for instance, such a thing as a bridge or a viaduct that has not been blown up.

Even in England we are aware that we need three million houses, and that the chances of getting them within measurable time seem rather slender. But how many houses will Germany need, or Poland, or the U.S.S.R., or Italy? When one thinks of the stupendous task of rebuilding Cologne, Essen, Hamburg, Warsaw, Budapest, Kharkov, Odessa, Leningrad, and scores or hundreds of other European cities, great and small—and rebuilding them at the end of six years, during which all available labour has been squandered on war production—one realises that a long period must elapse before even the standards of living of 1939 can be re-established.

We do not yet know the full extent of the damage that has been done to Germany, but judging from the areas that have been overrun hitherto, it is difficult to believe in the power of the Germans to pay any kind of reparations, either in goods or in labour. Simply to rehouse the German people, to set the shattered factories working, and to keep German agriculture from collapsing after the foreign workers have been liberated, will use up all the labour that the Germans are likely to dispose of.

If, as is planned at present, millions of them are to be deported to the victorious countries for reconstruction work, the recovery of Germany itself will be all the slower. After the last war the impossibility of obtaining substantial money reparations—in short, of making the enemy pay for the war—was finally grasped, but it was less generally realised that the impoverishment of any one country reacts unfavourably on the world as a whole. It would be no advantage to turn Germany into a kind of rural slum.[1]

1. The last three paragraphs were reprinted in *Forward*, 21 April 1945, under the title 'Europe's Homeless Millions.' It is a word-for-word reprint as far as '. . . will be all the slower' in the last paragraph. The rest of what Orwell wrote is summarised (probably to fit the space available) as: 'and its capacity both as a market and a source of manufactured goods correspondingly reduced.' In attributing the reprint to Orwell and *The Observer*, there is no indication that the text has been modified. *Forward* was the weekly paper of the Glasgow Labour Party. George Woodcock said it published 'Live criticism of political affairs, lately somewhat tamed owing to support of Labour govt. 2d weekly,' in his 'London Letter,' *Politics*, October 1946.

2655. Nellie Adam (née Limouzin) to Marjorie Dakin

8 April 1945   Handwritten

This is the first of two extremely long letters from Nellie Adam to Marjorie Dakin (see *2659* for the second). Nellie Adam was Orwell's aunt; she had lived in Paris when Orwell was working there, 1928–29; see *189, n. 1.*. Marjorie Dakin was his elder sister, married to Humphrey Dakin, a civil servant. The letters were written from 56A Craven Avenue, Ealing, London W5, where Nellie had the upper of two flats in a house belonging to her recently deceased sister (who had lived in the lower flat). The letters are chiefly concerned with Nellie's own family affairs, in particular her resentment that Humphrey Dakin had come to search for a will that would enable Nellie's niece, Dorothy, to inherit £2,000 following her mother's death. Nellie feared that this would enable Dorothy to sell the house, with the result that Nellie would be homeless. The situation is summed up towards the end of the letter:

Now, Marjorie dear, I think you will realise after all I have told you, that my sister being beyond all help, I am not in the least interested in seeing to it that D[orothy] acquires her wealth immediately. To H[umphrey] I am 'a spiteful old woman,' but I think in all this I have written you will find a little more to me than that!

Finally, she concludes with this reference to Orwell and the death of Eileen:

I was shocked to hear of poor old Eric's loss. How wonderful he is—there is his article in the Observer to-day and I know that he had to rush over for Eileen's funeral & then arrange a temporary haven for little R[ichard]. I could write much more about the situation, which seems to me now a hopeless impasse, but I have loaded enough of my dreadful handwriting on you for the nonce.

2656. To Anthony Powell
13 April 1945   Typewritten

Hotel Scribe
Rue Scribe
Paris 9e

Dear Tony,[1]
I tried to get in touch with you when I was in London last week, but failed. I don't know whether you will have heard from some other source about what has happened. Eileen is dead. She died very suddenly and unexpectedly on March 29th during an operation which was not supposed to be very serious. I was over here and had no expectation of anything going wrong, which indeed nobody seems to have had. I didn't see the final findings of the inquest and indeed don't want to, because it doesn't bring her back, but I think the anaesthetic was responsible. It was a most horrible thing to happen because she had had five really miserable years of bad health and overwork, and things were just beginning to get better. The only good thing is that I don't think she can have suffered or had any apprehensions. She was actually looking forward to the operation to cure her trouble, and I found among her papers a letter she must have written only about an hour before she died and which she expected to finish when she came round. But it was terribly sad that she should die when she had become so devoted to Richard and was making such a good job of his upbringing. Richard I am glad to say is very well and for the moment is provided for. He is staying with his sort of aunt[2] who lives in the same square as me and has a young baby of her own, and I hope within a fairly short time to find a good nurse whom I can take on as a permanency. As soon as I can get a nurse and a house I shall remove him to the country, as I don't want him to learn to walk in London. I just got him settled in and then came straight back here, as I felt so upset at home I thought I would rather be on the move for a bit. I was in Germany for a few days recently and am now going back there for a week or two.

What I partly wrote for was to ask if you know Malcolm Muggeridge's address. He has left Paris and I have no idea how to get in touch with him. I vaguely heard there had been some kind of row in which l'affaire Wodehouse was mixed up, but have no idea what it is. Letters generally take about a fortnight, but the above address will find me. Please remember me to Violet.[3]

Yours
George

1. Anthony Powell (1905–2000; CH, 1988), novelist, whose twelve-volume sequence *A Dance to the Music of Time* was published 1951–75. He served from 1939 to 1945 in the Welch Regiment and Intelligence Corps.
2. Doreen Kopp, half-sister of Dr. Gwen O'Shaughnessy, and wife of George Kopp, Orwell's POUM commander in Spain.
3. The Lady Violet Powell; Anthony Powell married The Lady Violet Pakenham, third daughter of the 5th Earl of Longford, in 1934.

2657. Allies Facing Food Crisis in Germany: Problem of Freed Workers

The Observer, 15 April 1945

Paris, 14 April

There are more and more reports, official and unofficial, telling of the difficulties now being experienced in dealing with the Allied and neutral deportees in German territory, generally referred to in the British Press as slave labour, but known officially as Displaced Persons.

The Displaced Persons do not include released prisoners of war, who are a separate problem and a somewhat easier one to handle.

When, only a few weeks ago, I visited a camp of 14,000 Displaced Persons in the Rhineland, I was struck by the sensible manner in which the American officers in charge were handling the job, and the obvious delight of the Displaced Persons at getting out of German hands. But at that time the problem was still of manageable proportions.

The extent to which it has swollen since then can be illustrated by a few figures. In France the Allied armies liberated 100,000 Displaced Persons, and in Germany west of the Rhine another 100,000. By the first week in April the number had risen to about 1,000,000, and it is now thought to be round about 2,000,000, with the prospect of many more to come; for there are at least 7,000,000 of these people in Germany and German-held territory, possibly as many as 10,000,000 or 12,000,000, exclusive of war prisoners.

Meanwhile, the number actually rounded up is fewer by several hundred thousand than the number estimated as being in the areas which the Allied armies have occupied. As the German administration collapses, more and more displaced persons simply escape and take to the roads, often with the idea of walking back to their own countries by the shortest route, and the Allied authorities have several difficult problems to solve.

Obviously, before these people can be repatriated, some kind of sorting-out process is needed, both to prevent epidemics and to eliminate the spies and saboteurs who exist among them. This means that even French and Belgian deportees, whose homes are near at hand, have to be detained for several days, while most of the Russians and Poles will probably have to wait for some months before it is practicable to repatriate them.

It is not easy to find accommodation for these vast numbers of people, who include many children born in captivity, and the food problem is likely to become acute within a few months. In principle the responsibility for feeding the Displaced Persons falls on Germany, but this is only a financial measure and does not necessarily mean that actual food will always be forthcoming. Evidently a great deal depends on finishing the war quickly enough to allow this year's German harvest to be gathered in.

The Germans, who have been plundering all Europe for several years, still have or had recently good stocks of food, but their agriculture is now disorganised by the defeat, all the more so because it depends for labour largely on the Displaced Persons, who are now escaping or being released. Unless it can be set on its feet again by the late summer, the result is likely to be a disastrous food shortage, which will react indirectly on the Allied countries.

The great majority of Displaced Persons remaining under Allied care are Russians, Ukrainians, Poles, and Italians.

The Western European deportees can usually be repatriated after only a short delay. Liaison officers drawn from the various countries concerned are attached to the military government.

It does not yet seem to have been definitely decided whether the return of a displaced person to his country of origin is or is not compulsory, and on this subject there are serious possibilities of disagreement between the Allied Governments.

Apart from stateless persons, of whom there are thousands in the German concentration camps, there is the minority of collaborators whose transference to Germany was voluntary, and the probably larger number of people who cannot be classed as collaborators but have their own reasons for not wanting to go home.

It seems to be admitted that the Germans did not in all cases treat their deportees badly. At any rate, since they needed them for manual labour, they had the wisdom to feed them adequately—much better, it is generally agreed, than they fed their prisoners of war—and they seem often to have deported whole families rather than individuals and to have allowed the deportees to get married while in captivity.

In the circumstances it will not be surprising if some of the Poles, especially those from Eastern Poland, and perhaps some of the Ukrainians as well, make efforts to remain where they are. The Soviet authorities are unlikely to acquiesce, and this awkward point will have to be settled in the near future.

In France this particular difficulty does not arise, but there has been much unfavourable comment on the failure of the Government to organise suitable ceremonies of welcome for returned prisoners and deportees.

2658. The French election will be influenced by the fact that
WOMEN WILL HAVE FIRST VOTE
Manchester Evening News, 16 April 1945

No date has yet been fixed for the General Election, but it has been officially stated that the municipal elections will take place at the end of this month provided that the date fixed does not coincide with some great external event, such as the ending of the war. In France the voting at municipal and cantonal elections usually follows party lines, and the forthcoming elections should, therefore, give, for the first time since 1936, a reliable picture of the balance of political forces in France.

Now, six months after the liberation, it is realised that until elections have been held certain urgently necessary decisions cannot be taken. Unavoidably, and very unfortunately, some three million men, prisoners or deportees in Germany, will be missing from the electoral roll. The absence of these men, who are mostly youngish, and include many who were deported for their political activities during the occupation, will tell chiefly against the parties of the Left. This is generally agreed, but there are several unknown factors about which there is much speculation.

It has not yet been decided what method of voting will be followed, i.e., whether proportional representation will be adopted. Nor have the Socialists and Communists yet decided in what manner, if at all, they will pool their candidatures in order to avoid splitting one another's votes. By far the most important unknown factor is the attitude of the women. In the forthcoming elections women will vote for the first time in French history, and, moreover, they will outnumber the men by ten or fifteen per cent. Since this is their first venture into political life, it has been laid down that women will be allowed to vote even if they have not registered beforehand: very large numbers of women, however, have already registered themselves as voters, especially in strongly Catholic or Communist areas.

Another unknown factor is the attitude of the Church. The old struggle between clericals and anti-clericals cooled down as a result of the occupation, but it has shown signs of flaring up again, the immediate cause of dispute being the continuance by the Provisional Government of State subsidies to Catholic schools. It is possible that the Church may, as in the past, make an authoritative pronouncement against certain political doctrines, especially Communism: in which case the large female vote might be a very serious handicap for the parties of the Left.

There is good reason for thinking that the forces of Conservatism are much stronger in France than they appeared in the first few months after the liberation. At the last general election, that of 1936, the Left-wing parties grouped together in the Popular Front polled something over five and a half million votes, while the parties of the Right polled nearly four and a quarter millions. Thereafter, up till the war, the Left probably lost ground as against the Right.

The follies of the Daladier Government,[1] and the discredit brought on the old regime by the defeat and the occupation, changed the picture, but it is admitted that the Pétain Government had popular support in some areas, especially among the peasants. Even now there are parts of the South of France where pro-Pétain literature is circulating illegally.

The Radical-Socialist party is also rapidly reviving, and other moderate parties are reappearing. These parties have at present no very clear-cut policy, but they can make an appeal to the peasants and other middling people who are not strongly opposed to the nationalisation of major industry but are frightened of Communism.

During recent months all the surviving political parties have increased their membership: it is considered that most of them now have more members than they had in 1939. The Communist party is still probably the biggest, and certainly the most cohesive and best organised party in France. Its greatest strength is in the Paris area, but of late, for the first time in its history, it has managed to get a foothold in some rural areas. The Communists are aware that even if they came to power they could hardly govern France single-handed, and they have tried very hard, and not absolutely without success, to come to terms with the Socialists on the one hand and the Catholics on the other. The Socialist party has a large and faithful following in various areas, particularly the industrial districts of Lille and Toulouse in the South. Finally there is the large and vital Resistance Movement, which has not yet crystallised into a definite party but is bound to play an important rôle in the elections, both through its own candidates and by its tendency to push the Socialist party further to the Left.

With so many unknown factors, even Dr. Gallup himself could hardly make an accurate forecast, but at least it seems clear that the impression which prevailed a few months ago, that France was on the edge of revolution, was exaggerated. There is no widespread opposition to certain measures of a semi-Socialistic kind, and all forms of Fascism are discredited: but the tone of the Press and of most public utterances since the liberation have made ordinary Conservatism seem deader than it is. Experienced observers point out that the four million people who voted for the parties of the Right in 1936 have not ceased to exist, and that when the elections come off, an overwhelming victory for the Left is not to be expected.[2]

1. Edouard Daladier (1884–1970) was three times Premier of France: 1933, 1934, and 1938–40; it is to his last term of office that Orwell refers. He signed the Munich pact in 1938 and fell from office after the defeat of Finland by the Soviet Union, being replaced on 21 March 1940 by Paul Reynaud (in whose cabinet he served). He was interned when France fell and released in 1945, when he returned to politics. See also 2667.
2. Elections to the National Assembly were held in October 1945. The Left won three-quarters of the seats: Communists 142; Socialists 140; Mouvement Républicain Populaire (the Catholic Left) 133. For the Municipal election results, see 2664.

2659. Nellie Adam to Marjorie Dakin

16 April 1945   Handwritten

For the background to this letter, see 2655. Only the opening is reproduced:

Thanks for your letter.

First, about Richard; I quite understand now that you did offer help, but must point out that what I wrote to H[umphrey] about it was based on his remark that he was afraid to take R[ichard] in case you would have him permanently fixed with you. That point I understood, although privately I thought that a time-limit could have been set. H[umphrey] did not speak to me of your offer. Eric wrote to me at some length of Eileen's death and appeared to me to be very grieved about it. It certainly was strange that he didn't do the same to you. Maybe a letter miscarried (as has occurred to both Mrs Briffa[1] and myself lately) or perhaps he deputed A[vril][2] to give you the news. Those days for him must have been pretty strenuous and ghastly. . . .

1. Unidentified; the name is uncertain.
2. Avril: Orwell's and Marjorie's younger sister.

2660. Bavarian Peasants Ignore the War: Germans Know They Are Beaten

The Observer, 22 April 1945

Nuremberg, 21 April

To judge by the demeanour of the civilian population in this part of Germany, it is an understatement to say that the Germans now know they are beaten.

Most of them seem to regard the war as something already in the past and its continuation as a lunacy in which they have no part, and for which they need feel no responsibility.

To a surprising extent village life continues as usual, even in the middle of the fighting. The oxen still trudge slowly in front of the harrow while the guns echo from all the surrounding hillsides, and most of the peasants seem more afraid of being attacked by wandering Displaced Persons—freed foreign workers—than of being hit by a stray shell. A day or two ago I entered the little village of Wimmelbach, west of Nuremberg, just after the leading units of the American Twelfth Armoured Division had passed through.

Just outside the village a smashed road-block, a corpse or two, an abandoned tank and an orchard cratered by mortar shells, marked the spot where the Germans had tried to make a stand. The village itself had been shelled. Several houses were burning. Immediately over the next hillside the self-propelled guns and heavy machine-guns had already opened fire on the next village and batches of miserably-dressed German prisoners, their hands locked behind their heads, were being brought in by bored soldiers with carbines.

Amid all this the villagers were almost completely unconcerned. A little knot of elderly people, two women and a man, seemed to be in a state of distress, but as for the others they watched the irruption of the American Army with probably less interest than they would have given to a passing circus. Someone was loading manure into a cart. There was the usual queue at the pump, and two old men were steadily sawing up logs on a trestle. Even the wretched parties of prisoners got hardly a glance of curiosity.

In this area what little civilian resistance there is (usually in the form of sniping) is almost entirely the work of youths between 12 and 20. The other age groups seem indifferent or even friendly and relieved to see secure government established again. In some places German civilians have applied to the military government not merely to protect them against the Displaced Persons, but even to provide anti-aircraft guns to keep the German planes away. The young men, who will obviously be the first source of trouble, are not much in evidence, most of them being in the army.

Almost anyone who is questioned, including prisoners, admits that the war is lost, and adds that resistance only continues because of a handful of fanatical Nazis, which is no doubt true. The decision to defend Nuremberg, for instance, was a political decision taken by the local S.S. commander against the wishes of both the army and the civilians.

This part of Germany has not suffered very greatly from the war, the people, especially the children, have obviously been very well fed, and the blitzing of Bavaria and Württemberg has not been so comprehensive as in the Rhineland and the Ruhr. It is true that with the solitary exception of Heidelberg the big towns have been flattened. Even the ancient university city of Wurzburg is now a mere mass of ruins though, fortunately, its medieval castle was too solid to be completely destroyed. But the villages and the pleasant little country towns, with their massive gateways, their baroque churches, and their cobbled squares, have mostly escaped damage, except when they stood in the direct path of the fighting and did not produce their white flags promptly enough.

Away from the main roads one would hardly know there was a war on if it were not for the occasional group of Displaced Persons who trudge past carrying bundles of rags on their backs and keeping one eye open for stray chickens.

As one drives through this peaceful countryside with its winding roads fringed by cherry trees, its terraced vineyards and its wayside shrines, there is one question that raises itself over and over again. It is: to what extent can these obviously simple and gentle peasants who troop to church on Sunday mornings in decent black be responsible for the horrors of the Nazis?

The Nazi movement actually started in this part of Germany, and there can be no question about the enormity of the crimes it has committed if only because the mass of evidence came in long before the war started.

But if one wants evidence of German cruelty, there is plenty of it here and now in the tales told by escaped prisoners and deportees.

Their condition partly depended on how long they had been prisoners, but the main dividing line was between those who did and those who did not receive Red Cross parcels. This camp contained some thousands of Russians, who were herded together in wretched tents without side flaps and with no covering on the ground, so that they had to make themselves burrows in the sandy soil. Universally they were ragged and filthy, their faces drawn with hunger and misery, and fresh typhus cases were occurring among them every day.

Even the British prisoners had been treated badly enough, most of them having been put to work in the Silesian coal mines and then when the Red Army approached were forced to march on foot all the way to Bavaria.

But they all spoke with indignation of the treatment given to the Russians. Only a few days before at this camp the German guards had opened fire and killed several Russians for crowding up to the wire when British and American prisoners tried to throw food over to them.

A British prisoner described how on his arrival he and his companions had thrown some soap over the wire to the Russians, and the starving Russians had promptly eaten it. Another told me of a camp in Silesia where, when a Russian prisoner died, his comrades would cover his body with a blanket and pretend that he was merely ill so that they could go on drawing his soup ration for a few days longer.

An American prisoner, an officer, summed up the situation by pointing to the scarecrow figures in the Russian encampment, and remarking: "The sole thing that has saved us from being in the same condition as those people there is our parcels from home."

2661. The Germans Still Doubt Our Unity: The Flags Do Not Help

The Observer, 29 April 1945

With the U.S. Third Army, Stuttgart, 28 April

The morning after the French First Army entered Stuttgart this week, the General commanding the 100th American Division sent a small detachment of tanks and infantry to make contact with them in the eastern suburbs of the town.

On the east bank of the Neckar a column found the French and turned back. It was impossible for vehicles to cross the river, every bridge in the 60 miles between Heilbronn and Tuebingen having been blown up. There was, however, a small footbridge which the Germans had not thought worth a charge of explosive, and two other correspondents and myself who were accompanying the Americans decided to go on foot.

On the other bank of the river groups of Displaced Persons, still delirious after 24 hours of liberty, were careering to and fro in looted cars and trucks, while others who had got hold of rifles were letting fly at pieces of driftwood in the stream.

The central part of the town, or what was left of it, had been thoroughly pillaged. The worst looting generally happens in the first hour or two after resistance collapses and is the work of German civilians and suddenly released prisoners and deportees.

Looting can be prevented, if at all, only by having the apparatus of military government ready before a town is captured, and in this case, no doubt owing to the unexpected suddenness with which Stuttgart collapsed, there was a long delay.

Seventy-two hours after the French entered no proclamations had been posted, and the whereabouts of the military government was undiscoverable, though some harmless-looking elderly men with armbands marked "Polizei" were occasionally to be seen on the streets.

The disorder after the fall of Stuttgart was probably worse than usual because of the large-scale looting of wine. Empty bottles, and even half-full bottles, were littered all over the place. I had entered the town to the sound of rifle shots, and stray shots were still reverberating when I left two days later, though all pockets of resistance had long since been cleared out. The shots were merely an unofficial *feu de joie.*

Meanwhile, the French, disregarding the deportees and concentrating on the Germans, were combing the town house by house and arresting not only every one in uniform but every male civilian suspected of having belonged either to the Wehrmacht or the Volkssturm. The toll of prisoners was so large that it was difficult to find places to put them in, and numbers of them had to be temporarily housed in the subway under the main railway station.

It is, above all, when one watches German prisoners being rounded up that a gulf seems to open between almost any Anglo-Saxon and almost any Continental European. One may recognise fully the need to destroy the German army and to use no matter what means to do it, but one has to have lived under German rule before one can get an actual pleasure out of these scenes of humiliation.

As the endless lines of prisoners trailed by, the deportees, and even some of the French soldiers, watched them with grins of quite frank delight.

"Just like us in 1940!" was a comment I heard several times. Some of these people even seemed to get a grim satisfaction in contemplating the ruin wrought by the bombs. I could not feel anything of the kind myself. Stuttgart, it is true, is a big town, and parts of it are still intact; but, as usual, it is the ancient central part of the town that has been flattened and the uninteresting residential suburbs which have escaped.

I had been billeted on some middle-class Germans in the suburbs. These people, like most of the Germans I have been able to talk to, were not only eager for the war to end quickly, but even more eager to see as much as possible of Germany occupied by the Americans and British and as little as possible by the Russians and French.

Evidently it is still necessary to make the Germans understand that the Governments of the United Nations are in substantial agreement. At present the idea seems widespread that Russia, France, and Anglo-America are more or less hostile to one another and stand for quite different policies.

It is obviously dangerous to let this idea take root, and the failure to define the zones of occupation in advance, and the practice followed by the various armies of hoisting only their own national flag in the areas they occupy, have done something to encourage it.

2662. Now Germany Faces Hunger

Manchester Evening News, 4 May 1945

It is generally agreed that up to date Allied Military Government has worked with unexpected smoothness in Germany, especially in the rural areas, where the peasants are so heartily sick of war that they often greet the advancing Allied forces as liberators rather than as conquerors.

Some Military Government officers say frankly that the ever-growing bands of escaped prisoners and foreign deportees who roam the country-side are a much bigger problem than the Germans themselves. But it is also recognised that within a fairly short time, probably within six months, the real difficulties will begin to make themselves felt, and that the present docility of the Germans is due to the fact that they are war-weary, that their food situation is still fairly good, and that they look to Anglo-America to protect them against the Eastern European peoples whom they are conscious of having wronged.

In principle Military Government exists only to facilitate the prosecution of the war. It keeps order, attends to food supply, public utilities, and the other needs of the population, and appoints a temporary German administration, merely in the interests of military efficiency and not with any long-term political objective. In practice, however, it is obliged to do things which have political implications and which will leave their mark on any German regime that finally emerges from the war.

One such measure—undesirable in itself but forced upon the occupying authorities by the nature of the Nazi regime—is the closing of schools. At present, apart from six kindergarten opened in Aachen on Tuesday, no schools are open in Allied-occupied Germany.

As early as possible it is hoped to reopen schools up to the fourth grade, but the choice of new teachers and provision of new textbooks are bound to impose a long delay. It would have been impossible to allow the existing educational system to remain in being, because its leading purpose was to disseminate Nazi doctrine. Another step, more doubtfully wise but considered necessary in the interests of military security, is the confiscation of civilian wireless sets. And in issuing German-language newspapers, in deciding which factories to reopen and what agricultural policy to favour, and in picking out politically reliable people as burgomasters and other officials, the Military Government is compelled to do many things that go beyond the narrow function of facilitating the passage of the armies.

However, the immediate and dangerous problem is that of food. Until recently the mass of the German people have been well nourished, they still have fairly large stocks of food, and such of the agricultural land as has not actually been fought over is in good condition. But this state of affairs is rapidly changing. Germany's war-time food supply depended largely on the plundering of occupied territories which have now been lost, and agriculture had come to depend more and more on war prisoners and deported foreign labourers.

Several millions of these slave workers have already been liberated by the advance of the Allied armies, and on many a farm where there were recently half a dozen sturdy Russian or Polish labourers there is now no one except an aged peasant and his wife.

This year's harvest has been sown, but whether it will be gathered in will depend on an early end to the war and the prompt return to the land of some millions of young Germans. There are also shortages of suitable seed (this year's potato crop, it is already calculated, will be much below the average), of fertilisers, of oil for agricultural machinery, and of horses, the peasants in most areas being obliged to use their milch cows as draught animals. Even if the chaos of war is cleaned up with unexpected speed, there is bound to be a severe food shortage this winter.

Apart from the difficulties with our Allies that this will involve—for if the U.S.A. and Britain are to feed Germany it will have to be at the expense of the Western European countries—discontent over the food situation is the likeliest starting-point for German resistance. At present the attitude of the people in occupied territory is friendly and even embarrassingly friendly.

The non-fraternisation order, the wisdom of which is doubted by many of the officers who have to enforce it, already works rather creakily. But there are three or four abnormal factors which probably make the task of governing Germany appear simpler than it is. To begin with, almost all the young men, and especially the active Nazis, are away from home—they are in the army, or have retreated along with the army, or they are already prisoners. Secondly, the German people are for the time being thoroughly well aware that they have lost the war, and in the big towns they are profoundly relieved that the bombing has stopped.

Thirdly, there is a widespread idea, for which the Allies themselves are partly to blame, that the U.S.S.R., France, and Anglo-America are not occupying Germany along prearranged lines, but that each is simply grabbing as much territory as possible. Many or most Germans are so terrified of the French and Russians that they actually welcome British or American occupation. Some of the popularity of Britain and the U.S.A. will probably wear off when it is better realised that the leading Allies are in substantial agreement.

Hitherto there has been surprisingly little sabotage or guerrilla activity, although the vast area overrun by the Allied armies is of necessity thinly held. Of strikes, demonstrations, or open opposition of any kind there has been hardly a trace. Hitler's birthday, for instance, passed off almost without incident,[1] and in the big towns there is a surprising lack of wall-chalking, sticky-backs, or other evidences of underground political activity. The "Werewolves" have accomplished little or nothing up to date, and the Volkssturm[2] is generally agreed to have been a miserable failure.

The chief concern of its members has been to get rid of their uniforms and disguise themselves as civilians, or, failing that, to surrender as promptly as possible—this in spite of the fact that the Volkssturm was fairly well armed, being supplied in large quantities with the panzerfaust,[3] the German equivalent of the bazooka.

But what one has to remember in this connection is that resistance movements and guerilla warfare take a long time to organise. The Germans had occupied France for six moths or more before the French resistance began to make itself felt, and in England it took a year or more to turn the Home Guard into a serious military organisation. Since about the middle of 1944 the Germans have collapsed very suddenly, and they do not appear to have made serious preparations beforehand for fighting on their own soil.

We cannot assume, therefore, that a serious resistance movement, difficult to deal with except by the repugnant method of mass reprisals, will not spring up in the coming winter. The conditions likely to favour it are continuation of war-time chaos, shortage of food, and serious differences, or even the semblances of differences, between the Allies. The present system by which each army administers the territory it has occupied more or less independently, and without even displaying the flags of its Allies, has already created a false impression among the Germans and has in it the seeds of danger.

1. Hitler's birthday was 20 April 1889; by the time this article was published, Hitler had committed suicide (30 April 1945). The surrender document was signed by German representatives on 7 May 1945.
2. The Werewolves were intended to be a guerrilla force; they were led by General Hans Pretzmann and proved ineffective. The Volksturm, a Home Guard, was formed in September 1944.
3. Anti-tank gun.

2663. Anarchist Trial

4 May 1945

On 27 April 1945, three of four anarchists, members of the editorial board of *War Commentary*, were sentenced by Mr. Justice Birkett to nine months' imprisonment for offences under the Defence Regulations. On 4 May 1945, *Tribune* published three letters of protest: one by Herbert Read, Chairman of the Freedom Press Defence Committee, one by George Woodcock, and one jointly signed by nine people, of whom Orwell was one.

Philip Sansom, Vernon Richards and Dr. John Hewetson, three members of the editorial board of *War Commentary*, were sentenced at the Old Bailey last Thursday[1] to nine months' imprisonment for actions arising out of their editorship of that British bi-monthly political journal. To stress, as the Court repeatedly did, that this was not a political trial and that the freedom of the Press was in no way involved is simply legal hair-splitting.

We concede the right of the Government to try these citizens, but our more serious concern is to emphasise the necessity of the whole body of Socialist opinion in this country to identify itself with these editors as did Herbert Read, an English poet, both in the witness-box and from a political platform, when he so magnificently said, in effect, that if these men were imprisoned, he did not wish to remain unmolested. The jury having returned their verdict of "guilty," the sentence was politically wise, as the maximum penalty is 14 years, but was it anything else but politics that caused these men to be arrested at this (seemingly unnecessary) moment when soldiers all over Europe are about to lay down their arms?

The things these men did which brought them standing, where thieves and murderers are wont to stand, inside the dock at the Old Bailey, spring from their love of justice and their concern for the victims and the poor. On trial with them were the teachings of Jesus, the philosophy of Peter Kropotkin, the politics of Tom Paine, the poetry of William Blake and the paintings of Van Gogh. No man who accepts these can remain true to them while rejecting the right of these three men to do the things they did.

LAZARUS AARENSON,
YANKEL ADLER,
GEORGE BAKER,
ALEX COMFORT,
NICHOLAS MOORE,

GEORGE ORWELL,
DYLAN THOMAS,
R. E. WATERFIELD,
PAUL POTTS.

1. 27 April was a Friday; Herbert Read gives the date of sentencing as 27 April in his letter.

2664. France's Interest In The War Dwindles: Back to Normal Is The Aim

The Observer, 6 May 1945

Paris, 5 May

Looking at the surface aspect of Paris, it is a little difficult to believe that only last week-end a third of its electorate voted Communist, whilst another quarter voted for other extremist parties of the Left.

Paris has brightened up in the spring sunshine. Solid food is no more plentiful than it was when I came here two months ago, but there are lettuces and spring onions, even strawberries if you can pay for them, and it is warm enough to sit at café tables out of doors.

Clothes are still shabby, but the women's hats are more flamboyant than ever. If it were not for the ever-present American soldiers one would hardly take this for the capital of a country at war. In a little while, no doubt, flags will be flying and bells ringing to celebrate the final victory, but no extra flags have appeared as yet, and though Hitler's death did cause a certain stir, I could not overhear many spontaneous comments on it. Life goes on pretty much as usual, and the quest for food, fuel, and amusement looms larger for most people than any external event.

And yet one could not truthfully say that there is no political activity. The municipal elections not only showed a nation-wide swing to the Left, but—what was perhaps even more significant—produced a very large poll. And there were also the May Day celebrations, when an enormous crowd of people filed through the streets chanting in unison: "Pétain au Poteau!"[1]

What is one to make of this seeming combination of apathy and revolutionary sentiment? First of all it is widely agreed that France is far more interested in internal affairs than in the war. France's principal act of war was the Resistance, which involved only a minority, and even now the number of people directly engaged in the war effort is tiny compared with that in Britain. Everyone wants France to be strong, to have a big army and reappear as a great Power, but the day-to-day detail of the war is not interesting.

Even the repatriated prisoners evoke very little enthusiasm. Every day hundreds of these men, in ragged discoloured uniforms, jolt through the streets in lorries. The authorities give them a warm meal and a ceremony of welcome, but the passing crowds hardly notice them.

International affairs do not arouse the passions that they do in Britain. San Francisco is not much discussed, and neither the Greek nor the Polish issue provoked any very violent controversy. The average Frenchman is interested first of all in France, and though he wants certain political reforms, what he wants above all things is to get back to normal, with enough to eat and better facilities for recreation.

Among the noticeable things in Paris are the long cinema queues and the large proportion of the dwindled Press given over to sport. Not only hunger, but boredom and the longing for a bit of amusement, make up the background of the political scene.

The municipal elections showed a general Leftward slide. Communists won votes from Socialists, Socialists won them from Radicals, and in many areas the parties of the Right were almost obliterated. But one certainly cannot infer from this that France is on the verge of revolution. One has only to glance down any street to see that the people are in no mood for violent effort of any kind. In some ways, in spite of all that has happened, pre-war habits of mind seem to have lingered more strongly than they have in England. Distinctions of wealth are greater, or at any rate they are more obtrusive, and a larger proportion of people are engaged in menial occupations. Fifty per cent. of the electorate have just voted Socialist or Communist, but the haberdashers still display top hats in their depleted windows, and sandwichmen still trudge to and fro bearing advertisements for manicurists. However it may be when France is less hungry, and when political discussion is less hampered by censorship and paper shortage, the general desire at present is for security and normality and not for drastic changes.[2]

Reading the posters before the elections I was struck by the fact that all parties now promise almost exactly the same things. People, nevertheless, turn their eyes towards the Left because the Left is felt to stand, *not* for bloody revolution but for security of employment, family allowances, and protection of the rights of labour. The Popular Front Government of 1936,[3] which gave France certain elementary reforms it had never before had, is still fairly vividly remembered.

On the other hand, the Right is associated with certain vague but menacing entities called "the trusts," which are held to be responsible for everything from the defeat of 1940 to the shortage of cigarettes.

The French Communist Party has a big membership as well as a strong hold on the general public, and it contains a nucleus of hardened long-term members who still probably look forward to violent revolution as their ultimate objective. But the mass of its followers do not appear to want any such thing, and certain points even in its declared policy are only doubtfully popular.

To begin with, in spite of "Pétain au Poteau!" it is doubtful whether the French masses wish for such a wholesale and vindictive persecution of collaborationists as the Communists demand. Certainly they are anxious that the biggest culprits shall not escape, but there seems to be a certain uneasiness about the moral aspects of the purge, which, if carried out in a thoroughgoing way, would be all too often the punishment of the guilty by the guilty.

The other feature of Communist policy which probably does not reflect popular opinion is its anti-British orientation. Apart from the Vichyites, who are now lying low, the Communists are the only French political faction who are anti-British (and to a less extent anti-American), and they show it as plainly as is possible in the general muffling of the Press.

This is probably a matter of high policy—Britain being the possible leader of the Western bloc, whose formation the U.S.S.R. opposes—rather than an expression of the sentiments of ordinary French people, working-class or middle-class.

1. In this context, *poteau* is the stake to which a person about to be executed by firing squad is tied.
2. This sentence is reproduced as in the original
3. Léon Blum (see *2627, n. 1*) led reformist Popular Front governments in 1936 and 1938. Daladier (see *2658, n. 1*) was Minister of War in Blum's 1936 cabinet and became Premier later in 1938.

2665. VE-Day

8 May 1945

This day officially marked the end of World War II in Europe.

2666. To Lydia Jackson

11 May 1945   Typewritten

Hotel Scribe
Rue Scribe
Paris 9eme

Dear Lydia,
I just had letters from you and Pat[1] about simultaneously. I don't want to relet the cottage, because for the time being I want to keep it on as a place to go down to for an occasional week end. I can however make either of the following arrangements with you. Either I will lend you the cottage for a month in the summer at any time you choose to name, or else you can continue to use the cottage at all times, but on the understanding that I can come and have it for a week or so any time I want to. In either case I don't want you to pay me anything. I should be back in London about May 25th and we can make any final arrangements then. You could have it for June or July or really whenever you like provided I know beforehand. At present it seems impossible to get a house in the country and for that reason I want to keep on the cottage so that Richard can get a few days of country air now and then. Eileen and I had hoped that it would not be necessary for him to learn to walk in London, but it seems unavoidable, so I am going to keep on the flat.

Gwen[2] says you borrowed a refrigerator of hers. Do you think we could have it back, because it is so hard to keep milk from going sour in the summer months and that makes it so difficult with the children.

I came straight back here after Eileen's death and have felt somewhat better for being at work most of the time. The destruction in Germany is terrifying, far worse than people in England grasp, but my trips there have been quite interesting. I am making one more trip, to Austria I hope, and then coming back about the end of next week. I get bulletins about Richard from Doreen[3] and it seems he is doing very well and had tripled his birth weight at 11 months. The next thing is to find a nurse for him which is next door to impossible at present. I don't know how long this letter will take getting to you—sometimes they take only 4 days, sometimes about 3 weeks—but if it gets to you before I get back, and you want to go down to the cottage, you can do so. Looking forward to seeing you both.

Yours
George

1. Patricia Donoghue shared Orwell's cottage at Wallington with Lydia Jackson (Elisaveta Fen).
2. Gwen O'Shaughnessy, Orwell's sister-in-law.
3. Doreen Kopp was taking care of Richard.

2667. Freed Politicians Return to Paris: T.U. Leader Sees de Gaulle

The Observer, 13 May 1945

Paris, 12 May
Paul Reynaud, Yvon Delbos, and Leon Jouhaux[1] arrived in Paris two days ago. Jouhaux, the former leader of the French Trade Union Movement, has already been called to confer with de Gaulle, but is somewhat cagey about his political future.

He will not say whether he is likely to be offered a post in the present Government. He says he supports the de Gaulle Government, and intends to return to political life immediately. At the coming general election he will stand as an independent candidate.

Reynaud, Premier up to June, 1940, and handed over by Pétain to the Germans after the Allied landings in North Africa in November, 1942, spent the first six months of his captivity in an isolation cell in Oranienburg, but was afterwards removed to a fortress in the Tyrol, where he was incarcerated with other French political leaders.

He was well treated, and spent his time in captivity writing a book on events leading up to the defeat.

There is, of course, a new political factor in the liberation of Herriot,[2] Daladier, Reynaud, and Blum. Of these, only Blum has fully maintained his reputation and his commanding position within his own party. Even when he had vanished into some concentration camp of unknown whereabouts, his name was still displayed on the front page of "Le Populaire" as editor-in-chief. Daladier is perhaps discredited for good. The Radicals have tried hard to build him up in recent months, but his internment of the Communist deputies in 1939 is not likely to be forgotten.

Nevertheless, all of these politicians are much better known to the general public than any member of the present Government, except de Gaulle himself, and Daladier and Reynaud share with Blum the prestige of the Riom Trial[3] at which they behaved with courage and dignity. By this half-hearted attempt at terrorism the Pétainists did much to rehabilitate the regime they had overthrown and it is thought that at the coming general elections the reappearance of Herriot, Reynaud, and Daladier may do something to revive the fallen fortunes of the Radical Socialist Party.

Those whose memories went back long enough declared that the victory celebrations in Paris "didn't come up to 1918," but they were certainly impressive, the more so because the news of the German surrender did not come with dramatic suddenness, but leaked out owing to various indiscretions after having been impatiently expected for weeks.

At least 24 hours before the official announcement everyone in Paris appeared to know the exact hour at which the cease fire would sound, and one evening paper was seized by the police for spilling the news prematurely. Apart from the much discussed misdemeanour of one of the news agencies, the German Radio at Flensburg had made an announcement which was repeated by the French Radio and then contradicted a little while later.

After all this it was hardly surprising that there was an unofficial celebration on Monday night, with songs and processions in the streets and aeroplanes dropping many coloured flares among the chimney-pots. But the real excitement began early on Tuesday morning. Bands of youths and girls marched to and fro in military formation, chanting, "Avec Nous! Avec Nous!" and gradually swelling their numbers until by midday the crowds were so enormous that many of the main streets and squares were quite impassable. They remained so the whole of Tuesday and the whole of Wednesday. Some people did go home for part of Tuesday night, while others subsided on to benches or patches of grass and snatched a few hours' sleep.

At three o'clock on Tuesday afternoon I managed to force my way near enough to a loudspeaker in the Place de la Concorde to listen to the official announcement.

There had been rumours that the whole thing might have to be postponed. Then came de Gaulle's voice: "The war is won. This is victory." The people did not break into a cheer, but listened attentively to the rest of the speech, and then stood in reverent silence while the National Anthems of all the leading Allies were played over.

For several days the newspapers maintained a kind of self-censorship, keeping unpleasant topics in the background as much as possible, but there are certain questions both of home and foreign policy that it is impossible to ignore for any length of time. It cannot be said that present-day French newspapers ever discuss foreign politics with much freedom, but there are obvious signs of discord over the San Francisco Conference and Russian policy generally. The question of the occupation of Germany, and especially of Berlin—who will occupy which areas, and how soon—is also discussed with evident uneasiness.

1. Paul Reynaud (1878–1966), politician, held many government posts, including, for a short time that of premier during the fall of France; see *2658, n. 1*. He participated in French political life from his release from captivity until losing his seat in 1962. Yvon Delbos (1885–1956), French journalist and politician. In 1936 and 1937–38 he served as Foreign Minister; in 1940 he was Minister of Education. He refused to agree to France's capitulation and was opposed to giving Pétain special powers. He returned to office in 1947. Léon Jouhaux (1879–1954), socialist trade union leader. He played a negotiating role between the Caballerista and Negrinista factions of the UGT, the Spanish socialist trade union in the autumn of 1936 (Thomas, 782, n. 5).
2. Edouard Herriot (1872–1957), leader of the Radical Socialists, presided over the National Assembly, 1947–54. See *1538, n. 1*.
3. In 1942 the Vichy government put on trial at the small town of Riom a number of France's political and military leaders, including Blum and Daladier, for having caused France to enter World War II without due preparation. The defendants turned successfully on their accusers, and the trial was postponed indefinitely.

2668. 'Notes on Nationalism'

Polemic: A Magazine of Philosophy, Psychology & Aesthetics, No. 1
[October] 1945[1]

Somewhere or other Byron makes use of the French word *longueur*, and remarks in passing that though in England we happen not to have the *word*, we have the *thing* in considerable profusion. In the same way, there is a habit of mind which is now so widespread that it effects our thinking on nearly every subject, but which has not yet been given a name. As the nearest existing equivalent I have chosen the word "nationalism," but it will be seen in a moment that I am not using it in quite the ordinary sense, if only because the emotion I am speaking about does not always attach itself to what is called a nation—that is, a single race or a geographical area. It can attach itself to a church or a class, or it may work in a merely negative sense, *against* something or other and without the need for any positive object of loyalty.

By "nationalism" I mean first of all the habit of assuming that human beings can be classified like insects and that whole blocks of millions or tens of millions of people can be confidently labelled "good" or "bad".★ But secondly—and this is much more important—I mean the habit of identifying oneself with a single nation or other unit, placing it beyond good and evil and recognizing no other duty than that of advancing its interests. Nationalism is not to be confused with patriotism. Both words are normally used in so vague a way that any definition is liable to be challenged, but one must draw a distinction between them, since two different and even opposing ideas are

★ Nations, and even vaguer entities such as the Catholic Church or the proletariat, are commonly thought of as individuals and often referred to as "she". Patently absurd remarks such as "Germany is naturally treacherous" are to be found in any newspaper one opens, and reckless generalisations about national character ("The Spaniard is a natural aristocrat" or "Every Englishman is a hypocrite") are uttered by almost everyone. Intermittently these generalisations are seen to be unfounded, but the habit of making them persists, and people of professedly international outlook, *e.g.* Tolstoy or Bernard Shaw, are often guilty of them [Orwell's footnote].

involved. By "patriotism" I mean devotion to a particular place and a particular way of life, which one believes to be the best in the world but has no wish to force upon other people. Patriotism is of its nature defensive, both militarily and culturally. Nationalism, on the other hand, is inseparable from the desire for power. The abiding purpose of every nationalist is to secure more power and more prestige, *not* for himself but for the nation or other unit in which he has chosen to sink his own individuality.

So long as it is applied merely to the more notorious and identifiable nationalist movements in Germany, Japan and other countries, all this is obvious enough. Confronted with a phenomenon like Nazism, which we can observe from the outside, nearly all of us would say much the same things about it. But here I must repeat what I said above, that I am only using the word "nationalism" for lack of a better. Nationalism, in the extended sense in which I am using the word, includes such movements and tendencies as Communism, political Catholicism, Zionism, anti-Semitism, Trotskyism and Pacifism. It does not necessarily mean loyalty to a government or a country, still less to *one's own* country, and it is not even strictly necessary that the units in which it deals should actually exist. To name a few obvious examples, Jewry, Islam, Christendom, the Proletariat and the White Race are all of them the objects of passionate nationalistic feeling: but their existence can be seriously questioned, and there is no definition of any one of them that would be universally accepted.

It is also worth emphasising once again that nationalist feeling can be purely negative. There are, for example, Trotskyists who have become simply the enemies of the U.S.S.R. without developing a corresponding loyalty to any other unit. When one grasps the implications of this, the nature of what I mean by nationalism becomes a good deal clearer. A nationalist is one who thinks solely, or mainly, in terms of competitive prestige. He may be a positive or a negative nationalist—that is, he may use his mental energy either in boosting or in denigrating—but at any rate his thoughts always turn on victories, defeats, triumphs and humiliations. He sees history, especially contemporary history, as the endless rise and decline of great power units, and every event that happens seems to him a demonstration that his own side is on the up grade and some hated rival on the down grade. But finally, it is important not to confuse nationalism with mere worship of success. The nationalist does not go on the principle of simply ganging up with the strongest side. On the contrary, having picked his side, he persuades himself that it *is* the strongest, and is able to stick to his belief even when the facts are overwhelmingly against him. Nationalism is power-hunger tempered by self-deception. Every nationalist is capable of the most flagrant dishonesty, but he is also—since he is conscious of serving something bigger than himself—unshakeably certain of being in the right.

Now that I have given this lengthy definition, I think it will be admitted that the habit of mind I am talking about is widespread among the English intelligentsia, and more widespread there than among the mass of the people. For those who feel deeply about contemporary politics, certain topics have become so infected by considerations of prestige that a genuinely rational approach to them is almost impossible. Out of the hundreds of examples that one might choose, take this question: Which of the three great allies, the U.S.S.R., Britain and the U.S.A., has contributed most to the defeat of Germany? In theory it should be possible to give a reasoned and perhaps even a conclusive answer to this question. In practice, however, the necessary calculations cannot be made, because anyone likely to bother his head about such a question would inevitably see it in terms of competitive prestige. He would therefore *start* by deciding in favour of Russia, Britain or America as the case might be, and only *after* this would begin searching for arguments that seemed to support his case. And there are whole strings of kindred questions to which you can only get an honest answer from someone who is indifferent to the whole subject involved, and whose opinion on it is probably worthless in any case. Hence, partly, the remarkable failure in our time of political and military prediction. It is curious to reflect that out of all the "experts" of all the schools, there was not a single one who was able to foresee so likely an event as the Russo-German Pact of 1939.* And when the news of the Pact broke, the most wildly divergent explanations of it were given, and predictions were made which were falsified almost immediately, being based in nearly every case not on a study of probabilities but on a desire to make the U.S.S.R. seem good or bad, strong or weak. Political or military commentators, like astrologers, can survive almost any mistake, because their more devoted followers do not look to them for an appraisal of the facts but for the stimulation of nationalistic loyalties.† And æsthetic judgements, especially literary judgements, are often corrupted in the same way as political ones. It would be difficult for an Indian Nationalist to enjoy reading Kipling or for a Conservative to see merit in Mayakovsky, and there is always a temptation to claim that any book whose tendency one disagrees with must be a bad book from a *literary* point of view. People of strongly nationalistic outlook often perform this sleight of hand without being conscious of dishonesty.

In England, if one simply considers the number of people involved, it is probable that the dominant form of nationalism is old-fashioned British jingoism. It is certain that this is still widespread, and much more so than most observers would have believed a dozen years ago. However, in this essay I am concerned chiefly with the reactions of the intelligentsia, among

---

* A few writers of conservative tendency, such as Peter Drucker,[2] foretold an agreement between Germany and Russia, but they expected an actual alliance or amalgamation which would be permanent. No Marxist or other left-wing writer, of whatever colour, came anywhere near foretelling the Pact [Orwell's footnote].

† The military commentators of the popular press can mostly be classified as pro-Russian or anti-Russian, pro-blimp or anti-blimp. Such errors as believing the Maginot Line impregnable, or predicting that Russia would conquer Germany in three months, have failed to shake their reputation, because they were always saying what their own particular audience wanted to hear. The two military critics most favoured by the intelligentsia are Captain Liddell Hart and Major-General Fuller,[3] the first of whom teaches that the defence is stronger than the attack, and the second that the attack is stronger than the defence. This contradiction has not prevented both of them from being accepted as authorities by the same public. The secret reason for their vogue in left-wing circles is that both of them are at odds with the War Office [Orwell's footnote].

whom jingoism and even patriotism of the old kind are almost dead, though they now seem to be reviving among a minority. Among the intelligentsia, it hardly needs saying that the dominant form of nationalism is Communism— using this word in a very loose sense, to include not merely Communist Party members but "fellow travellers" and Russophiles generally. A Communist, for my purpose here, is one who looks upon the U.S.S.R. as his Fatherland and feels it his duty to justify Russian policy and advance Russian interests at all costs. Obviously such people abound in England to-day, and their direct and indirect influence is very great. But many other forms of nationalism also flourish, and it is by noticing the points of resemblance between different and even seemingly opposed currents of thought that one can best get the matter into perspective.

Ten or twenty years ago, the form of nationalism most closely corresponding to Communism today was political Catholicism. Its most outstanding exponent—though he was perhaps an extreme case rather than a typical one—was G. K. Chesterton. Chesterton was a writer of considerable talent who chose to suppress both his sensibilities and his intellectual honesty in the cause of Roman Catholic propaganda. During the last twenty years or so of his life, his entire output was in reality an endless repetition of the same thing, under its laboured cleverness as simple and boring as "Great is Diana of the Ephesians." Every book that he wrote, every paragraph, every sentence, every incident in every story, every scrap of dialogue, had to demonstrate beyond possibility of mistake the superiority of the Catholic over the Protestant or the pagan. But Chesterton was not content to think of this superiority as merely intellectual or spiritual: it had to be translated into terms of national prestige and military power, which entailed an ignorant idealisation of the Latin countries, especially France. Chesterton had not lived long in France, and his picture of it—as a land of Catholic peasants incessantly singing the *Marseillaise* over glasses of red wine—had about as much relation to reality as *Chu Chin Chow* has to every-day life in Baghdad. And with this went not only an enormous over-estimation of French military power (both before and after 1914–18 he maintained that France, by itself, was stronger than Germany), but a silly and vulgar glorification of the actual process of war. Chesterton's battle poems, such as *Lepanto* or *The Ballad of Saint Barbara*, make *The Charge of the Light Brigade* read like a pacifist tract: they are perhaps the most tawdry bits of bombast to be found in our language. The interesting thing is that had the romantic rubbish which he habitually wrote about France and the French army been written by somebody else about Britain and the British army, he would have been the first to jeer. In home politics he was a Little Englander, a true hater of jingoism and imperialism, and according to his lights a true friend of democracy. Yet when he looked outwards into the international field, he could forsake his principles without even noticing that he was doing so. Thus, his almost mystical belief in the virtues of democracy did not prevent him from admiring Mussolini. Mussolini had destroyed the representative government and the freedom of the press for which Chesterton had struggled so hard at home, but Mussolini was an Italian and had made Italy strong, and that settled the matter. Nor did

Chesterton ever find a word to say against imperialism and the conquest of coloured races when they were practised by Italians or Frenchmen. His hold on reality, his literary taste, and even to some extent his moral sense, were dislocated as soon as his nationalistic loyalties were involved.

Obviously there are considerable resemblances between political Catholicism as exemplified by Chesterton, and Communism. So there are between either of these and, for instance, Scottish Nationalism, Zionism, Antisemitism or Trotskyism. It would be an over-simplification to say that all forms of nationalism are the same, even in their mental atmosphere, but there are certain rules that hold good in all cases. The following are the principal characteristics of nationalist thought:—

OBSESSION. As nearly as possible, no nationalist ever thinks, talks or writes about anything except the superiority of his own power unit. It is difficult if not impossible for any nationalist to conceal his allegiance. The smallest slur upon his own unit, or any implied praise of a rival organisation, fills him with uneasiness which he can only relieve by making some sharp retort. If the chosen unit is an actual country, such as Ireland or India, he will generally claim superiority for it not only in military power and political virtue, but in art, literature, sport, the structure of the language, the physical beauty of the inhabitants, and perhaps even in climate, scenery and cooking. He will show great sensitiveness about such things as the correct display of flags, relative size of headlines and the order in which different countries are named.* Nomenclature plays a very important part in nationalist thought. Countries which have won their independence or gone through a nationalist revolution usually change their names, and any country or other unit round which strong feelings revolve is likely to have several names, each of them carrying a different implication. The two sides in the Spanish civil war had between them nine or ten names expressing different degrees of love and hatred. Some of these names (*e.g.* "Patriots" for Franco-supporters, or "Loyalists" for Government-supporters) were frankly question-begging, and there was no single one of them which the two rival factions could have agreed to use. All nationalists consider it a duty to spread their own language to the detriment of rival languages, and among English-speakers this struggle reappears in subtler form as a struggle between dialects. Anglophobe Americans will refuse to use a slang phrase if they know it to be of British origin, and the conflict between Latinisers and Germanisers often has nationalist motives behind it. Scottish nationalists insist on the superiority of Lowland Scots, and Socialists whose nationalism takes the form of class hatred tirade against the B.B.C. accent and even the broad A. One could multiply instances. Nationalist thought often gives the impression of being tinged by belief in sympathetic magic—a belief which probably comes out in the widespread custom of burning political enemies in effigy, or using pictures of them as targets in shooting galleries.

---

* Certain Americans have expressed dissatisfaction because "Anglo-American" is the normal form of combination for these two words. It has been proposed to substitute "Americo-British" [Orwell's footnote].

INSTABILITY. The intensity with which they are held does not prevent nationalist loyalties from being transferable. To begin with, as I have pointed out already, they can be and often are fastened upon some foreign country. One quite commonly finds that great national leaders, or the founders of nationalist movements, do not even belong to the country they have glorified. Sometimes they are outright foreigners, or more often they come from peripheral areas where nationality is doubtful. Examples are Stalin, Hitler, Napoleon, de Valera, D'Israeli, Poincaré, Beaverbrook. The Pan-German movement was in part the creation of an Englishman, Houston Chamberlain. For the past fifty or a hundred years, transferred nationalism has been a common phenomenon among literary intellectuals. With Lafcadio Hearne the transference was to Japan, with Carlyle and many others of his time to Germany, and in our own age it is usually Russia. But the peculiarly interesting fact is that re-transference is also possible. A country or other unit which has been worshipped for years may suddenly become detestable, and some other object of affection may take its place with almost no interval. In the first version of H. G. Wells's *Outline of History*, and others of his writings about that time, one finds the United States praised almost as extravagantly as Russia is praised by Communists today: yet within a few years this uncritical admiration had turned into hostility. The bigoted Communist who changes in a space of weeks, or even days, into an equally bigoted Trotskyist is a common spectacle. In continental Europe Fascist movements were largely recruited from among Communists, and the opposite process may well happen within the next few years. What remains constant in the nationalist is his own state of mind: the object of his feelings is changeable, and may be imaginary.

But for an intellectual, transference has an important function which I have already mentioned shortly in connection with Chesterton. It makes it possible for him to be much *more* nationalistic—more vulgar, more silly, more malignant, more dishonest—than he could ever be on behalf of his native country, or any unit of which he had real knowledge. When one sees the slavish or boastful rubbish that is written about Stalin, the Red Army, etc. by fairly intelligent and sensitive people, one realises that this is only possible because some kind of dislocation has taken place. In societies such as ours, it is unusual for anyone describable as an intellectual to feel a very deep attachment to his own country. Public opinion—that is, the section of public opinion of which he as an intellectual is aware—will not allow him to do so. Most of the people surrounding him are sceptical and disaffected, and he may adopt the same attitude from imitativeness or sheer cowardice: in that case he will have abandoned the form of nationalism that lies nearest to hand without getting any closer to a genuinely internationalist outlook. He still feels the need for a Fatherland, and it is natural to look for one somewhere abroad. Having found it, he can wallow unrestrainedly in exactly those emotions from which he believes that he has emancipated himself. God, the King, the Empire, the Union Jack—all the overthrown idols can reappear under different names, and because they are not recognized for what they are they can be worshipped with a good conscience. Transferred nationalism, like the use of scapegoats, is a way of attaining salvation without altering one's conduct.

INDIFFERENCE TO REALITY. All nationalists have the power of not seeing resemblances between similar sets of facts. A British Tory will defend self-determination in Europe and oppose it in India with no feeling of inconsistency. Actions are held to be good or bad, not on their own merits but according to who does them, and there is almost no kind of outrage—torture, the use of hostages, forced labour, mass deportations, imprisonment without trial, forgery, assassination, the bombing of civilians—which does not change its moral colour when it is committed by "our" side. The Liberal *News Chronicle* published, as an example of shocking barbarity, photographs of Russians hanged by the Germans, and then a year or two later published with warm approval almost exactly similar photographs of Germans hanged by the Russians.* It is the same with historical events. History is thought of largely in nationalist terms, and such things as the Inquisition, the tortures of the Star Chamber, the exploits of the English buccaneers (Sir Francis Drake, for instance, who was given to sinking Spanish prisoners alive), the Reign of Terror, the heroes of the Mutiny blowing hundreds of Indians from the guns, or Cromwell's soldiers slashing Irishwomen's faces with razors, become morally neutral or even meritorious when it is felt that they were done in "the right" cause. If one looks back over the past quarter of a century, one finds that there was hardly a single year when atrocity stories were not being reported from some part of the world: and yet in not one single case were these atrocities—in Spain, Russia, China, Hungary, Mexico, Amritsar, Smyrna— believed in and disapproved of by the English intelligentsia as a whole. Whether such deeds were reprehensible, or even whether they happened, was always decided according to political predilection.

The nationalist not only does not disapprove of atrocities committed by his own side, but has a remarkable capacity for not even hearing about them. For quite six years the English admirers of Hitler contrived not to learn of the existence of Dachau and Buchenwald. And those who are loudest in denouncing the German concentration camps are often quite unaware, or only very dimly aware, that there are also concentration camps in Russia. Huge events like the Ukraine famine of 1933, involving the deaths of millions of people, have actually escaped the attention of the majority of English Russophiles. Many English people have heard almost nothing about the extermination of German and Polish Jews during the present war. Their own antisemitism has caused this vast crime to bounce off their consciousness. In nationalist thought there are facts which are both true and untrue, known and unknown. A known fact may be so unbearable that it is habitually pushed aside and not allowed to enter into logical processes, or on the other hand it

---

* The *News Chronicle* advised its readers to visit the news film at which the entire execution could be witnessed, with close-ups. The *Star* published with seeming approval photographs of nearly naked female collaborationists being baited by the Paris mob. These photographs had a marked resemblance to the Nazi photographs of Jews being baited by the Berlin mob [Orwell's footnote].

may enter into every calculation and yet never be admitted as a fact, even in one's own mind.

Every nationalist is haunted by the belief that the past can be altered. He spends part of his time in a fantasy world in which things happen as they should—in which, for example, the Spanish Armada was a success or the Russian Revolution was crushed in 1918—and he will transfer fragments of this world to the history books whenever possible. Much of the propagandist writing of our time amounts to plain forgery. Material facts are suppressed, dates altered, quotations removed from their context and doctored so as to change their meaning. Events which, it is felt, ought not to have happened are left unmentioned and ultimately denied.★ In 1927 Chiang Kai-Shek boiled hundreds of Communists alive, and yet within ten years he had become one of the heroes of the Left. The realignment of world politics had brought him into the anti-Fascist camp, and so it was felt that the boiling of the Communists "didn't count," or perhaps had not happened. The primary aim of propaganda is, of course, to influence contemporary opinion, but those who rewrite history do probably believe with part of their minds that they are actually thrusting facts into the past. When one considers the elaborate forgeries that have been committed in order to show that Trotsky did not play a valuable part in the Russian civil war, it is difficult to feel that the people responsible are merely lying. More probably they feel that their own version *was* what happened in the sight of God, and that one is justified in re-arranging the records accordingly.

Indifference to objective truth is encouraged by the sealing-off of one part of the world from another, which makes it harder and harder to discover what is actually happening. There can often be a genuine doubt about the most enormous events. For example, it is impossible to calculate within millions, perhaps even tens of millions, the number of deaths caused by the present war. The calamities that are constantly being reported—battles, massacres, famines, revolutions—tend to inspire in the average person a feeling of unreality. One has no way of verifying the facts, one is not even fully certain that they have happened, and one is always presented with totally different interpretations from different sources. What were the rights and wrongs of the Warsaw rising of August 1944? Is it true about the German gas ovens in Poland? Who was really to blame for the Bengal famine? Probably the truth is discoverable, but the facts will be so dishonestly set forth in almost any newspaper that the ordinary reader can be forgiven either for swallowing lies or for failing to form an opinion. The general uncertainty as to what is really happening makes it easier to cling to lunatic beliefs. Since nothing is ever quite proved or disproved, the most unmistakeable fact can be impudently denied. Moreover, although endlessly brooding on power, victory, defeat, revenge, the nationalist is often somewhat uninterested in what happens in the real world. What he wants is to *feel* that his own unit is getting the better of some other unit, and he can more easily do this by

---

★ An example is the Russo-German Pact, which is being effaced as quickly as possible from public memory. A Russian correspondent informs me that mention of the Pact is already being omitted from Russian year books which table recent political events [Orwell's footnote].[4]

scoring off an adversary than by examining the facts to see whether they support him. All nationalist controversy is at the debating-society level. It is always entirely inconclusive, since each contestant invariably believes himself to have won the victory. Some nationalists are not far from schizophrenia, living quite happily amid dreams of power and conquest which have no connection with the physical world.

I have examined as best I can the mental habits which are common to all forms of nationalism. The next thing is to classify those forms, but obviously this cannot be done comprehensively. Nationalism is an enormous subject. The world is tormented by innumerable delusions and hatreds which cut across one another in an extremely complex way, and some of the most sinister of them have not yet even impinged on the European consciousness. In this essay I am concerned with nationalism as it occurs among the English intelligentsia. In them, much more often than in ordinary English people, it is unmixed with patriotism and can therefore be studied pure. Below are listed the varieties of nationalism now flourishing among English intellectuals, with such comments as seem to be needed. It is convenient to use three headings, Positive, Transferred and Negative, though some varieties will fit into more than one category':—

POSITIVE NATIONALISM

(i.) NEO-TORYISM. Exemplified by such people as Lord Elton, A. P. Herbert, G. M. Young, Professor Pickthorne, by the literature of the Tory Reform Committee, and by such magazines as the *New English Review* and the *Nineteenth Century and After*. The real motive force of Neo-Toryism, giving it its nationalistic character and differentiating it from ordinary Conservatism, is the desire not to recognize that British power and influence have declined. Even those who are realistic enough to see that Britain's military position is not what it was, tend to claim that "English ideas" (usually left undefined) must dominate the world. All Neo-Tories are anti-Russian, but sometimes the main emphasis is anti-American. The significant thing is that this school of thought seems to be gaining ground among youngish intellectuals, sometimes ex-Communists, who have passed through the usual process of disillusionment and become disillusioned with that. The Anglophobe who suddenly becomes violently pro-British is a fairly common figure. Writers who illustrate this tendency are F. A. Voigt, Malcolm Muggeridge, Evelyn Waugh, Hugh Kingsmill, and a psychologically similar development can be observed in T. S. Eliot, Wyndham Lewis and various of their followers.

(ii.) CELTIC NATIONALISM. Welsh, Irish and Scottish nationalism have points of difference but are alike in their anti-English orientation. Members of all three movements have opposed the war while continuing to describe themselves as pro-Russian, and the lunatic fringe has even contrived to be simultaneously pro-Russian and pro-Nazi. But Celtic nationalism is not the same thing as Anglophobia. Its motive force is a belief in the past and future greatness of the Celtic peoples, and it has a strong tinge of racialism. The Celt is supposed to be spiritually superior to the Saxon—simpler, more creative, less vulgar, less snobbish, etc.—but the usual power-hunger is there under the surface. One symptom of it is the delusion that Eire, Scotland or even Wales could preserve its independence unaided and owes nothing to British protection. Among writers, good examples of this school of thought are Hugh MacDiarmid and Sean O'Casey. No modern Irish writer, even of the stature of Yeats or Joyce, is completely free from traces of nationalism.

(iii.) ZIONISM. This has the usual characteristics of a nationalist movement, but the American variant of it seems to be more violent and malignant than the British. I classify it under Direct and not Transferred nationalism because it flourishes almost exclusively among the Jews themselves. In England, for several rather incongruous reasons, the intelligentsia are mostly pro-Jew on the Palestine issue, but they do not feel strongly about it. All English people of good will are also pro-Jew in the sense of disapproving of Nazi persecution. But any actual nationalistic loyalty, or belief in the innate superiority of Jews, is hardly to be found among Gentiles.

TRANSFERRED NATIONALISM

(i.) COMMUNISM.

(ii.) POLITICAL CATHOLICISM.

(iii.) COLOUR FEELING. The old-style contemptuous attitude towards "natives" has been much weakened in England, and various pseudo-scientific theories emphasising the superiority of the white race have been abandoned.* Among the intelligentsia, colour feeling only occurs in the transposed form, that is, as a belief in the innate superiority of the coloured races. This is now increasingly common among English intellectuals, probably resulting more often from masochism and sexual frustration than from contact with the Oriental and Negro nationalist movements. Even among those who do not feel strongly on the colour question, snobbery and imitation have a powerful influence. Almost any English intellectual would be scandalised by the claim that the white races are superior to the coloured, whereas the opposite claim would seem to him unexceptional even if he disagreed with it. Nationalistic attachment to the coloured races is usually mixed up with the belief that their sex lives are superior, and there is a large underground mythology about the sexual prowess of Negroes.

(iv.) CLASS FEELING. Among upper-class and middle-class intellectuals, only in the transposed form—*i.e.* as a belief in the superiority of the proletariat. Here again, inside the intelligentsia, the pressure of public opinion is overwhelming. Nationalistic loyalty towards the proletariat, and most vicious theoretical hatred of the bourgeoisie, can and often do co-exist with ordinary snobbishness in every-day life.

(v.) PACIFISM. The majority of pacifists either belong to obscure religious

---

* A good example is the sunstroke superstition. Until recently it was believed that the white races were much more liable to sunstroke than the coloured, and that a white man could not safely walk about in tropical sunshine without a pith helmet. There was no evidence whatever for this theory, but it served the purpose of accentuating the difference between "natives" and Europeans. During the present war the theory has been quietly dropped and whole armies manœuvre in the tropics without pith helmets. So long as the sunstroke superstition survived, English doctors in India appear to have believed in it as firmly as laymen [Orwell's footnote].[5]

sects or are simply humanitarians who object to taking life and prefer not to follow their thoughts beyond that point. But there is a minority of intellectual pacifists whose real though unadmitted motive appears to be hatred of western democracy and admiration for totalitarianism. Pacifist propaganda usually boils down to saying that one side is as bad as the other, but if one looks closely at the writings of the younger intellectual pacifists, one finds that they do not by any means express impartial disapproval but are directed almost entirely against Britain and the United States. Moreover they do not as a rule condemn violence as such, but only violence used in defence of the western countries. The Russians, unlike the British, are not blamed for defending themselves by warlike means, and indeed all pacifist propaganda of this type avoids mention of Russia or China. It is not claimed, again, that the Indians should abjure violence in their struggle against the British. Pacifist literature abounds with equivocal remarks which, if they mean anything, appear to mean that statesmen of the type of Hitler are preferable to those of the type of Churchill, and that violence is perhaps excusable if it is violent enough. After the fall of France, the French pacifists, faced by a real choice which their English colleagues have not had to make, mostly went over to the Nazis, and in England there appears to have been some small overlap of membership between the Peace Pledge Union and the Blackshirts. Pacifist writers have written in praise of Carlyle, one of the intellectual fathers of Fascism. All in all it is difficult not to feel that pacifism, as it appears among a section of the intelligentsia, is secretly inspired by an admiration for power and successful cruelty. The mistake was made of pinning this emotion to Hitler, but it could easily be re-transferred.

NEGATIVE NATIONALISM

(i.) ANGLOPHOBIA. Within the intelligentsia, a derisive and mildly hostile attitude towards Britain is more or less compulsory, but it is an unfaked emotion in many cases. During the war it was manifested in the defeatism of the intelligentsia, which persisted long after it had become clear that the Axis powers could not win. Many people were undisguisedly pleased when Singapore fell or when the British were driven out of Greece, and there was a remarkable unwillingness to believe in good news, *e.g.* el Alamein, or the number of German planes shot down in the Battle of Britain. English left-wing intellectuals did not, of course, actually want the Germans or Japanese to win the war, but many of them could not help getting a certain kick out of seeing their own country humiliated, and wanted to feel that the final victory would be due to Russia, or perhaps America, and not to Britain. In foreign politics many intellectuals follow the principle that any faction backed by Britain must be in the wrong. As a result, "enlightened" opinion is quite largely a mirror-image of Conservative policy. Anglophobia is always liable to reversal, hence that fairly common spectacle, the pacifist of one war who is a bellicist in the next.

(ii.) ANTISEMITISM. There is little evidence about this at present, because the Nazi persecutions have made it necessary for any thinking person to side with the Jews against their oppressors. Anyone educated enough to have heard the word "antisemitism" claims as a matter of course to be free of it, and anti-Jewish remarks are carefully eliminated from all classes of literature. Actually antisemitism appears to be widespread, even among intellectuals, and the general conspiracy of silence probably helps to exacerbate it. People of Left opinions are not immune to it, and their attitude is sometimes affected by the fact that Trotskyists and Anarchists tend to be Jews. But antisemitism comes more naturally to people of Conservative tendency, who suspect the Jews of weakening national morale and diluting the national culture. Neo-Tories and political Catholics are always liable to succumb to antisemitism, at least intermittently.

(iii.) TROTSKYISM. This word is used so loosely as to include anarchists, democratic Socialists and even Liberals. I use it here to mean a doctrinaire Marxist whose main motive is hostility to the Stalin regime. Trotskyism can be better studied in obscure pamphlets or in papers like the *Socialist Appeal* than in the works of Trotsky himself, who was by no means a man of one idea. Although in some places, for instance in the United States, Trotskyism is able to attract a fairly large number of adherents and develop into an organised movement with a petty fuehrer of its own, its inspiration is essentially negative. The Trotskyist is *against* Stalin just as the Communist is *for* him, and, like the majority of Communists, he wants not so much to alter the external world as to feel that the battle for prestige is going in his own favour. In each case there is the same obsessive fixation on a single subject, the same inability to form a genuinely rational opinion based on probabilities. The fact that Trotskyists are everywhere a persecuted minority, and that the accusation usually made against them, *i.e.* of collaborating with the Fascists, is obviously false, creates an impression that Trotskyism is intellectually and morally superior to Communism; but it is doubtful whether there is much difference. The most typical Trotskyists, in any case, are ex-Communists, and no one arrives at Trotskyism except *via* one of the left-wing movements. No Communist, unless tethered to his party by years of habit, is secure against a sudden lapse into Trotskyism. The opposite process does not seem to happen equally often, though there is no clear reason why it should not.

In the classification I have attempted above, it will seem that I have often exaggerated, oversimplified, made unwarranted assumptions and left out of account the existence of ordinarily decent motives. This was inevitable, because in this essay I am trying to isolate and identify tendencies which exist in all our minds and pervert our thinking, without necessarily occurring in a pure state or operating continuously. It is important at this point to correct the oversimplified picture which I have been obliged to make. To begin with, one has no right to assume that *everyone*, or even every intellectual, is infected by nationalism; secondly, nationalism can be intermittent and limited. An intelligent man may half-succumb to a belief which attracts him but which he knows to be absurd, and he may keep it out of his mind for long periods, only reverting to it in moments of anger or sentimentality, or when he is certain that no important issue is involved. Thirdly, a nationalistic creed may be adopted in good faith from non-nationalist motives. Fourthly, several kinds of nationalism, even kinds that cancel out, can co-exist in the same person.

All the way through I have said "the nationalist does this" or "the nationalist does that", using for purposes of illustration the extreme, barely sane type of nationalist who has no neutral areas in his mind and no interest in anything except the struggle for power. Actually such people are fairly common, but they are not worth powder and shot. In real life Lord Elton, D. N. Pritt, Lady Houston, Ezra Pound, Lord Vansittart, Father Coughlin and all the rest of their dreary tribe have to be fought against, but their intellectual deficiencies hardly need pointing out. Monomania is not interesting, and the fact that no nationalist of the more bigoted kind can write a book which still seems worth reading after a lapse of years has a certain deodorising effect. But when one has admitted that nationalism has not triumphed everywhere, that there are still people whose judgements are not at the mercy of their desires, the fact does remain that the nationalistic habit of thought is widespread, so much so that various large and pressing problems—India, Poland, Palestine, the Spanish civil war, the Moscow trials, the American Negroes, the Russo-German pact or what-have-you—cannot be, or at least never are, discussed upon a reasonable level. The Eltons and Pritts and Coughlins, each of them simply an enormous mouth bellowing the same lie over and over again, are obviously extreme cases, but we deceive ourselves if we do not realise that we can all resemble them in unguarded moments. Let a certain note be struck, let this or that corn be trodden on—and it may be a corn whose very existence has been unsuspected hitherto—and the most fair-minded and sweet-tempered person may suddenly be transformed into a vicious partisan, anxious only to "score" over his adversary and indifferent as to how many lies he tells or how many logical errors he commits in doing so. When Lloyd George, who was an opponent of the Boer War, announced in the House of Commons that the British communiques, if one added them together, claimed the killing of more Boers than the whole Boer nation contained, it is recorded that Arthur Balfour rose to his feet and shouted "Cad!" Very few people are proof against lapses of this type. The Negro snubbed by a white woman, the Englishman who hears England ignorantly criticised by an American, the Catholic apologist reminded of the Spanish Armada, will all react in much the same way. One prod to the nerve of nationalism, and the intellectual decencies can vanish, the past can be altered, and the plainest facts can be denied.

If one harbours anywhere in one's mind a nationalistic loyalty or hatred, certain facts, although in a sense known to be true, are inadmissible. Here are just a few examples. I list below five types of nationalist, and against each I append a fact which it is impossible for that type of nationalist to accept, even in his secret thoughts:—

BRITISH TORY. Britain will come out of this war with reduced power and prestige.

COMMUNIST. If she had not been aided by Britain and America, Russia would have been defeated by Germany.

IRISH NATIONALIST. Eire can only remain independent because of British protection.

TROTSKYIST. The Stalin regime is accepted by the Russian masses.

PACIFIST. Those who "abjure" violence can only do so because others are committing violence on their behalf.

All of these facts are grossly obvious if one's emotions do not happen to be involved: but to the kind of person named in each case they are also *intolerable*, and so they have to be denied, and false theories constructed upon their denial. I come back to the astonishing failure of military prediction in the present war. It is, I think, true to say that the intelligentsia have been more wrong about the progress of the war than the common people, and that they were wrong precisely because they were more swayed by partisan feelings. The average intellectual of the Left believed, for instance, that the war was lost in 1940, that the Germans were bound to overrun Egypt in 1942, that the Japanese would never be driven out of the lands they had conquered, and that the Anglo-American bombing offensive was making no impression on Germany. He could believe these things because his hatred of the British ruling class forbade him to admit that British plans could succeed. There is no limit to the follies that can be swallowed if one is under the influence of feelings of this kind. I have heard it confidently stated, for instance, that the American troops had been brought to Europe not to fight the Germans but to crush an English revolution. One has to belong to the intelligentsia to believe things like that: no ordinary man could be such a fool. When Hitler invaded Russia, the officials of the M.O.I. issued "as background" a warning that Russia might be expected to collapse in six weeks. On the other hand the Communists regarded every phase of the war as a Russian victory, even when the Russians were driven back almost to the Caspian sea and had lost several million prisoners. There is no need to multiply instances. The point is that as soon as fear, hatred, jealousy and power-worship are involved, the sense of reality becomes unhinged. And, as I have pointed out already, the sense of right and wrong becomes unhinged also. There is no crime, absolutely none, that cannot be condoned when "our" side commits it. Even if one does not deny that the crime has happened, even if one knows that it is exactly the same crime as one has condemned in some other case, even if one admits in an intellectual sense that it is unjustified—still one cannot *feel* that it is wrong. Loyalty is involved, and so pity ceases to function.

The reason for the rise and spread of nationalism is far too big a question to be raised here. It is enough to say that, in the forms in which it appears among English intellectuals, it is a distorted reflection of the frightful battles actually happening in the external world, and that its worst follies have been made possible by the break-down of patriotism and religious belief. If one follows up this train of thought, one is in danger of being led into a species of Conservatism, or into political quietism. It can be plausibly argued, for instance—it is even probably true—that patriotism is an inoculation against nationalism, that monarchy is a guard against dictatorship, and that organised religion is a guard against superstition. Or again it can be argued that *no* unbiassed outlook is possible, that *all* creeds and causes involve the same lies, follies and barbarities; and this is often advanced as a reason for keeping out of politics altogether. I do not accept this argument, if only because in the modern world no one describable as an intellectual *can* keep out of politics in the sense of not caring about them. I think one must engage in politics—using the word in a wide sense—and that one must have preferences: that is, one must recognize that some causes are objectively better than others, even if they are advanced by equally bad means. As for the nationalistic loves and hatreds that I have spoken of, they are part of the make-up of most of us, whether we like it or not. Whether it is possible to get rid of them I do not know, but I do believe that it is possible to struggle against them, and that this is essentially a *moral* effort. It is a question first of all of discovering what one really is, what one's own feelings really are, and then of making allowance for the inevitable bias. If you hate and fear Russia, if you are jealous of the wealth and power of America, if you despise Jews, if you have a sentiment of inferiority towards the British ruling class, you cannot get rid of those feelings simply by taking thought. But you can at least recognize that you have them, and prevent them from contaminating your mental processes. The emotional urges which are inescapable, and are perhaps even necessary to political action, should be able to exist side by side with an acceptance of reality. But this, I repeat, needs a *moral* effort, and contemporary English literature, so far as it is alive at all to the major issues of our time, shows how few of us are prepared to make it.

On 26 March 1946, George Dilnot, Features Manager, Ministry of Information, wrote to Orwell to confirm 'one serial use in French and one in the Italian language' of this essay for a fee of £10.10.0 each, to include a special introduction written by Orwell. On 26 April 1946, J. H. McMillan of the Ministry of Information's Publications Division, writing chiefly about a digest in German of Orwell's four *Manchester Evening News* articles, 'The Intellectual Revolt' (24 January–7 February 1946; see *2874*), said he was enclosing 'a further £10.10.0 in respect of the Dutch rights in "Notes on Nationalism"'; presumably the same amount was paid for Finnish rights. The article was slightly abridged, mainly by the omission of detail of particular relevance to British readers, for example, the second half of the fifth paragraph; detail about G. K. Chesterton; some examples in the first pargraph of 'Indifference to Reality'; and the three lists of names given in 'Neo-Toryism' and 'Celtic Nationalism.' The word 'nationalism' is represented by 'chauvinisme' in French and Dutch versions; by 'sciovinismo' in the Italian, and by 'chauvinismi' and 'nationalismi' in Finnish. All the footnotes are omitted. The article was published in:

FRANCE: *Écho. Revue Internationale. Écrits, Faits et Idées de Tous Pays*, Tome 1, numéro 1, August 1946, pp. 66–74, as 'Remarques sur le Chauvinisme.'

NETHERLANDS: *Internationale Echo: Van Ideën en Gebeurtenissen uit Alle Landen*, 1e Jaargang, Nummer 1, August 1946, pp. 96–105, as 'Het Nieuwe Chauvinisme.'

ITALY: *Eco del Mondo: Opere, Fatti, Idee d'Ogni Paese*, Volume 1, numero 1, September 1946, pp. 75–82, as 'Il Nuovo Sciovinismo.'

FINLAND: *Parhaat*, Number 1, October–November 1946, pp. 4–14 as 'Chauvinismin Varjo.'

The translated abridgements were preceded by a short introduction. This was based on material supplied by Orwell—the fee included 'a special introduction' written by him—but the variations between the different language introductions and the third-person style show that what Orwell wrote was adapted.

Two examples of these introductions are given here. The first is a translation into English of that published in Finnish[5] and the second is the French introduction as it was published. The Italian and Dutch introductions are close to that in French.

THE SHADOW OF CHAUVINISM

The following article, which has been reprinted from the British periodical entitled *Polemic* (London), was written by a most prominent representative of the British intelligentsia. As a man of action, a novelist, a prolific and intelligent journalist, George Orwell is one of the men of the left, even of the extreme left—but, as he himself says, "What I saw in Spain . . . has given me a horror of politics . . . I think that the writer can remain honest only if he keeps aside from parties."

As the writer makes clear, he considers in this article a phenomenon which in his opinion has appeared generally throughout the world but he has restricted himself to its British variant. If this had originally been written for the French or German or American public, the points and names which he has chosen would have been different. Mr Orwell also says that he is not attempting to examine broadly-based national movements but only their subtler forms, whose manifestations can be observed in intellectual circles; because of this he directs his attention to such obviously less important branches of thinking as Trotskyism and pacifism, instead of to the more widely-spread and better known Nazism and Fascism.

REMARQUES SUR LE CHAUVINISME

L'article suivant a été publié dans la revue mensuelle Polemic, *de Londres, et est reproduit ici sous une forme quelque peu abrégée. Ainsi qu'il le souligne dans tout l'article, l'auteur étudie un phénomène qui, à son avis, s'étend au monde entier, mais dont toutefois il n'envisage ici que la variété plus particulièrement anglaise. Lorsqu'il parle du catholicisme, du communisme, etc., c'est donc toujours de la variété anglaise de ces doctrines religieuses ou politiques, et surtout de cette variété telle qu'elle est répandue parmi les intellectuels anglais, qu'il entend parler. Si cet article avait été écrit à l'origine pour un public français, allemand ou américain, les noms et les exemples choisis auraient été différents. L'auteur fait également ressortir qu'il ne cherche pas à étudier les mouvements qui s'appuient sur un large public, mais au contraire les formes sublimées qu'ils prennent parmi les intellectuels: d'où l'importance donnée à des courants de pensée apparemment aussi peu importants que le trotskysme ou le pacifisme, plutôt qu'à des maux plus étendus et plus évidents, tels que le nazisme et le fascisme.*

---

1. Nos. 1–8 of *Polemic*, 1945–47, were edited by Humphrey Slater; see *731, n. 1; 2314, n. 1; 2955, n. 4.* Orwell's Payments Book indicates that this was completed on 15 May 1945, and that he was paid a fee of £25.0.0.
2. Peter F. Drucker (1909–), author and university teacher. Born in Vienna, he emigrated to the United States 1937. He published books in German in the early thirties, but Orwell probably had in mind *The End of Economic Man: A Study of the New Totalitarianism* (1939) and *The Future of Industrial Man: A Conservative Approach* (New York, 1942; Toronto and London, 1943), which Orwell recommended to readers of the *Manchester Evening News* on 3 January 1946; see

2838. Of Drucker's more than twenty books, another that might later have attracted Orwell's attention was *The Concept of Corporation* (New York, 1946).

3. For Captain B. H. Liddell Hart, see *556, 16.7.39, n. 1*; for Major-General J. F. C. Fuller, see *1316, n. 1.*

4. The correspondent was Gleb Struve; see *2583.*

5. Orwell discussed the convention of wearing pith helmets in 'As I Please,' 45, 20 October 1944; see *2566.*

6. The translation from Finnish into English was made by Dr. John Screen, Librarian of the School of Slavonic and East European Studies, University of London.

2669. Danger of Separate Occupation Zones: Delaying Austria's Recovery

The Observer, 20 May 1945

In Austria, 19 May

Austria has not been ravaged by war to anything like the same extent as Germany. But for a moment the chaos is even greater, and the scenes accompanying the final round-up of the German Army are all the more fantastic because they occur against a background of snow-streaked mountains, unblitzed villages, and meadows filled with wild flowers.

In some places a newcomer must get the impression that Austria is being occupied not by the Allies but by the Germans.

The Germans are everywhere at every village inn, that knot of grey or green uniforms clustering round the porch, and half the traffic one passes on the roads has the characteristic wavy camouflage markings.

The toll of prisoners has been so enormous that in some cases it has been necessary to deal with them by simply depriving them of arms and then marking off an area on the map within which they are to remain. The other day I drove through an area south of Salzburg where it was estimated that there were 100,000 Germans, though to my eye the number seemed a good deal larger.

Save for its weapons, it was a complete army, seemingly well disciplined and in good shape. For mile after mile I drove past fields full of men sunbathing or laundering in the streams, and past tens of thousands of neatly parked vehicles and hundreds of corpses, cavalry chargers, and little piebald Cossack ponies. There were German military policemen directing the traffic at every crossroad.

Even more fantastic were the encampments of the Displaced Persons, some of them sharing barracks with derelict German soldiers, while others have seized railway trains and are living in the carriages. Every now and again some enterprising Displaced Person manages to get a locomotive running in the hope that if the points are right it may take him nearer to his homeland.

Then there are the camps of Allied prisoners of war now liberated and living under American care, and there are plenty of other prisoners who have grown sick of waiting and are trying to hitch-hike home.

At the moment, what with the glorious summer weather and the general relief that the war is ended, all this chaos seems almost funny, but it is widely realised that the underlying situation is not good. The task of feeding the civilian population and the Displaced Persons was a headache even before the Allies found themselves with several million extra prisoners on their hands, and one has only to glance at the mountainous landscape to see that Austria, even more than Western Germany, cannot be self-supporting in food.

By means of parachutes the Shaef[1] authorities are now distributing newspapers and leaflets in four languages, warning prisoners and Displaced Persons that it is in their own best interest to remain where they are, but not unnaturally there are signs of restiveness here and there, and in the rapidly changing situation the weaknesses inherent in military government are coming to light.

Military government was designed simply to keep order and facilitate rapid movement in the rear of fighting armies.

Indeed, military government has from a short-term viewpoint, been strikingly successful. The speed with which a bomb-wrecked city can be restored to some kind of order is often suprising, but military government has suffered from a serious handicap in having no long-term objectives.

Not to have a political policy—except of course the policy of not employing known Nazis—has been a matter almost of pride among officers. When asked any question that appears to touch on politics the stock reply is: "I wouldn't know."

To give just one example. I encountered one Military Government officer of the rank of captain who "wouldn't know" the difference between a Social Democrat and a Christian Socialist. Obviously this kind of thing can lead to trouble when political parties and movements begin to revive. In fact it is already happening. Two new Bavarian political parties have made their appearance, and the struggles now going on in various European countries appear to be raising echoes among the appropriate sections of Displaced Persons.

In an indirect way the administration of Germany and Austria is made harder by ignorant public opinion in Britain and the United States.

It often happens that some step which is an obvious military necessity on the spot would cause misunderstanding if revealed at home, and this works against the thorough thrashing out of major problems. But much the worst feature of the present situation is the arbitrary division of these countries into separate zones of occupation. There is very little contact between the Russians and the Western Allies, the armies being usually separated either by a river or a belt of No Man's Land, and the meagre reports that come in suggest that the Russians are following a different policy, at any rate in the treatment of prisoners, from that followed by the Anglo-Americans.

If the present rigid division continues it must set back the economic recovery of these countries, and it must lead to a competition for the allegiance of the German and Austrian peoples. This has already started and the new Austrian Government set up by the Russians in Vienna but unrecognised in western Austria is one symptom of it.

At present there cannot be much doubt about the state of popular feeling.

The Russians are feared and hated[2]—and the Vienna Government does not seem to evoke much enthusiasm, though the desire for separation from Germany is evidently strong.

But it would be very rash to assume that this frame of mind will be permanent. If it comes to a political struggle the Russians have several factors not obvious at present working on their side. While the feeling against them is partly a hangover of Nazi propaganda, it is difficult to believe that the administration of Austria and Germany can ever be successful unless it is a generally joint administration. And every day that this is delayed will make the final solution harder.

But the first indispensable necessity is that the United States and British Governments shall decide what they mean to do with the defeated countries and state their purpose clearly.

When that has happened certain dangerous misconceptions under which the Germans and Austrians now labour can be removed and the ordinary military commander or military government officer will have a clear line to go upon when he has to deal with problems which are every day more nakedly political.

1. Supreme Headquarters, Allied Expeditionary Force.
2. See 'Through a Glass, Rosily,' 23 November 1945, *2802*.

2670. Fredric Warburg to Leonard Moore

24 May 1945

Warburg told Moore in this letter that 'I saw George Orwell this morning just back from Europe and had a short talk with him.'

2671. Obstacles to Joint Rule in Germany

The Observer, 27 May 1945

It is too early to say that a genuinely joint occupation of Germany and Austria is impossible, but it has become obvious in recent weeks that powerful influences are working against it.

This is a disaster, but its worst results may be averted if the facts are faced and the necessary inferences drawn without delay.

Joint occupation, to be real, would imply four things.

First, delegation of as much authority as possible to German and Austrian Governments selected or approved by all the major Allies.

Secondly, an inter-allied controlling body in permanent session.

Thirdly, a clear agreement as to Germany's future development, political, military, and economic.

Fourthly, no "zoning"—that is, free circulation throughout the occupied countries, and as much intermingling as possible by the troops of the occupying Powers.

At present none of these conditions has been realised, and it is probably fair to say that most of the opposition has come from the Russian side. In the circumstances the Western Allies have only two courses between which to choose. One—which obviously they will not choose—is simply to move out and leave Germany and Austria to undivided Russian control.

The other is to accept the political challenge implied in the present situation and to try to make sure that the mass of the German people looks West and not East for guidance.

It should be realised that the competition for the allegiance of the German people has already started and had started before the fighting came to an end.

The division of the country into watertight "zones" was simply an expression of it: for if the Allies really had a joint policy, what was to prevent them from administering it jointly? And in addition it should be realised that *at present* most of the cards are in Anglo-American hands.

The majority of Germans dislike very much the prospect of being under Russian control, and have shown it in unmistakable ways. But the comparative popularity of Anglo-America rests on very shaky foundations. To begin with, the food situation is likely to be catastrophic in the coming winter, if not earlier, and it may turn out to be worse in Western Europe than in the mainly agricultural areas controlled by the Russians.

Secondly, the Russians can and probably will introduce much-needed reforms, such as the splitting-up of the East Prussian estates between landless peasants, which it would be difficult for the Western Allies to imitate even if they wanted to. Thirdly, the propaganda problems of the Russians are greatly eased by their exclusion of independent journalists and observers.

At present we have no real knowledge of what is happening in the Russian zone, and when discontent begins to accumulate in the Anglo-American zone the inevitably rosy reports issuing from the other side will have their influence.

At this moment, if the Western Allies chose to imitate the example of the Russians in Vienna and set up a German government by unilateral action, they could get overwhelming support for it.

Not of course, a government of Doenitz and Schacht,[1] but any moderately decent government sponsored by the United States and Britain, could be firmly established without any need to fake plebiscites, and the knowledge that it existed would have an immediate influence in the Russian zone. Presumably the governments of Britain and the United States will not take this drastic step, but what they could do, and indeed must do, is to make a prompt and clear declaration of policy.

Up to date the most enormous questions have been left unanswered. Is German industry to be dismantled, or is it to be restored? Are the Ruhr and the Rhineland to be annexed, or are they not? Will the war prisoners be retained as forced labourers, or will they be released as quickly as possible?

Which categories of Germans are to be treated as war criminals? There is not one of these questions to which the inquiring German can get a secure answer. And certain dangerous illusions—for instance, the widespread idea that the U.S.S.R. and the Western Powers will be at war in the near future—have sprung up and need to be contradicted by the highest authorities.

It is also necessary to make the German people realise how bad the prospective food situation is, and how much effort on their own part is needed to retrieve it.

Given some such declaration of policy, the political struggle which has already started would be happening in the open and the average German would know what to expect. At present the evident danger is that he will hope too much from the Western Powers and then, in disappointment, transfer his allegiance to the Russians.

Moreover, we are unlikely to come to a good understanding with the Russians unless we take up their challenge boldly. The present piecemeal occupation of Germany and Austria is exhausting and unsatisfactory to them as much as to us, but they may hope to elbow us out of these countries altogether if they oppose clear policies to feeble or divided ones.

On the other hand, if Anglo-America also produces a plan, and a workable plan, the Russian mood may change and it may be possible to work out the common policy without which this huge problem can hardly be solved.

1. Karl Doenitz (1891–1980) commanded the German submarine fleet until 1943, when he became chief of naval operations. He was named by Hitler as his successor, and almost immediately after becoming Führer, on Hitler's death, ordered the unconditional surrender of German forces. Tried at Nuremberg as a war criminal, he was sentenced to ten years' imprisonment. He was released in 1956. Hjalmar Horace Greeley Schacht (1877–1970), President of the Reichsbank, 1923–30 and 1934–39, was dismissed for disagreeing with Hitler. His skill in managing the German economy had done much to stabilize the currency and to enable Germany to rearm. He was not a member of the Nazi Party and participated in the plot to kill Hitler in 1944, which led to his being imprisoned in a concentration camp. He was acquitted of war crimes at the Nuremberg trials and in 1953 established his own bank.

Orwell's Payments Book records against 25 May 1945 that £10.3.4 was paid for this article after deduction of income tax. This is the first item to be entered after the absence of entries for March and April.

2672. London Letter, 5 June 1945

Partisan Review, Summer 1945[1]

Dear Editors,
I have spent the last three months in France and Germany, but I must devote this letter to British affairs, because if I touch directly on anything I saw abroad I shall have to submit the letter to SHAEF censorship.

The forthcoming general election is causing a fair amount of excitement, and many Labor Party supporters seem honestly confident that their party will win. Churchill is considered to have decided on an early election because this will probably mean a low poll. Millions of soldiers and others will still be away from home and, though not strictly speaking disenfranchised (the soldiers can vote by proxy, for instance), out of touch with their local political organizations. The votes lost in this way will be mostly potential Labor votes. I have predicted all along that the Conservatives will win by a small majority, and I still stick to this, though not quite so confidently as before, because the tide is obviously running very strongly in the other direction. It is even conceivable that Labor may win the election against the will of its leaders. Any government taking office now is in for an uncomfortable time, and a Left government especially so. Wartime controls will have to be continued and even tightened up, and demobilization will inevitably be slower than the general public expects. Then there is the coal problem, which is simply not soluble until the mines have been nationalized and then renovated by a process that will take several years. For the time being any government, of whatever color, will be obliged both to coerce the miners and to let the public shiver through the winter. There is also the impending show-down with Russia, which the people at the top of the Labor Party no doubt realize to be unavoidable, but which public opinion has not been prepared for. And above all there is India. The Conservatives might be able to stave off an Indian settlement for one more term of office, but a government calling itself Socialist could hardly attempt to do so, while at the same time it is very unlikely that Attlee, Morrison and the rest of them can make any offer that the Indian Nationalists would accept. Some people consider that a government taking office just at this moment does not risk much unpopularity, because the security and semi-prosperity produced by the war will still be operative, and that the really difficult time lies about two years ahead, when there will be full demobilization with consequent unemployment and a calamitous housing shortage. Nevertheless I believe that the fear of responsibility, which always weighs heavily on the Labor Party, will be particularly strong when the prospect ahead is of dragging an exhausted country through another two years of war, and that there will be some pulling of punches when the last-minute struggle begins. Of course one doesn't know what piece of trickery the Conservatives have in store this time. The election will be more or less a straight fight between Labor and the Conservatives. Both Common Wealth and the Communists are likely to increase their representation, but not to a significant extent, and the come-back which the Liberal Party is attempting is not likely to be much of a success. The Liberals have a big asset in Beveridge, but they no longer represent any definite block of interests or opinions, and they advocate several different policies which cancel out. It is thought that they may win another ten or twenty seats, but that their main achievement will be to split the Labor vote in town areas and the Conservative vote in rural ones.

I have only been home a week, and I cannot make up my mind whether the Russian mythos is as powerful as it was before. A good observer who has been in England throughout the past three months gives me his opinion that pro-Russian feeling is cooling off rapidly and that former sympathisers are much dismayed by Russian foreign policy and by such episodes as the arrest of the 16 Polish delegates.[2] Certainly the press is less adulatory than it was before, but this does not necessarily indicate a change in popular feeling. I have always held that pro-Russian sentiment in England during the past ten years has been due much more to the need for an external paradise than to any real interest in the Soviet regime, and that it cannot be countered by an appeal to the facts, even when these are known. A thing that has much struck me in recent years is that the most enormous crimes and disasters—purges, deportations, massacres, famines, imprisonment without trial, aggressive wars, broken treaties—not only fail to excite the big public, but can actually escape notice altogether, so long as they do not happen to fit in with the political mood of the moment. Thus it is possible *now* to rouse a certain amount of indignation about Dachau, Buchenwald etc., and yet before the war it was impossible to get the average person to take the faintest interest in such things, although the most horrible facts had had abundant publicity. If you could have taken a Gallup poll in 1939 I imagine you would have found that a majority, or at least a very big minority, of adult English people had not even heard of the existence of the German concentration camps. The whole thing had slid off their consciousness, since it was not what they then wanted to hear. So also with the USSR. If it could be proven tomorrow that the Russian concentration camps in the Arctic actually exist, and that they contain eighteen million prisoners, as some observers claim, I doubt whether this would make much impression on the Russophile section of the public. The Warsaw business last year[3] went almost unnoticed. And I don't see why the Russian behavior towards Poland should suddenly begin exciting indignation now.

It may be, however, that public opinion is beginning to alter for other reasons. One thing which, in a small way, probably affects working-class opinion is that latterly there has been more contact than before between British and Russians. From what I can hear, the British prisoners liberated by the Red Army in eastern Germany often bring back anti-Russian reports, and there has been a trickle of similar reports from the crews of the ships which go to Archangel and the air crews which were for a while operating in the USSR. What is probably involved here is the question of relative cultural levels, to which working-class people are usually very sensitive. In Germany I was struck by the attitude of the American G.I.s towards the hordes of Russian forced laborers, and of the British and American prisoners in liberated camps towards their Russian fellow-prisoners. It was not that there was hostility, merely that the western industrial worker, confronted with a Slav peasant, immediately feels him to be less civilized—which he is, according to the western worker's standards. However, this kind of thing takes effect on the big public very slowly, if at all. Meanwhile, so far as I can judge, pro-Russian sentiment is still strong and will be an appreciable factor in the general election. A lot of people remark that a real stand against Russian aggression in Europe can only be made by a government of the Left, just as, when Germany was to be opposed, it had to be under Conservative leadership.

I was not in England for V[E]-Day, but I am told it was very decorous—huge crowds, but little enthusiasm and even less rowdiness—just as it was in France. No doubt in both cases this was partly due to the shortage of alcohol. The ending of the European part of the war has made extraordinarily little difference to anybody. Even the blackout is almost as black as ever, since few of the street lights have been restored and most people don't possess any curtains other than blackout curtains. The basic petrol ration has been restored and there is a scramble for cars which are being sold at fantastic prices, but as yet the streets are comparatively empty. Certain wartime amenities, such as British Restaurants [4] and the excellent day nurseries at which working mothers can leave their children, are now to be scrapped, or at least there is talk of scrapping them, and already people are signing petitions against this. In general, people of leftwing views are in favour of continuing wartime controls (there were even some murmurs against the discontinuance of 18B),[5] while the Right makes play with such slogans as "No more bureaucracy." The ordinary people in the street seem to me not only to have become entirely habituated to a planned, regimented sort of life, in which consumption goods of all kinds are scarce but are shared out with reasonable fairness, but actually to prefer it to what they had before. Clearly one can't verify such impressions, but I have believed all along that England has been *happier* during the war, in spite of the desperate tiredness of some periods. It is usual to say that war simply causes suffering, but I question whether this is so when the casualties are small, as they have been for this country on this occasion. What happens in total war is that the acute suffering—not merely danger and hardship but boredom and home-sickness—is pushed on to the armed forces, who may number ten percent of the population, while the rest enjoy a security and a social equality which they never know at other times. Of course there is also bombing, the break-up of families, anxiety over husbands and sons, overwork and lack of amusements, but these are probably much more tolerable than the haunting dread of unemployment against a background of social competitiveness.

Having come back from the continent I can see England with fresh eyes, and I see that certain things—for instance, the pacifist habit of mind, respect for freedom of speech and belief in legality—have managed to survive here while seemingly disappearing on the other side of the Channel. But if I had to say what had most struck me about the behavior of the British people during the war, I should point to the *lack* of reaction of any kind. In the face of terrifying dangers and golden political opportunities, people just keep on keeping on, in a sort of twilight sleep in which they are conscious of nothing except the daily round of work, family life, darts at the pub, exercising the dog, mowing the lawn, bringing home the supper beer, etc., etc. I remember that during the worst moment of Dunkirk I was walking in a park with a friend,[6] and I pointed out to him that in the behavior of the crowds there was absolutely nothing to indicate that anything out of the ordinary was happening. Exactly as usual people were pushing their prams to and fro, young men were chasing girls, games of cricket were being played, etc. He said gloomily, "They'll behave like this until the bombs start dropping, and then they'll panic." Yet they didn't panic, and, as I noted at the time, they preserved the ordinary pattern of their lives to a surprising extent even amid the disorganization caused by the bombing. As William Empson puts it, "Three fathoms down the sea is always calm." I think it is well established that this time there has been far less feeling either for or against the war than there was last time. It is true that this time the number of men registering as Conscientious Objectors has about doubled itself, but I don't think this is significant, because, unless one actually wanted to be a martyr, being a C.O. has not entailed either ill-treatment or social ostracism this time. It has been made easy for C.O.s to choose non-military jobs, and the number refusing all kinds of national service has been tiny. One has to remember that last time the organized labor movement was more or less anti-war for the first two years, there was strong feeling against conscription, and by the end several parts of the country were not far from revolution. There were also military mutinies all over the place as soon as the fighting stopped. This time nothing of the kind has happened, but neither has there been anything like the insane enthusiasm of 1914, which I am old enough to remember, nor has hatred of the enemy gone to the same lengths. This time people haven't—except in the columns of the newspapers—referred to the Germans as Huns, they haven't looted German shops or lynched so-called spies in Hyde Park, and children's papers haven't been decorated with pictures of Germans wearing the faces of pigs: but on the other hand there has been less protest against the proposals to dismember Germany, make use of forced labor, etc., than there was against the Versailles settlement. Considering what has happened in Europe, I think it is worth noticing that almost no English people have changed sides in this war. At most a few dozen individuals, mostly with a prewar Fascist history, have quislingized. Towards the end of the war literally hundreds of thousands of Russians, Poles, Czechs and what-not were fighting for the Germans or serving in the Todt organization, but no British or Americans at all. It is the same with the development, or rather lack of development, on the home front. Never would I have prophesied that we could go through nearly six years of war without arriving at either Socialism or Fascism, and with our civil liberties almost intact. I don't know whether this semi-anaesthesia in which the British people contrive to live is a sign of decadence, as many observers believe, or whether on the other hand it is a kind of instinctive wisdom. It may well be that it is the best attitude when you live among endless horrors and calamities which you are powerless to prevent. Possibly we shall all have to develop it if war becomes continuous, which seems to me a likely development in the fairly near future.

I understand that with the ending of the war you are rearranging your foreign contributions, so this will be my last letter in this particular series, which started over four years ago. It doesn't seem worth making any winding-up remarks, since I did something of the kind in your last issue but one. I would merely like to finish up by telling you and your readers how much I have enjoyed writing these letters. In among the lunatic activities on which I have wasted the war years, they have given me a wonderful feeling of getting my nose above water. And finally, I think you all will agree that a word of praise is due to the censorship department, which has let these letters through with remarkably little interference. All the best.

George Orwell

An Editorial Note followed Orwell's letter: 'Mr. Orwell's London Letter will appear in every third issue of PARTISAN REVIEW as part of a series of letters from several European capitals. From time to time Mr. Orwell will also contribute special articles to the magazine.'

1. Orwell's Payments Book dates this 5 June 1945; his fee was £2.10.0.
2. See 2685.
3. The Warsaw Uprising, August–October 1944. The Russians were accused of deliberately holding back their advance in order that many of the Poles who had risen against the Nazis in Warsaw might be killed. See 'As I Please,' 40, 1 September 1944, 2541, and ensuing correspondence.
4. British Restaurants were established by the government during the war to provide adequate, well-balanced meals for the general public at reasonable prices.
5. In May and June 1940, under Regulation 18B, the government interned (chiefly on the Isle of Man) aliens, and British Fascists and Communists, whom it regarded as a threat to security and so liable to give aid to Germany. Some 30,000 Germans were interned; these were mainly those who had fled Nazi Germany in fear of their lives. A large number were held throughout the war.
6. Cyril Connolly; see 628, 30.5.40.

2673. Review of *The Fates are Laughing* by W. P. Crozier; *Cry Hylas on the Hills* by George Baker

Manchester Evening News, 7 June 1945

The historical novel—and perhaps most of all when it deals with classical antiquity—raises certain difficult problems which have seldom been solved by any novelist writing in the English language.

One difficulty is to make the characters appear human without giving the impression that they are simply modern people needlessly transferred to a remote setting.

Because of the slang of modern spoken English, this difficulty arises especially in connection with the dialogue. Here is a scrap of conversation taken at random from "The Fates are Laughing."

"If he's a philosopher," whispered Lucius to Metella, "he's the laughing sort, but that would never go down with Tiberius."

"He's on holiday from Tiberius," Metella replied. "So are Gaius and Drusilla—Isn't she lovely?—That's why they're all so gay. Listen to them."

"I like your frock, Lollia." It was Drusilla speaking, "There's nothing as smart as that down here."

"I can tell you," said Gaius, "it will shock the provincials if they see you in it—which, by the way, isn't difficult, Lollia. You had better not let the Emperor know about it; he's so severe in these days."

Can one imagine that these are Romans of A.D. 40 speaking? No, one can't, and one's instinctive feeling that ancient Romans would have been more dignified has some foundation, because the language that these people spoke had probably not been debased as ours has been.

On the other hand the old-style historical novel, such as those of Harrison Ainsworth, where all the characters are at home with the second person singular and indulge freely in expressions like "pish" and "tush," is no better.

It is partly this matter of language that makes French reconstructions of ancient life—for instance, Flaubert's "Salammbô," or the Greek scenes in Anatole France's "The White Stone"—seem more convincing than English ones. In French the spoken and the written tongue are nearer together, and it is easier for dialogue to be dignified without sounding stilted.

In spite of the considerable learning displayed—it would perhaps be fairer to say "implied," for it is never thrust in the reader's face—most of the characters in "The Fates are Laughing" give the impression of belonging to our own time.

It is the story of a Roman family in the troubled period of the early empire, and it proceeds against a background of palace intrigue. The sinister but efficient Tiberius is succeeded by the sadistic lunatic Caligula, who is succeeded in turn by Claudius, an enigmatic character who appears to have escaped assassination by systematically pretending to be a fool. . . . Nero, destined to become the next Emperor, is still a small boy.

The trouble is that the succession does not follow any dynastic principle, but is in each case a coup d'état. One never knows who will be the new Emperor until the old one is dead, and the newcomer always starts his reign by massacring his rivals and their more prominent supporters.

To spot the right claimant beforehand—soothsayers are much employed for this purpose—may make all the difference between losing one's head and being appointed governor of a province.

The story centres mainly round the adventures of Metella, a young Patrician girl who has taken the dangerous step of marrying the man of her choice and refusing a wealthier suitor who has influence in court circles. Her father, Publius Antonius, is an amiable old senator with a passion for Greek poetry.

He is the owner of a Greek slave named Pericles—one of those learned slaves whom wealthy Romans like to possess—who is always able to cap his quotations and who bears a rather marked resemblance to Mr. P. G. Wodehouse's "Jeeves."

During this period the empire was becoming more and more openly a military despotism, the Senate was being reduced to impotence, and the Roman aristocracy, swamped in a new world of money-lenders and adventurers, could only preserve their dignity by keeping out of public life.

All the more thoughtful characters in this book are haunted by the feeling that some disastrous change has overtaken the Roman civilisation and that the old, rustic life of the Republic, with its strict family ties and its austere religion, was better than the wealth and luxury of the empire.

But the beliefs on which the old life was founded cannot be restored, and a spate of new religions from the east, Christianity among them, is rushing in to fill the void. No doubt this was what was happening, but it is difficult not to feel that Mr. Crozier has read the thoughts of twentieth-century people into his characters.

They are too conscious of the historical processes amid which they live, and all but a few of them are lacking in the terrible cruelty which was in fact general in antiquity.

167

Metella does once order somebody to be flogged, but for the most part her opinions would be appropriate to a member of the Fabian Society. She is humane towards slaves, disbelieves in soothsayers, is in favour of equality of the sexes, disapproves of aggressive wars, and is disgusted by gladiatorial displays.

However, one of the great temptations of novels about ancient Rome, the temptation to make somebody turn Christian and suffer martyrdom, is resisted. The new religion is mentioned and Pontius Pilate, the well-meaning Governor of Judæa, makes a few appearances, but—and given the date, this is no doubt psychologically correct—no one is much interested.

"Cry Hylas on the Hills" is much slighter. The time of the book appears to be a generation or so before the fall of Troy, and the story is an extraordinary mixture of well-known myths and improbable adventures.

The two main characters are called Heracles and Hylas, and many other familiar names appear, but it never becomes completely clear whether or not these are the same people as one reads about in Lempriere's Classical Dictionary. Here, too, the dialogue is modernised, with effects that are sometimes even more disastrous than in "The Fates are Laughing."

[Fee: £8.8.0; 6.6.45]

2674. *Erewhon* by Samuel Butler

BBC Home Service, Talks for Schools, 8 June 1945

This talk was recorded on 6 June 1945. It is noted in Orwell's Payments Book against 4 June 1945. He was paid a fee of £12.12.0. The source of this text is a fair copy BBC script. The errors and resulting editorial amendments (see notes 1–8 and 10) probably stem from the BBC copy-typist. Reversals of letters have been corrected silently; punctuation has been reprinted as in typescript.

ANNOUNCER: Talks for Sixth Forms. Here is George Orwell to tell you about EREWHON by Samuel Butler.

GEORGE ORWELL: The first thing anyone would notice about EREWHON— which was by Samuel Butler and published round about 1870—is that it's a stupid title. You can see if you write it down, Erewhon, E.R.E.W.H.O.N. it's simply an anagram, or rearrangement, of the word "nowhere". It's a bad title, because one can't tell at a glance how it is supposed to be pronounced, a more experienced writer, who would know that people don't like to go into a library and ask for a book whose name they can't pronounce, would never have chosen it. This point isn't altogether unimportant, as I'll try to show later. However, the title tells you something about the book. It means "nowhere", and the book is what's called a Utopia—that is, a story about a country that doesn't exist. Samuel Butler, lived most of his life in England, but he spent a few years in New Zealand when he was a young man, and he chose to lay the scene of the story in New Zealand, which at that date was largely unexplored. In the story, the hero crosses a range of mountains and unexpectedly finds himself in a country inhabited by highly-civilized people, very similar to ourselves. They receive him hospitably—he is rather astonished to notice that they seem to think all the better of him because he has fair hair and a good complexion—and he soon succeeds in learning their language and settles down among them for several years. Most of the book is an account of their beliefs and customs—which, I don't need to say, had a considerable bearing on the beliefs and customs of England in Butler's own day.

All Utopia books are satires or allegories. Obviously if you invent an imaginary country you do so in order to throw light on the institutions of some existing country, probably your own. Erewhon is no exception, and though it won't, of course, bear comparison with a book like Gulliver's Travels, it is still one of the most original and penetrating Utopia books in the English language. It is a satire on Victorian society, but it is a very good-tempered satire, and Butler's aim is constructive rather than destructive. In so far as he is attacking anything, he is attacking the hypocrisy which is supposed to be our great national vice, and which was especially characteristic of that time. For instance, he satirises conventional religion. In Erewhon there are peculiar institutions known as Musical Banks. They are more or less like ordinary banks, with rows of counters, and cashiers sitting behind brass railings, and so on. But there is a solemn atmosphere and music is always playing in them. People go to the Musical Banks from time to time and go through a form of drawing out money, but it is not quite the same as ordinary money and it has no value outside the bank. Everybody claims that he values this special money more highly than ordinary money, but no one makes any attempt to spend it, and indeed a shop-keeper would be angry indeed if you offered him some of it in exchange for real goods. Of course, you can see what is meant here. The Musical Banks are churches and the worthless money represents the beliefs to which a lot of people pay lip-service on Sundays but which they don't allow to influence their everyday lives.

This is a fairly obvious piece of satire, which a lot of nineteenth century English writers would have been capable of.[1] But the queerest thing of all about the people of Erewhon is their attitude towards illness and disease. I have said already that when the hero of the book first arrives in Erewhon he notices that the people seem to admire him because he has a good physique and a clear complexion. A little later than this he catches a slight cold, instead of being pitied and sympathised with, as he naturally expects, he finds that everyone is extremely shocked and seems to feel that even if he does happen to be suffering from a cold he ought to keep quiet about it. He notices that the people of Erewhon are quite exceptionally handsome and healthy looking, and that practically no one is ever ill, or at any rate no one ever admits to being ill. On the other hand he is astonished to find that people admit without any sign of shame the things which we should regard as morally disgraceful.

For example, somebody will say "I stole a pair of socks off a shop counter yesterday", just as casually as we should say "I had a bad headache yesterday". A man who has a red nose will be careful to assure everybody that it is due to drunkenness, and spiteful people will say behind his back that it is probably due to indigestion. This state of affairs is taken for granted by everybody and is reflected in the laws of the country. Anyone who is known to have suffered from illness is prosecuted and may be sentenced to a long term of imprisonment, while on the other hand ordinary crime is looked on as something undesirable of course, but in no way disgraceful. As a result every sign of ill health is concealed with the most extraordinary cunning and hypocrisy. In Erewhon, in fact, crime is a disease and disease is a crime.

Now, what is Butler saying here? He is generally taken as meaning—and in part this is certainly what he did mean—that moral evil is simply something like disease, a misfortune due to heredity and mistakes in early training, and though, of course, you have to reform criminals as best we can and protect society against them, you should no more blame them than you should blame an invalid. Crime is simply a problem like smallpox or typhoid fever, which you can only get rid of by completely removing its causes and not by blaming and persecuting individuals. This does not sound very startling now, but it did seem so when Butler said it. A great deal that we realise to be due to bad environment was ascribed[2] by our grandparents to simple wickedness. For example, in nineteenth century England there was the most terrible drunkenness. Most of it was really due to the unbearable conditions in which the majority of the people lived: they crowded together in horrible slums, they worked what we should consider impossibly long hours, they had almost no chance for amusement, and great numbers of them could not even read. In such circumstances, it was quite natural that millions of people should get drunk just as often as they could afford it. This chain of cause and effect which seems obvious enough to us now, was not obvious until Samuel Butler and others like him had pointed it out. But when he draws this comparison between crime and disease, Butler is also saying something else. It is something much more personal to himself, but something which you have to grasp if you want to understand Butler's work as a whole. In Erewhon, people are not only prosecuted for being ill, but for suffering any kind of misfortune. For example, if one man swindled another out of a sum of money the one who is sent to prison is the one who is swindled, and not the swindler. This seems rather a curious idea, but it is bound up with a theory of human personality which is the basis of Butler's other well-known book, THE WAY OF ALL FLESH. Butler was very interested in the theory of evolution, and he spent a great deal of time and energy in having controversies with Charles Darwin. He believed that evolution takes place through exceptional individuals who have to pay in suffering for the advance which they make possible. He held that, at any given moment, the best representatives of any species, human or animal, are not those who are evolving, but those who have reached a dead end. I shall have a great deal to say about this next week in The Way of all Flesh. It followed that the people Butler most admired were not the brilliant, exceptional people, who might perhaps succeed in lifting society a stage higher, but the healthy, simple, middling people, who don't suffer misfortunes and who were fitted to enjoy life at its present stage. There is no doubt that Butler's admiration for the ordinary, healthy, successful, brainless person was exaggerated, partly because he wasn't at all that type of person himself. He was the other type, the gifted, badly adjusted type, who is capable of thinking of new ideas, but is not capable of making a success of his own life. He had very little worldly wisdom, and he knew it. I pointed out at the beginning of this talk that the title of Erewhon is a bad title, which would be liable to hamper the sale of the book. Now Butler didn't realise this until after the book was published and that little mistake is typical of his whole life. He had no conception of salesmanship, no business sense, and over his whole life his books, instead of giving him a livelihood, simply represented a dead loss. Except Erewhon itself, none of them ever sold more than a few hundred copies, and he [achieved][3] no reputation until after he was dead. Fortunately he had a small income to live on, but even so he lost a good deal of his money through unwise investments, and through being swindled by a friend whom he ought to have known better than to trust. In his own life he demonstrated the point which he made in Erewhon and elsewhere; that the people society can learn most [from][4] are not usually lucky or happy people. In the sequel, which he wrote years later, *Erewhon Revisited*, Butler has a lot more to say about the distinction between genius and worldly wisdom, and he touches on the subject again and again in his Notebooks. (By the way, if you read Samuel Butler's Notebooks, try to get hold of the edition which was published round about 1920:[5] there have been more recent editions, but a lot of the best passages are left out of them.) But in Erewhon there is one other idea which is of great importance and has influenced people's thoughts ever since, although it has the appearance of being pushed into the book for no particular reason. Apart from their curious attitude towards crime and disease, the people of Erewhon have another characteristic, which astonishes the hero very much. This is their hatred, perhaps not hatred, but suspicion of machinery. The hero finds them living comfortably, but at a rather low standard of mechanical efficiency. For instance, they don't have either railway trains or watches. Then one day he happens to go into a museum and finds to his astonishment that many of the machines used in Europe are preserved there—that they [have been][6] preserved merely as curiosities. In the past people possessed and used these machines, but they have deliberately abandoned them. On enquiry he finds out that it is forbidden by law to make use of any machine invented after a certain stated date. Mechanical progress has been stopped by deliberate intention.

The reason for this is explained in a long essay, which Butler had published the substance [of][7] in a New Zealand paper some years earlier. It is that the people of Erewhon have decided that the machine is the enemy of humanity. If you allow machinery to develop beyond a certain point, it is capable of destroying civilisation, and possibly of wiping out the human race altogether. Now once again, this doesn't now seem a particularly revolutionary idea. Nowadays we are all well aware that there is tremendous danger in allowing mechanical progress to continue without checking it by any international authority and without stopping to think where it is leading us. We realise this because it has been brought home to us in the[8] form of bombs and the frightful destruction of war altogether. However, when Butler wrote Erewhon it did need imagination of a very high order to see that machinery could be dangerous as well as useful. At that date, remember, the railway train was still a novelty, the aeroplane was barely dreamed of, and weapons of war were still almost where they had been a century earlier.[9] Butler is not so much concerned with the possible destructiveness of future wars as with the tendency of the machine to rob the human being of any kind of creative function and turn him into an unskilled labourer or even a kind of parasite. As he realised, it would be quite possible to develop machinery to such a point that no human being would need to use his arms or legs. Everything, even things [such][10] as blowing our noses or combing our hair, *could* be done for us by some kind of machine. But after all, if *everything* were done for you by machinery, what sort of life would you lead—what purpose or meaning could your life contain? This part of Erewhon needs to be read with care, because Butler chooses to exaggerate his case and gives the impression that he is merely joking. His joking part of the time doesn't do away with the truth of what he is saying. Unless it is carefully controlled, the machine can be the enemy of human life: and what's more, in order to control it we may even have to end by doing that fantastic thing which the people of Erewhon did—that is, to put a deliberate stop to mechanical invention. So far as I know, Samuel Butler was the first person to point out the dangers contained in mechanical progress, and he did it at a time when those dangers weren't actually operative, when in fact they had to be divined by imagination. A lot of what he says seems commonplace now, but it only seems so because his ideas influenced countless other people who pass them on to us. No doubt you've heard of the old lady who went to see Hamlet acted, and came away saying: "I didn't care for it. There are too many quotations in it". Well it's rather the same with Samuel Butler and certain other thinkers. Their ideas get popularised so completely that they end by getting no credit for them.

Erewhon is not one of the great books of the world. Except for a collection of letters which he wrote from New Zealand and afterwards printed, it was Butler's first book, and it is the work of an inexperienced writer. It is clumsily arranged and, as I've pointed out already, the device of having anagrammatic names—all the names in the book are anagrams of English names—is extremely tiresome. Also, like many other writers of Utopia books, Butler doesn't fully make up his mind whether he is writing pure satire, or whether he is making constructive suggestions. The book has a story, it's rather an unconvincing story, with a preposterous ending, but essentially it's a book of essays, and it would probably have been more successful if Butler had presented it simply as that. But it's still an extremely stimulating book and one of the few books of this type in English that have stood the test of time. Samuel Butler was born in 1835 and died in 1902. He did not write a large number of books, and there are only about five of them that are worth tackling today. I recommend Erewhon—though I don't recommend the sequel to it, 'Erewhon Revisited"—and perhaps even more I recommend the Notebooks, which are extremely amusing as well as containing most of what Butler had to say in a shortened form. But far and away his best book, the one he would certainly be remembered by even if all the rest were forgotten, is his autobiographical novel, THE WAY OF ALL FLESH, which I hope to talk to you about next week.

ANNOUNCER: :Today's talk was by George Orwell.

1. capable of.] capable of it.
2. ascribed] *an editorial conjecture for the typescript's* surprised
3. achieved] *editorial addition*
4. from] *editorial addition*
5. Despite the date of 1920, Orwell probably refers to the edition prepared by Henry Festing Jones, published in 1912. Orwell reviewed *Further Extracts from the Note-Books*, compiled by A. T. Bartholomew (1934) in *The Adelphi*, April 1934; see *197*. Bartholomew also published a series of selections in 1930.
6. have been] *editorial addition*
7. of] *editorial addition*
8. the] *editorial addition*
9. a century earlier] a century years earlier actually. *The typist may have confused a draft and a final version of the talk. This suggests that the typescript was produced as a fair-copy for BBC records after Orwell had given his talk using a rather untidy script.*
10. such] *editorial addition*

2675. Uncertain Fate of Displaced Persons

The Observer, 10 June 1945

Facts relating to the problem of the Displaced Persons—that is, the foreign forced labourers imported by the Germans during the war—continue to trickle in, but there has been no comprehensive statement, and, apparently, no official ruling on one or two very important points.

It is very much to be hoped that the relevant facts will be published in the fairly near future. Otherwise a valuable sociological opportunity may be missed, and decisions may be taken which public opinion in the United States and Britain would not tolerate if it knew the facts.

Unrra[1] is now at work in 230 camps in Western Germany, and the military authorities in a further number of camps unspecified, on the registration of these uprooted people. They are known to number some 4,500,000 in

Germany alone. According to present registrations, the bulk of this figure is made up of 1,500,000 Russians, 1,200,000 Frenchmen, and 600,000 Poles. There were about 100,000 Belgians—now nearly all repatriated—and there are some 100,000 Dutchmen, with smaller groups of Jugoslavs, Czechs, Scandinavians, and Greeks. By last week 1,800,000 had been registered, medically examined and repatriated.

Of the rest the majority are living under the care of the Military Government, which feeds them as best it can and in some cases employs them at road-mending and similar jobs. Great numbers, however, have refused to be rounded up and have endeavoured to walk home, or have simply lived on the countryside by begging and stealing. Others, though probably not many, have remained on the farms where they were working before the Allied invasion.

At the beginning most of the Displaced Persons welcomed their liberators with enormous enthusiasm, but this has been somewhat damped by the unavoidable delays in repatriation and the growing food shortage. It had been laid down in advance that in the matter of food supply the Army came first, the Displaced Persons second, and the Germans third; but in practice it is impossible to allow the Germans to starve, and in some areas the point has already been reached where it is necessary to reduce the rations of the Displaced Persons in order to keep those of the Germans up to subsistence level.

It is easy to imagine the ill-feeling that this causes, and in American-controlled areas it is not made better by the wastage of food which anyone in contact with the troops can observe for himself.

Meanwhile, various extremely interesting facts about the Displaced Persons have come to light. To begin with, the term "slave labour," habitually used in the British Press, is misleading. Some of these people—it might even be possible to determine the number with reasonable accuracy—were volunteers, and the rest, though they could be described as slaves in the sense that they were deported against their will, do not seem in most cases to have been badly treated.

Those employed on factory work lived in encampments in semi-prison conditions, but those employed on the land, usually on small farms, where all the younger menfolk were away at the war, seem to have fared reasonably well. In many cases they were not only paid wages but were enrolled in the German workers' insurance scheme, and all observers agree that as a whole the Displaced Persons have been well fed.

We can make only the vaguest guess as to how many of these people changed sides on ideological grounds, how many were mere adventurers, and how many were ignorant peasants to whom serving in one army was very like serving in another. Clearly this whole subject needs investigating for the sake of the light it may cast on the changes now occurring in the structure of nationalism. But the investigation must be made within the next few months or the data will have vanished.

One point that does not seem to have been decided—or at least, no authoritative pronouncement has been made—is whether a Displaced Person who does not wish to go home is obliged to do so. The people most affected here are the Poles. It is known that great numbers of Poles, especially from eastern Poland, want to remain abroad. If the Government of the U.S.S.R. decides that those of them who are now technically Soviet citizens must return, will the British and American Governments feel obliged to repatriate them? Quite obviously this question should not be decided without letting the British and American peoples understand what is happening. Moreover, if the Poles and others who prefer to remain abroad are allowed to do so, what exactly is their status to be?

[Fee: £10.3.4; 8.6.45]

1. United Nations Relief and Rehabilitation Administration.

2676. Review of *Christianity and Democracy* by Jacques Maritain

The Observer, 10 June 1945

M. Maritain is never a very easy writer, and his latest book is especially full of those cloudily abstract passages which seem to be so common in present-day French literature and which do not improve in translation. Here are two sentences picked almost at random:

> Democracy is a paradox and a challenge hurled at nature, at that thankless and wounded human nature whose original aspirations and reserves of grandeur it evokes.
>
> Nothing is easier for human weakness than to merge religion with prejudices of race, family or class, collective hatreds, passions of a clan and political phantoms which compensate for the rigours of individual discipline in a pious but insufficiently purified, soul.

Both of these sentences, and the hundreds of others like them that are strewn through this book, have a meaning, but one not only has to dig it out from beneath masses of verbiage, one also has to some extent to infer it from the general tenor of the book and from the known direction of M. Maritain's own thought. Considerable passages in the book read like the speeches of a non-belligerent statesman: one knows in advance which side he is on, but one would have some difficulty in proving it. An invisible censor hovers over the pages, and to outwit him it is often necessary to avoid using proper names and change concrete words into abstract ones.

What M. Maritain is saying is that Democracy and Christianity are not incompatible—indeed, they are necessary to one another. A Christian life can hardly be lived in an unjust society, while on the other hand a democracy which is purely secular in inspiration always ends by turning into slavery. Moreover, a Christian society is not necessarily a poverty-stricken one. The desire of the working classes not merely for political equality but for higher wages and better working conditions, is justifiable, and it is the needless starvation of this desire that has made possible the rise of atheistic Communism. Christianity, in short, can be reconciled with material progress.

In our ears this hardly sounds the kind of statement that needs to be uttered with circumspection, but M. Maritain has good reasons for his guarded manner of writing. To begin with, these essays were written in the middle of 1942, when the Axis still appeared capable of winning the war and the Pétain regime was not only still in power but was, to a considerable extent, approved of by Catholics outside France. Secondly, the species of Christian Socialism for which M. Maritain stands has only very recently begun to gain ground and is certainly not representative of the Church as a whole. Primarily M. Maritain is writing "at" his fellow-Catholics, and he is well aware of the existing tie-up between Catholicism and reaction. Towards the end of the nineteenth century, he says, "the working classes sought their salvation in the denial of Christianity; the Conservative Christian circles sought theirs in the denial of the temporal exigencies of justice and love." The position is no better now, though the defeat of the Axis powers has made it temporarily appear better, and when one remembers the lyrical praises of Fascism that were being uttered by Cardinals and Catholic apologists only a few years ago, it is not surprising if M. Maritain clothes his plea for Christian Socialism in soothing and rather indistinct language.

The thing he does not quite care to admit is the loneliness of his own position. How lonely it is could be seen at the time of the Spanish civil war, when he was one of the tiny handful of prominent Catholics who kept their heads and refused to make propaganda for Fascism. He is able to argue forcibly that democracy and social justice are inherent in Christian doctrine and have even been enjoined by the leaders of the Church, but it is difficult to feel that the people for whom he is specially writing will be much impressed. The fact is that the Catholic humanist is a rare animal, like an albino elephant, and must probably remain so. Humanism assumes that man is the measure of all things, Christian doctrine assumes that this world only has a meaning in reference to the next. On paper a reconciliation is possible, but it always breaks down when any concrete problem arises. M. Maritain sees that the drifting-away of the masses from a reactionary Church is inevitable, and would like to retrieve the situation not by the Fascist expedient of keeping the masses ignorant but by calling the rich to repentance. He is unwilling to admit, or at any rate he does not very clearly say, that religious belief is frequently a psychological device to *avoid* repentance.

Meanwhile the essential problem remains. Material progress, which is necessary if the average human being is to be anything better than a drudge, has only been achieved at a fearful price. Somehow the religious attitude to life must be restored, and yet the only body of doctrine available to the Western world is one which the great mass of people are obviously less and less willing to accept. M. Maritain makes the usual claim that a just society can only be founded on Christian principles. Before making statements of this kind one ought to reflect that only a quarter of the population of the world is nominally Christian, and that the proportion is constantly dwindling: also that Hindus or Chinese are not noticeably worse people than ourselves. M. Maritain is a voice crying in the wilderness and rather a muffled voice at that. Nevertheless, considering the people he was writing for and the pressures he was probably subjected to, it must have needed much courage to write such a book at such a time.

[Fee: £10.3.4; 1.6.45]

2677. To Fredric Warburg

13 June 1945   Typewritten

27B, Canonbury Square, London N. 1.

Dear Fred,

Thanks for your letter of June 12th. I will send the blurb[1] as soon as possible.

As to the contract for a novel, I was in France when the two contracts reached me and I probably did not explain adequately why I did not sign the novel contract and struck out references to it in the other contract. To begin with, the novel referred to did not exist and does not exist yet. Secondly there was the question of my existing contract with Gollancz. I still have a contract to give Gollancz the first refusal of my next two works of fiction, but I have no intention of keeping this as he has not kept his contract with me in spirit nor, I think, in the letter. However, I want to remain within my rights and this involves something which I had explained to Moore but which he had failed to understand. Gollancz was offered "Animal Farm", which of course I knew in advance he would refuse, and he was only offered it on his own insistence. Having refused it he refused to regard it as one of the two contracted novels on the ground that it was too short. It appeared that these two novels, of which he was to have first refusal, were to be of standard length. I then tried to get Moore to get from Gollancz a statement of what amounted to standard length. Moore failed to see what I was driving at and simply said that standard length is a trade expression meaning about 70,000 words and that 65,000 words could be regarded as a minimum. I then decided that I would make my next two novels, if any, less than 65,000 words, which would get me out of this contract. It was for that reason that I did not want to sign an ordinary novel contract with you, which might give Gollancz the chance to say I was defrauding him. If you like we can draw up another contract worded differently, but in any case you know I will bring you all my books except any which may be written for some special purpose.[2]

I don't think the list of review copies needs adding to. I think it is best if you send them out, as your office will be able to do them more systematically than I can. Have you fixed a definite date for publication yet?

Victor Serge now doesn't want to send his memoirs[3] across the Atlantic because it seems he has only one copy and he is frightened of their getting lost or seized on the way. I have written suggesting that he should get another copy typed.

I could have lunch on June 19th as you suggest. I'll ring up about this between now and then.

Yours,
George

1. For *Animal Farm*.
2. Against this sentence Warburg has written 'v good.'
3. See *2652*.

Warburg replied on 15 June, saying, 'On the whole I think we can regard the second paragraph of your letter as perfectly satisfactory.' He proposed to discuss the matter further when they had lunch (arranged for the Acropolis Restaurant) on 19 June. On that day he was also meeting Humphrey Slater to discuss Polemic 'and any relevant matters.' The carbon copy of the letter is annotated in Warburg's hand, 'Why not let Moore break off with VG on your behalf.' On 25 June they again had lunch together, after which Warburg wrote this 'Note on George Orwell':

> Further to my letter of June 15th to Orwell the matter was discussed at lunch today, and he is instructing Leonard Moore to obtain his release from V.G. on the grounds that V.G.'s list is now unsuitable for Orwell's books. If this fails, Orwell has a complicated scheme for non-fulfilment of his contract which I do not fully understand. But in any case, he stands on the sentence of his letter which reads:—
>
> "but in any case you know I will bring you (S.&W.) all my books except any which may be written for some special purpose."
>
> There is, therefore, no more to be done until we hear from him or Moore, and ANIMAL FARM will be published without an agreement.
>
> George Orwell has written the first twelve pages of his new novel, but, of course, disclaims knowledge of when it will be finished.

The new novel must be *Nineteen Eighty-Four*. This is the first reference to its having been started. See also *2694, n. 2*.

2678. Review of *Land Fit for Heroes* by George Sava; *Death of a Poet*, by Leonid Grossman

Manchester Evening News, 14 June 1945

"Land Fit For Heroes"[1] is not the kind of phrase that is likely to be used nowadays without irony, and Mr. George Sava's thesis is that the heroes got a very poor reward last time, and are in danger of faring no better this time.

In general terms his complaints are justified, and it is a pity that he should have chosen a very untypical case to illustrate them.

The story starts with a hideously burned fighter pilot—blind, deprived of speech, his back broken and encased in plaster, unable to communicate with the outer world, except by movements of a bandaged hand—lying on the bed of a cottage hospital and obstinately refusing to die. He has been shot down in flames after unparalleled feats of heroism, and he is a V.C. and a nine-days' wonder. He is pestered by publicity of every kind, including innumerable offers of marriage from totally unknown women. The bulk of the book consists of his memories, and an account of his rather improbable origins.

The young airman's name is Raymond Masters. His father had been one of the derelicts of the last war. He had had a brilliant war record, and had received the D.S.O. and the M.C., but he had also been gassed with chlorine, and, being unable to prove this, had received no pension. Raymond is, therefore, born into extreme poverty. His father goes through the usual ex-officer's progress of losing his savings and his gratuity in ill-judged attempts to start a garage, then trying to earn a living by selling things on commission, then lapsing into unemployment.

Finally he gets a job as caretaker in a small factory, and dies after a few years from the after-effects of the chlorine. Raymond's mother, Honor, presented at the beginning as a girl who had led "a life of leisure and a monotonous round of dances in the winter and tennis parties in the summer," becomes a charwoman. Raymond grows up in a slum, but is taught to pronounce his aitches. He is gifted with mechanical ability, and he gets a good start in life by being articled as apprentice in a motor-manufacturing firm—however, this engagement is terminated when he marries his employer's daughter, a worthless girl, who leaves him almost immediately.

When war breaks out Raymond joins the R.A.F. and serves with distinction for four years before being shot down. On the last page, overcome by the thought that yet another meaningless war may break out in twenty years' time, he puts an end to his life by throwing himself out of bed.

A good deal in this story is arbitrary and almost incredible. It is quite true that many of the heroes of the last war were swindled out of their gratuities and denied the chance of a decent livelihood, but in actual practice how many officers' wives ended up as charwomen? And—though such things do happen sometimes—how typical is the experience of a boy of middle-class origin brought up in an East End slum and having to fight with his fists almost daily because his accent is "different"? And how many apprentices in motor firms marry the boss's daughter?

In so far as this book is intended as social history, incidents of this kind defeat its purpose, and even as a story it wobbles somewhat. There is a peculiarly pointless incident when Raymond's mother, repelled by her war-worn husband, suddenly goes down to the country and spends two nights with a young farmer who had almost succeeded in seducing her when she was a Land Girl during the war. This escapade has no bearing on the story, since it is emphasised that Raymond, born about a year later, is not the son of the farmer. Mr. Sava has written many other books, but, as the dust jacket informs us, this is his first novel, and he has perhaps underrated the magnitude of the task.

"Death of a Poet" is a spirited and fairly convincing historical novel in which the author has followed the device of writing the fictitious memoirs of a real man. It deals with the death of Pushkin, the famous Russian poet and story-teller, who was killed in a duel in the thirties of the last century, aged ony 37. The memoirs are supposed to be those of the Vicomte D'Archiac, who was an attaché at the French Embassy at St. Petersburg and was the cousin of Georges D'Antes, the young Frenchman by whom Pushkin was killed. D'Archiac, who was a passionate admirer of Pushkin, somewhat unwillingly seconded his cousin in the duel, and afterwards, when the real meaning of the affair had dawned upon him, wrote down a full account of it, which he addressed to Prosper Mérimée.

The author's thesis is that Pushkin's untimely death was not simply a meaningless disaster, but was in effect a political assassination. Pushkin, who belongs to roughly the same current of thought as Byron, was looked upon as a Radical, almost a revolutionary, and his European reputation made him especially hateful in the eyes of the reactionary Czar. A plot to get rid of him was therefore hatched by the supporters of the Czar and of the equally reactionary Charles X, who had recently been exiled from France. The young man who did the actual killing was, more or less, innocent in the affair, but had been selected for the purpose and manœuvred into a quarrel with Pushkin because he was known to be a deadly shot with a pistol.

Is this a true interpretation? One would have to know a great deal about the history of the period to give an authoritative answer, but it could be true. Inconvenient people have often been got rid of in a similar manner, and in the struggle between progress and reaction which was then raging almost as fiercely as it is now Pushkin was in the progressive camp, though, like Byron, he was only rather doubtfully in it. On the other hand it is known that Pushkin was of a quarrelsome disposition and had been involved in at least one other duel.

Such incidents were common at that time, an almost equally famous poet, Lermontov, being killed in the same way a few years later. But this is a lively story, and with only a few lapses—just occasionally D'Archiac is made to talk about "The inevitable clash of historical forces" and "the aspirations of the toiling masses," in the modern Marxist manner—the author has successfully entered into the spirit of his period. So far as one can judge without knowing anything about the original, Miss Edith Bone's translation is excellent.

[Fee: £8.8.0; 13.6.44]

1. 'A Land Fit for Heroes' is the commonly-used form of what Lloyd George (1863–1945) seemed to promise returning servicemen when, as Prime Minister, he spoke at Wolverhampton on 24 November 1918. What he actually said was: 'What is our task? To make Britain a fit country for heroes to live in.' That 'promise' contrasted bitterly with the years of deprivation and unemployment that soon followed in the twenties and thirties.

2679. *The Way of All Flesh* by Samuel Butler

BBC Home Service, Talks for Schools, 15 June 1945[1]

On 13 June, Mrs. M. P. (Becky) Cocking[2] dictated this memorandum to the Director of Schools Broadcasts (signed in her absence by her secretary, J. Carson):

> Another that won't set the Thames on fire, I'm afraid. Mr. Orwell will accept minor alterations but is not, I fear, in a state to cope with rewriting. The virtue's gone out of him! . . .

I am uneasy about the references to family history—specific schools—etc. Though much more has been said in books on Butler. I have marked danger points with question marks in the margin. There are two minor points at A. on page 3. I feel "dosing and stuffing" are too close to be happy in this context, and at B. on page 4 it seems to me we should substitute "any other" for "the opposite".

The words 'dosing and stuffing' still appear in the script, but neither 'any other' nor 'the opposite' occurs on the next page. There seems, therefore, to have been some revision. Presumably details of family history and 'specific schools' have also been cut. Roughborough School was based on Shrewsbury School, which Butler attended, and several characters are based on members of his family; Alethea, in character if not in appearance, was suggested by Eliza Mary Anne Savage.

ANNOUNCER: [Blank.]

GEORGE ORWELL: Samuel Butler's novel, THE WAY OF ALL FLESH—it's the only novel among the dozen or more books that he wrote—was not published until several years after his death. This was by his own wish. It is an autobiographical novel containing a good deal of family history, and he had good reason for not wanting it to appear until all the people concerned in it were dead. I don't want, however, to convey the impression that THE WAY OF ALL FLESH is a scandalous book, or even that it is straightforward autobiography, taken directly from life. Actually it is based on Butler's own life to about the same extent as for instance David Copperfield is based on Charles Dickens' life. That is to say, it isn't necessarily relating things that actually happened, and even the real events in it have been altered and rearranged sufficiently to form them into a story. It is the story of a boy, and then a man, named Ernest Pontifex, the son of a country clergyman. But the story doesn't start with Ernest, it starts two generations back, and Ernest himself does not appear until chapter seventeen. The reason is that Butler understood, better than most of the people of his time, that a human being isn't simply an individual. A human being is what he is largely because he comes from certain surroundings, and no one ever fully escapes from the things that have happened to him in early childhood. To some extent your character depends on the way your parents have treated you, and their character depends on the way theirs have treated them, and so on. One can't, of course, follow this process very far, but it is probably true that you can't give a really revealing history of a man's life without saying something about his parents and probably his grandparents. In any case part of Butler's purpose in THE WAY OF ALL FLESH was to study the relationship between parents and children and to show up the stupidity of the educational methods of that time. Well, the Pontifexes were one of those many English families who suddenly grew rich at about the end of the eighteenth century, when world trade was expanding and Britain was developing from a second-rate nation into a powerful and important one. Ernest Pontifex's great grandfather had been a village carpenter. His grandfather, George Pontifex, had gone into business in London and become a wealthy man. His father, Theobald Pontifex, who was George's younger son, was a clergyman and had earlier been fellow of a Cambridge college. But it is very important to the story that Theobald hasn't entered his profession because of having any real vocation for it. He is not drawn towards the life of a clergyman, he doesn't even—as he would find out if he knew how to analyse his own feelings— really believe in the religious doctrines which he professes to hold.

He has simply been pushed into an unsuitable profession because he is no match for his father, and in those days it was usual in well-to-do families to send one son into the Church. In the same way, when Theobald marries, it isn't really by any will of his own. Just as he has been trapped into the Church, he is trapped into marrying someone he doesn't really care about, because the pressure of his parents and of the society round about him is too strong for him to stand up to. People who have been bullied have a way of becoming bullies themselves when they get the chance. As soon as Theobald becomes head of a family he tyrannises over his children in just the same way as his father had tyrannised over him. Ernest doesn't have a good childhood, though it is not quite as bad as it might be, because he has some good friends among the servants in his father's household, and also a very intelligent aunt who protects him to some extent while she remains alive. Still, he is bullied and beaten and prayed over—even when he is a tiny child he is beaten because he can't pronounce certain letters of the alphabet properly—he is dosed with calomel and Epsom Salts and stuffed up with Latin and Greek, until at the age of about twelve his spirit is almost broken already. At this time he is sent to a public school which is called Roughborough in the book. Ernest is just able to keep his feet in school life, but he is not suited to it. He is a rather backward boy, small and not good at games, and though obviously intelligent he[3] doesn't seem able to make any use of his brains. As for the regular curriculum of the school, the Latin and Greek and so forth, he just can't stomach it, try as he will. He thinks it is wicked to be idle, and yet somehow he goes on idling, by a kind of instinct. He has been taught that if you enjoy doing anything it must be wrong, whereas anything unpleasant—Latin grammar, say, or Epsom salts—must be good for you. He accepts this, because he's never heard it questioned, but somehow his actions don't square with it. The way Butler puts it is that Ernest has an inner self which he is only partly conscious of and which warns him against wasting his time on useless learning and against being what his schoolmasters would call a good boy: "You are not strong enough"—I am quoting Butler's words: this [is][4] Ernest's unconscious self speaking—"to attend to your bodily growth and to your lessons too. Besides, Latin and Greek are great humbug; the more people know of them the more odious they generally are; the nice people whom you delight in either never knew any at all or forgot what they had learned as soon as they could . . . Never learn anything until you find you have been made uncomfortable for a good long while by not knowing it; when you find you have occasion for this or that knowledge, or foresee that you will have occasion for it shortly, the sooner you learn it the better, but till then spend your time in growing bone and muscle; these will be much more useful to you than Latin and Greek, nor will you ever be able to make them if you do not do so now."

The "nice people"—Butler is fond of this phrase— means the middling, healthy, sensible people who get on in the world and are good-natured into the bargain, but are not necessarily clever and above all not priggish. These are the people that Ernest admires in his heart, though as yet he doesn't understand himself well enough to realise it.

When he is about fourteen his life takes a turn for the better and his health improves, because his aunt comes down to stay near the school and finds ways of encouraging his natural talents and giving him more self- confidence. But about a year later his aunt dies, and after this partly because they happen to catch him out in telling a lie, he falls more under the domination of his parents than ever.

At Cambridge he is happier than he had been at school, but he still seems to have no aim in life and no way of using his talents. His father has decided that Ernest must also become a clergyman. Ernest in fact doesn't want this, and he is more conscious of not wanting it than Theobald had been when he was in the same situation himself. He does make a few feeble efforts to escape, but his father promptly over-rules him. Even when, at twenty-one, he inherits five thousand pounds, he is still too much of a child in outlook to realise that he could live on the interest of this money and so become independent of his father. He prepares for his career as a clergyman without any real enthusiasm, but also without any active rebellion, and he goes through several violent but rather short-lived fits of piety. He has still not learned a very important lesson, and that is to know what he likes and what he dislikes.

Apart from allowing himself to be pushed into the Church against his real inclination, Ernest is also foolish enough to let a fellow-curate— whom he ought to have been able to recognize at a glance as a scoundrel—swindle him out of his five thousand pounds. But when he has actually been ordained a priest and seems all set for a career which he is totally unsuited to, he is saved by an accident. It is an accident which in any ordinary person's case would be an appalling disaster, but which in Ernest's case is a blessing in disguise.

Chiefly through ignorance of the world, he commits a criminal offence. It is not a terribly serious offence, and any really bad man would have had enough common sense to avoid committing it: but it is enough to earn him six months imprisonment. I should add, by the by, that this particular incident is NOT based on Butler's own life. That, of course, is the end of his career as a clergyman, and curiously enough it is also the point at which he really begins to grow up. His term of imprisonment is the first real education he has ever had. He comes out of prison cured for good of his dependence on his parents and of any respect for their standards or their way of life.

However, he has not altogether learned wisdom yet— perhaps I should say, he has not learned what Butler considered to be wisdom. For example, he does not yet understand the importance of money, a thing on which Butler felt strongly. "Money losses," Butler says—and he elaborates this at considerable length, money losses "are the hardest to bear of any by those who are old enough to comprehend them." Ernest has been through the folly of what is called respectability, but now his tendency is to go to the other extreme, and before the end he makes one more big mistake, that is to make a foolish marriage. In prison he has been taught tailoring, and when he comes out he tries—for of course he has now got to start life over again—to find work in a tailor's shop. He is making efforts to do this when he runs across a servant girl named Ellen who had been dismissed from his parents' house eight years earlier. Ellen is three years older than himself. She is a good-tempered and pretty girl, but obviously worthless in character. She suggests to him that instead of trying to find work, which is almost impossible for an inexperienced man, he should use the few pounds that he's got left setting up a second-hand clothes shop. This is a good idea and Ernest jumps at it: unfortunately he also takes it into his head to marry Ellen, and he promptly does so, lives with her for several years and has two children. Ernest is happier in the second-hand clothes shop, at any rate at first, than he had been at school or at Cambridge, but still his marriage was a mistake which he ought to have known better than to make. Ellen turns out to be a drunkard, she keeps him on the verge of ruin by selling the stock and the household goods to buy drink, and incidentally she has another husband still living. Ernest is at a very low ebb when he discovers this fact, and after another year or two with Ellen he would probably have given up hope altogether. However, his escape from her is the turning-point of his life. He has now committed all his mistakes and is fully grown-up at last.

Two years later it turns out that his aunt Alethea, the aunt who had taken an interest in him in his childhood has left him all her money, on the condition that he is not to inherit it or to hear about it until he is twenty-eight. Needless to say the rest of his relatives, who have treated him as an outcast ever since imprisonment, are promptly reconciled to him now that he has become a rich man. Ernest devotes the rest of his life to writing books, and his literary history is very similar to Butler's own. As for his two children, he puts them out to nurse in the family of a barge-captain, and though he gives them all the money they need, he gives them no education in the sense of book-learning. They will be happier, too, if he himself has little or no contact with them: for all fathers, he says, bully their children, and he himself, if he saw too much of his children, would behave no better towards them than his father had done to him.

So the book ends. You'll see that it is rather a weak ending, or at least an improbable ending compared with the rest of the book. This is because Butler's attitude to life, which he is trying to illustrate here, leaves certain things out of account. But just what is it that Butler is trying to say? Well, two things. First of all there is his notion, already set forth in a different form in other books which are not novels, that evolution, or progress, takes place only through individuals who suffer and make mistakes, and that at any given moment the finest specimens are people who are incapable of progressing further. Ernest Pontifex belongs to the type through whom progress can happen. He has no natural wisdom, he makes terrible mistakes and has to be saved by the skin of his teeth, but he is capable of growth. As a contrast to him there is in the book a young man named Towneley whom Ernest has known at Cambridge and who has every quality that Ernest lacks. He is good-looking, healthy, athletic, popular—the kind of person who is born to succeed in life and who has all the intelligence he needs without being troubled by any sort of intellectual curiosity. Ernest looks up to Towneley, well knowing that he can never be like him. But in the end, though he continues to admire him, he says that he doesn't want to see Towneley any more, nor to mix with his kind of person again. By this time he has got beyond Towneley: he has suffered and made mistakes, and by learning from his mistakes he has acquired a wisdom which is better than natural wisdom.

The unsatisfying ending to the book, which I've referred to, comes ultimately from Butler's lack of interest in politics. He implies in THE WAY OF ALL FLESH, as in various of his other writings, that one condition of living a good life is to inherit enough money to live on. He doesn't seem to see that this is only possible in a certain kind of society, and then only for a few people. Indeed, although he is trying to alter people's outlook and behaviour, he seems to assume that the kind of society he knew in the middle and late nineteenth century would last for ever. In that society, simply to live on an inherited income—enjoying yourself and doing no work in return—was looked on as normal, even creditable, and Butler accepts this. In so far as he had any politics he was a kind of Conservative. Ernest, towards the end, takes to writing books, but otherwise the characters who are presented as most admirable—Towneley, Alethea Pontifex, and Mr. Overton, who is supposed to be telling the story—are shown as doing no work and as not feeling the need for work. It is this lack of the sense of duty or function that makes the ending of the book seem inferior to the rest. Somehow the comfortable, irresponsible life which Ernest is shown as leading at the end—not even taking full responsibility for his own children—seems unworthy of the struggles that he has been through. But the other thing that Butler is doing is to satirise religious hypocrisy and the ghastly shams and tyrannies of the middle-class Victorian life. For all its good-temper, THE WAY OF ALL FLESH was a deadly blow at the old conception of parental authority. Books do in the long run influence public opinion, and if the relationship between parents and children is better and easier nowadays than it was a hundred years ago, I think Samuel Butler was partly responsible.

The book also has great value as social history, as what people call a period piece: especially the bits dealing with Butler's experiences at school and at Cambridge, which are described in some detail.

I am not fond of those dreary lists of the hundred best this and the twenty best that, but if you had to compile a list of the twelve best novels in English I think you would have to include THE WAY OF ALL FLESH. And this in spite of the fact that it has the weakness I have mentioned, and that it sometimes turns aside from the story to branch off into what is really an essay, and that it leaves certain themes right out. For instance, it doesn't contain what is usually called a love interest. Butler isn't trying to stir up the reader's emotions, there are no purple passages in the book, and it isn't even particularly subtle in a psychological sense.

It is a great book because it gives an honest picture of the relationship between father and son, and it could do that because Butler was a truly independent observer, and above all because he was courageous. He would say things that other people knew but didn't dare to say. And finally there was his clear, simple, straightforward way of writing, never using a long word where a short one will do, which makes him one of the best English prose writers of the past hundred years and has made his books wear well even when the ideas in them have ceased to seem important.

1. Orwell's Payments Book records that this script was completed on 11 June 1945; his fee is given as £12.12.0. The text is printed from a BBC fair copy. This is more accurately typed than was the first talk; see 2674, headnote. Obvious errors are noted below; one or two typing slips have been corrected silently.
2. See Eileen's letter to Mrs. Cocking, 25 March 1945, 2644.
3. though obviously intelligent he] typescript has though he obviously intelligent he
4. is] editorial addition

2680. John Morris to Geoffrey Trease

18 June 1945   Typewritten; carbon copy

On 16 June 1945, at Orwell's suggestion, Geoffrey Trease[1] wrote to John Morris, Far Eastern Service Director (with whom Orwell had worked when serving with the BBC), telling him that he was being stationed in India as a Warrant Officer in the Army Education Corps and inquiring as to the possibility of assisting with English radio programmes there. Morris replied on 18 June. He had run into Orwell on Friday, 15 June—presumably when his Schools Broadcast was being transmitted—and Orwell had told him that Trease would be writing. Morris suggested he make himself known to Professor A. S. Bokhari, Director-General of All India Radio, and Mr. Sayers, Director-General of the Far Eastern Bureau in New Delhi, who organised propaganda broadcasting to the Far East.

1. Geoffrey Trease (1909–1998), author, many of whose books were written for children. Orwell wrote to him on 1 May 1940 in connexion with writing for children, and in particular the possibility of there being newspapers for children; see 618.

2681. Review of *Another Shore* by Kenneth Reddin; *The Weeping Wood* by Vicki Baum[1]

Manchester Evening News, 21 June 1945

It is not the job of a mere book-reviewer to put on airs of snooty superiority, and yet any reviewer is failing in his duty to the public if he does not from time to time point out that the general run of books now appearing is unbelievably bad.

During the past year or two English literature, especially fiction, has achieved what one might describe as a depth record. No doubt the main reason is the war, for it is the same story almost everywhere. Not only in the Fascist countries, but in the countries newly liberated from Fascism, very few books have appeared, either clandestinely or since the liberation, and among those few there is very little of value.

In the U.S.S.R. the literary output is still large, but—to judge from the translations which pour from Messrs. Hutchinson—the emphasis is decidedly on quantity rather than quality. Only in the United States, where there are still leisure, peace of mind and abundant paper, has a certain standard been preserved throughout the war years.

So far as England goes, most of the novels now appearing would be regarded as not worth publishing in peace time, and this lowering of the average level ought to be borne in mind when one sees it stated that this or that book is "good," "brilliant," or what-not.

Thus, "Another Shore" is a fairly good book according to the standards now prevailing. That is to say, it is not illiterate. It has a story of sorts and it has been constructed and written with some care.

It is also a thoroughly silly, frivolous book—frivolous in the bad sense, in that it deals with a "whimsical", escapist, flagrantly impossible theme, which the reader is nevertheless expected to take seriously.

Its central character is a young man named Gulliver Sheils, whose great ambition is to go and live in the South Pacific, preferably on the island of Raratonga. Gulliver has inherited an income of about three pounds a week, but obviously he will need more than this—perhaps another £400 a year or thereabouts—if his dream is ever to be realised. He has, however, thought out a plan for raising the necessary money. He will rescue a rich man who has been the victim of an accident, and the grateful rich man will promptly reward him with a gift of several thousand pounds. With this end in view, Gulliver sits every day for several years on a public seat in St. Stephen's Green, at a spot where he judges it likely that an accident of some kind may happen. Later he changes his terrain, and stands every day for several months in the doorway of the North British and Mercantile Insurance Company.

In the meantime he has made the acquaintance of an Anglo-Irish girl whom the experienced reader would spot instantly as his future wife. Later the long-expected accident actually happens, and Gulliver is on the point of setting out for the Pacific, but in the end, partly as the result of another accident, he doesn't go. Instead, he stays at home and marries the Anglo-Irish girl. This, too, would be foreseen by every hardened novel reader.

A story of this kind might succeed as a fantasy in the manner of Evelyn Waugh, but it becomes merely irritating when it is presented as a fragment of real life. We are apparently expected to believe that the hero not only could exist, but is a rather admirable and exceptionally intelligent person. The "love interest" is presented more or less seriously, and there are even some spurious attempts at pathos, not to mention occasional excursions into politics. The result is to make one wonder whether the author has some talent and is deliberately squandering it, or whether he is merely trying to sound clever because he has nothing to say. And yet—such is the pass we have reached—this novel is somewhat better than most that have appeared recently.

Miss Vicki Baum's novel is about rubber—it is really an understatement to say that it is about rubber—and contains much quotable information for anyone who is not afraid of 500 closely printed pages. Did you know, for example, that the wild rubber-tree was originally native to Brazil and was from there introduced into the East Indies?

Probably you did, but it is less likely that you knew that well back in the eighteenth century the forest Indians were well acquainted with the properties of rubber and used it for making waterproof bags and small syringes with which they squirted one another at festivals. Like quinine, rubber was brought to the attention of the Europeans by a Jesuit missionary, and a pair of rubber boots is said to have been presented to Frederick the Great. Curiously enough, it seems to have been prized for its waterproof qualities rather than its elasticity, and the first large-scale use to which it was put was the making of galoshes.

Miss Vicki Baum follows up the story of rubber from the days when the gum was gathered from scattered trees in the jungle by underpaid Indian labourers, through the period when the seeds were transported to the East Indies, and great plantations, based on coolie labour, were built up in the East Indies, Malaya, and Ceylon, through the development of synthetic rubber, and up to the return of the rubber tree to its native Brazil.

Mainly with the idea of making the U.S. independent of supplies from Asia, Henry Ford and others have opened up plantations on the Amazon, and the labour difficulties and plant diseases which previously made it more practicable to grow rubber in Asia are within sight of being overcome. The various episodes in the history of rubber are strung together upon a sort of plot, but just why a book of this kind should be dressed up as a novel it is hard to see.

The title, by the way, is a translation of the Indian name for the rubber tree, which "weeps" the white latex when its bark is cut.

[Fee: £8.8.0; 20.6.45]

1. 'Vicki' in the heading and the text was printed as 'Vicky.'

2682. To Leonard Moore

23 June 1945   LMP/SH   Typewritten

27B Canonbury Square   Islington   London   N 1

Dear Mr Moore,

Many thanks for your letter of 21st June. I have already written to Warburg explaining about the contract, and I am going to see him and get it fixed on Monday.[1] It was a complicated matter which I did not feel equal to dealing with by the very unreliable mails between Britain and France, but I could not sign the contract just as it stood, so I left it unsigned and deleted references to it from the other contract. But I don't think there will be any further difficulty after I have seen him on Monday. I have already clearly explained by letter that he can have all my work from now on.

A long time ago Britain in Pictures commissioned me to write a short book (15,000 words), and duly passed the synopsis I showed them. When I presented the manuscript there was a certain amount of fuss and Collins's reader sent in a long report wanting me to make certain modifications, or suggesting that I should do so. I explained clearly to Turner that I could not make the alterations, as they would falsify the book and I had closely followed the synopsis which they had passed. Turner then assured me there was no question of compelling me to alter anything and that the book would go forward. Subsequently I learned that Britain in Pictures were contemplating a companion volume on the same subject (mine was on "The English People"), and that the two were to be published simultaneously or as a single volume. All this was months ago, in fact I sent them the manuscript about a year ago, and I have heard no more of it. I really don't care whether the book, which was a piece of propaganda for the British Council, gets published or not, but I think they ought in any case to pay me something as they signed a contract promising £50 plus additional royalties. I have lost the contract but they must have a copy. Could you tickle them up about this? The best person to approach would be W. J. Turner, who can be found care of the Spectator. He is the editor of the series.[2]

Yours sincerely
Eric Blair

1. See 2677.
2. A cryptic annotation made in Moore's office suggests that the publishers of 'B in P' (Collins) were contacted on 26 June 1945. Orwell noted in his Payments Books against 22 May 1944 that his contribution to the series 'Britain in Pictures,' *The English People*, had been completed. He asterisked the entry and recorded, 'Payment to be made later.' On 3 July 1945 Orwell wrote to Moore (see 2694), saying that he had seen W. J. Turner, the editor of the series, and he had agreed that an advance of £50 should be paid, £25 immediately. In his Payments Book for 14 July, Orwell records receiving £20 (not the £25 agreed). *The English People* (eventually published in August 1947), is reproduced here at the date of its completion, 22 May 1944; see 2475. W. J. Turner (1889–1946) was a poet, novelist, editor, and music critic; see 1743, n. 1.

2683. Review of *The Nigger of the Narcissus, Typhoon, The Shadow Line* by Joseph Conrad;[1] *Within the Tides* by Joseph Conrad

The Observer, 24 June 1945

It has been said that a creative writer can only expect to remain at the top of his form for about fifteen years, and the bibliography which is included in the Everyman reprint of Conrad's short stories seems to bear this out. Conrad's great period was from 1902 to 1915. Within those years he produced not only "The Secret Agent," "Chance," and "Victory," but a whole string of brilliant short and long-short stories, such as "Youth," "The End of the Tether," "Falk," and "Heart of Darkness." Also, it is only in this period that stories *not* dealing with the sea predominate in his work.

Of the tales now reprinted (the Penguin book contains four), only one, TYPHOON, shows Conrad at his best. His name is associated with the sea and with the "romance" of muddy islands in the eastern archipelagoes, and in a time of paper shortage it was no doubt inevitable that the more obviously picturesque of his stories should be selected for re-issue. But even if inevitable it was unfortunate. "The Planter of Malata," for instance, which occupies nearly half of WITHIN THE TIDES, was not worth reprinting. It simply illustrates the vulgar theatricality which was the reverse side of Conrad's feeling for *noblesse oblige.*

"The Partner," on the other hand, which is included in the same volume, is in essence a very fine story, though it is marred by the queer shyness or clumsiness which made it difficult for Conrad to tell a story straightforwardly in the third person. THE NIGGER OF THE NARCISSUS contains magnificent descriptive passages, but curiously enough the most memorable thing in it are certain irrelevant paragraphs in which Conrad goes out of his way to express his reactionary political and social opinions. In a penetrating essay published some years ago, the sailor writer, George Garratt,[2] pointed out that the whole story can probably be traced back to some encounter which Conrad, as an officer, had had with a rebellious seaman. THE SHADOW LINE is a goodish story, not better or worse than about a dozen others that Conrad wrote. TYPHOON, of course, was well worth reprinting, but one cannot help feeling sorry that it was not accompanied either by "Chance" or by "The Secret Agent" and some of the short stories of kindred subjects.

Nearly the whole of Conrad's charm springs from the fact that he was a European and not an Englishman. This is most obvious in his style of writing, which even at his best, and perhaps especially at his best, has the air of being a translation. It is said that for many years he was obliged to translate his thoughts from Polish into French and from French into English, and when he uses phrases like "his face of a sick goat," or puts the adjective after the noun ("it was a fate unique and their own"), it is possible to follow the process back at least as far as the French. But Conrad's romanticism, his love of the grand gesture and of the lonely Prometheus struggling against fate, is also somehow un-English. He had the outlook of a European aristocrat, and he believed in the existence of the "English gentleman" at a time when this type had been extinct for about two generations. As a result he was constantly creating characters in whom a capacity for having adventures, and a capacity for appreciating them, were combined in a way that is impossible in real life. "Lord Jim," for instance, is an absurdity as a whole, in spite of the brilliant passages describing the scuttling of the ship.[3] "The End of the Tether" is an example of a story in which Conrad's feeling for personal nobility produces a truly moving effect, but probably an Englishman could not have written it. To admire the English as much as Conrad did, one had to be a foreigner, seeing the English with fresh eyes and slightly misunderstanding them.

The other advantage Conrad derived from his European background was a considerable understanding of conspiratorial politics. He had an often-expressed horror of anarchists and nihilists, but he also had a species of sympathy with them, because he was a Pole—a reactionary in home politics, perhaps, but a rebel against Russia and Germany. His most colourful passages may have dealt with the sea, but he is at his most grown-up when he touches dry land.

[Fee: £10.3.4; 22.6.45]

1. Also reviewed in the *Manchester Evening News*; *see 2687.*
2. Orwell met George Garratt when he travelled north in 1936; see *287, n.2.* Orwell wrote out a passage from this article in his last literary note-book; see *3725.* The essay was published in *Adelphi*, June 1936.
3. In his letter to C. E. de Salis, 29 June 1945 (see *2690*), Orwell expressed regret that he had referred to the scuttling, rather than the abandonment, of the *Patna*. He also explains that, owing to lack of space, some 300 words had been cut from this review in which, among other things, he particularly praised *The Secret Agent*.

2684. Morrison and Bracken Face Stiff Fights: Heavy Poll Expected

The Observer, 24 June 1945

In all of the half-dozen London constituencies that I have visited up to date it is expected that a high percentage of the registered electorate will vote: otherwise considerable uncertainty reigns, and there are several areas where leading members of the various parties are by no means sure of their seats.

In Lewisham East, for example, Mr. Herbert Morrison has chosen to attack a constituency which had a 7,000 Tory majority in 1935, and the result is likely to be a close thing. In Paddington North Mr. Brendan Bracken is having a tough fight against General Mason-Macfarlane, the Labour candidate. Partly owing to the bombing, the Paddington area has changed its social composition since the last election, and if Mr. Brendan Bracken wins it will quite likely be because Mr. C. Groves, the Socialist Party of Great Britain candidate (this is the sole constituency the S.P.G.B. is contesting) has split the Labour vote.

In Marylebone Captain Cunningham-Reid is fighting against an official Conservative candidate, thus for the first time giving Labour some kind of chance in this strongly Conservative area. In Mile End it is sure to be a close finish between Mr. Dan Frankel, the Labour candidate, and the very energetic and popular Communist candidate, Mr. Phil Piratin. The situation is similar in Hackney South where Mr. William Rust, editor of the "Daily Worker," faces Mr. H. W. Butler, a Labour candidate, who is a well-known local figure. The only constituency I have visited where the result seemed to me a foregone conclusion is Limehouse, Mr. Attlee's seat: but even here the youthful Conservative candidate, Mr. Peter Woodard, is putting up a lively fight and is surprisingly confident about his chances.

Part of the present uncertainty arises from the shift of the population and the bad state of the electoral roll. Because of the bombing, in several East End constituencies the electorate has shrunk from about 40,000 to about 16,000. Moreover many votes are "lost." Some people have returned to their London homes to find that they are registered in the places to which they were evacuated, and would have to make a special journey if they wanted to vote. Others have been registered as living in premises which have been demolished in recent clearance schemes, and it is sometimes impossible to discover their whereabouts. A certain number of workers in special categories have not been registered at all because they still have the old identity cards, and considerable numbers of Service men abroad have failed to register. Hackney, for instance, has five thousand potential Service voters, of whom only two thousand have applied for papers.

Except in areas like Stepney, where the entire population is working class, the mechanical difficulties of the election probably operate in the Conservative interest. The "lost" votes are mostly working-class votes, and the fact that there is now almost no unemployment makes things harder for the Left-wing parties. Canvassing and other organisational work used to be done largely by unemployed men, but it is now very difficult, in a working-class area, to find anyone who has spare time on his hands before six in the evening.

The election is only just "warming up," and I have not yet overheard a spontaneous remark about it in the street, nor have I seen a single person stopping to look at an election poster. On the other hand the indoor meetings of all parties, though usually not large (the blitzing of many public buildings has had its effect here) are well-attended and lively, and even when there is rowdiness the questions and interruptions are generally to the point. Both speakers and audiences seem anxious to deal with the real issues—that is, nationalisation of industry, and the continuance of Mr. Churchill in office— and to disregard irrelevancies. The anti-Laski campaign for instance, seems to have made very little impression, and even Communist speakers put somewhat more emphasis on housing, old age pensions, etc., than on recriminations about the past. On the other hand there seems to be little interest in the war against Japan, and no feeling that this is an electoral issue.

No one can doubt that in London, at any rate, the political current is still running strongly leftward, and the Conservative meetings are usually the rowdiest. But the violence of feeling varies a good deal from constituency to constituency.

In Lewisham, for instance, the fighting is clean, whereas in Paddington it is distinctly dirty. On Thursday night there were concerted efforts to shout down Mr. Brendan Bracken, who, however, won in the end, because he had a loudspeaker and his interrupters had not. And in Mile End on Friday the Communist speaker was subjected to a certain amount of interruption which had the appearance of being organised. A few party agents have told me that in their opinion gangs of "professional hecklers" are being sent from meeting to meeting, but even among the Conservatives—the worst sufferers from interruption—this view is not general.

Many observers also believe that rowdiness tends to defeat its own purpose in the long run—or even in the short run—for a foolish interruption often gives a quick speaker the chance to score a cheap laugh. Within the next week we shall be able to see whether the big public has grasped the momentousness of this election, or whether the political apathy produced by a ten-years' Parliament is something that has come to stay. But up to date, among the section of the public that has entered into the struggle, the prevailing attitude is serious and democratic and gives evidence of a great advance in political intelligence.

[Fee: £10.3.4; 23.6.45]

2685. Unpublished letter to *Tribune*
26[?] June 1945

This letter was set up in type but, according to Orwell's marginal note on the galley slip, 'withdrawn because *Tribune* altered attitude in following week.'

POLISH TRIAL

I read with some disappointment your comment on the trial of the sixteen Poles in Moscow,[1] in which you seemed to imply that they had behaved in a discreditable manner and deserved punishment.

Early in the proceedings I formed the opinion that the accused were technically guilty: only, just what were they guilty of? Apparently it was merely of doing what everyone thinks it right to do when his country is occupied by a foreign power—that is, of trying to keep a military force in being, of maintaining communication with the outside world, of committing acts of sabotage and occasionally killing people. In other words, they were accused of trying to preserve the independence of their country against an unelected puppet government, and of remaining obedient to a government which at that time was recognised by the whole world except the U.S.S.R. The Germans during their period of occupation could have brought exactly the same indictment against them, and they would have been equally guilty.

It will not do to say that the efforts of the Poles to remain independent "objectively" aided the Nazis, and leave it at that. Many actions which Left-wingers do not disapprove of have "objectively" aided the Germans. How about E.A.M., for instance? [2] They also tried to keep their military force in being, and they, too, killed Allied soldiers—British in this case—and they were not even acting under the orders of a government which was recognised by anyone as legal. But what of it? We do not disapprove of their action, and if sixteen E.A.M. leaders were now brought to London and sentenced to long terms of imprisonment we should rightly protest.

To be anti-Polish and pro-Greek is only possible if one sets up a double standard of political morality, one for the U.S.S.R. and the other for the rest of the world. Before these sixteen Poles went to Moscow they were described in the Press as political delegates, and it was stated that they had been summoned there to take part in discussions on the formation of a new government. After their arrest all mention of their status as political delegates was dropped from the British Press—an example of the kind of censorship that is necessary if this double standard is to be made acceptable to the big public. Any well-informed person is aware of similar instances. To name just one: at this moment speakers up and down the country are justifying the Russian purges on the ground that Russia "had no quislings," at the same time as any mention of the considerable numbers of Russian troops, including several generals, who changed sides and fought for the Germans is being suppressed by cautious editors. This kind of whitewashing may be due to a number of different motives, some of them respectable ones, but its effect on the Socialist movement can be deadly if it is long continued.

When I wrote in your columns I repeatedly said that if one criticises this or that Russian action one is not obliged to put on airs of moral superiority. Their behaviour is not worse than that of capitalist governments, and its actual results may often be better. Nor is it likely that we shall alter the behaviour of the rulers of the U.S.S.R. by telling them that we disapprove of them. The whole point is the effect of the Russian mythos on the Socialist movement *here*. At present we are all but openly applying the double standard of morality. With one side of our mouths we cry out that mass deportations, concentration camps, forced labour and suppression of freedom of speech are appalling crimes, while with the other we proclaim that these things are perfectly all right if done by the U.S.S.R. or its satellite states: and where necessary we make this plausible by doctoring the news and cutting out unpalatable facts. One cannot possibly build up a healthy Socialist movement if one is obliged to condone no matter what crime when the U.S.S.R. commits it. No one knows better than I do that it is unpopular to say anything anti-Russian *at this moment*. But what of it? I am only 42, and I can remember the time when it was as dangerous to say anything pro- Russian as it is to say anything anti-Russian now. Indeed, I am old enough to have seen working class audiences booing and jeering at speakers who had used the word Socialism. These fashions pass away, but they can't be depended on to do so unless thinking people are willing to raise their voices against the fallacy of the moment. It is only because over the past hundred years small groups and lonely individuals have been willing to face unpopularity that the Socialist movement exists at all.

George Orwell

1. The British had called for a meeting of the leaders of the Polish underground to discuss the implementation of the Yalta decisions on the formation of a Polish Government of National Unity. The preliminary meeting was to be held in Moscow and a further meeting was planned for London. However, when the Poles reached Moscow they were put on trial.
2. E. A. M. (Ethnikon Apeleftherotikon Metopon), the National Liberation Front, was formed in Greece in 1941 after the German invasion. It started as a true resistance movement with nearly the whole population as members. By early 1942 it was discovered that it was in fact a Communist-organised movement. A national guerrilla army was then formed to fight the Germans, but found itself also fighting the E.A.M. When the British returned to Greece in 1945, they also found themselves fighting the E.A.M.

2686. To Hamish Hamilton

27 June 1945   Typewritten

27B Canonbury Square   Islington   London   N 1

Dear Mr Hamilton,[1]
Many thanks for your letter of 25.6.45. [2]

I don't think the book I have coming out in August is suitable for publication in the USA, as I had already sent a copy to an American agent who said that that kind of thing will not sell over there nowadays.[3] However, I have another book coming along about the end of this year, a book of reprinted critical essays. The Dial Press had been urging me for some time to send them something, and I sent them a copy of this one, which will be published over here by Secker & Warburg. If it turns out that the Dial people don't want it, perhaps Harper's would like to see it? It is a book of about 50,000 words, I think. I think it might be suitable for the USA because the editor of an American magazine told me that I ought to try and get some of my critical essays reprinted over there.[4]

Yours sincerely
[Signed] Geo. Orwell
George Orwell

1. Hamish Hamilton (1900–1988), barrister but distinguished as a publisher, was born in Indianapolis, brought up in Scotland, and educated in England at Rugby and Cambridge. After running the London office of Harper & Brothers, he established his own company in 1931, at first using the sign of the green bay tree (a reference to Psalm 34: 'I myself have seen the ungodly in great power: and flourishing like a green bay-tree'), but later adopted the oak. He was seconded to the American Division of the Ministry of Information, 1941–45. He built up an impressive list of authors, many of whom were American, but sold his publishing house in the 1960s.
2. Hamish Hamilton wrote to Orwell on that date to tell him that 'Cass Canfield, the head of Harpers, whom you may remember meeting some years ago shortly after the publication of DOWN AND OUT IN PARIS, LONDON AND NEW YORK,° was in London during the week-end on his way back to America after running the Paris office of The O[ffice of] W[ar] I[nformation] for some months. He asked me to write and let you know that he had been greatly impressed by your *Observer* articles and that he hopes he will some day have the pleasure of publishing something else of yours in the U.S.'
3. *Animal Farm*.
4. Orwell's letter is annotated (by Hamilton ?): 'Pl. ack, saying we feel sure Harpers wd. like to see—and inform Miss Fiske.' Hamilton wrote to Orwell on 28 June to tell him that he felt sure

Harpers would like to see his volume of essays if it should not be accepted by Dial Press. A letter from Hamilton to Miss D. B. Fiske of Harpers survives in the Harry Ransome Humanities Research Center, University of Texas, Austin, in a section of which Orwell's reply to Canfield's request is copied. He said that arrangements would be made to forward the book 'if it comes in.' Neither Dial nor Harpers published *Critical Essays*.

2687. Review of *The Nigger of the Narcissus, Typhoon, The Shadow Line* by Joseph Conrad;[1] *Poems of Our Time 1900–1942*, chosen by Richard Church and Mildred M. Bozman

Manchester Evening News, 28 June 1945

It was particularly fortunate that the reprinting of three of Conrad's tales in the Everyman Edition should coincide with the reprinting of four others ("Within the Tides" and other stories) as a Penguin.

Conrad's books, like nearly everybody else's books, are largely out of print, and it is a treat to be able to get hold of some of them again at a low price. But whether the present selection is the best that could have been made is a different question: most of Conrad's admirers would probably answer "Yes," but the minority who prefer Conrad when he sticks to dry land will answer "No."

There are two well-marked strains in Conrad. On the one hand he is a writer of stories about the sea and about adventures, sometimes very melodramatic adventures, in remote places at the edges of civilisation. At the time when he was writing there was a tendency for novelists to specialise in local colour and to be associated in their readers' minds with some particular locality, and it was felt that Conrad "belonged" to the Indian Ocean and the Malay Archipelago, just as Arnold Bennett "belonged" to the Five Towns, W. W. Jacobs to Wapping, Thomas Hardy to Wessex, and Barrie to Scotland.

But the other, less obvious source of Conrad's subject-matter was his Continental European origin. Although he went to sea early in life and ultimately became English by adoption he was by birth a Pole, a member of the small land-owning aristocracy. Traditionally anti-German and anti-Russian—his father, indeed, had been exiled to Siberia[1a] by the Czar.

He had a grasp of European history which an English writer of comparable gifts would probably not have had, and he also had a remarkable understanding of the atmosphere of conspiratorial politics. Politically he was a reactionary, and never pretended to be anything else, but he was also a member of an oppressed race, and he understood just why people throw bombs, even if he disapproved of such activities.

This comes out in several short stories dealing with Russian and Polish themes; but, above all, it comes out in his powerful but underrated novel, "The Secret Agent." It is very much to be hoped that "The Secret Agent" will be reprinted in the near future, and also "Chance," which, besides some first-rate passages dealing with the sea, is especially memorable for a portrait of a swindling financier.

The three tales now reprinted all deal with the sea. "Typhoon," it hardly needs saying, is one of the finest pieces of writing of this kind in English. It describes a ship battling for life in the China Seas, and the drama of the tropical storm is heightened by having for its background the impenetrable stolidity, not to say stupidity, of the captain. Captain MacWhirr, the commander of the "Nan-Shan," bears out the remark Conrad once made that adventures do not happen to adventurous people, but to ordinary decent people who go where their sense of duty leads them.

"The Nigger of the Narcissus" is a tale of rather the same type, but written earlier in Conrad's career (it was his third published book), more complex and on the whole, less successful. It is based on a voyage he himself had made between Australia and England as an ordinary seaman.

"The Shadow Line" describes a sailing ship trying to beat its way up the Gulf of Siam in an almost dead calm with the entire crew prostrated by malaria.

Its previous captain had died at about the spot where the ship is becalmed, and the superstitious mate believes that the dead man's ghost is haunting the ship. What the late captain has actually done, however, is to turn a dishonest penny by selling the whole of the ship's supply of quinine.

The Everyman Edition contains a bibliography of Conrad's work, and a short but useful introduction. It appears, by the way, that no definitive[2] biography of Conrad has been published, nor any full-length critical study of his work. It is about time that both these needs were met.

"Poems of Our Time" contains, as it was inevitable that it should, a lot of rubbish, but it is a wonderful three shillings' worth and a good book to have about the house. Within its 310 pages are contained more than seven hundred poems, ranging in point of time from Thomas Hardy, who was born in 1840, to Sidney Keyes, who was born in 1922 and was killed in action at the age of twenty-one.

The aim of an anthology of this kind is to be inclusive rather than selective, and in some cases the choice of poems has not been happy. Mr. T. S. Eliot, for instance, is not represented by any of his best poems except "The Hollow Men." [3] However, the selectors were not quite free agents, since in the interest of variety they were obliged to concentrate on very short poems.

There is also a certain tendency to overplay the Georgian poets at the expense of the less traditional writers who made their appearance from about 1920 onwards.

W. H. Davies, for instance, is represented by fifteen poems, Walter de la Mare by fourteen, Edward Thomas by eleven, and Rupert Brooke by seven, while Eliot only gets four, W. H. Auden three, Cecil Day Lewis six, and Louis MacNeice two.

Still, granted that the selectors' own tastes probably lie towards Georgianism, they have been remarkably open-minded. You can find here poems by very young writers who have only made their appearance during the war years—writers like Alex Comfort, Roy Fuller, Terence Tiller, Dylan Thomas, and George Barker—side by side with Rudyard Kipling, Edward Shanks, Robert Nichols, and Siegfried Sassoon.

The anthology only contains poems written since 1900, but in effect it stretches back into the 'nineties, and Francis Thompson, Alice Meynell, "A. E.," and John Davidson are all represented. W. B. Yeats gets the best showing of all, being represented by seventeen poems. The arrangement of the book leaves something to be desired, since it is based—always an unsatisfactory method with poetry—on subject-matter. It would have been better to stick to a chronological arrangement. However, there is a full index, from which one can discover not only the date of each writer's birth but the titles of the books drawn on and the publishers who have issued them.[4]

[Fee: £8.8.0; 27.6.45]

1. Also reviewed in *The Observer*, 24 June 1945; see *2683*.
1a. He was not exiled to Siberia but to Vologda, north of Moscow.
2. definitive] *printed as* 'definite'; *the error may be Orwell's*; compare *2794, n. 2*.
3. Besides 'The Hollow Men,' 'A Song for Simeon,' 'Gerontion,' and 'La Figlia che Piange' were chosen.
4. Nothing by Orwell was included in this anthology.

2688. To Gerry Byrne

28 June 1945   Typewritten

27B Canonbury Square   Islington   London N 1

Dear Mr Byrne,[1]

Many thanks for your letter. I am very sorry to tell you that my wife died three months ago, very suddenly and unexpectedly. She was to have an operation which should not have been very serious in itself and was expected to cure the trouble she suffered from, but she appears to have died as soon as the operation began, as a result of the anaesthetic. No one had anticipated anything going wrong, and I did not even hear she was to have the operation then till the last moment. I was in France at the time and I telegraphed my consent to the operation, only to get another telegram next day telling me she was dead. It was a horrible shock, and after seeing to everything as best I could I went straight back to France for another month or two, as I felt better when I was moving about. The only good thing about the whole business was that I don't think she herself had any uneasiness about what was going to happen. Also that the child was, I think, just too young to miss her. He is now 13½ months old and is extremely well. He has twelve teeth and is almost able to walk, and without being fat he weighs about 25 pounds, which I believe is pretty good as he started life a 7 pounds baby. I had great trouble finding a suitable nurse, but I have got one now[2] and he will come back here on Sunday. At present he is with an aunt at Greenwich.[3]

I can't possibly come and speak, because I am up to the eyes in the election myself, apart from other work. I don't even know of anyone suitable, but

Transport House[4] would no doubt send down somebody if you applied to them. I am sorry I can't be more helpful. Please give my best wishes to your wife.

Yours sincerely
Geo. Orwell

1. Gerry Byrne, second husband of Amy Charlesworth, with whom Orwell had corresponded in 1937 and 1944; see *384, n. 1* and *2569*. Writing to Orwell on 6 October 1937, she had said she was thirty-three and 'a bittock'—Scots for a small bit of a person—had been married at sixteen, 'when far too young to know anything about it.' In 1937, her children were a girl of sixteen and a boy of ten. She had separated from her first husband in 1929 because 'He hit me rather too often.' In 1937 she was 'on the way to earning a modest livelihood' as a health worker. She asked Orwell to tell her whether, in revealing these personal details, he was 'revolted by [her] frankness.'
2. Susan Watson (1918–) was Orwell's housekeeper from early summer 1945 to autumn 1946, caring also for Richard. She had married a Cambridge mathematician, but they were then in process of being divorced. She had a seven-year-old daughter, who was at boarding school. See her specially written memoir in *Orwell Remembered*, 217–25, and also *Remembering Orwell*, 156–62, 175–78.
3. Gwen O'Shaughnessy.
4. Transport House was at this time the headquarters of the Labour Party and was synonymous with the leadership of the party.

2689. To Ronald Boswell

29 June 1945   Typewritten

In a letter that has not been traced, Orwell wrote to Mrs. Rowland, of the BBC Schools Broadcasts Department, to say that he had not been paid for his broadcasts on *The Way of All Flesh* and *Erewhon*. Ronald Boswell (Talks Booking) replied on 27 June that Orwell had not been paid because he had not signed the contract dated 16 February; he enclosed a duplicate. Orwell replied:

27B Canonbury Square
Islington
London N 1

Dear Sir,
Herewith the signed copy of contract. I had not previously had a copy of the contract, and the one you refer to probably got mislaid during my absence in France: or it may have been sent on by my wife and lost in the post, which was very unreliable.

Yours faithfully
[Signed] Geo. Orwell
George Orwell

On his return from France until about the time he left for Jura in 1946, Orwell engaged Miss Siriol Hugh-Jones to type articles and letters for him. He was, of course, writing a great deal, and the additional earnings from his freelance work enabled him to finance this secretarial assistance. In this period, letters which have 'GEORGE ORWELL' or, less frequently, 'George Orwell' below Orwell's signature are almost certainly Miss Hugh-Jones's work. (See also *2902, n. 1.*) Siriol Hugh-Jones later became a much-loved journalist; she died when quite young. Orwell refers to his employing a secretary in his letter to Geoffrey Gorer, 22 January 1946; see *2870*. On 15 August 1944, Orwell told Leonard Moore that he (Orwell) would have to find someone to type 'Raffles and Miss Blandish' because he was so busy (*2533*). The essay was completed on 28 August 1944. It is not known if he engaged a typist then nor, if he did, whether it was Miss Hugh-Jones.

2690. To C. E. de Salis

29 June 1945   Typewritten

27B Canonbury Square   Islington   London   N 1

Dear Sir,

Your letter was sent on to me by the Observer. I am very sorry I made the bad slip of speaking of the scuttling of the ship in "Lord Jim." [1] Of course I meant to say abandonment of the ship, and would probably have corrected this if I had sent the article in early enough to see a proof.

With regard to the other points in your letter. The rest of Lord Jim° seems to me absurd, not because a young man who had behaved in that way would not seek redemption, but because the actual incidents of Jim's life among the Malays are of a kind I find incredible. Conrad could describe life in the far East from a sailor's angle, with the emphasis on jungle scenery and the life of seaport towns, but if one has actually lived in one of those countries his descriptions of life inland are not convincing. As a whole, Lord Jim seems to me to be a very distinguished version of the type of book in which the hero is expelled from his club for cheating at cards and goes off to Central Africa to shoot big game. Even the Dorothy Lamour figure[2] comes in. When I made that remark about people who could have adventures and also appreciate them, I thought of T. E. Lawrence, whom you mention, but after all how common or typical are such people? Marlow himself seems to me quite incredible. A person like that would not be a sea captain. Conrad himself was perhaps rather like that, but then the point is that he left the sea and took to writing. That way of writing a book also seems to me unsatisfactory, because one is so often brought up by the thought, "No one could possibly talk like this, or at such length."

The Observer article rather deformed what I meant to say about Conrad, because as so often happens they had to cut out about 300 words from lack of space. I had written a paragraph or two in elaborating the point that with his Polish background Conrad had a remarkable understanding of the atmosphere of revolutionary movements—an understanding which very few Englishmen would have, and certainly no Englishman with anything resembling Conrad's political outlook. I especially praised "The Secret

Agent," and suggested that this book, which now seems quite difficult to get hold of, should be reprinted.

Yours truly
[Signed] Geo. Orwell
George Orwell

1. This was in a review by Orwell published on 24 June 1945; see *2683*.
2. Dorothy Lamour (Dorothy Kaumeyer, 1914–) was first dressed by Hollywood in a sarong-like garment in *The Jungle Princess*, 1936, and came to typify exotic beauty, and especially so dressed in the 'Road' films to the point of self-parody. The film *Typhoon*, 1940, in which she appeared, had nothing to do with Conrad's novel of that title. Orwell very briefly reviewed her *Moon over Burma*, 5 July 1941 (see *828*), but devoted more attention to an elephant and a cobra than to Miss Lamour.

2691. 'Orwell and the Stinkers': A Correspondence

Tribune, 29 June–27 July 1945

On 29 June 1945, *Tribune* published a short review by Subramaniam[1] of *Million: Second Collection*,[2] edited by John Singer. This briefly summarised the contents and recommended the collection, but devoted half its length to an essay by J. E. Miller, 'George Orwell and Our Times,' which was said to deserve a separate paragraph:

This article, which is as provocative as any of Orwell's, is analytical, stimulating and almost brilliant. Mr. Miller, however, fails in one respect. He does not give enough importance to the fact that Orwell is one of the few writers who give political writing a literary form. Instead, he seems to be primarily concerned as to how far George Orwell has correlated his beliefs with correct Socialist behaviour and submits a long indictment with several counts. But since I hold a brief for George Orwell I should like to plead in mitigation of sentence that he is one of the best social, political and literary critics of our time, and I heartily concur with J. E. Miller in recommending "Shooting an Elephant in Burma" as an example of Orwell's vivid style at its best.

A lively correspondence followed, and *Tribune* clearly played it for all it was worth. Twice letters were given headings as provocative as the argument: 'Orwell and the Stinkers' and 'More Views on Stinkers.' The first letter, from Paul Potts, was published on 6 July 1945:

When reviewing *Million* last week Subramaniam mentioned an article on George Orwell by J. E. Miller. In this article Miller reiterates an old libel on Orwell, current at the time "The Road To Wigan Pier" first appeared, that Orwell said somewhere in that book that working-class folks stank. What he did say was that as a schoolboy at Eton he was brought up to believe they did. This error has been pointed out to Mr. Miller, who persists in circulating it. May one remind him that the particular version of socialism that he advocates is in no way aided by a mean untruth?

Mr. Miller has not even bothered to read widely the work he is trying to deprecate, else he would have discovered that "Shooting an Elephant in Burma" is not a part of the novel "Burmese Days" but is an entirely separate work.

This opened the floodgates. First, Gladys Bing wrote (*Tribune*, 13 July 1945), giving the reason why 'the people stink':

George Orwell is able to defend himself. But do not let us confuse the truth of this issue out of silly sentiment. Some thousands of the proletariat *do* stink—as we in the fresh air of the countryside discovered when the towns evacuated into our midst. Also, in spite of misguided denials in the House at the time, it was established beyond doubt that the proletariat also bred and harboured lice.

But what is not taught at Eton is that it is largely *Eton's* fault that the proletariat are thus. This is the point that matters. Eton is the hotbed that breeds the *élite* of our rulers: those world-famous men who hit the headlines in all our affairs of import. It is they who decree the pay and pensions of the proletariat. Hence the stink. The common phrase "it costs nothing to be clean" is grossly untrue. It costs a good bathroom; a nice little constant hot water boiler in the kitchen, and 4 to 5 cwt. of coke a week at £3 16s. a ton. It costs a wardrobe of at least a dozen shirts, vests and pants, and several changes of outer clothing in order that the stink of sweat be eliminated.

Eton is right. Rub it in. The people stink, as any London tram-ride will prove. And it is chiefly *Eton's* fault that they do.

James Miller defended his position in *Tribune*, 20 July 1945:

While it is true that Mr. Orwell, in *Wigan Pier*, links his most violent abuse of the working class with the mental climate of his adolescence, there is little to indicate that his attitude has changed much when he states his more "mature" views on the subject. He asks: "Meanwhile, *do* the 'lower classes' smell? Of course, as a whole, they are dirtier than the upper classes. They are bound to be, considering the circumstances in which they live . . . Besides, the habit of washing yourself all over every day is a very recent one in Europe, *and the working classes are generally more conservative than the bourgeoisie.*" (The italics are mine, though the implications of this last sentence scarcely need stressing.—J. E. M.)

Mr. Orwell goes on to state that the English people—ninety per cent. constituted by the working class—*are* getting cleaner, however—"visibly cleaner," he says—and "we may hope that in 100 years they will be almost as clean as the Japanese."

The real significance of Mr. Orwell's conception of a smelly proletariat, however, can only be fully appreciated when we learn of Mr. Orwell's other prejudices in this direction—that the working classes eat their peas, and their cheese, off knives, for instance; that they make horrible noises eating their soup, and that they are addicted to the foulest language and bawdiest jokes.

A last word. Mr. Orwell says I am reiterating an old libel; in other words, I am not alone in my criticism. In a preface to the Left Book Club edition of *Wigan Pier* Mr. Victor Gollancz reproached Mr. Orwell for his snobbish attitude. But perhaps one must not attack one's publishers. That sort of pastime must be reserved for critics and reviewers.

On 27 July 1945, two more readers wrote, and Orwell replied.

Why doesn't Mr. James E. Miller come out from behind Mr. Gollancz's skirts and say outright that, in the neatly catalogued list of writers which Mr. Miller and his like love to compile, George Orwell is labelled "Fascist . . . or as near as doesn't matter"?

Orwell said, in *The Road to Wigan Pier*, that the middle class believed that the working class smelled. If Mr. Miller had worked ten hours at a stretch, let us say, in a steel rolling mill, and, on getting home, had to choose between reading the paper and washing himself in sections in a tin bowl he might find it easier to understand how the idea that workers smell got about among the middle classes.

It ought to have dawned on Mr. Miller by this time that the admirable thing about Orwell is that he was not snob enough to stick by his Public school background and that he has not learned since to assimilate that other snobbery which Mr. Miller is trying so hard to palm off as "class consciousness."

Orwell's main trouble of late seems to be an irresistible attraction towards unpopular causes for their unpopularity's sake, but I am certain that he has not collected many ground axes in the course of his literary career, nor has he fallen for the hammer-and-sickly gruel that Mr. Miller believes to be criticism.

David Cole

How futile is this business of—do we stink, as a class! Do we eat peas with a knife—as a class! Must our views of each other—especially Socialist views—always be bedevilled by this labelling of mankind with a group label? He is a miner; he is a Civil Servant; he is a trade unionist; he is a Jew; he is a coloured man. Spoken as though each of these were some particular brand of being. As though one said, "He is a monkey," or a horse.

It is surely our business and worth the world's while to insist that first of all we are men. That, given the same type—and type is spread indiscriminately in every group—men placed in certain circumstances will react in certain ways. They are not certain sorts of creatures specially born to be working class, or belted earls, but men who would act just as the others act if they were placed in the other's circumstances.

This way of talking and thinking of men as though they were not men at all, but some sort of group creatures—stinks, and stinks pretty badly from a Socialist point of view.

E. S. Fayers

ORWELL REPLIES

I can hardly ask you to publish whole chapters of a book in your correspondence columns, but anyone who cares to look up the relevant passages in *The Road to Wigan Pier* will see that your correspondent, Mr. J. E. Miller, has misrepresented me seriously and, I think, intentionally.

He accuses me of "violently abusing" the working class and of thinking them "smelly," etc., because of such statements as (*a*) the working classes as a whole are dirtier than the bourgeoisie; (*b*) the habit of washing all over is a recent one in Europe and was more recently adopted by the working class; and (*c*) the English are dirtier than the Japanese. All of these are simply statements of well-known and easily observed facts which it would be merely dishonest to deny. Of course, the working classes, as a whole, are dirtier than the bourgeoisie. How can they be otherwise? The average person in this country still lives in a house where there is not even a bathroom, let alone an adequate water supply. Again, it is perfectly well known that personal cleanliness is only a recently adopted habit in Europe and, like most innovations, reached the poorer classes last. Well within the last ten years I have heard elderly or middle-aged miners and farm labourers maintain that hot baths are "weakening." And, of course, the English are dirtier than the Japanese or several other Oriental peoples. Thousands of observers would confirm this. Every Indian, for example, washes his teeth elaborately every day. Who would dare to say the same of the English? If I had *not* made the remarks objected to, while I was discussing the question at all, I should simply have been misstating known facts.

But what I was discussing in this chapter of *Wigan Pier* was the theory taught to us as children that the working classes are, as it were, smelly by nature. We were taught that the "lower classes" (as it was usual to call them) had a different smell from ourselves, and that it was a nasty smell; we were taught just the same about Jews, Negroes and various other categories of human beings. In the book, I explained elaborately how I was taught this, how I accepted it, and how and why I afterwards got rid of it. Mr. Miller ignores all this and simply picks out isolated sentences which seem to support his thesis, a method by which anybody can be made to say anything.[3]

Since Mr. Miller has chosen to drag in Mr. Gollancz (no longer my publisher, by the way), I will add that I discussed these passages with Mr. Gollancz before the book was printed, and that he does not "reproach" me in his preface but merely reinforced what I had said: that I had received a thoroughly snobbish education, which had left its mark on me but which I had done my best to struggle against.[4] After all, if the book had been simply the anti-working-class tirade that Mr. Miller seems to imply it was, why should it have been selected by the Left Book Club?

George Orwell

---

1. Unidentified.
2. *Million* ran for three issues. It was undated; they are assigned to 1943–45. It was published in Glasgow and carried one of two subtitles: 'New Left Writing' or 'The People's Review.'
3. Orwell wrote, 'That was what we were taught—*the lower classes smell*'; see *CW*, V, 119; the

italics are in the original. He then discussed this proposition on the following four pages. It was Maugham who unequivocally stated that the working man stank. Orwell quoted a dozen lines from Somerset Maugham's *On a Chinese Screen*, the only book, Orwell said, he knew in which this issue 'is set forth without humbug.' Maugham wrote, and Orwell quoted, 'I do not blame the working man because he stinks, but stink he does.' Orwell concluded his discussion by saying, 'Actually people who have access to a bath will generally use it. But the essential thing is that middle-class people *believe* that the working class are dirty' (VI, 122). Arnold Bennett, who had intimate experience of the world he describes in his novels set in the Potteries, refers in *Clayhanger* (1910) to the 'steamy whiff of humanity' as the Sunday School procession passes Edwin (Book 2, chapter 10, section 2), and to the smell of those attending a union meeting as 'nauseating' (Book 2, chapter 20, section 3).

4. Gollancz's Foreword is reprinted as an appendix to the *Complete Works* edition, Volume V. Although he thought Orwell was 'exaggerating violently,' he went on, 'I know, in fact, of no other book in which a member of the middle class exposes with such complete frankness the shameful way in which he was brought up to think of large numbers of his fellow men. This section will be, I think, of the greatest value to middle-class and working-class members of the Left Book Club alike. . . .'

2692. Liberal Intervention Aids Labour: 'Puzzle' Blocks of Voters

The Observer, 1 July 1945

Election feeling in London has not "hotted up" to the extent that had been expected, and the reactions of large blocks of the people are still unpredictable. The most one can say is that among those who are articulate, the Labour Party is still gaining ground. It also seems to be agreed that the intervention of the Liberals splits the Conservative and not the Labour vote, especially in middle-class areas. But the agents of all parties refuse to make detailed forecasts.

At Wandsworth Central, Mr. Ernest Bevin is fighting a hard and doubtful battle against his Conservative opponent, Brigadier-General Smyth, V.C. Mr. Bevin was returned to this seat unopposed during the war, but the Labour majority at the previous election was less than 500, and since then the electorate has dropped by 6,000 and altered in composition. Islington East is also anybody's fight. Mrs. Cazalet Keir, the outgoing Conservative member, had a majority of 4,000 at the last election and has won renown as the champion of equal pay for women teachers: on the other hand, her attitude on old age pensions is considered locally to be unsatisfactory, and Dr. Eric Fletcher, her Labour opponent, evidently has a good chance.

At Holborn Captain Max Aitken seems likely to win in a straight fight against Miss Marcousé, the Labour candidate. But even here there is considerable uncertainty because of the difficulty of canvassing in this area, with its mixed and shifting population.

At Hammersmith South a Conservative win by a small majority seems likely. In this constituency it is a straight fight between Labour and Conservative, and most of the blows are landing above the belt. It is distinctly different in Hammersmith North, a penny bus ride away, where the official Labour candidate, Mr. W. H. Church, is contending not only against the Conservative, Major L. Caplan, but against the outgoing member, Mr. D. N. Pritt. This is probably the most interesting as well as the most acrimonious contest now happening in the London area.

Mr. D. N. Pritt has held the seat for a number of years, but was expelled from the Labour Party in 1940. His posters have not made it altogether clear that he is not the Labour candidate, and Mr. Church has been obliged to spend much energy in establishing this point. Locally Mr. Pritt has a good record, and he probably started off with a big advantage, but Mr. Church seems to have been gaining ground during the past week. The situation is a curious one. If Mr. Church and Mr. Pritt run neck and neck, Major Caplan is quite likely to win, since the Labour majority at the last election was only 1,600. But the spirit in which the election has been fought has compelled Major Caplan to turn most of his guns against Mr. Pritt, and on Wednesday night he announced at a large and stormy meeting that he was issuing a writ for alleged libel. If his efforts to demolish Mr. Pritt succeed, the result will probably be a win for Mr. Church. Mr. Pritt and Major Caplan are both barristers and are close neighbours in the Temple.[1]

There is a somewhat similar situation in Putney, where there are five candidates—Mr. H. N. Linstead, the outgoing Conservative Member, Mr. P. Stewart, the Labour candidate, Sir Richard Acland for Common Wealth, a Liberal, and an Independent who represents the Never Again Association. Putney has always been strongly Tory, and Sir Richard Acland appears to have chosen this unpromising constituency under the impression that Labour was not contesting it. The Liberal and the Independent will capture some Conservative votes, but effectively the struggle is three-sided. Labour is thought to have a block vote of about a quarter of the electorate in the local factories, but Sir Richard Acland seems to be making good progress, and once again the effect of inter-Left rivalry may be to ensure a Conservative victory.[2]

Except for Hammersmith North and possibly Wandsworth Central, I have not yet seen a Labour seat which I thought the Conservative Party could win. But almost all observers of all parties agree on the impossibility of knowing what the big masses are thinking. Indoor meetings get good audiences, and in spite of some organised rowdiness the level of questions and discussion compares well with the mud-slinging in sections of the Press: but here only minorities are involved, and outdoor meetings, at any rate in the more thickly-populated parts of London, do not seem to be having much success.

More than once I have seen a loud-speaker wasting its efforts on an audience composed entirely of small boys and dogs. Just once during this week I have overheard a spontaneous comment on the election—from a Scotswoman whose sympathies appeared to be with Labour. Direct questioning sometimes elicits this disconcerting answer: "Well, you see, I don't know anything about politics." Canvassers in some areas report that "I haven't made up my mind yet" is a frequent answer. But when the time comes these seemingly uninterested masses will most of them cast their votes, and there is still the possibility that they will be swayed by some last-minute appeal.

The Laski campaign has now definitely failed, and some Conservative agents say frankly that they regard Lord Beaverbrook as a liability. The thing that is likeliest to influence the doubtful votes at the last moment is alarm at the thought of dropping Mr. Churchill, and it is a swing of this kind, possibly precipitated by events abroad, that Labour Party organisers are most afraid of.

[Fee: £10.3.4; 30.6.45]

1. D. N. Pritt (1887–1972) won the election as an Independent Socialist, but lost his seat in 1950.
2. Sir Richard Acland (1906–1990) lost the election, and his Common Wealth Party fared disastrously. It won only one of 23 seats contested and 16 candidates lost their deposits. For Orwell's 'Profile' of Acland, 23 May 1943, see *2095*; see also *2405, n. 2*.

2693. Bulletin of the Freedom Defence Committee

The first issue of the *Bulletin of the Freedom Defence Committee* was published from 17 St George Street, London, W. 1, in July 1945. Orwell served as the Committee's Vice-Chairman, spoke at its meetings, and was generous in supporting it financially. He also drafted its manifesto. See Crick, 497–98; Shelden, 435; U.S.: 399. See also Orwell's 'Freedom of the Park,' *Tribune*, 7 December 1945, *2813*.

2694. To Leonard Moore

3 July 1945   Typewritten

27B Canonbury Square
Islington, London N 1

Dear Mr Moore,

I had a talk with Warburg about the contract position. He is quite satisfied with my assurance that I will bring him all my future work, subject to books of a special nature (eg. that Britain in Pictures book)[1] being allowed to go elsewhere. He is not pressing for a hard and fast contract, but he would no doubt prefer to have one when the other business is settled.

The real trouble is with Gollancz. The contract to bring him my next two novels is still extant, and as he refused to regard ANIMAL FARM as working off one of these, it looks as if he wants to keep to it. At the same time I frankly would prefer not to give or offer him any more books if we can get out of it. I have no quarrel with him personally, he has treated me generously and published my work when no one else would, but it is obviously unsatisfactory to be tied to a publisher who accepts or refuses books partly on political grounds and whose own political views are constantly changing. When I wrote ANIMAL FARM for instance, I knew in advance that it would be a very difficult book to find a publisher for, and having to submit it to Gollancz simply meant that much time wasted. This might happen over and over again, and judging by some of the things he has published during the past year or two, I doubt whether I could now write anything that Gollancz would approve of. For instance, I recently started a novel.[2] Considering how much work I have to do elsewhere I don't expect to finish it till some time in 1947, but I am pretty sure Gollancz would refuse it when the time comes, unless by that time his views have altered again. He might say that so far as novels go he does not mind what views they express, but it is a bad arrangement to take novels to one publisher and non-fiction to another. For example, that Spanish war book, which is about the best I have written, would probably have sold more if published by Gollancz, as by that time I was becoming known to the Gollancz public. With Warburg these difficulties don't arise. He is less interested in propaganda and in any case his views are near enough to mine to prevent serious disagreement. From Gollancz's own point of view I do not imagine I am a good proposition either. Having me on his list means that from time to time he will publish a book which neither he nor his friends can disapprove° of. It seems to me that if he will agree it would be better to scrap the contract. If he won't agree I will keep to the strict letter, ie. as regards two more novels, and I have no doubt I can make this all right with Warburg. Perhaps you could approach Gollancz about this. You can quote this paragraph if you wish.

I saw W. J. Turner[3] the other day and asked him about the Britain in Pictures book. He said Edmund Blunden[4] is writing the companion volume and the two will be published simultaneously. I said that as they had had the MS a year I thought I ought to have some money. The agreed advance was £50 and I suggested they should give me £25 now. He said there would be no objection to this and I told him you would write to him, which you have perhaps done already.

Hamish Hamilton wrote to say Harper's would like to see something more of mine. I told him about the book of essays,[5] and perhaps if the Dial Press people turn it down it might be worth showing it to Harpers,° though I shouldn't think it is much in their line.

Yours sincerely
Eric Blair

1. *The English People*; see *2475*.
2. *Nineteen Eighty-Four*; see *2677*, n. 4.
3. See *2682*, n. 2 for Turner and for the matter of the advance.
4. Edmund Blunden (1896–1974; CBE), poet, editor, man of letters; see *1401*, n. 1. He worked with Orwell on broadcasts to India on English literature for the BBC. He contributed *English Villages* as No. 11 in the Britain in Pictures series, 1941.
5. *Critical Essays* (*Dickens, Dali & Others* in the United States).

2695. Contract with *Polemic*

3 July 1945

On 3 July 1945, Orwell entered into a contract with Rodney Phillips to contribute four articles to *Polemic: A Magazine of Philosophy, Psychology &*

Aesthetics, edited by Humphrey Slater. He had already contributed one article—
'Notes on Nationalism' (see *2668*)—to *Polemic*, 1, for which he had been paid
£25. The first manuscript was to be delivered on or before 1 October 1945 and the
next three at three-monthly intervals. Orwell was to be paid twenty-five guineas
for each article (£26.5.0) and he was to retain copyright. The witness to Phillips's
signature was Celia Mary Kirwan, described as Manager, Rodney Phillips &
Co. Celia Kirwan (later Celia Goodman) was the twin of Arthur Koestler's wife,
Mamaine. She was twenty-nine at this time, and she and Orwell became close
friends. See Crick, 483–84; Shelden, 442: U.S. 405. See also *3590A*

The first article under the terms of the contract was 'The Prevention of
Literature.' It was not submitted until 12 November 1945 (six weeks late) and
was published in *Polemic*, 2, January 1946; see *2832*. The other articles were:
'Second Thoughts on James Burnham,' *Polemic*, 3, May 1946, later reprinted as a
pamphlet entitled *James Burnham and the Managerial Revolution* (see *2989*);
'Politics vs. Literature,' *Polemic*, 5, September–October 1946 (see *3089*); 'Lear,
Tolstoy and the Fool,' *Polemic*, 7, March 1947 (see *3181*).

Orwell also wrote the Editorial for *Polemic*, 3, *(2988)* and annotated Randall
Swingler's 'The Right to Free Expression,' *Polemic*, 5. *(3090)*

2696. To Jack Hilton

4 July 1945   Typewritten

27B Canonbury Square   Islington   London N 1

Dear Mr Hilton,[1]

Thanks for your letter, just forwarded to me by the Observer. I don't believe
we ever met but we knew each other through Richard Rees[2] and others and
we were going to have met when I was in Yorkshire in 1936, but it fell
through somehow. Why don't you come in to tea some day at the above? If
you are working at Hackney I don't think it can be far—you take the bus that
goes up Balls Pond Road, which leads into St Paul's Road, which is just near
me. I am nearly always at home except on Wednesdays and Fridays and have
tea about half past six. You probably didn't know, but I am sorry to say I lost
my wife 3 months ago, and I have a little boy aged 14 months, and I have a
nurse-housekeeper who looks after him and me. On the other hand if you're
in the middle of London we can meet for lunch or dinner some day. I can
introduce you to the Tribune people, if you don't know them already, who
might be useful to you for a start, also to people on various other papers. Did
you know Warburg? I can't remember whether or not it was he who
published that book of yours. If there's anyone you specially want to meet tell
me and I'll try and fix it.

I've now just read the P.S. to your letter giving your times of work. How
about coming in to tea this coming Sunday, ie the 8th? If you're coming from
the WC area, the 19 and 30 buses both go to Highbury Corner which is 5
minutes walk from here.

I've lost touch with Richard Rees for over a year and the last letter I sent
him came back. He was in the Navy. I trust nothing has happened to him, but

I think I'd have seen it if it had. I think you knew Jack Common[3] too. I sometimes run into him, but I don't know where he is living at the moment. He is working at films.

Looking forward to seeing you.

Yours sincerely
Eric Blair

1. John (Jack) Hilton (1900–1983), author, born in Oldham, Lancashire, was the son of a general labourer. He published *Caliban Shrieks* (1935), *Champion* (1938), *English Ways* (1940), *Laugh at Polonius* (1942), and *English Ribbon* (1950), contributed to *Authors Take Sides on the Spanish War* (1937) and *Seven Shifts* (edited by Jack Common; 1938), and wrote for *The Adelphi*, 1934–39. Orwell reviewed *Caliban Shrieks* (see 240) and *English Ways* (see 647). He met Hilton several times in 1945. See Clive Fleay, ' "Voices in the Gallery." George Orwell and Jack Hilton,' *Middlesex Polytechnic History Journal*, 2 (Spring 1985), 55–81.
2. Sir Richard Rees (1900–1970), joint editor of *The Adelphi*, was Orwell's literary executor (with Sonia Orwell), and author of *George Orwell: Fugitive from the Camp of Victory* (1961). He gave Orwell much encouragement in his early days as a writer and remained a friend throughout Orwell's life. For a fuller note, see 95.
3. Jack Common (1903–1968), a Tyneside working-class man who worked on *The Adelphi*, 1932–36, wrote a number of books. He took Orwell's cottage in Wallington when Orwell was in Marrakech, and they remained friends until Orwell's death. See also *295, n. 1, 1086, n. 1.*

2697. 'Authors Deserve a New Deal'

Manchester Evening News, 5 July 1945

About a year ago Sir Osbert Sitwell published a little book, "A Letter To My Son," in which he discussed with great vigour—and perhaps also with a certain amount of perversity—the position of the artist in modern society. The result was a series of controversies, some of which turned upon a problem which Sir Osbert had only lightly touched—the economic position of the artist and the question of patronage.[1]

Now that the war period is ending and numbers of young men are presumably getting ready to start on a literary career this problem is more urgent than ever. For it ought to be realised that the bad state of present-day English literature is in part due to the difficulty of keeping alive simply by writing books.

The majority of full-length books before the war were sold at 7s. 6d., and at present 10s. 6d. would perhaps be an average price. Royalties vary as between the different publishing houses and the rate paid rises as the sales rise, but in general each copy that is sold does not bring the author much more than a shilling.

A novel, or some comparable type of book—that is to say, a book not needing a great deal of research, but on the other hand not written in the slapdash manner of a political pamphlet—generally takes round about a year to write. Sometimes it takes only six or eight months, but few serious writers can average more than one book a year. This means that a writer who devotes his whole time to books must be sure of a sale of 10,000 copies in order to earn a gross income of five or six hundred pounds a year.

But in practice 10,000 copies is far above the average sale. If a book sells 2,000 it has done respectably, and there are plenty of "established" writers whose average sales are round about 5,000. It is true that sales of 100,000 and even a million do sometimes occur, but such things are hardly likelier to happen to any serious writer than winning the Irish sweepstake. The upshot is that it is almost impossible to live simply by writing books—almost impossible, that is to say, to earn enough money to secure the spare time and peace of mind that writing books demands.

And in fact only a few score, or at most a few hundred, people in England do live solely by books, and a proportion even of those have private incomes. The rest earn the major part of their living by journalism or broadcasting or writing scripts for films, or have some alternative profession.

Now look at it from the reader's point of view. Compared with smoking, drinking, or going to the pictures, how much does reading cost you?

If you buy a book for 10s. 6d., spend three hours in reading it and don't re-sell it, you are paying for your amusement at about the same rate as you would pay in one of the more expensive seats at a theatre. But in fact the vast majority of people don't buy books to any great extent. There are many people who read several books a week but never think of buying a new book, other than a cheap reprint such as a Penguin. They take books out of the lending libraries, paying twopence a time—twopence, that is to say, for three hours' recreation. Very often, however, they borrow books from the public library, where they pay nothing except an infinitesimally small fraction of the sum they pay in rates.[2]

Books in the public libraries are in some cases review copies on which the author has received no royalty. If they are popular books they are generally rebound in a stout cover which makes them almost immortal, so that literally hundreds of people can read a book without the author receiving anything except the shilling or so which he had from the original sale.

It would seem that if book-writing is to survive as a means of livelihood the public must somehow be persuaded to spend more money on books. Either books must be made more expensive (this is obviously a bad solution), or people must acquire the habit of buying books rather than borrowing them, or some arrangement must be made by which the author draws his percentage every time a book is borrowed, the library rates being raised correspondingly.

No one demands that authors should receive incomes comparable to those of Chancery lawyers. You do not make a man into a better writer by raising his earnings from £1,000 a year to £5,000. On the other hand it is not to be expected that anyone can live on £4 a week and also produce books.

The present arrangement, by which the writers of books have to make their living mainly out of journalism, is a bad one. Journalism brings in more money, but it also entails a kind of life that requires more money and which makes concentration on one subject and prolonged spells of work very difficult. Good books have been written by people who, like Trollope, or James Joyce, or Joseph Conrad, were earning their living in another way, but for any ordinary person book-writing is a full-time job which it is difficult to combine with such exhausting work as journalism or broadcasting.

Writing, like every other activity, has to have an economic basis, and the writer's possible patrons are three—rich men, the State, and the big public. As for the first two, their undesirability hardly needs pointing out. But if the writer is to escape from their clutches, then the public which reads his books must pay him enough to give him reasonable security, a comfortable place to work in, and freedom from extraneous jobs—all of which, allowing for the present purchasing-power of money, adds up to not less than £500 a year.

The reading public, in fact, must expect to pay for its books, just as the drinking public expects to pay for its beer. And the fairest—though not, perhaps, the most easily organised—way of bringing this about would be to raise the price of library subscriptions and charge a small fee on books borrowed from the public libraries, passing some of the extra profit on to the author.[3]

Without doubt there are people who will grow indignant at this suggestion—yet the same people think nothing of spending half-a-crown on a seat at the pictures and two and four-pence on twenty cigarettes. Meanwhile, writers who might be doing good work are driven away from literature or forced to make it a part-time occupation, not because they are attracted elsewhere by "big money" (no one who was after big money would ever choose any branch of literature as a profession), but because books by themselves will not even yield a bare living.

Of late years there has been more and more tendency for the writer to be subsidised, directly or indirectly, by the State, which is primarily interested in propaganda and will not pay for experimental work. The direct support of the big public is a better basis for literature, and an extra twopence on library subscriptions would be the surest way of obtaining it.[4]

[Fee: £8.8.0; 4.7.45]

1. For Orwell's discussion of *A Letter to My Son*, see 'As I Please,' 41, 2547, and 44, 2562.
2. The *Manchester Evening News* gave details of 'Manchester's Book Bill' in a box within the text of Orwell's article:

    Last year Manchester Corporation bought 72,000 books (7,000 for the reference libraries, 61,000 for the Central and district lending libraries, and the remainder for hospitals, prison libraries, etc.). These books and binding charges cost £25,000.

    Three years ago, when costs were not so high, the same amount of money would have bought 100,000 volumes. The number of books withdrawn as worn out or out of date last year was 62,000, leaving a net increase to the libraries of only 10,000.

    Out of a total estimated income of £138,000 the Libraries' Committee propose to spend £26,000 this year on books and binding.

3. The law now allows that writers may receive a royalty based on the number of times their books are borrowed from public libraries.
4. The final two paragraphs are reproduced as printed in the *Manchester Evening News*, but it may be that they should be read in the reverse order.

2698. To Michael Meyer[1]

5 July 1945   Typewritten postcard

27B Canonbury Square   N 1
Thursday

O.K. The Czarda° Restaurant, Dean Street, Wednesday 11th at 12.30.

George

1. Michael Meyer was at the Operational Research Section of an R.A.F. station in High Wycombe; see *2008, n. 1.*

2699. Review of *Nine Tales from Les Contes Drolatiques* by Honoré de Balzac, translated by J. Plummer, R. Scutt, and J. P. Collas, illustrations by R. A. Brandt

The Observer, 8 July 1945

"The Contes Drolatiques," now newly translated, are usually considered to be in the tradition of Rabelais, and indeed are sometimes spoken of as though they were a kind of continuation of Rabelais. Balzac himself, in his Prologue, draws the mantle of "our good master . . . the prince of all wisdom and all comedy" very closely about him, and here and there attempts an imitation of certain of Rabelais's mannerisms; but the resemblance, if any, is superficial, and the motive for invoking Rabelais in the first place was probably to give a respectable colour to pornography.

The present collection contains nine tales, and the derivation of seven of them seems to be either from Boccaccio or from the narrative poems attributed to Villon. They turn on the immemorial themes of cuckoldry and the swindling of creditors. "Concerning a Provost who did not recognise things" is an ingenious story in this line. "The Sermon of the Merry Vicar of Meudon" is direct imitation of Rabelais, fairly successful so far as atmosphere goes, but somewhat pointless as a story, and suggesting, together with various remarks dropped here and there in the book, that Balzac thought of Rabelais as primarily a humorist. "The Succubus" is a longer story than the rest and different in character. It purports to be an account of the trial, torture and ultimate burning by the Inquisition of a young woman who was believed to be a demon in disguise. The story gives plenty of opportunities for salaciousness and Balzac takes full advantage of them, but his main purpose seems to have been to make a humanitarian protest against bigotry and superstition. The atmosphere and implied moral outlook of this story recall some of Anatole France's stories in the Abbé Coignard series.

It is difficult not to feel that in nearly all of these stories Balzac is simply indulging in dirt and making it respectable by a veneer of archaism. Rabelais was probably regarded as a pornographer in nineteenth-century France, as he certainly was in nineteenth-century England. Archdeacon Grantly, it will be remembered, kept his works in "a secret drawer beneath his table,"[1] and in a well-known poem of Browning's a "little edition of Rabelais" is part of the general racketiness of a bachelor's chambers. To this day, vilely-printed paper-covered editions of Urquhart's translation are sold together with "Mademoiselle de Maupin" and the "Complete Works of Aristotle." But for some reason it has always been the fashion to claim that Rabelais's obscenities are "healthy" and "natural," and altogether of a different order from those of, say, Sterne or Petronius. The word "Rabelaisian" is habitually used to indicate a sort of earthy coarseness which aims only at being funny, and is in no way demoralising: indeed, Rabelais has often been used as a stick to beat such writers as Swinburne, George Moore or D. H. Lawrence. Actually there are passages in his work that are among the most morbid and disgusting ever written, but since it was agreed that he was "healthy" he could be enjoyed by Puritans, and traces of his influence turn up in unexpected quarters, for instance, Charles Kingsley's "Water Babies." In declaring himself a disciple of Rabelais, Balzac was in effect proclaiming that his intentions were harmless, and was then free to go ahead with what as often as not are imitations of Boccaccio or the "Heptameron."[2]

The trouble was, as one is bound to feel when reading such stories as "How the Château d'Azay came to be built" or "The Monk Amador," that between Balzac and Boccaccio there lay the Reformation. In his Prologue Balzac explains that he has ("regretfully," he adds) eliminated the "old words" which are now regarded as unprintable. The result, almost all the way through, is an unbearable archness: nearly every paragraph refers to something which the reader understands perfectly well, but which can be mentioned only in a sniggering indirect way. When the "Decameron" was compiled, there was not much that could not be said, but in addition these stories were the product of a civilisation which had become almost pagan. There is naughty-naughtiness here and there in Boccaccio's tales, but in general their aim is not to be shocking. Religion is guyed in a manner that the most violent anti-clerical would not adopt in our own day. With centuries of Puritanism behind him, Balzac cannot attain the innocence of Boccaccio. He is conscious all the while of how naughty he is being, and how cleverly he is expressing unprintable meanings by innocent-seeming metaphors. The result is a rather laboured, distasteful facetiousness. At a time when many of Balzac's novels are unobtainable, it seems a pity to have wasted paper on this unsuccessful minor work.

[Fee: £10.0.0; 6.7.45]

1. In Anthony Trollope's *The Warden* (1855), Archdeacon Grantly (not 'Grantley', as in *The Observer*), makes ceremonial preparations for writing a sermon, locks the door of his study, takes 'a volume of Rabelais' from a secret drawer, and passes the morning by amusing himself with the 'witty mischief of Panurge' (chapter 8).
2. The *Heptameron* is a collection of love stories attributed to Marguerite of Navarre (1492–1549). The title means 'seven days' (compare Boccaccio's *Decameron*).

2700. To Maurice Hussey

10 July 1945   Typewritten

27B Canonbury Square   Islington   London N 1

Dear Mr Hussey,[1]

Many thanks for your letter of 6th July.

I am sorry, but I cannot possibly make any arrangements to lecture. I not only cannot find the time, but it is not at all easy for me to get out of London. Please forgive me.

Yours truly
[Signed] Geo. Orwell
George Orwell

1. Maurice P. Hussey (1925–) was, at this time, honorary secretary to the Doughty Society, Downing College, Cambridge. This invitation may have arisen from Dr. F. R. Leavis's suggestion that Orwell should have been asked to speak at Downing (8 January 1944); see *2402*. Hussey later edited and wrote a number of educational and academic books, including a modernised version of the *Chester Mystery Plays* (1957), an edition of Jonson's *Bartholomew Fair*, and a collection of essays, *Jonson and the Cavaliers* (both 1964); and he wrote *The World of Shakespeare and His Contemporaries* (1971).

2701. Review of *The English Way* by Pierre Maillaud; *A Steel Man in India* by John L. Keenan; *Joseph the Provider* by Thomas Mann

Manchester Evening News, 12 July 1945

At a time like the present, when the trouble in Syria[1] is still making headlines in the French Press, it is pleasant to be reminded that there are some Frenchmen who do not dislike us. But actually, friendly and even over-friendly though it is, M. Maillaud's book gives a truer picture of the contemporary French attitude towards England than one would gather from the utterances of certain public men.[2] Almost any Englishman who has been in France recently would agree that Anglophile feeling has never been so strong, and that now, if ever, is the moment for the two countries to move into closer partnership.

M. Maillaud's book, which is aimed at the British rather than the French public, is first and foremost a plea for Anglo-French co-operation and for an understanding of what that co-operation would mean.

However, it is also an analysis of English civilization and the English character, of the structure and peculiarities of British political parties, and of the policies and strategies that have been dictated by Britain's special position as a part of Europe and at the same time the centre of an extra-European empire. M. Maillaud has lived in England for the last fourteen or fifteen years and he knows our country quite exceptionally well. Throughout most of the war he was one of the small but brilliant team of

French broadcasters who succeeded in making the B.B.C. the most trusted source of news in occupied France.

Probably the most valuable part of his book is his examination of British foreign policy between the wars. Politically he is himself a Liberal, and the qualities he most admires in England are respect for minorities and the ability to make deep changes without either shedding blood or losing touch with tradition. But with the detachment of a foreigner he is able to see that these qualities spring out of Britain's insular position, which is also a cause of ignorance and complacency.

British conduct of foreign affairs between 1930 and 1940 is not a thing to be proud of, and M. Maillaud does not spare it. He rightly points out the part played by sheer class feeling in the Conservative party's appeasement of Fascism, but he also emphasises—what is less popular to mention nowadays—the pacifism of the British working class and the unrealistic outlook of the Left wing° parties who demanded an active foreign policy but were unwilling to back it up with adequate armies.

It is important that as many foreign critics as possible should point this out, for few people are aware of the disastrous effects that were produced in Europe by the Labour party's opposition to conscription. But M. Maillaud is looking deeper than the surface and he sees that part of the trouble is that nearly all classes in England are guilty of xenophobia. The strip of water which has given them security has also given them a conscious or unconscious contempt for foreigners—especially, M. Maillaud adds, those who are "noisiest and darkest-haired"—which leads to a lack of interest in foreign affairs and a too slow reaction to danger.

The appeasement policy was due partly to the apathy of the masses who, if they paid any attention to Europe at all, were inclined to prefer the Germans to the French. But it was also due in part to the British Government's need to consider the Dominions, who were none too willing to be mixed up in European quarrels.

The fact that M. Maillaud points this out is sufficient to stamp him as an exceptionally acute observer. Britain's special relationship with the United States, and the pull it exercises on British policy, is obvious enough, but there are very few Europeans indeed who realise that Australia and Canada are not simply provinces governed from Whitehall and that public opinion in those countries has to be considered when Britain makes any move in Europe.

M. Maillaud ends his book with an urgent plea to Britain to abandon the policy implied in the Teheran agreement (this book appears to have been written early in 1944) and to remember that she is part of Europe and that her main interests lie there. In 1940, he says, all Europe looked up to Britain as the defender of Western civilisation. But the special position then gained could be lost if Britain committed herself to a "Big Four" policy which would tie her to Russia and America and force her to be indifferent to the fate of the smaller nations.

What he would like to see is a federation of all the Western European States—an attractive project, but one which is less likely of realisation now than it may have seemed when the book was written. However, the first step towards it would be a better understanding between Britain and France, and this book should at least help in achieving that.

"A Steel Man in India" justifies the statement on its dust jacket that it is "an unusual book." Indeed, it would be difficult for a book about India to be freer from the familiar atmosphere and subject matter, although there is plenty of whisky in it, and not a few tigers. It is the story of the building-up of the great Tata steel mills at Jamahedpur, with which Mr. Kennan, a blast furnace engineer, was associated for twenty-five years. Not long before the other war, the Tatas, an extremely enlightened and enterprising family of Parsi business men (incidentally Mr. Saklatvala, for many years Communist M.P. for Battersea,[3] was a scion of this family), made up their minds that it was possible to produce steel in India and set to work to do so in face of considerable discouragement from the British. The Tata Steel Works are now the biggest in the British Empire.

As in the case of various other Indian industries, there was obstruction from British business interests which feared the possible competition and the Tatas had to go to America for their machinery and most of their experts. In the first world war, however, the extra steel was of great value to the Allied cause and during the present war the short-sighted policy of impeding the industrialisation of India has been largely abandoned.

Mr. Keenan writes in a slap-dash way, and his occasional comments on Indian politics are very shallow. All he is really interested in is steel and the men who produce it, and so long as he sticks to that subject he is always readable.

"Joseph the Provider" is the fourth and last volume of Thomas Mann's enormous paraphrase of the Book of Genesis. It runs to 447 pages and disciples of Thomas Mann will no doubt read every word of it, but the average reader may be inclined to ask what is the point of struggling through all this verbiage when one can get the substance of it from fifteen short chapters of the Bible.

[Fee: £8.8.0; 11.7.45]

1. In 1945, Syria sought independence from French control. In May there were clashes between local people and French troops, and the French bombarded Damascus. The British, who, as a result of World War II, had forces in Syria, intervened. France was forced to evacuate its troops from Syria and Lebanon in 1946.
2. At the head of this review were reproduced photographs of ten prominent Frenchmen, each with a two-word description: Charles Boyer (actor), 'Latin romance'; Edouard Herriot (radical socialist politician), 'stubby provincial'; General Charles De Gaulle, 'rigid dignity'; Paul Reynaud (politician and prime minister), 'intellectual subtlety'; Maurice Chevalier (actor and singer), 'saucy wit'; Marshal Pétain, 'the Ancien regime'; Edouard Daladier (politician and premier), 'smooth shrewdness'; Jean Borotra (tennis champion), 'wiry vigour'; Georges Bidault (resistance leader and foreign minister), 'keen-eyed strength'; General De Lattre de Tassigny, 'ironic nonchalance.' These were probably not Orwell's descriptions.
3. Shapurji Saklatvala (1874–1936), a wealthy Parsee who was born in Bombay, represented Battersea North as Independent Labour M.P., 1922–23 and 1924–29, but supported by the Labour Party. Then he stood for the Communist Party on a number of occasions, but was opposed by Labour and was not again elected. One of the British companies of the

International Brigade in the Spanish civil war (commanded by Tom Wintringham) was named after him.

2702. To George Woodcock

13 July 1945[1]   Postcard; handwritten

I hope you got my wire. I'm awfully sorry about Saturday, but on looking at my diary I found I had someone coming here. I could come next Friday (20th) if that's any good to you   G.O.

1. The message is undated, but the card was posted on 13 July 1945. It reproduces 'A Café in the Faubourg Montmartre' by Edgar Degas. Orwell sent Lydia Jackson a similar card on 31 March 1936; see *542A, n. 1.*

2703. Preparations for Second Edition of *Animal Farm*

Once a publisher had been found for *Animal Farm*, the chief reason for the delay in its publication was lack of paper caused by wartime shortages. The first edition was to be published on 17 August 1945, but a month earlier than this a second edition was being planned, because it was expected that more paper would become available. A letter of 19 July 1945 from Roger Senhouse, of Secker & Warburg, to Mr. W. Smith, of Morrison & Gibb, Ltd., printers of Tanfield, Edinburgh, refers to several of Secker's publications, including *Animal Farm* and *Critical Essays*:

> We have your sample of paper for approval in today—46 rms. 30 × 40. 50-lb. paper from W. Rolandson marked "For ANIMAL FARM and CRITICAL ESSAYS". Today we have heard from the makers that there is a further 10-cwts. manufactured, this being the increase in the present quota for the current period, and this too I will have sent up to you for one or other of the same titles. Let us take 20 rms. of the 46 now available and use this for a second edition of ANIMAL FARM and we can later decide whether to put the 10 extra cwts. into the CRITICAL ESSAYS, or some other title. I will give Mr. Norrington the order for this reprint tomorrow.
> . . . .
> George Orwell will be returning the proofs of his CRITICAL ESSAYS early next week, so that we may get on with this as the next title, after those already in progress.

An indication of how serious was the shortage of paper is given by a reference in the letter to copies of a book required for His Majesty's Stationery Office:

> It was unfortunate that we could not supply sufficient paper for WATER ON THE STEPS—2000 copies for the H.M.S.O. They will be coming before the end of the year.

2704. Review of *Freedom was Flesh and Blood* by José Antonio de Aguirre; *Personal Landscape: An Anthology of Exile*

Manchester Evening News, 19 July 1945

The Spanish civil war brought forth many strange stories, but few of the things that happened in the war itself can have been stranger than the subsequent adventures of the President of the Basque Republic.

The Basque country was overrun by Franco's forces, with large-scale Italian aid, early in 1937. From the start it had been isolated from the other territories held by the Republicans, and "non-intervention," plus Franco's superiority at sea, made it impossible for it to be supplied with food and weapons. However, Conservative opinion abroad was less hostile to the Basques than to the Central Spanish Government, and Senor Aguirre and some of his colleagues were able to remain in Paris as a Government-in-exile.

They were not even a government without subjects, since about 200,000 people, five per cent of the Basque population, had become refugees. Senor Aguirre had been lucky to escape from Spain with his life, but his real adventures began after the German invasion of May, 1940, which caught him in Belgium.

He and his family were cut off from returning to France, and though they had a front-seat view of the Dunkirk evacuation they failed to get a place on any of the boats. For a while they existed furtively in Brussels in acute danger of being identified by the Gestapo.

The Third Republic had given Senor Aguirre an asylum, but Franco had put a price on his head, and there could be no doubt what would happen if he fell into the hands of either the Germans or the Vichy French. He would be handed over to Franco and then shot, like Companys, the President of the Catalan Republic. Meanwhile all the ways into neutral or Allied territory seemed to be barred.

It then occurred to Senor Aguirre that much the best way out was through Germany. Apparently there is a Basque maxim to the effect that when you see a crowd going in one direction you should go in the other direction, and it was on this principle that he acted.

He grew a heavy moustache and renamed himself "Dr. Alvarez," a citizen of Panama, while his wife posed as a Venezuelan widow named "Senora Guerra." This name was chosen because if one of the children blurted out his real surname it would be taken as a mispronunciation. Through various friends at the South American consulates, it was not difficult to get hold of false papers, and after a certain amount of fuss and questioning the permit to enter Germany was given.

Senor Aguirre spent about six months in Germany and was rash enough to keep a diary, which he succeeded in bringing away with him. It was the period of the German victories in Greece and the Balkans, but even at that date the serious economic strain of the war was becoming apparent, and the British air offensive was growing in intensity.

Having once got the Gestapo stamp on their papers, neither Senor Aguirre nor his wife had much trouble with the authorities. The chief danger was the children, who were always liable to begin speaking in Basque.

A little before the German invasion of the U.S.S.R. the whole family managed to reach Sweden, whence they sailed for Rio de Janeiro, with their false papers in perfect order.

This is not a well-written book, but, apart from the interest of the German interlude, it is valuable because it expresses the outlook of a Catholic democrat. Throughout the past twenty years an impression has prevailed that a Catholic, as such, is bound to be pro-Fascist, and during the Spanish Civil War the Catholic press in nearly all countries did its best to give colour to this.

It almost escaped notice that the Basque country was solidly anti-Franco and at the same time one of the most Catholic parts of Spain. The Basque Republic, as Senor Aguirre points out, is the oldest democracy in Europe, and extremist doctrines of either Right or Left have never been able to gain a footing there. About a third of his book is given over to an examination of the issues in the world war and to a sincere but perhaps over-hopeful profession of faith in the future of democracy.

"Personal Landscape," compiled in Cairo by Robin Fedden, Terence Tiller, Lawrence Durrell, Hugh Gordon Porteous and others, does not profess to represent any group or "school." Its common denominator is homesickness, and it is not particularly surprising that one of its items should be an essay on "Finnegans Wake" and another an essay on Shakespeare's Sonnets (incidentally the last-named contribution, by Mr. Gwyn Williams, discusses the interesting theory that the Dark Lady of the Sonnets may have been a negress).

An introductory essay by Mr. Robin Fedden explains how the anthology came to be compiled and analyses the strange and rather unfriendly cultural atmosphere of modern Egypt.

It would seem that much of the valuable literary result of the Middle Eastern campaigns has been the opening-up of contemporary Greek literature to English readers. Contacts between Greek and English writers did exist before the war, but the war itself has naturally produced more of them, and this anthology contains translations from the works of several Greek poets, besides an essay on C. P. Cavafy, the Alexandrian poet, who died in 1933 and of whom most of us had probably not heard.

Most of us had not heard of Elie Papadimitriou either, but it is evident from the translations appearing here that we ought to have done so. The English poets who get the best showing are Terence Tiller, Keith Douglas and Lawrence Durrell. It would be untrue to say that this anthology contains no trivialities, but it is one of the most promising and interesting collections of work by writers in the Services that have yet appeared.

[Fee: £8.8.0; 18.7.45]

2705. 'Personal Notes on Scientifiction'

Leader Magazine, 21 July 1945

This article, entered in Orwell's Payments Book at 9 July 1945 (fee: £15) was described in the heading in *Leader*: 'Personal Notes. A New Feature by George Orwell.' The second article to be published, on 28 July 1945, 'Funny, But Not Vulgar,' was written much earlier. It is entered in the Payments Book at 1 December 1944 and reprinted in this edition at that date; see *2585*. Only these two articles in this 'new series' appeared. An announcement in *Leader* for 4 August 1945, at the bottom of the correspondence column, stated: 'We are sorry to say that Mr Orwell is not able to continue this feature which we have announced.' It is not known why Orwell did not continue. His letter to Mrs. Belloc Lowndes, 31 July 1945 (see *2711*), states that he had stopped writing for *Leader* and suggests he might start 'the column,' that is, such 'personal notes,' in *Tribune*. He did do so from 12 October 1945. He might also have felt that his *Leader* notes conflicted with his 'As I Please' column, though he did not take that up again until 8 November 1946. The essay 'Scientifiction' was illustrated by a reproduction of the cover of an American magazine with the caption '10 Cents a Sensation.' Until 21 October 1944, *Leader Magazine* had been called *The Leader* (and was popularly still so known).

Recently a friend in America sent me a batch of ten-cent illustrated papers of the kind which are known generically as "comics" and consist entirely of coloured strip cartoons. Although bearing such titles as *Marvel Comics* or *Famous Funnies*, they are, in fact, mainly given over to "scientifiction"—that is, steel robots, invisible men, prehistoric monsters, death rays, invasions from Mars, and such-like.

Seen in the mass these things are very disquieting. Quite obviously they tend to stimulate fantasies of power, and in the last resort their subject matter boils down to magic and sadism. You can hardly look at a page without seeing somebody flying through the air (a surprising number of the characters are able to fly), or somebody socking somebody else on the jaw, or an under-clad young woman fighting for her honour—and her ravisher is just as likely to be a steel robot or a fifty-foot dinosaur as a human being. The whole thing is just a riot of nonsensical sensationalism, with none of the genuine scientific interest of the H. G. Wells stories from which this class of fiction originally sprang.

Who reads these papers is uncertain. Evidently they are intended primarily for children, but the advertisements and the ever-present sex appeal suggest that they are read by adults as well.

What is strange, when one looks at this poisonous rubbish, is to remember that several generations of English children were brought up largely on American children's books, because on the whole those were the best. At the top of the list came *Uncle Tom's Cabin*, *Uncle Remus*, and *Tom Sawyer* and *Huckleberry Finn*: then, more in the nature of girls' books, there were Louisa M. Alcott's *Little Women*, *Good Wives* and *Little Men* (the last-named one was a bit *too* high-minded, however), and James Habberton's *Helen's Babies*: and also—these were definitely girls' books, but still not to be despised—*Rebecca of Sunnybrook Farm* and Susan Cooleridge's "Katy" books. Later in time there were Booth Tarkington's "Penrod" stories, Ernest Thompson Seton's *Wild Animals I have Known* and other similar books, and Jack London's *White Fang* and *Call of the Wild*: not to mention the Buffalo Bill stories and the Buster Brown comic supplements.

From these and kindred sources the English child acquired quite a detailed picture of the American scene. He knew a lot about woodchucks, gophers, chipmunks, raccoon hunting, buggy riding, keeping the woodpile full, prairie dogs, whip-poor-wills, coyotes, covered wagons and the mortgage on the old homestead. The peculiarity of the American books, and especially those written prior to about 1880, was their wholesome, high-spirited atmosphere, and the decent simple civilisation that they implied. The basis of nearly all of them was home life and the Bible. And though a book like *Little Women* may now seem over-civilised as well as faintly ridiculous, it is still a pleasant patch for one's memory to linger on.[1]

It is queer that, after so short an interval of time, the typical juvenile literature of America should be stuff that many English parents would actually hesitate to put into a child's hands.

Everyone has at least one story about the imbecilities of wartime censorship. My own favourite instance is a War Office pamphlet which I happen to possess, entitled *German Infantry Weapons* and giving a short account of the rifles, machine guns, etc. in use in the German army. It is marked on the cover: "Not to fall into enemy hands."

Now that the war, or at least a good part of it, is over, would it not be possible to let up on some of the sillier kinds of restrictions—for example, censorship of letters passing between allied countries? Letters from the United States usually reach me plastered with censor's stamps, and I know from the time they take to get there my outgoing letters are suffering the same fate.

Throughout the war I have been writing periodical articles for American magazines. All of them, of course, have been opened en route, and not only have a number been tampered with in the most pettifogging way, but in some cases the censors have actually cut passages without letting the recipient know that any deletion has been made.

War is war, and I do not mind this kind of thing very much, but I do mind the delay which trans-Atlantic censorship is still causing. Quite recently, airmail letters from London to New York were liable to take as much as six weeks. They could do the journey quicker than that in a sailing ship.

Another peacetime pleasure I am looking forward to is being able to buy decent maps again. The panic legislation of 1940 forbade the selling of maps larger in scale than one inch to the mile, and at that time even Home Guards trying to buy maps of their own areas had every kind of difficulty put in their way. Possibly the ban has now been lifted, but maps on even the smallest scale are still difficult to get. I wonder when it will again be possible to walk into a stationer's shop and buy the excellent 25 inch to the mile Ordnance maps, which show every cowshed and almost every tree and on which you can easily mark down a good blackberry bush or a root of sweetbriar with sufficient accuracy to be sure of finding it again the following year?

However, one cannot leave the subject of censorship without remarking that, in England, official censorship is not the only or the worst kind. It is wonderful what a number of good stories fail to get into the newspapers, *not* because of any official ban, but because they happen to conflict with the orthodoxy of the moment and there is consequently an all-round tacit agreement that it "wouldn't do" to print them.

For example, I am told that the last speech made to his ministers by Mr. Arciszewsky, the premier of the outgoing London Polish Government, began:

"In the words of a man whom we once trusted, I have nothing to offer you except blood, toil, tears and sweat. . . ." but I believe none of the papers had the guts to mention it.

As I passed the church door I paused for a moment to listen to the hymn that was being sung inside. The words that floated out to me—not the words as they would have appeared on paper, but as they were actually pronounced and as I transliterated them a few minutes later—were something like this:

> *Er*bide with me farce—falls the *ye*ventide—
> *Ther* darkness deeperns—Lord with me erbide—
> When *nuther* helpers—fail ern comforts flee—
> Help *pov* the helpless *so er*—bide with me!

And it struck me, not for the first time, that something really ought to be done about modern South-English pronunciation. It is a good general rule that one accent is not intrinsically better or worse than another, but something is clearly wrong when people's manner of speaking leads to misunderstanding, or when the sounds they make cannot be rendered by the existing methods of spelling.

Most of us now speak in so slovenly a way that if you ask for a threepenny bus ticket you are as often as not given a three-halfpenny one, or vice versa. And how exactly would one write down the mystic formula which any two Londoners invariably utter after concluding a transaction? The nearest you could come to it would be "nkew," or perhaps simply "N.Q.," Or take the current pronunciation of such words as "passionate," "deliberate," "vegetable," "actual" or "average." The closest possible renderings would, I should say, be: "pashnit," "delibrit," "vejtbl," "ackchl," "avridge."

In countless words ending in -ion, -ate, -ial and so forth, the vowel sounds have simply slipped out and been replaced by sounds for which there is no equivalent in our alphabet. What is the final vowel sound in "elephant," for instance? There just isn't one, the current pronunciation of the word being something like "elefnt": or at any rate it is certainly nearer to "ele*phunt*" than "elephant."

All of which suggests that if we are ever to have that rational spelling about which there is talk and controversy from time to time, more will be involved than a good system of phonetics and foolproof rules. The Oxford dictionary can give you an accurate phonetic rendering of a word like "culture," but it still spells it as though there were a "t" in it and ignores the fact that the current pronunciation is "culcher."

The spelling reformers will have to make up their minds whether to reform our pronunciation as well, or whether to accept spoken English as past praying for and adjust the written language accordingly.

These 'Personal Notes' prompted several letters, all but the last appearing in *Leader Magazine* on 4 August 1945; the final letter was published on 11 August.

Why does George Orwell in his amusing article this week accuse the Southern English, exclusively, of mispronunciation?

It is common enough all the world over wherever English is spoken and has, I fancy, been always so. I have in mind some correspondence on the subject appearing in the Melbourne *Argus* about 40 years ago, started by a letter which accused the townspeople of Ballarat of habitually clipping the word "Thank you" to "Ku."

This brought indignant letters from Ballarat and, a heated correspondence being raged for some days, the matter was finally clinched by a Ballarat man. He, after many years' residence in that town, was able to assert with confidence that people there neither said "Thank you" nor "Ku."

H. H. Levy

Mr. George Orwell must have remarkable hearing powers to listen outside a church and be able to say that each member of the congregation was singing "Abide with me" in the slipshod manner as printed in his article. If each person was not singing the same, then Mr. Orwell could not have heard with such precise definition. What he heard was a volume of sound, distorted probably by the acoustics of the building which he was not in, and muffled to some extent by the organ.

Has he listened to people in other parts of the country? Up in the north mispronunciation is glorified by being referred to as a brogue, but it is ungrammatically pronounced English. Maybe if Mr. Orwell listened at a church, again outside, in the north, he might hear something like this—

A = bahd wi' me = f-asst falls t'eventahd
T'darkness deepens = Lord wi' me abahd

and so on. Hardly any person speaks the King's English strictly according to rule. Indeed, I think it would sound pedantic and stilted, except in the case of an oration.

Maybe Mr. Orwell would be surprised if a record of his conversation was made without his knowing and he heard the result and then the same words spoken strictly according to rules of pronunciation.

E. Newton Bungey

Your correspondent, George Orwell, quotes as imbecile a War Office pamphlet on "German Infantry Weapons" because it is marked on the cover "Not to fall into enemy hands."

As there is still a war on, I feel that readers should be reminded that to guard against giving an enemy an idea of the extent of our knowledge of his own weapons is not imbecile. On the contrary, it is one of the most vital principles of security.

H. I. Parrott

It is plain that Mr. Orwell is confined too much to his study. His paragraph on Censorship is out of date.

Transatlantic censorship ceased some little time ago, and there is nothing to hinder him walking into any booksellers and buying as large a scale map as he wants. He can even get them of the recently most secret coastal areas at H.M. Stationery Office shops, where they are displayed in the windows.

J. R. K. Pirie

I hasten to inform all interested readers that real science-fiction has nothing to do with the lurid stuff mentioned in George Orwell's article.

I have been a reader of science-fiction for about 18 years and can testify to its high standard. The magazines which are devoted to science-fiction stories are excellent publications of very good literary standard. Scientists and university professors are among the authors whose work appears in these magazines.

The stories often contain much real scientific knowledge in a form made fascinating and understandable to the man in the street.

Norman Burgess

1. Orwell developed these reflections on American writing for children in 'Riding Down from Bangor,' *Tribune,* 22 November 1946, *3123.*

2706. Review of *Man the Measure* by Erich Kahler

The Observer, 22 July 1945

As its name implies, this enormous book (640 pages, with 30 pages of bibliography) is concerned with the problems of humanism, but it is also an attempt to summarise world history from the Bronze Age onwards. The author is himself a somewhat tentative or uneasy humanist. He sees the gradual elimination of religious belief as something necessary to human emancipation, and he accepts the principle of progress and evolution to the point of denying that there is something called "human nature" which is the same in all ages. Indeed, some of the most interesting passages in his book are those in which he asserts, against Marx and similar thinkers, that motives which we now assume to have almost the status of instincts did not operate until comparatively recently:—

Some modern economists and sociologists have tried to prove that there were traces of capitalism as far back as Babylon. But what they discovered is not capitalism. Capitalism is not identical with wealth and mobile property, it is not identical with money-making and money-lending, not even with a mere productive investment of property. All this is not capitalism in itself, for all this may serve a life principle, alien to economic aims, it may be done for a human end, a human purpose, for something a human being can enjoy.

The context for this passage is a brief biographical sketch of the first real capitalists, the Fuggers, who financed and almost controlled the Hapsburg Empire, but who, unlike the Italian merchant princes, were unable to use their money for any purpose except making more money. In a rather similar passage Mr. Kahler sets out to explain why it was that the physical sciences failed to develop in antiquity. The reason, he says, was not intellectual inferiority or even technical backwardness but simply a different habit of mind:

The Byzantine mathematician and architect, Anthemius . . . was even completely aware of the technical application of steam pressure. He could easily have invented the steam engine, but he used his knowledge only to organise an artificial earthquake as a jest to frighten his friends. . . . The prerequisite for the tremendous technical and industrial progress of our era is the modern concept of nature, and what prevented the ancient peoples from forming this concept was religion. . . . Religion is the one great antagonist of technology and economy.

Throughout most of his book Mr. Kahler maintains that the various epochs of human history have been shaped and governed by the ideas that happened to be inside men's heads at the time, and not, as it is now more fashionable to assume, that ideas are merely the reflection of external conditions. It follows that any improvement in human affairs will have to be preceded by a change of outlook and will not be brought about by a mere increase in mechanical efficiency. Even the quite simple problem of making sure that everyone has enough to eat cannot be solved without a "fundamental shift in the state of mind of people."

But at the end of his book Mr. Kahler seems to fall back upon the notion that human beings can learn nothing except through the suffering imposed on them by external events. A sane society, he says, "will not be created by the pure idea, it will be tortured out of men through cruel and bitter necessity—how bitter, coming generations alone may know. The idea of man, the counsel of a new humanism, are certainly the very last things to move the present world to a fundamental change."

Naturally, much of the later part of the book deals with the rise of totalitarianism. Some of the chapters which discuss this subject suffer from a certain distortion, owing to having been composed, apparently, in 1941 and 1942, when it was none too sure that Germany would be defeated. All the way through, indeed, there is a tendency to claim that all the evils of the modern world originated in Germany, and to discover the causes, even as far back as the days of Arminius.

But in the main this book is intended as history rather than propaganda, and the dilemma of the humanist is finally left unsolved. As long as supernatural beliefs persist, men can be exploited by cunning priests and oligarchs, and the technical progress which is the prerequisite of a just society cannot be achieved. On the other hand, when men stop worshipping God they promptly start worshipping Man, with disastrous results. The humanist has to decide whether what is needed is re-education and a "change of heart," or whether the indispensable first step is the abolition of poverty. Mr. Kahler hesitates between the two positions, but with a tendency to choose the first. The best sections of this book are the purely historical ones; the learning displayed is prodigious.

[Fee: £10.0.0.; 19.7.45]

2707. To Kathleen Raine

24 July 1945   Typewritten

> 27 B Canonbury Square
> Islington
> London   N 1

Dear Kathleen,[1]

Thank you for your letter. No one has taken the French rights of "Animal Farm," which is supposed to appear in early August. I am going to ring up Warburg's and ask them to send you a copy. But as they've already had to send out a lot of advance copies and we could only print a small number altogether, they may say they have no more to spare. In that case I have one set of proofs myself, also I think a copy of the MS, and could send you that.

I am not working for Tribune any more, at least for the time being. I was abroad for some months for the Observer, and I write for them and the Manchester Evening News, besides other odds and ends. I expect that you know my wife died four months ago. I think you met her once at the Empson's.[2] It was a terrible thing altogether. But happily my little boy now aged nearly 15 months is very well and happy, and I have a good nurse for him.

> Yours sincerely
> [Signed] Geo. Orwell
> George Orwell

1. Kathleen Raine (1908–), poet, scholar, critic, and translator from the French. In Orwell's lifetime she published *Stone and Flower* (1943), *Living in Time* (1946), *The Pythoness* (1949). Her many books written since include a number of memoirs, most recently *Autobiographies*, (1991). She had written to Orwell from the British Council in an undated letter to say that Editions de la Jeune Parque, Paris, had asked 'anxiously' for a copy of *Animal Farm* and she suggested that, if Orwell were interested, he should have Secker & Warburg send them a copy. See also *1526, n. 3*.

2. William Empson (1906–1984) and his wife. Empson, poet, critic, and academic, had been one of Orwell's colleagues at the BBC. He had taught at Tokyo and Peking Universities before the war and was Professor of English Literature at Sheffield, 1953–71. See *845, n. 3* and *2568, n. 9.*

2708. World Affairs, 1945

Junior: Articles Stories and Pictures, [1], 1945[1]

The following essay was written before the world at large learned of the existence of the atomic bomb.

Up to the moment of writing, two of these bombs have been dropped.[2] The first of them completely wiped out more than four square miles of a Japanese city and is said to have killed about fifty thousand people. It was a bomb weighing less than five hundred pounds, and of a type already described as out of date.

Although atomic energy may prove to be of great value to man, its first introduction to the public has been in the shape of a bomb—and it is hardly necessary to point out what the discovery of this terrible weapon means for the human race. It may be a turning-point in history as important as the invention of the steam engine. At present the process of making the bomb is a secret and is only fully known in the United States, but researches along similar lines have been proceeding elsewhere, and we may be sure that before long at least three nations, probably more, will possess the means of blowing one another to pieces. Only a few hundred such bombs, dropped on great cities and on important industrial areas, could push us back into conditions of primitive savagery.

This is all the more reason why every person who can read and think should interest himself in political affairs. Wars do not happen because of simple wickedness, they result from jealousies and frictions—over markets, over boundaries, over raw materials, over national minorities—which can be removed if we put our minds to it. To understand where the world is going, and what can be done to prevent disaster, is above all the concern of the young, because the future belongs to them. To make sure that there is never another war is even more important to someone who is now sixteen than it is to someone of sixty. The article that follows is an attempt to describe the actual state of the world and the immediate problems that face us. It sets out to show that those problems CAN be solved, but at the same time it emphasises that there is not much cause for optimism in the world to-day.

While I write this the leaders of the Big Three are still conferring in Potsdam,[3] and we have not as yet been told anything about the decisions that they may have reached. However, it is possible to make a good guess at what subjects they are discussing. To do so, one has only to stop and think what has happened to the world as a result of six years of war.

The first thing that has happened is that the world, by and large, is very much poorer. Most of its inhabitants are living, and will be living for years to come, at a much lower level of comfort than they enjoyed in 1939. The most obvious cause of this is the actual physical destruction. In Germany every big town that was within reach of the British and American bombers has been wrecked in a way that even we in England, badly bombed though we were, do not find it easy to imagine. Whole areas which once housed hundreds of thousands of people have been reduced to piles of plaster and broken bricks. German industry has perhaps not been smashed beyond repair, but it will certainly need many years of building before the German people have enough houses to live in. And this destruction has not only happened in Germany, but also in Poland, Italy, parts of Austria, Hungary and Greece, and in a large and important area of Soviet Russia. Wherever there has been ground fighting the destruction has been even worse than what was caused by the bombing-planes. Coal mines have been flooded, machinery has been smashed up or looted, locomotives and railway trucks have been destroyed in tens of thousands. One gets some idea of the work of repair that will have to be done if one realises, for instance, that between Paris and Berlin there is hardly a single bridge that has not been blown up.

But perhaps more important than the mere destruction is the fact that in wartime many kinds of necessary work are neglected. Every scrap of steel and every ounce of labour has to be used in the manufacture of weapons, which means not only that it is impossible to supply the public with such things as motor cars, watches, typewriters, refrigerators and wireless sets, but that machinery is not replaced unless it is of a kind to be useful to the war effort. Outside the range of the fighting, the amount of industrial plant may and probably does increase—it has certainly increased to an enormous extent in the United States, for instance—but it is all designed for war purposes and cannot be switched over at a moment's notice. Factories which were built to make tanks, machine guns, shell-cases and camouflage nets cannot start the next morning to make saucepans, vacuum cleaners, window frames and sewing machines: and meanwhile all of those things are in very short supply. War means taking millions of people away from productive work for years on end, and somehow or other the lost labour has to be made up.

There is also the loss of life, and the huge displacement of populations, which will take years to smooth out. We have no accurate information as to how many people have been killed in battle or in air raids, or have been massacred, or have died in the various famines caused by the war: but it is unlikely that they number less than twenty millions—that is, about one per cent. of the population of the world.[4] Besides this, in various parts of Asia and Europe, millions or tens of millions of people have been uprooted from their homes and dumped down somewhere else to begin life anew. The Germans transported at least seven million people, mostly Russians and Poles, in order to use them for forced labour on the land or in industry. Most of them are now finding their way home again, but merely to move them is an enormous undertaking. About two million Germans are in process of being expelled from Czechoslovakia, and millions more have been or will be expelled from East Prussia to make way for the Poles. At the same time large numbers of Poles, previously deported by the Russians, are moving back into Poland, and others are moving out of the eastern provinces of Poland which the U.S.S.R. has now taken over. One must remember that most of these people who have been shifted to and fro are peasants who cannot take their farm machinery and their animals with them when they move. Nearly every European country now has in it masses of homeless, destitute people, and how to feed them is a formidable problem: not only because food is none too plentiful anywhere, but still more because of the shortage of shipping and the all-round damage to communications. So the two countries which have been least damaged by the war—that is, the U.S.A. and Britain—will have to put their main energies to repairing the World.

We know, therefore, without needing to be told, what is the most urgent of the problems now being discussed in Potsdam. It is simply this: how to prevent millions of people in Europe from dying of hunger and cold during this coming winter. And beyond that lies the yet bigger problem of cleaning up the mess. Tens of millions of houses have to be built, hundreds of sunken ships replaced, wrecked coal mines and oil wells put in working order, war industries converted to peaceful purposes, agricultural machinery manufactured and distributed, and trade set flowing again between the continents—and all this after six years of destruction and waste. For several years nearly every country in the world will have to go on living in what are more or less wartime conditions. Industry will still have to be controlled by the state, food and clothes will still have to be rationed, travel will be restricted and long working-hours will be the rule. There is not likely to be much unemployment in the years immediately following the war, because there will be no difficulty in finding markets for such goods as can be produced and transported. Every kind of commodity—coal, oil, cloth, rubber, timber, machinery—is desperately needed by some country or other, and the main difficulties in the way of international trade will be first the lack of transport, and secondly the fact that the countries hardest hit by the war will have no goods to export. Perhaps in five years from the ending of the war with Japan the world will be reasonably prosperous again: and it is then that certain changes which have been happening under the surface from 1939 onwards will begin to make themselves felt.

One thing which the war has proved is that neither small nor large nations can be fully independent. Even when they are able to support themselves in an economic sense, they are utterly unable to defend themselves against an outside attack. During the past six years a whole string of small nations—Belgium, Jugoslavia, Denmark, Iran, Norway and others—have been overrun by some great power, usually after only a few days' fighting, and even countries of the size of France and Italy were unequal to making war on a big scale. To be able to make war you have to be able to turn out highly complicated weapons such as tanks and aeroplanes in enormous numbers, which means that only those countries which have big reserves of industrial plant, skilled labour and raw materials can be powerful in a military sense. In the nineteenth century wars were still fought with crude weapons which could be manufactured anywhere: military power was therefore a matter of numbers, and ten small nations whose combined populations added up to 100 millions were—at any rate potentially—stronger than one great nation of 50 millions. Today most of the small nations are unable to produce modern weapons, even in small quantities. High-speed aeroplanes, or large-calibre guns, or pieces of armour plate big enough for battleships, can only be produced in the main industrial areas, of which there are about a dozen in the whole world. It follows that every small nation has to live under the protection, and to some extent under the control, of some big nation, usually its nearest neighbour.

Poland or Finland, for instance, cannot remain even partially independent unless they keep on good terms with Russia. Belgium and Holland have to be protected by Britain and France, or both. The South American countries could and would be conquered by the Japanese or by some European power if they were not guarded by the United States. All this was known, in a sort of way, before the guns started firing in 1939, but the war has emphasised it. For the war has not only brought out the weakness of the small powers, it has also changed the attitude of the great powers. Not merely Germany and Japan, but Britain, Russia and the United States have on a number of occasions invaded small countries without provocation, or have interfered in their internal affairs in a way that few people would have approved of ten years ago. They have been compelled to do so, because otherwise these small countries could have been used as bases of attack against themselves. As a result of the war, all of the great powers have become less scrupulous about respecting neutrality, and less inclined to tolerate hostile governments on their borders. The present tendency is for the world to be cut up into what are called "zones of influence," with one big country all-powerful within each zone.

Therefore, again without being told, we can make a good guess at another of the subjects now being debated in Potsdam. It is: can the three great victors of the war administer the world as a single unit, or must it be permanently split up into three zones of influence? And if so, where are the boundaries of those zones to be drawn?

Before the war there were seven nations which were usually described as "great powers"—the United States, Britain, Soviet Russia, Germany, France, Italy and Japan. Now only the first three of these remain. France has been greatly weakened, and Italy even more so: Germany's military power has been broken for a long time to come, and Japan's as well, and China, in spite of its vast hard-working population, is still too backward to exert any power outside its own borders or even to defend itself unaided. India is even more backward than China. For the time being three nations are supreme, and the kind of future that is before us depends on whether they choose to co-operate or to remain rivals.

If we face the facts, we must realise that the chances are against any genuine organisation for world control being set up at this moment. For quite two years all the signs have pointed in the other direction. The three great powers differ very greatly in outlook and tradition, and when they have recovered from the war their material interests will clash as well. By considering the special position of each of the Big Three—its social and economic system, its resources and its weaknesses—one can get a good idea of the difficulties that are likely to arise.

Of the three great powers, Britain is the weakest. Its population is only 46 million, and within its own borders it has no large supply of any raw material except coal. This means that Britain has to live largely on imported goods, which in the long run have to be paid for by exports. But, because for six years it was compelled to use all its energy in producing weapons of war, Britain has lost most of its overseas markets and has failed to modernise its industries. During the period when war damage is being repaired, Britain will be able to sell anything it can produce, but after that it may be unable to compete with the bigger and more efficient industries of the United States. Without a steady flow of imports and exports, Britain could not keep its navy and air force at the necessary level of efficiency, and might not even be able to survive as an independent nation.

But to set against this, Britain has several great advantages. One is the possession of air and sea bases at important strategic spots such as Gibraltar and Aden. Another is the adherence of the English-speaking Dominions, which are not controlled by Britain but linked to it in a sort of permanent alliance. Britain's colonial possessions in Asia and Africa are a more doubtful asset. They provide a market for manufactured goods and pay for them with valuable products such as rubber, rice and tin, but in time of war they have to be defended, and the natural desire of their inhabitants for independence makes for constant political friction. By far the biggest of Britain's possessions, India, is likely to become independent in the fairly near future, and after a few years of re-adjustment the results will probably be beneficial to Britain. Britain has another less obvious but still real advantage in its democratic tradition, which allows it to make great changes without bloodshed and gives it a certain moral authority among the western European nations. Of the three great powers, Britain has the most to gain by international co-operation, and above all it cannot afford to quarrel with the United States.

Soviet Russia has the advantages of a huge and growing population and of unlimited resources of every kind of raw material inside its own territories. Its great size and poor communications make it a difficult country to invade successfully, and it is able to place its most important industries in areas where they cannot be bombed. Its economic system, in which everything is planned and controlled by the State, makes it possible to carry through huge reconstruction schemes, such as the first and second Five Year Plans, and to modernise agriculture and create new industries at short notice. It is therefore easy for Soviet Russia to control the governments and the policies of all the countries of Eastern Europe, and of certain Asiatic countries as well. From the point of view of a peasant who is overworked and permanently in debt, the Russian system means a very great improvement, and it is natural for the populations of the poorer European countries to look towards Russia for leadership. At the moment, however, the Russians have been greatly weakened and impoverished by the war. One of their best industrial areas has been devastated, and to get their agriculture on its feet again they will need quantities of tractors and other farm machinery which will have to be procured from the United States.

Alone among the big countries of the world, the United States has not suffered seriously from the war—indeed, has grown vastly stronger because of it. The industrial power of the United States is so enormous that it has been able to take the major share in two wars and at the same time maintain its own people at a standard of living that no other country could dream of. With existing weapons the United States cannot be directly attacked, no other power can build ships or planes in competition with it, and during the war it has acquired new sea and air bases all over the Atlantic and Pacific. The one great disability from which it suffers is the lack of a strong central government, which often allows its policies to be controlled by irresponsible business men. After the last war the Americans threw away their chance of becoming the leaders of the world by refusing to enter the League of Nations: This time they will not make precisely the same mistake, but they may make the equally bad one of refusing to co-operate with other powers in the matter of tariffs or of air transport.

When one considers the existing differences between the three great powers, one sees that it is not easy for them to combine in a single organisation for the reconstruction of the world. But if they do not do so, if they remain as separate, sovereign states, they are bound to be in constant friction with one another. "Zones of influence" are a very poor solution, because zones inevitably overlap. The British, for example, want a secure sea route to India and Australia, and therefore want control of the Mediterranean: the Russians want control of the Dardanelles. And if you look at the map you can see a dozen places at which the interests of the great powers are bound to clash: for example Persia, Afghanistan and Manchuria. If the great states are unready to give up some of their national sovereignty, then they are bound to develop into enemies of one another. That does not mean that there will immediately be another war. No belligerent nation is able or willing to fight another big-scale war at this moment. But it does mean that there will be first a scramble to secure as big a "zone of influence" as possible, and then a tightening-up of frontiers which will make trade and intercommunication on a world-wide scale impossible. The world will split into three camps, and ultimately into two, for Britain, not strong enough to stand alone, will become part of the American system. The smaller nations will be grouped about the bigger ones, on lines which it is already possible to draw with fair accuracy. Something of the kind has already happened in occupied Europe, where the Russian and the Anglo-American zones are divided by a no-man's land which makes it impossible to exchange either goods or ideas.

The leaders of the Big Three will have been discussing other topics besides those I have raised. They will have been discussing, for example, the war with Japan, and what to do with the German armament factories, and what to demand in the way of reparations. But their two most urgent and most difficult problems will be how to feed Europe and where to draw its frontiers. The answer to the first may affect the lives of millions, but there is not a human being on the face of the earth whose future will not be affected by the answer to the second. The days are gone when the world could consist of a patchwork of small and genuinely independent states. The choice is between a single world organisation and the survival of two or three giant states, all more or less hostile to one another. We do not yet know which alternative will prevail, but we can have a good idea what each of them would mean. The happiness of ordinary people everywhere is bound up with the first, and it is for them to use their votes, their voices and any other influence they have to bring it into being.

1. *Junior* was published by Children's Digest Publications, Ltd., London. Orwell's Payments Book shows that he was paid £13.2.6 for the article and it is dated 24 July 1945. It is placed at that date here, since it is not known when this number of *Junior* was issued. The introduction in italic must have been added after the main article was written, for it refers to the two atomic bombs dropped on Japan. As Orwell writes with only specific (if sketchy) knowledge of the first bomb, it is likely that the introduction was written soon after 9 August 1945. A search made of the files of *Junior* by Peter Tucker has not revealed any more articles by Orwell. In the Foreword to the issue in which Orwell's article appeared, there is this biographical note: 'GEORGE ORWELL has been a schoolmaster, a civil servant in Burma and fought in the Spanish civil-war. He has written many novels and is a great lover of Dickens. He is a journalist, and has visited Europe during and since the War. Is careless about his clothes and rolls his own cigarettes.'

2. Hiroshima was devastated on 6 August 1945; Nagasaki, three days later. Although usually thought of as bringing the war to an end, the entry of the Soviet Union into the war with Japan on 8 August (one result of the Potsdam Conference) and the invasion of Manchuria by Russian forces were also influential. Japan did not immediately surrender, even after the second atom bomb fell. It took the intervention of Emperor Hirohito to persuade a divided Japanese cabinet to agree to surrender five days later on 14 August 1945.

3. The Potsdam Conference was the last of the World War II meetings of the 'Big Three' (at that time, the United States, the Soviet Union, and Britain). It was held from 17 July to 2 August 1945, in Potsdam, Germany. It was hoped at this meeting to carry on the wartime collaboration into the years of peace and was attended principally by President Harry S Truman and Secretary of State James F. Byrnes; Premier Stalin and Foreign Secretary V. M. Molotov; and, initially, Prime Minister Churchill and Foreign Secretary Anthony Eden. The results of the British General Election were announced during the course of the conference, and to Stalin's evident surprise, and Churchill's chagrin, the new, Labour, Prime Minister, Clement Attlee, and his Foreign Secretary, Ernest Bevin, replaced Churchill and Eden. The conference discussed, among other things, final operations against Japan (with the use of the atom bomb in the offing, to which Britain had given agreement in principle on 4 July), large-scale reparations demanded by Stalin (and agreed), Soviet demands for certain territorial oversights (which were not all agreed), the removal of Franco (which was refused), the division of Germany into four zones of occupation, the western border of Poland (to be along the Oder-Neisse line), and the trial of war criminals (all three agreed). Treatment of Italy was noticeably more lenient than that meted out to Germany. The Chinese Nationalist leader, General Chiang Kai-shek, was co-opted (by radio) by Truman and Churchill to demand the unconditional surrender of Japan. The Potsdam Declaration was made public on 26 July 1945.

4. About fifty-five million people were killed, over 80% of whom were non-combatants.

2709. Unpublished Review

25 July 1945

Orwell's Payments Book has an entry for 25 July 1945 noting a review for the *Manchester Evening News* for which he was paid £8.8.0. This should have appeared on 26 July, but most of the paper is given over to listing the results of the General Election. There is no notice explaining the non-appearance of Orwell's feature, 'Life, People and Books,' and the review does not seem to have been published at a later date.

2710. Funny, But Not Vulgar

Leader Magazine, 28 July 1945

This article was recorded in Orwell's Payments Book at 1 December 1944 and is reprinted at that point in this edition; see *2585*.

2711. To Mrs. Belloc Lowndes

31 July 1945   Typewritten

Mrs. Belloc Lowndes, sister of Hilaire Belloc, wrote to Orwell on 28 July 1945. She apologised for sending a typed letter—'my writing is almost illegible,' she said—but she was keen to tell Orwell how touched and delighted she was by his 'charming paper' on her brother in *The Leader*, 'Funny, But Not Vulgar,' 28 July 1945; see *2585*. She had sent Hilaire Belloc a copy; he was far from well, she wrote, 'indeed in a sad state.' He had lost his eldest son in World War I and his youngest in World War II. She said she followed all Orwell's writing and hoped she could meet him on her return to London early in September.[1]

27 B Canonbury Square   Islington   London   N 1

Dear Mrs Belloc Loundes,°
Many thanks for your letter of July 28th. I am glad that Mr Belloc should see what I wrote about him in the "Leader", as I have always admired his work, much as I disagreed with him politically. It is a pity that the book I was quoting (from memory), "The Modern Traveller," has not been re-printed. It was a great favourite of mine in my boyhood, but I have not seen a copy for years. It is possible that you might be able to lend me (I would promise to return it) a copy of "The Servile State," which I have also been trying to get hold of. It is a long time since I read it, and I should like to consult it in connection with an essay I am projecting on James Burnham.

I would certainly like to meet you. I shall probably be out of London during the first half of September and back again in the second half. I have stopped writing for the "Leader," but it is possible I may start the column in "Tribune" again at some later time.

Yours sincerely
[Signed] Geo. Orwell
George Orwell

1. Offset on Orwell's letter, in Mrs. Lowndes's very distinctive handwriting, is the draft of an invitation to dine with her at the Queensborough Club at 6:45 P.M. on Sunday, the seventeenth. The seventeenth is crossed through, probably because, if this was written in September, the seventeenth was a Monday. The next Sunday, 17, was in February 1946. It is not certain that this invitation was intended for Orwell, though it seems likely, and it is not known whether he then met Mrs. Lowndes. For Hilaire Belloc, see *214, n. 1* and *2309, n. 2*.

2712. To Lydia Jackson

1 August 1945   Typewritten

Dear Lydia,
Of course use the cottage second half of August. Even if I did manage to go down there some time, it wouldn't be then.

I am still trying to take that cottage in the Hebrides. I don't know if it will materialise, but if it does, I shall send the Wallington furniture there. That wouldn't be until early next year, however.

I am frightfully busy, but I am glad to say I have got a good nurse who looks after Richard and cooks my meals as well. Richard is extremely well although he is teething rapidly. He is now 14½ months and weighs about 26 pounds. He can stand up without support but doesn't actually walk yet, and I don't want to hurry him as I am afraid he may be too heavy for his legs. He isn't talking yet, ie. he utters word-like sounds, but no actual words. He doesn't seem to have taken any harm from the many changes in his short life. When you are back, come over and see us both. I am nearly always at home in the afternoons. Richard has his tea about half past four and I have a high tea about seven. My love to Pat.

Yours
Eric

2713. Review of *Memoirs* by the Right Hon. Viscount Samuel; *Good-Bye to Berlin* by Christopher Isherwood; *A Room of One's Own* by Virginia Woolf; *Thomas Paine* by Chapman Cohen

Manchester Evening News, 2 August 1945

Lord Samuel is a reasonable man, and reasonable people are not always the most exciting companions. Those who read his Utopia book ("An Unknown Land," published about three years ago)[1] will remember it as a description of a country so well conducted and so faultless in every way that no ordinarily constituted person could bear to live there for even a fortnight.

It is, therefore, not surprising if his memoirs are less valuable as reading matter than as an accurate record of events, against which doubtful points in contemporary history can be checked.

Lord Samuel was born into a wealthy banking family, and was destined for the Bar, but decided very early in life on a political career. The big dock strike of 1889, William Booth's "In Darkest England," and some work on behalf of his elder brother in a County Council election in Whitechapel made him aware of the shameful conditions in which millions of English people had to live, and from then onwards he was a faithful supporter of the Liberal party, which until about 1900 was effectively the only party of the Left.

While he was at Oxford he took a lively interest in local politics, and was partly responsible for trade unionism getting a foothold, for the first time, among the downtrodden Oxfordshire farm labourers.

Activities of that kind were less fashionable in those days than they have since become, and Mr. Samuel (as he then was) sometimes had his door screwed up by rowdy undergraduates while celebrities from London were addressing meetings in his rooms. He was adopted as Liberal candidate for South Oxfordshire soon after he went down from Oxford, but failed to win the seat, and did not enter Parliament until 1902.

The part of this book that is certain to be read with most interest are the chapters dealing with the period between 1914 and 1916. Both before and during the war Lord Samuel held office in the Asquith Government, and he is able to give authoritative judgments on such men as Grey, Haldane, Kitchener, and Lloyd George, and to tell from the inside the story of the abrupt change of Government at the end of 1916.

When Lloyd George took over the Premiership he asked Lord Samuel to continue in his post as Home Secretary, which Lord Samuel refused to do, since he objected not only to the composition of the new Government but to the unscrupulous Press campaign by means of which Asquith had been overthrown.

He adds that Lloyd George, in manœuvring himself into power, was undoubtedly acting in what he believed to be the true interests of the country. This part of the book, consisting largely of extracts from a diary Lord Samuel kept at the time, is of great value as a corrective to the account written many years afterwards by Lloyd George himself.

For the rest these memoirs are rather slow going, though Lord Samuel has known every eminent person from 1890 onwards and has anecdotes about many of them.

He is at his best when he is simply discussing the political events of which he has had a front-seat view, and towards the end of the book there are some well-balanced passages on Munich, rearmament, and foreign policy generally.

It would be absurd to pretend that the sketches and stories assembled by Mr. Christopher Isherwood under the title "Good-bye to Berlin" are on the same level as that little masterpiece, "Mr. Norris Changes Trains," and since they deal with the same subject matter they even derive part of their charm from the memory of the earlier book.

But they are still very brilliant sketches of a society in decay. In a short foreword Mr. Isherwood explains that his original intention had been to write a huge novel about pre-Hitler Berlin—its projected title was "The Lost"—of which these stories were to form part. The best of them is "The Nowaks,"[2] which deals with a Berlin working-class family on the edge of destitution and contains a desolating description of a tuberculosis sanatorium in winter.

Reading such tales as this, the thing that surprises one is not that Hitler came to power, but that he did not do so several years earlier. The book ends with the triumph of the Nazis and Mr. Isherwood's departure from Berlin.

"Frl. Schroeder [his landlady] is inconsolable . . . It's no use trying to explain to her, or talking politics. Already she is adapting herself, as she will adapt herself to every new regime. This morning I even heard her talking reverently about 'Der Fuehrer' to the porter's wife. If anybody were to remind her that, at the elections last November, she voted Communist, she would probably deny it hotly, and in perfect° good faith. . . . Thousands of people like Frl. Schroeder are acclimatising themselves."

It is a long time since Mr. Isherwood wrote a novel, and during most of that time he has been sitting at the feet of Mr. Gerald Heard [3] in California. The reprinting of these sketches is a reminder of how good a writer he used to be, and will make a lot of people wish that he would abandon Hollywood and come back to Europe to have another look at Berlin.

Virginia Woolf's little book, a long essay, is a discussion of the handicaps which have prevented women, as compared with men, from producing literature of the first order. What she believes to be the main reason is alluded to in the title of the book. If a writer is to do his best, she says, he needs £500 a year and a room of his own, and far fewer women than men have enjoyed these advantages.

But there are other disabilities, and Miss Woolf invents, among other things, a sister for William Shakespeare,[4] not less fitted than her brother, but cut off by the very nature of the society she lives in from any chance of using her rights. At times this book rather overstates the drawbacks from which women suffer, but almost anyone of the male sex could read it with advantage.

"Thomas Paine" is a useful short biography of the great English Radical (for he was an Englishman, a fact that Americans are rather apt to forget) who championed the American colonists and the French revolutionaries, and who helped to draw up the Declaration of Independence.

[Fee: £8.8.0; 1.8.45]

1. Reviewed by Orwell anonymously in *The Listener*, 24 December 1942, *1768*.
2. Orwell wrote to John Lehmann on 12 June 1936, to say how much he had enjoyed this story when it was first published in *New Writing*; see *317*.
3. For Gerald Heard, see *2397, n. 2*; for Orwell's description 'the yogis of California'—Heard, Aldous Huxley, and Isherwood—see 'Looking Back on the Spanish War,' *1421, n. 8*. The review following Tosco Fyvel's of *Animal Farm* in *Tribune*, 24 August 1945, was of Heard's *A Preface to Prayer*. The 'hot sun of California' had not only hatched out Auden's *For the Time Being* and Aldous Huxley's *Time Must Have a Stop*, but also this, 'the most unrestrained of the mystical works of Mr. Gerald Heard.' Heard, it was said, described flagellation 'in succulent detail,' and the reviewer asked, 'What is the difference between flagellation practised by religious men [as described by Heard] and the flagellation paid for in brothels, recorded by Krafft-Ebing?' Since Orwell was no longer *Tribune*'s literary editor, he may not have seen this review in advance of publication. However, if the reviewer's initials, R. H., are those of Rayner Heppenstall, he may well have been reminded of Heard by Heppenstall.
4. Shakespeare had four sisters but three died in infancy. The sole survivor, the second to be given the name Joan, married William Hart; they had four children. Hart died on 17 April 1616, one week before Shakespeare. Shakespeare provided well for Joan in his will, and she outlived him by thirty years. See Samuel Schoenbaum, *William Shakespeare: A Documentary Life* (1975), 25. Because she lived for the rest of her life in the western wing of the double house

Shakespeare left her in Henley Street, her grandson Thomas coming into possession of both wings of the house in due time, she might be said to have had at least a part of the wherewithal to enable her to write had she wished to do so.

2714. Review of *The Rescue* by Edward Sackville-West; illustrated by Henry Moore; Limited Edition

The Observer, 5 August 1945

Radio programmes are meant to be heard and not read, and Mr. Sackville-West's Introduction (or "Preamble," as he prefers to call it) to "The Rescue" is somewhat more worth reading than the play itself. The play does indeed contain passages which were well worth printing, and the directions as to "effects" and fading have a technical interest: but anyone who did not listen to the actual broadcast will get more profit from the "Preamble," which is one of the few serious attempts that have yet been made to discuss the possibilities and the largely unsolved problems of radio drama.

"The Rescue," which was broadcast in two parts, each taking forty-five minutes, is a dramatised version of the last few books of the "Odyssey," sufficiently recast to give it a slightly melodramatic quality. With a few interludes definitely in verse, and a few others in colloquial prose, it is mostly written in a highly stylised language which trembles on the edge of verse and has an almost continuous musical accompaniment. Part I. shows Penelope hard pressed by the suitors, and Part II. culminates in the triumph of Odysseus. As nearly as possible the strict dramatic form is followed, and the dreary figure, the Narrator, is got rid of: his place is taken by Phemius the poet and the goddess Athene, who are able to give the necessary explanations while taking part in the action.

One would have to hear this play broadcast to know how well it "goes over," but even when one reads the text there are one or two objections. First, it is questionable whether the "Odyssey" lends itself to radio presentation. With so unfamiliar an art-form as the radio play it is probably wise to choose stories which the listener is likely to know already, but one fact which the microphone brings out is that some stories are much more visual than others. In this case, for instance, the scene in which Odysseus shoots down the suitors with his bow cannot be adequately presented: it has to occur "off" and be described to Penelope by Eumaeus. Moreover, it is a great pity that a serious piece of work such as this should be pervaded, even faintly, by official propaganda. The parallel between Ithaca occupied by the suitors and Greece occupied by the Germans, though it is not pressed, is definitely indicated in Part II., and there is even, in one place, what appears to be an identification of Odysseus with King George of the Hellenes.

In his "Preamble" Mr. Sackville-West is discussing chiefly the problems of musical accompaniment, but he also has some interesting things to say about radio drama in general. As he points out, radio has made it possible to revive the soliloquy (no longer tolerable on the realistic stage), and to play tricks with space and time which would be difficult even in a film. On the other hand, the difficulty, in any broadcast involving more than two or three voices, of making the listener understand what is happening where, and who is speaking to whom, has not been fully overcome. It is usually done by means of a Narrator, who ruins the dramatic effect, or by making the characters drop explanatory remarks, which are likely to hold up the action and have to be managed very skilfully if they are to be convincing.

As yet these problems have been very little studied. The basic reason is that in England, as in almost all countries, radio is a monopoly. There is only one source of radio programmes, the B.B.C., which is as though the entire Press, from "Comic Cuts" to the "Hibbert Journal,"[1] had to be contained within the pages of a single newspaper. Obviously very little time can be set aside for "highbrow" programmes, which the bulk of the listening public actively dislike, and because the B.B.C. is a semi-official organisation it is subject to interference from all kinds of busybodies who raise an outcry whenever they overhear a programme which strikes them as too intelligent. There is also the financial difficulty. A radio programme costs a great deal to produce—"The Rescue," with a cast of nearly 30 voices, must have cost hundreds of pounds—and it goes on the air only once, or at most two or three times. It is therefore impossible to have elaborate rehearsals, and indeed it is very unusual for the actors to know their parts by heart. It is also impossible to pay the script-writer a sum that would justify the weeks or months of work that go into the writing of a stage play. These conditions do not favour experimental work.

Meanwhile it is encouraging to see radio plays printed in book form, and on good quality paper. If they exist in print they are more likely to be revived, and if it became normal for radio programmes to make more than one appearance, it would be easier for those who write them to take them seriously.

[Fee: £10.0.0; 2.8.45]

1. *Hibbert Journal* (1902–1970), quarterly devoted to religion, philosophy, sociology and the arts.

2715. To Geoffrey Earle

8 August 1945   Typewritten

Geoffrey Earle, a programme assistant in the BBC's Services Educational Unit, recorded a note on 20 July 1945 that he had tentatively approached Orwell 'as to the possibility of his writing "Jack London" biography and interview arranged for Thursday, 26 July.' This is annotated by Earle indicating that on 26 July, Orwell agreed to submit a script. On 27 July, N. E. Wadsley of the Services Educational Unit wrote to Programme Copyright advising them that Orwell was writing a script, to be broadcast on 8 October 1945, which would be 'embodying two or three voices.' He asked whether this was sufficient information for the preparation of a contract or whether more details were required. A handwritten note states that these programmes may be relayed by 'our own networks in Italy and Germany to augment reception.' A requisition for the programme, with a fee of £15.15.0, is dated 7 August, and on that day, Earle wrote to Orwell to ask him to let him know fairly soon the number and type of voices he would need. He also asked him whether he had thought further 'along the lines of a dramatised short story.' Orwell replied on 8 August.

27 B Canonbury Square   Islington   London N 1[1]
Dear Mr Earle,
With reference to your letter dated August 7th.

I have only rather roughly projected the *Jack London* script so far, but the way I thought of it was as critical and biographical passages interspersed with fragments from two or three of the stories. The stories I should probably choose would be some or all of the following: "Just Meat," "A Piece of Steak," "The Chinago" and "Love of Life." Any of these could be managed by at most two voices plus narrator. So if we had three voices (capable of being fairly dramatic), that would be enough, and I could manage the critical passages myself, unless you think I am too bad a broadcaster. (I have occasionally broadcast on the Home Service and recently did two talks for the Schools Service.)

As to the dramatised short stories. I enclose a script of one, "Crainquebille." This was the first we did and not the most successful. I think the most successful was "A Slip under the Microscope" (by H. G. Wells), of which I have lost the script. They would probably have a copy at 200 Oxford Street, and possibly the discs. These broadcasts were done towards the end of 1943.

I should emphasise that these particular stories, besides being very long (half hour programmes), were chosen with an eye to the Indian student audience. I am only sending the enclosed script to show the technique we followed. I think the best of all was a fairy story, "The Emperor's New Clothes," which was done as a 15 minute programme and went out on other services besides the Indian. Stories by Kipling, Conan Doyle, Jack London and perhaps Maupassant would lend themselves well to this treatment.

Yours sincerely
[Signed] Geo. Orwell
George Orwell

PS. I've just found the script of "The Fox" so am enclosing that too.

1. Orwell usually gives his telephone number at Canonbury Square—CAN 3751—at the head of his letters. This is not reproduced from here on.

2716. To Leonard Moore

8 August 1945   Typewritten

27 B Canonbury Square   Islington   London   N 1

Dear Mr Moore,
Some French publishers are enquiring after the translation rights of BURMESE DAYS and ANIMAL FARM. They have been in communication about this with

Warburg, who apparently gave them your name but not your address. Can you send them copies of both books. Their address is:

    Editions Nagel Paris
    47 Rue Blanche
    Paris
    FRANCE.

A Penguin copy of BURMESE DAYS would do. If you haven't a copy I have one I can give you.[1]

They are also, of course, asking about terms. Please don't be hard on them, as there is never much money in that kind of thing any way, and it would be a great thing if these books could be translated, especially ANIMAL FARM.[2]

                        Yours sincerely
                     [Signed] Eric Blair
                          Eric Blair

1. The letter has been annotated in Moore's office: 'have we?' and 'our file copy sent to "Nagel" Paris.'
2. Nagel published *Burmese Days* (as *Tragédie Birmane*), 31 August 1946, but did not take *Animal Farm*.

2717. They Throw New Light on India [book reviews]
Manchester Evening News, 9 August 1945

One of the Penguin books listed as "recent or forthcoming" is "Coolie," by Mulk Raj Anand,[1] who is also the author of "The Village," "Two Leaves and a Bud," "The Sword and the Sickle," and other novels of Indian life.

Mr. Anand is one of the small group of Indian writers who prefers to write in English, and whose appearance during the past twenty years marks an important turning-point in Anglo-Indian relations. Others in this class are Ahmed Ali, Iqbal Singh, Narayana Menon, and the Eurasian novelist, Cedric Dover.[2]

Some of these writers have probably chosen English as their medium, because they can thus reach a larger audience, but they have made it very much their own, and even show signs of evolving a distinguishable dialect, comparable to Irish-English. Ahmed Ali's "Morning in Delhi," for instance, is an exquisite piece of writing, but one would probably know without being told that it had not been written by an Englishman.

The advantage that these writers derive from their double Orientation is that they can bring the real India direct to the British public. The "Sahibs," who used to loom so large in Anglo-Indian literature, but who in fact make up less than one in a thousand of India's population, do not dominate their stories.

And in addition to those who write in English, there are others—the short-story writer Prem Chand is an example—who stick to Hindustani but have been influenced by European writers such as Maupassant, and whose stories, when translated, are immediately intelligible to an English reader. From this group of writers one can get a picture of life in the village and the bazaar that one could not get from any English novelist or from any purely Indian source.

Before the time of Kipling the British dominion in India sometimes produced interesting documents such as diaries kept during the Mutiny, but very little imaginative literature.

Kipling seems to have been almost the first English writer to notice, or at any rate to exploit, the picturesqueness of the Indian scene. He is accused, justly enough, of a snobbish and crudely Imperialistic outlook, but what is best in his work derives from the fact that he did not really belong to the Anglo-Indian hierarchy.

As a very young man he was the ill-paid sub-editor of a newspaper in Lahore, and books like "Plain Tales From the Hills" and "Soldiers Three" draw their vitality from that period, and from his childhood memories. But Kipling's books are essentially about British India. Even "Kim," which tells—not very convincingly—the story of an Indian boy, is dominated by the godlike figure of a British official.

In writing of Indians, Kipling is never able to escape from a patronising attitude, which degenerates into brutal insensitiveness when any political issue arises. Flora Annie Steel, far less gifted than Kipling and now almost forgotten, made a more serious effort to appreciate the Indian point of view.[3]

The next milestone after Kipling was E. M. Forster's "A Passage to India," which was published in 1924. This still is, and probably will always remain, the best novel written about India by an English writer. It took an accidental circumstance to produce it, for Mr. Forster gathered his experiences not in British India proper but in an Indian State. But the change of outlook that it marks was the product of developments in England.

Belief in white superiority had been deflated to the point at which it was possible to think of an Indian not as a picturesque feudal retainer, nor even as a downtrodden victim, but simply as an individual. The strength of the book lies in the fact that though, in a political sense, Forster sides with the Indians against the British, he does not feel obliged to represent them morally or intellectually superior.

Almost all the characters, English and Indians alike, are shown as corrupted by Imperialism, capable of decent impulses and worthy of pity.

After Forster, "sophisticated" books about India became somewhat commoner. Examples are Edward Thompson's "An Indian Day." J. S. Collis's "Trials in Burma,"[4] and a very "light" novel, but displaying a lack of colour-consciousness which would have been impossible a few years earlier—J. R. Ackerley's "Hindoo Holiday."[5]

"A Passage to India" will survive as a novel if anything in contemporary literature survives, but what already "dates" it as a social document is its theme. It deals with the impossibility, inside the Imperialist framework, of true friendship between an Indian and an Englishman. At that time (the book was probably conceived round about 1913) this theme was almost forced upon any honest writer who touched the subject of India at all. In the near future, however, it is probable that we shall see novels about India which have a different approach.

For the uneasy relationship that Forster so delicately described is not likely to last much longer. India is bound to win its independence before many years are past, and at the same time a new kind of contact has been established through the presence of hundreds of thousands of British soldiers—not, as in the old days, illiterate mercenaries, but well-educated conscripts—on Indian soil. It is on their experiences that the next batch of Indian novels will probably be founded.

Meanwhile we can learn most about India from the little group of Indians who write in English. They are not very well known to the British public, and they have had almost no encouragement from the British Government, which has never grasped the importance of the English language as a link between Asia and Europe. In a way the most interesting of them is Cedric Dover, author of "Half-Caste," one of the very few writers who have told the outside world anything about the small but important Eurasian community.

Indeed, the only other books on this subject that come to mind are those of Peter Blundell—"Mr. Podd of Borneo" and others—which are "light" in the extreme, but still quite informative. Penguin Books would do a good service to Anglo-Indian relations if they would follow up "Coolie" with "Half-Caste" and a collection of Ahmed Ali's sketches of old Delhi.

[Fee: £8.8.0; 8.8.45]

1. For Mulk Raj Anand, see *905, n. 1*.
2. For Ahmed Ali, see *1103, n. 3*; Narayan Menon, *1118, n. 1*; Cedric Dover, *633, n. 1*.
3. Especially *On the Face of the Waters* (1896), a novel of the Indian Mutiny from British and Indian viewpoints.
4. Orwell was mistaken. *Trials in Burma* (1938; New York, 1945) is by Maurice Collis; the error possibly arose because Orwell seems to have been in correspondence with J. S. Collis about this time (see *2775*). Maurice and John Steuart Collis were born in Killiney, County Dublin, and educated at Rugby and Oxford. Maurice Collis (1889–1973), historian, biographer, and novelist, served in Burma, 1912–36, on much the same basis as Orwell, became in 1930 District Magistrate, Rangoon. After his retirement from the Indian Civil Service, he became a writer, achieving considerable success. *Trials in Burma*, an autobiography, was reviewed by Orwell in *The Listener*, 9 March 1938 (see *429*); Orwell also reviewed his account of Ma Saw, *She Was a Queen*, in the *Manchester Evening News*, 6 April 1944 (see *2449*).
5. *Hindoo Holiday* is a memoir, not a novel.

2718. To Eric Warman

11 August 1945

Sotheby's Catalogue for a sale on 21 February 1978 offers a letter by Orwell from Canonbury Square to Eric Warman, literary editor for the publishing firm Paul Elek. He agrees to write a preface to a volume of Jack London's stories—'I am rather a fan of Jack London's'—and asks for details of the length required and by when it is wanted: 'I can't do it if you wanted it, for instance, within the next month.'

It has not proved possible to trace the buyer of this letter. Orwell's introduction was published in *Love of Life and Other Stories* by Jack London (November 1946); see *2781*.

2719. London Letter, 15–16 August 1945[1]

Partisan Review, Fall 1945

Dear Editors,

I have put off starting this letter until today, hoping that some unmistakeable symptom might indicate what the Labor government intends doing. However, nothing very revealing has happened up to date, and I can discuss the situation only in general terms. In order to see what the Labor Party is up against, one has to consider the background against which it won its victory.

It is fashionable to say that all the causes we fought for have been defeated, but this seems to me a gross exaggeration. The fact that after six years of war we can hold a general election in a quite orderly way, and throw out a Prime Minister who has enjoyed almost dictatorial powers, shows that we *have* gained something by not losing the war. But still the general outlook is black enough. Western Europe is mostly on the verge of starvation. Throughout eastern Europe there is a "revolution from above," imposed by the Russians, which probably benefits the poorer peasants but kills in advance any possibility of democratic Socialism. Between the two zones there is an impenetrable barrier which runs slap across economic frontiers. Germany, already devastated to an extent that people in this country can't imagine, is to be plundered more efficiently than after Versailles, and some twelve million of its population are to be evicted from their homes. Everywhere there is indescribable confusion, mix-up of populations, destruction of dwelling-houses, bridges and railway tracks, flooding of coal mines, shortage of every kind of necessity, and lack of transport to distribute even such goods as exist. In the Far East hundreds of thousands of people, if the reports are truthful, have been blown to fragments by atomic bombs, and the Russians are getting ready to bite another chunk off the carcass of China. In India, Palestine, Persia, Egypt and other countries, troubles that the average person in England has not even heard of are just about ready to boil over.

And Britain's own situation is none too rosy. We have lost most of our markets and overseas investments, twelve million tons of our shipping have gone to the bottom, much of our industry is hopelessly antiquated, and our coal mines are in such a state that for years it will be impossible to get enough coal out of them. We have ahead of us the enormous job of reconstructing industry and recapturing markets in the teeth of overwhelming competition from the USA, and at the same time we have to build millions of houses and to keep up armed forces larger than we can afford in order to hold on to our precarious supplies of oil. No one, I think, expects the next few years to be easy ones, but on the whole people did vote Labor because of the belief that a Left government means family allowances, higher old age pensions, houses with bathrooms, etc., rather than from any internationalist consideration. They look to a Labor government to make them more secure and, after a few years, more comfortable, and the chief danger of the situation lies in the fact that English people have never been made to grasp that the sources of their prosperity lie outside England. The parochial outlook of the Labor Party itself is largely responsible for this.

I have already written on the election and I do not want to repeat what I said. But I must re-emphasise two points. One—not everyone agrees with me about this, but it is the impression I gathered in the London constituencies—is that the election was fought on domestic issues. Even Russophile feeling was a secondary factor. The other is that the turnover of votes was not enormous. Looking back at the last letter I sent you, I find that I was wrong on several points, and above all in predicting that the Conservatives would win. But everybody else, so far as I know, was also wrong, and even when the Gallup polls indicated that about 46 percent would vote Labor, the newspapers of the Left would go only so far as predicting a stalemate. The anomalies of the English electoral system usually work in favor of the Conservatives, and everyone assumed that they would do so again. Actually they worked the other way, for once, and everyone was stunned with surprise when the results were announced. But I was also wrong in suggesting that the Labor leaders might flinch from power and hence fight the election half-heartedly. It was a genuine enough fight, and it turned on issues that were serious so far as they went. Everyone who took an interest saw that the only chance of getting the Tories out was to vote Labor, and the minor parties were ignored. The twenty candidates put up by the Communists only won about 100,000 votes between them, and the Common Wealth did equally badly.[2] I think that the democratic tradition came out of the election fairly well. Tory efforts to turn the whole thing into a sort of plebiscite only excited disgust, and though the big masses appeared uninterested, they did go into the polling booths and vote at the last minute—against Churchill, as it turned out. But one cannot take this slide to the Left as meaning that Britain is on the verge of revolution. In spite of the discontent smouldering in the armed forces, the mood of the country seems to me less revolutionary, less Utopian, even less hopeful, than it was in 1940 or 1942. Of the votes cast in the election, at most 50 percent could be considered as outright votes for Socialism, and about another 10 percent as votes for nationalisation of certain key industries.

A Labor government may be said to mean business if it (a) nationalises land, coal mines, railways, public utilities and banks, (b) offers India immediate Dominion Status (this is a minimum), and (c) purges the bureaucracy, the army, the Diplomatic Service etc., so thoroughly as to forestall sabotage from the Right. The symptoms to watch for are an all-round swapping of ambassadors, the abolition of the India Office and, after Parliament reassembles, a battle with the House of Lords. If these don't happen, it is a good bet that no really radical economic change is intended. But the success or failure of the government does not depend solely on its willingness to fullfil its promises. It also has to re-educate public opinion at short notice, which to a large extent means fighting against its own past propaganda.

The weakness of all leftwing parties is their inability to tell the truth about the immediate future. When you are in opposition, and are trying to win support for a new economic and political programme, it is your job to make people discontented, and you almost inevitably do it by telling them that they will be better off in a material sense when the new programme is introduced. You probably don't tell them, what may very well be true, that they won't experience any benefit *immediately*, but only after, say, twenty years. The British people have never been warned, i.e. by the Left, that the introduction of Socialism may mean a serious drop in the standard of living. Nearly all left wingers, from Laborites to Trotskyists, would regard it as political suicide to say any such thing. Yet in my opinion it is probably true, at least in the case of a country like Britain, which lives partly by exploiting the colored peoples. To continue exploiting them is incompatible with the spirit of Socialism, while to stop doing so would entail a difficult reconstruction period during which our own standard of living might fall catastrophically. In one form and another this problem comes up again and again, and, except for the minority who have travelled outside Europe, I have never met an English Socialist who would face it. The stock answer is that we should lose nothing by liberating India and the colonies, since they would then develop more rapidly and their purchasing power would increase, which would be to our advantage—all true enough, but overlooking the interim period, which is the crux of the matter. The colored peoples themselves are not to be fobbed off with such easy answers, and indeed they are inclined to think of British prosperity as more dependent on imperialist exploitation than it actually is. When the Beveridge Report was first published, it had to be somewhat soft-pedalled in the news bulletins to India. There was danger that it would cause serious resentment, the likeliest Indian reaction being: "They are making themselves comfortable at our expense."

Similarly, the calamity of the war, and the impoverishment of the world as a whole, have not been fully brought home to the British people. I think they grasp that the reconversion of industry will be a big job, involving rationing and "direction" of labor over a long period, but are less well aware that the devastation of Europe must react badly on our own economy. It is extraordinary how little protest there has been against the proposal to turn Germany into a sort of overcrowded rural slum. In looking to the future, people think in terms of re-distributing the national income, and don't pause to reflect that that income is itself dependent on world conditions. They have had the Beveridge Scheme, raising of the school-leaving age, and so forth, whisked in front of their noses, and no one has told them that for a long time to come we may be unable to afford any improvement in our way of life. Sometimes at Labor meetings during the election I tried the experiment of asking at question time: "What is the Labor Party's policy towards India?" I always got some such perfunctory answer as "Of course the Labor Party is in the completest sympathy with the Indian people's aspiration towards independence," and there the subject dropped, neither speakers nor audiences having the faintest interest in it. I don't think throughout the election I heard a Labor speaker spontaneously mention India, and they rarely mentioned Europe except to make the demagogic and misleading claim that a government of the Left would be able to "come to an understanding with Soviet Russia." It is easy to see what dangers are contained in this optimism about home affairs and disregard of conditions abroad. The trouble could come to a head in dozens of ways—over India or the colonies, over the need to cut our rations further in order to prevent occupied Germany from starving, over mobility of labor, over the inevitable muddles and failures in re-housing, and so on and so forth. The great need of the moment is to make people aware of what is happening and why, and to persuade them that Socialism is a *better* way of life but not necessarily, in its first stages, a more comfortable one. I have no doubt they would accept this if it were put to them in the right way: but at present nothing of the kind is being attempted.

Up to date there has been no definite sign of a re-orientation in foreign policy. A Labor government has fewer reasons than a Conservative one for propping up unpopular monarchs and dictators, but it cannot disregard British strategic interests. I think it is an error to suppose, as the public was allowed to suppose during the election, that the Labor leaders will be more subservient to the USSR than the Tories were. After the first few months it will probably be the other way about. Most of them—Laski, for instance, is an exception—have no illusions about the Soviet system, they are involved, as the Tories are not, in the ideological struggle between the eastern and western conceptions of Socialism, and if they choose to stand up to Russia public opinion will support them, whereas Tory motives for opposing Russia were always justly suspect. One probable source of trouble in the near future is Palestine. The Labor Party, and the Left generally, is very strongly committed to support of the Jews against the Arabs, largely because it is only the Jewish case that ever gets a hearing in England. Few English people realize that the Palestine issue is partly a color issue and that an Indian nationalist, for instance, would probably side with the Arabs. As to the long-term aspects of international policy, they are largely governed by geography. Britain, not strong enough to compete singlehanded with Russia or America, has three alternatives. One is to carry on as at present, acquiescing in "spheres of interest" and holding the Empire together as well as possible; another is to move definitely into the orbit of the USA; and the other is to liberate India, cut the links with the Dominions, and form a solid bloc of the western European states and their African possessions. Various observers, including scientists, assure me that the third alternative is technically feasable and that such a bloc could be stronger than either the USA or the USSR. But it seems to me a pipe dream. The centrifugal forces in both France and Britain, the two countries that would matter most, are far too strong.

In spite of the difficulties and dangers I have outlined above, the new government starts off in a very strong position. Unless the Party suffers a major split, Labor is secure in office for at least five years, probably longer. Its one serious opponent, the Conservative Party, is discredited and bankrupt of ideas. Moreover the people who are in power this time are not a gang of easily-bribed weaklings like those of 1929. Like nearly everyone else in England, I know very little about Attlee. Someone who does know him tells me that he is in fact the colorless creature that he appears—one of those secondary figures who step into a leading position because of the death or resignation of somebody else, and hold on to it by being industrious and methodical. He certainly has not the magnetism that a statesman needs nowadays, and the cartoonists of the daily press are frankly puzzled to find some outstanding characteristic (cf. Churchill's cigar, Chamberlain's umbrella, Lloyd George's hair) by which they can popularize him. But the other people in a commanding position in the government, Bevin, Morrison, Greenwood, Cripps, Aneurin Bevan, are tougher and abler than their opposite numbers in the Conservative Party, Churchill's tendency having been to surround himself with yes-men. The composition of the House has altered greatly. For the first time the bulk of the Labor Party members are not trade union officials but come from the constituency parties. Of the 390 Labor members, about 90 are trade union officials and about another 40 are proletarians of one kind or another. The rest are mostly middle-class, and include large numbers of factory managers, doctors, lawyers and journalists. The salaried and professional middle class has now largely "gone left," and its votes were an important factor in swinging the election. It is difficult to believe that this government will collapse in the same ignominious way as those of 1929 and 1923. Five years should be long enough to tide over the worst period. Heaven knows whether the government has any serious intention of introducing Socialism, but if it has, I don't see what there is to stop it.

The news of the Japanese surrender came in yesterday about lunchtime, when I was in Fleet Street. There was quite a bit of jubilation in the streets, and people in upstairs offices instantly began tearing up old papers and throwing them out of the window. This idea occurred to everyone simultaneously, and for a couple of miles my bus travelled through a rain of paper fragments which glittered in the sunlight as they came down and littered the pavements ankle deep. It annoyed me rather. In England you can't get paper to print books on, but apparently there is always plenty of it for this kind of thing. Incidentally the British War Office alone uses more paper than the whole of the book trade.

The prompt surrender of Japan seems to have altered people's outlook on the atomic bomb. At the beginning everyone I spoke to about it, or overheard in the street, was simply horrified. Now they begin to feel that there's something to be said for a weapon that could end the war in two days. Much speculation as to "whether the Russians have got it too." Also, from some quarters, demands that Anglo-America should hand over the secret of the bomb to Russia, which does seem to be carrying trustfulness a bit far.

George Orwell

1. Orwell's Payments Book states that he was paid £2.10.0 for this article, and he dates it 11 August 1945. That date probably applies to the bulk of the article, but the penultimate paragraph states that 'news of the Japanese surrender came in yesterday about lunchtime.' Japan surrendered on 14 August, but the news was not announced in Britain until 0045 on the 15th (by the Prime Minister, Clement Attlee, in a BBC broadcast). The President of the United States, Harry S Truman, gave a simultaneous press conference. The 15th and 16th were declared public holidays in Britain, and the scenes Orwell describes are consonant with 15 August; that suggests a date of 16 August for the completion of this Letter. However, Orwell's reference to lunchtime must refer to the 14th, before the news was announced. The headline of the News Chronicle on the 15th was 'The World War is Over,' so by lunchtime on that date the news was hardly fresh. On the 14th, newspapers were reporting unofficially that

the Japanese were said to be negotiating with the U.S. Commander of the Pacific Fleet, Admiral Chester W. Nimitz. It may be that Orwell heard of the surrender twelve hours in advance of the announcement by Attlee and Truman; if so, that suggests the date for the completion of this Letter should be the 15th.
2. Labour won 394 seats; Conservatives 188; Independents 14; Liberal National 13; Liberals 12; Ulster Unionists 9; ILP 3; Communists 2; Irish Nationalists 2; Nationalists 2; Common Wealth 1; Total: 640

2720. Review of *That Hideous Strength* by C. S. Lewis; *We Mixed Our Drinks* by Nerina Shute

Manchester Evening News, 16 August 1945

On the whole, novels are better when there are no miracles in them. Still, it is possible to think of a fairly large number of worth-while books in which ghosts, magic, second-sight, angels, mermaids, and what-not play a part.

Mr. C. S. Lewis's "That Hideous Strength" can be included in their number—though, curiously enough, it would probably have been a better book if the magical element had been left out. For in essence it is a crime story, and the miraculous happenings, though they grow more frequent towards the end, are not integral to it.

In general outline, and to some extent in atmosphere, it rather resembles G. K. Chesterton's "The Man Who Was Thursday."

Mr. Lewis probably owes something to Chesterton as a writer, and certainly shares his horror of modern machine civilisation (the title of the book, by the way, is taken from a poem about the Tower of Babel) and his reliance on the "eternal verities" of the Christian Church, as against scientific materialism or nihilism.

His book describes the struggle of a little group of sane people against a nightmare that nearly conquers the world. A company of mad scientists—or, perhaps, they are not mad, but have merely destroyed in themselves all human feeling, all notion of good and evil—are plotting to conquer Britain, then the whole planet, and then other planets, until they have brought the universe under their control.

All superfluous life is to be wiped out, all natural forces tamed, the common people are to be used as slaves and vivisection subjects by the ruling caste of scientists, who even see their way to conferring immortal life upon themselves. Man, in short, is to storm the heavens and overthrow the gods, or even to become a god himself.

There is nothing outrageously improbable in such a conspiracy. Indeed, at a moment when a single atomic bomb—of a type already pronounced "obsolete"—has just blown probably three hundred thousand people to fragments, it sounds all too topical. Plenty of people in our age do entertain the monstrous dreams of power that Mr. Lewis attributes to his characters, and we are within sight of the time when such dreams will be realisable.

His description of the N.I.C.E. (National Institute of Co-ordinated Experiments), with its world-wide ramifications, its private army, its secret torture chambers, and its inner ring of adepts ruled over by a mysterious personage known as The Head, is as exciting as any detective story.

It would be a very hardened reader who would not experience a thrill on learning that The Head is actually—however, that would be giving the game away.

One could recommend this book unreservedly if Mr. Lewis had succeeded in keeping it all on a single level. Unfortunately, the supernatural keeps breaking in, and it does so in rather confusing, undisciplined ways. The scientists are endeavouring, among other things, to get hold of the body of the ancient Celtic magician Merlin, who has been buried—not dead, but in a trance—for the last 1,500 years, in hopes of learning from him the secrets of pre-Christian magic.

They are frustrated by a character who is only doubtfully a human being, having spent part of his time on another planet where he has been gifted with eternal youth. Then there is a woman with second sight, one or two ghosts, and various superhuman visitors from outer space, some of them with rather tiresome names which derive from earlier books of Mr. Lewis's. The book ends in a way that is so preposterous that it does not even succeed in being horrible in spite of much bloodshed.

Much is made of the fact that the scientists are actually in touch with evil spirits, although this fact is known only to the inmost circle. Mr. Lewis appears to believe in the existence of such spirits, and of benevolent ones as well. He is entitled to his beliefs, but they weaken his story, not only because they offend the average reader's sense of probability but because in effect they decide the issue in advance. When one is told that God and the Devil are in conflict one always knows which side is going to win. The whole drama of the struggle against evil lies in the fact that one does not have supernatural aid. However, by the standard of the novels appearing nowadays, this is a book worth reading.

"We Mixed our Drinks" is one of those books that are valuable in a different way from what the author intended. It is described on the dust jacket as "The autobiography of an odd, rebellious young woman," and the phrase conveys well enough the narcissistic atmosphere of the whole book. The authoress likes to refer to herself in the third person and by her surname— "Shute did this" and "Shute did that"—a habit which somehow calls to mind a little girl with a pink bow in her hair posing in front of a looking-glass and remarking: "Aren't I sweet?"

From a sociological point of view, however, the book has value as a sort of postscript to "Cavalcade," [1] a catalogue of all the fashionable follies from about 1930 onwards. Although earning her living mostly by writing film criticism and publicity for cosmetics, Miss Shute has had time to cast a fleeting glance at very nearly everything and to swallow quite a few political nostrums ranging from Soviet Communism to something called Christian Democracy.

Companionate marriage, Mosley's New Party, Buchmanism, Nudism, Communism, Balletomania, Surrealism, Common Wealth, and many other topics are given the "once-over," and the narrative is studded with brief comments on famous writers, some of whose names are incorrectly spelt. It all ends happily with a hard-won divorce, a fresh marriage and the conviction that as a result of the war Britain has been born anew.

This is a silly superficial book, but if you want to know something about Lord Beaverbrook's luncheon manners, or how many fur coats a film star is expected to possess or what the Archbishop of Canterbury said about the Duke of Windsor, Miss Shute is the person to tell you.

[Fee: £8.8.0; 15.8.45]

1. *Cavalcade*, a patriotic chronicle play by Noël Coward telling the story of a family from 1899 to 1930, was performed at Drury Lane, with great success, in 1931, with a very large cast; a film version was made in 1933.

2721. Publication of *Animal Farm*; 'The Freedom of the Press'

London, 17 August 1945; New York, 26 August 1946

Animal Farm was published in London by Secker & Warburg on 17 August 1945 and in New York by Harcourt, Brace on 26 August 1946. The first English edition was of 4,500 copies. A second impression, of 10,000 copies, was published in November 1945 (see *2766, n. 2*); a third, of 6,000 copies, in October 1946. These all sold at 6s 0d per copy. The first cheap edition—5,000 copies at 3s 6d—was published by Secker & Warburg in May 1949. Thus, by the time Orwell died, 25,500 copies of *Animal Farm* had been issued in Britain. The first American edition comprised 50,000 copies; two impressions, of 430,000 and 110,000 copies, were issued as Book-of-the-Month Club editions; and a separate Canadian edition of 2,000 copies appeared in November 1946. According to Ian Willison's thesis (1953), the copy in the American Library in London has an additional imprint (Kingsport Press, Kingsport, Tenn.) suggesting a second impression, but Harcourt, Brace, the publishers, advised Willison that they issued only one impression. Willison records translations into Portuguese, Swedish, Norwegian, German (in one Swiss and two German-national versions), Polish, Persian (via the British Central Office of Information), Dutch, French, Italian, Ukrainian, Danish, Estonian, Spanish, Korean, Japanese, Telugu, Icelandic, and Russian by the time Orwell died. Many editions and translations have followed, of which the Penguin edition is probably the most commonly available. The first Penguin edition, of 60,000 copies, was published on 27 July 1951, and a second impression, of 40,000 copies, was issued on 24 October 1952. These sold at 1s 6d and 2s 0d respectively. Secker & Warburg published a corrected edition in the *Complete Works* series, as Volume VIII, in 1987; a Penguin reprint of that edition was published in 1989.

Orwell wrote a preface for *Animal Farm*, under the title 'The Freedom of the Press,' and space was left for it, as the pagination of the proofs shows. However, it was not included. The typescript was found many years later by Ian Angus and first published in the *Times Literary Supplement*, 15 September 1972, and then in the *New York Times Magazine*, 8 October 1972, on each occasion with an introduction by Bernard Crick. In March 1947, Orwell wrote a special preface for the Ukrainian edition of *Animal Farm*. 'The Freedom of the Press' is reproduced here from Orwell's typescript; for the Ukrainian introduction, see *3198*. Full details of the publishing history of these prefaces are given in *CW*, VIII.

Animal Farm was widely reviewed and has been subject to much comment since. Two contemporary reviews might be mentioned here. Tosco Fyvel, in *Tribune*, 24 August 1945, called *Animal Farm* a 'gentle satire on a certain State and on the illusions of an age which may already be behind us.' On 7 September, Julian Symons responded:

> Is it not pulling punches a little to call George Orwell's *Animal Farm* a "gentle satire on a certain State"? Should we not expect, in *Tribune* at least, acknowledgment of the fact that it is a satire not at all gentle upon a particular State—Soviet Russia? I suggest that it is begging a central question which will certainly be raised elsewhere to view *Animal Farm* simply as a fairy story: it is in fact a political satire, which cannot be considered without reference to its truth or falsity to facts. It seems to me that (again I would say particularly in *Tribune*) a reviewer should have the courage to identify Napoleon with Stalin, and Snowball with Trotsky, and express an opinion favourable or unfavourable to the author, upon a political ground. In a hundred years' time perhaps, *Animal Farm*, which we can all agree is brilliantly written, may be simply a fairy story: today it is a political satire with a good deal of point.

Simon Watson Taylor, reviewing *Animal Farm* in *Freedom—Through Anarchism*, 25 August 1945, though he does not make identifications, does spell out what he calls the grim moral of this 'delightfully amusing and witty story of a Revolution that Went Wrong,' that (as anarchists had repeatedly stated), 'power corrupts all who succeed in achieving it, and no one with power in his hands escapes its taint. Further, not only is this corruption inevitable but it always shows itself on an increasingly virulent scale. . . . It is this all-important fact which our Tame Communists, living in their two-dimensional world of Party and Leadership, seem utterly unable to realize. . . . I am prepared to claim on behalf of Mr. Orwell that *Animal Farm* is of far greater significance than its unassuming title would suggest.'

Despite its great success, Orwell's earnings from *Animal Farm* were not as great as these long runs might suggest. On 23 January 1950, shortly after Orwell died, the *Evening Standard* stated: '*Animal Farm* made for him at least £12,000. This may seem a low figure, but the majority of the sales were at the low prices of the American Book of the Month Club.' It is not now possible to check the reliability of the figure given by the *Evening Standard*.

THE FREEDOM OF THE PRESS

This book was first thought of, so far as the central idea goes, in 1937, but was not written down until about the end of 1943. By the time when it came to be written it was obvious that there would be great difficulty in getting it published (in spite of the present book shortage which ensures that anything describable as a book will 'sell'), and in the event it was refused by four publishers. Only one of these had any ideological motive. Two had been publishing anti-Russian books for years, and the other had no noticeable political colour. One publisher actually started by accepting the book, but after making the preliminary arrangements he decided to consult the

Ministry of Information, who appear to have warned him, or at any rate strongly advised him, against publishing it. Here is an extract from his letter:

> I mentioned the reaction I had had from an important official in the Ministry of Information with regard to *Animal Farm*. I must confess that this expression of opinion has given me seriously to think. . . . I can see now that it might be regarded as something which it was highly ill-advised to publish at the present time. If the fable were addressed generally to dictators and dictatorships at large then publication would be all right, but the fable does follow, as I see now, so completely the progress of the Russian Soviets and their two dictators, that it can apply only to Russia, to the exclusion of the other dictatorships. Another thing: it would be less offensive if the predominant caste in the fable were not pigs.* I think the choice of pigs as the ruling caste will no doubt give offence to many people, and particularly to anyone who is a bit touchy, as undoubtedly the Russians are.

This kind of thing is not a good symptom. Obviously it is not desirable that a government department should have any power of censorship (except security censorship, which no one objects to in war time) over books which are not officially sponsored. But the chief danger to freedom of thought and speech at this moment is not the direct interference of the MOI or any official body. If publishers and editors exert themselves to keep certain topics out of print, it is not because they are frightened of prosecution but because they are frightened of public opinion. In this country intellectual cowardice is the worst enemy a writer or journalist has to face, and that fact does not seem to me to have had the discussion it deserves.

Any fairminded person with journalistic experience will admit that during this war *official* censorship has not been particularly irksome. We have not been subjected to the kind of totalitarian 'co-ordination' that it might have been reasonable to expect. The press has some justified grievances, but on the whole the Government has behaved well and has been surprisingly tolerant of minority opinions. The sinister fact about literary censorship in England is that it is largely voluntary. Unpopular ideas can be silenced, and inconvenient facts kept dark, without the need for any official ban. Anyone who has lived long in a foreign country will know of instances of sensational items of news—things which on their own merits would get the big headlines—being kept right out of the British press, not because the Government intervened but because of a general tacit agreement that 'it wouldn't do' to mention that particular fact. So far as the daily newspapers go, this is easy to understand. The British press is extremely centralised, and most of it is owned by wealthy men who have every motive to be dishonest on certain important topics. But the same kind of veiled censorship also operates in books and periodicals, as well as in plays, films and radio. At any given

---

* It is not quite clear whether this suggested modification is Mr . . .'s own idea, or originated with the Ministry of Information; but it seems to have the official ring about it [Orwell's footnote].

moment there is an orthodoxy, a body of ideas which it is assumed that all right-thinking people will accept without question. It is not exactly forbidden to say this, that or the other, but it is 'not done' to say it, just as in mid-Victorian times it was 'not done' to mention trousers in the presence of a lady. Anyone who challenges the prevailing orthodoxy finds himself silenced with surprising effectiveness. A genuinely unfashionable opinion is almost never given a fair hearing, either in the popular press or in the highbrow periodicals.

At this moment what is demanded by the prevailing orthodoxy is an uncritical admiration of Soviet Russia. Everyone knows this, nearly every-one acts on it. Any serious criticism of the Soviet régime, any disclosure of facts which the Soviet government would prefer to keep hidden, is next door to unprintable. And this nation-wide conspiracy to flatter our ally takes place, curiously enough, against a background of genuine intellectual tolerance. For though you are not allowed to criticise the Soviet government, at least you are reasonably free to criticise our own. Hardly anyone will print an attack on Stalin, but it is quite safe to attack Churchill, at any rate in books and periodicals. And throughout five years of war, during two or three of which we were fighting for national survival, countless books, pamphlets and articles advocating a compromise peace have been published without interference. More, they have been published without exciting much disapproval. So long as the prestige of the USSR is not involved, the principle of free speech has been reasonably well upheld. There are other forbidden topics, and I shall mention some of them presently, but the prevailing attitude towards the USSR is much the most serious symptom. It is, as it were, spontaneous, and is not due to the action of any pressure group.

The servility with which the greater part of the English intelligentsia have swallowed and repeated Russian propaganda from 1941 onwards would be quite astounding if it were not that they have behaved similarly on several earlier occasions. On one controversial issue after another the Russian viewpoint has been accepted without examination and then publicised with complete disregard to historical truth or intellectual decency. To name only one instance, the BBC celebrated the twenty-fifth anniversary of the Red Army without mentioning Trotsky. This was about as accurate as commem-orating the battle of Trafalgar without mentioning Nelson, but it evoked no protest from the English intelligentsia. In the internal struggles in the various occupied countries, the British press has in almost all cases sided with the faction favoured by the Russians and libelled the opposing faction, some-times suppressing material evidence in order to do so. A particularly glaring case was that of Colonel Mihailovich, the Jugoslav Chetnik leader. The Russians, who had their own Jugoslav protégé in Marshal Tito, accused Mihailovich of collaborating with the Germans. This accusation was promptly taken up by the British press: Mihailovich's supporters were given no chance of answering it, and facts contradicting it were simply kept out of print. In July of 1943 the Germans offered a reward of 100,000 gold crowns for the capture of Tito, and a similar reward for the capture of Mihailovich. The British press 'splashed' the reward for Tito, but only one paper mentioned (in small print) the reward for Mihailovich; and the charges of collaborating with the Germans continued.[1] Very similar things happened during the Spanish civil war. Then, too, the factions on the Republican side which the Russians were determined to crush were recklessly libelled in the English leftwing° press, and any statement in their defence even in letter form, was refused publication. At present, not only is serious criticism of the USSR considered reprehensible, but even the fact of the existence of such criticism is kept secret in some cases. For example, shortly before his death Trotsky had written a biography of Stalin. One may assume that it was not an altogether unbiased book, but obviously it was saleable. An American publisher had arranged to issue it and the book was in print—I believe the review copies had been sent out—when the USSR entered the war. The book was immediately withdrawn. Not a word about this has ever appeared in the British press, though clearly the existence of such a book, and its suppression, was a news item worth a few paragraphs.

It is important to distinguish between the kind of censorship that the English literary intelligentsia voluntarily impose upon themselves, and the censorship that can sometimes be enforced by pressure groups. Notoriously, certain topics cannot be discussed because of 'vested interests'. The best-known case is the patent medicine racket. Again, the Catholic Church has considerable influence in the press and can silence criticism of itself to some extent. A scandal involving a Catholic priest is almost never given publicity, whereas an Anglican priest who gets into trouble (e.g. the Rector of Stiffkey[2]) is headline news. It is very rare for anything of an anti-Catholic tendency to appear on the stage or in a film. Any actor can tell you that a play or film which attacks or makes fun of the Catholic Church is liable to be boycotted in the press and will probably be a failure. But this kind of thing is harmless, or at least it is understandable. Any large organisation will look after its own interests as best it can, and overt propaganda is not a thing to object to. One would no more expect the *Daily Worker* to publicise unfavourable facts about the USSR than one would expect the *Catholic Herald* to denounce the Pope. But then every thinking person knows the *Daily Worker* and the *Catholic Herald* for what they are. What is disquieting is that where the USSR and its policies are concerned one cannot expect intelligent criticism or even, in many cases, plain honesty from Liberal[3] writers and journalists who are under no direct pressure to falsify their opinions. Stalin is sacrosanct and certain aspects of his policy must not be seriously discussed. This rule has been almost universally observed since 1941, but it had operated, to a greater extent than is sometimes realised, for ten years earlier than that. Throughout that time, criticism of the Soviet régime *from the left* could only obtain a hearing with difficulty. There was a huge output of anti-Russian literature, but nearly all of it was from the Conservative angle and manifestly dishonest, out of date and actuated by sordid motives. On the other side there was an equally huge and almost equally dishonest stream of pro-Russian propaganda, and what amounted to a boycott on anyone who tried to discuss all-important questions in a grown-up manner. You could, indeed, publish anti-Russian books, but to do so was to make sure of being ignored or misrepresented by nearly the whole of the highbrow press. Both publicly and privately you were warned that it was 'not done'. What you said might possibly be true, but it was 'inopportune' and 'played into the hands of' this or that reactionary interest. This attitude was usually defended on the ground that the international situation, and the urgent need for an Anglo-Russian alliance, demanded it; but it was clear that this was a rationalisation. The English intelligentsia, or a great part of it, had developed a nationalistic loyalty towards the USSR, and in their hearts they felt that to cast any doubt on the wisdom of Stalin was a kind of blasphemy. Events in Russia and events elsewhere were to be judged by different standards. The endless executions in the purges of 1936–8 were applauded by life-long opponents of capital punishment, and it was considered equally proper to publicise famines when they happened in India and to conceal them when they happened in the Ukraine. And if this was true before the war, the intellectual atmosphere is certainly no better now.

But now to come back to this book of mine. The reaction towards it of most English intellectuals will be quite simple: 'It oughtn't to have been published.' Naturally, those reviewers who understand the art of denigration will not attack it on political grounds but on literary ones. They will say that it is a dull, silly book and a disgraceful waste of paper. This may well be true, but it is obviously not the whole of the story. One does not say that a book 'ought not to have been published' merely because it is a bad book. After all, acres of rubbish are printed daily and no one bothers. The English intelligentsia, or most of them, will object to this book because it traduces their Leader and (as they see it) does harm to the cause of progress. If it did the opposite they would have nothing to say against it, even if its literary faults were ten times as glaring as they are. The success of, for instance, the Left Book Club over a period of four or five years shows how willing they are to tolerate both scurrility and slipshod writing, provided that it tells them what they want to hear.

The issue involved here is quite a simple one: Is every opinion, however unpopular—however foolish, even—entitled to a hearing? Put it in that form and nearly any English intellectual will feel that he ought to say 'Yes'. But give it a concrete shape, and ask, 'How about an attack on Stalin? Is *that* entitled to a hearing?', and the answer more often than not will be 'No'. In that case the current orthodoxy happens to be challenged, and so the principle of free speech lapses. Now, when one demands liberty of speech and of the press, one is not demanding absolute liberty. There always must be, or at any rate there always will be, some degree of censorship, so long as organised societies endure. But freedom, as Rosa Luxembourg° said, is 'freedom for the other fellow'. The same principle is contained in the famous words of Voltaire: 'I detest what you say; I will defend to the death your right to say it.'³ª If the intellectual liberty which without a doubt has been one of the distinguishing marks of western civilisation means anything at all, it means that everyone shall have the right to say and to print what he believes to be the truth, provided only that it does not harm the rest of the community in some quite unmistakable way. Both capitalist democracy and the western versions of Socialism have till recently taken that principle for granted. Our Government, as I have already pointed out, still makes some show of respecting it. The ordinary people in the street—partly, perhaps, because they are not sufficiently interested in ideas to be intolerant about them—still vaguely hold that 'I suppose everyone's got a right to their own opinion.' It is only, or at any rate it is chiefly, the literary and scientific intelligentsia, the very people who ought to be the guardians of liberty, who are beginning to despise it, in theory as well as in practice.

One of the peculiar phenomena of our time is the renegade Liberal. Over and above the familiar Marxist claim that 'bourgeois liberty' is an illusion, there is now a widespread tendency to argue that one can only defend democracy by totalitarian methods. If one loves democracy, the argument runs, one must crush its enemies by no matter what means. And who are its enemies? It always appears that they are not only those who attack it openly and consciously, but those who 'objectively' endanger it by spreading mistaken doctrines. In other words, defending democracy involves destroying all independence of thought. This argument was used, for instance, to justify the Russian purges. The most ardent Russophile hardly believed that all of the victims were guilty of all the things they were accused of: but by holding heretical opinions they 'objectively' harmed the régime, and therefore it was quite right not only to massacre them but to discredit them by false accusations. The same argument was used to justify the quite conscious lying that went on in the leftwing press about the Trotskyists and other Republican minorities in the Spanish civil war. And it was used again as a reason for yelping against *habeas corpus* when Mosley was released in 1943.

These people don't see that if you encourage totalitarian methods, the time may come when they will be used against you instead of for you. Make a habit of imprisoning Fascists without trial, and perhaps the process won't stop at Fascists. Soon after the suppressed *Daily Worker* had been reinstated, I was lecturing to a workingmen's college in South London. The audience were working-class and lower-middle class intellectuals—the same sort of audience that one used to meet at Left Book Club branches. The lecture had touched on the freedom of the press, and at the end, to my astonishment, several questioners stood up and asked me: Did I not think that the lifting of the ban on the *Daily Worker* was a great mistake? When asked why, they said that it was a paper of doubtful loyalty and ought not to be tolerated in war time. I found myself defending the *Daily Worker*, which has gone out of its way to libel me more than once. But where had these people learned this essentially totalitarian outlook? Pretty certainly they had learned it from the Communists themselves! Tolerance and decency are deeply rooted in England, but they are not indestructible, and they have to be kept alive partly by conscious effort. The result of preaching totalitarian doctrines is to weaken the instinct by means of which free peoples know what is or is not dangerous. The case of Mosley illustrates this. In 1940 it was perfectly right to intern Mosley, whether or not he had committed any technical crime. We were fighting for our lives and could not allow a possible quisling to go free. To keep him shut up, without trial, in 1943 was an outrage. The general failure to see this was a bad symptom, though it is true that the agitation against Mosley's release was partly factitious and partly a rationalisation of other discontents. But how much of the present slide towards Fascist ways of thought is traceable to the 'anti-Fascism' of the past ten years and the unscrupulousness it has entailed?

It is important to realise that the current Russomania is only a symptom of the general weakening of the western liberal tradition. Had the MOI chipped in and definitely vetoed the publication of this book, the bulk of the English intelligentsia would have seen nothing disquieting in this. Uncritical loyalty to the USSR happens to be the current orthodoxy, and where the supposed interests of the USSR are involved they are willing to tolerate not only censorship but the deliberate falsification of history. To name one instance. At the death of John Reed, the author of *Ten Days that Shook the World*—a first-hand account of the early days of the Russian Revolution—the copyright of the book passed into the hands of the British Communist Party, to whom I believe Reed had bequeathed it. Some years later the British Communists, having destroyed the original edition of the book as completely as they could, issued a garbled version from which they had eliminated mentions of Trotsky and also omitted the introduction written by Lenin.[4] If a radical intelligentsia had still existed in Britain, this act of forgery would have been exposed and denounced in every literary paper in the country. As it was there was little or no protest. To many English intellectuals it seemed quite a natural thing to do. And this tolerance or[5] plain dishonesty means much more than that admiration of Russia happens to be fashionable at this moment. Quite possibly that particular fashion will not last. For all I know, by the time this book is published my view of the Soviet régime may be the generally-accepted one. But what use would that be in itself? To exchange one orthodoxy for another is not necessarily an advance. The enemy is the gramophone mind, whether or not one agrees with the record that is being played at the moment.

I am well acquainted with all the arguments against freedom of thought and speech—the arguments which claim that it cannot exist, and the arguments which claim that it ought not to. I answer simply that they don't convince me and that our civilisation over a period of four hundred years has been founded on the opposite notion. For quite a decade past I have believed that the existing Russian régime is a mainly evil thing, and I claim the right to say so, in spite of the fact that we are allies with the USSR in a war which I want to see won. If I had to choose a text to justify myself, I should choose the line from Milton:

By the known rules of ancient liberty.[6]

The word *ancient* emphasises the fact that intellectual freedom is a deep-rooted tradition without which our characteristic western culture could only doubtfully exist. From that tradition many of our intellectuals are visibly turning away. They have accepted the principle that a book should be published or suppressed, praised or damned, not on its merits but according to political expediency. And others who do not actually hold this view assent to it from sheer cowardice. An example of this is the failure of the numerous and vocal English pacifists to raise their voices against the prevalent worship of Russian militarism. According to those pacifists, all violence is evil, and they have urged us at every stage of the war to give in or at least to make a compromise peace. But how many of them have ever suggested that war is also evil when it is waged by the Red Army? Apparently the Russians have a right to defend themselves, whereas for us to do [so] is a deadly sin. One can only explain this contradiction in one way: that is, by a cowardly desire to keep in with the bulk of the intelligentsia, whose patriotism is directed towards the USSR rather than towards Britain. I know that the English intelligentsia have plenty of reason for their timidity and dishonesty, indeed I know by heart the arguments by which they justify themselves. But at least let us have no more nonsense about defending liberty against Fascism. If liberty means anything at all it means the right to tell people what they do not want to hear. The common people still vaguely subscribe to that doctrine and act on it. In our country—it is not the same in all countries: it was not so in republican France, and it is not so in the USA today—it is the liberals who fear liberty and the intellectuals who want to do dirt on the intellect: it is to draw attention to that fact that I have written this preface.

1. General Draža Mihailović (1893?–1946) led the Chetnik guerrillas against the Axis during World War II. He and Tito failed to agree, and Tito won Allied support. After the war, Mihailović was tried for treason and executed. See also *1579, n. 2*.
2. The Reverend Harold Davidson, when Rector of Stiffkey, Norfolk, though commended by the Bishop of London for his missionary work, was defrocked by Norwich Consistory Court for immoral practices. The case proved a field-day for the popular press. Davidson thereafter made a living by entertaining cinema audiences and then appearing in a barrel as an attraction at Blackpool Pleasure Beach. 'In the end, like the early Christians, he was thrown to the lions' (Malcolm Muggeridge, *The Thirties*, 1940, 1971 ed., 172): he was exhibited in 1937 in a circus cage of lions but was mauled and killed.
3. 'Liberal' is given a capital 'L' throughout the typescript.
3a. Attributed to Voltaire in S. G. Tallentyre, *The Friends of Voltaire* (1907).
4. There is no evidence that such a 'garbled' edition was issued by the British Communist Party or anyone else. Orwell may be confusing the attempt by the *News Chronicle* to serialise *Ten Days that Shook the World* in 1937 to mark the twentieth anniversary of the Russian Revolution. This the Party would only permit if all references to Trotsky were removed. See *The New Leader*, 19 November 1937 and *Evening Standard*, 12 November 1937. (Information from Clive Fleay and Mike Sanders.) See also Orwell's fourth annotation to Randall Swingler's 'The Right to Free Expression,' *Polemic*, 5, September–October 1946, *3090*.
5. or] *possibly* of
6. Compare the first two lines of the epigram from Euripedes' *The Suppliants* on the title-page of Milton's *Areopagitica* (1644): 'This is true Liberty when free born men / Having to advise the public may speak free.'

2722. To Geoffrey Earle

17 August 1945   Typewritten, with handwritten postscript

> 27 B Canonbury Square
> Islington
> London   N 1

Dear Mr Earle,

I hope this is the kind of thing you wanted.[1] Please excuse the paper; I was out of typing paper and could not buy any more during the holiday.

I make it about 2700 words. If that is too long it [ca]n be cut in the middle. In the two extracts I have followed the text as closely as possible, merely abridging a bit. If you want a copy of the book these stories come from to deal with the copyright people, I can send it you. I am sending back the biography of Jack London separately.

I understand this is to go out some time in October. I am going to be away for the first two or three weeks of September, so if you want to see me in connection with the script, perhaps it would be better if it were before the end of this month.

> Yours sincerely
> [Signed] Geo. Orwell
> George Orwell

PS. I wonder if we could get Laidman Brown° [2] for one of the caste°? He's always good.

1. N. E. Wadsley, Administrative Assistant in the BBC's Services Educational Unit, acknowledged the script, on Jack London (see *2715*), on 20 August; Earle, absent on leave, was to be back on 27 August. Wadsley suggested that Orwell ring, so that he and Earle could discuss the script on 27 August. Orwell entered this script in his Payments Book for 17 August 1945; the fee was £15.15.0.
2. Laidman Browne (1896–1961) made his debut in 1925, had much experience as a Shakespearian actor, and joined the BBC Repertory Company in September 1939. He did not take part in this broadcast.

2723. To Roger Senhouse

17 August 1945[1]   Typewritten

> 27 B Canonbury Square
> Islington
> London   N 1

Dear Roger,

Herewith list of answers to your corrections.[2] I suppose you have a carbon of the list you sent (if not I still have it.)

I've remarked a correction for p. 85 which I'm not sure whether I made in the corrected proof I sent back to you. I've put this in the list with the others.

> Yours
> George

CORRECTIONS — "CRITICAL ESSAYS"

P. 7, l. 12.	Yes.
P. 10, l. 4.	No. It is correct—ie. *de*structive, with only the de-italicised.
P. 23, par. 3, l. 5.	No. OED gives "mews" as singular.
P. 23, next line.	Yes.
P. 32, par. 2, l. 4.	Yes, "identify himself" is better.
P. 48, l. 8.	Yes.
P. 57, par. 2.	1. No. "Every" is singular.
ls. 4 & 6.	2. I feel "contents" has established itself as a singular.
P. 59, l. 4.	Yes.
P. 84, l. 12 from end.	As you like.

P. 85, par. 3. First sentence of this par. should be 2 sentences & should read thus: "Mr Wells, like Dickens, belongs to the non-military middle class. The thunder of guns, the jingle of spurs, the catch in the throat when the old flag goes by, leave him manifestly cold."

P. 92, mid-page 4 lines from end of para.	"anti trade-union" is better.
P. 101, last l.	As you like.
P. 108, footnote.	Yes.
P. 110, l. 6.	No. ("Other side of the fence" has the sense of "away from.")
P. 112, par. 2, l. 18.	Yes.

P. 113, 6 ls. from end. NO! Would sound intolerable pedantry to leave out the "to." As this is written in English a French phrase imported into it becomes for practical purposes English and must be governed by English grammar rules. Otherwise one would have, for instance, to decline Latin nouns used in English and say "We must find a modum vivendi" or "I consider him the fontem et originem of all the trouble" etc.

P. 123, 4 ls. from end 1st par. after quote. As you like.

P. 125 All right, leave the footnote in, but I'd like to verify it if you know anyone who has Miller's books. It'll be either, I think, in "Max & the White Phagocytes" or in some periodical.

P. 156. "June 25th 1941" is better, but in that case the other dates in the same par. should be altered accordingly.

The corrections were all made (so far as they can be identified) in *Critical Essays* except that on p. 92, 'trade-union' is printed as 'Trade Union' and the dates on p. 156 are given in the form 25th June 1941. The footnote on p. 125 was retained but a reference to *Max and the White Phagocytes* or some periodical is avoided. The U.S. edition, *Dickens, Dali & Others*, has these amendments except that 'Trade Union' was printed 'trade union,' without a hyphen.

1. Received by Secker & Warburg on the date written, according to their date stamp.
2. Orwell's letter is annotated (in Senhouse's hand?) with the name 'Salammbô' and 'pp 51, 132, 133.' This gives the name as spelt in *Critical Essays* and was presumably either a note to correct it or to check this spelling.

2724. To Leonard Moore

18 August 1945   Typewritten

27 B Canonbury Square   Islington   London   N 1

Dear Mr Moore,
I have a copy of "Inside the Whale" I can spare, and I think I can get hold of a copy of "Wigan Pier." If so I'll send these under separate cover. I haven't got a copy of "Homage to Catalonia", ie. I have only 1 which I don't wish to part with. Couldn't you get Warburg to send them one? I have no doubt he has some copies left.[1] Of the three, this is the book that would most lend itself to translation. You could perhaps explain to Nagel that two out of the three essays in "Inside the Whale" are going to be reprinted in "Critical Essays."
  I received a duplicate copy of Warburg's letter to you about the contracts.[2] I will see him before I go away for my holiday, which I intend doing in September.

Yours sincerely
Eric Blair

1. Although only 1,500 copies were printed in 1938, they had not all been sold by the time a second (Uniform) edition was printed in 1951.
2. See letter to Moore, 24 August 1945, *2731*.

2725. To Herbert Read

18 August 1945   Typewritten

27 B Canonbury Square
Islington
London   N 1

Dear Read,
Thanks for your letter.[1] I'm glad you liked "Animal Farm." If you're going to be back in London about the end of August we could perhaps meet shortly after that, as I would like to talk to you about this Freedom Defence Committee.[2] George Woodcock[3] asked me to be vice-chairman, which I agreed to, but I haven't been very active, because I am really not much good

at that kind of thing, and it's all still a bit vague in my mind. I am going away for my holiday about September 10th, but shall be in London till then.

I lost my wife in March. I cannot remember whether you ever met her. It was a beastly, cruel business, however I don't think she expected to die (it happened during an operation), so perhaps it was not so bad as it might have been. I was in France at the time and only got back after she was dead. My little son is now 15 months. Fortunately he has always had excellent health and I have got a very good nurse who looks after both him and me. I am trying to take a cottage on Jura and am going up to arrange about the rent and repairs in September. If I can fix it up and manage to transfer some furniture there, which is the most difficult thing, I can live there in the summers, and it would be a wonderful place for a child to learn to walk in.

Rayner Heppenstall is out of the army and is working at the BBC. Tribune is going through some changes now that Labour has won the election. Bevan and Strauss[4] are severing their official connection with it and Michael Foot[5] is going on to the editorial board. It will thus be able to continue as a critical organ and not have to back up the Government all the time. I am probably going to continue my column, or something similar, after I come back from my holiday. I stopped it, of course, while I was in France, and didn't start again because Bevan was terrified there might be a row over "Animal Farm," which might have been embarrassing if the book had come out before the election, as it was at first intended to.

Hoping to see you.

Yours
Geo. Orwell

1. Herbert Read (see *522, n. 1*) wrote to Orwell on 13 August, to say that he had read an advance copy of *Animal Farm* 'at a sitting with enormous enjoyment.' His son of 7½ had insisted on having a chapter read him each evening and had enjoyed it 'innocently as much as I enjoy it maliciously. It thus stands the test which only classics of satire like Gulliver survive.' Read was particularly impressed by its rare quality of completeness. 'The cap fits all round the head—everything is there & yet there is no forcing of the story—it is all completely natural & inevitable. I do most heartily congratulate you.' Read was anxious to meet Orwell when he, Read, returned from holiday in Scotland. He knew much had happened to Orwell since they had last met but was 'only vaguely informed about the tragic side of it.' He hoped Orwell had come through to some peace of mind and that his health was better.
2. The Freedom Defence Committee was founded in 1945. It was originally formed in 1944 as the Freedom Press Defence Committee—with Herbert Read as its chairman—to fight a court case affecting the editors of the Freedom Press. After the trial it was decided to enlarge the Committee and rename it. It was then that Orwell was asked to join, and he became vice-chairman on the understanding that it would not involve him in 'office work.' Read was still chairman; George Woodcock was secretary. The Committee fought innumerable cases of infringement of civil liberties, and many of these were reported in its *Bulletin*. The Committee was active until 1949. (Details from George Woodcock in a letter to Howard Fink, 8 May 1963.) The FDC was not connected with the National Council for Civil Liberties, established following the passing of the Disaffection Act (known as the Sedition Act) in 1934, of which E. M. Forster was the first president. By 1945 the NCCL was Communist-dominated.
3. George Woodcock (1912–1995), author, Anarchist, editor of *Now*, 1940–47, and later Professor of English at the University of British Columbia. After his controversy with Orwell (see *1270*), they corresponded and remained friends until Orwell's death. His books included *The Crystal Spirit: A Study of George Orwell* (1967) and *Orwell's Message: 1984 and the Present* (1984).

4. Aneurin (Nye) Bevan (1897–1960), Labour M.P., and Minister of Health, 1945–50, was one of Wales's greatest orators and the symbol of the Socialist aspirations of the Left. As a director of *Tribune* he had given Orwell complete freedom to write as he pleased, however unpopular or inexpedient his anti-Soviet line might be with the official Left. See *565, 28.8.39, n. 11; 1064, n. 3*; for Orwell's Profile of him in *The Observer*, see *2765*. George Russell Strauss (1901–; Baron Strauss, 1979), politician and, at this time, a co-director with Bevan of *Tribune*, had been Labour M.P., 1929–31, but was expelled from the Labour Party for supporting the Popular Front (a Communist-inspired, anti-Fascist alliance), 1939–40. In 1968 he introduced the Theatres Bill for the abolition of stage censorship.
5. Michael Foot (1913–), politician, writer, and journalist, on the extreme Left of the Labour Party. Labour MP for Devonport 1945–55. From 1960 until 1992 (when he retired) Labour MP for Ebbw Vale, the constituency formerly held by Bevan, whose official biography he wrote and whose close friend he had been. He was assistant editor of *Tribune*, 1937–38, editor, 1948–52 and 1955–60, and one of the ablest debaters in the post-war House of Commons. He was Leader of the Labour Party, 1980–83.

2726. Review of *A Forgotten Genius: Sewell of St. Columba's and Radley* by Lionel James

The Observer, 19 August 1945

If Freud did nothing else for humanity, he at least broke people of the habit of relating their dreams at the breakfast table. The diffusion of psychological knowledge has killed a lot of innocence, and if Dr. Sewell, founder of two public schools and headmaster of one, were writing his reminiscences to-day it is doubtful whether he would let slip such a remark as: "To this hour some of the most delightful, touching, blessed associations I have are connected with the Whipping Room at Radley." Not that this remark tells the whole story about Sewell, who seems to have done somewhat less flogging than was usual in the mid-nineteenth century: but it does typify the complete absence of self-knowledge which was the strength and weakness of so many of the great Victorians.

William Sewell was the founder of St. Columba's College, near Dublin, and later of Radley, of which he was also headmaster from 1853 to 1861. If he is now forgotten, this book, which is mostly a mass of ill-digested documentation, is not likely to make him less so, but the author does show good reason for thinking that Sewell, as much as, or even more than, Arnold, was responsible for giving the public schools their present character. He was a High Anglican and a strong Tory, with "a passionate conviction of the importance of birth," but he was also an educational theorist with considerable foresight, and even capable, when planning schools for the aristocracy, of contemplating "the creation and maintenance of analogous institutions for the poor." St. Columba's was frankly founded with the idea of breeding up an Anglo-Irish gentry which should be reliably loyal and Protestant, and Sewell, who realised that the language-difference was one of the roots of the trouble in Ireland, showed his originality by making Gaelic a compulsory subject. His Radley activities had a wider influence.

In the early nineteenth century the public schools were in a very bad way, and it was touch and go whether they survived or not. At even the best-known of them the neglect, disorder, squalor, and vice in which the boys lived would be incredible if countless people had not testified to the facts. As a result the number of their pupils was slumping rapidly. Mr. James gives some interesting figures bearing on this. Harrow had only 69 boys in 1844, having had 350 half a century earlier. Westminster dropped from 282 to 67 between 1821 and 1841. At Eton it was for a long time impossible even to keep up the complement of 70 King's Scholars, and as late as 1841 only two candidates presented themselves for 35 scholarships. Meanwhile the population was growing, the new moneyed class needed schools for their sons, and large day schools which took education seriously were beginning to appear. The older schools might well have vanished altogether if Arnold, Sewell, and a few other gifted men had not saved them by reforming them.

Sewell's eight years at Radley ended in disaster. "No one," says Mr. James, "pretends that finance was his strong point," and the school passed through a period of bankruptcy, thanks to some surprising extravagances. But meanwhile he had left his mark upon it, and his example had influenced other schools. His reforms seem to have been in the direction of stricter supervision, further development of the prefect system, more emphasis on religious teaching, and, above all, encouragement of athletics. He was consciously aiming at the creation of a ruling class, and was one of the first people to realise that it was necessary to train administrators for the newly won Empire. His political outlook was in some ways close to that of Disraeli, and his novel, "Hawkstone," was dedicated to the romantic aristocrat, Lord John Manners.

Mr. James tries hard, but unsuccessfully, to present Sewell as a sympathetic character. Actually he seems, apart from his financial indiscretions, to have been a circumspect person and rather unpopular with his contemporaries. At Winchester he was one of the seven boys who did not join in the famous rebellion; as a young man he was once engaged to be married, but broke off the engagement for reasons he prefers not to mention; at Oxford he had connections with the Oxford Movement, but neatly extricated himself when the storm broke over Tract 90.[1] His Oxford nickname, Suillus (little pig), although a play on his own name, hardly suggests esteem or affection. But Mr. James is justified in claiming that he was in his way an important figure, and that without his efforts compulsory games, the prefect system, and the Whipping Room would probably have played a smaller part in the education of the English upper classes.

[Fee: £10.0.0; 16.8.45]

1. Number ninety was the last tract published by the Tractarians (or Oxford Movement), 1841. Its subject was the Thirty-Nine Articles of the Church of England; it was written by John Henry Newman (1801–1890) and caused uproar among Anglicans because it pointed to the essential Catholicism of the Articles. Newman converted to Roman Catholicism and in 1879 was made a cardinal.

2727. To Leonard Moore

20 August 1945[1]   Typewritten postcard

Monday.
I'm sending on copies of "Wigan Pier" and "Inside the Whale" separately. Another French publisher has asked to see "Animal Farm."[2] What is the position about this? Would it be right to send him a copy, or should one wait until Nagel has made a decision?

[Unsigned]

1. The card has been stamped in Moore's office as having been received on 21 August and answered on 22nd. There is a very clearly visible post-franking mark, but this carries no date. Instead, in celebration of victory, the frank shows two bells suspended from a bold 'V' and the five wavy lines are broken to give the equivalent in Morse code: . . . —
2. This request was transmitted to Orwell in an undated letter from Kathleen Raine. She asked if she could have an advance copy for Les Editions de la Jeune Parque, if the rights were still available. See his letter to her on this matter, 24 July 1945, 2707, and n. 1 for Kathleen Raine.

2728. Reg Reynolds to Orwell

22 August 1945

One of Orwell's friends, Reg Reynolds,[1] who was then ill, wrote to him with humour and enthusiasm to congratulate him on the success of *Animal Farm*. 'It is GREAT—positively the *first* ANIMAL CLASSIC (no doubt Orwell is a pseudonym for Benjamin). If Fred [Warburg] doesn't allow you all the paper he's got for a long dynasty of editions, I'll never drink with him again.' After saying he would like to use it to re-educate some of his friends, he went on, 'Well George, I hand it to you. Wish I'd written it myself, though—not that I believe I could have made anything like such a good job of it. I've only one fault to find—"artificial manures" on p. 45.[2] Animals, subsistence farming, wouldn't need such nonsense, so that's a trap they *would* have avoided!' Reynolds's humour, despite his illness, breaks through in a short sequence of notes crammed into the margins, one of which (if not the venue) does suggest what was to happen in Orwell's lifetime and thereafter. 'Wot° price the Soviet Rights?' he asks. 'Can't you DRAMATISE it? (For the Unity Theatre[3] . . . ??)'; and 'How about the war now, though? Hasn't NAPOLEON [Stalin] won it?'

1. Reg Reynolds (1905–1958), journalist and author. Though a Quaker and a pacifist, he and Orwell were good friends. See *1060, n. 1* and *3206*.
2. *CW*, VIII, 42, line 20.
3. The Unity Theatre Club was formed in London in 1936 and offered left-wing drama in opposition to the conventional drama of the West End theatres. One of its best-known productions was *Waiting for Lefty* by Clifford Odets, but it produced some notable satirical revues and political pantomimes, as well as introducing the 'Living Newspaper' technique into British theatre, for example in John Allen's *Busmen*, 1938. *Animal Farm* would have proved suitable for the Unity Theatre had it been politically compatible with the theatre management.

2729. Review of *Chekov the Man* by Kornei Chukovsky;
translated by Pauline Rose

Manchester Evening News, 23 August 1945

Perhaps the following story, which has a bearing on the lives of literary men and artists generally, is not too well known to be worth repeating.

Some time in the mid-nineteenth century, when the clown Grimaldi was one of the delights of the London stage, a crushed, gloomy-looking man presented himself at a doctor's consulting room, and explained that he was suffering from chronic melancholia. The doctor examined him and could find nothing wrong with him.

"What you need," he said finally, "is something to cheer you up. Why not try and forget your troubles for a little while? Take my advice and go to the pantomime this evening. Go and see Grimaldi."

"I am Grimaldi," replied the patient.

A similar contrast exists, in the case of many writers, between the character which they display in private life and the character which seems to emanate from their published works, and Anton Chekov, the Russian playwright and short-story writer, was also—if Mr. Chukovsky is to be believed—a very different person from what most of us had imagined.

This little book is not a biography. It is merely, as its title implies, a study of Chekov's character. Chekov is known to the world as a delicate rather than a powerful writer, and as a chronicler of futility. He was one of the first short-story writers to break away from the bondage of the "plot," and to produce stories which were in effect sketches dependent on atmosphere and character rather than on a surprise at the end.

But his outstanding characteristic is that he writes of people who are charming but ineffectual. His last and best-known play, "The Cherry Orchard," shows a family of small landowners being turned out of their old home, which, because of their general fecklessness, they are no longer able to keep up.

The whole play is a sort of lament for the passing away of the old, semi-feudal rustic society, and the thudding of the axe against the trees, with which it ends, rubs in the impression. Although much of his work is comic, or even farcical, Chekov would strike the casual reader as being a sentimentalist of genius.

But, says Mr. Chukovsky, Chekov was not really that kind of person.

Chekov was not only kindly, generous, and high-spirited, which one might infer from his writings, but was also a man of iron will-power and almost superhuman energy. Much of Mr. Chukovsky's book is taken up with enumerating the various activities into which he flung himself, and they certainly make an impressive list when one remembers that Chekov died of tuberculosis at a not very advanced age, and that he practised as a doctor as well as producing a large body of writing.

He travelled all over the world, he interested himself in town-planning, he built four schools and founded a library to which he presented 2,000 books, he supported a considerable family from his student days onward, he supervised 25 villages during a cholera epidemic, he helped to compile the all-Russia census, he assisted innumerable struggling writers and not merely made them gifts of money but rewrote their [1] stories for them; all this in addition to leading an active social life and practising hospitality on a large scale.

But his most notable, though not his best-known, exploit was his journey to Sakhalin Island to study the conditions in the penal settlement.

Arrived at Sakhalin, Chekov not only made a detailed study of conditions in the prison camps but compiled single-handed a census of the whole island.

The book he wrote about it [2] did not bring him much renown, the atmosphere of Czarist Russia not being very friendly to revelations of this kind.

Towards the end of the book Mr. Chukovsky notes that his own estimate of Chekov's character is different from almost everybody else's. "I could," he says, "cover hundreds of pages with quotations from articles and booklets about Chekov, describing him as 'weak-willed,' 'passive,' 'characterless,' 'inactive', 'anæmic,' 'inert,' 'flabby,' 'impotent,' 'sluggish.'"

Certainly he answers these charges effectively, but one has all the time a feeling that Chekov's moral earnestness and social consciousness are being written up a little too strongly. Probably part of Mr. Chukovsky's purpose is to rehabilitate Chekov as so many of the famous figures of pre-revolutionary Russia have been rehabilitated during the past ten years.

The book ends with a dragged-in reference to Marshal Stalin and the great patriotic war, and Mr. Chukovsky is even careful to insist that Chekov, although born near the Sea of Azov and liking to describe himself as a "Khokol" (Ukrainian) was of pure Muscovite extraction and "typically Russian in all his tastes and habits." Nevertheless, this is a sympathetic book which proves its main point and will help many readers to approach Chekov's work with a more understanding eye.

[Fee: £8.8.0; 22.8.45]

1. their] *typeset as* the
2. *Ostrov Sakhalin* (Sakhalin Island), 1894.

2730. To Leonard Moore

23 August 1945   Typewritten postcard

The other French publisher who wanted to see a copy of ANIMAL FARM was Editions de la Jeune Parque. The address[1] is
M. Muller, Directeur des Editions de la Jeune Parque, 51 Chaussee° d'Antin, Paris 9eme.
I'm seeing Warburg on the 24th and will let you know what we fix up.[2]

Eric Blair

1. The address is not given in Kathleen Raine's letter asking about rights; see 2727, *n. 2*. Secker & Warburg wrote to Leonard Moore on 29 October 1945 indicating that yet another French

publisher, Gallimard, might publish *Animal Farm*, as a result of André Gide's interest in the book, 'even to the extent of translating it himself.' In the event, none of these three French publishers took *Animal Farm*. See *2787, n. 3*.

2. Warburg's diary at Secker & Warburg noted that he was to discuss the *Animal Farm* agreement.

2731. To Leonard Moore

24 August 1945   Typewritten

27 B Canonbury Square   Islington   London   N 1

Dear Mr Moore,

I have seen Warburg and it is all right about the contract, which covers ANIMAL FARM and future non-fiction books, but leaves the question of fiction open.

Warburg is sending a cheque for £100 as a further advance on royalties. The first edition of 5000 has sold out and they are doing another of 6000, but I suppose it will take some time to print. I should be obliged if you could send me on the money as soon as possible after deduction of commission etc., as I am going away for a holiday on September 10th and have some expenses to settle before then.[1]

Yours sincerely
Eric Blair

1. Warburg and Moore paid up before Orwell went on holiday. His Payments Book for 1 September 1945 records the sum of £87.16.4 from Secker & Warburg for royalties—the £100 less £12.3.4 agent's commission. The usual agent's commission is 10%; why Moore should have charged 12.125% is not known, nor whether he regularly charged so much. See also *2736, n. 1*.

2732. To Roger Senhouse

26 August 1945   Typewritten

27 B Canonbury Square
Islington
London   N 1

Dear Roger,

I've just remembered another serious misprint or rather slip in the book of essays. It has been carried forward from "Inside the Whale." P. 25, lines 10–11 from bottom, "Horace Skimpole" should be "Harold Skimpole." (The explanation of the original slip was that in the "Gem" there is a character called Horace Skimpole.)[1]

Yours
George [2]

1. This correction was made. *The Gem* was a periodical for boys. It was published as *The Gem Library*, 1907–29, and then as *The Gem*, to 1939, when it was incorporated in *Triumph*.
2. In a letter to John Carter at Scribner's, New York, 11 September 1945, Senhouse said, 'I have passed your letter [untraced] to George — Or Eric as we used to call him, though he has now become his pseudonym and even his friends call him George. . . .' This was hardly new to Senhouse, so presumably it was Carter who had referred to Orwell as Eric Blair. John Carter (1905–1975), bibliographer and bookman, would have known Orwell as Eric Blair at Eton; both were King's Scholars and they overlapped for nearly three years. (Senhouse was also at Eton, overlapping with Orwell for a year; see *375, n. 2*). Carter worked at the Ministry of Information, 1939–43, and the British Information Service, New York, 1944–45; was Managing Director, Charles Scribner's Sons Ltd., London, 1946–53, and Sandars Lecturer in Bibliography, University of Cambridge, 1947. Among his books were *Taste and Technique in Book-Collecting* (1948), the often-reprinted *ABC for Book-Collectors* (1952), and, with Percy H. Muir, *Printing and the Mind of Man* (1967). With Graham Pollard, he exposed the bibliographic forgeries of T. J. Wise in the nineteen-thirties.

2733. To Geoffrey Earle

29 August 1945   Typewritten

27 B Canonbury Square
Islington
London   N 1

Dear Mr Earle,
I hope the short biographical passage I have added will do.[1] It goes at the place marked A on page 4. I have cut out a corresponding number of words elsewhere. If we find it necessary to cut further, the passage dealing with "The Iron Heel" could be shortened greatly.

I am leaving London on September 10th and shall be away till about the 25th. I have made a note that the broadcast is to go out on October the 8th at 10 am, and that it will probably be rehearsed on Sunday the 7th.

Your sincerely
[Signed] Geo. Orwell
George Orwell

1. This was an addition to the script of his broadcast on Jack London, 8 October 1945. It may well be the first paragraph, which Orwell himself speaks. Earle acknowledged Orwell's letter on 3 September.

2734. Review of *Hammer or Anvil: The Story of the German Working-Class Movement* by Evelyn Anderson; *In Search of the Millennium* by Julius Braunthal

Manchester Evening News, 30 August 1945

These two books, though somewhat different in aim, are complementary to one another. Mrs. Anderson's book is a short history of the Left-wing movement in Germany,[1] with its main emphasis on events subsequent to 1918. "In Search of the Millennium" is less strictly historical and more autobiographical, and its author is an Austrian.

He played a leading part in the Austrian Socialist movement until the Schuschnigg Government drove him into exile in 1935, but he is especially interested in the period between 1905 and the end of the last war. From the two books together one can extract a good picture of the long chain of errors and disasters that culminated in Hitler's rise.

Before the other war, and throughout most of the nineteen-twenties as well, the German labour movement was by far the most impressive in the world. It was ultimately crushed by Hitler, but, as Mrs. Anderson's narrative shows, its real collapse had happened earlier, when it found itself in power at the end of the war and failed to put through the necessary reforms. The trouble, as Mrs. Anderson sees it, was that even before 1914 there was a veiled split in the movement.

The great mass of German Social Democrats were "reformist" in outlook, and their leaders were used to manœuvring for parliamentary positions and unready for drastic action.

The extremists, such as Karl Liebknecht and Rosa Luxemburg, had a far better grasp of world politics, but were out of touch with the masses and underrated the importance of trade unionism.

Rosa Luxemburg, however, had a passionate belief in democracy, and as early as 1905 she was struggling against Lenin's authoritarian conceptions. She and Liebknecht were murdered in a horrible manner early in 1919, and with her death there disappeared the one person who might conceivably have held the German Socialist movement together.

As it was, the Right and Left wings of the movement fought one another almost uninterruptedly until Hitler seized power and then crushed reformists and revolutionaries alike.

Mrs. Anderson recounts the lamentable story in some detail and with great impartiality. Naturally at the end the question arises: how completely have the Socialists, the Communists, and the other forces of the Left been destroyed by 12 years of Nazi terrorism? Mrs. Anderson devotes four chapters to the underground struggle. These were no doubt written before V(E) day, at a time when there was very little real data about internal conditions in Germany, but their general conclusions have been proved correct. Mrs. Anderson emphasises—what, indeed, was widely recognised towards the end—that the "unconditional surrender" terms published by the Allies made things a lot harder for resisters inside Germany.

She concludes that there now exists in Germany a whole generation of young people who are utterly disillusioned with Nazism, but so lacking in definite political ideas that they might develop in almost any direction, according to what leadership they get. Their re-education depends finally on a just peace settlement which will allow Germany to grow prosperous again and not drive it back into revengeful nationalism.

This point is taken up equally strongly by Mr. Braunthal, who notes sadly that the resolutions with which the British Labour party started the war—"There should be no dictated peace. We have no desire to humiliate, to crush, or to divide the German nation. There must be restitutions made to the victims of aggression, but all ideas of revenge and punishment must be excluded"—seem to have become rather dimmed during the past five years.

Mr. Braunthal was born in 1891, of strictly orthodox Jewish parents and was apprenticed to a book-binder when he was 14. That was the year of the abortive revolution in Russia, and it was partly this event that led him to devote his life to the Socialist movement.

In Austria, he says, and especially before the other war, Socialism was a way of life, a moral attitude, and not merely a political and economic theory. Persecution, failure, and exile have merely deepened his feeling that if Socialism does not mean a passionate belief in human brotherhood it means nothing. After being expelled from Austria he spent some time in Palestine, and then came to England.

He has a deep affection for England, and after some bewilderment he developed a respect for its political institutions as well. He ends his book with an earnest plea for the revival of the international outlook, and says truly that acquiescence in such things as the expulsion of 8,000,000 Germans from East Prussia threatens "the entire collapse of everything that Socialism stood for . . . it signifies the triumph of Machiavellian materialism in morals and politics."

[Fee: £8.8.0; 29.8.45]

1. Orwell had 'volunteered Eileen's help' in correcting Evelyn Anderson's English for this book (Crick, 446). Eileen completed her work not long before she died. For Evelyn Anderson, see *2638, n. 8*. The *Manchester Evening News* gave the title of the book incorrectly as *Hammer of Anvil*.

2735. E. M. Forster to Orwell; Evelyn Waugh to Orwell
30 August 1945

E. M. Forster wrote to Orwell asking for guidance in sending boys' magazines to a friend in France who wished to start a periodical of 'a sensible type' for boys of 10–13. He did not have by him the article Orwell had written on boys' magazines. He also had been asked 'what "passionant" literature, if any, boys in England read.' Forster said he was delighted with *Animal Farm* and had broadcast to India about it on 29 August—paraphrasing, not criticising it, so his talk would not appear in *The Listener*. He was off to India and asked if there were any young writers he should try to see. Orwell evidently replied (though his letter has not been traced), for on 17 September Forster wrote, thanking him for his information and commenting on Eileen's death. From his words, it would appear that Orwell was feeling Eileen's death more severely six months after the event than earlier. Forster wrote, 'These things do get worse afterwards, at least for a bit. A villager said down here the other day "You don't cry because people are dead but because you miss them"—awfully true.' He hoped to see Orwell on his return from India.

Evelyn Waugh wrote to thank Orwell for sending him a copy of his 'ingenious & delightful allegory,' which he had been seeking to buy but had found was sold out.

2736. To Leonard Moore

1 September 1945   Typewritten

27 B Canonbury Square
Islington
London   N 1

Dear Mr Moore,

Many thanks for your letter of 31st August.

Yes, naturally I am very pleased that World Digest° should featurise "Animal Farm", and should be obliged if you would go ahead with the arrangements.[1]

I am going away for a holiday on September 10th, but shall be back in London about the 25th.

Yours sincerely
[Signed] Eric Blair
Eric Blair

1. *World Digest* published the abridgement in January 1946, pages 83 to 94; see *2833*. The text was accompanied by an illustration by D. L. Ghilchik. In his Payments Book at 8 December 1945, Orwell recorded a payment of £14.15.5 for 'Second Rights' from L. P. Moore. He noted that this was for the *World Digest* abridgement of *Animal Farm*. If the fee paid by *World Digest* was £16.16 (16 guineas), and Moore deducted a commission of 12.125% (see *2731, n. 1*), that would account for such a curious payment as £14.15.5.

2737. To Gleb Struve

1 September 1945   Typewritten

Struve had written to Orwell on 28 August 1945, saying he had found *Animal Farm* 'delightful, even though I do not necessarily agree with what one of the reviewers described as your "Trotskyist prejudices."' He was teaching in the Russian section of a Summer School at Oxford and students were queuing for the book. He had been very amused 'by the *pudeur*' of those reviewers who had praised the book but had avoided mentioning its real target. He wished to translate *Animal Farm*, not for the benefit of Russian émigrés, but for Russians abroad who could read the truth about their country only when outside it. He asked Orwell whether he had severed his connection with *Tribune*; he missed his articles. His own book, on Soviet literature, was soon to be published in French with a special preface emphasising the fact that there was no freedom of expression in the Soviet Union.

27 B Canonbury Square
Islington
London   N 1

Dear Mr Struve,
Many thanks for your letter of August 28th.

I will keep in mind your suggestion about translating "Animal Farm," and naturally, if it could be in any way arranged, I should be highly honoured if it were you who made the translation. The thing is that I don't know what the procedure is. Are books in Russian published in this country, ie. from non-official sources? At about the same time as your letter a Pole wrote wanting to do the book into Polish. I can't, of course, encourage him to do so unless I can see a way of getting the book into print and recompensing him for his work, and ditto with yourself. If there is any way of arranging this that would allow a reasonable fee to the translators, I would be most happy to do it, as naturally I am anxious that the book should find its way into other languages. If translations into the Slav languages were made, I shouldn't want any money out of them myself.[1]

No, I haven't severed connection with Tribune, though I have stopped editing for them. I was away in France and Germany between February and May, and my affairs have been disorganised in other ways which obliged me to cut down my journalistic work for some time. However, I am going to start a weekly column again in Tribune in October, but not under the old title.

I am glad your book should be translated into French. My impression in France was that the Soviet mythos is less strong there than in England, in spite of the big Communist party.

I am leaving London shortly for a holiday, but shall be back about the 25th. I would like to meet you if you are in London any time. My phone number is CAN 3751.

Yours sincerely
[Signed] Geo. Orwell
George Orwell

1. Gleb Struve did translate *Animal Farm* into Russian, in conjunction with M. Kriger, as *Skotskii Khutor*. It first appeared as a serial in *Possev* (Frankfurt-am-Main), Nos. 7–25, 1949, and then in two book versions, one on ordinary paper for distribution in Western Europe and one on thin paper for distribution behind the Iron Curtain. See *3590A*.

2738. V-J Day and the End of World War II
15 August and 2 September 1945

On 10 August 1945, the Japanese offered to surrender. They accepted the Allied terms on 14 August (15 August), V-J Day. On 2 September, representatives of the Japanese government signed the instrument of capitulation on board the battleship USS *Missouri*, bringing to a formal conclusion World War II.

Also on 2 September, censorship of the press came to an end in the United Kingdom.

2739. Review of *Charles Dickens* by Una Pope-Hennessy

The Observer, 2 September 1945

The perfect book on Dickens, that is, a book which would show precisely the relationship between his life and his work, and between his work and his environment, is yet to come, but Dame Una Pope-Hennessy's book assembles so much material and is written in so fair-minded a spirit that it may make further studies of a purely biographical kind unnecessary.

Most of what is written about Dickens is either violently "for" or violently "against," according to whether he is being judged as a writer or as a husband. In the long run his reputation has probably been damaged by the fact that Forster's "Life,"[1] suppressed or slurred over various incidents which must have been known to a fairly large circle of people at the time. As a result of this, it was with something of a shock, indeed, with a feeling of having been deceived by Dickens himself, that the public finally learned that this champion of the domestic virtues had at least one mistress, separated from his wife after 22 years of marriage, and behaved in a distinctly tyrannical way towards several of his children. Dame Una's book falls into the "for" class, but she makes no attempt to cover up the facts, and even adds one or two details which have not seen the light before. On the other counts on which Dickens is sometimes attacked, such as his behaviour over money matters, his treatment of his parents and "in-laws," and his alleged willingness to pander to public opinion, she defends him, and generally with success.

The two governing facts in Dickens's make-up were his insecure childhood and his rocket-like rise to fame in very early manhood. He derived, says Dame Una, a "horror of patronage and distrust of the aristocratic system masquerading as representative government" from his very origins, for his grandfather had begun life as a footman and his father was brought up in the servants' quarters of a country house. But the interlude in his childhood, when his father was in a debtors' prison and he himself worked in a blacking factory in the Strand, must have been a far bitterer and more formative memory. It is clear from the two accounts which Dickens wrote of this episode that his feelings about it were partly snobbish, but were partly also the grief and loneliness of a child who believes himself to be unloved by his parents. Within a dozen years of leaving the blacking factory, however, he was already brilliantly successful, and after the age of about 25 he never again knew what it meant to be pinched for money. Only for a very brief period could he have been described as a "struggling author," and he did not pass through the normal development of first writing bitter books and then becoming "mellowed" by success. On the whole his books grew more radical as he grew older. "Little Dorrit," "Hard Times," or "Great Expectations" do not attack individual abuses more fiercely than "Oliver Twist" or "Nicholas Nickleby," but their implied outlook on society is more despondent.

Dame Una is less successful as a critic than as a biographer, and her attempts to summarise various of the novels would not be very helpful to anyone who had not read them already. She does, however, give an adequate account of Dickens's attitude to life and to society, and rescues him from the distortions which have been forced upon him by earlier critics. Dickens was neither a neo-Catholic, nor a Marxist, nor a time-serving humbug, nor a Conservative. He was a Radical who believed neither in aristocratic government nor in class warfare. His political outlook was summed up in his own statement: "My faith in the people governing is, on the whole, infinitesimal; my faith in the People governed is, on the whole, illimitable"— a statement which, thanks to the ambiguity of the English language, has sometimes been interpreted as meaning that Dickens was an enemy of democracy. Dickens's private character did undoubtedly deteriorate from about the middle 'fifties onwards, but it would be difficult to show that he ever sold his opinions or lost his tendency to side with the under-dog. The one act of his life which seems to contradict this is his acceptance of a baronetcy: but this was only a few weeks before his death, when he may already have been in an abnormal state.

Dame Una's narrative seems to show that the change in Dickens's character dates from his long stay in Paris during the early glittering days of the Second Empire. The society in which he then mingled was far more luxurious and sophisticated than any he had known, and the lymphatic Mrs. Dickens, mother of ten children, must have seemed very out of place in it. There was also the demoralising friendship of Wilkie Collins, and Dickens's growing interest in the stage, which took him away from home a great deal and threw him into contact with attractive young women. Like Gissing, Dame Una feels that the intense excitement which Dickens felt, and managed to communicate to his audiences, in his public readings, was somehow morbid and was bound up with the decline in his health. She seems, however, to underrate the morbid streak which had been in Dickens from the beginning. Speaking of his meeting with Edgar Allan Poe in 1842, she says that Poe's macabre stories would hardly have appealed to him "at this time," although Dickens had already written some intensely horrible scenes in "Oliver Twist," and also the madman's tale in "Pickwick," which might almost be an imitation of Poe.

[Fee: £10.0.0; 30.8.45]

1. *The Life of Charles Dickens* (3 volumes, 1872–74) by John Forster, a friend of Dickens's; it was revised and abridged in 1903 by George Gissing, whom Orwell mentions later in his review. Orwell owned the two-volume edition of 1927 (see *3734*).

2740. To Frank D. Barber

3 September 1945   Typewritten

> 27 B Canonbury Square
> Islington
> London N 1

Dear Mr Barber,

Many thanks for your letter, and thanks for the notice in the Yorkshire Evening News, which I had already seen. I am sorry you have left the Leeds Weekly Citizen,[1] as it is so important that there should be some Labour papers which are not taken in by Russian propaganda. However, I think the intellectual atmosphere is changing a bit. I have been surprised by the friendly reception "Animal Farm" has had, after lying in type for about a year because the publisher dared not bring it out till the war was over. I don't suppose there will be any more copies yet awhile, as the first edition sold out immediately. Warburg is printing a second edition of 6000 copies, but I suppose there will be the usual delays before they appear.

No, I haven't severed connection with Tribune, though I have given up the literary editorship. I was, of course, obliged to stop the column while I went abroad, but I am going to start doing another weekly article for them in October.

> Yours sincerely
> [Signed] Geo. Orwell
> George Orwell

1. See *2587* for correspondence with Barber when he was assistant editor of the *Leeds Weekly Citizen.*

2740A. To the Editor, *Commentary*

3 September 1945   Typewritten

> 27 B Canonbury Square
> Islington
> London N 1

Dear Sir,

In answer to your letter of August 17th,[1] the following is a short outline of my life:—

I was born in 1903 of a middle-class Anglo-Indian family, and was educated at Eton 1917–21. I was only at Eton because I had a scholarship, and I don't belong to the social stratum of most of the people who are educated there. From 1922 to 1927 I served in the Indian Imperial Police in Burma. This job was totally unsuited to me, and when I came home on leave at the end of 1927 I had already decided to take up journalism. I knew nobody and at first could get no footing. During 1928 and 1929 I lived in Paris, writing a novel which no one would publish and which I afterwards destroyed, and when my money gave out I worked for a time as a dishwasher in a hotel, and afterwards in a Russian restaurant. When I went back to England I worked at various ill-paid jobs. I was a teacher at cheap private schools for two years. Later, when I had begun to make enough to live on out of my books, I was a part-time assistant in a bookshop, and for a little while after I married I had a small grocer's shop. I was married in 1936, and at the end of that year my wife and I went to Spain. My wife worked in Barcelona and I served in the POUM militia on the Aragon front between December 1936 and June 1937. In the beginning it was chance that I had joined the POUM militia and not another, but afterwards I was glad of it, as it gave me an inside view of political events which I could not otherwise have had. I was wounded by a Fascist sniper near Huesca in early June, and soon afterwards we went back to England. That autumn I was seriously ill and spent some months in a sanatorium, and afterwards we went to Morocco for about 6 months. When war broke out I was rejected by the army (Class D), but I was in the Home Guard for 3 years. I worked 2 years in the Eastern Service of the BBC, organising English-language broadcasts aimed at the Indian students, then took over the literary editorship of "Tribune" for a year at the end of 1943. My wife spent 4 years in the Censorship Department and the Ministry of Food, and was very much overworked, which I am afraid was partly the cause of her death. In June of 1944 we adopted a little boy aged 3 weeks. At the beginning of 1945 I went to France for the "Observer," and while I was there my wife died suddenly and unexpectedly. I went back to France as soon as I could, and spent some time in Germany just before and just after the surrender. Since coming back I haven't resumed the literary editorship of "Tribune," but I am shortly going to start writing a column for them again, and I write regularly for several other papers. I have a housekeeper who looks after me and my little son, who is now nearly 16 months old and very healthy.

I have published 10 or 12 books. The better known ones are: "Down and Out in Paris & London" (1933), "Burmese Days" (1934), "The Road to Wigan Pier" (1937), "Homage to Catalonia" (1938), "Animal Farm" (1945). "Animal Farm," which is very short, is the first book I had managed to write since 1940. I have recently started another novel,[2] but with the pressure of journalistic work, which one has to do in order to stay alive, I don't expect to finish it before 1947.

You can use any of the above material. I hope this is the kind of thing you wanted.

Yours truly
[Signed] Geo. Orwell
George Orwell

1. Presumably in connexion with the article 'The British General Election,' which Orwell was to contribute to the first issue of *Commentary*, November 1945; see *2777*.
2. *Nineteen Eighty-Four*. He can have made little progress for, writing to Humphrey Slater, 26 September 1946 (see *3084*), he said he had by then completed only fifty pages. See also *2677*, n. 4.

2741. Jacques B. Brunius to Orwell

3 September 1945

Orwell (and, it would appear, some other contributors) had not received his complimentary copy of *Fontaine*, in which 'Grandeur et décadence du roman policier anglais' had been published; see *2357*. Brunius claimed they had been despatched in May and July, but apparently they had not been delivered. Whilst making these explanations, he asked Orwell if *Fontaine* could acquire the rights of *Animal Farm* for publication in French in a series of English novels, beginning in October with Rex Warner's *The Aerodrome*, which they were to issue. If Orwell preferred to have one of his earlier books translated for the series, Brunius was prepared to discuss that and he also asked Orwell if he would contribute to a series of talks on English literature for the French Service of the BBC. No reply has been traced, but Orwell must almost certainly have replied: he took up the proposition with Moore on 8 September 1945; see *2747*.

1. Jacques B. Brunius was London correspondent of *Fontaine: Revue mensuelle des lettres françaises et de la littérature internationale*. Among Orwell's collection of pamphlets was a copy of *Idolatry and Confusion* by Brunius and E. L. T. Mesens (1944).

2742. Review of *Britain and Her Birth-Rate* by Mass Observation

Manchester Evening News, 6 September 1945

It is well known—though Mass-Observation's Report shows that plenty of people are not yet aware of [it]—that Britain's population is now in danger of a serious decline. The birth-rate has risen slightly during the later war years, but the general curve has been downwards for the past half-century, and the point has been reached, or nearly reached, when deaths will outnumber births.

The comments reported by Mass-Observation show that comparatively few people grasp what this means. It is thought of as meaning merely a smaller population, which is often welcomed on the ground that it would solve the housing problem or even reduce unemployment. Actually, however, what it means is not merely fewer people, but a constantly shrinking population—the economic effects of which are bound to be disastrous—and a rapidly ageing population. Beyond a certain point the vital statistics cannot be predicted, because something may happen to alter the trend, but we do know what will happen if the present trends continue. Thus, if fertility rates continue to fall as fast as they fell during the nineteen-thirties, by A.D. 2015, only 70 years hence, Britain's population will be about ten and a half million, of whom more than half will be people of over 60 years of age.

Even if the fertility rate should [not][1] fall any further, but remains as it is now, there will still be a catastrophic drop in the population, and by the end of the century nearly a third of the British people will be over 60, while only 11 per cent will be young children.[2]

With these figures as their background Mass-Observation set out to discover *why* the birth-rate dwindles and what inducement or what change in the social atmosphere might send it up again. At present the increase that is needed is not enormous. If each family had one extra child the population would be once again at the replacement level: but if that increase does not happen in the very near future a far more drastic rise in the birth-rate will be needed at a later date.

Mass-Observation's inquiry shows, however, that people not only do not want larger families but are inclined to want smaller ones. Two children—which is below the present average and far below replacement level—is almost universally regarded as the ideal family. On the other hand, deliberately childless marriages are not common.

One fact that the whole survey brings out is that the causes of the dropping birth-rate are *not* directly economic. The commonest explanation is that people nowadays "can't afford" to bring up children, but in fact the birth-rate is always highest among the poorest groups. This is true all over the world—the low standard countries are always the fastest breeders—and the enormous increase in the population of Victorian England occurred against a background of unbearable poverty.

A rising standard of living goes with diminishing fertility, partly because there are other attractions—films, radios, and so forth—which compete with children, partly because people learn to expect more from life and women do not wish to be worn-out drudges from the age of 25 onwards. Also, the children themselves are taken more seriously than they used to be. Everyone is anxious to give his own children the best possible education and upbringing, and with families of more than three or four, a certain amount of neglect is unavoidable.

All in all the social pressure against big families is overwhelming, and the mother of 10 children is as much pitied or laughed at, as the childless old maid.

It is therefore very doubtful, the Mass-Observers point out, whether much can be achieved by subsidising maternity. Certain minor improvements, such as more up-to-date and considerate treatment in maternity hospitals would help, but family allowances, day nurseries, baby-minders, the free diaper services and the like may actually accelerate the downward trend of the birth-rate.

All social services of this kind raise the standard of living, directly or indirectly, and hitherto every rise in the standard of living has led to a drop in fertility. The more people are accustomed to comfort and leisure, the less likely they are to surround themselves with hordes of children. On the other hand economic security, in the sense of freedom from unemployment, is favourable to larger families: and at present the housing shortage is a direct cause of childlessness in many cases.

The Mass-Observers' conclusion is that the situation can only be saved by restoring a belief in the future. People are likelier to have large families if they feel that they are doing children a favour by bringing them into the world—if they believe, that is, that life in 1970 will be better worth living than it is now.

Actually there is no such belief abroad at present. Instead there is a widespread fear that mass unemployment will return, an almost equally widespread fear of another world war within the next generation, and a tendency to suspect that efforts at raising the birth-rate have "cannon fodder" as their real object. It is significant that religious believers, both Catholic and Anglican, have a slightly higher birth-rate than unbelievers.

This survey was presumably compiled before the General Election, and it perhaps over-emphasises the prevalence in Britain of political apathy and cynicism about the future. But its main conclusions, product of hundreds of interviews with middle-class and working-class women, are hard to escape.

People have small families because there is no accepted aim which can outweigh comfort and social prestige, and merely to make them better off in an economic sense will not reverse the trend. Meanwhile a certain amount can be done by minor measures such as rapid rehousing and reduction of infant mortality, and, above all, by educating public opinion.

As the Mass-Observers remark, within a few decades the dwindling and ageing of our population may seem to us the most urgent of all problems. The sooner people realise where they are heading and the sooner they stop believing such monstrous fallacies, as, for instance, that a smaller population means less [un]employment,[3] the better. This is a disquieting book, but anyone who can get hold of a copy should read at least the first few chapters.

[Fee: £8.8.0; 5.9.45]

1. The omission of 'it' in the first sentence, and the almost certain omission of 'not' here are surprising instances of error in what is generally very accurate typesetting of these reviews. See also *n. 3*.
2. According to the Office of Population Censuses and Surveys, on the basis of the 1981 census, over-55s account for 14.8 million of the population, or one quarter. By the end of the century, 55–65-year-olds will have remained much the same in number, but over 75s will have increased by 25%. Although the proportion of older people will not be very greatly less than that suggested in 1945 (which speaks of over 60s), the population will be almost six times as great as that forecast.
3. In the original the negative prefix is mistakenly omitted.

2743. *The Observer* to Orwell

6 September 1945

On 6 September 1945, Orwell was asked by *The Observer* whether he wished to review *García Lorca* by Edwin Honig (Editions Poetry, London). For whatever reason—because he was about to go on holiday; because he was disinclined to review the book—no review was published.

2744. Review of *Quiver's Choice* by Sagittarius

Tribune, 7 September 1945

No one is at the top of his form every week, and some of the verses of Sagittarius (who appears under this name in the *New Statesman* and under others in *Tribune* and *Time and Tide*)[1] are better than others, but she is the only political versifier of our time who does manage to combine technical skill with intelligent comment. Curiously enough, she is at her best when she makes use of a form of parody which was popular in Victorian days but has rather gone out in later years—the parody not of a writer or a school of writers, but of an individual poem. For example:

> It was a peacetime evening,
> Old William's watch was done,
> And he before his sandbagged cave
> Was polishing his gun;
> While by him scavenged on the green
> The little war-child, Wavelline.
>
> She rummaged in a refuse pile
> And found a rusty tin,
> Exclaiming with a thrifty smile,
> 'That's for the salvage bin.'
> But he replied. 'No, little maid,
> I'll use it for a hand-grenade.'

There is another poem on President Inonu,[2] modelled on Ernest Dowson, with the refrain "I have been faithful to the Allies in my fashion," and an exceptionally happy one, after William Allingham, on the Countryside Control recommended by the Scott Commission:

> Up the scheduled mountain,
> Down the earmarked glen,
> The Board of Education
> Is fanning out its men—
> Urchins of the green belt
> Rambling with the schools,
> Youth Groups and their leaders,
> Rambling by the rules.
> Bye-laws on the hillside,
> Fences round the heather,
> Lovers and their lasses
> Marching all together.

By contrast, the more serious poems sometimes have a rather forced air, and the incorporation of foreign names and phrases, unavoidable in verse of this type, is not always very successful. It is rather a pity that these poems were not arranged in chronological order, but even so, ranging as they do from 1935 to 1945, they form quite a comprehensive record of political events. A minor attraction of the book is the game the reader can play with himself, of trying to determine which poems were written for which periodical.

[Fee: £1.1.0; 3.9.45]

1. Sagittarius, the pseudonym of Olga Katzin (1896–1987), wrote under this pseudonym in *The New Statesman & Nation*; in *Time and Tide*, she was Fiddlesticks; and in *Tribune*, Roger Service. Many of her parodies are brilliant, and they can still be read to advantage, giving an ironic twist to political and war news fifty years later, for example, 'Cherchez La Femme' on the Fall of France (152–53) and 'The Passionate Profiteer to his Love' (190–91). Her *Sagittarius Rhyming* was published in 1940. She visited Orwell at Cranham Sanatorium with the Fyvels in 1949 (then as Olga Miller; see Tosco Fyvel, *George Orwell*, 162).

2. Ismet Inönü (formerly Ismet Paza; 1884–1973), Turkish soldier and Chief of Staff to President Atatürk in the war against Greece, 1919–22 (twice defeating the Greeks at Inönü), was Prime Minister of Turkey, 1923–24 and 1925–37, and President, 1938–50. He kept Turkey out of World War II until 1 March 1945, when war was declared on Germany and Japan.

2745. Article for *The Observer*

7 September 1945

Orwell's Payments Book records an 800-word article for *The Observer* against the date of completion of 7 September 1945, for which he was paid £10.0.0. This article has not been traced.

2746. Review of *The French Cooks' Syndicate* by W. McCartney

Freedom—through Anarchism, 8 September 1945

Mr. McCartney's pamphlet[1] is incidentally a revelation of the dirt, the crowding, the bullying and the overwork that are to be found behind the service doors of almost any hotel or restaurant, but in the main it is a highly expert study of the technique of the lightning strike. Before the other war he and others were instrumental in forming a union of kitchen workers on syndicalist lines (there were no permanent officials, and such officials as existed were unpaid), and managed to form a working agreement with the Waiters' Union which already existed. They were then ready to stage their first strike. The method was a sudden stoppage of work in the very middle of dinner, and its success depended on secrecy, discipline and accurate timing:

> "Five minutes before 6.30 the dinner gong sounded, calling all the well-fed parasitical guests to 'dine'. They took their seats, ushered by smiling, bowing waiters, who were treated with contempt by the guests. 6.30 p.m. Hors d'Oeuvres were served, then soup, then fish. The entree arrived, and that was the lot. 7 p.m. A stranger walked into the dining room, he wiped his forehead with a white handkerchief—the signal agreed upon at the secret meeting. Waiters stood like statues, except one or two. The kitchen got the 'wire' and everyone stopped work at once . . . The guests are calling for the head waiter, for God, the devil, anyone who will serve them! Never before had the sacred dining room seen such a sight in all its long history. Guests forgot, being only half-fed, that they were gentlemen, and even began swearing. They began to leave the hotel, but had to find their own hats and coats, and call their own cabs or carriages. This

reminded me of other hungry, angry men on London's streets a short time previously, but those were batoned."

This wallop, literally below the belt, took effect promptly. When the manager discovered that he was up against a big union whose existence he had not suspected, but which included all his own staff, he signed a long list of demands which included T.U. rates for all workers, the abolition of tipping, a forty-eight hour week and a week's paid holiday every year.

Other successful strikes followed, in spite of a certain amount of blacklegging. The movement had originated among the kitchen workers, who were largely foreign-born, and the blacklegs were to be found mostly among the waiters, who were British. There were thirty-eight such strikes between 1905 and 1914, all of them successful. The immediate aim, of course, was to improve working conditions and put an end to such scandals as, for instance, workers being employed without wages and having to depend on tips; but the ultimate objective was to get rid of profit-making catering firms altogether and establish "the owning and controlling of all catering firms for the benefit of the workers and not for the profit of a few idle parasites."

The movement was naturally not liked by the leaders of the T.U.C., but it prospered and retained its solidarity until the war of 1914. The war broke it up by effecting a change of personnel throughout the catering trade, and the mass unemployment that followed produced armies of blacklegs. Working conditions were forced down to the level of 1910, and when a new union was formed it followed half-hearted tactics which led to disaster. Mr. McCartney, marked down by the employers' organisation as a dangerous man, was driven out of the trade, and was ultimately expelled from the General Workers' Union for a too-revolutionary speech at a May Day demonstration.

I have only had brief glimpses of hotel work, and Mr. McCartney has been in and out of it for fifty years, so what he says hardly needs confirmation from me: but I should like to add that his account of life below stairs, with its heat, dirt, quarrelling and turmoil, exactly agrees with my own experiences as a kitchen porter in Paris in 1929.

1. This little pamphlet was sold for only threepence (not much more than 1p in current coinage). Orwell's review was boldly headlined as 'A Review by the Author of "Down and Out in Paris and London." ' Orwell entered the review in his Payments Book for 12 August 1945 and gave the journal's name as *War Commentary*—predecessor of *Freedom—through Anarchism*—which became simply *Freedom*. His entry is marked with an asterisk and 'Unpaid.'

2747. To Leonard Moore

8 September 1945   Typewritten

27 B Canonbury Square
Islington
London   N 1

Dear Mr Moore,

I understand Scribners of New York have written for "Critical Essays." I think they would be very good people to tie up with, so if they definitely want the book it would be well to let them have it. I believe the Dial people still have a copy of the MS, but as they have had it for so long without reacting, they presumably don't want it.

Meanwhile there is the question of "Animal Farm." I don't fancy it will be easy to find an American publisher for this book. However I have just given a copy to a Polish-American named Kister who represents a firm called Roy Publications. I believe Warburg had given him a copy earlier on, but at any rate he will send the copy I gave him to his firm in New York. The point about this firm having the book is that if they did decide to do it they might also publish a Polish translation. I am extremely anxious that the book should be translated into one Slav language at least, but this will obviously not be easy to arrange. Various people are anxious to translate it into both Polish and Russian, but the job is to make it financially feasible. If therefore Kister's firm did decide to take the book and were willing to print a Polish translation, I would much rather they had it than some other firm which might give better terms but would not translate.

Brunius, one of the people who edits "Fontaine", wrote asking for the rights in "Animal Farm" and also saying "Fontaine" are going to publish translations of a series of English books and wanted to include one of mine. I explained to him that Nagel already had copies of the books which seemed most worth translating. But as presumably Nagel won't accept all of them, we might possibly get one off onto the "Fontaine" people.[1]

I am going away on the 10th and shall be back about the 25th.

Yours sincerely
Eric Blair

P.S. If this business of translating "Animal Farm" into the Slav languages comes to anything, I don't mind about the money side, as there would not be much in it anyway. I want it to exist in those languages if possible.

1. A note written in Moore's office indicates that the Nagel copy of *Burmese Days* be sent to *Fontaine*.

2748. To George Woodcock

8 September 1945   Typewritten

> 27 B Canonbury Square
> Islington
> London N 1

Dear Woodcock,

I found that cutting (from Lady Listowel's Bulletin[1] of 15.8.45.)° It doesn't say what source the information comes from, but presumably from monitoring some radio or other. Enclosed cutting from Vernon Bartlett's article[2] in todays° News-Chronicle shows that even the News-Chron. has got round to admitting some of the facts.

I am going away on Monday and shall be back about the 25th.

> Yours
> Geo. Orwell

1. Judith Listowel (née de Marffy-Mantuaro; b. Budapest, 1904) married the Earl of Listowel in 1933; the marriage was dissolved in 1945. He was Labour Whip in the House of Lords, 1940–44, and Deputy Leader, 1944–45. Thereafter, he held various offices under Labour including that of Secretary of State for Burma, 1947–48. Her bulletin was variously titled *SEEC Bulletin* (Seven East European Countries), *East Europe and Soviet Russia*, and *Soviet Orbit*, from 1945 onwards, the titles accurately indicating its concerns. Only Nos. 43 and 44 were called *Listowel's Bulletin*, the issue of 15.8.45 being No. 43. Most of pages 12 and 13 deal with Poland, and the last of 13 topics is concerned with 'Return of Soviet Troops.' It is this that probably interested Orwell, for it is only this subject that coincides with one item in Bartlett's report (see *n. 2*). Bartlett states that in spite of the efforts of their officers, 'the behaviour of the men leaves much to be desired.' People living in the areas through which the Soviet troops are marching home are 'instructed to evacuate all their belongings and cattle and to hide their women.'
2. Bartlett's report, which is on the front page of the *News Chronicle*, is mainly devoted to the efforts of Mikolajczk, the Polish Vice-Premier, and Witos, a veteran leader of the old Polish Peasant Party, to revive that party in opposition to the one set up by the Lublin administration. It aimed to replace the secret police by a constitutional force, give freedom to the press, establish land reform that would not develop into collectivisation, and mitigate the severest forms of nationalisation, as proposed by Lublin. He reported also that those who had fought in the Polish Home Army were having the confidence to come out of hiding in the forests. The last two paragraphs were devoted to 'the ruthlessness with which Soviet troops help themselves to Polish produce and possessions on their way home.' The 'rapid deterioration of discipline in the Red Army' in Germany and in East European countries was becoming a 'grave handicap to Soviet policy in Eastern Europe' and a strain on good relations with the Allies. See also 'Through a Glass, Rosily,' *2802*.

2749. Julian Symons to Orwell

After 8 September 1945

Kingsley Martin reviewed *Animal Farm* in *The New Statesman & Nation*, 8 September 1945. Shortly afterwards, Julian Symons wrote to Orwell and remarked: 'I admired *Animal Farm* very much—I thought Kingsley Martin's review very unjust to you personally, although I suppose the most intelligent review I've seen. Which is not saying much.'[1]

1. Not a great deal of love was lost between Martin and Orwell. Crick records that when Orwell was lunching at the Little Akropolis with Malcolm Muggeridge he asked Muggeridge to change seats with him. 'Kingsley Martin had come in and Orwell said that he could not bear to have to look at "that corrupt face" all through a good meal' (500). For Martin, see *424* and *496, n. 9.*

2750. To S. McGrath

9 September 1945   Typewritten

> 27 B Canonbury Square
> Islington
> London   N 1

Dear Sir,[1]
I was not certain whether your letter dated 7th August, setting forth the terms for my 20-minute script on Jack London, required an answer, or whether I should await a contract. But if the letter was intended to serve as a contract, then I would like to state that the terms are quite agreeable to me.

> Yours faithfully
> [Signed] Geo. Orwell
> George Orwell

1. S. McGrath worked in the BBC Copyright Department.

2751. To George Woodcock

9 September 1945   Typewritten

> 27 B Canonbury Square
> Islington
> London   N 1

Dear Woodcock,
I've written an identical letter on Olday's case to 3 papers, the Herald, News-Chronicle and Manchester Guardian.[1] I hope some of them will print it. I couldn't pitch it very strong because he is evidently guilty on 2 counts, desertion and the false identity card, and in those circumstances all one can say is that this is a hard case and he has been sufficiently punished already.

I thought those were the likeliest papers. The Guardian will nearly always print a letter, and the News-Chron seems to print a fairly large number. It's no use trying the Times. I've been writing letters to them for years and never got one in yet. Tribune would print a letter but that doesn't get much publicity. Ditto the New Statesman, who probably wouldn't print a letter coming from me any way.

> Yours
> Geo. Orwell

1. John Olday (A. W. Oldag; 1905–1977) was described in *Freedom Defence Committee Bulletin*, No. 3, April–May 1946, as 'a militant anti-Nazi' who had 'served sentences' in Germany before 1939 for political activities. He served in the Pioneer Corps in the British army during the war but deserted in 1943 because 'he felt he was not serving the anti-fascist cause by remaining in the forces.' He was arrested in December 1944 and sentenced to a year's imprisonment in January 1945 for 'stealing by finding an Identity Card.' After serving eight months in Brixton Prison, he was charged in a military court with desertion and, despite already having served a prison term, was given two years' detention. The Freedom Defence Committee made representations to the War Office on 9 January and 28 February 1946 and was advised in the middle of April that Olday had had his sentence suspended and had been released. None of Orwell's letters was published. He contributed anti-war cartoons to the anarchist press, some of which were collected in *The March to Death* (1943).

2752. Extract of letter from Malcolm Muggeridge to Orwell

13 September 1945

My Dear George,
The enclosed came this evening. It's slightly self-conscious, and not as good as Johnny's[1] conversation with me on the subject. Even so, I quite like it, and I fancy you will. His enjoyment of "Animal Farm" was quite authentic. I found him in bed with it, very sleepy, but he hadn't wanted to put out the light. It's the supreme test of all good allegory that it appeals to children. "Don Quixote" and "Gulliver's Travels" are obvious examples. We read them as children, and then we read them again but not quite with the same enjoyment. . . .

Yours
M. M.

1. Muggeridge's son, John, had presumably written, or drawn something suggested by *Animal Farm*. Muggeridge wrote on *Daily Telegraph* headed paper (and perhaps from Fleet Street, hence 'The enclosed came this evening').

2753. To Leonard Moore

24 September 1945   Typewritten

27 B Canonbury Square
Islington
London   N 1

Dear Mr Moore,
I enclose a letter from the Dial Press people. I don't know what they are up to. So far as I know they had a copy of the essays book ages ago and didn't react in any way. Now they write once again asking for a manuscript. I think it would be much better to tie up with Scribner's if they are willing to do the essays book. Perhaps you will let me know if anything has come of this.
   Someone has written asking leave to translate "Animal Farm" into German. I don't know whether this is financially feasible in any way. He

seems to think publication of books in German will start again soon. I have told him to get in touch with you, so perhaps he will do so if he is really anxious to make the translation. His name is Eugen Brehm.[1]

Yours sincerely
Eric Blair

1. Brehm did not translate *Animal Farm*. A German translation was made by N. O. Scarpi (Fritz Bondy) and published as *Farm der Tiere*, October 1946.

2754. To Kay Dick

26 September 1945   Typewritten

27 B Canonbury Square
Islington
London   N 1

Dear Kay,

I was very glad to get your letter because I had been trying to get in touch with you. When I rang up John o' London[1] they just said you had left, and I had lost your home address.

I simply haven't any ideas for a story at this moment, and I don't want to force one. Later on I don't know. I did one time contemplate a story about a man who got so fed up with the weeds in his garden that he decided to have a garden just of weeds, as they seem easier to grow. Then of course as soon as he started to do this he would find the garden being overwhelmed with flowers and vegetables which came up of their own accord. But I never got round to writing it.

I note that you will be back in London about the 4th and will get in touch with you after that. I'll try and not lose your address this time. I wish you would come round here some time and see my little boy, who is now aged nearly 17 months. If you come from Hampstead you have to go to the Angel and then take a bus, or if you come from the City you come on the 4 bus to Highbury Corner. I am almost always at home because I don't go to an office now. The child goes to bed about 6 and after that I have high tea about 7.

You may be interested to hear that poor old Wodehouse was most pathetically pleased about the article in the Windmill.[2] I met him in Paris and afterwards heard from him once or twice.

Looking forward to seeing you,

Yours
[Signed] Geo. Orwell
George Orwell

1. *John o' London's Weekly* was a popular literary journal, founded in 1919.
2. Kay Dick, under the name Edward Lane, was a co-editor of *The Windmill*; see *2618, n. 1*.

2755. Review of *The Midnight Court* by Bryan Merryman; translated from the Irish by Frank O'Connor

Manchester Evening News, 27 September 1945

We have been very much out of touch with Eire during the war years, and Mr. O'Connor's book is to be welcomed for the light it incidentally casts on present-day Irish letters, as well as for introducing us to a little-known poet of the eighteenth century.

Bryan Merryman was a village schoolmaster in County Clare, a part of the world which, according to Mr. O'Connor, was at that time "as barbarous as any in Europe." Later he removed to Limerick, where he seems to have lived by teaching mathematics, and died, completely obscure, in 1805. The long poem which Mr. O'Connor has translated is a sort of farcical allegory purporting to be a description of a dream. Perhaps it will be better to summarise the poem first and outline Mr. O'Connor's explanation of it afterwards.

The poet professes to have fallen asleep one day in the bracken and to have been awakened by the Queen of Fairyland (who does not resemble Titania but is a giantess of extreme ugliness). The Fairy Court is about to try the case of a young woman, married to an old man, who has given birth to a child on the day of her wedding. The case develops into a sort of slanging match between women and men, with the author's sympathies heavily on the side of the women.

First to speak is a girl who complains bitterly that men nowadays are too cautious to get married, and that property is always preferred to youth and beauty:

A boy in the blush of his youthful vigour,
With a gracious flush and a passable figure,
Finds a fortune the best attraction,
And sires himself off on some bitter extraction,
Some fretful old maid with her heels in the dung
And pious airs and venomous tongue,
Vicious and envious, nagging and whining,
Snoozing and snivelling, plotting, contriving—
Hell to her soul, an unmannerly sow,
With a pair of bow legs and hair like tow,
Went off this morning to the altar,
And here am I without hope of the halter!
Couldn't some man love me as well?
Amn't I plump and sound as a bell,
Lips for kissing and teeth for smiling,
Blossomy skin and forehead shining?

She goes on to describe her other attractions with considerable freedom, and ends up with some interesting information about the love philtres which were at that time in favour in Ireland. She is followed by the old man whose wife has deceived him. He delivers a violent tirade against marriage in general and his own wife in particular, and declares that it would be better for the Irish race if it were replenished entirely by bastards. The girl who spoke first defends the errant wife, and denounces clerical celibacy as one of the chief reasons why girls go without husbands. The priests, she says, usually have mistresses, and it would be better if they were compelled to marry. The Queen of Fairyland gives judgment for the women and decrees that men who have deliberately remained unmarried are to be punished. The poet, who is 30 and still single, is sentenced to be flogged, but wakes from his vision just in time.

What is one to make of this strange and, in places, bawdy poem? It is, says Mr. O'Connor, a deliberate attack on Irish puritanism and clericalism, delivered by a man who was in outlook a Continental European and had been influenced by the teaching of Rousseau. Although writing in Gaelic he imitated contemporary English verse, and was, according to Mr. O'Connor, the first Irish poet to get away from mere lyricism.

Before Merryman, Mr. O'Connor says, "of drama, prose, criticism, or narrative poetry there was nothing. Intellectually Irish literature did not exist. What Merryman aimed at was something that had never even been guessed at in Gaelic Ireland; a perfectly proportioned work of art on a contemporary subject, with every detail subordinated to the central theme. The poem is as classical as the Limerick Custom House; and, fortunately, the Board of Works had not been able to get at it."

Since one is dealing with a translation it is hard to know whether this judgment is correct in strictly literary terms, and the rollicking metre used by Mr. O'Connor does not suggest the traditional smoothness of classical verse.

His statement that "the religious background of 'The Midnight Court' is Protestant" should, perhaps, be taken as a reaction against the atmosphere of Catholic Dublin. Clerical celibacy is not a Protestant institution, but neither is sexual libertinism—and, in effect, the poem is a plea for that. The man and the woman who are the principal speakers, though they approach the subject from different angles, are both attacking puritanism, which Ireland apart, is somewhat less rampant in the Catholic countries than in the Protestant ones.

But Mr. O'Connor is probably right in saying that the poem reflects the "enlightenment," the cult of the "natural man," which had been preached in their different ways by Rousseau and Voltaire, and which, at the time when Merryman was writing, was about to find political expression in the French Revolution.

Merryman, says Mr. O'Connor, "was writing in an Irish-speaking village in the eighteenth century things which even Yeats himself might have thought twice of writing in English-speaking Dublin of the twentieth," and we may guess that he only got away with it because of his obscurity.

After "The Midnight Court" he wrote nothing more, but went to teach mathematics in Limerick, where he perhaps hoped to find kindred spirits among the Protestant community. If so he was disappointed, and his attack on puritanism and clericalism was a failure, especially in his chosen city. As Mr. O'Connor puts it:

"Nowhere else in Ireland has Irish puritanism such power. Leaning over the bridge in the twilight, looking up the river at the wild hills of Clare, from which old Merryman came down so long ago, you can hear a Gregorian choir chanting *Et expecto resurrectionem mortuorum,*★ and go back through the street where he walked, reflecting that in Limerick there isn't much else to expect."

[Fee: £8.8.0; 9.9.45]

★ 'I expect the resurrection of the dead' [Orwell's, or newspaper sub-editor's, footnote].

2756. To Leonard Moore

29 September 1945   Typewritten

> 27 B Canonbury Square
> Islington
> London   N 1

Dear Mr Moore,

Many thanks for your letter.[1] The Nagel contract is herewith, duly signed.

I think I wrote personally to a man named Erval in the Nagel firm about this, but could you request of them that whoever does the translation should consult with me about any difficulties that arise, and also let me see either the complete proofs or a complete draft of the translation. I know that difficulties are bound to come up over Burmese words that occur in the text, and over local colour generally. My French is far from perfect, but I should always detect a mistranslation. I am very glad the translation of this book has been arranged, as I always thought it would stand translation.[2]

I haven't any more copies of "Animal Farm" either, in fact my own last copy has gone. Warburg is doing a second edition, but I see from the advertisement that this is not expected till Xmas.[3]

> Yours sincerely
> Eric Blair

1. Orwell records in his Payments Book against 29 September 1945 the payment of royalties from L. P. Moore of £5.17.9.
2. *Tragédie Birmane*, translated by Guillot de Saix, was published by Nagel, in Paris, 31 August 1946, in a run of 7,800 copies.
3. A second edition of 10,000 copies was published in November 1945.

2757. Review of *The Earth Remains* by Crichton Porteous; *Gvadi Bigva* by Leo Kiacheli

Manchester Evening News, 4 October 1945

One more illustration of the fact that almost anything can be described as a novel is provided by "The Earth Remains." It is simply a series of episodes, singularly pointless if regarded as a story and not working up to any kind of crisis, but redeemed by a few good descriptive passages and numerous scraps of out-of-the-way information.

The hero is a novelist with a passionate love of "the country" and a belief that farm life is the best as well as the most useful of all lives. So far so bad, for novelists ought not to write about novelists, and a sentimental reverence for "nature" and "the soil" is one of the curses of modern English literature.

However, Mr. Porteous does not fall into any of the ordinary traps. He knows a great deal about farming and farm management and he is not inclined to idealise either the land or the men who work on it.

He knows all about the dreariness of hoeing turnips and the coldness of milk churns in the early morning; he can explain why a four-acre small-holding does not pay and can inventory the depressing muddle of the average farmyard; he can even describe a ferreting expedition with a realism that extends to noting that wild rabbits are frequently infested by tapeworms.

Indeed, one can pick up quite a lot of miscellaneous knowledge from his book, especially from the latter part of it, which deals with the war agricultural committees and the competition for man power between the farms and the armed forces.

At the beginning of the book the hero, Grant Scott, is still living the comparatively comfortable life of a literary man, but with the coming of war he feels it his duty to go back to farm work, to which he was bred, and for a while he works on a dairy farm, where he is in charge of the milk round.

Later he gets the chance of a job on the Agricultural Committee, and promptly takes it, though still with an uneasy feeling that his proper place is on the land.

The account of the working of the committee, with its red tape and good intentions, and its endless struggles with the farmers, who are constantly in need of more labour and will resort to almost any dodge to keep their sons out of the army, is obviously taken from life, and is in places exceedingly interesting.

In spite of the great rise in productivity during the war the picture which Mr. Porteous gives of the future of British farming is a gloomy one. The basic fact is the drift away from the land of the young people, who will not put up with village life, and would probably find it no more endurable even if agriculture were the best paid instead of the worst paid industry.

The end of the story, if it can be called a story, finds Grant Scott still convinced that we have a duty towards the English soil, but far from certain whether that duty will be carried out in future.

When one comes upon a book like this, so full of accurate observation and so deficient in narrative power, one feels strongly the need for some kind of recognised art-form which could be a repository for sketches and anecdotes as opposed to stories. A book which in essence is a collection of scraps—some of the works of W. H. Hudson are an illustration of this—is ruined if it has to pretend to be a novel.

The things that are real in "The Earth Remains" are all incidental. Such things as the description of the milk round, the conversations with harassed farmers and slippery conscientious objectors, the ripple of a field of oats with the wind blowing over it, or a glimpse of a pyramid of freshly made cheeses in a farmhouse cellar.

The author feels, quite rightly, that things like this are worth recording, but if he simply set them down without attempting to string them together into a story the resulting collection would not, according to our current ideas, rank as a book. Hence much padding and wastage of talent.

However, this book is always worth reading when the author forgets about the plot.

Many contemporary Russian books have been translated into English during the past five years, but nearly all of them have been the product of Russia proper, and it is interesting to come upon a specimen from one of the minor Soviet nationalities. "Gvadi Bigva," which is a Stalin Prize novel, deals with Georgia, and is a translation of a Russian translation of the Georgian original.

Gvadi Bigva is a middle-aged peasant with an enlarged spleen, product of malaria, and four motherless children. He is a bit of [a] rogue, but kindly enough at heart.

His attitude towards collectivisation, which has happened fairly recently (the date is probably 1936 or thereabouts), is opportunist though not actually hostile. He will work for the collective farm and pile up a few "labour days" for himself when he is absolutely obliged to, but he prefers to slip away to the nearest market town and do a little private trading, sometimes with stolen goods.

By chance he is brought into contact with some scoundrels of a bigger calibre than himself, the remnants of the local "Kulaks," who have recently been dispossessed and are still making efforts to sabotage the regime.

The fright that these people give him, and a growing sense of responsibility towards his four children, cause Gvadi to turn over a new leaf, and in the end he wins a glorious reputation for himself by frustrating the burning-down of a sawmill.

As is usual in contemporary Soviet literature, this book does not lack a moral, but it is presented in a good-tempered way, with real humour and with a central character who can be accepted as credible.

One would like to hear more of this remote and sunny corner of the Soviet Union, where the vast changes of the last twenty-five years have not caused the peasants to abandon their picturesque garments or lose their pride of ancestry.

[Fee: £8.8.0; 3.10.45]

2758. Royalties for *Talking to India*

In his Payments Book for 6 October 1945, Orwell noted a payment of £16.0.0 for royalties for *Talking to India* from Allen & Unwin.

2759. To Leonard Moore

6 October 1945   Typewritten

27 B Canonbury Square
Islington
London N 1

Dear Mr Moore,
What are the facts about the enclosed? I thought it was Scribners who were doing the book of essays. At need I can think of another title, but would like to be clear just who has got the book.[1]

Yours sincerely
Eric Blair

1. The letter has been annotated in Moore's office: 'See letter from Jones 27/9/4<5> attached.' Reynal & Hitchcock published *Critical Essays*, as *Dickens, Dali & Others*; see Orwell's letter of 10 October 1945, *2762*.

2760. Review of *The Brothers Karamazov* and *Crime and Punishment* by Fyodor Dostoevsky; translated by Constance Garnett

The Observer, 7 October 1945

Constance Garnett's translations, now to be re-issued, were the first full translations of Dostoevsky to be made direct from Russian into English, and they appeared in the years immediately preceding the last war. At that date it must have been a wonderful experience to read Dostoevsky. It must have given many readers the feeling that an earlier generation had had from Flaubert and a later one was to get from Joyce—the feeling that here was a country of the mind which one had always known to exist, but which one had never thought of as lying within the scope of fiction. More than almost any novelist, Dostoevsky is able to give his reader the feeling: "He knows my secret thoughts; he is writing about *me*." It is hard to think of anything in English fiction to compare, for instance, with the scene near the beginning of CRIME AND PUNISHMENT, in which the drunken official Marmeladov describes how his daughter Sonia has been driven on to the streets to support the rest of the starving family.

In the eyes of an English reader Dostoevsky gained something by his foreignness—Marmeladov's remark that he got drunk in order to repent afterwards was, as people used to say, "very Russian"—but his basic quality was his enormous capacity for pity. He was sympathetic towards all his characters, even the respectable ones. The breakdown of the hero-villain antithesis, combined with a strict moral code, was something new, and it is not surprising that for a while he seemed a great thinker as well as a great novelist.

At this date, especially when one has just waded through the 800 pages of

THE BROTHERS KARAMAZOV, one can see faults which were less apparent thirty years ago. The impression one often gets from Dostoevsky is of looking at a series of pictures which are incredibly lifelike except that they are all in monochrome. In a way, all his characters are the same kind of person, there are no exceptional people, or perhaps it would be truer to say there are no ordinary people. Priests, peasants, criminals, policemen, prostitutes, business men, ladies of fashion, soldiers, all seem to mingle easily in the same world: above all, everybody tells everybody else about the state of his soul. It is worth comparing the conversations that take place in "Crime and Punishment" between Raskolnikov and the police official, Porfiry Petrovitch, with the kind of conversation that might actually take place, in England, between a neurotic university student and an inspector of police. One enormous hurdle which every novelist has to face—the problem of bringing the man of thought and the man of action into the same picture—has been simply by-passed.

Apart from the famous chapter, entitled "The Grand Inquisitor," "The Brothers Karamazov" is heavy going. Its theme does not seem to justify its vast bulk, about a third of which consists of introductory matter, and passages in it make it easy to believe that Dostoevsky habitually wrote on a corner of the kitchen table and corrected nothing. "Crime and Punishment" is quite another matter. It is an illustration of the extraordinary psychological insight of this book that one takes Raskolnikov's actions entirely for granted although, before the murder is committed, no sufficient motive for it is indicated. It seems quite credible that an intelligent and sensitive young man should suddenly commit a disgusting and almost purposeless crime: and the reason for this must be that Dostoevsky knew exactly what it feels like to be a murderer. A more conscious piece of artistry, forming a wonderful enclave in the book, is the dream of the dying horse by which Raskolnikov's crime is foreshadowed.

Messrs. Heinemann intend to re-issue the whole series of Constance Garnett's translations, and at eight and sixpence a volume they are good value. One volume to look out for—it is one of the less well known of Dostoevsky's books and not easy to obtain during recent years—is "The House of the Dead": this describes, under a thin disguise of fiction, Dostoevsky's own experiences as a prisoner in Siberia, and contains the never-to-be-forgotten short story, "The Husband of Akulka."

[Fee: £10.0.0; 4.10.45]

2761. 'Jack London'

Forces Educational Broadcast, Light Programme, BBC, 8 October 1945,
1000–1020

Correspondence in the BBC Archive shows that agreement was reached on 11 September that Orwell should be paid £15.15.0 for the script of 'Jack London.' At the rehearsal, it was decided that Orwell would act as Narrator, and on 10

October the Talks Booking Manager was asked to pay an additional fee of £3.3.0; a talks booking form was then issued.

On 1 October, Geoffrey Earle, who was responsible for making the arrangements for the programme, wrote to Orwell to say that the producer and an 'advisor' felt strongly that the opening of the script would not broadcast well. Their objections, with which Earle agreed, were:

> That there isn't quite enough of the story to plant it firmly with the listener; that it will not be quite clear to the listener what is happening between Jim and Matt; and that the dramatic value of the extract is in any case too much interrupted by the narrator to make good radio drama. There are several instances where one or other character speaks only one short line before being interrupted by the narrator and thus losing the sequence of it.
>
> What I should like to do, with your consent, is to substitute at the beginning of the programme a reading from the opening of the "The Apostate", which you mention as being a wonderful story, which will be very effective I think, and which is in fact a description of Jack London's own boyhood, and I do want to get something of this into the programme.

Earle asked Orwell to discuss this with him on the following day, 2 October. Rehearsals were to be held on 5 October at 3:15 and, if the producer believed it necessary, at 10:00 on Saturday, 6 October, in Studio C, Film House, Wardour Street.

The script reproduced is one prepared by the BBC; Earle was originally to have been the Narrator. It has no markings and has the cast list as originally arranged: READER—Staff Sergeant Wilfred Davidson; Robert Marsden, Stuart Latham, Frank Atkinson; NARRATOR: Geoffrey Earle. At the rehearsal it was decided that Orwell should be the Narrator; on 10 October, the Talks Booking Manager was asked to pay Orwell a fee of £3.3.0 for taking this part in addition to his fee of £15.15.0 for writing the script. The details in Programmes as Broadcast are as above, but with the addition of Orwell, described as 'Script and reading.' A 1,331–word extract from 'The Apostate' (from *When God Laughs and Other Stories*, 1910) was reported to have been read. Two effects records were used: DLO 81572, the sound of a pulley, and DLO 81571, the sound of a guillotine. Atkinson was shown to be a member of the BBC Repertory Company. The producer was Captain Royston Morley.

The programme was repeated on the Light Programme on 22 November 1946 in the Forces Educational Service. In Programmes as Broadcast Orwell was listed only as Scriptwriter; the cast was Roger Snowdon, Margot Van Der Burgh, Derick Randall, Martin Lewis, and Preston Lockwood. Lewis and Lockwood were members of the BBC Repertory Company. The producer was George Steedman. The extract from 'The Apostate' was counted as 1,400 words. The script was modified to take in the producer's and the advisor's suggestion.

Later in the year, Geoffrey Earle asked Orwell to lend him a book of London's short stories. Orwell did so, and Earle returned the book on 29 November saying, 'I wanted it because I was using an extract from "A Piece of Steak" in a broadcast on Monday and I should have been very stuck without the book. Again many thanks.'

ANNOUNCER:
(from Violet
continuity)

This is a Forces Educational Broadcast. A programme by George Orwell about Jack London.

1st VOICE: Jack London? The American? When he was a kid of eleven he was selling newspapers to get food for his family.

2nd VOICE: Used to work in a canning factory too—10 hours a day and more—eighteen sometimes.

3rd VOICE: London? He was a pirate when he was 16—and tough! running raids on the oyster beds in 'Frisco Bay.

1st VOICE: Yeah—He loved the sea. In the fo'cstle of the old Sophie Sutherland he worked his way all over the South Pacific.

2nd VOICE: Seal fisher? You know, I thought he was a tramp.

3rd VOICE: Tramp? Sure he was a tramp! —King of the Hoboes. He jumped freight cars on the railroad, 3,000 miles clear across Canada.

1st VOICE: That's right. And he was in the Yukon Gold rush too— never found an ounce of gold though.

2nd VOICE: Don't forget the time when the Japs were fighting the Russians in '04, Jack London covered that as a reporter. He was a writer then.

ORWELL: He was a writer. Yes. Born at San Francisco on January 14th, 1876, he died at his Californian Ranch in 1916 and by then he had written nearly 50 novels and collections of short stories—a pretty big output in 16 years, for he didn't publish his first book till he was 25. He came of very poor parents, indeed he never knew for certain who his father was. From his earliest childhood he knew the meaning of insecurity, hunger and hard work.

Before trying to give you any general account of Jack London's work, I'd like you to listen to a fragment from one of his stories. It's a picture of his own boyhood—he calls it "The Apostate."

READER: "If you don't git up, Johnny, I won't give you a bite to eat!"

The threat had no effect on the boy. He clung stubbornly to sleep, fighting for its oblivion as the dreamer fights for his dream. The boy's hands loosely clenched themselves, and he made feeble, spasmodic blows at the air. These blows were intended for his mother, but she betrayed practised familiarity in avoiding them as she shook him roughly by the shoulder.

"Lemme 'lone!"

It was a cry that began, muffled, in the deeps of sleep, that swiftly rushed upward, like a wail, into passionate belligerence, and that died away, and sank down into an inarticulate whine. It was a bestial cry, as of a soul in torment, filled with infinite protest and pain.

But she did not mind. She was a sad-eyed, tired-faced

woman, and she had grown used to this task, which she repeated every day of her life. She got a grip on the bedclothes and tried to strip them down; but the boy, ceasing his punching, clung to them desperately. In a huddle, at the foot of the bed, he still remained covered. Then she tried dragging the bedding to the floor. The boy opposed her. She braced herself. Hers was the superior weight, and the boy and bedding gave, the former instinctively following the latter in order to shelter against the chill of the room that bit into his body.

As he toppled on the edge of the bed it seemed that he must fall head-first to the floor. But consciousness fluttered up in him. He righted himself and for a moment perilously balanced. Then he struck the floor on his feet. On the instant his mother seized him by the shoulders and shook him. Again his fists struck out, this time with more force and directness. At the same time his eyes opened. She released him. He was awake.

"All right," he mumbled.

She caught up the lamp and hurried out, leaving him in darkness.

'You'll be docked,'' she warned back to him.

He did not mind the darkness. When he had got into his clothes, he went out into the kitchen. His tread was very heavy for so thin and light a boy. His legs dragged with their own weight, which seemed unreasonable because they were such skinny legs. He drew a broken-bottomed chair to the table.

"Johnny!" his mother called sharply.

He arose as sharply from the chair, and, without a word, went to the sink. It was a greasy, filthy sink. A smell came up from the outlet. He took no notice of it. That a sink should smell was to him part of the natural order, just as it was a part of the natural order that the soap should be grimy with dish-water and hard to lather. Nor did he try very hard to make it lather. Several splashes of the cold water from the running faucet completed the function. He dried himself on a greasy towel, damp and dirty and ragged, that left his face covered with shreds of lint.

"I wish we didn't live so far away," she said, as he sat down. "I try to do the best I can. You know that. But a dollar on the rent is such a savin', an' we've more room here. You know that."

"A dollar means more grub," he remarked sententiously. "I'd sooner do the walkin' an' git the grub."

He ate hurriedly, half-chewing the bread and washing the unmasticated chunks down with coffee. The hot and muddy liquid went by the name of coffee. Johnny thought it was coffee—and excellent coffee. That was one of the few of life's illusions that remained to him. He had never drunk real coffee in his life.

In addition to the bread, there was a small piece of cold pork. His mother refilled his cup with coffee. As he was finishing the bread, he began to watch if more was forthcoming. She intercepted his questioning glance.

"Now, don't be hoggish, Johnny," was her comment. "You've had your share. Your brothers an' sisters are smaller'n you."

A distant whistle, prolonged and shrieking, brought both of them to their feet. She glanced at the tin alarm-clock on the shelf. The hands stood at half-past five. The rest of the factory world was just arousing from sleep. She drew a shawl about her shoulders, and on her head put a dingy hat, shapeless and ancient.

"We've got to run," she said, turning the wick of the lamp and blowing down the chimney.

They groped their way out and down the stairs. It was clear and cold, and Johnny shivered at the first contact with the outside air. The stars had not yet begun to pale in the sky, and the city lay in blackness. Both Johnny and his mother shuffled their feet as they walked. There was no ambition in the leg muscles to swing the feet clear of the ground.

After fifteen silent minutes, his mother turned off to the right.

"Don't be late," was her final warning from out of the dark that was swallowing her up.

He made no response, steadily keeping on his way. In the factory quarter, doors were opening everywhere, and he was soon one of a multitude that pressed onward through the dark. As he entered the factory gate the whistle blew again. He glanced at the east. Across a ragged sky-line of housetops a pale light was beginning to creep. This much he saw of the day as he turned his back upon it and joined his work gang.

ORWELL: That was the background of young Jack London. He was almost completely self-educated, but he packed an enormous amount of reading into his short life, and along certain lines, such as the history of the Socialist movement, he could almost have been called a learned man. He made a great deal of money out of his writings, but he spent it or gave it away almost as fast as he got it. He was essentially an active, full-blooded, life-loving sort of man, he had a magnificent physique, and he was passionately interested in boxing, as you might infer from his books. But above all things he was a Socialist. On and off he was an active worker and lecturer in the Socialist movement and the basis of all his best work is a feeling of indignation against the cruel, sordid misery in which the modern world often forces people to live. Some of his best stories spring straight out of the experiences of his childhood. But he doesn't write tracts: nearly always the story comes first and the "moral", if you like to call it that, is merely implied. His work falls into three fairly well-defined groups, and I'll try to mention the most important books in each class.

First of all there are the books by which—unfortunately, because they're not his best—he is still best known, his animal books, such as White Fang and The Call of the Wild, each of which is the life history of a dog done in a vivid and interesting way. I don't want to discuss these now.

Secondly there are his directly Socialistic books, such as The Iron Heel, which I'll come back to in a moment. Another example is The People of The Abyss, a remarkable and horrible book about the London slums, which Jack London had explored systematically. Then there is an extraordinarily readable book, The Road, about his experiences as a tramp in America when he was a very young man. There are some wonderful prison scenes in this book. There are also some excellent prison scenes in another book called The Jacket. In this class you could also place a book called Before Adam, which is an attempt to popularise Darwin. It's a reconstruction highly incorrect, I've no doubt, but extremely vigorous and convincing, of the life of prehistoric man, before the discovery of fire or even of stone implements.

Thirdly there are his novels and short stories, such as The Valley of the Moon, Burning Daylight, The Sea Wolf and— this is the best of all—the collection of short stories published under the title of When God Laughs.

Now let me come back to The Iron Heel. About 1934, when Jack London's reputation was rather low, there was a sudden search all over Europe for copies of this book, which had become a rarity. The reason was that The Iron Heel, written in 1907, had made what was in some ways a surprisingly accurate forecast of Fascism. It's a book about the future, about the world revolution which Jack London believed was going to break out quite soon. I don't want to give the impression that as a whole it's a truthful prophecy. Much of the detail in it, especially the dates and the geography, is ridiculous, and Jack London doesn't even mention Russia, the country where revolution did actually break out. But unlike most of the Socialist writers of his time, he argued that the capitalist class would not just let itself be abolished, but would be capable of organising itself, and would stop at nothing in defence of its possessions. He therefore builds up a picture of an appalling, organised reign of terror which at moments has surprising resemblances to the Nazi regime in Germany. Here and there he anticipated very closely the sort of thing that would happen. And I think the reason why he could do so was that he had a Fascist streak, or at any rate a strain of brutality, in himself. This had its disadvantages, but it did help him to understand something that the book-trained Socialist generally fails to understand: that the possessors of great wealth are not simple scoundrels, but that they honestly believe themselves to be the defenders of civilisation, and draw all their strength from that. As a result, the most interesting thing in The Iron Heel is a passage—it's Chapter XXI of the book—analysing the mentality of the new rulers of the world. It's one of the best statements of the outlook of a ruling class—of the outlook that a ruling class must have if it's to survive—that has ever been written.

But finally Jack London's best works are the novels and short stories in which his Socialist convictions have been digested, so to speak, and are not on the surface. His long novel, The Valley of the Moon, is still worth reading; and so are almost all the stories, such as Smoke Bellew, that he wrote about the Alaskan goldfields. But above all, if you can get hold of them, read the stories collected in When God Laughs. You've already heard a bit of "The Apostate," describing child labour as Jack London had seen it. And there's another very effective story on a grim and sordid theme called "Just Meat". It's about two burglars who've got away with a haul of jewellery worth half a million dollars, killing a man in doing it. Each poisons the other in an attempt to get the whole of the swag and the story ends with the two men stretched dead on the floor—"just meat".

There's another called "Love of Life" which describes a prospector struggling against starvation somewhere in the Arctic. Day after day, as he plods along the trail, a wolf, also half dead from starvation, is following him, hoping to wear him down. But in the end the man's stamina turns out to be the greater, and the story ends not with the wolf eating the man but the man eating the wolf. Incidentally, when Lenin was in his last illness, and his wife Krupskaya used to sit at his bedside reading to him, this was the very last story she read.

To end with, here's a fragment from another story from this collection, called "The Chinago." Chinago is a nickname used on some of the Pacific islands for a Chinese.

NARRATOR: This story concerns a French island, and some minor officials have received orders to guillotine a Chinese coolie named Ah Chow, C,H,O,W, who has committed a murder. The official who signs the order has had too much to drink, and he leaves out the last letter, with the result that another coolie named Ah Cho, C,H,O, is taken to the place of execution. On the way he keeps trying to explain that he is not Ah Chow, but without success. The guard, a rather stupid policeman called Cruchot—who has charge of him merely laughs at him and tells him not to worry, because the blade of the guillotine won't hurt: most probably it will only tickle, he says.

When they arrive the overseer, who is also the executioner, is just trying out the hastily erected guillotine on the trunk of a banana tree. Cruchot hands over his prisoner and goes. Ah Cho glanced at the sergeant who was standing by and saw his opportunity.

AH CHO: The honourable judge said that Ah Chow was to have his head cut off.

NARRATOR: The sergeant nodded impatiently. He was thinking of the fifteen-mile ride before him that afternoon, to the windward side of the island, and of Berthe, the pretty half-caste daughter of Lafiere, the pearl trader, who was waiting for him at the end of it.

AH CHO: Well, I am not Ah Chow. I am Ah Cho. The honourable jailer has made a mistake. Ah Chow is a tall man, and you see I am short.

SERGEANT: That's true! Schemmer! Come here.
(puzzled)

SCHEMMER: Is your Chinago ready?

SERGEANT: Look at him. Is he the Chinago?

SCHEMMER: No, he isn't. (Pause) Look here, we can't postpone this
(pause) affair. I've lost three hours work already out of those five hundred Chinagos. I can't afford to lose it all over again for the right man. Let's put the performance through just the same. It's only a Chinago. They'll blame it on Cruchot—if it's discovered. But there's little chance of its being discovered. Ah Chow won't give it away, at any rate.

SERGEANT: The blame won't lie with Cruchot, anyway. It must have been the jailer's mistake.

SCHEMMER: Then let's go on with it. They can't blame us. Who can tell one Chinago from another? We can say we merely carried out instructions with the Chinago that was turned over to us. Besides, I really can't take all those coolies a second time away from their labour.

NARRATOR: They spoke in French, and Ah Cho, who did not understand a word of it, nevertheless knew that they were determining his destiny. He knew also, that the decision rested with the sergeant, and he hung upon that official's lips.

SERGEANT:	All right. Go ahead with it. He's only a Chinago.
SCHEMMER:	I'm going to try out the guillotine once more, just to make sure.
NARRATOR:	Schemmer moved the banana trunk forward under the knife, which he had hoisted to the top of the derrick. Ah Cho tried to remember maxims from "The Tract of the Quiet Way." "Live in Concord", came to him: but it was not applicable. He was not going to live. He was about to die. Schemmer leant forward to test the drop of the knife. With a quick movement he jerked the cord.
SERGEANT: (to himself)	Beautiful! Beautiful, my friend.
SCHEMMER:	Come on, Ah Chow.
AH CHO:	But I am not Ah Chow—
SCHEMMER:	Shut up! If you open your mouth again, I'll break your head.
NARRATOR:	The overseer threatened him with a clenched fist, and he remained silent. What was the good of protesting? He allowed himself to be lashed to the vertical board that was the size of his body. Then he was aware that the board had come to rest, and from muscular pressures and tensions he knew that he was lying on his back. He opened his eyes. Straight above him he saw the suspended knife blazing in the sunshine. He saw the weight which had been added, and noted that one of Schemmer's knots had slipped. Then he heard the sergeant's voice in sharp command. Ah Cho closed his eyes hastily. He did not want to see that knife descend. But he felt it—for one great fleeting instant. And in that instant he remembered Cruchot and what Cruchot had said. But Cruchot was wrong. The knife did not tickle. That much he knew before he ceased to know.
ORWELL:	I haven't been able to mention all of Jack London's work. In his short life he travelled all over the world and had many wild adventures, and—as I've said—he wrote an enormous amount. He made a rule of writing a thousand words a day, and he kept to it a great deal of the time. If you write at that speed you don't always do your best, and much of Jack London's work is hardly worth bothering with today. But read, if you can get hold of them, The Valley of the Moon, When God Laughs, The Road, The Jacket, The Iron Heel, and Before Adam. If you read those six books, you've read the best of Jack London.
ANNOUNCER: (from Violet Continuity)	That programme about Jack London was written by George Orwell. The reader of the first story was Staff Sergeant Wilfred Davidson, the narrator was Geoffrey Earle; and parts were played by Robert Marsden, Stuart Latham and Frank Atkinson.

2762. To Leonard Moore

10 October 1945   Typewritten

27 B Canonbury Square
Islington
London N 1

Dear Mr Moore,

The contract is herewith duly initialled at the bottoms of the pages.[1] I am very glad Nagel are going to do "Animal Farm" as well. I don't suppose many difficulties will arise about the translation of this one, but if any do, perhaps whoever is doing the work would consult me, as in the other case.

If Reynal & Hitchcock are going to do "Critical Essays," a new name will have to be found for the American edition, as they asked for one. I'll try and think of one within the next week. I suppose they will send me some proofs? I don't remember whether they had a copy of the MS or a set of the proofs from Warburg, but in either case there might be some minor alterations.

Another person has written asking if he may translate "Animal Farm" into French. I suppose I can tell him that the arrangement with Nagel is definitely fixed?

Yours sincerely
[Signed] Eric Blair
Eric Blair

1. Annotated in Moore's offices: 'Dealt with.'

2763. Review of *Edwin and Eleanor* by C. E. Vulliamy; *At Mrs. Lippincote's* by Elizabeth Taylor; *To the Boating* by Inez Holden

Manchester Evening News, 11 October 1945

Some years ago Mr. James Laver wrote a history of fashion, in which he showed that almost anything can become elegant after the appropriate lapse of time, which can even be calculated within a few decades.

A garment or a piece of furniture is first "all the rage," then it is out-of-date, then it is ugly, then ridiculous, then it takes on the charm of antiquity, and, finally, it may even return as a fashion.

The crinoline is now seen to have been a distinctly attractive garment, though perhaps rather an inconvenient one, and the black lacquered furniture inlaid with mother-of-pearl, which our parents threw on to the junk heap, is sought after by collectors. Indeed, nearly every aspect of Victorian life has undergone a revaluation during the past ten or 20 years, and one can no longer get a laugh by the mere mention of pegtop trousers or the Prince Consort as one could when Lytton Strachey wrote "Eminent Victorians."

This change of viewpoint makes a large and elaborate joke like "Edwin and

Eleanor" seem rather pointless. It is a story of Victorian life, ostensibly occurring in the years 1854–56, and told in the form of diaries and letters. Implicit all the way through it is the notion that our grandparents were in some way funnier than ourselves: to anyone who cannot accept this, the book will appear primarily a waste of talent.

It concerns an elopement in what used to be known as "good society." A rather foolish young couple who seem well enough suited to one another—the husband dabbles in painting, the wife works spasmodically at a romantic novel entitled "Sir Florio Ponsonby"—gradually drift apart, the husband developing sentimental attachments to other women, the wife succumbing to the charms of a young literary dilettante, for whom she finally leaves home.

It is a rather empty story, though in real life it would be rather a painful one. In our own day the seduction would be accomplished more rapidly, otherwise the sequence of events is familiar enough. The joke lies in these events occurring against a background of whiskers, Tennyson's poetry, and the fashionable fads of the period, such as ornamenting glass jugs with paper patterns stuck on by means of gelatine.

Landseer and other nineteenth-century painters come in for a good deal of guying, and there are some parodies of Tennysonian verse. Some real research has gone into this book, however, and the best things in it are some passing references to the Crimean war, and to the slow, dirty, and dangerous railway trains which were then beginning to be the normal means of travel.

"At Mrs. Lippincote's" is a waste of talent in a different way. It was written with real distinction, and the author gives the impression of feeling very strongly about something or other, but just what are the meaning· and purpose of the book it would be hard to say. It concerns the wife—for the wife is the chief figure—of an R.A.F. officer who has come to join her husband in the rather dreary provincial town where he is stationed, taking a furnished house in order to do so.

Her cousin has come with her and in a rather meaningless way gets mixed up with the local Communist party. The wife, Julia, is represented as unpractical and quarrelsome, and her thoughts often flit vaguely in the direction of infidelity. In the end it turns out that her husband has been unfaithful for some time past, and this, it seems, is much worse than anything that Julia herself has done, or contemplated doing.

In the background there are the enigmatic figures of the Wing Commander, whose peacetime occupation nobody knows, and of Mrs. Lippincote, the owner of the house. There is also Julia's little boy, aged seven and very precocious. Probably this book means something, but the meaning fails to get through.

Inez Holden[1] is an uneven writer, but she is at the top of her form in several of the stories in "To the Boating," notably "Musical Chairman" and "Theme Song for a Drunken Uncle." The former story, which is the longest in the book, describes—very convincingly and no doubt from first-hand experience—the working of the Appeals Board at a Labour Exchange.

The Board is extremely conscientious and, in intention, just, but by an unerring instinct it does the wrong thing in every case, because of the inability of comfortably placed people to imagine what a wage-earner's life is like. There is a rather similar picture of the impersonal cruelty of authority in "Shocking Weather, Isn't It?" which describes visiting day at a prison. But these stories are not merely "social documents." Like Miss Holden's sketches of factory life, they give accurate detail and remarkably lifelike dialogue, but they make a pattern, in some cases by means of a single phrase which recurs like the refrain of a song.

This is one method by which a piece of writing which is in reality only a sketch—a description, for example, of a single person's character, or of the atmosphere of a house—can be made to stand on its own feet without having to masquerade as an ordinary story with a "denouement."

Thus, in "Theme Song for a Drunken Uncle," the recurring motif is the fact that the uncle always accuses everybody else of being drunk, and after his death the story is neatly rounded off by one more accusation contained in his will.

About half a dozen of the stories in the book are constructed on a similar plan: one or two, such as "Soldiers' Chorus," are simply descriptive sketches. At the end (these are linguistic curiosities, but one of them is quite a good story in itself) are three very short stories written in basic English.[2]

[Fee: £8.8.0; 10.10.45]

1. Inez Holden was one of Orwell's friends; see *1326, n. 1*.
2. Basic English (the review should have a capital 'B' for 'basic') was devised in 1929–30 by C. K. Ogden; see *1746, n. 1*. Its vocabulary was restricted to 850 words. These can conveniently be found in David Crystal, *The Cambridge Encyclopedia of Language* (1987), 356.

2764. Review of *Freedom of Expression*, edited by Hermon Ould

Tribune, 12 October 1945

I have never actually seen a polar bear in boxing gloves trying to pick up a bead of quicksilver, but [I] imagine the spectacle must be very similar to what is usually presented by a so-called "symposium." A "symposium" (literally a drinking party, but that side of it was scrapped a long time ago) means a discussion, or a series of talks on the same subject, by a circle of people who may be held to represent the various possible viewpoints. It is generally at its vaguest and most evasive when it takes place on the radio, but the talks delivered to the P.E.N. Club a year ago and now printed under the title of *Freedom of Expression* are certainly remarkable for the way in which they *don't* deal with their alleged subject matter. Indeed there seem to have been at least two schools of opinion as to what the P.E.N. conference was about.

The purpose, we are told on the cover, was to "commemorate the tercentenary of the publication of Milton's *Areopagitica*." The *Areopagitica*, it will be remembered, was a pamphlet written in 1644 in defence of freedom of the press, and the book of collected talks is entitled *Freedom of Expression*. You might be forgiven, therefore, for imagining that it is mainly concerned with freedom of expression. But not a bit of it! The purpose of the conference, writes Mr. Hermon Ould in the introduction, was "to provide a platform for the untrammelled expression of views and convictions on perhaps the most important subject that can exercise our minds at the present time—'The Place of Spiritual and Economic Values in the Future of Mankind.'" Just what this has to do with *Areopagitica* is hard to see: and in fact about half of the thirty or forty speakers left Milton unmentioned.

Of the rest, about a dozen did from time to time utter a remark bearing on the question of liberty, and a few others touched upon it by implication. The statements really relevant to the position of the press at this time and in this country are so few that they can be summarised in a few lines. Thus, Mr. E. M. Forster, in his inaugural address, takes a very mild crack at the M.O.I.[1] and the British Council. Mr. Ifor Evans points out that to permit real freedom of the press involves great dangers. Professor J. B. S. Haldane discusses the effects of censorship on radio and the films and mentions the suppression of the *Daily Worker*. Mr. John R. Baker states that the British press is to some extent censored in the interests of Russian propaganda, and that bodies like the National Council for Civil Liberties have been captured from within by people sympathetic to totalitarianism. Mr. Herbert Read urges that Milton's plea for unlicensed printing has not lost its relevance. Mr. Mulk Raj Anand denounces the press censorship existing in India. Mr. Harold Laski admits that during the war the British press has enjoyed more freedom than might have been expected. Mr. Kingsley Martin points out that to defend liberty you have to deny liberty to the people who would destroy liberty if they got the chance. Mr. Alec Craig attacks the laws relating to obscenity in literature. That is really about all the relevant matter—relevant, that is, to the issues Milton raised—to be found in nearly 200 closely printed pages.

Now, nearly all of the speakers at this conference, and probably a large part of the audiences, were people directly concerned with the writing trade. Considering the age we live in and the kind of things that have been happening to writers and journalists during the past fifteen years, wouldn't you expect such a gathering of people to be a bit more vehement and a bit more precise in their accusations? Here are some of the subjects that were *not* mentioned, or barely mentioned:—The centralised ownership of the British press, with its consequent power to suppress any bit of news that it chooses; the question of who really controls the B.B.C., the buying-up of young writers by film units, the M.O.I., etc.; the methods by which British correspondents in foreign countries are squeezed into telling lies or concealing truths; the corruption of literary criticism by the publishing trade; the vague semi-official pressure that prevents books on unpopular themes from getting published; the spread of totalitarian ideas, mostly emanating from the U.S.S.R., among English intellectuals. One could extend the list, but it is that kind of influence that now menaces all that we have hitherto meant by intellectual liberty. Except in the talk given by Mr. John Baker, and here and there in those given by Mr. Ifor Evans and Professor Haldane, hardly one of these issues received an unmistakable mention.

What is one to think of a gathering of over thirty literary men of whom barely one can say plainly that freedom means the freedom to criticise and oppose, and that in consequence freedom is non-existent in the U.S.S.R., unless one gives the word a totally different meaning from what it held for Milton and for almost every Englishman between his day and ours? Is it not blatantly obvious that if there is freedom of the press in the U.S.S.R., then there is no freedom here, so that all talk about "defending our hard-won liberties" etc., becomes meaningless? Yet hardly a single speaker could point this out, just as hardly a single speaker could give Beaverbrook or Rothermere[2] the sort of kick in the pants that they would be likely to feel.

A discussion of this kind, which might have been lively forty years ago, and might be lively now if it were conducted in some obscure periodical by people who have not much to lose, is killed by two separate though interacting influences. On the one hand there is the general drift towards a planned and centralised but not democratic society, in which the writer or journalist tends to become a sort of minor official. On the other hand, there is the pressure of totalitarian propaganda. How many people, making their living out of writing, can afford to insult simultaneously the M.O.I, the B.B.C., the British Council, the press lords, the film magnates, the leading publishing houses and the editors of all the principal newspapers? Yet you have to insult all of those if you want to speak up for the freedom of the press. And how many people have—or had in the late summer of 1944—the courage to utter genuine criticism of Soviet Russia? So, in order to commemorate Milton's great plea for liberty, you get this vague bumbling, in which the liberty which is supposedly being defended is never clearly defined—in which, indeed, it is not even certain what subject is being discussed. On the whole this is a depressing book.[3]

[Fee: £5.0.0; 5.10.45]

1. Ministry of Information, which was based for much of the war in Senate House, University of London, a combination which suggested Minitrue in *Nineteen Eighty-Four*.
2. Two of the press lords to whom Orwell refers later: Lord Beaverbrook (1879–1964), associated especially with the *Daily Express*, and Minister of Supply and of Production, 1941–42; and Lord Rothermere (1868–1940), associated especially with the *Daily Mail*.
3. See the 'Prevention of Literature' (*2792*) which begins by discussing this meeting of the P.E.N. Club.

2765. Aneurin Bevan, Profile

The Observer, 14 October 1945 Anonymous, but chiefly written by Orwell[1]

This week's debate on Housing will certainly bring a major speech from the new Minister of Health.[2]

For several of the war years Aneurin Bevan—"that architect of disloyalty," as Mr. Churchill once called him in a heated moment—was known as the most turbulent M.P. on the Opposition benches, and it is only sixteen months since [3] his own Party came near to expelling him for voting against the Government on a major issue. His weekly paper "Tribune," whose editorship in-chief he had inherited from Sir Stafford Cripps, also criticised the conduct of the war, and British foreign policy, with a freedom that sometimes bordered on irresponsibility. These activities have tended to stamp him in the public mind as the naughty boy of the Labour Party and to obscure the solid achievements that actually lie behind him. Yet in the job of re-housing Britain his experience in local government and in trade union administration may be as important as the restless energy of his temperament. [4]

Aneurin Bevan was born in 1897, the son of a coalminer. He himself left school at 13 and went to work in the pit. In spite of his powerful physique he was a shy, bookish boy, left-handed, and troubled by a severe stammer, which still has a slight tendency to return in moments when he is overtired. In such spare time as he could get he read voraciously, making a speciality of books on philosophy. He had the chance to educate himself, he says, quite largely because the Tredegar public library happened to be an exceptionally good one and the librarian took a personal interest in him. As for his stammer and his nervousness, he got rid of them by deliberately involving himself in street-corner meetings and other situations where he knew he would be compelled to speak extempore.

Some years later he was able to leave the pit and study at the Central Labour College. He was only 19 when he was chairman of the largest Miners' lodge in South Wales, and was still a very young man when he became a member of the local Urban District Council. He was a miners' disputes agent in 1926, and has held the Ebbw Vale seat since 1929. With this background his natural affinity might seem to be with the trade union end of the Labour Party, but in fact he has until lately been looked on with some suspicion by the chiefs of the T.U.C.

His following, outside his own constituency, has been chiefly among the "intellectuals" of the Party branches and the growing body of middle-class people whose sympathies have turned leftward during the past five or ten years. He was the close associate of Sir Stafford Cripps until Cripps joined the Churchill Government, and he has many foreign refugee Socialists among his friends and advisers. He is more of an extremist and more of an internationalist than the average Labour M.P., and it is the combination of this with his working-class origin that makes him an interesting and unusual figure.

On any issue of domestic policy—on housing, social security, education, public health—Bevan thinks and feels as a working man. He knows how the scales are weighted against anyone with less than £5 a week, and during the war he has defended the right of the workers to strike, even at moments when strikes did or could seriously hamper the war effort. But he is remarkably free—some of his adversaries would say dangerously free—from any feeling of personal grievance against society. He shows no sign of ordinary class consciousness. He seems equally at home in all kinds of company. It is difficult to imagine anyone less impressed by social status or less inclined to put on airs with subordinates. Everyone who has more than a nodding acquaintance with him calls him by his nickname of "Nye." He has the temperament that used to be called "mercurial"—a temperament capable of sudden low spirits but not of settled pessimism. His boisterous manner sometimes gives casual observers the impression that he is not serious, and his warmest admirers do not claim that punctuality is his strong point. But in fact he has a huge capacity for work and manages to put in a great deal of time at his rather inaccessible constituency.

Some of Bevan's qualities may be traceable to his Welsh blood. Though only tepidly interested in Welsh Nationalism, he has not lost touch with his origins and retains traces of his Welsh accent. His infrequent holidays are always devoted to climbing in his native hills. He is a typical Celt not only in his quickness of speech and abrupt alternations of mood but in his respect for the intellect. He does not have the suspicion of "cleverness" and anaesthesia to the arts which are generally regarded as the mark of a practical man. Those who have worked with him in a journalistic capacity have remarked with pleasure and astonishment that here at last is a politician who knows that literature exists and will even hold up work for five minutes to discuss a point of style.

Bevan's campaign against Churchill, in Parliament and in the Press, was very bitter, and sometimes undignified. There were moments when Bevan seemed to be actuated by personal dislike, and Churchill, too, was more easily "drawn" by Bevan than by any other opponent. Some observers have remarked that the two men are natural antagonists "because they are so alike." In fact, there are points of resemblance. Both men are naturally genial but capable of sudden anger and rough speech, both of them have been held back in their careers by the "cleverness" which did not commend itself to more stolid colleagues. Whether Bevan is fully Churchill's equal in obstinacy remains to be seen.

The post he now holds, a post in which he is responsible not only for public health but for rehousing, is a thankless and difficult one. In the matter of houses the public expects miracles and is certain to be disappointed at not getting them. Bevan is well aware of this and knows all about the fight with local authorities, with the building trade and with the B.M.A.[5] that lies ahead of him. He has clear ideas about what is desirable and what is possible in the matter of housing. His own private preference is for a house and not a flat, and he holds it as a principle that everyone should have the right to choose between the two. But he also realises that if people are to live in big conglomerations they must spread themselves vertically, and he would like, if he can, to popularise the idea of the small town which is a single building— the "skyscraper in open country."[6]

He sought out his present job because he feels strongly about slum clearance, about the effects of the housing shortage on the birth-rate, and about the need to put the practice of medicine on a non-commercial basis. Those who know him believe that he can make decisions boldly, will get results, and will soon return to the headlines as a quite different figure from the fiery debater of the last five years.[7]

1. Orwell's major contribution to this Profile was attested by David Astor. There is no record in Orwell's Payments Book in October 1945 which might refer to it, but Orwell does list £10.0.0 for an article in *The Observer* against 7 September which has not otherwise been traced; it might therefore refer to this Profile. The bulk of the Profile was reprinted in *English Digest*, Vol. 20, No. 3, January 1946; paragraphs 1 and 7, and the last sentence of paragraph 8 were omitted and some minor style changes were made. The article was included in *Observer Profiles*, with an introduction by Ivor Brown (1948); authorship of Profiles is not given. The verbal changes then made are given in the notes below. For a short biographical note on Bevan, see *2725, n. 4.*
2. The first paragraph is omitted from *Observer Profiles* (as *OP* hereafter).
3. it is only sixteen months since] at one time   *OP*
4. Yet in the job of re-housing Britain . . . energy of his temperament] *omitted   OP*
5. British Medical Association: the general practitioners' 'trade union.'
6. and knows all about . . . in open country"] *omitted   OP*
7. return . . . five years] be more than just a fiery debater in the public eye   *OP; the last two paragraphs are combined as one in OP*

2765A.   To Arthur Koestler, 17 October 1945: see Vol XX last appendix

2766.   To Fredric Warburg

17 October 1945   Typewritten

27 B Canonbury Square
Islington
London   N 1

Dear Fred,

I had some conversation with Frank Horrabin, who told me [he] had shown a copy of "Animal Farm" to David Low,[1] and the latter said something suggesting he would like to illustrate it. If he would really do so this would be a winner, and would be a way of placing the book in the USA, which I have not succeeded in doing. (It's going to be translated into French, by the way.)

The trouble is I don't know Low and don't know how to approach him. Do you know him? Horrabin said he had mentioned this idea to you.[2]

I have had a stinking cold but it is a bit better now. I'll read that MS and let you have an opinion as soon as possible, but I am very busy as usual. I am sending back the proofs of the essays book separately.

Yours
George

1. David Low (1891–1963; Kt., 1962), outstanding political cartoonist, was born in New Zealand and began work in London in 1919. His cartoons were published in many countries but banned in Germany from 1936. In England, his left-wing-orientated work was published in the right-wing *Evening Standard* and the liberal-inclined *Manchester Guardian*. Many collections of his cartoons were published but, at the time Orwell wrote, the most remarkable were his 'cartoon histories,' published by Penguin: *Europe Since Versailles* (1940), *Europe at War* (1941), and *The World at War* (1942), comprising 220 cartoons with facing-page narratives.
2. Warburg replied on 18 October, saying he knew of Low's reaction to *Animal Farm* and quoting Low's letter to Horrabin in full: 'I have had a good time with ANIMAL FARM—an excellent bit of satire. As you say, it would illustrate perfectly.' Low could not have given concrete consideration to illustrating the book, however, since 'he could have no information as to whether we were anxious for an illustrated edition.' Warburg and Senhouse were in

favour of an illustrated edition: 'it is the timing . . . that presents the problem.' He hoped to discuss this with Orwell and Low at a lunch in the New Year. A second edition, of 10,000 copies, of *Animal Farm* was promised for delivery in December, in time for Christmas; this might last 'through to the spring, though this is doubtful.' This second edition actually appeared earlier, in November. Orwell was evidently suffering from a cold, and Warburg warned him to be careful during the winter (as he must also be). Warburg also sought a report 'on Fitzgerald's novels' when Orwell had time. No report of this has been traced. An edition illustrated by Low was not published but one illustrated by the cartoonist, Ralph Steadman, was published by Secker & Warburg in 1995 to celebrate the fiftieth anniversary of the first edition of *Animal Farm*.

2767. To Roger Senhouse

17 October 1945   Typewritten

27 B Canonbury Square
Islington
London   N 1

I have made further corrections on the following pages:—
    Title page, both sides (date.) Contents page. 25. 85. 98. 109 (2). 145. 153.
    The one on p. 25 is important. I believe I may have misdirected you about this before. It should be definitely HAROLD Skimpole, not Horace.[1]

Geo. Orwell

1. These corrections are to *Critical Essays*. Orwell had already written to Senhouse about the Horace/Harold change two months before; see *2732*. The correction, to Harold, was made in the text. One of the changes to be made to p. 109 ('nine and sixty' for 'nine and fifty,' in line 3 of the footnote) is specified in Orwell's letter to Moore of 17 November 1945; see *2797*.

2768. Review of *Selected Stories* by Rhys Davies

Manchester Evening News, 18 October 1945

There is only a small handful of successful short-story writers in England at this moment and Mr. Rhys Davies is one of them. He has lightened the dreary pages of so many a magazine that it seems almost ungrateful to criticise him too closely.

Nevertheless an examination of the stories in his present book brings out once again the peculiar difficulty under which this genre has laboured during the past twenty years or so—the difficulty, that is, of producing something which is a real story with action and development in it, and which at the same time is readable and has a clear connection with real life.

This can be sufficiently illustrated by the subject-matter of Mr. Davies's stories. Of the ten pieces in his present book two are less definitely stories than the others and are, so to speak, off his usual beat. The other eight deal, like most of his work, with his native Wales.

The first deals with a corpse who comes to life just before burial, to the dismay of her sisters, who have spent a lot of money on the funeral.

The second deals with the refusal of some old women in an alms-house to use a newly installed water-closet.

The third deals with a young miner who has never seen his wife with her clothes off.

The fourth describes a Welsh family squabbling over their father's belongings while he lies dying upstairs.

The fifth deals with an eccentric old maid who insists on taking her cow to church with her.

The sixth describes an insurance agent whose home life temporarily improves because he is getting tenderer meat for his meals, which is really due to the fact that his wife is having an affair with the butcher.

The seventh deals with a dwarf with a gift for drawing who rapes and murders a girl who has treated him in a heartless way.

The eighth deals with a fatuous poet whose wife ends by chopping up for firewood the oak throne he has won at an Eisteddfod.

Obviously it is unfair to summarise even the shortest story in this manner, but these brief notes perhaps give some idea of the atmosphere which pervades almost all of Mr. Rhys Davies's work. Almost invariably his themes are grotesque—sometimes in a humorous way, sometimes in a gruesome way, but at any rate with a tendency to avoid the every-day incident and the humdrum character.

As a story-teller Mr. Rhys Davies is nearer to Hans Andersen than to Maupassant. His stories do not actually deal with the supernatural, but they habitually deal with the improbable, and some of them are a kind of prose poem. And after all this is one way in which the writer of short stories can escape from his dilemma. He can preserve form and style by sacrificing credibility.

As every editor and publisher knows, present-day short stories which attempt to deal faithfully with real life are almost invariably dreary and eventless. A lonely woman sits in her maisonette waiting for the telephone to ring; it doesn't ring. That, spun out to two or three thousand words, is the type of the modern short story.

There appears to be something in this phase of civilisation that makes it very difficult to imagine an incident which is dramatic and at the same time can be thought of as actually happening. In a full-length novel character interest can make up for absence of plot, but in a short story one practically has to choose between the pointless and the abnormal. Mr. Rhys Davies, obviously, is a specialist in the abnormal.

After all, how often does it happen that a dead woman sits up after she has been put in her coffin? And how many people take cows to church with them? These tiny grotesques, like carvings on nut shells, are excellent of their kind, but they have not, and are not meant to have, much to do with every-day life.

The longest story in the book, "Arfon," the story of the gifted dwarf, deals with an incident that could happen, but in the telling it is turned into a species of poem, and realistic detail is avoided. The story of the cow that went to church illustrates in a slightly different way Mr. Rhys Davies's instinctive avoidance of the commonplace. The point of the story is that the old lady's foible had to be tolerated because her contributions to the church funds were too important to be sacrificed.

A generation or more ago Jack London, H. G. Wells, D. H. Lawrence, and others could produce stories which contained action and surprise and yet stuck fairly closely to ordinary life. Somehow that has ceased to be possible and the stories which are most truly stories tend to be exercises in the fantastic. It is a pity, for to specialise in the fantastic inevitably means narrowing one's range.

[Fee: £8.8.0; 17.10.45]

2769. Randolph Churchill to Orwell

19 October 1945

Randolph Churchill (1911–1968) son of Winston Churchill, returned to Orwell a copy of *Animal Farm* which he had lent him, with thanks for Orwell's kindness.

2770. 'You and the Atom Bomb'

Tribune, 19 October 1945

On 12 October 1945, *Tribune* published a letter from Miss S. D. Wingate to which it gave the title 'An Atom Dictatorship?' This argued that 'socialists would be well advised to do some serious thinking now about the implications of the discovery of atom-fission for the structure of the future society—if there is one.' She continued:

> For the last century or more real power, potentially at least, was in the hands of the masses. This was true not only in the field of production but also in the military field. During the age of mass, conscript armies, which began at the time of the French Revolution, the basis of military power was the ordinary man with a rifle in his hand. The reflection of this basic fact in the political sphere was the trend towards democracy observable throughout the western world in the century leading up to this war. We are now, however, moving into the atomic age, when neither productive nor military power will be any longer in the hands of the masses, but both will be concentrated in a small group of highly qualified scientists and technicians, with a handful of skilled workers operating under their direction, the latter, moreover, tending to shrink in numbers as the process of discovery goes on.
>
> Logically, the appropriate political organisation for such an age might well be the dictatorship (no doubt "enlightened" from its own point of view) of a small class, highly specialised in its training, and increasingly so, I suggest, in its social origins, tending to feel itself more and more separate from and out of touch with the needs and desires of the common man, with a considerable contempt for his ignorance and prejudices, and without any sanction for a

code which would impose on this hierarchy the obligation to respect the rights and liberties of subordinate classes and groups.

If this is a nightmare without any real foundation, what are the grounds for thinking that this time a drastic change in the productive process will not be followed by a corresponding change in the balance of social forces? If, on the other hand, there is at least a probability of the sort of development I have outlined, what do we do about it?

In the next issue of *Tribune*, 19 October 1945, Mr. J. Stewart Cook responded to this letter, and, either prompted by her letter (if Orwell had seen it before it was published; his essay is dated 11 October in his Payments Book) or coincidentally, Orwell published 'You and the Atom Bomb.' On 26 October, Miss Wingate replied to Cook, and Orwell, prompted by Cook's letter, published a second essay, 'What is Science?' Orwell's essays sparked a considerable correspondence. In order to co-ordinate this material here, the chronology has been disturbed. Randolph Churchill's letter, *2769*, has been placed before 'You and the Atom Bomb,' and the review for the *Manchester Evening News* of 25 October, *2773*, has been placed after 'What is Science?' and its correspondence. The sequence begins, therefore, with Cook's response to Miss Wingate's initial letter and her reply (19 and 26 October respectively), followed by Orwell's two essays and relevant correspondence, *2770* and *2771*.

Miss Wingate is, I suggest, wrong in believing that the number of skilled workers operating scientific or technological processes "tends to shrink in numbers as the process of discovery goes on." On the contrary, every new development, such as radio, the internal combustion engine, the development of the modern machine tool industry, and many other similar applications of scientific knowledge, have resulted in the formation of a new and growing class of skilled workers who can handle the specialised operations involved, usually with far greater competence and confidence than the scientists themselves could possibly hope to achieve.

The development of atomic energy as a major source of motive power would inevitably result in the creation of an even larger class of skilled workers who were trained in the practical technical work that would have to be carried out on a very wide basis before atomic energy could ever be utilised to any effective extent.

Nevertheless, the danger of the development of a kind of "scientific hierarchy" remains and Miss Wingate is right in asking what we are going to do about it. May I, as a scientist, make one or two suggestions?

Firstly, we must see to it that the attainment of a proper understanding of science is universally accepted by all teachers, schools and universities as a fundamental aim of modern education. By which I mean that every pupil in every school must be taught to understand and appreciate the meaning of science irrespective of whether it is going to help him to earn a living directly or not.

Secondly, a similar purpose must also be accepted by those responsible for adult education, which has hitherto tended to neglect scientific studies in favour of literary, economic and social subjects.

Thirdly, some endeavour should be made by the Labour Movement in particular to give scientists the fullest opportunity of taking part in its affairs, as local Councillors, as M.P.s, as delegates to Party gatherings and in all other ways possible.

These suggestions are all derived from the belief that, if we are to avoid a hierarchy of scientists, the important point to realise is that such a hierarchy would be based on the possession by its members of exclusive knowledge of certain processes. The more we spread knowledge and understanding of science on the one hand and the more we succeed in drawing scientific workers into public affairs on a democratic basis on the other hand, the more likely we are to avoid the sort of thing Miss Wingate fears.

J. Stewart Cook

Mr. Stewart Cook differs from me on the probability that the numbers engaged in producing atom energy will tend to grow less. (I did not, incidentally, suggest that there was any general rule to this effect. I was referring only to the results of atomic-fission; and I should have said that the diminution I expected was relative rather than absolute.)

But on the point I am mainly concerned that we should discuss, the danger of the development of a "scientific hierarchy," he agrees with me, and goes on to suggest two remedies, firstly, "the attainment of a proper understanding of science as a fundamental aim of modern education," and, secondly, the encouragement of scientists to take their place in the machinery of democratic government.

It is difficult to see how either of these can do anything to avert the danger in question. The sort of general scientific knowledge which even the best system of education could give, in Mr. Cook's words, "to every pupil in every school," while it would enlarge his outlook and enrich his mind, could do nothing to limit the monopoly of power possessed by those whose training fitted them for research into nuclear physics, or even to put the ordinary citizen on a level with the average scientifically trained technician.

As to the second suggestion, that the Labour Movement should invite scientists into the seats of democratic government, local and national, I would say that this is bound to happen anyway. My doubt is whether the government is to remain democratic when the process is finished. If the fundamental nature of the productive process and the structure of class relationships based upon it had undergone a radical change in an anti-democratic direction, I doubt if the consequences could be averted, or democracy artificially maintained, by the fact that Labour had itself invited scientists to take their share in the actual work of government. The question would remain: What is their share? Anything less than one hundred per cent.?

The proposal for a race of eugenically produced supermen to control the production of atomic energy, which Sunday's papers reported as having been put before the Military Affairs Committee of the American House of Representatives, may be regarded as fantastic at this stage, but it is a pointer to the sort of lines on which the world may develop if it does not first destroy itself.

S. D. Wingate

YOU AND THE ATOM BOMB

Considering how likely we all are to be blown to pieces by it within the next five years, the atomic bomb has not roused so much discussion as might have been expected. The newspapers have published numerous diagrams, not very helpful to the average man, of protons and neutrons doing their stuff, and there has been much reiteration of the useless statement that the bomb "ought to be put under international control." But curiously little has been said, at any rate in print, about the question that is of most urgent interest to all of us, namely: "How difficult are these things to manufacture?"

Such information as we—that is, the big public—possess on this subject has come to us in a rather indirect way, apropos of President Truman's decision not to hand over certain secrets to the U.S.S.R. Some months ago, when the bomb was still only a rumour, there was a widespread belief that splitting the atom was merely a problem for the physicists, and that when they had solved it a new and devastating weapon would be within reach of almost everybody. (At any moment, so the rumour went, some lonely lunatic in a laboratory might blow civilisation to smithereens, as easily as touching off a firework.)

Had that been true, the whole trend of history would have been abruptly altered. The distinction between great States and and small States would have been wiped out, and the power of the State over the individual would have been greatly weakened. However, it appears from President Truman's remarks, and various comments that have been made on them, that the bomb is fantastically expensive and that its manufacture demands an enormous industrial effort, such as only three or four countries in the world are capable of making. This point is of cardinal importance, because it may mean that the discovery of the atomic bomb, so far from reversing history, will simply intensify the trends which have been apparent for a dozen years past.

It is a commonplace that the history of civilisation is largely the history of weapons. In particular, the connection between the discovery of gunpowder and the overthrow of feudalism by the bourgeoisie has been pointed out over and over again. And though I have no doubt exceptions can be brought forward, I think the following rule would be found generally true: that ages in which the dominant weapon is expensive or difficult to make will tend to be ages of despotism, whereas when the dominant weapon is cheap and simple, the common people have a chance. Thus, for example, tanks, battleships and bombing planes are inherently tyrannical weapons, while rifles, muskets, longbows and hand grenades are inherently democratic weapons. A complex weapon makes the strong stronger, while a simple weapon—so long as there is no answer to it—gives claws to the weak.

The great age of democracy and of national self-determination was the age of the musket and the rifle. After the invention of the flint-lock, and before the invention of the percussion cap, the musket was a fairly efficient weapon, and at the same time so simple that it could be produced almost anywhere. Its combination of qualities made possible the success of the American and French revolutions, and made a popular insurrection a more serious business than it could be in our own day. After the musket came the breech-loading rifle. This was a comparatively complex thing, but it could still be produced in scores of countries, and it was cheap, easily smuggled and economical of ammunition. Even the most backward nation could always get hold of rifles from one source or another, so that Boers, Bulgars, Abyssinians, Moroccans—even Tibetans—could put up a fight for their independence, sometimes with success. But thereafter every development in military technique has favoured the State as against the individual, and the industrialised country as against the backward one. There are fewer and fewer foci of power. Already, in 1939, there were only five States capable of waging war on the grand scale, and now there are only three—ultimately, perhaps, only two. This trend has been obvious for years, and was pointed out by a few observers even before 1914. The one thing that might reverse it is the discovery of a weapon—or, to put it more broadly, of a method of fighting— not dependent on huge concentrations of industrial plant.

From various symptoms one can infer that the Russians do not yet possess the secret of making the atomic bomb; on the other hand, the consensus of opinion seems to be that they will possess it within a few years. So we have before us the prospect of two or three monstrous super-States, each possessed of a weapon by which millions of people can be wiped out in a few seconds, dividing the world between them. It has been rather hastily assumed that this means bigger and bloodier wars, and perhaps an actual end to the machine civilisation. But suppose—and really this is the likeliest development—that the surviving great nations make a tacit agreement never to use the atomic bomb against one another? Suppose they only use it, or the threat of it, against people who are unable to retaliate? In that case we are back where we were before, the only difference being that power is concentrated in still fewer hands and that the outlook for subject peoples and oppressed classes is still more hopeless.

When James Burnham wrote *The Managerial Revolution* it seemed probable to many Americans that the Germans would win the European end of the war, and it was therefore natural to assume that Germany and not Russia would dominate the Eurasian land mass, while Japan would remain master of East Asia. This was a miscalculation, but it does not affect the main argument. For Burnham's geographical picture of the new world has turned out to be correct. More and more obviously the surface of the earth is being parcelled off into three great empires, each self-contained and cut off from contact with the outer world, and each ruled, under one disguise or another, by a self-elected oligarchy. The haggling as to where the frontiers are to be drawn is still going on, and will continue for some years, and the third of the three super-States—East Asia, dominated by China—is still potential rather than actual. But the general drift is unmistakable, and every scientific discovery of recent years has accelerated it.

We were once told that the aeroplane had "abolished frontiers"; actually it is only since the aeroplane became a serious weapon that frontiers have become definitely impassable. The radio was once expected to promote international understanding and co-operation; it has turned out to be a means of insulating one nation from another. The atomic bomb may complete the process by robbing the exploited classes and peoples of all power to revolt, and at the same time putting the possessors of the bomb on a basis of military equality. Unable to conquer one another, they are likely to continue ruling the world between them, and it is difficult to see how the balance can be upset except by slow and unpredictable demographic changes.

For forty or fifty years past, M[ess]rs. H. G. Wells and others have been warning us that man is in danger of destroying himself with his own weapons, leaving the ants or some other gregarious species to take over. Anyone who has seen the ruined cities of Germany will find this notion at least thinkable. Nevertheless, looking at the world as a whole, the drift for many decades has been not towards anarchy but towards the reimposition of slavery. We may be heading not for general breakdown but for an epoch as horribly stable as the slave empires of antiquity. James Burnham's theory has been much discussed, but few people have yet considered its ideological implications—that is, the kind of world-view, the kind of beliefs, and the social structure that would probably prevail in a State which was at once *unconquerable* and in a permanent state of "cold war"[1] with its neighbours.

Had the atomic bomb turned out to be something as cheap and easily manufactured as a bicycle or an alarm clock, it might well have plunged us back into barbarism, but it might, on the other hand, have meant the end of national sovereignty and of the highly-centralised police State. If, as seems to be the case, it is a rare and costly object as difficult to produce as a battleship, it is likelier to put an end to large-scale wars at the cost of prolonging indefinitely a "peace that is no peace."

[Fee: £3.3.0, written over £5.5.0; 11.10.45]

On 26 October 1945, *Tribune* published this letter from Alex Comfort (see *1195*, n. 10):

Orwell puts his finger, as usual, on the wider analytical point when he describes how weapons have tended to produce "democratic" or tyrannical societies, but I feel that another conclusion is possible besides mere resignation to the omnipotence of tyrants equipped with nuclear energy. Not only are social institutions dictated by weapon-power: so are revolutionary tactics, and it seems to me that Orwell has stated the case for the tactical use of disobedience which he has tended to condemn in the past as pacifism.

The conception of resistance, by which any society complex enough to produce atom bombs can be controlled and its rulers defeated, has to become an individual one. Armed revolutions stand less, not more, chance of success in an armed world. To my mind, the efficacy of disobedience as a technique depends not on any mystical argument about its moral force, since moral force never made anyone bullet-proof, but because few if any new techniques have been devised or can be devised to counter it. You cannot use atom-bombs against individuals—they are essentially national rather than ideological weapons. The weapons available to the rulers against the ruled, in the sphere of resistance rather than war, are exactly what they were in 2000 B.C.—terrorism, secret police, wholesale execution, and propaganda. It seems to me that the entire case for "pacifist" action, interpreting that to mean the avoidance of military conflict, is made out in this, even for those who cannot see that any cause which submits itself to military discipline ceases to be a libertarian cause.

The following week, L. R. Borsley wrote:

Mr. George Orwell's views on the atom bomb, in your issue of October 19, hold water on the assumption that the Soviet Union is nothing more than one of what he calls "two or three monstrous super-States." It is significant that he quotes Burnham's *The Managerial Revolution* in support of his thesis, for Burnham's main argument is an anti-Soviet one.

With the aid of *The Managerial Revolution* those who want to can bring themselves to believe the worst. For example, "All the evidence indicates that the autocracy of the Russian regime is the most extreme that has ever existed in human history, not excepting the regime of Hitler" (Pelican edition, p. 43). All the evidence! What simpletons Sidney and Beatrice Webb must have been.

This lurid nonsense seems to boggle some of us. But it isn't that there is any mystery as to what Burnham was up to when he wrote his book. In the light of Stalin's obvious success in the building of a Socialist economy, the Trotskyists (of whom Burnham was one) were beginning to realise the inadequacies of Trotskyism as originally formulated (Burnham describes the "theoretical jam," p. 45). A new anti-Soviet line-up was needed. Burnham supplied it: Accept the fact of Stalin's success, but deny that his success was Socialism. And, in case of objections, one crushing finality: the Socialist revolution "cannot take place in our time" (p. 185).

If, as Mr. Orwell suggests, Burnham's main argument is a sound one, then Socialists had better think again. And not only the Soviet Union, but also our own Labour Government, had better consider with Mr. Orwell the "ideological implications" of Burnham's theory.

'Orwell and the A-bomb' was the subject of a letter from Harold T. Bers published on 16 November 1945:

In his article on the atom bomb, Mr. Orwell admits, for a change, that one of his generalities may have exceptions—"that ages in which the dominant weapon is expensive or difficult to make will tend to be ages of despotism, whereas when the dominant weapon is cheap and simple, the common people have a chance." Starting with Spartacus and continuing through the General Election of 1945 the common people have continuously asserted themselves with such simple weapons as clubs and words and ideas. Yet

Mr. Orwell uses this flimsy generality, in which he himself seems to have little faith and which he does little to justify, as superstructure for his article.

Mr. Orwell then theorises about how atomic power concentrated in a few hands makes the cause of oppressed classes still more hopeless. But the fact of the matter is that the atomic secret is at present in the hands of Britain and the United States, which two nations, despite all we can find wrong with them, are the two most democratic big nations in the world and the two great powers least likely to wage a war of aggression for years to come.

Mr. Orwell says patly that radio "has turned out to be a means of insulating one nation from another." But surely if you were to choose the one tangible thing that did most to keep a tie between the oppressed people of Europe during the war with the forces fighting for their liberation, you must choose the B.B.C.

Mr. Orwell further contends that if the smaller nations could economically produce atom bombs they would have military equality with the larger nations. Let us take an example: should Bulgaria somehow decide to bomb the U.S.S.R. out of existence and should destroy Odessa with one blow—as we know it, the atomic bomb can destroy a city: surely with only one-sixth of the earth at her disposal, the Soviet Union would sue for peace. In, as we say in my homeland, a pig's eye.

L. R. Borsley's letter of 2 November on the atom bomb and James Burnham and *The Managerial Revolution* was taken up in *Tribune* on 9 November by F. D. Barber,[2] who argued that Borsley misrepresented Burnham on three counts; Borsley responded to Barber on 23 November as did R. Mitchell, who maintained that Burnham did not merit such attention; all Burnham did was 'state glibly a glib thesis.'

1. Although Bernard Baruch, U.S. financier, is often credited with coining this phrase on 16 April 1947, and Walter Lippmann with giving it wider currency (e.g., by *The Fontana Dictionary of Modern Thought*, edited by Alan Bullock and Oliver Stallybrass (1977), 110) in the title, *The Cold War: A Study of U.S. Foreign Policy* (1947), Orwell is cited by *OED* as being the first to use it, in this essay.
2. For F. D. Barber, see *2587*, and *2789*.

2771. 'What is Science?'

Tribune, 26 October 1945

See headnote to *2770*.

In last week's *Tribune*, there was an interesting letter from Mr. J. Stewart Cook, in which he suggested that the best way of avoiding the danger of a "scientific hierarchy" would be to see to it that every member of the general public was, as far as possible, scientifically educated. At the same time, scientists should be brought out of their isolation and encouraged to take a greater part in politics and administration.

As a general statement, I think most of us would agree with this, but I notice that, as usual, Mr. Cook does not define Science, and merely implies in passing that it means certain exact sciences whose experiments can be made under laboratory conditions. Thus, adult education tends "to neglect scientific studies in favour of literary, economic and social subjects," economics and sociology not being regarded as branches of Science, apparently. This point is of great importance. For the word Science is at present used in at least two meanings, and the whole question of scientific education is obscured by the current tendency to dodge from one meaning to the other.

Science is generally taken as meaning either (a) the exact sciences, such as chemistry, physics, &c., or (b) a method of thought which obtains verifiable results by reasoning logically from observed fact.

If you ask any scientist, or indeed almost any educated person, "What is Science?" you are likely to get an answer approximating to (b). In everyday life, however, both in speaking and in writing, when people say "Science" they mean (a). Science means something that happens in a laboratory: the very word calls up a picture of graphs, test tubes, balances, Bunsen burners, microscopes. A biologist, an astronomer, perhaps a psychologist or a mathematician, is described as a "man of science": no one would think of applying this term to a statesman, a poet, a journalist or even a philosopher. And those who tell us that the young must be scientifically educated mean, almost invariably, that they should be taught more about radioactivity, or the stars, or the physiology of their own bodies, rather than that they should be taught to think more exactly.

This confusion of meaning, which is partly deliberate, has in it a great danger. Implied in the demand for more scientific education is the claim that if one has been scientifically trained one's approach to *all* subjects will be more intelligent than if one had had no such training. A scientist's political opinions, it is assumed, his opinions on sociological questions, on morals, on philosophy, perhaps even on the arts, will be more valuable than those of a layman. The world, in other words, would be a better place if the scientists were in control of it. But a "scientist," as we have just seen, means in practice a specialist in one of the exact sciences. It follows that a chemist or a physicist, as such, is politically more intelligent than a poet or a lawyer, as such. And, in fact, there are already millions of people who do believe this.

But is it really true that a "scientist," in this narrower sense, is any likelier than other people to approach non-scientific problems in an objective way? There is not much reason for thinking so. Take one simple test—the ability to withstand nationalism. It is often loosely said that "Science is international," but in practice the scientific workers of all countries line up behind their own governments with fewer scruples than are felt by the writers and the artists. The German scientific community, as a whole, made no resistance to Hitler. Hitler may have ruined the long-term prospects of German Science, but there were still plenty of gifted men to do the necessary research on such things as synthetic oil, jet planes, rocket projectiles and the atomic bomb. Without them the German war machine could never have been built up.

On the other hand, what happened to German literature when the Nazis came to power? I believe no exhaustive lists have been published, but I imagine that the number of German scientists—Jews apart—who voluntarily exiled themselves or were persecuted by the regime was much smaller than the number of writers and journalists. More sinister than this, a number of German scientists swallowed the monstrosity of "racial Science". You can find some of the statements to which they set their names in Professor Brady's *The Spirit and Structure of German Fascism*.

But, in slightly different forms, it is the same picture everywhere. In England, a large proportion of our leading scientists accept the structure of capitalist society, as can be seen from the comparative freedom with which they are given knighthoods, baronetcies and even peerages. Since Tennyson, no English writer worth reading—one might, perhaps make an exception of Sir Max Beerbohm—has been given a title.[1] And those English scientists who do not simply accept the *status quo* are frequently Communists, which means that, however intellectually scrupulous they may be in their own line of work, they are ready to be uncritical and even dishonest on certain subjects. The fact is that a mere training in one or more of the exact sciences, even combined with very high gifts, is no guarantee of a humane or sceptical outlook. The physicists of half a dozen great nations, all feverishly and secretly working away at the atomic bomb, are a demonstration of this.

But does all this mean that the general public should *not* be more scientifically educated? On the contrary! All it means is that scientific education for the masses will do little good, and probably a lot of harm, if it simply boils down to more physics, more chemistry, more biology, etc., to the detriment of literature and history. Its probable effect on the average human being would be to narrow the range of his thoughts and make him more than ever contemptuous of such knowledge as he did not possess: and his political reactions would probably be somewhat less intelligent than those of an illiterate peasant who retained a few historical memories and a fairly sound æsthetic sense.

Clearly, scientific education ought to mean the implanting of a rational, sceptical, experimental habit of mind. It ought to mean acquiring a *method*—a method that can be used on any problem that one meets—and not simply piling up a lot of facts. Put it in those words, and the apologist of scientific education will usually agree. Press him further, ask him to particularise, and somehow it always turns out that scientific education means more attention to the exact sciences, in other words—more *facts*. The idea that Science means a way of looking at the world, and not simply a body of knowledge, is in practice strongly resisted. I think sheer professional jealousy is part of the reason for this. For if Science is simply a method or an attitude, so that anyone whose thought-processes are sufficiently rational can in some sense be described as a scientist—what then becomes of the enormous prestige now enjoyed by the chemist, the physicist, etc., and his claim to be somehow wiser than the rest of us?

A hundred years ago, Charles Kingsley described Science as "making nasty smells in a laboratory." A year or two ago a young industrial chemist informed me, smugly, that he "could not see what was the use of poetry." So the pendulum swings to and fro, but it does not seem to me that one attitude is any better than the other. At the moment, Science is on the up-grade, and so we hear, quite rightly, the claim that the masses should be scientifically educated: we do not hear, as we ought, the counter claim that the scientists themselves would benefit by a little education. Just before writing this, I saw in an American magazine the statement that a number of British and American physicists refused from the start to do research on the atomic bomb, well knowing what use would be made of it. Here you have a group of sane men in the middle of a world of lunatics. And though no names were published, I think it would be a safe guess that all of them were people with some kind of general cultural background, some acquaintance with history or literature or the arts—in short, people whose interests were not, in the current sense of the word, purely scientific.

[Fee: £3.3.0, written over £5.5.0; 18.10.45]

Tribune published a letter from Kenneth Most on 2 November and one from Edward R. Ward on 9 November; Orwell replied on 23 November.

Your correspondent's writing on the moral responsibility of the world's scientists for the use of the atom bomb, and Mr. Orwell's article on the same theme, raise very interesting questions.

A more important subject for discussion, because more immediately related to the present, is the lack of social responsibility which seems to be strongly marked in the scientific hierarchy, and which is related, I feel, to the remark of Mr. Orwell that "those who do not simply accept the status quo are frequently Communists." The term "science" is, as Mr. Orwell remarks, indicative of a method rather than of a subject, and this is the method of reasoning which works in logical sequence from the known to the unknown, subjecting the results from time to time to whatever proof seems necessary. That the conclusions reached by this method are correct, depends upon whether the premises on which the arguments are based are correct.

But when we come to apply scientific method to the problems of living, whether as individuals or as members of society, or combining the two, we are faced with an entirely different state of affairs. For our workings can only be proved in the light of results: there is no way of making out a *pro forma*, of having a "trial run."

We have very few historical laws, the subject being in its infancy, and constantly troubled by the healthy winds of controversy. The codification of living must wait—but upon whom, the scientists or the artists? Here is the crux, and if I may be excused the highly unscientific generality with which I use those two labels, perhaps the matter resolves itself as follows: It is for the scientists to perform the practical tasks and duties of mankind, but only the artists have the vision to show how their accomplishments may best be utilised. We want more poets in Parliament and more scientists on the sewage committee of the Borough Council.

Kenneth Most

Mr. Orwell finds that the invention of the atomic bomb will render null and void all possibilities of overthrowing a despotic social system. This is utterly defeatist and untenable as a product of a scientific analysis of the situation. In Cromwell's time the feudal knights must have looked upon Oliver's cannon balls, which sent their impregnable castle walls crashing, as similar agents of perpetual tyranny. But Oliver (after he had over-thrown the basis of feudal England and cleared the ground for the new social order) was thrown down in his turn.

Apart from the obvious fact that defence weapons against the atomic bomb will emerge, the possibility exists of developing small individual weapons of a devastating character. More than this; we shall expect their production: to each tyrannical age belongs the appropriate weapon that has caused its disruption. The human race has an uncanny way of saving itself at the last moment, as witness the outcome of the conflict which has just ended.

Mr. Orwell compliments the scientists who refused to participate in atom bomb research and thereby condemns those that did. But if the Allied scientists had refused to participate the Germans or more likely the Japs (with German aid) would at this very moment have been completing their preparations to cast atomic bombs on to our cities. The scientists who took this "insane decision" did so with no ill motives against society, but in the face of stark facts.

Mr. Orwell's conclusions are remarkable for one feature only, namely, that they have all been reached before by the progressive scientists themselves. Already the scientists are taking action themselves to see that science is taught as a method of thinking, as an approach to the understanding of external reality, and not as a meaningless confusion of isolated facts.

Mr. Orwell would object if I started assessing the contribution that cheap-jack journalists and writers have made to the present "disorder of society," hence I strongly object when Mr. Orwell takes it upon himself to examine the social relations of science. The scientific hierarchy (including the atom bomb cyclotron wallahs) have been remarkably tolerant about the abuse that has come their way. I think the time has come for a one-day token strike to convince people of their social necessity.

Edward R. Ward

Your correspondent, Mr Edward R. Ward, says: "Mr. Orwell would object if I started assessing the contribution that cheap-jack journalists have made to the present 'disorder of society,' hence I strongly object when Mr. Orwell takes it upon himself to examine the social relations of science."

Why should he think that I would object? The more the folly and dishonesty of present-day journalism are shown up, the better I am pleased.

And on the other hand, why should not the layman be allowed to criticise the social relations of science? Since they affect him very nearly, it is his right and duty to have ideas about them. If the physicists decide to blow us all to pieces, are we expected to acquiesce in the process simply because we do not understand the nature of atomic energy?

The rest of Mr. Ward's letter forces me to reiterate what I said in the article. I am well aware—and I said—that scientists will agree that "science" ought to mean a method of thinking. But when asked, "What do you mean by scientific education?" they usually define it as meaning more training in the exact sciences to the detriment of what used to be called "humane" studies. But, as I also pointed out, even a prolonged training in one of the exact sciences does not necessarily inculcate either political intelligence or, outside certain narrow limits, the power to examine evidence. One could name a long list of scientists who have been the dupes of spiritualists, who have subscribed to Nazi "racial science," who are Roman Catholics (believers, therefore, in levitating saints, etc.), who swallow Communist propaganda without inquiry, or who are so enmeshed in the English social system that they see no objection to accepting titles.

It is no answer to say that these people are not "real" scientists. They are very much more scientists, in the present sense of the word, than any ordinary member of the public could ever be. Clearly the problem is to get the scientific spirit out of the laboratory and infuse it into journalism, sociology and politics. But in that we must all of us take a hand. It is no use leaving it to the "atom bomb cyclotron wallahs," who, I fear, are little better than the rest of us.

George Orwell

1. Possibly a slight modification is demanded here. One author whom Orwell certainly thought 'worth reading' (whatever reservations he had about him) was Rudyard Kipling. In May 1917 Stanley Baldwin sent a message to Kipling that he might have 'any honour he will accept' but he replied he would accept none. Later he warned Bonar Law that 'it must not be' that he be knighted and he twice declined to be appointed a Companion of Honour. See Charles Carrington, *Rudyard Kipling: His Life and Work* (1955, 1970), 526–27.

2772. To Edward R. Ward

9 January 1946   Typewritten

Ward's response to Orwell's article had evidently been cut, unknown to Orwell, and Ward complained to *Tribune*. Orwell sent him a personal letter; this is reproduced here, out of chronological order, for ease of reference.

27 B Canonbury Square   Islington   N 1.

Dear Mr. Ward,
Your letter has been passed on to me by "Tribune". I am sorry that in their correspondence columns I should have answered what was really an abridgement of your original letter; but I had not seen the latter, and I did not know that what was printed was a shortened version.

I cannot enter into what might become a prolonged controversy, but I must stick to two of my original points: (a) that many scientists, including some of those you name, appear to adopt an extremely unscientific attitude towards problems in which their emotions and loyalties are involved; and (b) that members of the general public, such as myself, have a right to form and express their own opinions on the relationship between science and society. I do not know in what way your original letter was mutilated, but you did state quite clearly that I, as a journalist, had no right to express an opinion on matters that were the sole concern of scientists. It was this remark in your letter that led me to reply. The theologians make exactly similar claims—for example, that a member of the lay public has no right to air his opinions on such questions as the existence of God—and the one claim seems to me to be about as well founded as the other.

Yours truly,
[Signed] Geo. Orwell
George Orwell

2773. Review of *Human Guinea Pigs* by Kenneth Mellanby

Manchester Evening News, 25 October 1945

Medical science, which has learned how to deal with such terrible scourges as typhoid fever and bubonic plague, has remained almost helpless before some of the minor illnesses.

Chilblains and the common cold are still almost as mysterious as they were in the days of our grandparents, and though there was talk a year or two ago of a cure for seasickness nothing seems to have come of it. Another minor disease which has long baffled the doctors is scabies, popularly known as "the itch."

Although not, of course, fatal, scabies is painful, disgusting and, like all skin diseases, profoundly depressing when it is not cured quickly.

Its cause—a mite which burrows under the surface of the skin—is well known, but until recently not much was known about the manner of its dissemination and epidemics of it were very hard to check. Dr. Mellanby's unpretentious little book is an account of some experiments in the treatment of scabies, conducted in highly unusual circumstances during the war years.

Early in the war, when Dr. Mellanby was investigating the incidence of head-lice among school children, he was struck by the alarming increase in scabies, and managed to get a grant from the Ministry of Health for some experimental work on this subject. Scabies had been growing steadily commoner since about 1926 (its increase was not, as experiments were to show, in any way due to the war) and was causing a perceptible loss of efficiency in the armed Forces.

His first idea was to use horses as "subjects," but it was obviously more desirable to study the human form of the disease, and it then struck him that he might find willing co-operators among conscientious objectors.

Even those who objected to any form of National Service could justifiably undertake such work as this, which benefited humanity as a whole and was not merely intended to further the war effort; and from Dr. Mellanby's point of view conscientious objectors had the advantage that they were not liable to be called up or directed to some other work in the middle of an experiment.

In the event he had no difficulty in finding over forty suitable volunteers, who were installed in a large house in Sheffield and cheerfully endured the painful and disagreeable things that were asked of them.

The experiments involved, of course, infecting most of the men with scabies and sometimes allowing the disease to persist long enough to cause unbearable irritation, sleeplessness, and septic infections. At the end several important facts not known before had been established.

One was that scabies is almost invariably contracted by intimate contact with another human being and not, as had previously been believed, from infected clothing or bedding. Another was that the incubation period of the scabies mite is a very long one. And another was that a soldier suffering from scabies could almost invariably be shown to have caught it during a period of leave and not from his fellow soldiers.

The upshot was that the preventive measures then in use in the armed forces—that is, "de-infesting" clothes and bedding by means of heat—were a waste of labour and fuel. To check the spread of the disease it was necessary, wherever a case occurred, to submit the entire family to treatment, including those who seemed uninfected.

How to cure scabies was already known, but the current treatment was so drastic that it was liable to frighten patients away. Dr. Mellanby gives a graphic account of it.

The patient was first rubbed all over with soft soap, then boiled for 20 minutes in a bath as hot as he could bear, then scrubbed with a rough brush, then anointed with sulphur ointment. This nearly always effected a cure, but it was so painful and exhausting that the patient often fainted. It was found that the comparatively mild expedient of painting the body all over with an emulsion of benzyl benzoate was equally effective.

The team of conscientious objectors submitted themselves to other experiments besides those connected with scabies. Most of these were dietetic experiments, and one, the purpose of which was to study the effects of thirst on shipwreck survivors, involved drinking no liquid of any kind for three or four days.

At the end of this book Dr. Mellanby makes the suggestion that the use of "human guinea pigs" might with advantage be greatly extended, and that at the start the volunteers might once again be conscientious objectors. If conscription is to be continued in peace-time there will, he says, presumably be plenty of these. Other people may be willing to offer themselves as "subjects" for short periods, and there may even be some, anxious to serve the cause of science, who would undertake such work as a full-time career.

Dr. Mellanby is not a conscientious objector himself, and he appears to have no strong feelings either "for" or "against" on the subject of compulsory military service.

His work brought him into contact with conscientious objectors in large numbers, and he considers that a proportion of them are naturally aggressive people who are not so much reluctant to shed blood as unwilling to submit to authority. But he is convinced that all but a few are subjectively honest, and that though pacifism may be traceable to a number of different motives, cowardice is very rarely one of them. Those who took part in his experiments were almost without exception willing, reliable, and intelligent.

Although written without much literary grace, this is an interesting book, and it touches on quite a number of controversial questions in its 96 pages. In his preface Dr. Mellanby puts in a word for the independent scientific investigator as against the State-controlled teamwork which is now generally considered to be more desirable. In these days of all-round planning this is a question which is likely to be often debated, and Dr. Mellanby's experiments on scabies, carried out on his own initiative and with very little official interference, are a strong argument for allowing the scientist, like the artist, to retain his independent status.

[Fee: £8.8.0; 24.10.45]

2774. Review of *Drums under the Windows* by Sean O'Casey

The Observer, 28 October 1945

W. B. Yeats said once that a dog does not praise its fleas, but this is somewhat contradicted by the special status enjoyed in this country by Irish nationalist writers. Considering what the history of Anglo-Irish relations has been, it is not surprising that there should be Irishmen whose life-work is abusing England: what does call for remark is that they should be able to look to the English public for support and in some cases should even, like Mr. O'Casey himself, prefer to live in the country which is the object of their hatred.

This is the third volume of Mr. O'Casey's autobiography, and it seems to cover roughly the period 1910 to 1916. In so far as one can dig it out from masses of pretentious writing, the subject matter is valuable and interesting. Mr. O'Casey, younger son of a poverty-stricken Protestant family, worked for years as a navvy, and was at the same time deeply involved in the nationalist movement and the various cultural movements that were mixed up with it. Several of his brothers and sisters died in circumstances of gaunt poverty which would excuse a good deal of bitterness against the English occupation. He was the associate of Larkin, Connolly, the Countess Markievicz, and other leading political figures, and he had a front-seat view of the Easter Rebellion in 1916. But the cloudy manner in which the book is written makes it difficult to pin down facts or chronology. It is all in the third person ("Sean did this" and "Sean did that"), which gives an unbearable effect of narcissism, and large portions of it are written in a simplified imitation of the style of "Finnegans Wake," a sort of Basic Joyce, which is sometimes effective in a humorous aside, but is hopeless for narrative purposes.

However, Mr. O'Casey's outstanding characteristic is the romantic nationalism which he manages to combine with Communism. This book contains literally no reference to England which is not hostile or contemptuous. On the other hand, there is hardly a page which does not contain some such passage as this:

> Cathleen ni Houlihan, in her bare feet, is singing, for her pride that had almost gone is come back again. In tattered gown, and hair uncombed, she sings, shaking the ashes from her hair, and smoothing out the bigger creases in her dress; she is
>
> *Singing of men that in battle array*
> *Ready in heart and ready in hand,*
> *March with banner and bugle and fife*
> *To the death, for their native land.*

Or again:

> Cathleen, the daughter of Houlihan, walks firm now, a flush on her haughty cheek. She hears the murmur in the people's hearts. Her lovers are gathering round her, for things are changed, changed utterly: "A terrible beauty is born."

If one substitutes "Britannia" for "Cathleen ni Houlihan" in these and similar passages (Cathleen ni Houlihan, incidentally, makes her appearance several times in every chapter), they can be seen at a glance for the bombast that they are. But why is it that the worst extremes of jingoism and racialism have to be tolerated when they come from an Irishman? Why is a statement like "My country right or wrong" reprehensible if applied to England and worthy of respect if applied to Ireland (or for that matter to India)? For there is no doubt that some such convention exists and that "enlightened" opinion in England can swallow even the most blatant nationalism so long as it is not British nationalism. Poems like "Rule, Britannia!" or "Ye Mariners of England" would be taken seriously if one inserted at the right places the name of some foreign country, as one can see by the respect accorded to various French and Russian war poets to-day.

So far as Ireland goes, the basic reason is probably England's bad conscience. It is difficult to object to Irish nationalism without seeming to condone centuries of English tyranny and exploitation. In particular, the incident with which Mr. O'Casey's book ends, the summary execution of some twenty or thirty rebels who ought to have been treated as prisoners of war, was a crime and a mistake. Therefore anything that is said about it has to pass unchallenged, and Yeats's poem on the subject, which makes a sort of theme song for Mr. O'Casey's book, has to be accepted uncriticised as a great poem. Actually it is not one of Yeats's better poems. But how can an Englishman, conscious that his country was in the wrong on that and many other occasions, say anything of the kind? So literary judgment is perverted by political sympathy, and Mr. O'Casey and others like him are able to remain almost immune from criticism. It seems time to revise our attitude, for there is no real reason why Cromwell's massacres should cause us to mistake a bad or indifferent book for a good one.

There is no entry for this review in Orwell's Payments Book. An entry was made for 18 October, but it is scored through and no fee is recorded.

On 29 October 1945, Sean O'Casey wrote from Devon to the Editor of *The Observer* castigating Orwell's review. The letter, reproduced here, by kind permission of Shivaun O'Casey, was not then published. O'Casey headed his letter, <u>Orwell and the Green Flag.</u>

It is sad to think that my book filled Mr. Orwell with such fury, so, it isnt° any wonder that he contradicts himself, and makes misstatements. He writes like a spiteful kid when he says that my "life-work is abusing England," and that she is "the object of my hatred." What England has he in his troubled mind? Is it the England of poets, painters, scientists, saints, and great warriors, the England of those who till her fields, sail her ships, herd her cattle, carry her transport, weave her textiles, and hew her coal? If this be the England he has in his mind, then, simply, he is libelling me, and he knows it. Does he think that those who ruled so long in Dublin Castle, and those who sent them to rule there, are England, the whole England, and nothing but England? Is this England, his England? Doesnt° he know that "England" is wider than herself, and that within the broader circle are Scotland, Wales, and (by England's own force and determination) Ireland, too? It is certainly a queer evidence of "hostility to England," on the part of one who has built up the greater part of his educated view of life on Shakespeare, Marlowe, Webster, Herrick, Milton, Shelley, Keats, Blake, Dickens, the English bible and prayerbook, Hogarth, Gainsborough, Wilson, Turner, Constable, and Crome[1] (let Mr. Orwell read Sir Charles Holmes[2] to see how some of these great men were treated by his England), Darwin, and Huxley. So leaving out all Welsh poetical tinges and the prose, poetical, and scientific influences of Scotland (Scott, Burns, and James Frazer), and confining my choice to pure English influences, there stands a fair array to show an admiration for England's achievements that Orwell himself could hardly excel. I'll venture the statement that I know far and away more about England than he knows about my country. Mr. Orwell complains that in my book that Cathleen ni Houlihan appears in most chapters (he is seemingly unaware that this is a name for Ireland), and that in the book "Sean does this and Sean does that," which is hardly surprising, since the book is part history of Ireland seen through the vision of this irritating "Sean," and that the fellow wasnt°, happily, born deaf, dumb, and blind. But a laughable thing is that the name of Cathleen ni Houlihan was forced on us by Mr. Orwell's England, who, for many centuries, made it a penal thing to write down the name of the country, so her poets were forced to adopt the allegorical ones, one of which so annoys the reviewer. It looks now, if Mr. Orwell has his way, that the use of the name will again become a penal offence once more. In one breath he snarls at O'Casey as "a blatant nationalist," and in the next tells everyone that "he has managed (managed, mind you!) to combine his nationalism with Communism," thus telling us (through the term 'combine') that the Nationalist is an internationalist, too. The fact is, Mr. Orwell doesnt° know the difference between nationality and nationalism. Again, Irish writers "enjoy no special status" in England: Yeats tells us that he never got more than two hundred pounds a year for his books. Less than Mr. Orwell gets for his reviews, I'll wager. And what about Joyce? Let Mr. Orwell read James Joyce's letter to his American publishers, and he will see something about the "status" of this great writer in Orwell's "England." How often has° Synge's plays been performed here? How long ago is it since even The Abbey Theatre has toured his England? Apart from Mr. Bernard Shaw, will Mr. Orwell give us the names of Irish nationalist authors who "enjoy a special status" here? Perhaps, Mr. Orwell thinks we shouldnt° get published at all; or, if we do, then we should be careful not to say what we think; that we should not portray life as we see it, even in our own country; or that we should write to please him. Where, then, is the principle of freedom of thought, which, I daresay, Mr. Orwell holds in honour, like red wax berries in a glass case. As for O'Casey living in England, the plain facts are that he gets near as much from his own country as from England, and much more from America; so that, actually, he has often given back in tax more than he got. But this is an odd thing to be brought to the fore by a critic.

In the end of his article, he quotes from my book an example of what, to him is "blatant nationalism," but he doesnt° give the sentence that follows—the very last in the book—which shows that what has gone before is meant to be sadly ironical. Why doesnt° he give this last sentence? Because, if he did, it would go to disprove his point. He is out to prove O'Casey a "blatant nationalist" at any cost.

But what are we to think of a critic quoting the poem,

"Singing of men that in battle array . . .
Marching° with banner and bugle and fife
To the death for their native land,"

as those written by an Irish nationalist, when as a matter of fact they were written by a famous and most respectable poet who was English of the English![3] Well, that's maudern° English literary criticism for you!

1. John Crome (1768–1821), landscape painter influenced by Constable; he and John Sell Cottman were the major figures of the Norwich School of landscape painting.
2. Sir Charles J. Holmes (1868–1936), editor of *Burlington Magazine*, 1903–09; Director of the National Gallery, 1916–28, wrote a number of books, several on the National Gallery's collections, but O'Casey may have had in mind *Constable and his Influence on Landscape Painting* (1902).
3. These lines are from 'A passionate ballad gallant and gay, / A martial song like a trumpet's call!' sung by Maud in Tennyson's poem of that name, lines 169–72. 'March' in line 171 (as in the review) is the correct reading, not 'Marching.' O'Casey gives the source in his chapter 'Rebel Orwell' in his autobiography, *Sunset and Evening Star* (1954), 124–42. This is largely a swingeing attack on Orwell, seemingly prompted by Orwell's review. Thus: 'Self-preservation was the first law of nature to Orwell as well as to all the sorts of men. And Orwell had quite a lot of feeling for himself; so much, that, dying, he wanted the living world to die with him' (126).

2775. J. S. Collis to Orwell
29 October [1945]

John Steuart Collis (1900–c.1980) was born in Ireland, educated at Rugby and

Balliol and worked as an author, lecturer, and journalist. From 1940 until 1945 he worked on the land. Among his books were *Following the Plough* (he gave his recreations as tennis and ploughing) and *An Irishman in England*. He wrote to Orwell, addressing him as 'Dear Orwell' and starting his letter abruptly— 'About Wodehouse: what I want to know is, is he even funny?'—as if he had already been in correspondence with Orwell. That this might be so is also suggested by Orwell's confusing John Steuart Collis for Maurice Collis in his survey of books about India; see *2717* and *2717, n. 3*).

Collis wrote that he found Dickens exceedingly amusing and recognised that Wodehouse had 'good phrases' from time to time, 'but can a man be seriously funny minus *body* to his work?' He wondered whether Wodehouse was not another 'frightful fake swallowed by the highbrows in exactly the same way as they swallow "dog-fight" as an adequate description of two aeroplanes engaged in combat.' Unfortunately, no reply by Orwell has been traced.

2776. To Eric Warman

30 October 1945

On 21 February 1978, Sotheby's sold a letter by Orwell, written from 27B Canonbury Square, to Eric Warman, Literary Editor for the publishing firm Paul Elek. The catalogue summary states that Orwell apologizes 'for the fact that his introduction to "Jack London" will be about a week late, owing to a recent spell of illness, and offering to let him see the section he has written so far (". . . about a quarter of it . . .").' This letter has not been traced. See also *2718*.

2777. 'The British General Election'

Commentary, November 1945

The Labor Party's victory was overwhelming. It has a clear majority of more than 150 seats over all other parties combined, while the Conservatives and their satellites have lost nearly 200 seats and the minor parties have been simply obliterated. So far as I know, not a soul in England foresaw any such outcome. Before the election began, my own forecast had been a small Tory majority, and after polling day—this as a result of observing the strong leftward swing in the London area—a small Labor majority. Most of the people I know were of the same way of thinking, while the newspapers alternated between giving the Tories a majority of about 50, and predicting a stalemate. The Liberals, who put up 300 candidates, were expected to increase their representation considerably (actually it has dwindled from 18 seats to 10),[1] and most of the discussion between polling day and the announcement of the results turned on what would happen if there were a minority government and the Liberals had the casting vote. The belief that the election would be a very near thing, and that we should be left with a weak government which would be forced to form some kind of coalition, was almost universal. Before giving any opinion as to what this landslide means, I should like to record the impressions I picked up while the election was on.

I saw the election only in London, but I followed its developments fairly closely, as I was "covering" the London constituencies for a Sunday paper. The thing that principally struck me, as it struck others who were watching events in the streets and not in the newspapers, was that the masses were not interested. It is true that a high percentage voted (actually higher than it seems, since hundreds of thousands of people were disenfranchised owing to defects in the electoral register), but people always do vote in a general election, as opposed to a by-election, because of the last-minute pressure put upon them by newspapers and radio.

During a fortnight of electioneering, in which most of my waking hours were spent in the streets or in pubs, buses and tea-shops, with my ears pricked all the time, I only twice overheard a spontaneous comment on the election. Outdoor meetings, especially in the more crowded and noisy parts of London, were often a complete failure. Indoors, in church halls, schools and dance-palaces, you had lively and sometimes very turbulent meetings of five hundred or a thousand people, but in the streets the great crowds drifted to and fro as usual, seemingly indifferent to the whole thing and never, in my experience, stopping to look at the election posters which were pasted all over the walls. Nearly all the agents and organizers whom I interviewed remarked on the difficulty of canvassing and the impossibility of finding out what the masses were thinking. Canvassers reported that "I haven't made up my mind yet" was a frequent answer. There was also a certain amount of feeling that there ought not to have been an election at this time, i.e., when the Japanese end of the war was uncompleted, and both Tory and Labor candidates did their best to transfer the odium of "forcing" the election on to the other party.

On the other hand, among the minority who did take an interest, I was struck by the comparative seriousness and decency with which the whole thing was conducted. The behavior of candidates and audiences seemed to me a good deal better than the behavior of the press. It is so long since we have had a general election in England that people have forgotten the libels and buffooneries that used to be taken for granted, and there were angry protests from some quarters that Britain was presenting an undignified spectacle to Europe. Actually I believe that this election was an exceptionally quiet and an exceptionally clean one, and several party agents with long experience confirmed this. The only real attempt to drag the contest down to the level of 1931 or 1924 was the short-lived campaign of the Beaverbrook press against Professor Laski. This failed even to become an election issue, and was simply one more demonstration of the inability of the big press lords to influence public opinion by direct means. So far as my observation went anti-Semitism was not a factor in the election, and certainly no overt attempt at stirring up anti-Semitism was made in the press, though the Laski affair could obviously have been given some such twist. (Anti-Semitism, although it is probably on the upgrade, isn't really a political issue at all in England, and can't be made to appear so when there is no Fascist party functioning. There are Jews in all political parties, though they are distributed a bit thicker in the parties of the left, and there were Jewish candidates on all the tickets. Incidentally, the one new Communist who got in—they now have two seats—was a Jew, but as he was elected in what is practically an all-Jewish quarter of London and his Labor opponent was also a Jew, it's a bit difficult to see deep significance in this.)

At public meetings, the attempts to shout down the speakers were usually the work of small groups of Communists or near-Communists, who were countered with similar tactics by small groups of Conservatives. All the Labor Party meetings I went to were quiet and serious, and the level of the questions asked was fairly high. Much the worst feature of the election, if one regards it in broad terms, was the exploitation of Churchill's record and personality by the Conservatives. But in the end this recoiled against themselves, and the leader-worship and ballyhoo were nothing to what goes on in Continental countries. Symptomatically, the photographs of Churchill which were plastered everywhere were only about a quarter the size of the photographs of Stalin, de Gaulle, etc., which are to be seen in the appropriate parts of Europe.

The third thing that struck me was that this election was fought almost wholly on domestic issues. This ought to be emphasized, because such foreign press comments as I have seen hitherto point to [a] serious misconception. Obviously, the Labor Party and the Conservative Party stand for quite different policies, and British policy all over the world will be affected by the change of government: but the mass of the electorate, during the actual struggle, showed no interest in anything outside the British Isles. The war with Japan, foreign policy, relations with the U.S.A., the Dominions, Palestine and India were not election issues. Even relations with the USSR only had an indirect effect because of the widespread vague belief that a Labor government would "get on better with Russia." The questions on which the election turned were nationalization of industry, social security, demobilization, housing, old age pensions, continuation of wartime controls and also of wartime facilities such as day nurseries, and the raising of the school-leaving age. The Conservatives, unable simply to keep silent about home affairs, were forced to come out openly as the champions of *laissez-faire*, and did their best to make this policy a little more acceptable by tying Churchill's name to it. They would have liked to put more emphasis on the Pacific war and the need to recapture Britain's foreign markets, but their audiences would not let them. Labor candidates sometimes talked as though Britain's internal prosperity need be in no way affected by the outside world. Significantly, the handbook issued to Labor speakers gives, out of its 218 pages, only a single rather uninformative page to India.

These were my main impressions, and I think many other observers would confirm them. But now one must ask, what did this nationwide swing to the Left actually mean?

The first thing to notice is that in terms of votes the swing was not nearly so big as it looks if one considers it in terms of seats. The English electoral system is capable of producing all kinds of anomalies, and would in theory be capable of giving every single seat in Parliament to a party which had won only 51 per cent of the votes. Over the past twenty-five years—largely because the rural areas, where people used to vote Conservative, were over-represented—the anomalies have worked in the Conservative interest, and it has needed many more votes to elect a Labor man than to elect a Conservative. In the present election the position has been reversed, and it has needed, on average, 46,000 votes to elect a Conservative and only 30,000 to elect a Labor man. The upshot is that though Labor has won 392 seats as against 195 won by the Conservatives, the number of votes won was roughly 12 million as against 9 million. If one takes into account the minor parties which can be lumped with one or other of the two main ones, then the figures are approximately twelve and a half millions and ten millions: which means that the preponderance of votes was in the ratio of six and a half to five, while the preponderance of seats was in the ratio of two to one.

There were various complicating factors which should be mentioned but are not worth discussing in detail, since they probably did not alter the over-all result. The most important were the large-scale intervention of the Liberals (who polled over 2 million votes though they only won 10 seats), and the very large number of "lost" votes, nearly all of them working-class votes, due to the bad state of the electoral register and the inadequate facilities for men and women serving overseas. (Men and women in the services could vote either by post or by proxy. Many who had applied to vote by post did not get their voting papers in time, while others had not been adequately informed by their unit commanders about the steps it would be necessary to take beforehand. This may not have been entirely due to carelessness. The non-commissioned ranks in all three services would mostly vote Labor if they voted at all.) According to the very rough calculations that I have been able to make, the wastage of votes on one side and on the other would either cancel out, or would slightly benefit the Conservatives.

Had Proportional Representation been in force in England, the division of votes would have given Labor about 300 seats, the Conservatives and their satellite parties about 250 seats, and the Liberals 55 seats. This is to say that the Labor Party would not have had a reliable working majority: and similarly, on a basis of Proportional Representation, the Conservatives would hardly have had a working majority after the election of 1935. In that election the Conservatives polled something over 10 million votes and the Labor Party something over 8 million. If one compares the figures for 1935 and 1945, it can be seen that a comparatively small turnover of votes may bring about a complete reversal of the political situation. This often means that the House of Commons is not genuinely representative of the electorate, but it does have the advantage of producing governments which are strong enough to act but which can be fairly easily got rid of when their five-years' term is over.

In the present election, the defeat of the Conservatives is sufficiently accounted for by two things that were bound to happen sooner or later: the penetration of the Labor Party into the rural areas, and the defection of the middle class. Labor members have been returned by rustic constituencies and by prosperous "dormitory suburbs" where only ten years ago it would have been quite hopeless for any leftwing candidate to present himself. But though I have emphasized above that the turnover of votes is not enormous, the general drift in England *is* leftward, as innumerable observers have pointed out from 1940 onwards. In spite of the general apathy and ignorance, there is a gathering discontent which cannot be fitted into any "ism" but which springs from a desire for more dignity and decency in everyday life, more opportunities for the young, and, above all, more security.

It would be absurd to imagine that Britain is on the verge of violent revolution, or even that the masses have been definitely converted to Socialism. Most of them don't know what Socialism means, though public opinion is quite ready for essentially socialistic measures such as nationalization of mines, railways, public utilities, and land. Again, it is doubtful whether there is any widespread desire for complete social equality. There is considerable class feeling, which is never quite dormant and sometimes sharpens to acute resentment, but if a plebiscite could be taken, the mass of the people would not vote for rigid equalization of incomes, nor for the abolition of the monarchy, nor even, possibly, for the abolition of hereditary titles. The Labor Party, in the average man's mind, does not stand for republicanism, and still less does it stand for red flags, barricades and reigns of terror: it stands for full employment, free milk for school-children, old-age pensions of thirty shillings a week, and, in general, a fair deal for the working man.

The same drift towards the Left, not accompanied by any strong revolutionary yearnings or any sudden break-up of class system, can be observed in France. Recently, after the municipal elections in which half the electorate of Paris voted either Communist or Socialist, it appeared to me that Paris was in fact less revolutionary, more pre-1939 in outlook, even than London. People voted for the Left partly because the collaborators had belonged to the Right, but above all because the Left stood for social security. In England the mythos of the USSR and the victories of the Red Army have been helpful to the Labor Party, but there is little real interest in the Soviet system. Russia is dimly thought of as a country where "they" (the upper classes) do not usurp all the privileges and where there is no unemployment. After the experience of the between-wars years, mass unemployment— unemployment against a background of social competitiveness—is the worst horror the English people can imagine, and they have turned towards the Labor Party because, more convincingly than its opponents, it promised a way out.

Meanwhile, unless it suffers a major split, the Labor Party has a completely free hand for five years. Just like any other government at this time, it will have to do unpopular things: it will have to continue with military conscription, to "direct" labor into hated jobs such as coal-mining, to crush sabotage on both Right and Left, to soothe the inevitable disappointments over demobilization and re-housing, and, in general, to clean up the mess left over from the war. But it starts out with great advantages, especially in dealing with foreign affairs. It has no strong motive for backing up such indefensible figures as Franco or King George of Greece, and on the other hand it is not obliged to adopt an appeaser attitude towards the USSR. At some point or another a stand against Russian aggression will have to be made, and when the moment comes a Labor government will be able to unite the country behind it, which a Conservative government for obvious reasons could not. It is, I believe, a mistake to imagine that the new government's foreign policy will be diametrically opposed to that of the old one.

A Labor government will approach such problems as the occupation of Germany with more common sense than has been shown hitherto, it will look with a friendlier eye on the Italian Socialists and the Spanish Republicans, and it will go somewhat further towards satisfying Jewish aspirations in Palestine: but Britain's strategic interests, in a world of competing nationalisms, remain the same, whether the government at home is called Socialist or capitalist.

By far the hardest problem for a Labor government—and it is all the harder because the mass of the people never give the subject a thought—is India. The Labor Party will now have to decide, once and for all, whether the promises it has made to India are to be kept or broken. It cannot simply postpone the question as a Conservative government might succeed in doing, because with Labor in power the Indian Nationalists will expect a decision promptly.

Underneath this problem lies the fact I mentioned above—that the election was fought on domestic issues and that the bulk of the British people are almost completely uninterested in foreign or imperial affairs. Immersed in their struggle with the Tories, the Labor leaders have never made clear to their followers the extent to which British prosperity depends on the exploitation of the colored peoples. It has always been tacitly pretended that we could "set India free" and raise our own wages simultaneously. The first task of the Labor government is to make people realize that Britain is not self-contained, but is part of a world-wide network. Even the problem of introducing Socialism is secondary to that. For Britain cannot become a genuinely Socialist country while continuing to plunder Asia and Africa; while on the other hand no amount of nationalization, no cutting-out of profits and destruction of privilege, could keep up our standard of living if we lost all our markets and our sources of raw materials at one blow. It is not yet certain whether the Labor Party will make a genuine effort to introduce Socialism: but if it does, the period of reconstruction will probably be a very uncomfortable one for almost everyone. By its success or otherwise in educating people for that period, in making them see that it has to be faced, just as the war had to be faced, the Labor Party will stand or fall.

The most difficult moment will probably be about two years hence, when the war boom is over and demobilization is complete. But the Labor government has at least five years in hand, and the men at the top of it, as a body, are at least as able and determined as any government we have had for decades past. It is too early to cheer, but a hopeful attitude is justified. As a sign of the vitality of democracy, of the power of the English-speaking peoples to get along without fuehrers, the outcome of this election is a thing to be rejoiced at, even if the men it has brought to power should utterly fail.

Right now Parliament is in recess, and though the ministerial appointments were made some time back, there has not as yet been any statement of policy. The government has addressed a not-too-friendly note to the Greek government, there have been shufflings in Spain which may be partly due to British pressure, and a Secretary of State for India has been appointed, which suggests that the India Office is *not* to be abolished. Otherwise there is nothing very revealing.

So far as foreign policy goes, no very violent or sudden change should be expected because of Labor's accession to power. The Labor Party has to play out the hand left to it by its predecessor, and one must remember that the Labor leaders helped to frame, or at any rate concurred in, Churchill's policy. In the matter of Greece, for instance, the people at the top of the Labor Party are very much less favorable to EAM than the rank and file. So also with Yugoslavia, Poland, the Baltic states, Finland and Turkey. With regard to all these countries there is a sort of left-wing orthodoxy which is accepted unreservedly by the big mass of Labor Party supporters, and which is perhaps best expressed by the Liberal *News-Chronicle*. One has only to look back two or three years at the earlier speeches and writings of the men who now form the government, to realize that their views on foreign policy are not always what their followers imagine. A Labor government has not the same motive as a Conservative one for automatically backing reaction everywhere, but its first consideration must be to guard British strategic interests, which are the same whatever government is in power. Ernest Bevin, the new Foreign Minister, is a very much tougher person than Anthony Eden.

The one part of the world, outside Britain, in which the Labor government's policy *may* diverge sharply from that of its predecessor is Palestine. The Labor Party is firmly committed to the establishment of the Jewish National Home, and indeed almost all shades of radical opinion in England are "pro-Jewish" on the Palestine issue. I think it would be rash, however, to assume that the Labor government will live up to the promises it made when it was in opposition. Left-wing opinion in England is pro-Jewish partly because the Arab case gets no hearing, and it is not always realized that the colored peoples almost everywhere are pro-Arab. Unreserved support of the Jews might have repercussions in the other Arab countries, in Egypt and even in India, of a kind that a newly-elected government could hardly be expected to face.[2]

1. Liberals dwindled from seventeen in 1935 to twelve; for accurate figures of party representation, see *2719, n. 2*.
2. This article, which appeared in the first issue of *Commentary*, was not entered in the Payments Book (see *2831*) in which Orwell listed articles written and payments received for them. At the top of the first column of the article this note about Orwell was printed: 'George Orwell is recognized as one of the most acute observers of the British scene today. An intellectual and a man of action, the writer joined the POUM militia during the Spanish civil war, served with the British Home Guard and worked for the B.B.C. during the recent conflict, and has been literary editor of the independent labor London *Tribune*. As a literary critic, he is a frequent contributor to the English magazine *Horizon*. Since 1928 Mr. Orwell has published 10 or 12 books, of which the better known are *Burmese Days*, *Inside the Whale*, a volume of critical essays, *The Road to Wigan Pier* and *Homage to Catalonia*. He is now at work on a new novel.' The new novel upon which Orwell was working was, presumably, *Nineteen Eighty-Four*.

2778. 'Catastrophic Gradualism'

C.W. Review, November 1945[1]

There is a theory which has not yet been accurately formulated or given a name, but which is very widely accepted and is brought forward whenever it is necessary to justify some action which conflicts with the sense of decency of the average human being. It might be called, until some better name is found, the Theory of Catastrophic Gradualism. According to this theory, nothing is ever achieved without bloodshed, lies, tyranny and injustice, but on the other hand no considerable change for the better is to be expected as the result of even the greatest upheaval. History necessarily proceeds by calamities, but each succeeding age will be as bad, or nearly as bad, as the last. One must not protest against purges, deportations, secret police forces and so forth, because these are the price that has to be paid for progress: but on the other hand "human nature" will always see to it that progress is slow or even imperceptible. If you object to dictatorship you are a reactionary, but if you expect dictatorship to produce good results you are a sentimentalist.

At present this theory is most often used to justify the Stalin régime in the USSR, but it obviously could be—and, given appropriate circumstances, would be—used to justify other forms of totalitarianism. It has gained ground as a result of the failure of the Russian Revolution—failure, that is, in the sense that the Revolution has not fulfilled the hopes that it aroused twenty-five years ago. In the name of Socialism the Russian régime has committed almost every crime that can be imagined, but at the same time its evolution is *away* from Socialism, unless one re-defines that word in terms that no Socialist of 1917 would have accepted. To those who admit these facts, only two courses are open. One is simply to repudiate the whole theory of totalitarianism, which few English intellectuals have the courage to do: the other is to fall back on Catastrophic Gradualism. The formula usually employed is "You can't make an omelette without breaking eggs." And if one replies, "Yes, but where is the omelette?", the answer is likely to be: "Oh well, you can't expect everything to happen all in a moment."

Naturally this argument is pushed backward into history, the design being to show that every advance was achieved at the cost of atrocious crimes, and could not have been achieved otherwise. The instance generally used is the overthrow of feudalism by the bourgeoisie, which is supposed to foreshadow the overthrow of Capitalism by Socialism in our own age. Capitalism, it is argued, was once a progressive force, and therefore its crimes were justified, or at least were unimportant. Thus, in a recent number of the *New Statesman*, Mr. Kingsley Martin, reproaching Arthur Koestler for not possessing a true "historical perspective," compared Stalin with Henry VIII. Stalin, he admitted, had done terrible things, but on balance he had served the cause of progress, and a few million "liquidations" must not be allowed to obscure this fact. Similarly, Henry VIII's character left much to be desired, but after all he had made possible the rise of Capitalism, and therefore on balance could be regarded as a friend of humanity.

Now, Henry VIII has not a very close resemblance to Stalin; Cromwell would provide a better analogy; but, granting Henry VIII the importance given to him by Mr. Martin, where does this argument lead? Henry VIII made possible the rise of Capitalism, which led to the horrors of the Industrial Revolution and thence to a cycle of enormous wars, the next of which may well destroy civilization altogether. So, telescoping the process, we can put it like this: "Everything is to be forgiven to Henry VIII, because it was ultimately he who enabled us to blow ourselves to pieces with atomic bombs." You are led into similar absurdities if you make Stalin responsible for our present condition and the future which appears to lie before us, and at the same time insist that his policies must be supported. The motives of those English intellectuals who support the Russian dictatorship are, I think, different from what they publicly admit, but it is logical to condone tyranny and massacre if one assumes that progress is inevitable. If each epoch is as a matter of course better than the last, then any crime or any folly that pushes the historical process forward can be justified. Between, roughly, 1750 and 1930 one could be forgiven for imagining that progress of a solid measurable kind was taking place. Latterly, this has become more and more difficult, whence the theory of Catastrophic Gradualism. Crime follows crime, one ruling class replaces another, the Tower of Babel rises and falls, but one mustn't resist the process—indeed, one must be ready to applaud any piece of scoundrelism that comes off—because in some mystical way, in the sight of God, or perhaps in the sight of Marx, this is Progress. The alternative would be to stop and consider (a) to what extent is history pre-determined? and (b) what is meant by progress? At this point one has to call in the Yogi to correct the Commissar.

In his much-discussed essay, Koestler is generally assumed to have come down heavily on the side of the Yogi. Actually, if one assumes the Yogi and the Commissar to be at opposite points of the scale, Koestler is somewhat nearer to the Commissar's end. He believes in action, in violence where necessary, in government, and consequently in the shifts and compromises that are inseparable from government. He supported the war, and the Popular Front before it. Since the appearance of Fascism he has struggled against it to the best of his ability, and for many years he was a member of the Communist Party. The long chapter in his book in which he criticises the USSR is even vitiated by a lingering loyalty to his old party and by a resulting tendency to make all bad developments date from the rise of Stalin: whereas one ought, I believe, to admit that all the seeds of evil were there from the start and that things would not have been substantially different if Lenin or Trotsky had remained in control. No one is less likely than Koestler to claim that we can put everything right by watching our navels in California.[2] Nor is he claiming, as religious thinkers usually do, that a "change of heart" must come *before* any genuine political improvement. To quote his own words:

Neither the saint nor the revolutionary can save us; only the synthesis of the two. Whether we are capable of achieving it I do not know. But if the answer is in the negative, there seems to be no reasonable hope of preventing the destruction of European civilization, either by total war's successor Absolute War, or by Byzantine conquest—within the next few decades.

That is to say, the "change of heart" must happen, but it is not really happening unless at each step it issues in action. On the other hand, no change in the structure of society can by itself effect a real improvement. Socialism used to be defined as "common ownership of the means of production," but it is now seen that if common ownership means no more than centralised control, it merely paves the way for a new form of oligarchy. Centralised control is a necessary pre-condition of Socialism, but it no more produces Socialism than my typewriter would of itself produce this article I am writing. Throughout history, one revolution after another—although usually producing a temporary relief, such as a sick man gets by turning over in bed—has simply led to a change of masters, because no serious effort has been made to eliminate the power instinct: or if such an effort has been made, it has been made only by the saint, the Yogi, the man who saves his own soul at the expense of ignoring the community. In the minds of active revolutionaries, at any rate the ones who "got there," the longing for a just society has always been fatally mixed up with the intention to secure power for themselves.

Koestler says that we must learn once again the technique of contemplation, which "remains the only source of guidance in ethical dilemmas where the rule-of-thumb criteria of social utility fail." By "contemplation" he means "the will not to will," the conquest of the desire for power. The practical men have led us to the edge of the abyss, and the intellectuals in whom acceptance of power politics has killed first the moral sense, and then the sense of reality, are urging us to march rapidly forward without changing direction. Koestler maintains that history is not at all moments predetermined, but that there are turning-points at which humanity is free to choose the better or the worse road. One such turning-point (which had not appeared when he wrote the book), is the Atomic Bomb. Either we renounce it, or it destroys us. But renouncing it is both a moral effort and a political effort. Koestler calls for "a new fraternity in a new spiritual climate, whose leaders are tied by a vow of poverty to share the life of the masses, and debarred by the laws of the fraternity from attaining unchecked power"; he adds, "if this seems utopian, then Socialism is a utopia." It may not even be a utopia—its very name may in a couple of generations have ceased to be a memory—unless we can escape from the folly of "realism." But that will not happen without a change in the individual heart. To that extent, though no further, the Yogi is right as against the Commissar.[3]

1. The 'C. W.' stood for Common Wealth. Arthur Koestler's 'The Yogi and the Commissar,' the title-essay of a volume of essays published in 1945, was reviewed in C. W. Review by Orwell and Reg Bishop in parallel . The pair of reviews was headed 'Which Way to Heaven?' and was introduced by a boldly-displayed editorial statement: 'Koestler's "The Yogi and The Commisar" has excited violent controversy. The Yogi and the Commissar are philosophical and political opposites. The Commissar "believes in Change from Without, and the end justifies all means." To the Yogi, "the Means alone count: all Change must come by the individual from Within." Which is Right?' Orwell's review, headed 'Catastrophic Gradual-

ism,' started on the left-hand page of the opening; Bishop's, titled 'The Liberty of Anarchy,' began on the facing right-hand page. Bishop's stance was that of hard-line Soviet Communism of the period, so much so that he concludes by accusing Koestler of rolling the ammunition for fascism, a statement that incensed at least one reader, Peter Harris, whose protest was published in a later issue of *C.W. Review*. Bishop had been the *Daily Worker* correspondent in Moscow, 1934–35 and had edited *Russia To-day*; at this time he was Secretary of the Russia Today Society and Chairman of the Trade and Periodicals Branch of the National Union of Journalists. With Dr. John Lewis he had just completed *Philosophy of Betrayal*.

2. For Isherwood and Heard and others whom Orwell regarded as contemplating their navels in California, see *2397, n. 2* and *2713, n. 2*.

3. Orwell's Payments Book recorded a fee of £2.12.6 for this article against 21 October 1945. The essay was reprinted in *Politics*, September 1945. The versions are identical except that in the fifth sentence *Politics* has 'this is' for 'these are.' In a box within the article is this note about its author: 'GEORGE ORWELL is 42 and spent 5 years in the Indian Imperial Police. He fought in the P.O.U.M. militia in the Spanish Civil War and was wounded in 1937. Has been school teacher and bookseller, lived in France, and was recently the "Observer's" Special Correspondent in Paris. Author of a number of books, the latest of which is "Animal Farm," a political fantasy.'

2779. Review of *Dead Ground* by Howard Clewes; *Giuseppe Mazzini: Selected Writings*, edited and arranged with an introduction by Professor N. Gangulee;[1] *The Trial of Jones and Hulten*, edited and with a foreword by C. E. Bechhofer Roberts

Manchester Evening News, 1 November 1945

The war of 1914–18 produced few, if any, first-rate novels until six or eight years after it was over, and the war of 1939–45 looks like conforming to the same pattern.

Later on we may or may not get something corresponding to the stream of excellent war books that appeared between 1925 and 1930, but, at any rate, no book has been published so far that seems to place the war in its true perspective. The best things have been slight or fragmentary: pieces of "reportage" like "The Scum of the Earth," anecdotes arising out of isolated incidents like "A Bell for Adano,"[2] or studies in loneliness and boredom like the short stories of Alun Lewis and Maclaren Ross.

"Dead Ground" is one of the better English war books to appear so far, and it falls roughly into the same class as "A Bell for Adano"; that is to say, it used a truthful account of Army life as the background for a highly improbable incident, and in spite of a hard-boiled attitude and much realistic detail it does not escape a tinge of whimsiness. Its implied outlook on the war, however, and on the causes for which the war has been fought, is much more disillusioned.

In a small seaport in some unnamed part of England—Yorkshire or Northumberland, perhaps—an old steamship is lying at anchor, with the captain and one engineer on board, waiting to be sunk as a blockship at the harbour mouth if the expected German invasion should come.

It has been lying there, with steam always up, for eighteen months, and the captain, who has been at sea all his life and believes that ships were made to be sailed and not sunk, has reached the point of mutiny. The engineer, who is only doubtfully sane, has reached this point some months earlier and has ever since remained locked in the engine room after posting a manifesto in the local pub.

The story turns upon the efforts of the military authorities to induce the captain to obey orders by allowing his holds to be filled with ballast. In the end, goaded beyond endurance, he sails his ship into the minefield outside and there blows her up. There are various complicating factors, but that is the essential story.

It is the kind of thing that could possibly happen—at any rate, countless human beings, struggling against vast forces that they do not understand, are destroyed in equally stupid and pathetic ways—but it is somewhat vitiated as a story by the amount of sympathy that the captain receives from the other characters.

We are given to understand that nearly every one is on the captain's side: even among the officers who are supposed to see to the loading of the blockship only the adjutant, a fussing blimp of the old type, is really in favour of getting the job done. The whole notion of sinking a ship across a harbour mouth is made to appear as an absurd manœuvre which the captain is right to sabotage. It is doubtful, however, whether many people would have taken this view at the time—that is, in 1941.

We know now that the German invasion did not come off, but there was a period of a year or more during which it was hourly expected, and throughout that time defence precautions were taken more seriously than Mr. Clewes seems to suggest. Mr. Clewes is the author of one other novel. He could write a better book than his present one, and he probably will do so: his future works are worth looking out for.

Mazzini was perhaps the greatest of the nineteenth-century Liberal Nationalists. He spent his life struggling for the liberation and unification of Italy, but he did not share the narrow racialism and the dreams of revenge and conquest in which subject peoples are too apt to indulge. He wanted Italy to be not only independent but also republican and anticlerical, and he wanted the other oppressed nations of Europe to be free as well.

Also, though he rejected Marx's economic interpretation of history, he knew that mere freedom from foreign rule would be valueless unless it was followed by the emancipation of the proletariat. His vision of Europe was of a free federation of socialist republics, Christian in their moral code and, perhaps, even in their beliefs, but owing no allegiance to the Papacy.

There is much in Mazzini's writings that has a relevance today, but his activities, and those of all others like him, were partly wasted because of the then unperceived fact that nationalism is of its nature a reactionary force.

As long as nationalism meant the struggle of the subject peoples against the Austrian, Russian, and German empires, it appeared to be synonymous with progress; but when the oppressed are set free they have a way of setting up as oppressors on their own account, and Mazzini and his followers[3] must bear some of the[4] blame for the hideous growth of nationalism in the epoch that followed them.

Some of his books have an all too modern ring—"Place the young at the head of the insurgent masses; you do not know what strength is latent in those young bands, what magic influence the voices of the young have on the crowd. . . . Youth lives on movement, grows great in enthusiasm and faith. Consecrate them with a lofty mission, inflame them with emulation and praise, spread through their ranks the word of fire, the word of inspiration; speak to them of country, of glory, of power, of great memories."

Mussolini spoke to the young Italians of just those things, with the results we have seen. The flame of nationalism now burns fiercest in Asia, and Dr. Gangulee, the editor of this book, himself an Indian, remarks in his introduction on the prestige enjoyed by Mazzini's writings among Indian nationalist students.

Verbatim accounts of trials are often fascinating reading, not only because crime is interesting but because the evidence brings out masses of authentic information about people's daily lives. But the "Cleft Chin Murder" case, which made something of a stir at the beginning of this year, was a peculiarly sordid and uninteresting crime.

An American deserter and an 18-year-old girl, by profession a strip-tease dancer, robbed and murdered a taxi driver after committing various other violent robberies. If the case has any interest, it is that it illustrates the power of films and cheap fiction to cast a glamour round gangsterism. But the court proceedings were not very dramatic, and most readers will be able to learn as much as they want from the summary which Mr. Bechhofer Roberts gives in his foreword.[5]

[Fee: £8.8.0; 31.10.45]

1. Dr. Nagendranath Gangulee had worked with Orwell at the BBC in the series 'In Your Kitchen' in 1943. He had been Professor of Agriculture and Rural Economics at the University of Calcutta and was active in the 'Free India' Movement in England. He was a son-in-law of Rabindranath Tagore. See also *1861, n. 1.*
2. *The Scum of the Earth*, by Arthur Koestler, was reviewed by Orwell within his essay 'Arthur Koestler,' written September 1944; published in *Focus*, 2, 1946; see *2548*; *A Bell for Adano*, by John Hersey (1944; as a film, 1947).
3. followers] 'fellows' *in printed text*
4. the] their *in printed text*
5. Orwell discussed the implications of this case in 'Decline of the English Murder,' *2900*.

2780. 'Good Bad Books'

Tribune, 2 November 1945

Not long ago a publisher commissioned me to write an introduction for a reprint of a novel by Leonard Merrick. This publishing house, it appears, is going to re-issue a long series of minor and partly-forgotten novels of the twentieth century. It is a valuable service in these bookless days, and I rather envy the person whose job it will be to scout round the threepenny boxes, hunting down copies of his boyhood favourites.

A type of book which we hardly seem to produce in these days, but which flowered with great richness in the late nineteenth and early twentieth centuries, is what Chesterton called the "good bad book": that is, the kind of book that has no literary pretentions but which remains readable when more serious productions have perished. Obviously outstanding books in this line are *Raffles* and the Sherlock Holmes stories, which have kept their place when innumerable "problem novels," "human documents" and "terrible indictments" of this or that have fallen into deserved oblivion. (Who has worn better, Conan Doyle or Meredith?) Almost in the same class as these I put R. Austin Freeman's earlier stories—*The Singing Bone, The Eye of Osiris* and others—Ernest Bramah's *Max Carrados*, and, dropping the standard a bit, Guy Boothby's Tibetan thriller, *Dr. Nikola*, a sort of schoolboy version of Huc's *Travels in Tartary*, which would probably make a real visit to Central Asia seem a dismal anti-climax.

But apart from thrillers, there were the minor humorous writers of the period. For example, Pett Ridge—but I admit his full-length books no longer seem readable—E. Nesbit (*The Treasure Seekers*), George Birmingham, who was good so long as he kept off politics, the pornographic Binstead ("Pitcher" of the *Pink 'Un*), and, if American books can be included, Booth Tarkington's Penrod stories. A cut above most of these was Barry Pain. Some of Pain's humorous writings are, I suppose, still in print, but to anyone who comes across it I recommend what must now be a very rare book—*The Octave of Claudius*, a brilliant exercise in the macabre. Somewhat later in time there was Peter Blundell, who wrote in the W. W. Jacobs vein about Far Eastern seaport towns, and who seems to be rather unaccountably forgotten, in spite of having been praised in print by H. G. Wells.

However, all the books I have been speaking of are frankly "escape" literature. They form pleasant patches in one's memory, quiet corners where the mind can browse at odd moments, but they hardly pretend to have anything to do with real life. There is another kind of good bad book which is more seriously intended, and which tells us, I think, something about the nature of the novel and the reasons for its present decadence. During the last fifty years there has been a whole series of writers—some of them are still writing—whom it is quite impossible to call "good" by any strictly literary standard, but who are natural novelists and who seem to attain sincerity partly because they are not inhibited by good taste. In this class I put Leonard Merrick himself, W. L. George, J. D. Beresford, Ernest Raymond, May Sinclair, and—at a lower level than the others but still essentially similar— A. S. M. Hutchinson.

Most of these have been prolific writers, and their output has naturally varied in quality. I am thinking in each case of one or two outstanding books: for example. Merrick's *Cynthia,* J. D. Beresford's *A Candidate for Truth,* W. L. George's *Caliban,* May Sinclair's *The Combined Maze,* and Ernest Raymond's *We, the Accused.* In each of these books the author has been able to identify himself with his imagined characters, to feel with them and invite sympathy on their behalf, with a kind of abandonment that cleverer people would find it difficult to achieve. They bring out the fact that intellectual refinement can be a disadvantage to a story-teller, as it would be to a music-hall comedian.

Take, for example, Ernest Raymond's *We, the Accused*—a peculiarly sordid and convincing murder story, probably based on the Crippen case. I think it gains a great deal from the fact that the author only partly grasps the pathetic vulgarity of the people he is writing about, and therefore does not despise them. Perhaps it even—like Theodore Dreiser's *An American Tragedy*—gains something from the clumsy, long-winded manner in which it is written; detail is piled on detail, with almost no attempt at selection, and in the process an effect of terrible, grinding cruelty is slowly built up. So also with *A Candidate for Truth*. Here there is not the same clumsiness, but there is the same ability to take seriously the problems of commonplace people. So also with *Cynthia* and at any rate the earlier part of *Caliban*. The greater part of what W. L. George wrote was shoddy rubbish, but in this particular book, based on the career of Northcliffe, he achieved some memorable and truthful pictures of lower-middle class London life. Parts of this book are probably autobiographical, and one of the advantages of good bad writers is their lack of shame in writing autobiography. Exhibition and self-pity are the bane of the novelist, and yet if he is too frightened of them his creative gift may suffer.

The existence of good bad literature—the fact that one can be amused or excited or even moved by a book that one's intellect simply refuses to take seriously—is a reminder that art is not the same thing as cerebration. I imagine that by any test that could be devised, Carlyle would be found to be a more intelligent man than Trollope. Yet Trollope has remained readable and Carlyle has not: with all his cleverness he had not even the wit to write in plain straightforward English. In novelists, almost as much as in poets, the connection between intelligence and creative power is hard to establish. A good novelist may be a prodigy of self-discipline like Flaubert, or he may be an intellectual sprawl like Dickens. Enough talent to set up dozens of ordinary writers has been poured into Wyndham Lewis's so-called novels, such as *Tarr* or *Snooty Baronet*. Yet it would be a very heavy labour to read one of these books right through. Some indefinable quality, a sort of literary vitamin, which exists even in a book like *If Winter Comes*, is absent from them.

Perhaps the supreme example of the "good bad" book is *Uncle Tom's Cabin*. It is an unintentionally ludicrous book, full of preposterous melo-dramatic incidents; it is also deeply moving and essentially true; it is hard to say which quality outweighs the other. But *Uncle Tom's Cabin*, after all, is trying to be serious and to deal with the real world. How about the frankly escapist writers, the purveyors of thrills and "light" humour? How about *Sherlock Holmes, Vice Versa, Dracula, Helen's Babies* or *King Solomon's Mines*? All of these are definitely absurd books, books which one is more inclined to laugh *at* than *with*, and which were hardly taken seriously even by their authors; yet they have survived, and will probably continue to do so. All one can say is that, while civilisation remains such that one needs distraction from time to time, "light" literature has its appointed place; also that there is such a thing as sheer skill, or native grace, which may have more survival value than erudition or intellectual power. There are music-hall songs which are better poems than three-quarters of the stuff that gets into the anthologies:

> Come where the booze is cheaper,
> Come where the pots hold more,
> Come where the boss is a bit of a sport,
> Come to the pub next door!

Or again:

> Two lovely black eyes—
> Oh, what a surprise!
> Only for calling another man wrong,
> Two lovely black eyes!

I would far rather have written either of those than, say, *The Blessed Demozel°* or *Love in a Valley*. And by the same token I would back *Uncle Tom's Cabin* to outlive the complete works of Virginia Woolf or George Moore, though I know of no strictly literary test which would show where the superiority lies.[1]

[Fee: £3.3.0, written over £5.5.0; 26.10.45]

Two letters in response to this article were printed in *Tribune*, 9 November 1945, and in the following issue, 16 November, a reader corrected Orwell's recall of the two songs.

How can you waste space on such mischievous rubbish as George Orwell writes this week? To prefer "Two Lovely Black Eyes" to "Love in a Valley" is simply to write himself down an ass. (He isn't one, but then why did he do it? If it is a joke, it is a pretty poor one, and certainly calculated to mislead those sincerely in search of literary guidance.)

Again, why condemn novelists (two distinguished ones, Beresford and May Sinclair, among them) for doing exactly what most *great* novelists do?—taking "seriously the problems of commonplace people," etc. If "intellectual refinement" is a bar to this, which, of course, it isn't, then let his "cleverer people" take their cleverness elsewhere than into the pages of novels. They will never be missed.

V. H. Friedlaender

George Orwell, I think, did not follow through to its conclusion his essay on the survival of "bad" books.

The point is really that what might be termed second-rate authors—storytellers pure and simple—often tend to survive because the author *was* second-rate; he wrote on his own level. And that level is the level of the vast majority of readers to-day.

As George Orwell says, "Uncle Tom's Cabin" will probably outlast the complete works of Virginia Woolf. The reason? Like most highly intellectual writers, Virginia Woolf wrote on her own intellectual level; the result is that large parts of her works are—to put it mildly—a little bewildering to the average reader. And who can blame the average reader for fighting shy of what he does not understand?

I don't pretend to offer a solution. But a higher standard of artistic appreciation—that is, the normal critical faculties allowed to develop—might make the second-rate authors less popular. So would a more stable world.

But in any case, it might be better to make all works of art of some temporary substance; those of little worth could then be allowed to die a natural death, while those of genuine value could be deliberately preserved. The only difficulty lies in deciding what is of value and what is not. I would rather leave a question like that to George Orwell.

J. F. Hayes

The reference in George Orwell's article on Good Bad Books to the Blessed Demosel may be a printer's error; but in the old-time songs "Come where the boss is a bit of a *sport*" should be "bit of a *joss*," and "Only for *calling another man wrong*" should be "Only for *telling a man he was wrong.*"[2]

W. G. Priest

1. An abridged version of this essay was published in *World Digest*, February 1946.
2. 'The Blessed Damozel' is a poem by Dante Gabriel Rossetti (1850; many times revised). 'Love in the Valley' (not 'a') is a poem by George Meredith (1851). Both music-hall songs were once immensely popular. The third line of the second song should be 'Only for telling a man he was wrong'; Orwell, as so often, quotes from memory. The song was first sung by Charles Coburn in 1886 and was a parody of the Christy Minstrel favourite 'My Nellie's Blue Eyes.' It was an incredible success. Coburn sang it at the Trocadero in London in a two-week engagement which, because of the song's appeal, was extended to fourteen *months*. The other correction is not quite accurate. It should be 'Come where the boss is a deuce of a joss,' but 'deuce' was usually softened in Victorian times and the original word has almost been lost to memory. 'Joss' is a colloquialism for 'boss.' This song was also very popular, and Queen Victoria enjoyed the tune without knowing what the song was called. She heard it played by a military band at Windsor Castle and asked its name. An equerry is said to have informed her, with an absolutely straight face (Christopher Pulling, *When They Were Singing*, 1952, 133).

2781. Introduction to *Love of Life and Other Stories* by Jack London

October or November 1945

This introduction, written in October or November 1945, was published by Paul Elek in 1946. It exists in typescript and in printed form. There is an obvious error; see *n. 1*. It is corrected in the typescript, but not by Orwell. The text below is the printed version, checked against the typescript. Orwell entered the fee for this introduction, £21.0.0., in his Payments Book against the date 5 November 1945.

In her little book, *Memories of Lenin*, Nadezhda Krupskaya relates that when Lenin was in his last illness she used to read aloud to him in the evenings:

> Two days before his death I read to him in the evening a tale by Jack London, *Love of Life*—it is still lying on the table in his room. It was a very fine story. In a wilderness of ice, where no human being had set foot, a sick man, dying of hunger, is making for the harbour of a big river. His strength is giving out, he cannot walk but keeps slipping, and beside him there slides a wolf—also dying of hunger. There is a fight between them: the man wins. Half dead, half demented, he reaches his goal. That tale greatly pleased Ilyich (Lenin). Next day he asked me to read him more Jack London.

However, Krupskaya goes on, the next tale turned out to be "saturated with bourgeois morals," and "Ilyich smiled and dismissed it with a wave of his hand." These two pieces by Jack London were the last things that she read to him.

The story, *Love of Life*, is even grimmer than Krupskaya suggests in her short summary of it, for it actually ends with the man eating the wolf, or at any rate biting into its throat hard enough to draw blood. That is the sort of theme towards which Jack London was irresistibly drawn, and this episode of Lenin's deathbed readings is of itself not a bad criticism of London's work. He was a writer who excelled in describing cruelty, whose main theme, indeed, was the cruelty of Nature, or at any rate of contemporary life; he was also an extremely variable writer, much of whose work was produced hurriedly and at low pressure; and he had in him a strain of feeling which Krupskaya is probably right in calling "bourgeois"—at any rate, a strain which did not accord with his democratic and Socialist convictions.

During the last twenty years Jack London's short stories have been rather unaccountably forgotten—how thoroughly forgotten, one could gauge by the completeness with which they were out of print. So far as the big public went, he was remembered by various animal books, particularly *White Fang* and *The Call of the Wild*—books which appealed to the Anglo-Saxon sentimentality about animals—and after 1933 his reputation took an upward bound because of *The Iron Heel*, which had been written in 1907, and is in some sense a prophecy of Fascism. *The Iron Heel* is not a good book, and on the whole its predictions have not been borne out. Its dates and its geography are ridiculous, and London makes the mistake, which was usual at that time, of assuming that revolution would break out first in the highly industrialised countries. But on several points London was right where nearly all other prophets were wrong, and he was right because of just that strain in his nature that made him a good short-story writer and a doubtfully reliable Socialist.

London imagines a proletarian revolution breaking out in the United States and being crushed, or partially crushed, by a counter-offensive of the capitalist class; and, following on this, a long period during which society is ruled over by a small group of tyrants known as the Oligarchs, who are served by a kind of S.S. known as the Mercenaries. An underground struggle against dictatorship was the kind of thing that London could imagine, and he foresaw certain of the details with surprising accuracy: he foresaw, for instance, that peculiar horror of totalitarian society, the way in which suspected enemies of the régime *simply disappear*. But the book is chiefly notable for maintaining that capitalist society would not perish of its "contradictions," but that the possessing class would be able to form itself into a vast corporation and even evolve a sort of perverted Socialism, sacrificing many of its privileges in order to preserve its superior status. The passages in which London analyses the mentality of the Oligarchs are of great interest:

> They, as a class (writes the imaginary author of the book), believed that they alone maintained civilization. It was their belief that, if they ever weakened, the great beast would engulf them and everything of beauty and joy and wonder and good in its cavernous and slime-dripping maw. Without them, anarchy would reign and humanity would drop backward into the primitive night out of which it had so painfully emerged . . . In short, they alone, by their unremitting toil and self-sacrifice, stood between weak humanity and the all-devouring beast: and they believed it, firmly believed it.

> I cannot lay too great stress upon this high ethical righteousness of the whole Oligarch class. This has been the strength of the Iron Heel, and too many of the comrades have been slow or loath to realise it. Many of them have ascribed the strength of the Iron Heel to its system of reward and punishment. This is a mistake. Heaven and hell may be the prime factors of zeal in the religion of a fanatic; but for the great majority of the religious, heaven and hell are incidental to right and wrong. Love of the right, desire for the right, unhappiness with anything less than the right—in short, right conduct, is the prime factor of religion. And so with the Oligarchy . . . The great driving force of the Oligarchs is the belief that they are doing right.

From these and similar passages it can be seen that London's understanding of the nature of a ruling class—that is, the characteristics which a ruling class must have if it is to survive—went very deep. According to the conventional left-wing view, the "capitalist" is simply a cynical scoundrel, without honour or courage, and intent only on filling his own pockets. London knew that that view is false. But why, one might justly ask, should this hurried, sensational, in some ways childish writer have understood that particular thing so much better than the majority of his fellow Socialists?

The answer is surely that London could foresee Fascism because he had a Fascist streak in himself: or at any rate a marked strain of brutality and an almost unconquerable preference for the strong man as against the weak man. He knew instinctively that the American business-men would fight when their possessions were menaced, because in their place he would have fought himself. He was an adventurer and a man of action as few writers have ever been. Born into dire poverty, he had already escaped from it at sixteen, thanks to his commanding character and powerful physique: his early years were spent among oyster pirates, gold prospectors, tramps and prizefighters, and he was ready to admire toughness wherever he found it. On the other hand he never forgot the sordid miseries of his childhood, and he never faltered in his loyalty to the exploited classes. Much of his time was spent in working and lecturing for the Socialist movement, and when he was already a successful and famous man he could explore the worst depths of poverty in the London slums, passing himself off as an American sailor, and compile a book (*The People of the Abyss*) which still has sociological value. His outlook was democratic in the sense that he hated exploitation and hereditary privilege, and that he felt most at home in the company of people who worked with their hands: but his instinct lay towards acceptance of a "natural aristocracy" of strength, beauty and talent. Intellectually he knew, as one can see from various remarks in *The Iron Heel*, that Socialism ought to mean the meek inheriting the earth, but that was not what his temperament demanded. In much of his work one strain in his character simply kills the other off: he is at his best where they interact, as they do in certain of his short stories.

Jack London's great theme is the cruelty of Nature. Life is a savage struggle, and victory has nothing to do with justice. In the best of his short stories there is a startling lack of comment, a suspension of judgment, arising out of the fact that he both delights in the struggle and perceives its cruelty. Perhaps the best thing he ever wrote is *Just Meat*. Two burglars have got away with a big haul of jewellery: each is intent on swindling the other out of his share, and they poison one another simultaneously with strychnine, the story ending with the two men dead on the floor. There is almost no comment, and certainly no "moral." As Jack London sees it, it is simply a fragment of life, the kind of thing that happens in the present-day world: nevertheless it is doubtful whether such a plot would occur to any writer who was not fascinated by cruelty. Or take a story like *The "Francis Spaight."* The starving crew of a waterlogged ship has decided to resort to cannibalism, and have° just nerved themselves to begin when another ship heaves in sight. It is characteristic of Jack London that the second ship should appear after and not before the cabin boy's throat has been cut. A still more typical story is *A Piece of Steak*. London's love of boxing and admiration for sheer physical strength, his perception of the meanness and cruelty of a competitive society, and at the same time his instinctive tendency to accept *vae victis* as a law of Nature, are all expressed here. An old prizefighter is fighting his last battle: his opponent is a beginner, young and full of vigour, but without experience. The old man nearly wins, but in the end his ring-craft is no match for the youthful resilience of the other. Even when he has him at his mercy he is unable to strike the blow that would finish him, because he has been underfed for weeks before the fight and his muscles cannot make the necessary effort. He is left bitterly reflecting that if only he had had a good piece of steak on the day of the fight he would have won.

The old man's thoughts all run upon the theme: "Youth will be served." First you are young and strong, and you knock out older men and make money which you squander: then your strength wanes and in turn you are knocked out by younger men, and then you sink into poverty. This does in fact tell the story of the average boxer's life, and it would be a gross exaggeration to say that Jack London *approves* of the way in which men are used up like gladiators by a society which cannot even bother to feed them. The detail of the piece of steak—not strictly necessary, since the main point of the story is that the younger man is bound to win by virtue of his youth—rubs in the economic implication. And yet there is something in London that takes a kind of pleasure in the whole cruel process. It is not so much an approval of the harshness of Nature, as a mystical belief that Nature *is* like that. Nature is "red in tooth and claw." Perhaps fierceness is bad, but fierceness is the price of survival. The young slay the old, the strong slay the weak, by an inexorable law. Man fights against the elements or against his fellow man, and there is nothing except his own toughness to help him through. London would have said that he was merely describing life as it is actually lived, and in his best stories he does so: still, the constant recurrence of the same theme—struggle, toughness, survival—shows which way his inclinations pointed.

London had been deeply influenced by the theory of the Survival of the Fittest. His book, *Before Adam*—an inaccurate but very readable story of pre-history, in which ape-men and early and late Palæolithic men are all shown as existing simultaneously—is an attempt to popularise Darwin. Although Darwin's main thesis has not been shaken, there has been, during the past twenty or thirty years, a change in the interpretation put upon it by the average thinking man. In the late nineteenth century Darwinism was used as a justification for laissez-faire capitalism, for power politics and for the exploiting of subject peoples. Life was a free-for-all in which the fact of survival was proof of fitness to survive: this was a comforting thought for successful business men, and it also led naturally, though not very logically, to the notion of "superior" and "inferior" races. In our day we are less willing to apply biology to politics, partly because we have watched the Nazis do just that thing, with great thoroughness and with horrible results. But when London was writing, a crude version of Darwinism was widespread and must have been difficult to escape. He himself was even capable at times of succumbing to racial mysticism. He toyed for a while with a race theory similar to that of the Nazis, and throughout his work the cult of the "Nordic" is fairly well marked. It ties up on the one hand with his admiration for prizefighters, and on the other with his anthropomorphic view of animals: for there seems to be good reason for thinking that an exaggerated love of animals generally goes with a rather brutal attitude towards human beings. London was a Socialist with the instincts of a buccaneer and the education of a nineteenth-century materialist. In general the background of his stories is not industrial, nor even civilized. Most of them take place—and much of his own life was lived—on ranches or South Sea islands, in ships, in prison or in the wastes of the Arctic: places where a man is either alone and dependent on his own strength and cunning, or where life is naturally patriarchal.

Nevertheless, London did write from time to time about contemporary industrial society, and on the whole he was at his best when he did so. Apart from his short stories, there are *The People of the Abyss*, *The Road* (a brilliant little book describing London's youthful experiences as a tramp), and certain passages in *The Valley of the Moon*, which have the tumultuous history of American trade unionism as their background. Although the tug of his impulses was away from civilisation, London had read deeply in the literature of the Socialist movement, and his early life had taught him all he needed to know about urban poverty. He himself was working in a factory at the age of eleven, and without that experience behind him he could hardly have written such a story as *The Apostate*. In this story, as in all his best work, London does [not]¹ comment, but he does unquestionably aim at rousing pity and indignation. It is generally when he writes of more primitive scenes that his moral attitude becomes equivocal. Take, for instance, a story like *Make Westing*. With whom do London's sympathies lie—with Captain Cullen or with George Dorety? One has the impression that if he were forced to make a choice he would side with the Captain, who commits two murders but does succeed in getting his ship round Cape Horn. On the other hand, in a story like *The Chinago*, although it is told in the usual pitiless style, the "moral" is plain enough for anyone who wants to find it. London's better angel is his Socialist convictions, which come into play when he deals with such subjects as coloured exploitation, child labour or the treatment of criminals, but are hardly involved when he is writing about explorers or animals. It is probably for this reason that a high proportion of his better writings deal with urban life. In stories like *The Apostate, Just Meat, A Piece of Steak* and *Semper Idem*, however cruel and sordid they may seem, something is keeping him on the rails and checking his natural urge towards the glorification of brutality. That "something" is his knowledge, theoretical as well as practical, of what industrial capitalism means in terms of human suffering.

Jack London is a very uneven writer. In his short and restless life he poured forth an immense quantity of work, setting himself to produce 1,000 words every day and generally achieving it. Even his best stories have the curious quality of being well told and yet not well written: they are told with admirable economy, with just the right incidents in just the right place, but the texture of the writing is poor, the phrases are worn and obvious, and the dialogue is erratic. His reputation has had its ups and downs, and for a long period he seems to have been much more admired in France and Germany than in the English-speaking countries. Even before the triumph of Hitler, which brought *The Iron Heel* out of its obscurity, he had a certain renown as a left-wing and "proletarian" writer—rather the same kind of renown as attaches to Robert Tressall, W. B. Traven or Upton Sinclair. He has also been attacked by Marxist writers for his "Fascist tendencies." These tendencies unquestionably existed in him, so much so that if one imagines him as living on into our own day, instead of dying in 1915, it is very hard to be sure where his political allegiance would have lain. One can imagine him in the Communist Party, one can imagine him falling a victim to Nazi racial theory, and one can imagine him the quixotic champion of some Trotskyist or Anarchist sect. But, as I have tried to make clear, if he had been a politically reliable person he would probably have left behind nothing of interest. Meanwhile his reputation rests mainly on *The Iron Heel*, and the excellence of his short stories has been almost forgotten. A dozen of the best of them are collected in this volume, and a few more are worth rescuing from the museum shelves and the second-hand boxes. It is to be hoped, too, that new editions of *The Road*, *The Jacket*, *Before Adam* and *The Valley of the Moon* will appear when paper becomes more plentiful. Much of Jack London's work is scamped and unconvincing, but he produced at least six volumes which deserve to stay in print, and that is not a bad achievement from a life of only forty-one years.

1. 'not' is omitted from the typescript and printed texts.

2782. To Roger Senhouse

6 November 1945   Typewritten

27 B Canonbury Square
Islington
London   N 1

Dear Roger,
The Correction in "Critical Essays" is the following:—
    Page 7, lines 13–16. Delete "when Lenin was in his last . . . . . abandon it" and substitute
        "towards the end of his life Lenin went to see a dramatised version of *The Cricket on the Hearth*, and found Dickens's 'middle-class sentimentality' so intolerable that he walked out in the middle of a scene."
    Page 7, line 17. Delete "bourgeois" and substitute "middle-class."[1]
I think this only makes a difference of about a line.

Yours
George

1. These changes were made.

2783. The Amnesty Campaign

7 November 1945

Issue 2 of the *Freedom Defence Committee Bulletin*, February–March 1946, reported that on 7 November 1945 the Committee had, with a meeting at the Conway Hall, publicly launched its campaign for the granting of an amnesty to military and political prisoners held under wartime legislation. Fenner Brockway was in the chair and among the speakers were Ernest Silverman and George Orwell. An advertisement in *Freedom—Through Anarchism*, 20 October 1945, stated that other speakers would include George Padmore and Philip Sansom.[1] One probable result of this campaign was a half-hour adjournment debate in the House of Commons on 28 November 1945. In this the Secretary of State for War announced some mitigation of sentences, so that by 5 November

1945, of 3,156 soldiers under sentence in Britain, nearly 59% had been released, and of 6,751 serving sentences overseas, nearly 37½ had been released.

In an account of the meeting, *Freedom—Through Anarchism* for 7 November 1945 gave this report of Orwell's contribution:

George Orwell, the novelist and critic, spoke on non-fraternisation [of British servicemen with Germans], and said that there were still people suffering terms of imprisonment who had been sentenced in the period before the non-fraternisation laws were modified. These laws had been recognised to be ridiculous by all the war correspondents, like himself, who had seen them in operation. Yet although the laws had been relaxed, men sentenced under them were still kept in prison.

Issue 2 also prints a long list of those who sent donations to support the work of the Committee between May and September 1945. Some 230 individual donations are listed, mainly against the initials of the donor, though some of these may have been group donations. By far the majority are of ten shillings or less. Two of the larger donations can be identified: £10 from the singer Peter Pears and £2.2.0 from G.O.—almost certainly Owell. It is difficult to put a contribution of two guineas into perspective, but it was among the twenty largest contributions. In issue 3, April–May 1946, G.O. donated £10; there was only one larger donation from an individual: £20 from P.W. for 1947, see *3144*.

1. Philip Sansom (1916–1999), writer, editor, cartoonist and public speaker (especially in Hyde Park). He was associated with *Freedom* and was involved in Syndicalism, the sex-reform movement, and campaigns against capital punishment and for those held in Franco's jails. He worked as a journalist on trade papers.

2784. Review of *Mind at the End of Its Tether* by H. G. Wells

Manchester Evening News, 8 November 1945

Mr. Wells explains in his preface that his new book "Mind at the End of Its Tether" is intended to supersede "'42 to '44," a book of essays which was published last year and which had been flung together rather hurriedly, because at that time he did not expect to live much longer.

The present book (it is only 34 pages) brings to a conclusive end the series of essays, memoranda, pamphlets through which the writer has experimented, challenged discussion, and assembled material bearing upon the fundamental nature of life and time. So far as fundamentals go, he has nothing more and never will have anything more to say.

It is, indeed, hard to see how Mr. Wells could add much to his present message, since that message is to the effect that—if his reasoning is correct—life on this planet is now due to come to an end.

"This world," he says, "is at the end of its tether; and the end of everything we call life is close at hand and cannot be evaded." It is not completely clear whether this means all life or merely human life, but, at any rate, homo sapiens is doomed.

A series of events has forced upon the intelligent observer the realisation that the human story has already come to an end, and that homo sapiens, as he has been pleased to call himself, is, in his present form, played out. The stars in their courses have turned against him and he has to give place to some other animal better adapted to face the fate that closes in more and more swiftly upon mankind.

One could hardly have anything more final than that. A little later, however, Mr. Wells seems to suggest that the inheriting species may belong to the hominidæ.* A small minority of adaptable human beings may survive if they are capable of turning into something else: the new animal may be an entirely alien strain, or it may arise as a new modification of the hominidæ, and even as a direct continuation of the human phylum,† but it will certainly not be human. There is no way out for man but steeply up or steeply down. Adapt or perish, now as ever, is nature's inexorable imperative.

In other words, the price of survival is an evolutionary leap so abrupt that the product of it will not be a human being. However, in the last sentence of the book it is once again stated that life itself is coming to an "inevitable end," so that it hardly seems to matter whether or not a few transformed hominidæ are present at the final death-agony.

The fact is that this is an incoherent book, and, in spite of its shortness, probably unfinished. And yet the issues it raises are interesting. This is not a moment at which one can simply disregard the statement that humanity is doomed. It quite well may be doomed. Mr. Wells does not give his reasons for thinking that life itself is coming to an end, but so far as mankind is concerned he is presumably thinking of the power of modern weapons and our complete failure to produce a social and political organisation capable of controlling them.

It is interesting to learn that he wrote this book before the arrival of the atomic bomb—which, however, he himself prophesied years ago in "The World Set Free."

It is certainly true that man must either alter his habits quickly or see civilisation blown to pieces—and it may be true, as Mr Wells suggests, that the great mass of mankind is simply unteachable and the necessary change can only happen through an evolutionary change in a chosen minority.

But one is obliged to ask—where is this minority to come from? We ourselves are the only hominidæ on this planet, and there are no great differences between the various races of man—and as for an evolutionary change so drastic that the resulting creature would be definitely "not human," it is hardly likely to happen in a few generations. So it would seem that the necessary new species is not in sight, in which case life is finished. And yet a faint doubt, not due entirely to wish-thinking, keeps intruding itself.

Are we really done for? If the worst came to the worst and a shower of atom bombs descended on every great city in the world, would that necessarily be the end? The end of machine civilisation—yes, but probably not of human life. It is worth remembering how numerous the human race has become in recent centuries. The population of Europe is probably ten times what it was in Roman times, and that of North America a hundred times what it was in the days of Columbus. One could kill off 95 per cent of

---

* HOMINIDAE: A family of mammals represented by the single genus Homo (man) [Orwell's footnote].

† PHYLUM: A race of organisms descended from common ancestral form [Orwell's footnote].

humanity, and the world would still be more populous than it was in the Stone Age. The survivors would revert to savagery, but they would probably retain knowledge of the use of metals—and at any rate it would be a long time before they had another chance of monkeying with atomic bombs.

It would be simply dishonest to pretend that this is one of Mr. Wells's better books.

Indeed, it is hardly a book at all, merely a series of short, disjointed essays which have probably been written with considerable effort between bouts of illness. And yet it has the power that Mr. Wells's writings have always had— the power of arresting the reader's attention and forcing him to think and argue. The thesis that it puts forward may be far-fetched, it may even be slightly absurd, but it has a sort of grandeur.

It calls up that world of cooling stars and battling dinosaurs which Mr. Wells has made so peculiarly his own. Mr. Wells is 79 and may not, he thinks, live very much longer. Nevertheless, while writing this book he has been contemplating another, to be entitled "Decline and Fall of Monarchy and Competitive Imperialisms." Let us hope that he writes it.[1] Meanwhile, in spite of its incoherence, the present book is well worth the hour or so that it takes to read it.

[Fee: £8.8.0; 7.11.45]

1. H. G. Wells died nine months later, on 13 August 1946. *Mind at the End of Its Tether* was his last book.

2785. Leonard Moore to Roger Senhouse, and Senhouse to Moore

8 November 1945 and 14 November 1945

Roger Senhouse had evidently drawn Leonard Moore's attention to the importance of George Orwell. In his reply, Moore gave as evidence that he had been alive to this long before Senhouse by pointing out 'that it was I who saved Orwell's first manuscript [*Down and Out in Paris and London*] from destruction by the author, and took it personally to Victor Gollancz.' Mabel Fierz saved the book, for it was she who took it to Moore. Senhouse's reply to Moore reads:

Thank you for your letter of November 8th with the information about Scribner and the French rights in ANIMAL FARM. I must say that it does surprise me that the Americans have cold feet about taking this title, and one would think that its resounding success in this country would overrule their personal prejudice to touch anything that is a dangerous commodity while the Russian situation is so uncertain. You do not tell me whether Roy Publishers are definitely out of the market, and I would like to be certain on this point.[1]

We will certainly let you have six copies of the second edition of ANIMAL FARM, early in December. In fact, they may be through in the last week in

November, but nothing can be guaranteed until the books are actually in this office.

There were a few corrections to be made in the book proofs of CRITICAL ESSAYS, and I would rather that these did not go out for commercial purposes until the corrections are made. I am sending you, however, one copy of the proofs, which have not the author's final corrections, and will ask you to wait for further copies of this book, which is at present printing.

1. Roy Publishers was 'out of the market.'

2786. 'Revenge Is Sour'

Tribune, 9 November 1945

Whenever I read phrases like "war guilt trials," "punishment of war criminals," and so forth, there comes back into my mind the memory of something I saw in a prisoner-of-war camp in South Germany, earlier this year.

Another correspondent and myself were being shown round the camp by a little Viennese Jew who had been enlisted in the branch of the American army which deals with the interrogation of prisoners. He was an alert, fair-haired, rather good-looking youth of about twenty-five, and politically so much more knowledgeable than the average American officer that it was a pleasure to be with him. The camp was on an airfield, and, after we had been round the cages, our guide led us to a hangar where various prisoners who were in a different category from the others were being "screened."

Up at one end of the hangar about a dozen men were lying in a row on the concrete floor. These, it was explained, were S.S. officers who had been segregated from the other prisoners. Among them was a man in dingy civilian clothes who was lying with his arm across his face and apparently asleep. He had strangely and horribly deformed feet. The two of them were quite symmetrical, but they were clubbed out into an extraordinary globular shape which made them more like a horse's hoof than anything human. As we approached the group the little Jew seemed to be working himself up into a state of excitement.

"That's the real swine!" he said, and suddenly he lashed out with his heavy army boot and caught the prostrate man a fearful kick right on the bulge of one of his deformed feet.

"Get up, you swine!" he shouted as the man started out of sleep, and then repeated something of the kind in German. The prisoner scrambled to his feet and stood clumsily to attention. With the same air of working himself up into a fury—indeed he was almost dancing up and down as he spoke—the Jew told us the prisoner's history. He was a "real" Nazi: his party number indicated that he had been a member since the very early days, and he had held a post corresponding to a general in the political branch of the S.S. It could be taken as quite certain that he had had charge of concentration camps and had presided over tortures and hangings. In short, he represented everything that we had been fighting against during the past five years.

Meanwhile, I was studying his appearance. Quite apart from the scrubby, unfed, unshaven look that a newly captured man generally has, he was a disgusting specimen. But he did not look brutal or in any way frightening: merely neurotic and, in a low way, intellectual. His pale, shifty eyes were deformed by powerful spectacles. He could have been an unfrocked clergyman, an actor ruined by drink, or a spiritualist medium. I have seen very similar people in London common lodging-houses, and also in the Reading Room of the British Museum. Quite obviously he was mentally unbalanced—indeed, only doubtfully sane, though at this moment sufficiently in his right mind to be frightened of getting another kick. And yet everything that the Jew was telling me of his history could have been true, and probably was true! So the Nazi torturer of one's imagination, the monstrous figure against whom one had struggled for so many years, dwindled to this pitiful wretch, whose obvious need was not for punishment, but for some kind of psychological treatment.

Later, there were further humiliations. Another S.S. officer, a large brawny man, was ordered to strip to the waist and show the blood-group number tattooed on his under-arm; another was forced to explain to us how he had lied about being a member of the S.S. and attempted to pass himself off as an ordinary soldier of the Wehrmacht. I wondered whether the Jew was getting any real kick out of this new-found power that he was exercising. I concluded that he wasn't really enjoying it, and that he was merely—like a man in a brothel, or a boy smoking his first cigar, or a tourist traipsing round a picture gallery—*telling* himself that he was enjoying it, and behaving as he had planned to behave in the days when he was helpless.

It is absurd to blame any German or Austrian Jew for getting his own back on the Nazis. Heaven knows what scores this particular man may have had to wipe out: very likely his whole family had been murdered; and, after all, even a wanton kick to a prisoner is a very tiny thing compared with the outrages committed by the Hitler regime. But what this scene, and much else that I saw in Germany, brought home to me was that the whole idea of revenge and punishment is a childish daydream. Properly speaking, there is no such thing as revenge. Revenge is an act which you want to commit when you are powerless and because you are powerless: as soon as the sense of impotence is removed, the desire evaporates also.

Who would not have jumped for joy, in 1940, at the thought of seeing S.S. officers kicked and humiliated? But when the thing becomes possible, it is merely pathetic and disgusting. It is said that when Mussolini's corpse was exhibited in public, an old woman drew a revolver and fired five shots into it, exclaiming, "Those are for my five sons!" It is the kind of story that the newspapers make up, but it might be true. I wonder how much satisfaction she got out of those five shots, which, doubtless, she had dreamed years earlier of firing. The condition of her being able to get near enough to Mussolini to shoot at him was that he should be a corpse.

In so far as the big public in this country is responsible for the monstrous peace settlement now being forced on Germany, it is because of a failure to see in advance that punishing an enemy brings no satisfaction. We acquiesced in crimes like the expulsion of all Germans from East Prussia—crimes which in some cases we could not prevent but might at least have protested against—because the Germans had angered and frightened us, and therefore we were certain that when they were down we should feel no pity for them. We persist in these policies, or let others persist in them on our behalf, because of a vague feeling that, having set out to punish Germany, we ought to go ahead and do it. Actually there is little acute hatred of Germany left in this country, and even less, I should expect to find, in the army of occupation. Only the minority of sadists, who must have their "atrocities" from one source or another, take a keen interest in the hunting-down of war criminals and quislings. If you ask the average man what crime Goering, Ribbentrop and the rest are to be charged with at their trial, he cannot tell you. Somehow the punishment of these monsters ceases to seem attractive when it becomes possible: indeed, once under lock and key, they almost cease to be monsters.

Unfortunately, there is often need of some concrete incident before one can discover the real state of one's feelings. Here is another memory from Germany. A few hours after Stuttgart was captured by the French army,[1] a Belgian journalist and myself entered the town, which was still in some disorder. The Belgian had been broadcasting throughout the war for the European Service of the B.B.C., and, like nearly all Frenchmen or Belgians, he had a very much tougher attitude towards "the Boche" than an Englishman or an American would have. All the main bridges into the town had been blown up, and we had to enter by a small footbridge which the Germans had evidently made efforts to defend. A dead German soldier was lying supine at the foot of the steps. His face was a waxy yellow. On his breast someone had laid a bunch of the lilac which was blossoming everywhere.

The Belgian averted his face as we went past. When we were well over the bridge he confided to me that this was the first time he had seen a dead man. I suppose he was thirty-five years old, and for four years he had been doing war propaganda over the radio. For several days after this, his attitude was quite different from what it had been earlier. He looked with disgust at the bomb-wrecked town and the humiliations the Germans were undergoing, and even on one occasion intervened to prevent a particularly bad bit of looting. When we left, he gave the residue of the coffee we had brought with us to the Germans on whom we were billeted. A week earlier he would probably have been scandalised at the idea of giving coffee to a "Boche." But his feelings, he told me, had undergone a change at the sight of "*ce pauvre mort*" beside the bridge: it had suddenly brought home to him the meaning of war. And yet, if we had happened to enter the town by another route, he might have been spared the experience of seeing even one corpse out of the—perhaps—twenty million that the war has produced.

[Fee: £3.3.0; 2.11.45]

A less sympathetic view of 'innocent Germany' was expressed in a letter from Mrs. S. Rose printed in *Tribune*, 16 November 1945:

Of course everyone knows that revenge can be sour—if too long delayed and too long anticipated. But it can also be sweet if it takes the form of just, sure retribution. Why does Mr. Orwell seek to damp down the just indignation of the still suffering victims of fascism? Is it that he sympathises with it more than he pretends to do with the millions it has outraged? Is he so kind to Germany because he hates Russia and the other Slav countries who won't let him forget and forgive and so resume his comfortable existence writing for progressive journals?

His poor withers are wrung with pity for innocent Germany because by a "monstrous" peace settlement she is suffering the "crime" of dismemberment. He would not punish her at all for twice in one generation hurling the world into the ruin of world war, because "punishment brings no satisfaction." The man who can write like this has lost all sense of justice and reality.

On 7 December 1945, *Tribune* published a response to Mrs. Rose's letter from H. Duncan Littlechild:

Is it not Mrs. Rose rather than Mr. Orwell who has lost all sense of justice and reality? There are still millions in Spain and Portugal suffering from fascism, and I am certain that Mr. Orwell is at least as disturbed as Mrs. Rose; but disgust with a regime does not entail blood lust.

I would like to remind Mrs. Rose that justice does not mean, as she appears to think, the Mosaic law of an eye for an eye, but rather the socialist interpretation. When justice for miners, or other workers, is called for, it means that their needs should be understood, and, being understood, should be satisfied. It was this failure, twenty-five years ago, to deal *justly* with the people of Germany that was wholly responsible for the recent holocaust. As for the cry that Germany has twice plunged the world into the ruin of world war, this statement may be convenient to the Tory capitalists, but it is simply not true.

Perhaps Mrs. Rose is not aware that until September, 1939, we were supplying Germany with munitions of war, and Japan long after the date. As one who saw German dead at Passchendaele and in France, I can assure your correspondent that such a sight brings no feeling of exultation. Only a dead fellow human is seen, and that brings angry bitterness and a feeling of nausea for those who still laud the glories of war.

We want peace, and that can only be secured by interpreting justice as Mr. Orwell does, and not by the damnable Mosaic interpretation of Mrs. Rose.

On 31 December 1945, Dwight Macdonald wrote from the United States to tell Orwell that this article made a point which was new to him and very important: 'when I have been angry with people, I too have felt just the same lack of interest, later, in scoring off them. Stalin, however, apparently is a horse of another color!'

1. For Orwell's despatch from Stuttgart (dated 28 April 1945) see *2661*.

2787. To Leonard Moore

9 November 1945   Typewritten

27 B Canonbury Square
Islington
London   N 1

Dear Mr Moore,

Many thanks for your two letters. I have written to Mr Allwood[1] and made it clear that any business arrangements must be made through you. I have not here a copy of either "Down & Out" or "Wigan Pier," but I think there may be copies at my sister's flat and I hope to find out within the next day or two. I am glad you sent them "Animal Farm" as I fancy this would go well in Sweden if translated.[2] Did anything further transpire about a French translation?[3]

As to the Portuguese translation.[4] I see that the publishers are called Livraria Popular de Francisco Franco. Has this any connection with the Spanish (Franco) government? I mean is it either a concern maintained in Portugal by the Spanish government, or is it so named to show sympathy with Franco? Or is the name merely a coincidence? It is important to know, because I could not consider letting the firm have the book if they have any connection with the Spanish fascists. Not to put it on any other ground, it could do me a great deal of harm in this country if it got out, as it would. I know of course that Portugal itself has a semi-fascist regime and censorship of books must be pretty strict there, but it is a different matter to be definitely used as propaganda by Franco's lot.

I enclose a proof copy of the essays for Reynal & Hitchcock. This is an uncorrected proof, ie. it contains a few printer's errors, but the two mistakes which it was important not to leave in it have been corrected in ink.

Yours sincerely
Eric Blair

1. Unidentified.
2. The Swedish translation of *Animal Farm*, *Djurfarmen: saga*, was translated by Nils Holmberg, who also translated *Nineteen Eighty-Four*, and was published on 8 March 1946 in a run of 2,000 copies by Albert Bonniers Förlag, Stockholm, in their *Panache* series of foreign 'avant-garde' works (Willison).
3. The French translation of *Animal Farm*, *Les Animaux Partout!*, was translated by Sophie Dévil, with a Preface by Jean Texcier, a pseudonymous Resistance writer, and published by Editions Odile Pathé, Paris, on 15 October 1947. 'Napoleon' was translated as 'César.' The publication of a French translation was the subject of considerable correspondence and delay (Willison).
4. The Portuguese translation of *Animal Farm*, *O Porco Triunfante*, was translated by Almirante Albert Aprá and published by Livraria Popular de Francisco Franco, Lisbon, [February] 1946. The publisher described the book as 'um livro hilariante' (a very funny book), a response to *Animal Farm* repeated on the soft card cover, which showed comically, but not satirically, a 'pig with umbrella and briefcase, and civil decoration hanging over [a] prominent stomach' (Willison).

2788. To Miss J. G. Manton

10 November 1945   Typewritten

27 B Canonbury Square
Islington
London   N 1

Dear Sir,
With reference to your letter of the 2nd November.[1]
   I could not speak on either of the books you name, as I have not read them and have not been in the USSR and only a very short time in Germany.

Yours truly
[Signed] Geo. Orwell
George Orwell

1. The letter was signed 'Jo Manton.' Orwell, evidently uncertain as to the writer's sex, replied formally. Miss Manton was an assistant in the School Broadcasting Department of the BBC. Orwell had been asked to discuss *Virgin Soil Upturned* (1932; translation, 1935) by Mikhail Sholokhov (1905–1984) and *Little Man, What Now?* (1932; translation, 1933) by Hans Fallada (pseudonym of Rudolf Ditzen; 1893–1947).

2789. To Frank Barber

10 November 1945   Typewritten

27 B Canonbury Square
Islington
London   N 1

Dear Barber,[1]
Yes, I did get the pamphlets, for which very many thanks. Please forgive me for not answering earlier. I have been ill, and struggling to keep up with my routine work at the same time.
   Look me up if you're in London any time.

Yours
[Signed] Geo. Orwell
George Orwell

1. Frank D. Barber was at one time an assistant editor of the *Leeds Weekly Citizen*; see *2587*; see also *2740* and *2770*.

2790. Review of *A Harp with a Thousand Strings* compiled by Hsiao Ch'ien[1]

The Observer, 11 November 1945

Mr. Hsiao Ch'ien has no official status and no directly political aim, but the books he has published during the past few years have done their bit towards improving Anglo-Chinese relations. His present book is a mixed anthology of a rather curious kind. It consists partly of translations from Chinese literature and folk lore, partly of appreciations of Chinese life and culture by European writers. The Chinese extracts are mostly from biographies or autobiographies; though there are also poems, proverbs, fairy stories, and samples of popular humour; the European writers deal with subjects as diverse as philosophy and entomology, and range in time between Sir John Mandeville and William Empson.

A large part of Mr. Hsiao's purpose is to show the variations in the European attitude towards China from the days of Marco Polo onwards. China enters fully into the European consciousness about the end of the seventeenth century, and is the subject of a ferocious attack in "Robinson Crusoe," some passages from which are quoted here. Defoe had previously written a pro-Chinese pamphlet, but one gets the impression in "Robinson Crusoe" that he is angry and frightened at the thought that there should exist a large, powerful and highly-civilised country which is not Christian. However, as Mr. Spraigue Allen's essay shows, China gets on the whole a good Press in the eighteenth century; so good, indeed, as to provoke protests from both Wesley and Dr. Johnson.

The conception of the Chinese as both wicked and comic comes later, and is perhaps not unconnected with the Opium Wars and commercial penetration generally. Mr. Hsiao quotes a hostile essay by de Quincey, some mildly disparaging remarks by John Stuart Mill, and also Lamb's "Dissertation upon Roast Pig," which expresses the kind of amused patronage which was to be one of the normal attitudes for nearly a hundred years. Lytton Strachey's attitude in the Chinese passages in his essay on Gordon is essentially the same as Lamb's. On the other hand, there are Lowes Dickinson's "Letters from John Chinaman," whose sentimental praise of China is insulting in a more subtle way. It is only in the last few years that the Chinese have begun to be regarded as human beings, and perhaps the obsolescence of the word "Chinaman" marks the change of outlook.[2]

There is a pleasant essay on Marco Polo by Miss Eileen Power, two essays on Chinese literature by Mr. Arthur Waley, and a great deal of varied information about musical instruments, porcelain, gardening, butterflies, alligators, and much else. Among the fragments of travel literature, the account of Lord Macartney's journey to Jehol in 1793 is an exceptionally vivid and readable piece of reporting.

The bulk of the translations from the Chinese are arranged under the headings "The Evolution of Chinese Women" and "The Evolution of Chinese Men." They start in the third century A.D. and they end in the 1940's. Among other things they include the surprising story, told by himself, of Sun Yat-sen's kidnapping at the Chinese Embassy in London in 1896. The most charming piece of all is the story of the married life of the painter Shen Fu in the late eighteenth century, a period when China was peaceful and prosperous and "men strove to be refined and women accomplished." Other extracts show the clash between the family and the individual, and the baleful influence of the mother-in-law. A poem of the third century, so skilfully translated that the allusions are easy enough to follow, describes the suicide of a young couple who are in effect sacrificed on the altar of filial piety. How hard the fight against the family system has been one can gather from the crudely iconoclastic attitude of some of the later writers.

Although they include an occasional gem like "He who rides a tiger cannot dismount," the Chinese proverbs are rather disappointing, and many of them would be better described as precepts. They do not have the crude earthy quality of European proverbs, the aim of which is usually to puncture fine attitudes. The book includes a selection of Chinese songs with music, numerous plates illustrating the date marks and symbolic signs on Chinese pottery, and a table showing the landmarks in the development of Chinese culture from Neolithic times onward. It is a scrappy book which will not please the scholarly, but there can be few people who would not get profit by dipping into it here or there.

[Fee: £10.0.0; 8.11.45]

1. Hsiao Ch'ien had given talks for Orwell in the Far Eastern Service of the BBC; see *919* and *919, n. 1.*
2. For Orwell's comments on the shift from 'Chinaman' to 'Chinese,' see 'As I Please,' 2, 10 December 1943, *2391.*

2791. To Dudley Cloud

Proofs of 'The Prevention of Literature' 27 January 1947

Orwell records against 12 November 1945 the following article for *Polemic* and a fee of £26.5.0. A full version of the article was published in *Polemic* No.2 in January 1946 and an abridged, amended version by *The Atlantic Monthly* in March 1947. There has also survived most of Orwell's typescript, as amended for the United States, and proofs of that version, dated 22 January 1947. It might, at first sight, seem appropriate simply to reproduce the full version published by *Polemic.* However, the changes suggested by the staff of *The Atlantic Monthly* were in part accepted by Orwell. The proofs also give his responses to proposed modifications, some of which are improvements in expression. See the notes at the end of the essay, *2792.*

Orwell returned the proofs to *The Atlantic Monthly* on 27 January 1947. His covering letter to Dudley Cloud, Managing Editor, has survived and is reproduced here rather than in its chronological place. This discusses in detail his use of the term 'modern physics' (see *n. 23*). Since he indicated what he did not want changed, it is reasonable to assume that the other modifications, whether or not they originated with him, had his approval, though some were made with American readers in mind. Thus, 'in this country' is changed to 'in England' with Orwell's approval. However, 'Although' and 'question' were silently changed to 'Though' and 'matter' *after* the proof stage and cannot have had his approval. A short summarising paragraph is omitted from the U.S. version; that may also have been cut with American readers in mind, as was, quite certainly, the omission of a reference to the beginning of the essay, for that looks back to the opening section cut from the U.S. version. The removal of the quotation marks from around 'reportage' was resisted by Orwell and agreed only if it was appropriate for U.S. readers. There are changes in spelling and in capitalisation to suit U.S. conventions. The U.S. version is broken down into shorter paragraphs than Orwell used, which were followed in *Polemic*. The essay was also divided into five numbered sections in *The Atlantic Monthly*.

Many thanks for your letter of the 24th. There are no errors in the proofs, but I have answered a few queries in the margin. "Physics" is not a misprint and should stand. The point is that the existence of the electronic world, where the ordinary rules of space and time to which we are accustomed appear not to work, is now often used as an argument to show that all our ideas about the macroscopic world are illusions. Thus for example, if I know anything definitely, I know that my inkpot is on the table in front of me. But in fact this is an illusion. The inkpot, the table and myself are not solid objects but merely wavering masses of electrons, and what appear to me as shapes and colours are in fact illusions. The real world, in fact, is something quite other than what it appears to be to our senses. But in that case all our ideas about objective reality are mistaken, and to say that we know that such and such an event happened in such and such a manner is what is called "naive realism." So that it isn't a falsification to say (for instance) that Trotsky fought on the side of the Whites in the Russian civil war. I have heard this argument put forward, almost as crudely as that, again and again. I haven't seen it in print yet, but no doubt it will get there before long. The unpredictability of events in the electronic world is also used as an argument for the freedom of the will, though it seems to me that it could equally well be used to prove the opposite. My point is that we live on the macroscopic plane and must not be argued into denying the evidence of our senses because the sub-microscopic world is in fact different from what our senses tell us.

I am air-mailing these proofs today and hope they will get to you in time. To make sure I will also cable—at least I will if I can do it over the phone, as I have been confined to my bed with 'flu and don't want to go out into the snow.

Yours sincerely
Geo. Orwell

2792. 'The Prevention of Literature'

Polemic, January 1946   *The Atlantic Monthly*, March 1947

CEJL reprinted 'The Prevention of Literature' as it had appeared in *Polemic*. The version printed here gives the full text of the original but incorporates those changes Orwell specifically or implicitly accepted for the U.S. version apart from those designed to suit American publication. It should be noted that the verbal changes written into Orwell's typescript are in the hand of the American sub-editor, 'M.F.M.' This typescript was returned to Orwell for his approval though without pages 1, 2, and 16, which were cut, and have not survived. It would not be appropriate to follow the shorter paragraphing of the U.S. version, because this would lead to a mixture of styles of paragraphing, Orwell's original having to be retained for the lengthy sections (totalling about one fifth of the whole essay) cut from the version printed in *The Atlantic Monthly*. Because one of the numbered sections falls in the middle of a paragraph, and a large portion of the first numbered section is cut, the numbering would be inappropriate here. For the record, section 2 began with 'The organised lying practised by totalitarian states . . .'; 3 with 'Literature has sometimes flourished under despotic regimes . . .'; 4 with 'It is not certain whether the effects of totalitarianism upon verse . . .'; and 5 with 'Meanwhile totalitarianism has not fully triumphed anywhere.'

Verbal changes are recorded in the notes; differences in spelling, punctuation, capitalisation, and paragraphing are not noted. The reading given first is that reproduced in this text. *P* = *Polemic*; *AM* = *The Atlantic Monthly*; *TS* = Typescript; Pf = Proof. Only the origin of a change is usually noted. Thus, if it is indicated that a change has been introduced into TS, then it is implied that it was made in Pf and *AM*, unless (as in 46) the change is not followed through. *Polemic* followed TS in its text and style very closely. Thus, Orwell's lack of initial capitals for 'civil war' in 'Spanish civil war' and his use of initial capitals for 'Displaced Persons' is followed by *Polemic*; *The Atlantic Monthly* adopted the opposite practice.

The marked-up typescript, the proof, and the letter to Cloud are reproduced by kind permission of the New York Public Library.

The essay was published in Polish in *Kultura* (Paris), 5, May 1948.

Fifty years after Orwell wrote this essay, 'the prevention of literature' at its most extreme was revealed in specific detail in *The KGB's Literary Archive* by Vitaly Shentalinsky, translated by John Crowfoot (1995). Some 1,500 writers perished at the hands of the NKVD and thousands of manuscripts were burnt.

About a year ago I attended a meeting of the P.E.N. Club, the occasion being the tercentenary of Milton's *Areopagitica*—a pamphlet, it may be remembered, in defence of freedom of the Press. Milton's famous phrase about the sin of 'killing' a book was printed on the leaflets advertising the meeting which had been circulated beforehand.

There were four speakers on the platform. One of them delivered a speech which did deal with the freedom of the Press, but only in relation to India; another said, hesitantly, and in very general terms, that liberty was a good thing; a third delivered an attack on the laws relating to obscenity in literature. The fourth devoted most of his speech to a defence of the Russian purges. Of the speeches from the body of the hall, some reverted to the question of obscenity and the laws that deal with it, others were simply eulogies of Soviet Russia. Moral liberty—the liberty to discuss sex questions frankly in print—seemed to be generally approved, but political liberty was not mentioned. Out of this concourse of several hundred people, perhaps half of whom were directly connected with the writing trade, there was not a single one who could point out that freedom of the Press, if it means anything at all, means the freedom to criticise and oppose. Significantly, no speaker quoted from the pamphlet which was ostensibly being commemorated. Nor was there any mention of the various books that have been 'killed' in this country and the United States during the war. In its net effect the meeting was a demonstration in favour of censorship.*

There was nothing particularly surprising in this. In our age, the idea of intellectual liberty is under attack from two directions. On the one side are its theoretical enemies, the apologists of totalitarianism, and on the other its immediate, practical enemies, monopoly and bureaucracy. Any writer or journalist who wants to retain his integrity finds himself thwarted by the general drift of society rather than by active persecution. The sort of things that are working against him are the concentration of the Press in the hands of a few rich men, the grip of monopoly on radio and the films, the unwillingness of the public to spend money on books, making it necessary for nearly every writer to earn part of his living by hackwork, the encroachment of official bodies like the M.O.I. and the British Council, which help the writer to keep alive but also waste his time and dictate his opinions, and the continuous war atmosphere of the past ten years, whose distorting effects no one has been able to escape. Everything in our age conspires to turn the writer, and every other kind of artist as well, into a minor official, working on themes handed to [him][1] from above and never telling what seems to him the whole of the truth. But in struggling against this fate he gets no help from his own side: that is, there is no large body of opinion which will assure him that he is in the right. In the past, at any rate throughout the Protestant centuries, the idea of rebellion and the idea of intellectual integrity were mixed up. A heretic—political, moral, religious, or æsthetic—was one who refused to outrage his own conscience. His outlook was summed up in the words of the Revivalist hymn:

Dare to be a Daniel,
Dare to stand alone;
Dare to have a purpose firm,
Dare to make it known.

To bring this hymn up to date one would have to add a "Don't" at the beginning of each line. For it is the peculiarity of our age that the rebels against the existing order, at any rate the most numerous and characteristic of them, are also rebelling against the idea of individual integrity. "Daring to stand alone" is ideologically criminal as well as practically dangerous. The independence of the writer and the artist is eaten away by vague economic forces, and at the same time it is undermined by those who should be its defenders. It is with the second process that I am concerned here.[2]

Freedom of speech[3] and of the Press are[4] usually attacked by arguments which are not worth bothering about. Anyone who has experience in[5] lecturing and debating knows them backwards.[6] Here I am not trying to deal

---

* It is fair to say that the P.E.N. Club celebrations, which lasted a week or more, did not always stick at quite the same level. I happened to strike a bad day. But an examination of the speeches (printed under the title *Freedom of Expression* [see 2764]) shows that almost nobody in our own day is able to speak out as roundly in favour of intellectual liberty as Milton could do 300 years ago—and this in spite of the fact Milton was writing in a period of civil war [Orwell's footnote].

with the familiar claim that freedom is an illusion, or with the claim that there is more freedom in totalitarian countries than in democratic ones, but with the much more tenable and dangerous proposition that freedom is undesirable and that intellectual honesty is a form of anti-social selfishness. Although[7] other aspects of the question[8] are usually in the foreground, the controversy over freedom of speech and of the Press is at bottom a controversy over the desirability, or otherwise,[9] of telling lies. What is really at issue is the right to report contemporary events truthfully, or as truthfully[10] as is consistent with the ignorance, bias and self-deception from which every observer necessarily suffers. In saying this I may seem to be saying that straightforward 'reportage'[11] is the only branch of literature that matters: but I will try to show later that at every literary level, and probably in every one of the arts, the same issue arises in more or less subtilised forms. Meanwhile, it is necessary to strip away the irrelevancies in which this controversy is usually wrapped up.

The enemies of intellectual liberty always try to present their case as a plea for discipline versus individualism. The issue truth-versus-untruth is as far as possible kept in the background. Although the point of emphasis may vary, the writer who refuses to sell his opinions is always branded as a mere egoist. He is accused, that is, either of wanting to shut himself up in an ivory tower, or of making an exhibitionist display of his own personality, or of resisting the inevitable current of history in an attempt to cling to unjustified privileges. The Catholic and the Communist are alike in assuming that an opponent cannot be both honest and intelligent. Each of them tacitly claims that 'the truth' has already been revealed, and that the heretic, if he is not simply a fool, is secretly aware of 'the truth' and merely resists it out of selfish motives. In Communist literature the attack on intellectual liberty is usually masked by oratory about "petty-bourgeois individualism," "the illusions of nineteenth-century liberalism", etc.,[12] and backed up by words of abuse such as "romantic" and "sentimental", which, since they do not have any agreed meaning, are difficult to answer. In this way the controversy is manœuvred away from its real issue. One can accept, and most enlightened people would accept, the Communist thesis that pure freedom will only exist in a classless society, and that one is most nearly free when one is working to bring about[13] such a society. But slipped in with this is the quite unfounded claim that the Communist party is itself aiming at the establishment of the classless society, and that in the U.S.S.R. this aim is actually on the way to being realised. If the first claim is allowed to entail the second, there is almost no assault on common sense and common decency that cannot be justified. But meanwhile, the real point has been dodged. Freedom of the intellect means the freedom to report what one has seen, heard, and felt, and not to be obliged to fabricate imaginary facts and feelings. The familiar tirades against "escapism", "individualism", "romanticism" and so forth, are merely a forensic device, the aim of which is to make the perversion of history seem respectable.

Fifteen years ago, when one defended the freedom of the intellect, one had to defend it against Conservatives, against Catholics, and to some extent—

for in England[14] they were not of great importance—against Fascists. To-day one has to defend it against Communists and 'fellow travellers'. One ought not to exaggerate the direct influence of the small English Communist party, but there can be no question about the poisonous effect of the Russian *mythos* on English intellectual life. Because of it, known facts are suppressed and distorted to such an extent as to make it doubtful whether a true history of our times can ever be written. Let me give just one instance out of the hundreds that could be cited. When Germany collapsed, it was found that very large numbers of Soviet Russians—mostly, no doubt, from non-political motives—had changed sides and were fighting for the Germans. Also, a small but not negligible proportion of the Russian prisoners and Displaced Persons refused to go back to the U.S.S.R., and some of them, at least, were repatriated against their will. These facts, known to many journalists on the spot, went almost unmentioned in the British Press, while at the same time Russophile publicists in England continued to justify the purges and deportations of 1936–38 by claiming that the U.S.S.R. "had no quislings". The fog of lies and misinformation that surrounds such subjects as the Ukraine famine, the Spanish civil war, Russian policy in Poland, and so forth, is not due entirely to conscious dishonesty, but any writer or journalist who is fully sympathetic to the U.S.S.R.—sympathetic, that is, in the way the Russians themselves would want him to be—does have to acquiesce in deliberate falsification on important issues. I have before me what must be a very rare pamphlet, written by Maxim Litvinoff in 1918 and outlining the recent events in the Russian Revolution. It makes no mention of Stalin, but gives high praise to Trotsky, and also to Zinoviev, Kamenev, and others. What could be the attitude of even the most intellectually scrupulous Communist towards such a pamphlet? At best, he would take the obscurantist attitude that[15] it is an undesirable document and better suppressed. And if for some reason it should be[16] decided to issue a garbled version of the pamphlet, denigrating Trotsky and inserting references to Stalin, no Communist who remained faithful to his party could protest. Forgeries almost as gross as this have been committed in recent years. But the significant thing is not that they happen, but that even when they are known,[17] they provoke no reaction from the Left-wing intelligentsia as a whole. The argument that to tell the truth would be "inopportune" or would "play into the hands of" somebody or other is felt to be unanswerable, and few people are bothered by the prospect that[18] the lies which they condone will get[19] out of the newspapers and into the history books.

The organised lying practised by totalitarian states is not, as is sometimes claimed, a temporary expedient of the same nature as military deception. It is something integral to totalitarianism, something that would still continue even if concentration camps and secret police forces had ceased to be necessary. Among intelligent Communists there is an underground legend to the effect that although the Russian government is obliged now to deal in lying propaganda, frame-up trials, and so forth, it is secretly recording the facts[20] and will publish them at some future time. We can, I believe, be quite certain that this is not the case, because the mentality implied by such an action is that of a liberal historian who believes that the past cannot be altered and that a correct knowledge of history is valuable as a matter of course. From the totalitarian point of view history is something to be created rather than learned. A totalitarian state is in effect a theocracy, and its ruling caste, in order to keep its position, has to be thought of as infallible. But since, in practice, no one is infallible, it is frequently necessary to rearrange past events in order to show that this or that mistake was not made, or that this or that imaginary triumph actually happened. Then, again, every major change in policy demands a corresponding change of doctrine and a revaluation of prominent historical figures. This kind of thing happens everywhere, but clearly it is[21] likelier to lead to outright falsification in societies where only one opinion is permissible at any given moment. Totalitarianism demands, in fact, the continuous alteration of the past, and in the long run probably demands a disbelief in the very existence of objective truth. The friends of totalitarianism in this country[22] usually tend to argue that since absolute truth is not attainable, a big lie is no worse than a little lie. It is pointed out that all historical records are biased and inaccurate, or, on the other hand, that modern physics[23] has proved that what seems to us the real world is an illusion, so that to believe in the evidence of one's senses is simply vulgar philistinism. A totalitarian society which succeeded in perpetuating itself would probably set up a schizophrenic system of thought, in which the laws of common sense held good in everyday life and in certain exact sciences, but could be disregarded by the politician, the historian, and the sociologist. Already there are countless people who would think it scandalous to falsify a scientific textbook, but would see nothing wrong in falsifying a historical fact. It is at the point where literature and politics cross that totalitarianism exerts its greatest pressure on the intellectual. The exact sciences are not, at this date, menaced to anything like the same extent. This difference[24] partly accounts for the fact that in all countries it is easier for the scientists than for the writers to line up behind their respective governments.

To keep the matter in perspective, let me repeat what I said at the beginning of this essay: that in England the immediate enemies of truthfulness, and hence of freedom of thought, are the Press lords, the film magnates, and the bureaucrats, but that on a long view the weakening of the desire for liberty among the intellectuals themselves is the most serious symptom of all.[25] It may seem that all this time I have been talking about the effects of censorship, not on literature as a whole, but merely on one department of political journalism. Granted that Soviet Russia constitutes a sort of forbidden area in the British Press, granted that issues like Poland, the Spanish civil war, the Russo-German pact, and so forth, are debarred from serious discussion, and that if you possess information that conflicts with the prevailing orthodoxy you are expected either to distort it or to keep quiet about it—granted all this, why should literature in the wider sense be affected? Is every writer a politician, and is every book necessarily a work of straightforward 'reportage'?[26] Even under the tightest dictatorship, cannot the individual writer remain free inside his own mind and distil or disguise his unorthodox ideas in such a way that the authorities will be too stupid to recognise them?

And[27] if the writer himself is in agreement with the prevailing orthodoxy, why should it have a cramping effect on him? Is not literature, or any of the arts, likeliest to flourish in societies in which there are no major conflicts of opinion and no sharp distinctions[28] between the artist and his audience? Does one have to assume that every writer is a rebel, or even that a writer as such is an exceptional person?

Whenever one attempts to defend intellectual liberty against the claims of totalitarianism, one meets with these arguments in one form or another. They are based on a complete misunderstanding of what literature is, and how—one should perhaps rather say *why*[29]—it comes into being. They assume that a writer is either a mere entertainer or else a venal hack who can switch from one line of propaganda to another as easily as an organ grinder changes[30] tunes. But after all, how is it that books ever come to be written? Above a quite low level, literature is an attempt to influence the views[31] of one's contemporaries by recording experience. And so far as freedom of expression is concerned, there is not much difference between a mere journalist and the most 'unpolitical' imaginative writer. The journalist is unfree, and is conscious of unfreedom, when he is forced to write lies or suppress what seems to him important news: the imaginative writer is unfree when he has to falsify his subjective feelings, which from his point of view are facts. He may distort and caricature reality in order to make his meaning clearer, but he cannot misrepresent the scenery of his own mind: he cannot say with any conviction that he likes what he dislikes, or believes what he disbelieves. If he is forced to do so, the only result is that his creative faculties dry up. Nor can the imaginative writer[32] solve the problem by keeping away from controversial topics. There is no such thing as genuinely non-political literature, and least of all in an age like our own, when fears, hatreds, and loyalties of a directly political kind are near to the surface of everyone's consciousness. Even a single tabu[33] can have an all-round crippling effect upon the mind, because there is always the danger that any thought which is freely followed up may lead to the forbidden thought. It follows that the atmosphere of totalitarianism is deadly to any kind of prose writer, though a poet, at any rate a lyric poet, might possibly find it breathable. And in any totalitarian society that survives for more than a couple of generations, it is probable that prose literature, of the kind that has existed during the past four hundred years, must actually *come to an end*.[34]

Literature has sometimes flourished under despotic regimes, but, as has often been pointed out, the despotisms of the past were not totalitarian. Their repressive apparatus was always inefficient, their ruling classes were usually either corrupt or apathetic or half-liberal in outlook, and the prevailing religious doctrines usually worked against perfectionism and the notion of human infallibility. Even so it is broadly true that prose literature has reached its highest levels in periods of democracy and free speculation. What is new in totalitarianism is that its doctrines are not only unchallengeable but also unstable. They have to be accepted on pain of damnation, but on the other hand they are always liable to be altered at a moment's notice. Consider, for example, the various attitudes, completely incompatible with one another, which an English Communist or 'fellow traveller' has had to adopt towards the war between Britain and Germany. For years before September 1939 he was expected to be in a continuous stew about "the horrors of Nazism" and to twist everything he wrote into a denunciation of Hitler;[35] after September 1939, for twenty months, he had to believe that Germany was more sinned against than sinning, and the word 'Nazi', at least so far as print went, had to drop right out of his vocabulary. Immediately after hearing the 8 o'clock news bulletin on the morning of June 22, 1941, he had to start believing once again that Nazism was the most hideous evil the world had ever seen. Now, it is easy for a politician to make such changes: for a writer the case is somewhat different. If he is to switch his allegiance at exactly the right moment, he must either tell lies about his subjective feelings, or else suppress them altogether. In either case he has destroyed his dynamo. Not only will ideas refuse to come to him, but the very words he uses will seem to stiffen under his touch. Political writing in our time consists almost entirely of prefabricated phrases bolted together like the pieces of a child's Meccano set.[36] It is the unavoidable result of self-censorship. To write in plain, vigorous language one has to think fearlessly, and if one thinks fearlessly one cannot be politically orthodox. It might be otherwise in an 'age of faith', when the prevailing orthodoxy has been long established and is not taken too seriously. In that case it would be possible, or might be possible, for large areas of one's mind to remain unaffected by what one officially believed. Even so, it is worth noticing that prose literature almost disappeared during the only age of faith that Europe has ever enjoyed. Throughout the whole of the Middle Ages there was almost no imaginative prose literature and very little in the way of historical writing: and the intellectual leaders of society expressed their most serious thoughts in a dead language which barely altered during a thousand years.

Totalitarianism, however, does not so much promise an age of faith as an age of schizophrenia. A society becomes totalitarian when its structure becomes flagrantly artificial: that is, when its ruling class has lost its function but succeeds in clinging to power by force or fraud. Such a society, no matter how long it persists, can never afford to become either tolerant or intellectually stable. It can never permit either the truthful recording of facts, or the emotional sincerity, that literary creation demands. But to be corrupted by totalitarianism one does not have to live in a totalitarian country. The mere prevalence of certain ideas can spread a poison[37] that makes one subject after another impossible for literary purposes. Wherever there is an enforced orthodoxy—or even two orthodoxies, as often happens—good writing stops. This was well illustrated by the Spanish civil war. To many English intellectuals the war was a deeply moving experience, but not an experience about which they could write sincerely. There were only two things that you were allowed to say, and both of them were palpable lies: as a result, the war produced acres of print but almost nothing worth reading.

It is not certain whether the effects of totalitarianism upon verse need be so deadly as its effects on prose. There is a whole series of converging reasons why it is somewhat easier for a poet than for a prose writer to feel at home in an authoritarian society. To begin with, bureaucrats and other 'practical' men usually despise the poet too deeply to be much interested in what he is saying. Secondly, what the poet is saying—that is, what his poem 'means' if translated into prose—is relatively unimportant even to himself. The thought contained in a poem is always simple, and is no more the primary purpose of the poem than the anecdote is the primary purpose of a picture. A poem is an arrangement of sounds and associations, as a painting is an arrangement of brush-marks. For short snatches, indeed, as in the refrain of a song, poetry can even dispense with meaning altogether. It is therefore fairly easy for a poet to keep away from dangerous subjects and avoid uttering heresies: and even when he does utter them, they may escape notice. But above all, good verse, unlike good prose, is not necessarily an individual product. Certain kinds of poems, such as ballads, or, on the other hand, very artificial verse forms, can be composed co-operatively by groups of people. Whether the ancient English and Scottish ballads were originally produced by individuals, or by the people at large, is disputed; but at any rate they are non-individual in the sense that they constantly change in passing from mouth to mouth. Even in print no two versions of a ballad are ever quite the same. Many primitive peoples compose verse communally. Someone begins to improvise, probably accompanying himself on a musical instrument, somebody else chips in with a line or a rhyme when the first singer breaks down, and so the process continues until there exists a whole song or ballad which has no identifiable author.

In prose, this kind of intimate collaboration is quite impossible. Serious prose, in any case, has to be composed in solitude, whereas the excitement of being part of a group is actually an aid to certain kinds of versification. Verse—and perhaps good verse of its kind, though it would not be the highest kind— might survive under even the most inquisitorial regime. Even in a society where liberty and individuality had been extinguished, there would still be need either for patriotic songs and heroic ballads celebrating victories, or for elaborate exercises in flattery: and these are the kinds of poetry[38] that can be written to order, or composed communally, without necessarily lacking artistic value. Prose is a different matter, since the prose writer cannot narrow the range of his thoughts without killing his inventiveness. But the history of totalitarian societies, or of groups of people who have adopted the totalitarian outlook, suggests that loss of liberty is inimical to *all* [39] forms of literature. German literature almost disappeared during the Hitler regime, and the case was not much better in Italy. Russian literature, so far as one can judge by translations, has deteriorated markedly since the early days of the Revolution, though some of the verse appears to be better than the prose. Few if any Russian novels that it is possible to take seriously have been translated for about fifteen years. In western Europe and America large sections of the literary intelligentsia have either passed through the Communist party or been warmly sympathetic to it, but this whole leftward movement has produced extraordinarily few books worth reading. Orthodox Catholicism, again, seems to have a crushing effect upon certain literary forms, especially the novel. During a period of three hundred years, how many people have been at once good novelists and good Catholics? The fact is that certain themes cannot be celebrated in words, and tyranny is one of them. No one ever wrote a good book in praise of the Inquisition. Poetry *might*[40] survive in a totalitarian age, and certain arts or half-arts, such as architecture, might even find tyranny beneficial, but the prose writer would have no choice between silence and death. Prose literature as we know it is the product of rationalism, of the Protestant centuries, of the autonomous individual. And the destruction of intellectual liberty cripples the journalist, the sociological writer, the historian, the novelist, the critic, and the poet, in that order. In the future it is possible that a new kind of literature, not involving individual feeling or truthful observation, may arise, but no such thing is at present imaginable. It seems much likelier that if the liberal culture that we have lived in since the Renaissance actually comes to an end, the literary art will perish with it.

Of course, print will continue to be used, and it is interesting to speculate what kinds of reading matter would survive in a rigidly totalitarian society. Newspapers will presumably continue until television technique reaches a higher level, but apart from newspapers it is doubtful even now whether the great mass of people in the industrialised countries feel the need for any kind of literature. They are unwilling, at any rate, to spend anywhere near as much on reading matter as they spend on several other recreations. Probably novels and stories will be completely superseded by film and radio productions. Or perhaps some kind of low-grade sensational fiction will survive, produced by a sort of conveyor-belt process that reduces human initiative to the minimum.

It would probably not be beyond human ingenuity to write books by machinery. But a sort of mechanising process can already be seen at work in the film and radio, in publicity and propaganda, and in the lower reaches of journalism. The Disney films, for instance, are produced by what is essentially a factory process, the work being done partly mechanically and partly by teams of artists who have to subordinate their individual style. Radio features are commonly written by tired hacks to whom the subject and the manner of treatment are dictated beforehand: even so, what they write is merely a kind of raw material to be chopped into shape by producers and censors. So also with the innumerable books and pamphlets commissioned by government departments. Even more machine-like is the production of short stories, serials, and poems for the very cheap magazines. Papers such as the *Writer* abound with advertisements of Literary Schools, all of them offering you readymade plots at a few shillings a time. Some, together with the plot, supply the opening and closing sentences of each chapter. Others furnish you with a sort of algebraical formula by the use of which you can construct your plots for yourself. Others offer packs of cards marked with characters and situations, which have only to be shuffled and dealt in order to produce ingenious stories automatically. It is probably in some such way that the literature of a totalitarian society would be produced, if literature were still felt to be necessary. Imagination—even consciousness, so far as possible—would be eliminated from the process of writing. Books would be planned in their broad lines by bureaucrats, and would pass through so many hands that when finished they would be no more an individual product than a Ford car at the end of the assembly line. It goes without saying that anything so produced would be rubbish; but anything that was not rubbish would endanger the structure of the state. As for the surviving literature of the past, it would have to be suppressed or at least elaborately rewritten.[41]

Meanwhile totalitarianism has not fully triumphed anywhere. Our own society is still, broadly speaking, liberal. To exercise your right of free speech you have to fight against economic pressure and against strong sections of public opinion, but not, as yet, against a secret police force. You can say or print almost anything so long as you are willing to do it in a hole-and-corner way. But what is sinister, as I said at the beginning of this essay,[42] is that the conscious enemies of liberty are those to whom liberty ought to mean most. The public[43] do not care about the matter one way or the other. They are not in favour of persecuting the heretic, and they will not exert themselves to defend him. They are at once too sane and too stupid to acquire the totalitarian outlook. The direct, conscious attack on intellectual decency comes from the intellectuals themselves.

It is possible that the Russophile intelligentsia, if they had not succumbed to that particular[44] myth, would have succumbed to another of much the same kind. But at any rate the Russian myth is there, and the corruption it causes stinks. When one sees highly educated men looking on indifferently at oppression and persecution, one wonders which to despise more, their cynicism or their short-sightedness. Many scientists, for example, are uncritical[45] admirers of the U.S.S.R. They appear to think that the destruction of liberty is of no importance so long as their own line of work is for the moment unaffected. The U.S.S.R. is a large, rapidly developing country which has acute need of scientific workers and, consequently, treats them generously. Provided that they steer clear of dangerous subjects such as psychology, scientists are privileged persons. Writers, on the other hand, are viciously persecuted. It is true that literary prostitutes like Ilya Ehrenburg or Alexei Tolstoy are paid huge sums of money, but the only thing which is of any value to the writer as such—his freedom of expression—is taken away from him. Some, at least, of the English scientists who speak so enthusiasti-cally of the opportunities enjoyed by scientists in Russia are capable of understanding this. But their reflection appears to be: "Writers are persecuted in Russia. So what? I am not a writer". They do not see that any[46] attack on intellectual liberty, and on the concept of objective truth, threatens in the long run every department of thought.

For the moment the totalitarian state tolerates the scientist because it needs him. Even in Nazi Germany, scientists, other than Jews, were relatively well treated, and the German scientific community, as a whole, offered no resistance to Hitler. At this stage of history, even the most autocratic ruler is forced to take account of physical reality, partly because of the lingering-on of liberal habits of thought, partly because of the need to prepare for war. So long as physical reality cannot be altogether ignored, so long as two and two have to make four when you are, for example, drawing the blueprint of an aeroplane, the scientist has his function, and can even be allowed a measure of liberty. His awakening will come later, when the totalitarian state is firmly established. Meanwhile, if he wants to safeguard the integrity of science, it is his job to develop some kind of solidarity with his literary colleagues and not regard it as a matter of indifference when writers are silenced or driven to suicide, and newspapers systematically falsified.

But however it may be with the physical sciences, or with music, painting, and architecture, it is—as I have tried to show—certain that literature is doomed if liberty of thought perishes. Not only is it doomed in any country which retains a totalitarian structure; but any writer who adopts the totalitarian outlook, who finds excuses for persecution and the falsification of reality, thereby destroys himself as a writer. There is no way out of this. No tirades against "individualism" and "the ivory tower", no pious platitudes to the effect that "true individuality is only attained through identification with the community", can get over the fact that a bought mind is a spoiled mind. Unless spontaneity enters at some point or another, literary creation is impossible, and language itself becomes ossified. At some time in the future, if the human mind becomes something totally different from what it now is, we may learn to separate literary creation from intellectual honesty. At present we know only that the imagination, like certain wild animals, will not breed in captivity. Any writer or journalist who denies that fact—and nearly all the current praise of the Soviet Union contains or implies such a denial—is, in effect, demanding his own destruction.[47]

1. [him]] *omitted from* P; *this section not reproduced in AM nor found in TS*
2. *From the start of the essay to . . .* I am concerned here. *is omitted from* Pf, AM; *first two pages of* TS *were not returned to Orwell as, with first two-thirds of p. 3, they were omitted from AM (and surviving p. 3 is so marked for omission). These two pages of* TS, *and p. 16 (see note 41) appear now to be lost.*
3. speech] thought   P; *revision written into* TS
4. are] *The sub-editor of AM notes on* TS, *'should be a singular verb,' referring back to* Freedom. *Orwell evidently had in mind the silent repetition of* Freedom *before* of the Press. *Suggestion not taken up.*
5. in] of   P; *revision written into* TS
6. backwards] off backwards   P; *revision marked in* TS
7. Although] Though   AM; Pf *has* Although
8. question] matter   AM; Pf *has* question
9. otherwise] Pf *suggests* undesirability *which Orwell rejected*
10. truthfully] AM *sub-editor notes on* TS; *'noun instead of adverb needed?' Ignored.*
11. 'reportage'] TS *suggests omission of quotation marks;* Pf *shows them as set but marked for omission with query; Orwell comments, 'I should leave "reportage" in quotes unless this has ceased to be a technical expression in the U.S.A.   G.O.' They were omitted from AM. See also n. 26.*
12. etc.] TS *suggests 'and so forth as elsewhere?' Ignored.*
13. bring about such a society] bring such a society about   P; *transposition marked in* TS
14. in England] *followed* importance *in* P; *transposition suggested in* TS *and* Pf; *accepted by Orwell,* Pf
15. at best . . . that] the obscurantist attitude of saying that   P; *revision written into* TS
16. should be] were   P; *revision written into* TS
17. known.] known about   P; *revision written into* TS
18. that] of   P; *revision written into* TS
19. will get] getting   P; *revision written into* TS

20. facts] true facts   *P; omission suggested in TS and marked in Pf*
21. clearly it is] is clearly   *P; revision marked into TS*
22. this country] England   *AM; need to specify 'which country?' suggested in TS and* England *written into TS*
23. modern physics] *TS and Pf both have a sub-editor's note, 'Author, do you mean "modern physics"? Whose physics? Physics is usually thought of as one of the "exact sciences."' Orwell replied, on Pf only, 'Yes, I mean "physics". See letter. I have also cabled about this. G.O.' For Orwell's letter, see 2791; the cable may not have been sent.*
24. This difference] This   *P; difference written into TS*
25. To keep the matter in perspective . . . most serious symptom of all.] *cut marked in TS and passage omitted from Pf, AM*
26. 'reportage'] *TS amended from single to double quotes (presumably by AM sub-editor); Pf has* "reportage"; *AM has* reportage; *see also n. 11*
27. And] And, in any case,   *P; cut marked in TS*
28. distinctions] distinction   *P; plural suggested in TS, Pf; Orwell's acceptance noted in Pf*
29. why] WHY   *TS; bold in P; TS marked for italic, which AM prints*
30. changes] changing   *P; revision written into TS*
31. views] viewpoints   *P; revision written into TS*
32. the imaginative writer] he   *P; revision written into TS*
33. tabu] taboo   Pf, AM; tabu *written into TS; TS (and P) gave Orwell's spelling,* taboo *(which appears in* Burmese Days)
34. come to an end] *bold in P; TS marked for italic; italic in AM*
35. *The AM sub-editor queried the date of the Soviet-Nazi Pact, giving 'August 23' [1939]. Orwell did not follow this suggestion. It was signed in Moscow by Molotov and Ribbentrop on 23 August 1939 and made public on 24/25 August. However, its Secret Protocol, which dealt with the division of Eastern Europe between the Soviet Union and Germany, was kept secret until discovered by the Americans in Nazi archives at the end of the war; it was not officially published until 1948. Soviet judges at the Nuremberg Trials refused to admit as evidence anything that referred to this Secret Protocol. Another Secret Protocol was signed by the Soviet Union and Germany on 28 September 1939; that settled Germany's eastern frontier. The American sub-editor was right to point out that changes in attitudes of western communists and fellow travellers should date from 23 August, but evidently Orwell thought September 1939 more clearly represented to general memory the communist change of line.*
36. *TS is here annotated 'OK,' presumably by sub-editor and probably referring to Meccano set*
37. a poison] a kind of poison   *P; revision written into TS*
38. poetry] poem   *P; revision written into TS*
39. all] *bold in P; marked for italic in TS; italic in AM*
40. might] *bold in P; marked for italic in TS; italic in AM*
41. Of course, print will continue to be used . . . at least elaborately rewritten.] *omitted from Pf, AM; p. 16 removed from text, also pp. 1 and 2, when TS returned to Orwell for checking and top two-thirds of p. 17 marked for omission. At the end of this cut, 'accepted' has been written, possibly by Orwell.*
42. , as I said at the beginning of this essay,] *marked to be cut from TS and omitted from Pf, AM. This refers back to the penultimate sentence of the opening passage dropped from AM.*
43. public] big public   *P; cut marked in TS*
44. that particular] the Russian   *AM; no change shown in TS, Pf*
45. uncritical] the uncritical   *P; revision marked in TS*
46. any] ANY   *TS; bold in P; TS marked for italic but Pf has* ANY; *change to italic made in AM*
47. Pf, *AM have:* 'English novelist and critic, George Orwell served as a volunteer in the Spanish Civil War, and in fighting against Franco came to detest tyranny, whether of Communist or Fascist origin. His latest novel, *Animal Farm*, was a sweeping success last autumn, and in it, as in this vigorous essay, he derides the captivity of the Party line.' *Against this in Pf is written,* 'Facts OK?,' *against which is written* 'O.K.,' *presumably by Orwell.*

2793. To Leonard Moore

14 November 1945   Typewritten

27 B Canonbury Square
Islington
London N I

Dear Mr Moore,
I enclose the two contracts duly signed, also the letter from the Portuguese people. From their advertisements I infer they are an ordinary publishing house.
   I haven't another proof copy of the essays, but Warburg must have plenty. As soon as I can find time to go in there I'll pick up a copy and make the two important corrections before sending it on to you.

Yours sincerely
Eric Blair

2794. Review of *The True Conan Doyle* by Aerian Conan Doyle; with a Preface by General Sir Hubert Gough

Manchester Evening News, 15 November 1945

The late Sir Arthur Conan Doyle was not a great writer. Indeed, he was not even a writer whom it is possible to take seriously, and yet he did something that no one else in our time has succeeded in doing: he created one of those characters that can escape from the pages and become a household word in the remotest parts of the earth.

And though the Sherlock Holmes stories are by far his greatest achievements, his other books, at least, have the merit of covering an extraordinarily wide range of subjects. He wrote detailed and accurate histories of the Boer War and the war of 1914–18, several lively and well-documented historical romances, an excellent boxing novel, some reminiscences of medical life, and numerous adventure stories, besides devoting many years to psychical research.

Clearly he was a man of unusual mental make-up, and it is interesting to gather some fresh facts about his private life and family history.

This pamphlet, written by his son, is not a biography. It is an "answer" to the recent biography by Mr. Hesketh Pearson,[1] and it has the air of pained indignation that such writings are apt to have. One would gather from it that Conan Doyle came nearer to perfection than it is given to ordinary mortals to do, and there are some of his activities—for instance, his spiritualism—which his son is inclined to soft-pedal.

Nevertheless one can dig a lot of facts out of these 23 pages, and there is at least one piece of information which will be cherished by Sherlock Holmes fans all the world over.

Conan Doyle was of Irish stock and was brought up as a Catholic, but he later lapsed from the faith, and it seems to have left curiously little mark on his intellect. He started life as a doctor and his early struggles produced not only the excellent stories in "Round the Red Lamp," but a book written in diary form which has now become a rarity and which is of great interest. His son is at pains to emphasise that his ancestry was originally noble and that his upbringing was "entirely feudal."

Even in childhood he was an expert on heraldry (one of his uncles incidentally compiled the "Official Baronetage of England") and no doubt his early reading partly accounted for his facility in writing historical romances. He was a man of violent temper, quixotically generous, and punctilious in his manners to an almost unheard-of degree.

On one occasion he smashed his son's pipe to pieces because he had committed the offence of smoking it in the presence of women. On another he took his shoes off and gave them to a tramp. At the age of 70 he set out to thrash with an umbrella someone who had insulted him. And, as is well known, he spent years working for the release of the wrongfully convicted Oscar Slater, refusing to make any profit from his writings on the subject. He also, according to his son, sacrificed a peerage rather than withdraw his public championship of spiritualism.

Conan Doyle was a gigantic, powerful man, of enormous energy, both physical and intellectual. He excelled at many kinds of sport, especially boxing.

There is a story—and it is a story that ought to be true, even if it is not—of an old prize-fighter to whom, on his death-bed Doyle's "Rodney Stone" was being read aloud by some charitable visitor. At the climax of the big fight the dying man was so excited that he raised himself to a sitting position and exclaimed, "By God, he's got him." This tribute, it is said, pleased Conan Doyle more than any praise he ever received from the literary critics.

Doyle was capable of immense bouts of work, and before writing "The White Company" he spent a year reading sixty-five works of reference dealing with the fourteenth century. He was also, although absent-minded, very observant of details, and his son claims that Sherlock Holmes was in the main a self-portrait and not, as is usually thought, based on Dr. Joseph Bell, under whom Doyle had studied in his medical days.

Doyle used even, it appears, to work in a dressing-gown similar to Holmes's, though it is not recorded that he kept his tobacco in a Persian slipper. One surprising and hitherto unpublished fact which his son reveals is that Dr. Watson was conceived before Holmes. There exists an unprinted draft of "A Study In Scarlet" (its first title was "The Angels of Darkness") in which Holmes does not appear. It would be worth something to see Watson tackle a mystery single-handed, and it is to be hoped that the manuscript will be printed when paper becomes more plentiful.

It is a pity that Doyle's activities as a spiritualist, although not actually unmentioned in this pamphlet, are somewhat slurred over. His son is on the defensive when it comes to this subject, and anxious to clear his father of the charge of credulity.

"My father began his investigations," he says, "as a bitter opponent of any

383

belief in a life after death, and—this is of paramount importance—he refused to pronounce any final judgment before he had devoted *thirty-three* years to his researches." Possibly: still, the fact remains that Doyle was sometimes deceived in very crude ways, as in the notorious case of the "fairies,"[2] and championed mediums who were almost unmistakable frauds. Combined with his wide knowledge and great acuteness of mind, this blind spot on one subject makes an interesting psychological puzzle, and any serious study of Doyle ought to attempt a solution of it.

Doyle's many-sided life was well symbolised by the litter of objects on his writing table, among which his son lists—"Boer War medals and Mauser bullets, Greeks coins, dum-dum bullets from a German sniper, the tooth of an ichthyosaurus, an Iron Cross, ancient Egyptian statuettes, a large crystalline growth from the stomach of a whale, pieces of Roman glass and pottery, and a vast coin gripped in the lava that destroyed Pompeii."

It is evident that he was a very lovable man and he would still seem an interesting one even if he had not written "Sherlock Holmes." But there is need of a definitive[3] biography of him, a biography which would be neither patronising, nor, like the present pamphlet, simply a labour of piety.[4]

[Fee: £8.8.0; 14.11.45]

1. Orwell's review prompted Hesketh Pearson to write the following letter, which the *Manchester Evening News* published on 27 November 1945:
   'In an article which appeared in your issue of November 15 Mr. George Orwell implied that my biography of Conan Doyle was "patronising." He also stated that Doyle "was not even a writer whom it is possible to take seriously." But as I took Doyle quite seriously as a writer in my book it seems to me that Mr. Orwell's attitude is patronising, not mine.'
2. In 1920 Doyle (and many others) was deceived that two teenage girls at Cottingley, near Bradford, had been photographed with fairies in their garden. One of them, Elsie Wright, admitted the hoax in 1983.
3. definitive] set as 'definite.' The error may be Orwell's—compare *2687, n. 2.*
4. The sections of this review were separated by small representations of three Sherlock Holmes deerstalker hats and three pipes, used alternately.

2795. To Katharine, Duchess of Atholl

15 November 1945   Typewritten; carbon copy

27 B Canonbury Square
Islington
London N 1

Dear Duchess of Atholl,[1]
I have only just received your letter dated November 13th.

I am afraid I cannot speak for the League for European Freedom. I could easily get out of it by saying that the date is impossible or—what is quite true—that I know nothing about Jugoslavia, but I prefer to tell you plainly that I am not in agreement with the League's ultimate objectives as I understand them. I went to the first public meeting, or one of the first, and wrote something about it in "Tribune"[2] which you may have seen. Certainly

Confidence

what is said on your platforms is more truthful than the lying propaganda to be found in most of the press, but I cannot associate myself with an essentially Conservative body which claims to defend democracy in Europe but has nothing to say about British imperialism. It seems to me that one can only denounce the crimes now being committed in Poland, Jugoslavia etc. if one is equally insistent on ending Britain's unwanted rule in India. I belong to the Left and must work inside it, much as I hate Russian totalitarianism and its poisonous influence in this country.

Yours truly
[Unsigned]
George Orwell

The Duchess's invitation has survived and also her response to Orwell's letter. Writing on 23 November 1945, she thanked Orwell for his frankness and explained that only one meeting had lacked a Labour speaker and then only because the League was unable to find one. She went on:

> I note what you say about the limitation of our work to Europe, but surely, to restore freedom to countries who have enjoyed it and therefore realise how precious it is, is something very different from joining in a task which is already being undertaken by our Government—i.e that of helping the various countries of the British Commonwealth and Empire towards self-government. I want personal freedom before the law for everyone everywhere, but just as I do not think children or young people are ready for a share in self-Government, so I think we have to recognise that there are races in the Empire which are more youthful than our own in these matters, and therefore must be led gradually along the path that leads to self-rule.

1. The Duchess of Atholl (1874–1960), a Unionist M.P., 1923–38, became in 1924 one of the first two women to be a minister in a British government. She was known as 'The Red Duchess' for her very strong anti-Franco feelings during the Spanish civil war. Her book *Searchlight on Spain* was published as a Penguin Special (1938); for Orwell's review of it, see *469*. Throughout her life she campaigned for various 'causes.'
2. See 'As I Please,' 56, 26 January 1945, *2609*.

2796. Review of *The Prussian Officer* by D. H. Lawrence

Tribune, 16 November 1945

Reviews ought not to consist of personal reminiscences, but perhaps it is worth recording how I first became acquainted with D. H. Lawrence's work, because it happened that I read him before I had heard of him, and the qualities which then impressed me were probably the essential ones.

In 1919 I went into my schoolmaster's study for some purpose, and, not finding him there, picked up a magazine with a blue cover which was on the table. I was then sixteen and wallowing in Georgian poetry. My idea of a good poem would have been Rupert Brooke's *Grantchester*. As soon as I opened the magazine I was completely overwhelmed by a poem which describes a woman standing in the kitchen and watching her husband approaching across the fields. On the way he takes a rabbit out of a snare and kills it. Then he comes in, throws the dead rabbit on the table, and, his hands still stinking of rabbit's fur, takes the woman in his arms. In a sense she hates him, but she is utterly swallowed up in him. More than the sexual encounter, the "beauty of Nature" which Lawrence deeply felt, but which he was also able to turn on and off like a tap, impressed me; especially the lines (referring to a flower):

> Then her bright breast she will uncover
> And yield her honeydrop to her lover.

But I failed to notice the name of the author, or even of the magazine, which must have been the *English Review*.[1]

Four or five years later, still not having heard of Lawrence, I got hold of the volume of short stories now reprinted as a Penguin. Both "The Prussian Officer" and "The Thorn in the Flesh" impressed me deeply. What struck me was not so much Lawrence's horror and hatred of military discipline, as his understanding of its nature. Something told me that he had never been a soldier, and yet he could project himself into the atmosphere of an army, and the German army at that. He had built all this up, I reflected, from watching a few German soldiers walking about in some garrison town. From another story, "The White Stocking" (also in this collection, though I think I read it later), I deduced the moral that women behave better if they get a sock on the jaw occasionally.

Clearly there is more in Lawrence than this, but I think these first impacts left me with a broadly true picture of him. He was in essence a lyric poet, and an undisciplined enthusiasm for "Nature," i.e., the surface of the earth, was one of his principal qualities, though it has been much less noticed than his preoccupation with sex. And on top of this he had the power of understanding, or seeming to understand, people totally different from himself, such as farmers, gamekeepers, clergymen and soldiers—one might add coalminers, for though Lawrence himself had worked in the pit at the age of thirteen,[2] clearly he was not a typical miner. His stories are a kind of lyric poem, produced by just looking at some alien, inscrutable human being and suddenly experiencing an intense imaginative vision of his inner life.

How true these visions were is debatable. Like some Russian writers of the nineteenth century, Lawrence often seems to by-pass the novelist's problem by making all his characters equally sensitive. All the people in his stories, even those to whom he is hostile, seem to experience the same kind of emotions, everyone can make contact with everyone else, and class barriers, in the form in which we know them, are almost obliterated. Yet he does often seem to have an extraordinary power of knowing imaginatively something that he could not have known by observation. Somewhere in one of his books he remarks that when you shoot at a wild animal, the action is not the same as shooting at a target. You do not look along the sights: you aim by an instinctive movement of the whole body, and it is as though your will were driving the bullet forward. This is quite true, and yet I do not suppose Lawrence had ever shot at a wild animal. Or consider the death scene at the end of "England my England" (which is not in the present collection, unfortunately), Lawrence had never been in circumstances remotely similar to those he was describing. He had merely had a private vision of the feelings of a soldier under fire. Perhaps it is true to experience, perhaps not: but at least it is emotionally true, and therefore convincing.

With few exceptions Lawrence's full-length novels are, it is generally admitted, difficult to get through. In the short stories his faults do not matter so much, because a short story can be purely lyrical, whereas a novel has to take account of probability and has to be cold-bloodedly constructed. In *The Prussian Officer* there is an extraordinarily good, longish story called "Daughters of the Vicar." An Anglican clergyman of the ordinary middle-class type is marooned in a mining village where he and his family are half-starved on a tiny stipend, and where he has no function, the mining folk having no need of him and no sympathy with him. It is the typical impoverished middle-class family in which the children grow up with a false consciousness of social superiority dragging upon them like a ball and fetter. The usual problem arises: how are the daughters to get married? The elder daughter gets the chance to marry a comparatively well-to-do clergyman. He happens to be a dwarf, suffering from some internal disease, and an utterly inhuman creature, more like a precocious and disagreeable child than a man. By the standards of most of the family she has done the right thing: she has married a gentleman. The younger daughter, whose vitality is not to be defeated by snobbishness, throws family prestige overboard and marries a healthy young coalminer.

It will be seen that this story has a close resemblance to *Lady Chatterley's Lover*. But in my opinion it is much better and more convincing than the novel, because the single imaginative impulse is strong enough to sustain it. Probably Lawrence had watched, somewhere or other, the underfed, downtrodden, organ-playing daughter of a clergyman wearing out her youth, and had a sudden vision of her escaping into the warmer world of the working class, where husbands are plentiful. It is a fit subject for a short story, but when drawn out to novel length it raises difficulties to which Lawrence was unequal. In another story in this book, "The Shades of Spring," there is a gamekeeper who is presented as a wild natural creature, the opposite of the over-conscious intellectual. Such figures appear again and again in Lawrence's books, and I think it is true to say that they are more convincing in the short stories, where we do not have to know too much about them, than in the novels (for example, *Lady Chatterley's Lover* or *The Woman Who Rode Away*), where, in order to be set into action, they have to be credited with complex thoughts which destroy their status as unspoiled animals. Another story, "Odour of Chrysanthemums," deals with the death of a miner in a pit accident. He is a drunkard, and up to the moment of his death his wife has wanted nothing so much as to be rid of him. Only when she is washing his dead body does she perceive, as though for the first time, how beautiful he is. That is the kind of thing Lawrence could do, and in the first paragraph of the story there is a wonderful example of his power of visual description. But one could not make a full-length novel out of such an episode, nor, without other more prosaic ingredients, out of a series of such episodes.

This is not quite the best volume of Lawrence's short stories, and it is to be hoped that the Penguin Library will follow it up by reprinting *England My England*. That contains, apart from the name story, "Fannie and Annie," "The Horse-dealer's Daughter," and, above all, "The Fox." This last story is perhaps the best thing Lawrence ever did, but it has the unusual quality of centring round an idea that might have occurred to anybody, so that one can enjoy the mental exercise of imagining the same story as it might have been told by Tolstoy, Maupassant, Henry James or Edgar Wallace. But the present volume contains at least six stories of the first rank, and only one ("A Fragment of Stained Glass") that is definitely a failure.

[Fee: £3.3.0; 9.11.45]

1. The couplet is from D.H. Lawrence's 'Cruelty and Love.' Lawrence's early poems were published in *The English Review*. This poem was included in *Love and Other Poems* (1913) but retitled, 'Love on the Farm' in *Collected Poems of D.H. Lawrence* (volume 1, 1928).
2. Lawrence never worked in a coal mine.

2797. To Leonard Moore

17 November 1945   Typewritten

> 27 B Canonbury Square
> Islington
> London N 1

Dear Mr Moore,

The following corrections should be inserted in the proof copies of the "Essays:"

Page 7. Second paragraph, lines 13–16. Delete "when Lenin was in his last illness . . . to abandon it" and substitute: "towards the end of his life Lenin went to see a dramatised version of *The Cricket on the Hearth* and found Dickens's 'middle-class sentiment' so intolerable that he walked out in the middle of a scene."

Next line. Delete "bourgeois" and substitute "middle-class."[1]

Page 25. First paragraph, line 30. Delete "Horace" and substitute "Harold."[2]

Page 109. Third line of footnote. Delete "nine and fifty" and insert "nine and sixty."[3]

> Yours sincerely
> Geo. Orwell

1. See letter to Roger Senhouse, 6 November 1945, *2782*.
2. See letter to Senhouse, 17 October 1945, *2767*.
3. The letter to Senhouse of 17 October 1945 refers to two corrections on p. 109. All these corrections were made.

2798. Review of *Novels and Stories* by Robert Louis Stevenson; selected with an Introduction by V. S. Pritchett

The Observer, 18 November 1945

When one is confronted with a selection, an abridgment or an anthology, it is always difficult not to start off with a complaint. Why, one is tempted to ask, has such a brilliant masterpiece as A been omitted, while something so obviously second-rate as B has been included? And complaints are liable to be particularly bitter in the case of a writer like Stevenson, about whom there are two opposite and even hostile schools of thought, the one regarding him as a serious novelist and the other as a master of burlesque.

The present selection—which is certainly good value so far as bulk goes—includes "The Suicide Club," "Thrawn Janet," "Travels with a Donkey," "Kidnapped," "The Beach of Falesa," "The Master of Ballantrae," and "Weir of Hermiston." It will be seen that Mr. Pritchett inclines very strongly towards Stevenson's more serious work, although in his introduction he analyses with some severity Stevenson's shortcomings as a novelist and a thinker. He has included only one example of the burlesques (it is hard to know just what to call these writings: perhaps highbrow thrillers would be the right expression), and that one, "The Suicide Club," is only a part of "The New Arabian Nights." "Treasure Island" is rejected on the ground that it is a boy's book, and "Dr. Jekyll and Mr. Hyde" because it is "available in a recent edition"—a rather unsatisfactory reason at a time when no book is reliably available. Apart from "The Beach of Falesa" there is nothing from the "Island Nights Entertainments," though surely any selection from Stevenson should have included "The Bottle Imp"; also, in a less fantastic and more genuinely horrible vein, "The Body Snatcher." On the other hand it seems doubtful whether "Travels with a Donkey" should come under "novels and stories."

Mr. Pritchett treats Stevenson primarily as a novelist, and considers that he was always at his best when writing of his native Scotland. He claims, rightly, that Stevenson's gift for narrative was quite outstanding, and admits that he had irritating tricks of style, though he appears to find them bearable. He also admits that Stevenson's range of thought was narrow and deeply marked by his puritanical origins. What he does not say, however, is that just this combination of qualities made Stevenson a superb writer of semi-comic melodramas, while making him tiresome and sometimes even morally disagreeable in his serious moments. Stevenson is to be seen at his very worst in his essay on Villon, where thoroughly bad writing and hypocritical indignation are combined. There is a sort of empty strenuousness about him, a temperamental puritanism, not richened by any definite religious belief, which comes out in his laboured manner of writing. He seems to be constantly saying to the reader "Look what an effort I am making!" and the cumulative effect is very trying to anyone who likes his English plain.

In his burlesque[s] Stevenson tends to write in a somewhat plainer manner, but in any case a touch of the baroque does no harm when he is dealing with figures like Mr. Malthus and Prince Florizel. And the horror themes, which answered to some deep need in his nature, set his imagination free and temporarily cured his moralising tendency. Neither "The Bottle Imp" nor "Dr. Jekyll and Mr. Hyde" has any discernible moral, and that is part of their charm.

The more orthodox of Stevenson's devotees will be glad to get "Kidnapped" and "The Master of Ballantrae" in one volume: the heretics will be chiefly sorry that the whole of "The New Arabian Nights" was not printed, but they will also be thankful for the inclusion of "The Beach of Falesa," which not only has a sort of poetic touch in its "Tyrolean harps" but contains some shrewd character touches of a kind that Stevenson did not often achieve. The fragment of "Weir of Hermiston" is well worth reading for the portrait of the hanging judge. Mr. Pritchett speculates on the possible ending of the book, and concludes that if Stevenson had finished it he would probably have spoiled it. A more important problem, an answer to which would cast much light on the nature of puritanism, is whether Stevenson does or does not admire the disgusting brute whom he is depicting. Mr. Pritchett decided that this book must be "pure Stevenson" and that he must leave out the various books which were written in collaboration: a pity, for any selection of Stevenson's best work ought to include "The Ebb Tide," a powerful and sinister story in which his narrative gift and his equivocal moral attitude are both at their most marked.

[Fee: £10.0.0; 15.11.45]

2799. Balraj Sahni to Orwell

20 November 1945

On 20 November 1945, Balraj Sahni wrote to Orwell from the Theosophical Colony, Juhu, Bombay, sympathising with him on Eileen's death, about which he and his wife had just learned from Mulk [Raj Anand] (see *905, n. 1*). The Sahnis had worked with Orwell at the BBC, particularly in the series with Norman Marshall, 'Let's Act It Ourselves' (see *1639*). Balraj Sahni wrote, 'We saw little of you two but you endeared yourselves to us greatly, through your work and your sincerity. This news has made us very sad indeed.' He said they were both working in the Indian People's Theatre movement, 'work which doesn't bring us money but a lot of happiness.' He added that the People's Theatre had had nearly fifty new plays written for it, which it had performed to audiences totalling more than a million people. He and his wife made their living by acting in films and on the professional stage. For his wife, Damyanti Sahni, see *861, n. 1*.

2800. Review of *Farewell Campo 12* by Brigadier James Hargest;
Immortal Years by Sir Evelyn Wrench; *Corn on the Cob:
Popular and Traditional Poetry of the U.S.A.*, selected
by A. L. Lloyd

Manchester Evening News, 22 November 1945

Prison stories are almost always readable, and never more so than when they deal with an escape. Even the most pedestrian account of an escape from captivity has its fascinating moments, and one's sympathy is invariably with the fugitive, even when he is an ordinary criminal whose imprisonment one more or less approves of.

"Farewell Campo 12" is on the pedestrian side. Brigadier Hargest was a New Zealander with a distinguished fighting record both in this war and the last.

After fighting in Greece and Crete he was taken prisoner near Tobruk in the unsuccessful offensive at the end of 1941, and sent to Italy by submarine along with several other senior officers who had been captured about the same time.

Even before leaving African soil, and, indeed, within an hour or two of being captured, his thoughts were running on escape, and he and various brother officers made a whole series of attempts, which were often baulked by their being moved to another camp before their preparations were completed.

His chance finally came when he was moved to the Castello Vincigliata, near Florence, where a number of British generals were incarcerated. He had managed, in spite of being searched countless times, to keep a compass and some money, and about a year later, after months of gruelling work, he and five other generals got away. Four of them were recaptured after a day or two, but Brigadier Hargest got safely to Switzerland, and thence via France and Spain to Gibraltar.

After a few unsuccessful attempts at simply getting over the wall, they realised that the only hope lay in digging a tunnel. In making the castle into a prison the Italians had sealed off parts of it by bricking up the doors, and among the disused parts was a chapel which would evidently make a good place for storing the excavated earth.

To get into the chapel the prisoners had to bore a hole through the side of a lift shaft. This hole they covered up with a sheet of plywood plastered to resemble the rest of the wall.

Once in the chapel they sank a vertical shaft 10 feet deep, then drove a horizontal one towards the outer wall, tunnelling gradually deeper as they went. As the subsoil was largely rock, and their only tools were an ice trowel, a large knife, and some lengths of iron bar, it is not surprising that they were only able to move at the rate of a few feet a week.

By the early months of 1943 they had got well beyond the outer wall and could drive a shaft towards the surface. It was then necessary to wait for a dark and stormy night on which with luck, the sentries posted on the wall would not see them. Finally a suitable night came.

The prisoners left dummies in their beds, broke through the last crust, and climbed to the surface, covering up the hole they had made with a board on which they strewed earth and pine needles.

Among those who got away but were recaptured was the well-known V.C., General Carton de Wiart, hero of Narvik and other places.

As soon as Brigadier Hargest reached Switzerland he surrendered himself to the police and was soon set at liberty by the Swiss authorities.

At the cost of severely tearing himself with barbed wire he managed to cross the French frontier, and then the resistance movement took him under its wing, and the rest of his journey was comparatively plain sailing.

His observations of Vichy France and of Franco Spain, at that time almost openly dominated by the Nazis, are of some interest.

This is an unpretentious book; but at any rate the middle chapters, which describe the detail of the escape, are well worth reading.

Sir Evelyn Wrench has travelled enormously, more widely than Brigadier Hargest, but in a more peaceful style. His book, based on diaries, starts in 1937, but deals mainly with the war years.

In 1940 he went on a lecture tour to the then neutral United States, expecting to be away only four months—actually his travels took him to Mexico, New Zealand, Australia, Malaya, India, and Palestine before he finally got home in 1944.

He had a good chance of observing the struggle between isolationism and pro-British sentiment in the autumn of 1940, and he talked with almost every Indian political leader during the bad period of 1942, when an Axis victory seemed possible and a Japanese invasion of India highly probable.

Probably the Indian interludes are the most interesting in the book. Sir Evelyn believes firmly that Dominion status is the best solution of the Indian problem, and he shows a not unjustified exasperation at the attitude of the Congress Party leaders in the moment of crisis.

This perhaps leads him to overestimate the importance of the Moslem League and the danger of civil war when the British have left.

But it was a great advantage to him that he knew Gandhi personally and could have several interviews with him on a friendly footing.

He came away feeling rather less certain of Gandhi's saintliness than he had felt at the time of the round table conference 10 years earlier.

In the chapters dealing with Palestine he gives a fair minded account of both sides of the case and is not completely unhopeful of a peaceful settlement.

This is a hastily written book and would be better if it were about half as long, but the student of contemporary history can dig some valuable scraps out of it.

"Corn on the Cob" is unreasonably expensive (3s.6d. for a paper-covered book of about 60 pages), but it is pleasant to be able to get hold of full versions of such half-known songs as "Frankie and Johnny" or "The Big Rock Candy Mountains."

Songs of this kind have no author and travel from generation to generation, no two versions ever being quite the same. Some of them are extremely ancient in origin; but it is interesting to see that they are still being made up, several in this collection dealing with Hitler and Roosevelt.

Mr. Lloyd contributes a useful introduction, in which he suggests contrary to what is generally believed, that the radio may help to keep popular poetry alive.

[Fee: £8.8.0; 21.11.45]

2801. Background to 'Through a Glass, Rosily'

Tribune, 2 and 16 November 1945

In its issue for 2 November 1945, *Tribune* published 'Report on the State of Austria by a Special Correspondent.' This sharply criticised the way the Russians, as one of the four occupying powers, were running occupied Austria. The following extracts and the sentences from the angry correspondence that followed in *Tribune*, 16 November 1945, give some background to Orwell's essay 'Through a Glass, Rosily.'

Immediately on arrival in Vienna, one is exposed to a series of shocks. The airport is inside the Russian zone, south-east of the capital, but entirely under R.A.F. control. Here one receives the first impression of emptiness and the absence of life that is the keynote of all Russian-controlled districts.

. . .

International relations in Austria hinge entirely on Russia. The Red Army was first on the spot, and it holds certain power positions which, so far, it has not relinquished and which dictate the actions also of the other occupying powers. There is no point in beating about the bush: too many people know what has happened. The Russians have between 600,000–800,000 troops in Austria. They live on the land in more senses than that they requisition food and cattle. In the zones they have occupied, they have left behind them a trail of economic and moral devastation. Life is insecure, rations have never yet reached a fraction of the nominal allowance, and looting is rampant.

In Vienna, the number of officially recorded cases of rape within the Russian-controlled zones exceeds 100,000. Few women venture out alone after dark in this area. In Lower Austria, the number of recently infected cases of venereal disease officially reported to the medical officer is above 50,000, and almost entirely confined to women; one adult woman in five is presumed to be thus affected. In Eastern Styria, which was first occupied by the Russians and then by the British, and where British doctors have supervised the inquiry, it has been established that 20,000 women were raped (about 80 per cent. of the total number of adult women) and between 25–40 per cent. have been reported as V.D. cases. This mass assault on women was accompanied by a similar one on property; and this was no

393

mere looting; it frequently took the form of sheer wanton damage to clothing, furniture and houses.

. . .

The Russian soldier is essentially likeable when one meets him without inhibitions on either side; but he is extraordinarily primitive, naïve and almost childlike, and he was psychologically unprepared for Europe outside Russia. Many a poor Austrian peasant or worker lost his belongings during the Soviet advance because the Russian soldier was told he was a bourgeois; many a British soldier or Austrian Communist suffered almost as great a shock when the reality of the Red Army stood before him—not the propagandist picture.

. . .

In yet one further way was the Russian impact felt by the people. The nominal Vienna rations are as follows: 300 grams (about 11 oz.) of bread per day; 350 grams of meat, 80 grams of fats, and 400 grams of peas or beans per week; 400 grams of sugar; 200 grams of salt and 125 grams of coffee per month. Children get 250 grams of bread per day and $\frac{1}{8}$ litre (about $\frac{1}{4}$ of a pint) of milk between 3–6 years; $\frac{1}{4}$ litre for those between 1–3, and $\frac{3}{8}$ litre for babies.

Until about six weeks ago, none of these rations was fully distributed. Then, for the first time, the British reached the scale and began to distribute them regularly. The Americans followed; the French still further behind. But in the Russian zone there has never been anything except bread and beans. These are the kind of politics that every housewife understands.

. . .

The overall picture of Austria is of a country in search of a policy and a nation in search of itself; and, unfortunately, the victorious Allies who have occupied—not liberated—the country seem to be in that same state of uncertainty. The consequences are severe. They have produced estrangement with the Russians on an unprecedented scale and they may produce disaster and disruption for Austria unless the problems are met squarely and with the minimum of delay.

In response, Tom Gittins, who explained that he was not a Communist, said that recent issues of *Tribune* had touched 'a new low in anti-Soviet propaganda,' in particular the 'Report on the State of Austria.' This, he said, amounted to 'a vicious slander on the Red Army' and was 'well calculated to increase that Russian "suspiciousness" which [*Tribune*] so frequently deplore[s].' It was a 'tissue of ill-natured, irresponsible racial rubbish' which was offered as 'a sober, factual statement of Russian policy and conduct in Austria!' R. Zerner described himself as 'disgusted to find nothing but the same old anti-Soviet stuff,' and F. C. White was 'amazed that a Left paper should publish such a slander on the Red Army without a single verifiable fact' and by a correspondent 'without the courage to sign his or her name.' A more sympathetic reaction, with an explanation of Russia's behaviour came from Miss D. H. Spalding, and the

Special Correspondent was given space for a rejoinder, both in the issue of 16 November.

According to your correspondent's report the state of affairs in Austria is deplorable and indefinable; and his moderate and understanding attitude encourages belief in his accuracy.

But, without condoning the conduct of the Russians, may I point out what may be an explanation? For hundreds of years before the revolution in Russia, the "upper" classes, aided and abetted by a degraded church, kept the masses in a state of complete serfdom, illiteracy, ignorance and superstition. Is it not too much to expect a total change-over to western ideas and ideals in little more than 25 years?

The colossal achievements of Lenin and Stalin and their friends in so short a time have perhaps led us to expect miracles.

Our Special Correspondent writes:—

In essence, all my critics who have written to the Editor say in effect two things: What I have written cannot be true because it is a slander on the Red Army: I produce no supporting evidence.

That is just the point that I sought to convey in my article. There are certain facts about the Red Army that are not in harmony with the war-time propaganda picture we were given. The shock when one comes up against this contrast is great—at least I found it so; so did the rank and file of the British troops in Vienna. The evidence is there on the spot. This is not a question of quoting this or that page out of a report but of talking to people, to comrades one has known, to officials who allow access to the day-by-day records that are available. There is no question about the genuineness of the evidence—I spoke to a number of high Russians. They don't deny the facts—though they seek to explain; and I quoted their explanation in my account of Austria.

The real issue almost unconsciously raised by your correspondents is not my veracity which in any case they are in no position to challenge, what they say in effect is that *Tribune* should not publish such accounts—even if true—because they bring grist to reactionary mills, because they increase Russian suspicions. But I wonder whether this is not a dangerously short-sighted policy, for the truth is bound to come out and then it will harm not only the reputation of the Red Army but also that of the Left press here who suppressed this knowledge.

What I sought to show is that here is a real problem that needs to be recognised, whatever its explanation or justification; cynical jokes about rape will not help the Russians, nor the Austrians who have suffered it, nor give socialism that standing in Europe which it so urgently needs.

Orwell's article appeared in the issue following the Special Correspondent's response.

2802. 'Through a Glass, Rosily'

Tribune, 23 November 1945

The recent article by *Tribune's* Vienna correspondent provoked a spate of angry letters which, besides calling him a fool and a liar and making other charges of what one might call a routine nature, also carried the very serious implication that he ought to have kept silent even if he knew that he was speaking the truth. He himself made a brief answer in *Tribune*, but the question involved is so important that it is worth discussing it at greater length.

Whenever A and B are in opposition to one another, anyone who attacks or criticises A is accused of aiding and abetting B. And it is often true, objectively and on a short-term analysis, that he *is* making things easier for B. Therefore, say the supporters of A, shut up and don't criticise: or at least criticise "constructively," which in practice always means favourably. And from this it is only a short step to arguing that the suppression and distortion of known facts is the highest duty of a journalist.

Now, if one divides the world into A and B and assumes that A represents progress and B reaction, it is just arguable that no fact detrimental to A ought ever to be revealed. But before making this claim one ought to realise where it leads. What do we mean by reaction? I suppose it would be agreed that Nazi Germany represented reaction in its worst form, or one of its worst. Well, the people in this country who gave most ammunition to the Nazi propagandists during the war are exactly the ones who tell us that it is "objectively" pro-Fascist to criticise the U.S.S.R. I am not referring to the Communists during their anti-war phase: I am referring to the Left as a whole. By and large, the Nazi radio got more material from the British Left-wing press than from that of the Right. And it could hardly be otherwise, for it is chiefly in the Left-wing press that serious criticism of British institutions is to be found. Every revelation about slums or social inequality, every attack on the leaders of the Tory party, every denunciation of British imperialism, was a gift for Goebbels. And not necessarily a worthless gift, for German propaganda about "British plutocracy" had considerable effect in neutral countries, especially in the earlier part of the war.

Here are two examples of the kind of source from which the Axis propagandists were liable to take their material. The Japanese, in one of their English-speaking magazines in China, serialised Briffault's *Decline and Fall of the British Empire*. Briffault, if not actually a Communist, was vehemently pro-Soviet, and the book incidentally contained some cracks at the Japanese themselves: but from the Japanese point of view this didn't matter, since the main tendency of the book was anti-British. About the same time the German radio broadcast shortened versions of books which they considered damaging to British prestige. Among others they broadcast E. M. Forster's *A Passage to India*. And so far as I know they didn't even have to resort to dishonest quotation. Just because the book was essentially truthful, it could be made to serve the purposes of Fascist propaganda. According to Blake,

> A truth that's told with bad intent
> Beats all the lies you can invent,[1]

and anyone who has seen his own statements coming back at him on the Axis radio will feel the force of this. Indeed, anyone who has ever written in defence of unpopular causes or been the witness of events which are likely to cause controversy, knows the fearful temptation to distort or suppress the facts, simply because any honest statement will contain revelations which can be made use of by unscrupulous opponents. But what one has to consider are the long-term effects. In the long run, can the cause of progress be served by lies, or can it not? The readers who attacked *Tribune's* Vienna correspondent so violently accused him of untruthfulness, but they also seemed to imply that the facts he brought forward ought not to be published even if true. 100,000 rape cases in Vienna are not a good advertisement for the Soviet regime: therefore, even if they have happened, don't mention them. Anglo-Russian relations are more likely to prosper if inconvenient facts are kept dark.[2]

The trouble is that if you lie to people, their reaction is all the more violent when the truth leaks out, as it is apt to do in the end. Here is an example of untruthful propaganda coming home to roost. Many English people of good will draw from the Left-wing press an unduly favourable picture of the Indian Congress Party. They not only believe it to be in the right (as it is), but are also apt to imagine that it is a sort of Left-wing organisation with democratic and internationalist aims. Such people, if they are suddenly confronted with an actual, flesh-and-blood Indian nationalist, are liable to recoil into the attitudes of a blimp. I have seen this happen a number of times. And it is the same with pro-Soviet propaganda. Those who have swallowed it whole are always in danger of a sudden revulsion in which they may reject the whole idea of Socialism. In this and other ways I should say that the net effect of Communist and near-Communist propaganda has been simply to retard the cause of Socialism, though it may have temporarily aided Russian foreign policy.

There are always the most excellent, high-minded reasons for concealing the truth, and these reasons are brought forward in almost the same words by supporters of the most diverse causes. I have had writings of my own kept out of print because it was feared that the Russians would not like them, and I have had others kept out of print because they attacked British imperialism and might be quoted by anti-British Americans. We are told *now* that any frank criticism of the Stalin regime will "increase Russian suspicions," but it is only seven years since we were being told (in some cases by the same newspapers) that frank criticism of the Nazi regime would increase Hitler's suspicions. As late as 1941, some of the Catholic papers declared that the presence of Labour Ministers in the British Government increased Franco's suspicions and made him incline more towards the Axis. Looking back, it is possible to see that if only the British and American peoples had grasped in 1933 or thereabouts what Hitler stood for, war might have been averted. Similarly, the first step towards decent Anglo-Russian relations is the dropping of illusions. In principle most people would agree to this: but the dropping of illusions means the publication of facts, and facts are apt to be unpleasant.

The whole argument that one mustn't speak plainly because it "plays into the hands of " this or that sinister influence is dishonest, in the sense that people only use it when it suits them. As I have pointed out, those who are most concerned about playing into the hands of the Tories were least concerned about playing into the hands of the Nazis. The Catholics who said, "Don't offend Franco because it helps Hitler" had been more or less consciously helping Hitler for years beforehand. Beneath this argument there always lies the intention to do propaganda for some single sectional interest, and to browbeat critics into silence by telling them that they are "objectively" reactionary. It is a tempting manœuvre, and I have used it myself more than once, but it is dishonest. I think one is less likely to use it if one remembers that the advantages of a lie are always short-lived. So often it seems a positive duty to suppress or colour the facts! And yet genuine progress can only happen through increasing enlightenment, which means the continuous destruction of myths.

Meanwhile there is a curious back-handed tribute to the values of liberalism in the fact that the opponents of free speech write letters to *Tribune* at all. "Don't criticise," such people are in effect saying: "don't reveal inconvenient facts. Don't play into the hands of the enemy!" Yet they themselves are attacking *Tribune*'s policy with all the violence at their command. Does it not occur to them that if the principles they advocate were put into practice, their letters would never get printed?

[Fee: £3.3.0; 16.11.45]

1. From *Auguries of Innocence*. Blake continues, 'It is right it should be so; / Man is made for Joy & Woe . . .'.
2. See also *2748, ns. 1* and *2*.

2803. To Fredric Warburg

24 November 1945   Typewritten

27 B Canonbury Square
Islington
London N 1

Dear Fred,
Ref your letter of the 20th. I'm sorry, but I just can't do any more work. I'm SWAMPED with it. Also that reading of MS takes up such a lot of time and I'm not good at it. Please forgive me.[1]

Yours
George

1. The manuscript has not been identified. On 18 October, Warburg refers to a report he seeks from Orwell 'on Fitzgerald's novels'; see *2766, n. 2.*

2804. To E. Lyon Young, Latin-American Service, BBC

24 November 1945   Typewritten

> 27 B Canonbury Square
> Islington
> London N 1

Dear Mr Young,

Many thanks for your letter of November 19th.[1] I am afraid I must refuse your offer. I don't in any case get much spare time, and I have never read Benjamin Franklin's Autobiography. Please forgive me.

> Yours sincerely
> [Signed] Geo. Orwell
> George Orwell

1. Young's letter was less perfunctory than were the usual BBC letters, suggesting, perhaps, Orwell's closer, more personal relationship with the Latin-American section than with other departments. Young wrote that Orwell's 'name is well known in Latin America and your broadcasts have been so much appreciated by listeners.' He hoped Orwell would write a fifteen-minute script on Franklin's *Autobiography*; the script would be 'very carefully translated into Spanish so as not to lose the style'; it would be broadcast in January 1946.

2805. Review of *London Belongs to Me* by Norman Collins

Manchester Evening News, 29 November 1945

There are some writers whose line of literary descent is so clear as to remind one of those chapters of the Old Testament which consist entirely of "and so-and-so." Thus, Cervantes begat Smollett, and Smollett begat Dickens, and Dickens begat Walpole (also several other novelists, of course), and Walpole begat Priestley, and Priestley begat Mr. Norman Collins,[1] whose "London Belongs to Me" must be one of the bulkiest novels published in this country in recent years.

Not that it has no qualities apart from its bulk. Mr. Collins is, in fact, superior to his two immediate forerunners, and in comparison with Mr. Priestley, in particular, he scores heavily by not having any strong leaning towards optimism. But readers of both books will at once notice a general resemblance to Priestley's "Angel Pavement."

"London Belongs to Me" is just the same kind of large, disorderly book, telling a whole series of stories simultaneously and trying to obtain a cross-section of London life by following up the fortunes of the people who happen to be grouped round one locality.

Both books are mainly humorous in intention and rather over-facetious in detail, and both are founded more or less consciously on the theory that the novel ought to follow Dickens and not, say, Flaubert—that is, that it ought to be long, shapeless, eventful, and crammed with burlesque characters.

The locality Mr. Collins takes as his starting-point is No. 10, Dulcimer-street, in South London, somewhere near Kennington Oval.

It is an "apartments" house, and it contains five sets of lodgers and the landlady. Perhaps the most important is Mr. Josser, who at the age of 65 has just retired from a city clerkship with a pension of £2 a week and who has a worthy but rather masterful wife and two grown-up children.

Then there is Mrs. Boon, whose son Percy works in a garage and is a bit of a rogue, and Mr. Puddy, an elderly widower, whose sole interest in life is food, and Connie, who is cloakroom attendant in a night club, and Mr. Squales, a spiritualist medium, and the landlady, Mrs. Vizzard, who is a bit of a miser but is also interested in spiritualism and ends by becoming infatuated with Mr. Squales.

One could infer in advance the general tone of the book from the slightly fantastic names of the characters. The time covered is from the end of 1938 to the beginning of 1941.

The two main events are a murder—or perhaps it ought really to have been classed as manslaughter—and a breach of promise case. Percy Boon, in whose job the handling of stolen cars is almost a routine matter, ends up by stealing a car himself, and in getting away with it he kills, not quite intentionally, a girl with whom he has been entangled.

His trial, like that of Joseph Smith, of "Brides in the bath" fame, coincides with the opening period of the war, and several of the other characters are involved in the preparation of the defence and of the petition for clemency after Percy has been condemned.

In handling the murder and the trial Mr. Collins is at his best. He knows all about the fees of lawyers and the unfairness of court procedure, and he contrives to leave the impression that Percy, though he has behaved callously enough, is not guilty of the actual deed for which he has been condemned.

Mr. Squales, the medium, is a drifting, worthless creature who has also been a fortune-teller, a phrenologist, and an astrologer, and has failed at everything. He calls himself by the high-sounding name of Professor Qualito. Curiously enough he has real mediumistic powers which come upon him at odd moments and merely seem to him unpleasant and disturbing.

His one remaining hope is to find some woman who will support him, and he makes an easy conquest of Mrs Vizzard. Almost simultaneously, however, he comes across a much more attractive victim, a Mayfair widow of enormous bulk and considerable wealth, and he deserts Mrs. Vizzard when the banns have already been proclaimed three times, afterwards being sued for breach of promise.

By a piece of poetic justice he ends up in the Isle of Man. It turns out that his name is really Qualito and that he is of Italian nationality, and he is duly interned.

These and various other stories are kept going simultaneously by means of short chapters which switch from character to character. The shortness of the episode[s] marks the difference between a book of this kind and the three-decker Victorian novels which it is attempting to emulate.

In Dickens's most characteristic novels you also have several plots proceeding simultaneously and sometimes almost independently; but each episode is long enough to carry the story a good distance, and the wealth of characters and complication of sub-plots is not solely due to Dickens's fertility of invention.

In those days it was usual to issue a novel serially in monthly parts, and one way of making sure that subscribers did not drop off was to keep them in continual suspense as to what was going to happen next.

Thus the switch from character to character, each episode raising fresh problems which could not be solved for at least another month, was a method that arose naturally out of the manner of publication. In those of his novels that were not published in monthly parts Dickens tended to stick more closely to a single story.

It is also questionable whether anyone nowadays is genuinely in the mood to write so voluminously and so carelessly as Dickens. Mr. Collins's book is 300,000 words long—the length of four ordinary novels. It does contrive to give an impression of London's vastness, and it brings in episodes from an operation for pleural congestion to a raid on a night-club, and from a heavyweight boxing contest to the "blitz" of 1940.

But it contains a lot of dead wood, and has probably been written at high speed. However, the spiritualistic scenes and most of the passages dealing with the murder are excellent, and since the arrangement of the book facilitates skipping, this can be numbered among the few novels published this year that are worth reading.

[Fee: £8.8.0; 28.11.45]

1. Orwell had crossed swords with Norman Collins when the latter worked for Victor Gollancz Ltd at the time *Keep the Aspidistra Flying* was prepared for the press in the early months of 1936. They had a slightly edgy relationship when both worked for the BBC during the war. For a biographical note on Collins, see *236*, paragraph 5. Orwell reviewed Priestley's *Angel Pavement* in *The Adelphi*, October 1930 (*98*).

2806. To Leonard Moore

29 November 1945   Typewritten

27 B Canonbury Square
Islington
London   N 1

Dear Mr Moore,
I have just heard from Erval of Nagel Paris.[1] He says that the contract you drew up for "Animal Farm" provides for publication in not less than a year, and says that this is an impossible condition. The main reason he gives is that it is not usual in France to publish two books by a foreign writer within 18 or 20 months of one another. "Burmese Days" is supposed to appear about February, so "Animal Farm" would clash with it if published in 1946. He also hints that from a political point of view this may not be a happy moment for producing a book like "Animal Farm" and says Nagel Paris would like to be

able to judge the right moment. I fancy the second objection is the real one, as they are so short of books of any kind in France at present that the first consideration would not be likely to carry much weight.

I am going to tell him that I leave the matter in your hands. The point is that we don't want the publication of A.F. put off for 18–20 months if it is at all avoidable. I have no doubt that *now* such a book would be likely to get a hostile reception in France, but it would in any case be a question of publishing it some time late in 1946, by which time pro-Russian feeling may have worn thin as it seems to be doing here. I don't fancy the book would be suppressed while Malraux has the Ministry of Information. I met him when in Paris and found him very friendly, and he is far from being pro-Communist in his views. Could we at need take it to another French publisher? The Fontaine people asked for it, you may remember. How does the contract stand with Nagel? Have they an option on all my books? I should be glad to hear what you are doing about this.

I had to make a new will when my wife died, and I am just having it put into proper legal form. It is not that there is likely to be much to leave, but I must think of copyrights and reprints. I am naming Christy & Moore as my literary agents and Sir Richard Rees as my literary executor, and I am leaving it to him to sort out whatever unpublished or reprintable material I may leave behind and decide what is worth preserving. I am also leaving records of anything I publish in periodicals, as there might at any given moment be a good deal that was worth salvaging for some kind of reprint.[2] It is just as well to get all this cleared up, what with atomic bombs etc.

Yours sincerely
Eric Blair

1. See *2727* and *2730*, *n. 1*.
2. See *2648*.

2807. Review of *A Coat of Many Colours: Occasional Essays* by Herbert Read[1]

Poetry Quarterly, Winter 1945

The essays and reviews in this moderate-sized volume cover such subjects as Anarchism, War Books, Toulouse-Lautrec, Paul Klee, Eric Gill, Havelock Ellis, prose style, Lawrence of Arabia, Gerard Manley Hopkins, Socialist Realism, George Saintsbury, Verlaine, Stendhal, Wordsworth's *Prelude*, Marlowe's *Faustus*, Chinese painting, Salvador Dali, Kierkegaard and Henry James. Those I have named make up roughly a quarter of the subjects that Herbert Read discusses, and obviously such a book cannot be exhaustively dealt with in a thousand or fifteen hundred words. I prefer to concentrate mainly on one point—the clash between Read's political beliefs and his æsthetic theory. But the multiplicity of subjects is in itself a point to be noticed. Even if one regards Read simply as a critic of painting the range of his interests and sympathies is very wide, and his open-mindedness has been his strength and weakness as a writer.

Read is an Anarchist, and an Anarchist of an uncompromising kind; he admits that the ideal society cannot be realized at this moment, but he refuses to be satisfied with anything less or to abandon the belief that Man is perfectible. He is also an acceptor of the Machine Age and a defender, on æsthetic grounds, of the products of the machine. In some of the essays in this book, notably 'Art and Autarky' and the essay on Eric Gill, he seems to hedge a little, but in general he sticks to it that an anarchistic form of society is compatible with a high level of technical development:

> 'Anarchism implies a universal decentralization of authority, and a universal simplification of life. Inhuman entities like the modern city will disappear. But anarchism does not necessarily imply a reversion to handicraft and outdoor sanitation. There is no contradiction between anarchism and electric power, anarchism and air transport, anarchism and division of labour, anarchism and industrial efficiency. Since the functional groups will all be working for their mutual benefit, and not for other people's profit or for mutual destruction, the measure of efficiency will be the appetite for fullness of living.'

The vague generalization contained in the last sentence avoids the enormous question: how are freedom and organization to be reconciled? If one considers the probabilities one is driven to the conclusion that Anarchism implies a low standard of living. It need not imply a hungry or uncomfortable world, but it rules out the kind of air-conditioned, chromium-plated, gadget-ridden existence which is now considered desirable and enlightened. The processes involved in making, say, an aeroplane are so complex as to be only possible in a planned, centralized society, with all the repressive apparatus that that implies. Unless there is some unpredictable change in human nature, liberty and efficiency must pull in opposite directions. Read will not admit this, and he will not fully admit that the machine has frustrated the creative instincts and degraded æsthetic feeling. Indeed, he takes what looks like a perverse pleasure in praising the things that are mechanically and collectively produced as against the achievement of the individual craftsman:

> 'The new æsthetic must be based on the fundamentally new factor in modern civilization—large-scale machine production. That method of production involves certain characteristics which contradict the accepted notion of beauty—they are generally indicated by the word *standardisation*. In itself, standardisation is not an æsthetic question. If a thing is beautiful you do not diminish that beauty by reproducing it. . . . Standardised machine products are exact replicas of one another, and if one is beautiful, the rest are beautiful. . . . We may admit that certain forms of personal expression are not suitable for mechanical reproduction as standardised objects, but we claim that the creative will of the artist can and should be adapted to the new conditions. We draw attention to a certain type of modern art (abstract, non-representational or constructivist art) which,

while still remaining a very personal expression of the individual artists who produce it, is nevertheless the prototype of machine art. Such works of art could be reproduced without losing any of their æsthetic qualities.'

At first glance this looks reasonable and the objections likely to be urged against it look sentimental and arty-and-crafty. But just test it by a few concrete examples. 'If a thing is beautiful you do not diminish that beauty by reproducing it.' I suppose that 'Whether on Ida's shady brow' is beautiful.[2] (If you don't care for that particular poem, substitute some other that you do care for.) Well, would you like to hear it read aloud five thousand times running? Would it still be beautiful at the end of such a process? On the contrary, it would seem the most hideous collection of words that has ever existed. Any shape, any sound, any colour, any smell becomes odious through too much repetition, because repetition fatigues the senses to which beauty must make its appeal. Read often speaks of beauty as though it were a kind of Platonic Absolute existing somewhere or other in its own right and in no way dependent on human appreciation. If one takes this view, one must assume that the value of, say, a picture resides in the picture itself, and that the method by which it has been produced is irrelevant. It may be produced by machinery, or, like certain surrealist pictures, by accident. But how about books? It is just thinkable that books may some day be written by machinery, and it is quite easy to imagine poems being produced partly by fortuitous means—by some device similar to the kaleidoscope, for instance. And if they were 'good' poems I do not see how Read could consistently object to such a process. It is a queer position for an Anarchist to be driven into.

But of course Read is not consistent in his acceptance of the machine. In this book we find him praising the beauties of modern car design, and we find him pointing out that the masses in the industrialized countries have been brought into a state of 'mental sickness' by 'deadening labours and devitalized environment.' We find him writing sympathetically of Paul Klee and Ben Nicholson, but also of Ruskin and Walter de la Mare. We find him saying 'personally, I am against the grandiose in art,' and we find him praising the Pyramids. The fact is, as anyone who has been reviewed by him knows, that Read is too kind a critic. The range of his sympathies, as I pointed out earlier, is very wide, perhaps too wide. The only thing he acutely dislikes is Conservatism, or, to put it more precisely, academicism. He is always on the side of the young against the old. He is in favour of abstract painting and streamlined teapots because the æsthetic Conservatives don't like them: and he is in favour of Anarchism because the political Conservatives, including the official Left, don't like that. The contradiction into which this leads him remains unresolved.

It would be difficult to over-praise Read as a popularizer and as a champion of unfashionable causes. I suppose no one in our time has done more to encourage young poets and keep the British public informed about artistic developments in Europe, and no one of equal standing has had the guts to speak out against the Russo-mania of the last ten years. But all the same, wide sympathies have their penalty. It is probably a mistake for any kind of artist, even a critic, to endeavour to 'keep up' beyond a certain point. This does not mean that one has to accept the normal academic assumption that literature and art came to an end about forty years ago. Clearly the young and the middle-aged ought to try to appreciate one another. But one ought also to recognize that one's æsthetic judgment is only fully valid between fairly well-defined dates. Not to admit this is to throw away the advantage that one derives from being born into one's own particular time. Among people now alive there are two very sharp dividing lines. One is between those who can and those who can't remember the period before 1914; the other is between those who were adult before 1933 and those who were not. Other things being equal, who is likelier to have the truer vision at this moment, a person of twenty or a person of fifty? One can't say, though on some points posterity may decide. Each generation imagines itself to be more intelligent than the one that went before it, and wiser than the one that comes after it. This is an illusion, and one should recognize it as such, but one ought also[3] to stick to one's own world-view, even at the price of seeming old-fashioned: for that world-view springs out of experiences that the younger generation has not had, and to abandon it is to kill one's intellectual roots.

If I apply to Read the simple test, 'How much of it sticks?' I find that none of his critical work has left so deep an impression on me as certain passages in his writings about his childhood, and a handful of poems. At this moment I recall particularly a passage describing the making of lead buckshot in a bullet-mould—and the joy of the act, he said, was not in the usefulness of the bullet but in the beauty of the silvery new-minted lead—and a poem written early in this war, 'The Contrary Experience'. In these and similar writings Read is simply speaking out of his experience: he is not trying to be open-minded, or up-to-date, or cosmopolitan, or public-spirited. In politics Read is an Anarchist, in æsthetic theory he is a Europeanizer, but in his origins he is a Yorkshireman—that is, a member of a small, rustic, rather uncouth tribe whose members secretly believe all the other peoples of the earth to be just a little inferior to themselves. I think his best work comes from the Yorkshire strain in him. I am not decrying his critical activities. They have been a civilizing influence which it would be ungrateful not to acknowledge. But in contrast to his autobiographical writings, and to some of his poems and certain passages in his political pamphlets, his purely critical work has a sort of diffuseness, a wateriness, which comes from being too open-minded, too charitable, too civilized, too anxious to keep abreast of modern thought and remain in touch with all movements simultaneously, instead of giving expression to the vehement likes and dislikes which must be present in his mind, just as much as in any other writer's.

[Fee: £3.3.0; 30.11.45]

Herbert Read wrote to Orwell from Broom House, Seer Green, Beaconsfield, Bucks, on 19 January 1946:

You know as well as I do that a writer can't afford the time to acknowledge all the criticism, favourable or otherwise, that he gets, but I find that sometimes, when it is a critic one likes and respects, he may come to the conclusion that the writer has been offended unless he makes some response. Let me hasten to say, therefore that nothing in the review of my Coat in PQ offends me in the least. I like it. But there is one point, your main point, which seems to me to rest on a logical fallacy. You confuse reproduction (a quantitative process) with repetition or reiteration (a qualitative process). The *diffusion* of the identical product is one thing (whether it is a picture or a book or a coffee-pot). It is not to be confused with the *consumption* of an identical product (shape, sound or colour, poem or picture). I want to see a million copies of "Animal Farm" diffused by the most efficient mechanical means possible: but I don't want myself to consume a million copies.

Otherwise, of course, you are right. I would love to retire to Yorkshire and write the kind of things you like and I like, but you know as well as I do that you can't support a large family on that sort of thing.

1. The typescript of this review survives. The printed version follows the typescript in word, spelling, and capitalisation precisely, except for the addition of 'also', in footnote 3.
2. The first line of Blake's 'To the Muses.'
3. 'also' does not appear in the typescript.

2808. Review of *Huis Clos* by Jean-Paul Sartre; *The Banbury Nose* by Peter Ustinov; *Twilight Bar* by Arthur Koestler

Tribune, 30 November 1945

There may be some deep significance in the fact that these three plays, one of them an unworthy squib by a well-known novelist, another a sentimental costume piece by a talented young actor, the third a baffling fantasy by a philosopher, all take leave of probability and of the ordinary laws of space and time. If so, I don't perceive it, though I suppose it could be plausibly said that many people now tend to write about imaginary worlds, or about the remote past, because existing problems are too much for them. I propose simply to summarise Sartre's play and let the reader draw his own conclusions. This is perhaps not useless, since we are certainly going to hear more of Sartre, and this and others of his works will be translated into English before long. He is one of the tiny handful of new French writers who made a reputation for themselves during the German occupation, and besides being a novelist and dramatist he is the leading exponent of the Existentialist school of philosophy. The writer generally associated with him is Camus, also a dramatist and for several years the editor of *Combat*, the best of the Resistance newspapers. If only because we all like to have the illusion of keeping up to date, some advance information about Sartre's most successful play may be acceptable.

There are only four characters in the play—in effect only three—and the action, as the reader perceives after a page or two, takes place in Hell. Hell, it appears, is a hot and stuffy drawing-room furnished with exceeding ugliness in the style of the Second Empire. There are no windows or looking-glasses in the room, the door is locked on the outside and the bell does not ring. Certain details in the furniture are calculated to increase the sense of boredom and futility: for example, there is a paper knife in the room, but no books or papers to use it on. The climax is reached when the three damned souls about whom the action revolves realise that they are in this room *for ever*, with no power to alter their condition.

The three people are Ines, a girl who has been a post-office clerk; Estelle, a girl more or less from the fashionable world, and Garcin, a journalist. They have never met while on earth, and it only gradually dawns on them that they have been thrown together because they are by temperament exactly qualified to inflict torture on one another. Once they have grasped their predicament, they are incapable of further development. All their thoughts are turned towards the world they have left, and they are even able to see and hear this world at the moments when people happen to be talking about them.

The actions for which they have been damned are revealed little by little. Ines, who is the most cynical and perhaps the most intelligent of the three, is a homosexual. She has been responsible for the suicide of another woman and indirectly responsible for the death of the latter's husband. Estelle, when she first appears, puts on airs of innocence, but it later appears that she has had an illegitimate baby which she disposed of by drowning it, as a result of which the child's father committed suicide. Garcin's case is more complicated. He is a pacifist journalist who has been shot for continuing with his pacifist activities when his country is at war: to all appearances, therefore, a hero and martyr. He has been damned, as he is well aware, for the cruelties he has inflicted on his wife. He has deliberately tortured her over a period of years, enjoying the process "because it was so easy." But his real secret is the fact that even his pacifism was partly a sham. When war came he forgot his principles and simply fled to escape military service, and at his execution he behaved in a cowardly fashion. It is not, of course, implied that these three people have been damned *for* such specific actions as murder or adultery, but because *through* such actions they have become rotten and irredeemable.

The temperaments of the three people set up a sort of triangle of forces which makes the emergence of any new pattern impossible. Ines, the homosexual, pursues Estelle. Estelle, whose surface delicacy hides a coarse temperament, pursues Garcin. Garcin, in a brutal way and without pretence of affection, is ready to succumb to her, but cannot do so while the jeering Ines is looking on. Lust, jealousy, hatred and remorse go round and round like the tunes in a musical box, and it is implied that this futile repetition must continue for ever. I translate as best I can the closing passage:—

Garcin. . . . . It's no good; I can't make love to you while she's looking on.
Estelle. All right! Then she shan't look on any longer!
(She picks up the paper knife from the table, flings herself upon Ines and stabs her several times.)
Ines. (Struggling with her and laughing.) What are you doing? Are you mad? You know very well I'm dead.
Estelle. Dead? (She drops the paper knife. A pause. Ines picks up the knife and stabs herself furiously.)

Ines. Dead! Dead! Dead! The knife, poison, the rope—it's no use. *It's been done already*, don't you understand? And we're together for ever. (She laughs.)

Estelle. (Bursting out laughing.) For ever! Isn't it comic? For ever!

Garcin. (Looking at them and laughing.)

(They fling themselves down, each on his own sofa. A long silence. They stop laughing and look at one another. Garcin stands up.)

(Curtain.)

The question is, what the devil is this all about? Hard though it is to judge anything written in a foreign language, I am certain that this is a powerful play, and remarkable for its economy of method and psychological precision. Whether it has any meaning that is relevant from the point of view of living human beings is more doubtful. It is convincing as a picture of ghosts, that is of creatures unable to develop. But ghosts, so far as we know, do not exist, and human beings continue to develop, or at least to change, up to the moment of death. Or do they? What Sartre is possibly saying is that there is such a condition as living death and that it cannot be escaped if one kills the good that is within oneself. Though there is no "next world," there may be something analogous to damnation in this one, and when one reaches it one is doomed to repeat the same pattern over and over again. That is the only meaning, of a moral or political or psychological kind, that I can extract from this play: otherwise it is simply a cold and skilful manoeuvre like a series of moves on a chessboard. One must remember that the play was produced in Paris under the German occupation, at a time, presumably, when any writer who wanted to preserve his integrity, and also to get published, had to choose themes remote from every-day life.

Peter Ustinov is a brilliant actor and will no doubt develop into a first-rate dramatist if he sticks to the burlesque themes which really suit him. He is just the man to bring out the enormous latent possibilities of the revue and the pantomime. His present play, though no doubt it went well on the stage, would seem rather empty if it were not enlivened by a trick. The story of a "county" family, the usual Kiplingesque family of soldiers and foxhunters, is told backwards. We see them in their final decay in 1943, and then backwards by successive stages till 1884, with the weight of family tradition warping each generation in turn. At the start each character is almost the opposite of what he is to become later: the youthful poet becomes a blimp, the unbeliever becomes a clergyman, the cynic becomes an idealist. It is fairly convincing, but it is the kind of story that would hardly seem worth telling if it started at the right end.

The drama is not Arthur Koestler's line. He wrote this play years ago, then had it seized by the Hungarian police, and re-wrote it recently. Two travellers arrive from another planet and announce that the human race is to be exterminated unless it can be shown, before a certain hour, that the happiness existing on earth outweighs the unhappiness. The inhabitants of the earth then make desperate and not altogether successful efforts to be happy. At the end their fate is left in doubt, and it is not even certain that the two travellers are not impostors. No definite conclusion is reached, partly because Arthur Koestler, like most of us, is unable to imagine what happiness would be like if it were attainable. The dialogue is mediocre, and, in general, the play demonstrates the gap that lies between having an idea and working it up into dramatic shape.[1]

[Fee: £3.3.0; 23.11.45; Orwell lists this as an article, not a review]

1. Orwell, with Richard (then eighteen months old), spent Christmas 1945 with the Koestlers at Bwylch Ocyn near Blaenau Ffestiniog. Celia Kirwan, Mamaine Koestler's twin sister, was also present. Arthur Koestler and Orwell managed to avoid recriminations over his recent castigation of Koestler's play—which says much for both men. Koestler recalled the occasion in an interview he gave Ian Angus, 30 April 1964. He said the episode was typical of Orwell's 'uncompromising integrity.' Koestler asked Orwell, 'jocularly, why, though it was a lousy play, he couldn't have softened the review just a little.' Orwell replied that that hadn't occurred to him. At the end of the weekend, when Koestler was driving Orwell to the station, Orwell said, 'Yes, perhaps it had been a bit too severe' and he thought he ought to have softened the review slightly in some way.

2808A. 'The Song of the Beasts'

Compass: Current Reading, December 1945

'The Song of the Beasts' from *Animal Farm* (*CW*, VIII, 7–8), was reprinted on page 45 of this journal. No record of payment to Orwell nor of permission being given has been traced.

2809. 'Bare Christmas for the Children'

Evening Standard, 1 December 1945

The toyshops are not quite so empty as they were this time last year, but that is about the most one can say.

Among the classes of toys that still seem to be completely "out" are rubber and celluloid articles of every kind—no balloons, no swans or goldfish to float in your bath—wax dolls, Meccano sets, and of course, the ingenious clockwork toys that once used to come to us from Germany.

Toy tricycles, if they still exist, are second-hand rarities, though scooters are fairly numerous, and also dolls' prams of very poor quality. Bows and arrows may still be procurable, but I have not seen any, and even pocket knives are hard to come by.

The rag dolls and the wooden toys—carts, tommy guns and the like—are as badly made and expensive as ever. Rag books seem to have vanished years ago. On the other hand, lead soldiers are fairly common again. They are lead soldiers of the inferior kind, flat and gilded all over, but perhaps they seem thrilling enough to the seven-year-old child who has never seen those realistic models, complete with gasmask and blancoed gaiters, that were on sale before the war.

Fretsaws are also procurable, though spare blades are not easy to get. And you can buy Plasticine once again, and other kinds of modelling wax, and kaleidoscopes; also paint-boxes and brushes of not absolutely bad quality. But good drawing paper is not so easy to find, and it still seems impossible to get hold of a BB pencil.

Here and there you can find those agreeable little grocer's shops with scales, tin canisters and a wooden counter; and a very welcome feature is the reappearance of chemistry outfits, one of the most absorbing of all toys for an intelligent boy of about 12.

In one London shop I saw quite elaborate sets with test tubes, flasks and spirit lamps—though I admit that when I learned the price I felt as though I had been hit over the head with a rubber club.

It will once again be rather a bare Christmas from the child's point of view, but one ought to remember that the importance of manufactured toys is exaggerated. Very young children hardly need toys.

It is absurd, for instance, to give a doll to a baby, as people habitually do. To the baby a doll is merely a soft object, in no way superior to a knotted towel, and even at the toddling age it is generally happier with the fire tongs, or a stone inside a tin can, than with anything that comes out of a shop.

Certain toys you can make for yourself if you have the tools. A wooden truck, or even the simpler kind of hobby-horse, is stronger as well as cheaper if you make it yourself, and you can buy the wheels at any wood shop.

Beyond a quite low age children often seem to get their greatest enjoyment out of things that cannot strictly be called toys: for instance, carpentering tools, sewing materials, beads, linoleum for making lino-cuts, china-clay and plaster of paris. It is curious that though carpentering and fretwork have been adapted for play purposes, tin-smithing and black-smithing have not.

From the age of about eight onwards a bright child wants to be either making something or breaking something. A boy of twelve gets almost inexhaustible pleasure out of a catapult, which he makes for himself at the cost of about sixpence.

It was because of this universal passion that the Belisha beacons had to be made out of metal instead of glass.

For children who live in the country, one of the most fascinating toys, during about two-thirds of the year, is a pond-water aquarium, for which one uses a small accumulator jar or a 7lb. pickle jar. The creatures that live in it—tadpoles, caddis flies and water fleas—need little attention, and the aquarium is a more interesting object in the middle of the dinner table than a bowl of flowers.

When the toy trade becomes normal again, I hope that several old favourites which had already vanished before the war will come back again. Whip tops are still in fashion, but peg tops seem to have dropped out in recent years. There were two kinds: a coloured one which you threw over your shoulder, and a white one, much harder to handle, which you threw underhand.

One of the greatest joys of my own childhood were those little brass cannons on wooden gun-carriages which are now hardly to be found outside an antique shop. The smallest had barrels the size of your little finger, the largest were six or eight inches long, cost ten shillings and went off with a noise like the Day of Judgment.

To fire them you needed gunpowder, which the shops sometimes refused to sell you, but a resourceful boy could make gunpowder for himself if he took the precaution of buying the ingredients from three different chemists.

One of the advantages of being a child 30 years ago was the lighter-hearted attitude that then prevailed towards firearms. Up till not long before the other war you could walk into any bicycle shop and buy a revolver, and even when the authorities began to take an interest in revolvers, you could still buy for 7s. 6d. a fairly lethal weapon known as a Saloon Rifle. I bought my first Saloon Rifle at the age of 10, with no questions asked.

Normal healthy children enjoy explosions. I think I have heard more explosions—though not such large ones, certainly—since VE Day[1] than I heard in the six years preceding it.

Meanwhile you would have difficulty even in buying an airgun, and such as exist are mostly poor things.

Let us hope that this time next year it will be different, and all the rare or unprocurable toys will be back in the shops again; not only airguns, but motorcars with pedals and a chain drive, clockwork mice to frighten your aunt, locomotives with real boilers in them, doll's sewing machines, wooden bricks square enough to stand on one another, ninepins whose balls are round instead of being egg-shaped, and—not strictly toys, but no child's upbringing is complete without them—new editions of Struwwelpeter and the Beatrix Potter books, now only obtainable by much searching through the shelves of second-hand book-shops.

[Fee: £20.0.0; 30.11.45]

1. Victory in Europe Day, 8 May 1945, marking the end of hostilities in Europe.

2810. To Leonard Moore

    1 December 1945   Typewritten

27 B Canonbury Square
Islington
London N 1

Dear Mr Moore,

Many thanks for your letter of 30th November. I return the statement of Reynall° & Hitchcock's payments, and also enclose the biographical notes you asked for in an earlier letter. The only photograph I have is a passport one which is attached. The only big ones I have seem to be copyright. Do R. & H. want a large photo? If so I shall have to have one taken, which is a great bore.

As to this title. I don't approve of these catchy titles, but I should think TO MAKE A SHORT STORY LONG is a just possible title, not completely unconnected with the subject-matter of the book. THE FACE BEHIND THE PAGE is another possible one and refers to something in the text.[1]

I suppose they'll put the titles of some of my previous books on the flyleaf. The ones I should like them to mention are "Down and Out in Paris and London," "The Road to Wigan Pier," "Homage to Catalonia" and "Animal Farm." It is important they should mention the last-named, which they will probably try not to do.[2]

When the Portuguese translation of A.F. comes out, shall I be able to get some copies?[3]

Yours sincerely
Eric Blair

1. The U.S. title of *Critical Essays* was at issue. The title chosen was *Dickens, Dali & Others: Studies in Popular Culture.*
2. All four were listed by R[eynal] & H[itchcock].
3. In Orwell's Payments Book against 1 December 1945 is noted the receipt of £77.1s.0d for royalties. A note on the facing page states, 'American edition of "Critical Essays" & Portuguese rights of "Animal Farm." '

2811. Review of *The Condemned Playground* by Cyril Connolly

The Observer, 2 December 1945

The playground that Mr. Connolly is referring to is the lost world of the nineteen-thirties (some of what he says would apply better to the 'twenties, perhaps), when literature had not become sodden with politics, and one could play the fool with a good conscience. The pieces reprinted in this book range in date between 1927 and 1944, and though the manner of writing varies remarkably little, the approach becomes more serious and less purely literary as time goes on. Among the earlier pieces are essays on Joyce, Gide, Swift, Sterne, and Chesterfield: among the later, essays on psycho-analysis, Barcelona during the Spanish civil war and the early death of the late Lord Knebworth, and a brilliant article written in 1943 looking back on the achievements of 1843.

In between are some relics of Mr. Connolly's short and turbulent career as a novel-reviewer, including a blistering parody of Aldous Huxley entitled "Told in Gath." "Like most critics," he says, "I drifted into the profession through a lack of moral stamina . . . Not that I despise criticism. . . . But I wish I had been a better critic and that I had not written brightly, because I was asked to, about so many bad books." He did, however, contrive to speak his mind about some of the bad books, even when he was a regular contributor to a weekly paper. Here are some excerpts from an article entitled "Ninety Years of Novel-Reviewing":

> The reviewing of novels is the White Man's Grave of journalism; it corresponds, in letters, to building bridges in some impossible tropical climate. . . . For each scant clearing made wearily among the springing vegetation the jungle overnight encroaches twice as far. . . . An unpleasant

sight in the jungle is the reviewer who goes native. Instead of fighting the vegetation he succumbs to it, and running perpetually from flower to flower, he welcomes each with cries of "genius"!

This is followed by some rather more serious articles on the contemporary English novel, and later in the book there are appreciations of E. M. Forster and Somerset Maugham. Some of Mr. Connolly's judgments on the English novel are extremely acute. Almost certainly he is right in saying that the rigid English class system, which narrows the range of nearly everyone's experience, is responsible for the thinness of subject matter in the average novel, and indirectly responsible for the present decadence of the English language. But at this stage of his career Mr. Connolly rather marred his critical writings by an indiscriminate admiration for everything American. "The American novelists, Hemingway, Hammett, Faulkner, Fitzgerald, O'Hara, for instance," he says, "write instinctively for men of their own age, men who enjoy the same things. . . . English novels always seem to be written for superiors or inferiors, older or younger people, or for the opposite sex.'

This is too sweeping. To begin with, since he excepts a number of English writers from his general condemnation, Mr. Connolly is in effect comparing the best American novels with the worst English ones. And in any case the violence of American novels, which he seems to admire, means in most cases that the characters are detached from the circumstances in which the average human being has to live. Nor is the sham-simple style, with the word "and" pushed in at every opportunity like the pellets in potted grouse, much more bearable than the "Mandarin" style which Mr. Connolly justly despises.

Several of the essays on novels and novel-reviewing were written in a phase of Anglophobia, and it is interesting throughout this book to follow the ups and downs of Mr. Connolly's affection for his own country. His relationship with England resembles a marriage in which tears and broken crockery are followed by exhausting reconciliations, but which is bound to end in the divorce court sooner or later. In 1929 he repudiates England altogether, in 1940 he rather admires her, but in 1943 he finds France superior in the things that matter most. Spain is perhaps the country that he loves best of all. Some of what he says is shallow and unfair, and too much coloured by the assumption that civilisation exists in order to produce works of art. But that is the reverse side of the urbane hedonism which makes him so readable a writer. This is an intelligent and amusing book, doubly welcome at a time when high thinking and low writing are the general rule.

[Fee: £10.0.0; 29.11.45]

2812. Review of *The Saturday Book*, [5], edited by Leonard Russell

Manchester Evening News, 6 December 1945

All lovers of the "Gem" and "Magnet"—and both papers have their followers in tens of thousands, both here and in the Dominions—will be delighted to see that Frank Richards is back on the job and has written a long autobiographical article in this year's "Saturday Book."[1]

We may hope that the "Gem" and "Magnet" themselves, after having been "amalgamated" with other papers for the last five years owing to the paper shortage, will reappear before long.

Frank Richards—so he calls himself when he writes in the "Magnet": in the "Gem" he is Martin Clifford—is the creator of those imaginary schools, Greyfriars and St. Jim's, and between 1909 and 1940 he was writing weekly stories about them to the tune of one and a half million words a year.

No one who made their acquaintance in his boyhood will forget Bob Cherry and the rest of the Famous Five at Greyfriars, or Tom Merry and the Honourable Arthur A. D'Arcy at St. Jim's; but without a doubt the greatest of Mr. Richards's creations is the fat boy Billy Bunter.

In Bunter—with his vast, spherical form, his spectacles, his endless search for food and his postal orders which never turn up—Mr. Richards has achieved something that is denied to most imaginative writers: he has created a character able to travel outside the bounds of the reading public.

I have known a barrage balloon nicknamed Billy Bunter by its crew and I have known the same name given to a promising porker on a farm.

In neither case, probably, did the people who used the name know its origin. That is fame, and in his interesting article Mr. Richards tells how he achieved it.

However, he also uses a paragraph or two in delivering a rap over the knuckles to me, and I must answer him. Some years ago I wrote, in a monthly magazine, a long article on the "Gem" and "Magnet," and Mr. Richards answered me vigorously the following month.[2] I made the mistake of assuming that Frank Richards's stories were written by relays of hack-writers, and this seems to have rankled. In "The Saturday Book" he raises the point again.

"What is the use of telling the public that the 'Magnet' was 'specially written' in a style 'easily imitated'? How many wretched imitators have tried to imitate it I could not count without going into high figures—but not one ever succeeded.

"The proof of the pudding is in the eating. The stuff sold like hot cakes—Frank Richards was incessantly dunned for twice or thrice as much copy as he could produce. . . . A good many tried—alternately amusing and exasperating their victim. Not one ever got away with it. George is a very good writer in his own line—but in this matter he simply did not know what he was talking about."

In reprinting the essay I have corrected the original error,[3] but, in case this should reach Mr. Richards's eyes, I should like to explain how I came to make it. The fact is that it just did not strike me as possible that any one human being could write a long complete story—let alone two or three such stories—every week for 30 years.

In that time Mr. Richards produced something like 45,000,000 words. As a journalist who works fairly hard to produce about 150,000 words a year, I find this just unimaginable. However, it is quite true, as I now know from several sources.

And, incidentally, I also know a comic strip artist who has produced his "piece" without a break six days a week for 29 years.

Mr. Richards adds that one of his ambitions is to write a book on religion. I look forward to that book. Meanwhile, good luck to him and soon may the "Gem" and "Magnet" reappear. Who would not rejoice to hear Bob Cherry's cheery "Hullo, hullo, hullo" again, or see some disaster happen to Gussy's top hat?[4]

All the same, there has been a change in the social atmosphere of this country in the five years since the two papers were suspended. If I were Mr. Richards I would be inclined to introduce a little Left wing ideology into my stories and perhaps even transfer the heroes to some more "advanced" kind of school.

How about turning St. Jim's into a co-educational establishment, or sending Billy Bunter and the Famous Five to Dartington Hall?

Mr. Richards's contribution is not of course the whole of "The Saturday Book," which is as full of unexpected things as ever.

There is an article by A. L. Rowse on All Souls College; a long article by Stephen Spender, explaining the successive stages by which a poem is written; an appreciation of Lombroso, the Italian criminologist, by another criminologist; a study of the Empress Eugenie, by Miss C. V. Wedgwood; short stories by Norah Hoult and J. MacLaren-Ross; an article on the mistakes of historians, by Ernest Newman; and much else.

Two contributions which stand out by reason of their queerness are those of Julian Symons and Mr. Fred Bason. Mr. Bason is a second-hand bookseller who has had a long acquaintance with Somerset Maugham, the novelist and playwright, and here writes his reminiscences of him.

Julian Symons, the brother of the late A. J. A. Symons, provides some astonishing and hitherto unpublished information about the mysterious "Baron Corvo"—author of "Hadrian the Seventh"—to whom A. J. A. Symons devoted so much research.

There are 12 caricatures by Low—of Bertrand Russell, Aneurin Bevan, T. S. Eliot, Sir William Beveridge, and others—and two large sections of the book are given over to photographs. One section, which contains several very beautiful compositions, consists of photographs of furniture and other household appliances.

The other is a panorama of the England of 50 years ago. Here you can see Keir Hardie in his deerstalker, the Prince of Wales (Edward VII) in his high-crowned bowler, Bernard Shaw with only a moderate-sized beard, young women in the first short skirts learning to ride fixed wheel bicycles, Aubrey

Beardsley in a check suit, and a whole gallery of actors, politicians, scientists and what-not.

There is also a series of photographs illustrating the evolution of the ballet, and in another part of the book Miss Olive Cook demonstrates with coloured illustrations the interrelation between English and French painting.

This book has a ragged, messy dust-jacket, but otherwise it would make an excellent Christmas present.

[Fee: recorded as £8.0.0—an error for £8.8.0?; 5.12.45]

1. *The Saturday Book,* 5, was the annual immediately following that for 1944, from which Orwell's essay 'Benefit of Clergy: Some Notes on Salvador Dali,' was excised at the last moment—indeed, after the book was in print and the title listed on the Contents page; see *2481.*
2. The article was 'Boys' Weeklies,' *Horizon,* March 1940 (abridged); see *598.* Frank Richards's reply, with this correction, was published in *Horizon,* May 1940; see *599, n. 7.*
3. Orwell added a footnote acknowledging his error when the essay was printed in *Critical Essays* (1945); see *598.*
4. *The Gem* was incorporated in *Triumph* in 1939 and *The Magnet* in *Knock-Out* in 1940. Neither regained its independence and the comics into which they were incorporated were themselves subsumed in others.

2813. 'Freedom of the Park'

Tribune, 7 December 1945

A few weeks ago, five people who were selling papers outside Hyde Park were arrested by the police for obstruction. When taken before the magistrate they were all found guilty, four of them being bound over for six months and the other sentenced to forty shillings' fine or a month's imprisonment. He preferred to serve his term, so I suppose he is still in jail at this moment.

The papers these people were selling were *Peace News, Forward* and *Freedom,* besides other kindred literature. *Peace News* is the organ of the Peace Pledge Union, *Freedom* (till recently called *War Commentary*) is that of the Anarchists: as for *Forward,* its politics defy definition, but at any rate it is violently Left. The magistrate, in passing sentence, stated that he was not influenced by the nature of the literature that was being sold: he was concerned merely with the fact of obstruction, and that this offence had technically been committed.

This raises several important points. To begin with, how does the law stand on the subject? As far as I can discover, selling newspapers in the street *is* technically obstruction, at any rate if you fail to move on when the police tell you to. So it would be legally possible for any policeman who felt like it to arrest any newsboy for selling the *Evening News.* Obviously this doesn't happen, so that the enforcement of the law depends on the discretion of the police.

And what makes the police decide to arrest one man rather than another? However it may have been with the magistrate, I find it hard to believe that in this case the police were not influenced by political considerations. It is a bit too much of a coincidence that they should have picked on people selling just those papers. If they had also arrested someone who was selling *Truth*, or the *Tablet*, or the *Spectator*, or even the *Church Times*, their impartiality would be easier to believe in.

The British police are not like a continental gendarmerie or Gestapo, but I do not think one maligns them in saying that, in the past, they have been unfriendly to Left-wing activities. They have generally shown a tendency to side with those whom they regarded as the defenders of private property. There were some scandalous cases at the time of the Mosley disturbances. At the only big Mosley meeting I ever attended, the police collaborated with the Blackshirts in "keeping order," in a way in which they certainly would not have collaborated with Socialists or Communists. Till quite recently "red" and "illegal" were almost synonymous, and it was always the seller of, say, the *Daily Worker*, never the seller of, say, the *Daily Telegraph*, who was moved on and generally harassed. Apparently it can be the same, at any rate at moments, under a Labour government.

A thing I would like to know—it is a thing we hear very little about—is what changes are made in the administrative personnel when there has been a change of government. Does the police officer who has a vague notion that "Socialism" means something against the law carry on just the same when the government itself is Socialist? It is a sound principle that the official should have no party affiliations, should serve successive governments faithfully and should not be victimised for his political opinions. Still, no government can afford to leave its enemies in key positions, and when Labour is in undisputed power for the first time—and therefore when it is taking over an administration formed by Conservatives—it clearly must make sufficient changes to prevent sabotage. The official, even when friendly to the government in power, is all too conscious that he is a permanency and can frustrate the short-lived Ministers whom he is supposed to serve.

When a Labour Government takes over, I wonder what happens to Scotland Yard Special Branch? To Military Intelligence? To the Consular Service? To the various colonial administrations—and so on and so forth? We are not told, but such symptoms as there are do not suggest that any very extensive reshuffling is going on. We are still represented abroad by the same ambassadors, and B.B.C. censorship seems to have the same subtly reactionary colour that it always had. The B.B.C. claims, of course, to be both independent and non-political. I was told once that its "line," if any, was to represent the Left wing of the government in power. But that was in the days of the Churchill Government. If it represents the Left Wing of the present Government, I have not noticed the fact.

However, the main point of this episode is that the sellers of newspapers and pamphlets should be interfered with at all. Which particular minority is singled out—whether Pacifists, Communists, Anarchists, Jehovah's Witness or the Legion of Christian Reformers who recently declared Hitler to be Jesus Christ—is a secondary matter. It is of symptomatic importance that these people should have been arrested at that particular spot. You are not allowed to sell literature inside Hyde Park, but for many years past it has been usual for the paper-sellers to station themselves just outside the gates and distribute literature connected with the open-air meetings a hundred yards away. Every kind of publication has been sold there without interference.

As for the meetings inside the Park, they are one of the minor wonders of the world. At different times I have listened there to Indian nationalists, Temperance reformers, Communists, Trotskyists, the S.P.G.B.,[1] the Catholic Evidence Society, Freethinkers, vegetarians, Mormons, the Salvation Army, the Church Army, and a large variety of plain lunatics, all taking their turn at the rostrum in an orderly way and receiving a fairly good-humoured hearing from the crowd. Granted that Hyde Park is a special area, a sort of Alsatia[2] where outlawed opinions are permitted to walk—still, there are very few countries in the world where you can see a similar spectacle. I have known continental Europeans, long before Hitler seized power, come away from Hyde Park astonished and even perturbed by the things they had heard Indian or Irish nationalists saying about the British Empire.

The degree of freedom of the press existing in this country is often over-rated. Technically there is great freedom, but the fact that most of the press is owned by a few people operates in much the same way as a State censorship. On the other hand freedom of speech is real. On the platform, or in certain recognised open-air spaces like Hyde Park, you can say almost anything, and, what is perhaps more significant, no one is frightened to utter his true opinions in pubs, on the tops of buses, and so forth.

The point is that the relative freedom which we enjoy depends on public opinion. The law is no protection. Governments make laws, but whether they are carried out, and how the police behave, depends on the general temper of the country. If large numbers of people are interested in freedom of speech, there will be freedom of speech, even if the law forbids it; if public opinion is sluggish, inconvenient minorities will be persecuted, even if laws exist to protect them. The decline in the desire for intellectual liberty has not been so sharp as I would have predicted six years ago, when the war was starting, but still there has been a decline. The notion that certain opinions cannot safely be allowed a hearing is growing. It is given currency by intellectuals who confuse the issue by not distinguishing between democratic opposition and open rebellion, and it is reflected in our growing indifference to tyranny and injustice abroad. And even those who declare themselves to be in favour of freedom of opinion generally drop their claim when it is their own adversaries who are being persecuted.

I am not suggesting that the arrest of five people for selling harmless newspapers is a major calamity. When you see what is happening in the world today, it hardly seems worth squealing about such a tiny incident. All the same, it is not a good symptom that such things should happen when the war is well over, and I should feel happier if this, and the long series of similar episodes that have preceded it, were capable of raising a genuine popular clamour, and not merely a mild flutter in sections of the minority press.

[Fee: £3.3.0; 3.12.45]

An abridged version of 'Freedom of the Park' was published in *Freedom Defence Committee Bulletin*, No. 2, February–March 1946.

1. The Socialist Party of Great Britain, a Marxist organisation having no connection with the Labour Party.
2. The French edition of *Down and Out in Paris and London* (1935) had a footnote by Orwell explaining Alsatia. This read (translated into English): 'A name once given to the district of Whitefriars, which was, in the seventeenth century, a regular refuge for all kinds of wrongdoers by virtue of a right of sanctuary which was finally abolished in 1697'. See *CW*, I, 171 and 228, note to that page.

2814. 'The Case for the Open Fire'

Evening Standard, 8 December 1945

Before long the period of hurriedly constructed prefabs will be over, and Britain will be tackling on a big scale the job of building permanent houses.

It will then be necessary to decide what kind of heating we want our houses to have, and one can be sure in advance that a small but noisy minority will want to do away with the old-fashioned coal fire.

These people—they are also the people who admire gaspipe chairs and glass-topped tables, and regard labour-saving as an end in itself—will argue that the coal fire is wasteful, dirty and inefficient. They will urge that dragging buckets of coal upstairs is a nuisance and that raking out the cinders in the morning is a grisly job, and they will add that the fogs of our cities are made thicker by the smoking of thousands of chimneys.

All of which is perfectly true, and yet comparatively unimportant if one thinks in terms of living and not merely of saving trouble.

I am not arguing that coal fires should be the sole form of heating, merely that every house or flat should have at least one open fire round which the family can sit. In our climate anything that keeps you warm is to be welcomed, and under ideal conditions every form of heating apparatus would be installed in every house.

For any kind of workroom central heating is the best arrangement. It needs no attention, and, since it warms all parts of the room evenly, one can group the furniture according to the needs of work.

For bedrooms, gas or electric fires are best. Even the humble oilstove throws out a lot of heat, and has the virtue of being portable. It is a great comfort to carry an oilstove with you into the bathroom on a winter morning. But for a room that is to be lived in, only a coal fire will do.

The first great virtue of a coal fire is that, just because it only warms one end of the room, it forces people to group themselves in a sociable way. This evening, while I write, the same pattern is being reproduced in hundreds of thousands of British homes.

To one side of the fireplace sits Dad, reading the evening paper. To the other side sits Mum, doing her knitting. On the hearthrug sit the children, playing snakes and ladders. Up against the fender, roasting himself, lies the dog. It is a comely pattern, a good background to one's memories, and the survival of the family as an institution may be more dependent on it than we realise.

Then there is the fascination, inexhaustible to a child, of the fire itself. A fire is never the same for two minutes together, you can look into the red heart of the coals and see caverns or faces or salamanders, according to your imagination: you can even, if your parents will let you, amuse yourself by heating the poker red-hot and bending it between the bars, or sprinkling salt on the flames to turn them green.

A gas or electric fire, or even an anthracite stove, is a dreary thing by comparison. The most dismal objects of all are those phoney electric fires which are so constructed as to look like coal fires. Is not the mere fact of imitation an admission that the real thing is superior?

If, as I maintain, an open fire makes for sociability and has an æsthetic appeal which is particularly important to young children, it is well worth the trouble that it entails.

It is quite true that it is wasteful, messy and the cause of avoidable work: all the same things could be said with equal truth of a baby. The point is that household appliances should be judged not simply by their efficiency but by the pleasure and comfort that one gets out of them.

A vacuum cleaner is good because it saves much dreary labour with brush and pan. Gaspipe furniture is bad because it destroys the friendly look of a room without appreciably adding to one's comfort.

Our civilisation is haunted by the notion that the quickest way of doing anything is invariably the best. The agreeable warming-pan, which warms the whole bed as hot as toast before you jump into it, went out in favour of the clammy, unsatisfying hot-water bottle simply because the warming-pan is a nuisance to carry upstairs and has to be polished daily.

Some people, obsessed by "functionalism," would make every room in the house as bare, clean and labour-saving as a prison cell. They do not reflect that houses are meant to be lived in and that you therefore need different qualities in different rooms. In the kitchen, efficiency; in the bedrooms, warmth; in the living-room, a friendly atmosphere—which in this country demands a good, prodigal coal fire for about seven months of the year.

I am not denying that coal fires have their drawbacks, especially in these days of dwindled newspapers. Many a devout Communist has been forced against all his principles to take in a capitalist paper merely because the Daily Worker is not large enough to light the fire with.

Also there is the slowness with which a fire gets under way in the morning. It would be a good idea, when the new houses are built, if every open fireplace were provided with what used to be called a "blower"—that is, a removable sheet of metal which can be used to create a draught. This works far better than a pair of bellows.

But even the worst fire, even a fire which smokes in your face and has to be constantly poked, is better than none.

In proof of which, imagine the dreariness of spending Christmas evening in sitting—like the family of Arnold Bennett's super-efficient hero in his novel The Card—round a gilded radiator!

[Fee: £20.0.0; 6.12.45]

> 'The Case for the Open Fire' was reprinted in SEAC (the South-East Asia Command newspaper for the forces), 2 January 1946. On 23 January, the case against the open fire was made in a letter from Major L. Fermaud. He pointed out that whereas the person sitting close to the fire might be so warm as to have his or her shins burnt, there would be a terrible chill at that same person's back, and the flowers on the table might be standing in ice. He listed faults of supplementary heating aids—'Little Joan has fainted in the boxroom which is filled with fumes from her oil heater'—and only in 'the centrally heated workroom, George is doing his homework in comfort.' Orwell does not seem to have replied. He must have seen Fermaud's letter, because the Labour M.P. Tom Driberg (see *1931, n. 1*) on 7 February 1946 sent him a cutting from SEAC for 23 January believing it 'may amuse you.' SEAC, edited by Frank Owen (see *1141, n. 4*), reprinted seven of Orwell's ten *Evening Standard* articles between 2 January and 20 April 1946. (The three not reprinted were 'Bare Christmas for the Children' (see *2809*), 'Banish This Uniform' (see *2827*), and 'Just Junk—But Who Could Resist It?' (see *2842*).)

2815. 'Politics and the English Language'

Payments Book, 11 December 1945; *Horizon*, April 1946[1]

Most people who bother with the matter at all would admit that the English language is in a bad way, but it is generally assumed that we cannot by conscious action do anything about it. Our civilization is decadent, and our language—so the argument runs—must inevitably share in the general collapse. It follows that any struggle against the abuse of language is a sentimental archaism, like preferring candles to electric light or hansom cabs to aeroplanes. Underneath this lies the half-conscious belief that language is a natural growth and not an instrument which we shape for our own purposes.

Now, it is clear that the decline of a language must ultimately have political and economic causes: it is not due simply to the bad influence of this or that individual writer. But an effect can become a cause, reinforcing the original cause and producing the same effect in an intensified form, and so on indefinitely. A man may take to drink because he feels himself to be a failure, and then fail all the more completely because he drinks. It is rather the same thing that is happening to the English language. It becomes ugly and inaccurate because our thoughts are foolish, but the slovenliness of our language makes it easier for us to have foolish thoughts. The point is that the process is reversible. Modern English, especially written English, is full of bad habits which spread by imitation and which can be avoided if one is willing to take the necessary trouble. If one gets rid of these habits one can think more clearly, and to think clearly is a necessary first step towards political regeneration: so that the fight against bad English is not frivolous and is not the exclusive concern of professional writers. I will come back to this presently, and I hope that by that time the meaning of what I have said here will have become clearer. Meanwhile, here are five specimens of the English language as it is now habitually written.

These five passages have not been picked out because they are especially bad—I could have quoted far worse if I had chosen—but because they illustrate various of the mental vices from which we now suffer. They are a little below the average, but are fairly representative samples. I number them so that I can refer back to them when necessary:

'(1) I am not, indeed, sure whether it is not true to say that the Milton who once seemed not unlike a seventeenth-century Shelley had not become, out of an experience ever more bitter in each year, more alien (*sic*) to the founder of that Jesuit sect which nothing could induce him to tolerate.'

Professor Harold Laski (Essay in *Freedom of Expression*).

'(2) Above all, we cannot play ducks and drakes with a native battery of idioms which prescribes such egregious collocations of vocables as the Basic *put up with* for *tolerate* or *put at a loss* for *bewilder*.'

Professor Lancelot Hogben (*Interglossa*).

'(3) On the one side we have the free personality: by definition it is not neurotic, for it has neither conflict nor dream. Its desires, such as they are, are transparent, for they are just what institutional approval keeps in the forefront of consciousness; another institutional pattern would alter their number and intensity; there is little in them that is natural, irreducible, or culturally dangerous. But *on the other side*, the social bond itself is nothing but the mutual reflection of these self-secure integrities. Recall the definition of love. Is not this the very picture of a small academic? Where is there a place in this hall of mirrors for either personality or fraternity?'

Essay on psychology in *Politics* (New York).

'(4) All the "best people" from the gentlemen's clubs, and all the frantic fascist captains, united in common hatred of Socialism and bestial horror of the rising tide of the mass revolutionary movement, have turned to acts of provocation, to foul incendiarism, to medieval legends of poisoned wells, to legalize their own destruction of proletarian organizations, and rouse the agitated petty-bourgeoisie to chauvinistic fervour on behalf of the fight against the revolutionary way out of the crisis.'

Communist pamphlet.

'(5) If a new spirit *is* to be infused into this old country, there is one thorny and contentious reform which must be tackled, and that is the humanization and galvanization of the B.B.C. Timidity here will bespeak canker and atrophy of the soul. The heart of Britain may be sound and of strong beat, for instance, but the British lion's roar at present is like that of Bottom in Shakespeare's *Midsummer Night's Dream*—as gentle as any sucking dove. A virile new Britain cannot continue indefinitely to be traduced in the eyes, or rather ears, of the world by the effete languors of Langham Place, brazenly masquerading as "standard English". When the Voice of Britain is heard at nine o'clock, better far and infinitely less ludicrous to hear aitches honestly dropped than the present priggish, inflated, inhibited, school-ma'amish arch braying of blameless bashful mewing maidens!'

Letter in Tribune.

Each of these passages has faults of its own, but, quite apart from avoidable ugliness, two qualities are common to all of them. The first is staleness of imagery: the other is lack of precision. The writer either has a meaning and cannot express it, or he inadvertently says something else, or he is almost indifferent as to whether his words mean anything or not. This mixture of vagueness and sheer incompetence is the most marked characteristic of modern English prose, and especially of any kind of political writing. As soon as certain topics are raised, the concrete melts into the abstract and no one seems able to think of turns of speech that are not hackneyed: prose consists less and less of *words* chosen for the sake of their meaning, and more and more of *phrases* tacked together like the sections of a prefabricated hen-house. I list below, with notes and examples, various of the tricks by means of which the work of prose-construction is habitually dodged:

Dying metaphors. A newly invented metaphor assists thought by evoking a visual image, while on the other hand a metaphor which is technically 'dead' (e.g. *iron resolution*) has in effect reverted to being an ordinary word and can generally be used without loss of vividness. But in between these two classes there is a huge dump of worn-out metaphors which have lost all evocative power and are merely used because they save people the trouble of inventing phrases for themselves. Examples are: *Ring the changes on, take up the cudgels for, toe the line, ride roughshod over, stand shoulder to shoulder with, play into the hands of, no axe to grind, grist to the mill, fishing in troubled waters,[rift within the lute],*[2] *on the order of the day, Achilles' heel, swan song, hotbed.* Many of these are used without knowledge of their meaning (what is a 'rift', for instance?), and incompatible metaphors are frequently mixed, a sure sign that the writer is not interested in what he is saying. Some metaphors now current have been twisted out of their original meaning without those who use them even being aware of the fact. For example, *toe the line* is sometimes written *tow the line*. Another example is *the hammer and the anvil*, now always used with the implication that the anvil gets the worst of it. In real life it is always the anvil that breaks the hammer, never the other way about: a writer who stopped to think what he was saying would be aware of this, and would avoid perverting the original phrase.

Operators, or *verbal false limbs.* These save the trouble of picking out appropriate verbs and nouns, and at the same time pad each sentence with extra syllables which give it an appearance of symmetry. Characteristic phrases are: *render inoperative, militate against, prove unacceptable, make contact with, be subjected to, give rise to, give grounds for, have the effect of, play a leading part (role) in, make itself felt, take effect, exhibit a tendency to, serve the purpose of,* etc., etc. The keynote is the elimination of simple verbs. Instead of being a single word, such as *break, stop, spoil, mend, kill,* a verb becomes a *phrase,* made up of a noun or adjective tacked on to some general-purposes verb such as *prove, serve, form, play, render*. In addition, the passive voice is wherever possible used in preference to the active, and noun constructions are used instead of gerunds (*by examination of* instead of *by examining*). The range of verbs is further cut down by means of the *-ize* and *de-* formations, and banal statements are given an appearance of profundity by means of the *not un*-formation. Simple conjunctions and prepositions are replaced by such phrases as *with respect to, having regard to, the fact that, by dint of, in view of, in the interests of, on the hypothesis that*; and the ends of sentences are saved from anticlimax by such resounding commonplaces as *greatly to be desired, cannot be left out of account, a development to be expected in the near future, deserving of serious consideration, brought to a satisfactory conclusion*, and so on and so forth.

Pretentious diction. Words like *phenomenon, element, individual* (as noun), *objective, categorical, effective, virtual, basic, primary, promote, constitute, exhibit, exploit, utilize, eliminate, liquidate*, are used to dress up simple statement[s] and give an air of scientific impartiality to biased judgements. Adjectives like *epoch-making, epic, historic, unforgettable, triumphant, age-old, inevitable, inexorable, veritable*, are used to dignify the sordid processes of international politics, while writing that aims at glorifying war usually takes on an archaic colour, its characteristic words being: *realm, throne, chariot, mailed fist, trident, sword, shield, buckler, banner, jackboot, clarion*. Foreign words and expressions such as *cul de sac, ancien régime, deus ex machina, mutatis mutandis, status quo, gleichschaltung, weltanschauung*, are used to give an air of culture and elegance. Except for the useful abbreviations *i.e., e.g.*, and *etc.*, there is no real need for any of the hundreds of foreign phrases now current in English. Bad writers, and especially scientific, political and sociological writers, are nearly always haunted by the notion that Latin or Greek words are grander than Saxon ones, and unnecessary words like *expedite, ameliorate, predict, extraneous, deracinated, clandestine, subaqueous* and hundreds of others constantly gain ground from their Anglo-Saxon opposite numbers.* The jargon peculiar to Marxist writing (*hyena, hangman, cannibal, petty bourgeois, these gentry, lacquey, flunkey, mad dog, White Guard*, etc.) consists largely of words and phrases translated from Russian, German or French; but the normal way of coining a new word is to use a Latin or Greek root with the appropriate affix and, where necessary, the -ize formation. It is often easier to make up words of this kind (*deregionalize, impermissible, extramarital, non-fragmentary*[3] and so forth) than to think up the English words that will cover one's meaning. The result, in general, is an increase in slovenliness and vagueness.

Meaningless words. In certain kinds of writing, particularly in art criticism and literary criticism, it is normal to come across long passages which are

---

* An interesting illustration of this is the way in which the English flower names which were in use till very recently are being ousted by Greek ones, *snapdragon* becoming *antirrhinum*, *forget-me-not* becoming *myosotis*, etc. It is hard to see any practical reason for this change of fashion: it is probably due to an instinctive turning-away from the more homely word and a vague feeling that the Greek word is scientific [Orwell's footnote].

almost completely lacking in meaning.* Words like *romantic, plastic, values, human, dead, sentimental, natural, vitality*, as used in art criticism, are strictly meaningless, in the sense that they not only do not point to any discoverable object, but are hardly even expected to do so by the reader. When one critic writes, 'The outstanding feature of Mr. X's work is its living quality', while another writes, 'The immediately striking thing about Mr. X's work is its peculiar deadness', the reader accepts this as a simple difference of opinion. If words like *black* and *white* were involved, instead of the jargon words *dead* and *living*, he would see at once that language was being used in an improper way. Many political words are similarly abused. The word *Fascism* has now no meaning except in so far as it signifies 'something not desirable'. The words *democracy, socialism, freedom, patriotic, realistic, justice*, have each of them several different meanings which cannot be reconciled with one another. In the case of a word like *democracy*, not only is there no agreed definition, but the attempt to make one is resisted from all sides. It is almost universally felt that when we call a country democratic we are praising it: consequently the defenders of every kind of régime claim that it is a democracy, and fear that they might have to stop using the word if it were tied down to any one meaning. Words of this kind are often used in a consciously dishonest way. That is, the person who uses them has his own private definition, but allows his hearer to think he means something quite different. Statements like *Marshal Pétain was a true patriot, The Soviet Press is the freest in the world, The Catholic Church is opposed to persecution*, are almost always made with intent to deceive. Other words used in variable meanings, in most cases more or less dishonestly, are: *class, totalitarian, science, progressive, reactionary, bourgeois, equality*.

Now that I have made this catalogue of swindles and perversions, let me give another example of the kind of writing that they lead to. This time it must of its nature be an imaginary one. I am going to translate a passage of good English into modern English of the worst sort. Here is a well-known verse from *Ecclesiastes*:

'I returned, and saw under the sun, that the race is not to the swift, nor the battle to the strong, neither yet bread to the wise, nor yet riches to men of understanding, nor yet favour to men of skill; but time and chance happeneth to them all.'

Here it is in modern English:

'Objective consideration of contemporary phenomena compels the conclusion that success or failure in competitive activities exhibits no tendency to be commensurate with innate capacity, but that a considerable element of the unpredictable must invariably be taken into account.'

---

* Example: 'Comfort's catholicity of perception and image, strangely Whitmanesque in range, almost the exact opposite in aesthetic compulsion, continues to evoke that trembling atmospheric accumulative hinting at a cruel, an inexorably serene timelessness. . . . Wrey Gardiner scores by aiming at simple bullseyes with precision. Only they are not so simple, and through this contented sadness runs more than the surface bitter-sweet of resignation' (*Poetry Quarterly*) [Orwell's footnote].

This is a parody, but not a very gross one. Exhibit (3), above, for instance, contains several patches of the same kind of English. It will be seen that I have not made a full translation. The beginning and ending of the sentence follow the original meaning fairly closely, but in the middle the concrete illustrations—race, battle, bread—dissolve into the vague phrase 'success or failure in competitive activities'. This had to be so, because no modern writer of the kind I am discussing—no one capable of using phrases like 'objective consideration of contemporary phenomena'—would ever tabulate his thoughts in that precise and detailed way. The whole tendency of modern prose is away from concreteness. Now analyse these two sentences a little more closely. The first contains 49 words but only 60 syllables, and all its words are those of everyday life. The second contains 38 words of 90 syllables: 18 of its words are from Latin roots, and one from Greek. The first sentence contains six vivid images, and only one phrase ('time and chance') that could be called vague. The second contains not a single fresh, arresting phrase, and in spite of its 90 syllables it gives only a shortened version of the meaning contained in the first. Yet without a doubt it is the second kind of sentence that is gaining ground in modern English. I do not want to exaggerate. This kind of writing is not yet universal, and outcrops of simplicity will occur here and there in the worst-written page. Still, if you or I were told to write a few lines on the uncertainty of human fortunes, we should probably come much nearer to my imaginary sentence than to the one from *Ecclesiastes*.

As I have tried to show, modern writing at its worst does not consist in picking out words for the sake of their meaning and inventing images in order to make the meaning clearer. It consists in gumming together long strips of words which have already been set in order by someone else, and making the results presentable by sheer humbug. The attraction of this way of writing is that it is easy. It is easier—even quicker, once you have the habit—to say *In my opinion it is a not unjustifiable assumption that* than to say *I think*. If you use ready-made phrases, you not only don't have to hunt about for words; you also don't have to bother with the rhythms of your sentences, since these phrases are generally so arranged as to be more or less euphonious. When you are composing in a hurry—when you are dictating to a stenographer, for instance, or making a public speech—it is natural to fall into a pretentious, Latinized style. Tags like *a consideration which we should do well to bear in mind* or *a conclusion to which all of us would readily assent* will save many a sentence from coming down with a bump. By using stale metaphors, similes and idioms, you save much mental effort, at the cost of leaving your meaning vague, not only for your reader but for yourself. This is the significance of mixed metaphors. The sole aim of a metaphor is to call up a visual image. When these images clash—as in *The Fascist octopus has sung its swan song, the jackboot is thrown into the melting pot*—it can be taken as certain that the writer is not seeing a mental image of the objects he is naming; in other words he is not really thinking. Look again at the examples I gave at the beginning of this essay. Professor Laski (1) uses five negatives in 53 words. One of these is superfluous, making nonsense of the whole passage, and in addition there is the slip *alien* for akin, making further nonsense, and several avoidable pieces of clumsiness which increase the general vagueness. Professor Hogben (2) plays ducks and drakes with a battery which is able to write prescriptions, and, while disapproving of the everyday phrase *put up with*, is unwilling to look *egregious* up in the dictionary and see what it means. (3), if one takes an uncharitable attitude towards it, [it] is simply meaningless: probably one could work out its intended meaning by reading the whole of the article in which it occurs. In (4), the writer knows more or less what he wants to say, but an accumulation of stale phrases chokes him like tea leaves blocking a sink. In (5), words and meaning have almost parted company. People who write in this manner usually have a general emotional meaning—they dislike one thing and want to express solidarity with another—but they are not interested in the detail of what they are saying. A scrupulous writer, in every sentence that he writes, will ask himself at least four questions, thus: What am I trying to say? What words will express it? What image or idiom will make it clearer? Is this image fresh enough to have an effect? And he will probably ask himself two more: Could I put it more shortly? Have I said anything that is avoidably ugly? But you are not obliged to go to all this trouble. You can shirk it by simply throwing your mind open and letting the ready-made phrases come crowding in. They will construct your sentences for you— even think your thoughts for you, to a certain extent—and at need they will perform the important service of partially concealing your meaning even from yourself. It is at this point that the special connection between politics and the debasement of language becomes clear.

In our time it is broadly true that political writing is bad writing. Where it is not true, it will generally be found that the writer is some kind of rebel, expressing his private opinions and not a 'party line'. Orthodoxy, of whatever colour, seems to demand a lifeless, imitative style. The political dialects to be found in pamphlets, leading articles, manifestos, White Papers and the speeches of under-secretaries do, of course, vary from party to party, but they are all alike in that one almost never finds in them a fresh, vivid, home-made turn of speech. When one watches some tired hack on the platform mechanically repeating the familiar phrases—*bestial atrocities, iron heel, bloodstained tyranny, free peoples of the world, stand shoulder to shoulder*—one often has a curious feeling that one is not watching a live human being but some kind of dummy: a feeling which suddenly becomes stronger at moments when the light catches the speaker's spectacles and turns them into blank discs which seem to have no eyes behind them. And this is not altogether fanciful. A speaker who uses that kind of phraseology has gone some distance towards turning himself into a machine. The appropriate noises are coming out of his larynx, but his brain is not involved as it would be if he were choosing his words for himself. If the speech he is making is one that he is accustomed to make over and over again, he may be almost unconscious of what he is saying, as one is when one utters the responses in church. And this reduced state of consciousness, if not indispensable, is at any rate favourable to political conformity.

In our time, political speech and writing are largely the defence of the indefensible. Things like the continuance of British rule in India, the Russian purges and deportations, the dropping of the atom bombs on Japan, can indeed be defended, but only by arguments which are too brutal for most people to face, and which do not square with the professed aims of political parties. Thus political language has to consist largely of euphemism, question-begging and sheer cloudy vagueness. Defenceless villages are bombarded from the air, the inhabitants driven out into the countryside, the cattle machine-gunned, the huts set on fire with incendiary bullets: this is called *pacification*. Millions of peasants are robbed of their farms and sent trudging along the roads with no more than they can carry: this is called *transfer of population* or *rectification of frontiers*. People are imprisoned for years without trial, or shot in the back of the neck or sent to die of scurvy in Arctic lumber camps: this is called *elimination of unreliable elements*. Such phraseology is needed if one wants to name things without calling up mental pictures of them. Consider for instance some comfortable English professor defending Russian totalitarianism. He cannot say outright, 'I believe in killing off your opponents when you can get good results by doing so'. Probably, therefore, he will say something like this:

'While freely conceding that the Soviet régime exhibits certain features which the humanitarian may be inclined to deplore, we must, I think, agree that a certain curtailment of the right to political opposition is an unavoidable concomitant of transitional periods, and that the rigours which the Russian people have been called upon to undergo have been amply justified in the sphere of concrete achievement.'

The inflated style is itself a kind of euphemism. A mass of Latin words falls upon the facts like soft snow, blurring the outlines and covering up all the details. The great enemy of clear language is insincerity. When there is a gap between one's real and one's declared aims, one turns as it were instinctively to long words and exhausted idioms, like a cuttlefish squirting out ink. In our age there is no such thing as 'keeping out of politics'. All issues are political issues, and politics itself is a mass of lies, evasions, folly, hatred and schizophrenia. When the general atmosphere is bad, language must suffer. I should expect to find—this is a guess which I have not sufficient knowledge to verify—that the German, Russian and Italian languages have all deteriorated in the last ten or fifteen years, as a result of dictatorship.

But if thought corrupts language, language can also corrupt thought. A bad usage can spread by tradition and imitation, even among people who should and do know better. The debased language that I have been discussing is in some ways very convenient. Phrases like *a not unjustifiable assumption, leaves much to be desired, would serve no good purpose, a consideration which we should do well to bear in mind*, are a continuous temptation, a packet of aspirins always at one's elbow. Look back through this essay, and for certain you will find that I have again and again committed the very faults I am protesting against. By this morning's post I have received a pamphlet dealing with conditions in Germany. The author tells me that he 'felt impelled' to write it. I open it at random, and here is almost the first sentence that I see: '(The Allies) have an opportunity not only of achieving a radical transformation of

Germany's social and political structure in such a way as to avoid a nationalistic reaction in Germany itself, but at the same time of laying the foundations of a co-operative and unified Europe.' You see, he 'feels impelled' to write—feels, presumably, that he has something new to say—and yet his words, like cavalry horses answering the bugle, group themselves automatically into the familiar dreary pattern. This invasion of one's mind by ready-made phrases (*lay the foundations, achieve a radical transformation*) can only be prevented if one is constantly on guard against them, and every such phrase anaesthetizes a portion of one's brain.

I said earlier that the decadence of our language is probably curable. Those who deny this would argue, if they produced an argument at all, that language merely reflects existing, social conditions, and that we cannot influence its development by any direct tinkering with words and constructions. So far as the general tone or spirit of a language goes, this may be true, but it is not true in detail. Silly words and expressions have often disappeared, not through any evolutionary process but owing to the conscious action of a minority. Two recent examples were *explore every avenue* and *leave no stone unturned*, which were killed by the jeers of a few journalists. There is a long list of flyblown metaphors which could similarly be got rid of if enough people would interest themselves in the job; and it should also be possible to laugh the *not un-* formation out of existence,* to reduce the amount of Latin and Greek in the average sentence, to drive out foreign phrases and strayed scientific words, and, in general, to make pretentiousness unfashionable. But all these are minor points. The defence of the English language implies more than this, and perhaps it is best to start by saying what it does *not* imply.

To begin with, it has nothing to do with archaism, with the salvaging of obsolete words and turns of speech, or with the setting-up of a 'standard English' which must never be departed from. On the contrary, it is especially concerned with the scrapping of every word or idiom which has outworn its usefulness. It has nothing to do with correct grammar and syntax, which are of no importance so long as one makes one's meaning clear, or with the avoidance of Americanisms, or with having what is called a 'good prose style'. On the other hand it is not concerned with fake simplicity and the attempt to make written English colloquial. Nor does it even imply in every case preferring the Saxon word to the Latin one, though it does imply using the fewest and shortest words that will cover one's meaning. What is above all needed is to let the meaning choose the word, and not the other way about. In prose, the worst thing one can do with words is to surrender to them. When you think of a concrete object, you think wordlessly, and then, if you want to describe the thing you have been visualizing, you probably hunt about till you find the exact words that seem to fit it. When you think of something abstract you are more inclined to use words from the start, and unless you make a conscious effort to prevent it, the existing dialect will come rushing in and do the job for you, at the expense of blurring or even changing

---

* One can cure oneself of the *not un-* formation by memorizing this sentence: *A not unblack dog was chasing a not unsmall rabbit across a not ungreen field* [Orwell's footnote].

429

your meaning. Probably it is better to put off using words as long as possible and get one's meaning as clear as one can through pictures or sensations. Afterwards one can choose—not simply *accept*—the phrases that will best cover the meaning, and then switch round and decide what impression one's words are likely to make on another person. This last effort of the mind cuts out all stale or mixed images, all prefabricated phrases, needless repetitions, and humbug and vagueness generally. But one can often be in doubt about the effect of a word or a phrase, and one needs rules that one can rely on when instinct fails. I think the following rules will cover most cases:

(i) Never use a metaphor, simile or other figure of speech which you are used to seeing in print.

(ii) Never use a long word where a short one will do.

(iii) If it is possible to cut a word out, always cut it out.

(iv) Never use the passive where you can use the active.

(v) Never use a foreign phrase, a scientific word or a jargon word if you can think of an everyday English equivalent.

(vi) Break any of these rules sooner than say anything outright barbarous.

These rules sound elementary, and so they are, but they demand a deep change of attitude in anyone who has grown used to writing in the style now fashionable. One could keep all of them and still write bad English, but one could not write the kind of stuff that I quoted in those five specimens at the beginning of this article.

I have not here been considering the literary use of language, but merely language as an instrument for expressing and not for concealing or preventing thought. Stuart Chase[4] and others have come near to claiming that all abstract words are meaningless, and have used this as a pretext for advocating a kind of political quietism. Since you don't know what Fascism is, how can you struggle against Fascism? One need not swallow such absurdities as this, but one ought to recognize that the present political chaos is connected with the decay of language, and that one can probably bring about some improvement by starting at the verbal end. If you simplify your English, you are freed from the worst follies of orthodoxy. You cannot speak any of the necessary dialects, and when you make a stupid remark its stupidity will be obvious, even to yourself. Political language—and with variations this is true of all political parties, from Conservatives to Anarchists—is designed to make lies sound truthful and murder respectable, and to give an appearance of solidity to pure wind. One cannot change this all in a moment, but one can at least change one's own habits, and from time to time one can even, if one jeers loudly enough, send some worn-out and useless phrase—some *jackboot, Achilles' heel, hotbed, melting pot, acid test, veritable inferno* or other lump of verbal refuse—into the dustbin where it belongs.

1. Orwell records against 11 December 1945 in his Payments Book that this article would be entered in his Payments Book for 1946; see *2831*. Unfortunately, this and any later books have not been traced. Later he added the note 'See 18.4.46,' presumably when he knew *Horizon* for April 1946 had appeared. Although he replied to the questionnaires on 'The Cost of Letters' (September 1946; see *3057*) and 'The Three Best Books of 1947' (December 1947; see *3311*),

this was to be Orwell's last major article for *Horizon*. The article has been reprinted many times. On 9 April 1946, the publisher Stanley Unwin wrote congratulating him on the essay and saying he hoped it would be included in a volume of Orwell's essays. The first two reprintings were private. The Observer Foreign News Service published it (as 'What Do You Mean?') and the *News of the World* reprinted it as an undated pamphlet (using Orwell's title) for the benefit of their staffs. A preliminary note in the OFNS reprint stated: 'We reproduce it for private circulation—without insinuation or apology—among those who write in The Observer and O.F.N.S.' It appeared, abridged, in *The New Republic*, 17 and 24 June 1946, and, more severely cut, in *World Digest*, August 1946 (as 'Do You Use Prefabricated Phrases?'). It was included in *Modern British Writing*, edited by Denys Val Baker (New York, 1947), and, as *Politics and the English Language* (abridged), was printed as three Christmas Keepsakes (Evansville, Indiana, 1947): one was for Herbert W. Simpson (100 copies), another for the Typophiles (320 copies), and one 'For the Friends of Paul Bennett' (50 copies): see *3077, n. 1*. The version used was that published by *The New Republic* and it carried the line 'The author has obliged with his consent from Scotland.' Whether Orwell realised that three separate printings were involved, not one, is unclear. As Unwin had hoped, the essay was included in the next collection of Orwell's essays, *Shooting an Elephant* (1950). Since then it has been included in many selections of Orwell's essays and in collections of essays compiled by others. The version reproduced here is that published in *Horizon*.

At the end of the exercise book in which Orwell wrote his Domestic Diary for 1946 are sixteen pages of notes which are clearly related to this essay. They cannot be dated precisely, but the first is a cutting from *Tribune* dated 31 August 1945. For convenience of comparison with the essay, these notes follow as the next item (*2816*).

Orwell's Payments Book indicates that this article was at first intended for *Contact*. He crossed through *Contact* and substituted *Horizon*; see *2831*, 11.12.45. *Contact* was founded and edited by George Weidenfeld (1919–); seventeen numbers were published between 1946 and 1949, and four more from May to December 1950 as *Contact: The Magazine of Pleasure*. Orwell and Weidenfeld met when both were working at the BBC at 200 Oxford Street. Since they worked on different floors and in different services—Weidenfeld worked in the Monitoring and the Empire & North American services, 1939–46—they did not come to know each other well, though Weidenfeld recalls 'a very agreeable luncheon,' probably at Bertorelli's, with Orwell and Tosco Fyvel. Philip Toynbee (1916–1981), literary editor of *Contact*, was briefed by Weidenfeld to commission a series of articles by distinguished writers, keeping rigidly to the modes and canons of 'reportage'; what was wanted for this part of *Contact* were factual narratives and investigative articles. It was Weidenfeld who 'committed the sacrilegious mistake of asking Philip to turn it [Orwell's article] down on these grounds,' as he himself put it in a letter to the editor, 6 May 1992. In his autobiography, Weidenfeld explained that the article 'did not fit in with the purist formula' he had evolved for *Contact* (*Remembering My Good Friends* (1995), 129). See also *2990, n. 2*. Weidenfeld founded the publishing house of Weidenfeld & Nicolson in 1948 and has ever since been its chairman. His *The Goebbels Experiment* was published in 1943. He was knighted in 1969, and in 1976 created a life peer as Baron Weidenfeld of Chelsea.

2. '*rift within the lute*' is given after 'fishing in troubled waters' in Orwell's list of Metaphors in his notes; see *2816*. Not all the metaphors in this list are in the essay, but in his next sentence Orwell asks 'what is a "rift", for instance?' He must have intended to include this metaphor, since his question does not make sense without it; it has therefore been added here in square brackets. The line comes from Tennyson's *Idylls of the King*, 'Merlin and Vivien.' Vivien sings to Merlin a song she heard Sir Launcelot once sing. It includes these two stanzas, which make the meaning plain:

It [want of faith] is the little rift within the lute,
That by and by will make the music mute,
And ever widening slowly silence all.

The little rift within the lover's lute,
Or little pitted speck in garner'd fruit,
That rotting inward slowly moulders all. [Lines 388–93]

3. Neither 'non-fragmentary' nor 'deregionalize' appear in the 1991 edition of the *Oxford English Dictionary*, though 'regionalize' and 'deruralize' do.
4. Stuart Chase (1888–1985), economist who investigated the U.S. meat-packing industry and served with the Labor Bureau Inc. Orwell probably refers to his *The Tyranny of Words* (1938). He also wrote, *Men and Machines* (1929), *The Economy of Abundance* (1934), and *Rich Land, Poor Land* (1936).

2816. Notes for 'Politics and the English Language'

February to October 1945?

At the end of the exercise book in which Orwell wrote his Domestic Diary III, 7 May to 8 October 1946 and 4 and 5 January 1947 (*3147*), are notes for 'Politics and the English Language.' They follow immediately the entry for 5 January 1947, but it should not be supposed that because of their position these notes were written after 5 January 1947. Not only are they directly related to 'Politics and the English Language' but the entry for 5 January is, exceptionally, on a verso page, facing the list of metaphors. Had that list of metaphors not already been written into the notebook, the entry for 5 January would have been written on the recto page. There is also with the notebook a loose sheet of paper showing a garden layout. The other sketches form part of the notebook and, had there been space available at this point, it would be expected that this loose sketch would have been included here—but see last paragraph below.

Because these notes are so closely related to 'Politics and the English Language,' they are reproduced directly following the essay. Some pages in the sequence of notes are blank; to conserve space, blank and partly filled pages are not reproduced as such here. Page breaks are indicated by rows of dots. Question marks in the text are Orwell's. The notes at the end are editorial. There is much cross-marking between facing pages listing Operators and Cliché Phrases other than metaphors; this cross-marking cannot be represented here exactly. One metaphor, '*rift within the lute*,' has been included in the essay because it seems to have been omitted by accident from the essay as printed; see *2815, n. 2.*

It is not possible to date these notes precisely. However, 'As I Please,' 58, 9 February 1945 (*2616*) refers to 'worn-out and useless metaphors.' Orwell there mentions 'explore every avenue,' 'leave no stone unturned,' 'ring the changes on,' ° 'take up the cudgels for,' and the alternative spellings in 'toe/tow the line'; all are listed in these notes, the first four being the first four given in Orwell's list. 'As I Please' also refers to 'cross swords with' and alternative spellings in 'plain/plane sailing,' neither of which is listed here (nor in 'Politics and the English Language'). This suggests that these notes were started in about February 1945. The cutting from *Tribune* was published on 31 August 1945, suggesting a concluding date between then and the completion of the article on 11 December 1945.

The entries are written in blue-black and various shades of blue ink; pencil; blue crayon; and, for the 'Propaganda tricks,' blue-black Biro and a paler shade of Biro. This section could not have been written until after February 1946, when Orwell ordered a Biro (though the supplier was out of stock at the time;

see *2375*). The section 'Propaganda tricks' is not part of 'Politics and the English Language.'

Metaphors

Ring the changes
Take up the cudgels for
⎧Explore every avenue ⎫
⎨Leave no stone unturned ⎬
⎩No axe to grind ⎭
Grist to the mill (Q. what is grist?)
Toe the line   (tow the line)
Fishing in troubled waters   (meaning?)
Rift within the lute   (Rift?)
Fly in the ointment
Ride roughshod over
Stand shoulder to shoulder with
Achilles heel
Hotbed
Swan song
Play into the hands of.
Order of the day.

....

Operators   (artificial limbs?)

Serve the purpose of $\times$[1]
render (with adjective) promote $\times$ Phenomenon
not un-   Sphere/Realm
militate against   Element
                       Exhibit[2]
Show a tendency to   Effective[3]
The fact that
-ise & -isation, de-
With regard to, with respect to, etc.
Play a leading part (role) in $\times$
Inoperative (render inoperative)
Make contact with   Prove unacceptable
                                                       Reach . . . point (that — of)?

Make itself felt
Subjected to   Take effect $\times$
Have the effect of $\times$ Effect $\times$
                                $\times$ five° good grounds for
Exploit — utilise[4] $\times$
In the interests of
Compels the conclusion that

433

By dint of		The fact that	
Development	†₅	In view of	Passive
Give rise to⁶	†	Form	×
Prove		Constitute⁷	×
Noun formation — The substitution of (substituting)			

....

Cliché phrases other than metaphors

Individual (noun)
Sorely tempted
On the order of the day
Forge (unity etc.)
Would serve no good purpose⁸
Veritable (inferno etc.)⁹
All hell was let loose   Promote
Adding insult to injury   Exhibit
Epic (adj.)
Historic
Quietus (gave him his   etc.)⁹
Swan song⁹   Veritable inferno¹⁰

Epoch-making.
Unforgettable   Basic
Inveterate   Primary   Stale metaphors
Veritable   Operators
Categorical   Clichés
Inevitable   Meaningless word.
Virtual   Foreign words
Archaisms?
(weapons)

....

Misuses & narrowed meanings

Egregius¹¹
Infer (for imply — but also bad currency in the past)
Element (eg. unreliable elements)

Sex words (misconduct, improper, suggestive, intimate, immoral, interfere with, association, dubious, of a certain nature¹²) Sensual, sensuous, fraternise, glamour,¹³ association.¹⁴

....

434

Jargons

Marxist
Art-criticism
Strayed scientific words
....

Meaningless words etc

Human (eg. "human values")
Sentimental
Dead (in art criticism)
Vitality
Classical
Romantic
Values
Plastic (?)
Natural
....

Words consciously used in variable meanings.

Fascism
Democracy
Socialism
Patriotic
Realistic
Romantic[15]
God
Good
Bad/Evil
Objective
Freedom/Liberty
....

Mixed metaphors
....

Abstract words etc.

Phenomenon
Noun formation in place of verb. Eg. "By the substitution of" for "by substituting". "The fact that" in place of gerund.
....

Barnacle adjectives

Undiluted (tripe etc.)
Invert[16]
Inveterate (hatred)
Veritable (inferno etc.)

……..

Archaisms

Jackboot (& weapons generally)

……..

Loose statements

……..

EXAMPLES

[Cutting from *Tribune*, 31 August 1945]

GALVANISE THE B.B.C.!

Speaking as one who wished to see Winston Churchill continue in the direction of affairs for the present, and who, therefore, unhesitatingly voted Conservative in the recent election, I freely concede that there are certain undoubted and manifest benefits to be derived from Labour rule.

For example, the real realisation of the hard facts governing the situation in the post-war world must come to millions as an unpleasant dose of medicine. It is well that the doctors administering it should not only have a mandate from the people, but themselves be sprung from the people.

Even so, a new Government must walk warily. I imagine that there is nothing like coming into power in a democratic state for making a man realise how limited are the powers of the princes of this (modern) world. Nevertheless, if a new spirit *is* to be infused into this old country, there is one thorny and contentious reform which must be tackled, and that is the humanisation and galvanisation of the B.B.C. Timidity here will bespeak canker and atrophy of the soul. The heart of Britain may be sound and of strong beat, for instance, but the British lion's roar at present is like that of Bottom in Shakespeare's 'Midsummer Night's Dream"—as gentle as any sucking dove. A virile new Britain cannot continue indefinitely to be traduced in the eyes, or rather ears, of the world by the effete languors of Langham Place, brazenly masquerading as "standard English." When the Voice of Britain is heard at nine o'clock, better far and infinitely less ludicrous to hear aitches honestly dropped than the present priggish, inflated, inhibited, school-ma'amishly arch braying of blamelessly bashful mewing maidens!

George Richards.

Above all, we cannot play ducks & drakes with a native battery of idioms which prescribes such egregius[11] collocations of vocables as the Basic *put up with* for *tolerate* & *put at a loss* for *bewilder.*

(Lancelot Hogben, "Interglossa.")

I am not, indeed, sure whether it is not true to say that the Milton who once seemed not unlike a seventeenth-century Shelley had not become, out of an experience even more bitter in each year, more alien to the founder of that Jesuit sect which nothing could induce him to tolerate. (53)

Harold Laski ("The Areopagitica of Milton after 300 years"
in "Freedom of Expression" (P.E.N. Club 1945).

....

Propaganda tricks.

I. "I do not claim that everything (in the USSR etc.) is perfect, but —"
   Technique. The intention to eulogise is disclaimed in advance, but in no specific instance is it ever admitted that anything is wrong. Thus the writer in effect does what he has declared he will not do—ie. claims that everything is perfect.

II. The balancing technique. When it is intended to eulogise A & denigrate B, anything detrimental which has to be admitted about A is balanced by a dragged-in reference to some scandal about B, while on the other hand unfavourable references to B are not so balanced. Especially common in pacifist literature, in which unavoidable references to Belsen, Buchenwald etc, are always carefully balanced by a mention of the Isle of Man, etc., whereas hostile references to Britain/USA are left unbalanced.

   ....

III. "I should be the last to deny that there are faults on both sides"
   Technique. Where the aim is to whitewash A. & discredit B.,[17] admissions are made about both, but the admission made about A. is a damaging one, while the one made about B. is trivial & may even redound to B.'s credit.
   Example: the writer will start by saying that the conduct of all of the Big Three leaves much to be desired, & proceed to accuse Britain of imperialist greed, the USA of being dominated by Big Business, & the USSR of "suspicion."
   He will then probably add that Russian suspicions are justified. But in any case, after a preliminary declaration of impartiality, one of the three is accused of a pecadillo, the other two of serious misdeeds.

IV. "Playing into the hands of."
   Technique. If A is opposed to B, & B. is held in general opprobrium, then all who oppose A. are declared to be on the side of B. This is applied only to the actions of one's opponents, never to one's own actions.
   ....

V.   Verbal colorations. (Innumerable—write down instances as they occur.)

VI.   The unwilling witness.
(Cf. the Daily Worker's statement that the New Statesman is an "anti-Soviet organ." In practice the N.S.'s reference° to the USSR are almost always favourable, hence the N.S. can be quoted as an unwilling & therefore trustworthy witness.)

VII.   Tu quoque, or two blacks make a white.

VIII. Swear words. (Fascist, antisemitic, reactionary, imperialist, etc.)

IX.   Transition from the moral to the practical phase, & back again.

1. The diagonal crosses are Orwell's.
2. Marked to be placed in left-hand column.
3. This group of four lines is ringed and marked for insertion in the list of clichés.
4. Ringed and marked for inclusion in the list of clichés.
5. The two upright crosses are placed indefinitely above and below 'Development.'
6. Ringed, probably with 'Development,' and marked for inclusion in the list of clichés.
7. Ringed for inclusion in the list of clichés.
8. Ringed for inclusion in the list of operators.
9. Crossed through.
10. Ringed and marked to follow 'All hell was let loose.'
11. Seemingly so written (twice) but 'Egregious' may be intended. Orwell makes particular reference to this word in his article.
12. 'of a certain nature' crossed through.
13. 'glamour' marked to precede 'fraternise.'
14. 'association' crossed through.
15. Crossed through.
16. Crossed through (possibly a false start for 'Inveterate').
17. Orwell should, presumably, have written 'Where the aim is to whitewash B. & discredit A.'

2817. Review of *The Firing Squad* by F. C. Weiskopf; *The Siren's Wake* by Lord Dunsany

Manchester Evening News, 13 December 1945

"The Firing Squad" is advertised as "something entirely new in war fiction," which is, perhaps, an overstatement, but it is certainly an unusual book. It is about war, but not about fighting, and its interest is mainly psychological. It is a tale of occupied territory—most of the action takes place in Prague—told from the point of view of a German.

The least credible thing about the story, which claims to be based on authentic material, is the manner in which it came to be told.

The narrator, a young German soldier who is wounded and a prisoner in Russian hands, is supposedly describing his experiences to a hospital nurse, who is taking them down in writing.

He had previously kept a diary, which he has now lost, and he is trying in this way to replace it. It seems rather strange that any hospital should be able to afford nurses for such a job in wartime, and the expressions of penitence with which the narrative starts off are not very convincing—

"How could you possibly realise what it means to a soldier in the German Wehrmacht to have a friend with him, a friend to whom he can speak openly, at least as far as hints and inflections can be open? That's what they've made of us, thanks to their spying, intimidation, and brutality. They got us to the point where we didn't dare commune with our own thoughts except in a whisper. . . ."

It is difficult to imagine anyone talking like this, and it is also difficult to believe that anyone who had been so elaborately spied upon would have risked keeping a diary in which he wrote down his secret thoughts. But the note of exaggerated self-disgust fades out a little later, and for the most part the story is straightforwardly told, with only an occasional generalisation or a paragraph or two in which the reader is reminded of the political and military situation.

In essence it is a story of disintegration. The young man who tells it, Hans Holler, is a Sudeten German. He has been wounded, or rather injured in Yugo-Slavia, and in the winter of 1941 he is posted to a unit in the occupation troops in Czecho-Slovakia.

The other members of his squad are a mixed lot, but most of them are potentially decent enough. They are more interested in having a good time than in oppressing the Czechs, and at the beginning they are frankly disgusted by such jobs as executing saboteurs.

But, somehow, as the war drags on those of them who are not killed—for one man after another is sent away to die in the interminable Russian campaign—go to pieces morally.

One commits suicide, another becomes a spy of the Gestapo, others are shot for real or imaginary offences. All of them become more and more brutalised by looting and "reprisals," and even family life in untouched parts of Germany seems to be disintegrating under the strain of war.

Hans is forced into marriage with a girl who is about to bear a child which he well knows is not his own, and he has no sooner married her than he finds himself involved in a sordid love affair with her sister. This girl, a mere child and already suffering from a venereal disease, has been corrupted by a period at a Hitler Youth camp.

Hans has more and more the feeling of living in a nightmare. The final touch comes when he sees the face of a Czech girl whom he had loved before the war, and has lost touch with for years, looking out at him from a poster with the caption, "Wanted—dead or alive."

Three things gradually break down the spirit of the soldiers. One is the quiet, contemptuous hatred of the Czech population, on which neither brutality nor spasmodic attempts to fraternise make any impression. Another is the endlessness of the war and the mounting tide of deaths, in every family.

Another, operating only occasionally but with dramatic effect, is the discovery that the German news bulletins are untruthful. The implication— and no doubt it is true enough—is that it needed military defeat to arouse a sense of guilt in the German people.

The book ends with some fearful but probably authentic descriptions of atrocities in Russia.

At moments, especially at the beginning and towards the end, this book lapses into the cruder kind of propaganda, and becomes psychologically false, but it is above the average level of contemporary war stories.

Lord Dunsany's book might almost stand as a demonstration of how not to use good material. It is a book of reminscences, covering the period between 1930 and 1942, but so carelessly thrown together as to be almost unreadable.

A good deal happened to Lord Dunsany during those years, especially the last three of them, but he is not content to concentrate on his major experiences. Instead, every page is cluttered up with trivial details and with reprintings of the topical poems which he seems to have produced to meet every possible occasion. One instance of his facility in that line is worth mentioning.

When Yugo-Slavia made its one-day pact with Hitler Lord Dunsany, then in Greece, wrote a denunciatory poem, which was declaimed over the Greek wireless. The next day, after the King's coup d'etat, he wrote another, praising the heroism of the Yugo-Slavs, which was also broadcast.

About the end of 1940 Lord Dunsany was sent on a mission to Greece. He had to get there by sailing to Capetown and then flying to Egypt, passing on his way over the upper reaches of the Nile, where herds of hippopotami have their baths with crocodiles watching from the bank.

He was not long in Greece before the Germans drove him out again, and he re-crossed the Mediterranean in a bombed and crowded ship, where the passengers were warned in advance that there were only enough lifeboats for the women.

On his way home he visited various other parts of Africa and even made a trip to the battlefield of Modder River, where he had fought in the Boer War. All in all it is an eventful story, and it is a pity that it has not been worked up into a better book.

[Fee: £8.8.0; 12.12.45][1]

1. This is, as usual, given as being 800 words long in Orwell's Payments Book, but it is over fifty percent longer. The *Manchester Evening News* allowed for the greater length by using particularly small type (newsprint then being severely rationed).

2818. 'The Sporting Spirit'

Tribune, 14 December 1945

Now that the brief visit of the Dynamo football team[1] has come to an end, it is possible to say publicly what many thinking people were saying privately before the Dynamos ever arrived. That is, that sport is an unfailing cause of ill-will, and that if such a visit as this had any effect at all on Anglo-Soviet relations, it could only be to make them slightly worse than before.

Even the newspapers have been unable to conceal the fact that at least two of the four matches played led to much bad feeling. At the Arsenal match, I am told by someone who was there, a British and a Russian player came to blows and the crowd booed the referee. The Glasgow match, someone else informs me, was simply a free-for-all from the start.[2] And then there was the controversy, typical of our nationalistic age, about the composition of the Arsenal team. Was it really an all-England team, as claimed by the Russians, or merely a league team, as claimed by the British? And did the Dynamos end their tour abruptly in order to avoid playing an all-England team? As usual, everyone answers these questions according to his political predilections. Not quite everyone, however. I noted with interest, as an instance of the vicious passions that football provokes, that the sporting correspondent of the Russophile *News Chronicle* took the anti-Russian line and maintained that Arsenal was *not* an all-England team. No doubt the controversy will continue to echo for years in the footnotes of history books. Meanwhile the result of the Dynamos' tour, in so far as it has had any result, will have been to create fresh animosity on both sides.

And how could it be otherwise? I am always amazed when I hear people saying that sport creates goodwill between the nations, and that if only the common peoples of the world could meet one another at football or cricket, they would have no inclination to meet on the battlefield. Even if one didn't know from concrete examples (the 1936 Olympic Games, for instance) that international sporting contests lead to orgies of hatred, one could deduce it from general principles.

Nearly all the sports practised nowadays are competitive. You play to win, and the game has little meaning unless you do your utmost to win. On the village green, where you pick up sides and no feeling of local patriotism is involved, it is possible to play simply for the fun and the exercise: but as soon as the question of prestige arises, as soon as you feel that you and some larger unit will be disgraced if you lose, the most savage combative instincts are aroused. Anyone who has played even in a school football match knows this. At the international level sport is frankly mimic warfare. But the significant thing is not the behaviour of the players but the attitude of the spectators: and, behind the spectators, of the nations who work themselves into furies over these absurd contests, and seriously believe—at any rate for short periods—that running, jumping and kicking a ball are tests of national virtue.

Even a leisurely game like cricket, demanding grace rather than strength, can cause much ill-will, as we saw in the controversy over body-line bowling and over the rough tactics of the Australian team that visited England in 1921. Football, a game in which everyone gets hurt and every nation has its own style of play which seems unfair to foreigners, is far worse. Worst of all is boxing. One of the most horrible sights in the world is a fight between white and coloured boxers before a mixed audience. But a boxing audience is always disgusting, and the behaviour of the women, in particular, is such that the Army, I believe, does not allow them to attend its contests. At any rate, two or three years ago, when Home Guards and regular troops were holding a boxing tournament, I was placed on guard at the door of the hall, with orders to keep the women out.

In England, the obsession with sport is bad enough, but even fiercer passions are aroused in young countries where games-playing and national-ism are both recent developments. In countries like India or Burma, it is necessary at football matches to have strong cordons of police to keep the crowd from invading the field. In Burma, I have seen the supporters of one side break through the police and disable the goalkeeper of the opposing side at a critical moment. The first big football match that was played in Spain, about fifteen years ago, led to an uncontrollable riot. As soon as strong feelings of rivalry are aroused, the notion of playing the game according to the rules always vanishes. People want to see one side on top and the other side humiliated, and they forget that victory gained through cheating or through the intervention of the crowd is meaningless. Even when the spectators don't intervene physically, they try to influence the game by cheering their own side and "rattling" opposing players with boos and insults. Serious sport has nothing to do with fair play. It is bound up with hatred, jealousy, boastfulness, disregard of all rules and sadistic pleasure in witnessing violence: in other words it is war minus the shooting.

Instead of blah-blahing about the clean, healthy rivalry of the football field and the great part played by the Olympic Games in bringing the nations together, it is more useful to inquire how and why this modern cult of sport arose. Most of the games we now play are of ancient origin, but sport does not seem to have been taken very seriously between Roman times and the Nineteenth century. Even in the English public schools the games cult did not start till the later part of the last century. Dr. Arnold, generally regarded as the founder of the modern public school, looked on games as simply a waste of time. Then, chiefly in England and the United States, games were built up into a heavily-financed activity, capable of attracting vast crowds and rousing savage passions, and the infection spread from country to country. It is the most violently combative sports, football and boxing, that have spread the widest. There cannot be much doubt that the whole thing is bound up with the rise of nationalism—that is, with the lunatic modern habit of identifying oneself with large power units and seeing everything in terms of competitive prestige. Also, organised games are more likely to flourish in urban communities where the average human being lives a sedentary or at least a confined life, and does not get much opportunity for creative labour. In a rustic community a boy or young man works off a good deal of his surplus energy by walking, swimming, snowballing, climbing trees, riding horses, and by various sports involving cruelty to animals, such as fishing, cock-fighting and ferreting for rats. In a big town one must indulge in group activities if one wants an outlet for one's physical strength or for one's sadistic impulses. Games are taken seriously in London and New York, and they were taken seriously in Rome and Byzantium: in the Middle Ages they were played, and probably played with much physical brutality, but they were not mixed up with politics nor a cause of group hatreds.

If you wanted to add to the vast fund of ill-will existing in the world at this moment, you could hardly do it better than by a series of football matches between Jews and Arabs, Germans and Czechs, Indians and British, Russians and Poles, and Italians and Jugoslavs, each match to be watched by a mixed audience of 100,000 spectators. I do not, of course, suggest that sport is one of the main causes of international rivalry; big-scale sport is itself, I think, merely another effect of the causes that have produced nationalism. Still, you do make things worse by sending forth a team of eleven men, labelled as national champions, to do battle against some rival team, and allowing it to be felt on all sides that whichever nation is defeated will "lose face".

I hope, therefore, that we shan't follow up the visit of the Dynamos by sending a British team to the U.S.S.R. If we must do so, then let us send a second-rate team which is sure to be beaten and cannot be claimed to represent Britain as a whole. There are quite enough real causes of trouble already, and we need not add to them by encouraging young men to kick each other on the shins amid the roars of infuriated spectators.

[Fee: £3.3.0; 7.12.45]

Orwell's essay prompted considerable correspondence in *Tribune*. In the issue for 28 December, E. S. Fayers wrote:

George Orwell is always interesting. But he does write some bilge. Of course, he can't help that. Like the rest of us, a journalist cannot know everything, and that means he must constantly write about things from the outside. It would take more space than I shall get to deal in general with the picture of "The Sporting Spirit" as delineated by "G.O." I will say only that it is like a jig-saw puzzle pushed at one corner.

It is obvious from the article that George has never played football for the love of it[3]—and nobody, except perhaps a few schoolboys and professionals, ever plays for any other reason. Let me assure George that football does not consist of two young men kicking one another's shins. Nor do the knocks and bruises of a hard game rouse passions of hatred or a vicious desire to atomise some distant fellow-creature. If you have not played and loved football, you are no more competent to talk about it than you are about musical composition if you are ignorant of music and that's all that need be said.

As to the spectators, with the greatest possible diffidence I suggest that George is in danger of falling into the error of intellectual contempt for the "mob." These football crowds, if only he got among them, he would find are not great ignorant mobs of sadistic morons. They are a pretty good mixture of just ordinary men. A little puzzled, a little anxious, steady, sceptical, humorous, knowledgeable, having a little fun, hoping for a bit of excitement, and definitely getting quite a lot of enjoyment out of that glorious king of games—football. I'm sorry for George. He's missed a lot of fun in life.

In *Tribune* for 4 January 1946, J. A. Mills wrote:

From George Orwell's article on the tour of the Russian football team in your issue dated December 14, it appears that not only does he have his statements regarding the games concerned on secondhand information, but also that his experience of sport in general is limited. A few games of football in which he himself took part might help to convince him that Atlantic Charters, U.N.O.'s, and what have you, do not and cannot by themselves create the spirit that is necessary if man is to co-operate with men of other countries and creeds.

International sports, even in their present commercially prostituted form, are a potential source of vast streams of good-will, provided they are not polluted by ill-informed outpourings of politicians and intellectuals. Orwell's informant on the "Dynamo" games might also have told him that the cheers of the vast crowds that gathered to witness them were given impartially to their own teams and to the Russians—often, indeed, to the latter's advantage, while the players engaged in the "miniature warfare" were no less sporting and no rougher than those to be found on the village-green games praised by Mr. Orwell.

Tribune for 18 January 1946 had two letters on the subject:

The letter from E. S. Fayers seems to have dealt rather superficially with Orwell's article on "The Sporting Spirit" (*Tribune*, 14.12.45). Quite a lot of evidence piles up in favour of Orwell's view, as well as support from competent psychologists and sociologists.

Dr. W. A. Brend, in his book *Foundations of Human Conflict* (A Study in Group Psychology) deals at length with the competitiveness in games and sports generally. He refers to the "encouragement of sport in which the competitive element predominates," and in schools "of the keen desire of the teams to triumph over each other," p. 31. "In the larger world, interest in sport has been sedulously fostered. Organisations have been formed to govern the different sports; newspapers devote much of their space to recording the results of matches; football clubs pay large sums to secure the services of the best players, and masses of people identify themselves with one or other of the teams, wear their colours, travel long distances, and are elated or chagrined according to the fortunes of their champion. Real bitterness may be aroused; fights may occur between the rival teams, referees may be attacked and crowds may show their hostility by 'barracking.'

The very use of the word 'beat' in an athletic contest is notable. The original meaning of the words 'to beat' is 'to strike repeatedly,' yet the word is now applied to actions from which in theory all elements of deliberate hurting have been excluded. The exceptional meaning attached to the word 'good' in the phrase 'a good sportsman' is also significant. These words do not connote one who excels at a particular sport—he may indeed be quite the reverse—but one who can be relied upon not to adopt illegitimate methods to win a game, and who will accept defeat without showing resentment, i.e., will keep under control the real hostility he is assumed to possess."

Playing the game to win, and not for its own sake, is the dominating motive in sport today, as any accurate observation will reveal. As Brend continues, "When we see how strongly the group spirit can be canalised into maintaining a competitive activity in a matter of so little intrinsic importance as sport, we shall have no difficulty in realising the part it may be made to play in the hands of skilful men in arousing the emotions of patriotism, national aggression and religious or other antagonisms."

Thos. Wm. Brown

I wish to thank George Orwell for his article on "The Sporting Spirit," the most intelligently written on the subject I have read. Such a reply as that of E. S. Fayers was altogether too obvious and to be expected. The fallacy, that one who has not played and enjoyed football is incompetent to talk about it, should not require exposition. Football as an exercise, or simply a game, is all right for those who enjoy trying to manœuvre a leather enclosed sphere of air between two posts against the efforts of people trying to do the same thing in the opposite direction, but the type of interest and spirit which George Orwell wrote about are indeed to be deplored. For an illustration, I recommend to friend Fayers a visit to Glasgow and a study of the relations existing in general between the respective supporters of Rangers and Celtic.[4]

Re the patronising remark that George has missed a lot of fun in life, this is pointless, as George may say the same of Fayers, in other respects. It is an elementary fact in psychology that behaviour is the result of instincts basically the same but differently developed and modified in every individual. Football provides an outlet for those with well developed or little modified instincts of self-assertiveness and aggressiveness; in other words, for the less civilised!

J. M.

Finally, on 25 January 1946, E. S. Fayers was allowed to reply:

I plead guilty, of course, Mr. Brown. Yet I stated very clearly in my letter that in the space available no answer was possible to the broad contentions of George Orwell's article; with which, indeed, in some superficial respects, I agree. I wished merely to say something in defence of football and football "fans." Despite strong temptation I again refrain from tackling the larger issue. No adequate reply is possible in a short letter.

A word to "J. M." Orwell is well able to take care of himself and it is absurd to regard myself as patronising him. He scourged football players and spectators pretty energetically and his humour will not turn sour at a gentle gibe from the scourgees. I have not the good fortune to be a psychologist. And, sticking to my last, I am very sure I am not competent to pronounce upon the findings of psychologists nor upon the satisfactions enjoyed by them in the pursuit of their interest. But it does sometimes seem that the devotees of the various schools of psychology carry on their disharmonies with almost the exacerbation of football fans. This leads me to the confident hope that in time psychology will add as much to the richness of living as football itself has. In the meantime it seems already to have enabled friend "J. M." to decide what one had thought, until now, to be in some doubt—who is and isn't civilised.

1. The Moscow Dynamos, a Russian soccer team, toured Britain in the autumn of 1945 and played a number of leading British clubs. 'Guest players' were allowed into teams at this time because of wartime conditions, but, even allowing for that, it was claimed that Britain's Arsenal team had been unduly strengthened.
2. The editor was present at Ibrox Park, Glasgow, for this match. There was an enormous crowd, and memory suggests that it was orderly and that the game was not unduly 'robust'—but Orwell was pointing accurately to the way sport, especially international contact sport, would develop.
3. Orwell had, of course, played football (and the Wall Game) with some success and with evident enjoyment, especially at Eton; see *40* for his poem 'Wall Game'—a parody of Kipling's 'If' and *40, n. 1* for a brief account of his prowess. For his own experience of 'international football,' see the first paragraph of 'Shooting an Elephant,' *326*, describing the animosity between Burmese and British players and the attitude of spectators. Orwell played football for the police in Burma so he had personal experience of games between British and local players.
4. Glasgow Rangers and Glasgow Celtic are divided on religious lines, Protestant and Catholic, with rare exceptions, even half a century later. Violence erupts from time to time at these games. J.M. wrote from Scotland.

2819. 'In Defence of English Cooking'

Evening Standard, 15 December 1945

We have heard a good deal of talk in recent years about the desirability of attracting foreign tourists to this country. It is well known that England's two worst faults, from a foreign visitor's point of view, are the gloom of our Sundays and the difficulty of buying a drink.

Both of those are due to fanatical minorities who will need a lot of quelling, including extensive legislation. But there is one point on which public opinion could bring about a rapid change for the better: I mean cooking.

It is commonly said, even by the English themselves, that English cooking is the worst in the world. It is supposed to be not merely incompetent, but also imitative, and I even read quite recently, in a book by a French writer, the remark: "The best English cooking is, of course, simply French cooking."

Now that is simply not true. As anyone who has lived long abroad will know, there is a whole host of delicacies which it is quite impossible to obtain outside the English-speaking countries. No doubt the list could be added to, but here are some of the things that I myself have sought for in foreign countries and failed to find.

First of all, kippers, Yorkshire pudding, Devonshire cream, muffins and crumpets. Then a list of puddings that would be interminable if I gave it in full: I will pick out for special mention Christmas pudding, treacle tart and apple dumplings. Then an almost equally long list of cakes: for instance, dark plum cake (such as you used to get at Buszard's before the war), shortbread and saffron buns. Also innumerable kinds of biscuit, which exist, of course, elsewhere, but are generally admitted to be better and crisper in England.

Then there are the various ways of cooking potatoes that are peculiar to our own country. Where else do you see potatoes roasted under the joint, which is far and away the best way of cooking them? Or the delicious potato cakes that you get in the north of England? And it is far better to cook new potatoes in the English way—that is, boiled with mint then served with a little melted butter or margarine—than to fry them, as is done in most countries.

Then there are the various sauces peculiar to England. For instance, bread sauce, horseradish sauce, mint sauce, and apple sauce, not to mention red currant jelly, which is excellent with mutton as well as with hare, and various kinds of sweet pickle, which we seem to have in greater profusion than most countries.

What else? Outside these islands I have never seen a haggis, except one that came out of a tin, nor Dublin prawns, nor Oxford marmalade, nor several other kinds of jam (marrow jam and bramble jelly, for instance), nor sausages of quite the same kind as ours.

Then there are the English cheeses. There are not many of them, but I fancy that Stilton is the best cheese of its type in the world, with Wensleydale not far behind. English apples are also outstandingly good, particularly the Cox's Orange Pippin.

And finally, I would like to put in a word for English bread. All bread is good, from the enormous Jewish loaves flavoured with caraway seeds to the Russian rye bread which is the colour of black treacle. Still, if there is anything quite as good as the soft part of the crust from an English cottage loaf (how soon shall we be seeing cottage loaves again?), I do not know of it.

No doubt some of the things I have named above *could* be obtained in continental Europe, just as it is *possible* in London to obtain vodka or bird's nest soup. But they are all native to our shores, and over huge areas they are literally unheard of.

South of, say, Brussels, I do not imagine that you would succeed in getting hold of a suet pudding. In French there is not even a word that exactly translates "suet." The French, also, never use mint in cookery, and do not use black currants except as the basis of a drink.

It will be seen that we have no cause to be ashamed of our cookery, so far as originality goes, or so far as the ingredients go. And yet, it must be admitted that there is a serious snag from the foreign visitor's point of view. This is, that you practically don't find good English cooking outside a private house. If you want, say, a good, rich slice of Yorkshire pudding, you are more likely to get it in the poorest English home than in a restaurant, which is where the visitor necessarily eats most of his meals.

It is a fact that restaurants which are distinctively English, and which also sell good food, are very hard to find. Pubs, as a rule, sell no food at all, other than potato crisps and tasteless sandwiches. The expensive restaurants and hotels almost all imitate French cookery and write their menus in French, while if you want a good cheap meal you gravitate naturally towards a Greek, Italian or Chinese restaurant.

We are not likely to succeed in attracting tourists while England is thought of as a country of bad food and unintelligible by-laws. At present one cannot do much about it, but sooner or later rationing will come to an end, and then will be the moment for our cookery to revive. It is not a law of nature that every restaurant in England should be either foreign or bad, and the first step towards an improvement will be a less long-suffering attitude in the British public itself.

[Fee: £20.0.0; 13.12.45]

Reprinted in *SEAC*, 9 March 1946, under the heading 'Bird's Nest Soup? George Orwell Speaks Up For Our English Delicacies.' Compare Orwell's unpublished booklet on 'British Cookery' (see *2954*), which may have been commissioned as a result of the publication of this essay.

2820. Review of *Science and the Creative Arts* by William Bowyer Honey

The Observer, 16 December 1945

During the last few years a number of writers have attempted, in no case very satisfactorily, to bring about a reconciliation between the scientist and the artist. The controversy is obscured by all kinds of jealousies and misunderstandings, and vitiated from the start by the fact that modern men can neither stop worshipping Science nor imagine a genuinely scientific civilisation. Mr. Honey attacks the problem from several angles, but, though he says some useful things incidentally, he appears to contradict himself, and ends up with what is almost a surrender to the scientific attitude which he starts out by attacking.

The first and longest essay in the book is devoted to showing that human nature contains a large irrational streak with which Science is not competent to deal. The very existence of Art, especially the most "useless" arts, poetry and music, proves this. Art serves no discoverable biological purpose, it cannot be satisfactorily related to the struggle for survival, and, above all, works of art cannot be produced synthetically. It is easy enough to explain away the artistic impulse in Freudian or Marxian terms, but this brings us no nearer to understanding the difference between a good work of art and a bad one. The difference is perceived, as it were, instinctively, and the only practical test that can be applied is that of survival. In other words, aesthetic feeling is extra-logical, and the failure of the scientist to explain or control it weakens his claim to be a legislator for mankind. Most people who are capable of being moved by poetry, music, or the plastic arts would agree with this, though it is a pity that this essay should be written largely "at" Dr. C. H. Waddington,[1] who can hardly be accused of scientific arrogance or philistinism.

The second essay is entitled "Science and Ethics," and here Mr. Honey is on much more shaky ground. Ethical values, he says, are as irrational as aesthetic ones, and cannot be explained as the product of the evolutionary process:

Energy may be rewarded, like intelligence and the power of planning, but (the other moral virtues) are positive handicaps in the struggle for existence. Nature puts a premium on treachery and cunning, not on trustworthiness or fair dealing; on aggressive and possessive self-assertion, not unselfishness, compassion, and love for our fellow-men; on predatory competitiveness and a ruthless destruction of our rivals, not tolerance and disinterested service. If Science is to say that it cannot accept any standard of value not discoverable in nature and the process of evolutionary advance, then these must be the values in question.

It is very doubtful whether this is true. Even in the animal world, the gregarious and peaceful creatures are usually the most successful. The sheep will outlive the wolf. Among human beings, almost every quality looked on as "good" is a quality tending to make it possible for men to live together in communities: or else it is a relic of some earlier attitude which was once supposed to have a utilitarian purpose, such as warding off the vengeance of jealous gods. In this section of the book Mr. Honey does not make out a satisfactory case, and he is inclined to overplay the duality of matter and spirit.

The final essay is called "Science and the Arts in a new social order," and the words "new social order" bring with them their usual implication. We are to have a planned, rationalised world with no wastage, no exploitation, no disorder, no poverty, no gross inequalities—in short, the sort of world that we all want and may even get if the atom bombs do not blow us to pieces first. But at the same time "the State is not to be an end in itself," and there is to be the most complete freedom of thought so long as it does not issue in open rebellion.

It is perhaps rather hopeful to expect that intellectual liberty will exist in a highly-organised society: but, what is more to the point, in this context, is that the artistic impulse must suffer, or at least must change, if the machine triumphs as completely as Mr. Honey wants it to do. He is rightly contemptuous of those who idealise the past, but he does not seem to see that, by destroying the creative element in ordinary labour, the machine has altered the status of the artist. In a fully mechanised age, art must either cease to be an individual activity, or it must finally sever its connection with usefulness. Presumably the machine has come to stay, and presumably Art in some form will survive. The question is *how* it will survive, and it is just there, where the real problem begins, that Mr. Honey stops. The outlook implied in this final essay is not easy to reconcile with that of the first one. This is an inconclusive book, and in places none too readable, but it raises some good talking points.

[Fee: £10.0.0; 13.12.45]

1. C. H. Waddington (see *993, n. 1*) gave talks under Orwell's aegis at the BBC. Orwell included one of his broadcasts in *Talking to India*; see *2359*.

2821. W. J. Turner to Orwell

19 December 1945

W. J. Turner, editor of 'Britain in Pictures,' wrote to Orwell from the offices of *The Spectator* to say that he had waited in vain for Orwell on that day for their lunch appointment at Vaiani Desio, 8 Charlotte St., London, W1 (listed as a café, rather than a restaurant, in *Kelly's Directory*). He suggested they make another appointment, after Christmas.

2822. Review of *Cellar*, a play in three acts, by William Russell

Manchester Evening News, 20 December 1945

Just recently rather a large number of plays have been published in book form. For example, Edward Sackville-West's radio play, "The Rescue"; a not very successful little fantasy by Arthur Koestler, entitled "Twilight Bar"; and a more workmanlike piece, "The Banbury Nose," by Peter Ustinov, which has already appeared on the stage. "Huis Clos," a powerful play by Jean-Paul Sartre,[1] one of the small handful of French writers who have made a reputation for themselves during the war years, was also published recently in this country in French, and will probably appear in an English version before long.

It is a curious fact that plays, although primarily written for the stage, are often at least as readable in book form as the average novel. Bernard Shaw used to publish his plays in book form with such elaborate stage directions as practically to turn them into novels. Sir James Barrie, with "The Admirable Crichton," did the same.

It is questionable whether this is necessary or desirable. The stage directions in a Shaw play inevitably contain a great deal that cannot be brought out by the actors, and the effect after reading the book is often the feeling that something has been left out. It is probably better to publish a play in the form in which it would be used by the producer.

William Russell may be remembered as the author of "Robert Cain," a rather unusual novel published about a year ago,[2] and dealing with the colour problem in the Southern States of America. In his present play the colour theme is again important, though not completely dominant. There are only five characters, and all the action occurs in the same place, the cellar of an empty house where five men are hiding from the police. They have just made their escape in a gaol mutiny, and they are waiting for an accomplice who is supposedly coming with a truck to carry them to safety, but who never turns up.

In breaking out of the gaol one of the men has killed a warder, and another, Johnson, a negro, has been seriously wounded. He has a bullet in his side and is suffering tortures of thirst as well as pain. A point is finally reached when it becomes clear that if help is not brought for Johnson he will die.

By this time the characters of the various men have become clear. One of them, Ted, is an ordinary gangster. Another, Archie, a bank clerk, is by nature gentle and thoughtful. Another, Sidney, the one who has been responsible for the death of the warder, is merely a scoundrel and loafer.

There is also a young boy, Leslie, who is capable of developing according to the influences he meets with; and there is the wounded man, Johnson, who is a southern negro, and pathetically conscious that people like himself are not regarded as full human beings.

The central action of the play is a struggle between Ted and Archie. Ted, contemptuous of "niggers," as he calls them, would simply let Johnson die. It would also be impossible for the fugitives to fetch help without betraying their whereabouts.

Sidney, of course, sides with Ted. Leslie at first sides with Archie but is later won over by Ted. The governing fact is that Archie, the only one of the gang who is capable of a decent impulse, is also a coward.

When dawn comes on the morning of the third day Johnson is seen to be lying dead in a corner of the cellar. The four survivors crawl out through the grating to escape as best they can. They have sacrificed Johnson's life without gaining more than a very slender advantage.

The implication—again not definitely stated—is that all of them, even Archie, would have been willing to take a risk for Johnson's sake if he had not happened to be a negro. Archie's last reflection is that though we may escape from physical prisons we all continue to be the prisoners of our temperament and upbringing.

This play has weak spots, but it is decidedly readable and a good deal more mature than "Robert Cain." The Unity Theatre or some similar organisation might well give it a trial.

[Fee: £8.8.0; 19.12.45]

1. Orwell reviewed these three plays in their printed form in *Tribune*, 30 November 1945; see *2808*.
2. This was reviewed by Orwell in the *Manchester Evening News*, 15 June 1944; see *2489*.

2823. Nonsense Poetry: *The Lear Omnibus* edited by R. L. Megroz

Tribune, 21 December 1945

In many languages, it is said, there is no nonsense poetry, and there is not a great deal of it even in English. The bulk of it is in nursery rhymes and scraps of folk poetry, some of which may not have been strictly nonsensical at the start, but have become so because their original application has been forgotten. For example, the rhyme about Margery Daw:

> See-saw, Margery Daw,
> Dobbin shall have a new master
> He shall have but a penny a day
> Because he can't go any faster.

Or the other version that I learned in Oxfordshire as a little boy:

> See-saw, Margery Daw.
> Sold her bed and lay upon straw.
> Wasn't she a silly slut
> To sell her bed and lie upon dirt?

It may be that there was once a real person called Margery Daw, and perhaps there was even a Dobbin who somehow came into the story. When Shakespeare makes Edgar in *King Lear* quote "Pillicock sat on Pillicock hill," and similar fragments, he is uttering nonsense, but no doubt these fragments come from forgotten ballads in which they once had a meaning. The typical scrap of folk poetry which one quotes almost unconsciously is not exactly nonsense but a sort of musical comment on some recurring event, such as "One a penny, two a penny, Hot-Cross buns," or "Polly put the kettle on, we'll all have tea." Some of these seemingly frivolous rhymes actually express a deeply pessimistic view of life, the churchyard wisdom of the peasant. For instance:

> Solomon Grundy,
> Born on Monday,
> Christened on Tuesday,
> Married on Wednesday,
> Took ill on Thursday,
> Worse on Friday,
> Died on Saturday.
> Buried on Sunday,
> And that was the end of Solomon Grundy

which is a gloomy story, but remarkably similar to yours or mine.

Until Surrealism made a deliberate raid on the Unconscious, poetry that aimed at being nonsense, apart from the meaningless refrains of songs, does not seem to have been common. This gives a special position to Edward Lear, whose nonsense rhymes have just been edited by Mr. R. L. Megroz, who was also responsible for the Penguin edition a year or two before the war. Lear was one of the first writers to deal in pure fantasy, with imaginary countries and made-up words, without any satirical purpose. His poems are not all of them equally nonsensical; some of them get their effect by a perversion of logic, but they are all alike in that their underlying feeling is sad and not bitter. They express a kind of amiable lunacy, a natural sympathy with whatever is weak and absurd. Lear could fairly be called the originator of the Limerick, though verses in almost the same metrical form are to be found in earlier writers, and what is sometimes considered a weakness in his Limericks—that is, the fact that the rhyme is the same in the first and last lines—is part of their charm. The very slight change increases the impression of ineffectuality, which might be spoiled if there were some striking surprise. For example:

> There was a young lady of Portugal,
> Whose ideas were excessively nautical;

> She climbed up a tree
> To examine the sea,
> But declared she would never leave Portugal.

It is significant that almost no Limericks since Lear's have been both printable and funny enough to seem worth quoting. But he is really seen at his best in certain longer poems, such as "The Owl and the Pussy-cat" or "The Courtship of the Yonghy-Bonghy-Bo":

> On the Coast of Coromandel,
> Where the early pumpkins blow,
> In the middle of the woods
> Lived the Yonghy-Bonghy-Bo.
> Two old chairs, and half a candle—
> One old jug[1] without a handle—
> These were all his worldly goods:
> In the middle of the woods,
> These were all the worldly goods,
> Of the Yonghy-Bonghy-Bo,
> Of the Yonghy-Bonghy-Bo.

Later there appears a lady with some white Dorking hens, and an inconclusive love affair follows. Mr. Megroz thinks, plausibly enough, that this may refer to some incident in Lear's own life. He never married, and it is easy to guess that there was something seriously wrong in his sex life. A psychiatrist could no doubt find all kinds of significances in his drawings and in the recurrence of certain made-up words such as "runcible." His health was bad, and as he was the youngest of twenty-one children in a poor family, he must have known anxiety and hardship in very early life. It is clear that he was unhappy and by nature solitary, in spite of having good friends.

Aldous Huxley, in praising Lear's fantasies as a sort of assertion of freedom, has pointed out that the "They" of the Limericks represents commonsense, legality and the duller virtues generally. "They" are the realists, the practical men, the sober citizens in bowler hats who are always anxious to stop you doing anything worth doing. For instance:

> There was an Old Man of Whitehaven,
> Who danced a quadrille with a raven:
> But they said, "It's absurd
> To encourage this bird!"
> So they smashed that Old Man of Whitehaven.

To smash somebody just for dancing a quadrille with a raven is exactly the kind of thing that "They" would do. Herbert Read has also praised Lear, and is inclined to prefer his verse to that of Lewis Carroll, as being purer fantasy. For myself, I must say that I find Lear funniest when he is least arbitrary and when a touch of burlesque or perverted logic makes its appearance. When he gives his fancy free play, as in his imaginary names, or in things like "Three Receipts for Domestic Cookery," he can be silly and tiresome. "The Pobble who has no Toes" is haunted by the ghost of logic, and I think it is the element of sense in it that makes it funny. The Pobble, it may be remembered, went fishing in the Bristol Channel—

> And all the sailors and Admirals cried,
> When they saw him nearing the further side—
> "He has gone to fish, for his Aunt Jobiska's
> Runcible Cat with crimson whiskers!"

The thing that is funny here is the burlesque touch, the Admirals. What is arbitrary—the word "runcible," and the cat's crimson whiskers—is merely rather embarrassing. While the Pobble was in the water some unidentified creatures came and ate his toes off, and when he got home his aunt remarked—

> "It's a fact the whole world knows,
> That Pobbles are happier without their toes,"

which once again is funny because it has a meaning, and one might even say a political significance. For the whole theory of authoritarian government is summed up in the statement that Pobbles were happier without their toes. So also with the well-known Limerick:

> There was an Old Person of Basing,
> Whose presence of mind was amazing;
> He purchased a steed,
> Which he rode at full speed,
> And escaped from the people of Basing.

It is not quite arbitrary. The funniness is in the gentle implied criticism of the people of Basing, who once again are "They," the respectable ones, the right-thinking, art-hating majority.

The writer closest to Lear among his contemporaries was Lewis Carroll, who, however, was less essentially fantastic—and, in my opinion funnier. Since then, as Mr. Megroz points out in his Introduction, Lear's influence has been considerable, but it is hard to believe that it has been altogether good. The silly whimsiness of present-day children's books could perhaps be partly traced back to him. At any rate, the idea of deliberately setting out to write nonsense, though it came off in Lear's case, is a doubtful one. Probably the best nonsense poetry is produced gradually and accidentally, by communities rather than by individuals. As a comic draughtsman, on the other hand, Lear's influence must have been beneficial. James Thurber, for instance, must surely owe something to Lear, directly or indirectly. With large numbers of Lear's own illustrations, and an informative Introduction, this book should make a first-rate Christmas present.

[Fee: £3.3.0; 14.12.45]

Reprinted in an abridged form in *The Literary Digest*, Autumn 1948, this review was preceded by this note: 'The lively author of "Animal Farm" makes a

Commonsense assessment of a Master of Nonsense finding that if "the sober citizens in bowler hats" had not invaded the Coromandel Coast they at least had reached Whitehaven.' Orwell gave permission for this reprinting in a letter to the editor, John Gawsworth, 2 June 1947; see *3234*.

1. 'jug' was set as 'pug.'

2824. Olaf Stapledon to Orwell

21 December 1945

Olaf Stapledon's[1] letter praising *Animal Farm* has a postscript which shows how Orwell came to write to G. H. Bantock (see *2825*); it also enables that letter to be approximately dated.

Dear George Orwell,
I have just read *Animal Farm*, and feel I must say how much I enjoyed it. Every page is delightful. The social satire is devastating, and the animal characters stick in the memory. I don't myself believe that Russia is as bad as all that, but there's that side to Russia, and of course a corresponding element here in this country.
Congratulations!

Yours sincerely
Olaf Stapledon
By the way, a friend of mine, G. H. Bantock,[2] is doing a biography of L. H. Myers,[3] You knew Leo fairly well, I think. I forget whether Bantock has been in touch with you already, but I am sure you could help him by telling him how you reacted to Leo. I knew Leo well, and greatly admired him.

1. William Olaf Stapledon (1886–1950) was a writer and lecturer. Among his books were *Latter-Day Psalms* (1914), *A Modern Theory of Ethics: A Study of the Relations of Ethics and Psychology* (1929), *Last and First Men: A Story of the Near and Far Future* (1930; New York, 1931), *New Hope for Britain* (1939), *Beyond the 'isms,'* a Searchlight Book, the series Orwell and Tosco Fyvel jointly initiated and edited (1942), and a pamphlet, *The Seven Pillars of Peace* (1944). His *Old Man in New World*, a P.E.N. Book (1944), was advertised in *Tribune* (for example, 16 June 1944) as 'A brilliant fantasy of the future. A World Federation has been achieved and we witness the great pageant in celebration of the New World Order.' He attended the Cultural and Scientific Conference for World Peace in New York, May 1949; see *3610, n. 2*.
2. See *2825*.
3. L. H. Myers (1881–1944), poet and novelist, had secretly funded Orwell's visit to Marrakech in 1938–39; see *449*. His books include *The Orissers* (1922), *The 'Clio,'* (1925), *Strange Glory* (1936). He began publishing a sequence of quasi-historical novels (he disclaimed their historicity) in 1929; these were collected in one volume, *The Near and the Far* (1940). They were set in sixteenth-century India in order, he explained in his Preface, to 'give prominence to certain chosen aspects of life, and illustrate their significance.' See G. H. Bantock, *L. H. Myers: A Critical Study* (1956). When Arnold Bennett met Myers in 1924, he described him as 'a thin dark man, *silencieux, un peu précieux,* but apparently of a benevolent mind'; the last quality was exemplified by his kindness to Orwell. (*The Journals of Arnold Bennett*, edited by Frank Swinnerton, 1954, 358.)

2825. To G. H. Bantock

Late 1945–early 1946   Typewritten

These extracts are from a letter Orwell wrote to G. H. Bantock (1914–), who was then doing research for his *L. H. Myers: A Critical Study*, published in 1956.

I was staying with him when war broke out. He spoke with the utmost bitterness of the British ruling class and said that he considered that many of them were actually treacherous in their attitude towards Germany. He said, speaking from his knowledge of them, that the rich were in general very class-conscious and well aware that their interests coincided with the interests of the rich in other countries, and that consequently they had no patriotism— "not even *their* kind of patriotism," he added. He made an exception of Winston Churchill. . . .

. . . I didn't see Leo very frequently during the war. I was in London and he was generally in the country. The last time I saw him was at John Morris's flat.[1] We got into the usual argument about Russia and totalitarianism, Morris taking my side. I said something about freedom and Leo, who had got up to get some more whisky, said almost vehemently, "I don't believe in freedom." (NB. I think his exact words were "I don't believe in liberty.") I said, "All progress comes through heretics," and Leo promptly agreed with me. It struck me then, not for the first time, that there was a contradiction in his ideas which he had not resolved. His instincts were those of a Liberal but he felt it his duty to support the USSR and therefore to repudiate Liberalism. I think part of his uncertainty was due to his having inherited a large income. Undoubtedly in a way he was ashamed of this. He lived fairly simply and gave his money away with both hands, but he could not help feeling that he was a person who enjoyed unjustified privileges. I think he felt that because of this he had no right to criticise Russia. Russia was the only country where private ownership had been abolished, and any hostile criticism might be prompted by an unconscious desire to protect his own possessions. This may be a wrong diagnosis, but that is the impression I derived. It was certainly not natural for such a sweet-natured and open-minded man to approve of a regime where freedom of thought was suppressed.[2]

1. John Morris was one of Orwell's colleagues at the BBC. Their relations were rather sour; see *1965, n. 1* and *2373, n. 1*. For an unfavourable account of Orwell by Morris, see his 'Some Are More Equal than Others,' *Penguin New Writing*, No. 40 (1950); as 'That Curiously Crucified Expression,' in *Orwell Remembered*, 171–76, and Crick's comments thereon, 419–20.
2. The last sentence was crossed through and then marked 'stet.' No signature survives at the end of the extracts.

2826. Negotiations for the U.S. Edition of *Animal Farm*

Frank Morley, of Harcourt, Brace and Company, Inc., met Fredric Warburg on 21 December 1945 with Leonard Moore, Orwell's agent. On the following day, Morley wrote to Warburg setting out the terms for the book rights for *Animal*

Farm in the USA: an advance of £100 against a straight 10% royalty on the understanding that Harcourt, Brace's publication would be sold at not more than $2.00. It was assumed by Morley that Warburg would 'wish to control Canada,' though Harcourt, Brace would be glad to have that market. He did ask that if *Animal Farm* were chosen by a recognised book club—'an off-chance'—the club should have the 'right of entry into Canada for their edition.' He asked for copies of *Animal Farm* to secure United States copyright and concluded: 'As you know I have been very much interested in Orwell's work and I want to launch him properly in America. *Animal Farm* seems to provide that opportunity. But my interest extends beyond that. Whether we ring the bell or not with this book, I want to have the chance at future ones. I understand about Scribner & the critical essays°; but I shall hope to prove that we are the right firm for at any rate the bulk of Orwell's future work.'

Warburg acknowledged Morley's letter on 27 December 1945 and said he had put the Harcourt, Brace offer to Christy & Moore. He was sending to New York three copies of *Animal Farm* together with a selection of the best reviews and some promotional material. Warburg's letter of the same day to Leonard Moore is also extant. This conveys the terms and repeats the last paragraph of Morley's letter (quoted here). Moore acknowledged Warburg's letter on 31 December 1945. He thought the proposals for the entry to the Canadian market seemed confused, especially in the matter of copyright. He also pointed out that *Critical Essays* would be published by Reynal & Hitchcock, not Scribner's, and that they would have an option on Orwell's next work.

Animal Farm was published very successfully in the United States, particularly in the Book-of-the-Month Club edition. The Harcourt, Brace edition came out on 26 August 1946. Some copies of the Book-of-the-Month Club edition were made available for members in Canada. The Canadian publisher, Saunders, also distributed some copies of the Secker & Warburg edition, and then printed its own edition of 2,000 copies in November 1946. When it sold out, in September 1947, instead of reprinting its own edition, some 1,500 copies of the Book-of-the-Month Club edition were purchased for sale in Canada. By April 1953 that stock had not been exhausted, according to Willison.

2827. 'Banish This Uniform'

Evening Standard, 22 December 1945

A few weeks ago I received a dinner invitation (it was for some kind of public function) marked with the words "Informal Dress."

At a time like the present, when "informal" would be a very polite term for such clothes as most of us have left, these words might seem superfluous; but what they really meant, of course, was, "You don't have to wear a dinner jacket."

Already, therefore, there are people who need to be told this—even, perhaps, people who would actually welcome the chance of buckling themselves into boiled shirts again. It is easy to foresee that I shall soon get another invitation marked "Evening Dress Optional," and then it will only be a short step before the dreary black-and-white uniform will be just as compulsory at theatres, dances and expensive restaurants as it was seven years ago.

At this moment no one—no man, that is to say—would buy himself a complete evening outfit. Without bootleg clothing coupons, it would be impossible to do so. But not all the pre-war "dress" suits have been devoured by moths or cut down into two-piece suits for ladies, and some of them are beginning to emerge from their obscurity again.

This is the moment, therefore, to decide once and for all whether evening dress for men is to revive, and if so, in what form.

In principle, evening clothes are a civilised institution. To change into special garments before going to a friend's house, or to some kind of recreation, freshens you up and cuts the evening off from the working part of the day.

But evening clothes, as they existed before the war, were only satisfactory from the feminine point of view. A woman chooses an evening dress with the object of beautifying herself, and, if possible, of being different from other women. She can do this with comparative cheapness, so that for many years past female evening dress extended to nearly every social level.

For men, on the other hand, evening clothes have always been a nuisance and even their devotees have valued them chiefly for snobbish reasons.

To begin with, men's evening clothes are fantastically expensive. To buy yourself the complete outfit—tails, dinner jacket, black overcoat, patent-leather shoes and all—would have cost £50 at the least, even at pre-war prices.

And because these clothes were expensive, and were also supposedly uniform, they were hedged round with all kinds of petty conventions, which you could only disregard at the price of being made to feel uncomfortable. To wear a white waistcoat with a dinner jacket or a soft shirt with tails, to have two studs in your shirt-front when other people were wearing only one, even to have too broad or too narrow a stripe of braid down your trouser-leg was enough to make you into an outcast.

Even the correct tying of an evening tie needed years of practice before one could master it. The whole thing was a snobbish ritual which terrified the inexperienced and repelled anyone of democratic outlook.

Secondly, men's evening clothes are far from comfortable. A boiled shirt is a misery, and for dancing one could hardly have a less suitable neckwear than a high, stiff collar which becomes a sodden rag half-way through the evening.

And lastly, these clothes are quite unnecessarily ugly. They are all in black and white, a colour scheme which only suits an ash blond or an exceptionally dark negro. But it must be admitted that the green or purple dinner jackets in which a few bold spirits sometimes made their appearance were not much better. The change of colour could not do away with the ugly lines which are common to most of the clothes worn by modern men.

Our clothes are ugly, and have been so for nearly a hundred years, because they are a mere arrangement of cylinders and do not either follow the lines of the body or make use of the flow of draperies. The least ugly clothes are usually those that are functionally designed, such as a boiler suit or a reasonably well-fitting battledress.

Could we not, then, evolve a style of evening dress which it would be a pleasure to put on, and which at the same time would have no snobbish implications?

It is no use saying "Let everyone wear what he chooses." Men in order to feel comfortable have to feel that they are not strikingly different from other men. Our imaginary evening dress would have to be truly national, like battledress, which is practically the same for all ranks from general to private. Secondly, it would have to be cheap. Thirdly, it would have to be comfortable—that is to say, definitely more comfortable, more suited to relaxation, than the clothes worn in the daytime.

And finally it would have to be decorative, which is not in the least incompatible with cheapness, as one can see in any Eastern country, where the poorest peasant is a pleasanter object to look at, so far as his clothes go, than the most expensively-dressed European.

If we are ever to escape by conscious effort from the ugliness of modern masculine attire, now—when existing stocks are near rock bottom—is surely the time to do it. But if we can't design a new and agreeable form of evening dress at least let us see to it that the old one, with its vulgarity, its expensiveness and its attendant misery of hunting for lost collar studs under the chest of drawers, does not come back.

[Fee: £20.0.0; 20.12.45]

On 28 December 1945, the *Evening Standard* published a letter from Francis G. Bennett, M.A., in which he said: 'Evening dress need not be uncomfortable, and is certainly the reverse of ugly. I don't know who George Orwell is, but, to my mind, he is lacking in knowledge of the things that count. His article will meet with the ridicule it deserves.'

2828. Payment for Second Rights to 'Grandeur et décadence du roman policier anglais'

28 December 1945

Against 28 December 1945 in his Payments Book (see *2831*) Orwell recorded a payment of £3.3.0 for 'Second Rights' from the Ministry of Information for reprinting his essay from *Fontaine*, 'Grandeur et décadence du roman policier anglais;' *2357*. The second appearance of this essay has not been traced despite an exhaustive search through Ministry of Information foreign periodicals. It may have been for a Russian translation. In an annotated handwritten list of his articles, probably prepared about mid-1947 to early 1948 (see *3323*), Orwell noted against this article, 'Russian translation.'

2829. 'Old George's Almanac¹ by Crystal-Gazer Orwell'

Tribune, 28 December 1945

Some weeks ago *Tribune* accepted an advertisement from Lyndoe, the world-famous astrologer. The advertisement was for Lyndoe's book of forecasts for 1946. It struck me at the time that it would be interesting at the end of the year to go through the book and test Lyndoe's predictions against the reality: and, if I should be spared until that date, I intend to do so. But it seems fairer all round to utter my own prophecies for the coming year at the same time. They will not be so comforting nor, probably, so detailed as Lyndoe's, but here they are for what they are worth:—

International Relations. The conference of Foreign Ministers now proceeding in Moscow will be a flop, leading only to high-sounding statements and an all-round increase of ill-will. Thereafter the international situation will continue to deteriorate, though with a few deceptive intervals when things seem to improve. The governing facts will be that no one intends to surrender sovereignty and no one is yet ready for another war, and the general tendency will always be towards "zones of influence" and away from co-operation. After much delay, work will be half-heartedly started on the building of the United Nations Organisation, but no one will believe that the U.N.O. is actually going to amount to anything. As the year goes on there will be more and more tendency for the U.S.A. and the U.S.S.R. to do a deal at the expense of Britain, the general terms of the bargain being American non-interference in Europe and the Middle East in return for Russian non-interference in China and Japan. Nevertheless the armaments race between Russia and America will continue without a check. There will be violent diplomatic battles over such strategic points as the Kiel Canal, Tangier, the Suez Canal and Formosa, but in each case the real control of the disputed area will remain with the power that happens to be nearest. The Dardanelles will pass under Russian control. Trieste will be declared an international port and later (probably not in 1946) annexed by Italy or Yugoslavia.

The Atomic Bomb. The Americans will continue to guard the secret, and the clamour for its revelation will continue. If at any moment it appears that some scientist or body of scientists is about to spill the beans, the cry will then be that the secret must be revealed only to the U.S.S.R. and not to the world at large. Towards the end of the year there will be strong rumours that the Russians have the bomb already. There will then be other rumours to the effect that the real subject of dispute is not the bomb itself but a rocket capable of carrying it several thousand miles. Attempts to apply atomic energy to industry will get nowhere, but the piling-up of bombs will continue. Professor Joad and others will sign manifestoes demanding that the bomb be put under international control, and many pamphlets will be published pointing out that atomic energy, properly used, could be "a boon to mankind." Unsuccessful efforts will be made to persuade the Government to dig shelters 500 feet deep. In all countries the general public will gradually lose interest in the subject.

And here are my forecasts for individual countries, or such of them as I have space for:—

The U.S.A. For some months an all-round orgy of spending, followed by a sudden economic crisis and huge-scale unemployment, complicated by over-rapid demobilisation. Growth of a formidable fascist movement, probably under military leadership, and, parallel with and hostile to this, growth of a Negro fascist movement, affiliated to kindred movements in Asia. All-round increase in anti-British feeling, which will be the one point on which all American factions will be in agreement. Increase— simultaneously and in the same people—in isolationism and in imperialist sentiment.

The U.S.S.R. Continued mobilisation and armaments production on a huge scale, with resulting privation for the people at large. Starvation and homelessness throughout the devastated areas. Serious trouble with military deserters and returned prisoners, large numbers of whom will end by being deported to Siberia. Increase in Pan-Slav feeling, and, simultaneously with this, a reversion to more revolutionary slogans for export purposes. Publication of new decrees guaranteeing freedom of speech and of the press. Continued exclusion of foreign observers, other than stooges.

Britain. No improvement in the conditions of daily life. Growing discontent over continuation of controls, slowness of demobilisation, and shortage of houses. Slight increase in antisemitism, growth of anti-American feeling, gradual waning of pro-Russian feeling. Renewed stew about the birth-rate, leading to proposals—neither of which will be carried out—to subsidise maternity heavily and to encourage immigration from Europe. Chronic coal shortage, numerous unofficial strikes, and savage battles, unintelligible to the ordinary man, over the reconversion of industry. Towards the end of the year the Opposition will begin to gain ground in by-elections, but there will be no come-back by the Conservatives. Instead there will appear a small but fairly active fascist movement, manned largely by ex-officers, and there will be symptoms of a serious split in the Labour Party.

Germany. Stagnation enlivened by banditry. At some time in the year the Allies will decide that Germany is a liability and begin a drive to restore the industrial plant which they have previously dismantled. The Czechs will also re-admit some of the Germans whom they have expelled. A powerful Resistance movement will grow up, led at first by ex-Nazis but drawing into it former anti-Nazis of every colour. By the end of the year the majority of Germans will look back on the Nazi regime with regret. There will be renewed rumours that Hitler is alive.

France. Slow economic recovery, intellectual stagnation. Growth in the power of the Catholics as against the other factions. Increasing estrangement between Socialists and Communists. All-round growth of xenophobia. The one great political issue will be the question of the Western Bloc, but the forces will be so perfectly balanced that no decision will be reached.

India. One deadlock after another. Rioting, civil disobedience, derailment of trains, assassination of prominent Europeans, but no large-scale revolt. Sporadic fighting in Burma which will be attributed to dacoits and bands of uncaptured Japanese. Famine or near-famine conditions in South India, Malaya and parts of the Indonesian Archipelago. Appearance all over Asia of fascist movements proclaiming the racial superiority of the coloured peoples. Within a few months Nehru will announce that the Labour Party is worse than the Conservative Party.

I could go on, but space is running out. Gazing into my crystal, I see trouble in China, Greece, Palestine, Iraq, Egypt, Abyssinia, Argentina and a few dozen other places. I see civil wars, bomb outrages, public executions, famines, epidemics and religious revivals. An exhaustive search for something cheerful reveals that there will be a slight improvement in the regimes of Spain and Portugal and that things will not go too badly in a few countries too small or remote to be worth conquering.

Messages for the New Year are supposed to sound a note of uplift and encouragement, and it may be objected that my forecasts are unduly gloomy. But are they? I fancy it will turn out that I have been over-optimistic rather than the contrary. And to those who just can't face the future without a cheer-up message to aid them, I present this consideration: that even if everything I have predicted comes to pass—yes, and a lot of other horrors that I didn't get round to mentioning—1946 will still be appreciably better than the last six years.

[Fee: £3.3.0; 20.12.45]

1. The essay title is a play on a cheap almanac, known as *Old Moore's*, still on the market. It derives from one first published in 1699 by Francis Moore (1657–1715), who offered weather predictions for the year as a way of publicising the pills he manufactured. It has had many successors related only in name to the original and offering predictions on a wide range of social and political aspects of life. It is, by the more sophisticated at least, taken as a joke (if they have even come across it). Lyndoe was a rather more serious astrologer, whose work was published regularly in popular newspapers.

2830. Dwight Macdonald to Orwell

31 December 1945

Macdonald wrote to congratulate Orwell on *Animal Farm*, which he thought 'absolutely superb,' and to comment on his essay 'Revenge Is Sour' (see 2786). In *Animal Farm*, Macdonald wrote, 'The transposition of the Russian experience into farm equivalents is done with perfect taste and skill, so that what might have been simply a witty burlesque becomes something more—really a tragedy. The pathos of the Russian degeneration comes out more strongly in your fairy tale than in anything I've read in a long time. The ending is not a letdown, as I should have thought it would have had to be, but is instead one more triumph of inventiveness. Congratulations on a beautifully done piece of writing.'

He thought 200 to 300 copies might be sold to readers of *Politics*, 'perhaps more—depends on the price.' He asked Orwell to inquire of Secker & Warburg the terms for the sale of 200 copies. 'I want,' he wrote, 'to do what I can to help distribute the book.'

APPENDIX

2831. Orwell's Payments Book
July 1943 to December 1945

Orwell kept a record of the articles he submitted and of royalties due; when payment was received, he noted this. He also gave the approximate number of words of the articles and books listed. Although this served as a record of what he had written and what payments he was due, the chief purpose of this log was to enable Orwell and his accountants, Harrison, Son, Hill & Co (see *2901*), to complete his tax returns. That this is so is clearly shown by the omission from the total of amounts received in May and June 1945 from *The Observer*, from which tax had been deducted at source (see note following 25.5.45). (The basic rate of tax in 1943 until October 1945 was 50%; it was then reduced to 45%.)

The Payments Book measures 17.2 by 10.7 cm; the pages are feint-ruled, ten squares to the square inch. The book was originally Eileen's, for it contains two pages (see last page here) recording items received in the Censorship Department in Whitehall, where she worked from shortly after the start of the war until about April 1941—dates ironically and coincidentally bounded by Orwell's two brushes with censorship. The first, early in August 1939, was when detectives called at The Stores and took away 'forbidden books' from Obelisk Press, in Paris (Shelden, 345–47; U.S.: 316–17) and the censorship on 21 April 1941 of his second letter to *Partisan Review* (see 787, *n. 1* and Shelden, 365–66; U.S.: 334–35). On the cover Orwell wrote 'ARTICLES' and the right-hand pages were ruled by him in the manner reproduced here. On the facing, verso, pages he added explanatory notes; these have been taken into the text, as indicated by the asterisks and the figure one that he used. The entries are written in variously coloured inks—blue-black, greenish-blue, royal blue—and some in pencil. At the foot of each page Orwell totalled, rather inaccurately, the amounts received and, on all but the first page, the number of words written. Editorial additions, notes, and corrections to Orwell's figures are in square brackets. Six longer notes, follow the transcription of the Payments Book. When giving dates in 1945, Orwell included the year—e.g. 3.1.45; the '45' has been omitted here. Some of his entries are slightly out of chronological order.

The record is not complete. For example, the cheque for the first royalty for *Talking to India* (see *2368*) is not recorded, nor is whatever payment he received from *Commentary* (see *2777*). The Payments Book does not list Orwell's salary as literary editor of *Tribune* (which, presumably, included the writing of his column, 'As I Please'); tax was presumably deducted at source.

Collation of the dates in the Payments Book and dates of publication of articles and reviews for *Tribune*, *The Observer*, and the *Manchester Evening News* indicates that the dates in the Payments Book were those when such items were completed. A check against correspondence indicates that dates against royalties and other payments were those on which payment was received. Internal evidence shows that Orwell later added the amounts paid him for items submitted.

This is the only Payments Book to have survived; Mrs. Sonia Orwell, with the help of Orwell's accountants, failed to trace others in the early sixties. Orwell may not have kept an income-tax record of his freelance writing before July 1943, perhaps because he wrote less frequently for newspapers and journals when earning an income from the BBC which attracted high tax; note his use of 'earlier' in the 1943 date column. He certainly kept such a log in 1946, as his notes 'See book for 1946' and 'See 18.4.46' (written in a different ink, presumably the one he was using in April 1946) demonstrate. Of course, it would have been sensible of him to keep such an account, and the books may well have been passed to his accountants and not been-returned, having served their prime purpose.

Apart from enabling a number of Orwell's articles to be traced (for example, 'Can Socialists be Happy?', written under the name John Freeman, see *2397*) and giving an indication of his free-lance earnings, the Payments Book offers a number of pointers about Orwell. It can be seen that his willingness to contribute a carefully thought-out article was not dictated by the size of his fee. It is noticeable how many important articles were written for very modest fees, among them the London Letters for *Partisan Review*, 'Catastrophic Gradualism,' 'You and the Atom Bomb,' and 'Good Bad Books.' It is clear that Orwell was anxious (notwithstanding his arithmetical errors) to make an accurate return to the Inland Revenue for tax purposes. Some articles were apparently rejected, and at 28.12.45 there is a curious break in the sequence of articles for the *Evening Standard*. It also looks as if Orwell was negotiating with George Weidenfeld to contribute to his new journal, *Contact* (see *2815, n. 1*).

The first four columns of the transcript printed here reproduce Orwell's manuscript with, for readers' convenience, his facing-page notes included in the columns. The fifth and sixth columns are editorial additions. These give the item numbers of each entry and brief details—authors' names, short titles, references—to assist in identification of what is reviewed or written about. When several books are discussed in the same review, the topic is given.

SUMMARY OF WORD COUNTS AND RECEIPTS:

	Orwell's Figures		Corrected Figures	
	Word Counts	*Receipts*	*Word Counts*	*Receipts*
1943	c. 24,750	£154–19–0	c. 24,750	£154–19–0
1944	99,850[1]	586– 4–0	113,150[1]	586–18–8
1945	109,850	961– 8–6	106,750[2]	967– 3–4
	234,450	£1,702–11–6	244,650	1,709– 1–0

Word counts do not include the 59 'As I Please' columns written in this period; these amounted to some 80,000 words. A further 5,400 words were excluded from the totals (see *n. 2* below). The poem (*2409*) is not counted. Including *Animal Farm* (as did Orwell), this brings the number of words written, according to Orwell's calculations, to some 330,000.

Payments do not include the first royalty (of an undisclosed amount) for *Talking to India* (*2368*), nor the fees for which tax was deducted at source totalling £100 before tax was deducted. No fee is recorded for the article published by *Commentary* (2777).

1. Includes 4,000 words for the *Focus* article, 11.9.44, which Orwell included.
2. Excludes 18.10.45 (700 words), item *2777* (3,800), and 28.12.45 (900); if included, these would bring the total to 112,150. The poem (*2409*) and Orwell's interview on Burma (*2540*) have been disregarded in these counts.

ARTICLES etc

Date	To whom	Particulars	Payment [£. s. d]	[Item]	[Notes]
[1943]					
12.7	Spectator	Review (500)	2-12-6	2208	Lehmann: *New Writing & Daylight*
5.7	Horizon	Article (3–4000)	6-6-0	2257	Gandhi in Mayfair
(earlier)	Observer	Second Rights	2-2-0	—	Not identified
..	"Betrayal of the Left"	Royalty	10-6	737, 753	Two chapters of this publication
..	"Donald McGill"	Reprint (Strand)	8-8-0	2211	First pub. Sept. 1941; 850A
5.8	N. Statesman	Review (900)	3-14-0	2236	Red Moon Rising; A Million Died
9.8	Observer	Review (800)	5-5-0	2237	Hulton: *The New Age*
16.8	Tribune	Review (900)	2-2-0	2271	Th. Mann: *Order of the Day*
30.8	Observer	Review (900)	6-6-0	2272	Lévy: *France Is a Democracy*
31.8	Listener	Review (600)	2-2-0	2327	Joad: *Adventures of a Young Soldier*
15.9	Partisan Review	Letter (2000)	2-2-0	—	Not pub.; see *n. 1*
earlier	Partisan Review[1]	Letter	2-10-0	2096	Compltd. 233.5.43; pubd. Jul–Aug. 43
4.10	Observer	Review (900)	6-6-0	2309	Laski: *Reflections on the Revolution*
18.10	Tribune	Review (2250)	5-5-0	2328	Cassius: *Trial of Mussolini*
27.10	Nation (USA)	Review (1000)	4-0-0	2365	Brailsford: *Subject India*
5.11	Observer	Review (800)	5-5-0	2347	*Lest We Regret; I Sit and I Think . . . .*
10.11	Observer	Review (600)	5-5-0	2380	Peers, Dundas: Spain
earlier	Observer	Second Rights	1-1-0	—	Not identified
17.11	Fontaine	Article (2000) (H)	– –	2357	Detective Story; H = Held over?
22.11	Tribune	Article (1500)	2-2-0	2379	Mark Twain
27.11	M. Evening News	Review (600)	– –	2389	Koestler: *Arrival & Departure*
6.12	Penguin Books	Royalty[2]	45-0-0	—	? *Burmese Days:* see *n. 2.*
8.12	M. Evening News	Review (300)	8-8-0	2389	Jordan: *Tunis Diary* (with 27.11)
11.12	Warburg	Reader's fee	2-2-0	—	Not identified
13.12	Observer	Review (900)	7-7-0	2394	W. H. Davies: *Collected Poems*
Carried Forward		[20,450–21,450]	£133-19-0		

Date	To whom	Particulars	Payment	[Item]	[Notes]
	Carried Forward	[20,450–21,450]	£133–19–0		
			£. s. d.		
20.12	Tribune	Special art. (2000)	5–5–0	2397	(Freeman) Can Socialists be Happy?
20.12	M. Evening News	Review (900)	8–8–0	2395	Hogben: Interglossa
27.12	Observer	Review (900)	7–7–0	2399	Chorley: Art of Revolution
	Total earnings to end of 1943		£154–19–0 [+ royalty for Talking to India, see 2368, n. 1]		
		[24,250–25,250]			
1944					
4.1	M. Evening News	Review (900)	8–8–0	2400	Wavell: Allenby in Egypt
..	..	Review (900)	8–8–0	2419	Elisabet Ney; see 2419, n. 2
6.1	"Poetry" Reprint [in Little Reviews Anthology]		1–1–0	1526	T. S. Eliot: [Three] Quartets
14.1	"Observer"	Review (750)	7–7–0	2406	Democracy and the Individual; Disraeli
15.1	"Partisan Review"	London Letter (2500)	3–10–0	2405	Pub. Spring 1944
17.1	"Tribune"	Poem (36 lines)	10–6	2409	Memories of the Blitz
19.1	"M. Evening News"	Review (1000)	8–8–0	2407	Burnham: The Machiavellians
26.1	Observer	Review (650)	7–7–0	2413	Trachtenberg, Fleg: on the Jews
1.2	Gollancz	Royalty	18–6	—	Not identified
2.2	M. Evening News	Review (900)	8–8–0	2415	T. Sawyer/H. Finn; Off the Record
9.2	Observer	Review (800)	7–7–0	2418	Martin Chuzzlewit
21.2	Observer	Review (800)	7–7–0	2425	Noyes: Edge of the Abyss
28.2	M. E. News	Review (900)	8–8–0	2428	Levin: James Joyce
9.3	Observer	Review (800)	5–5–0	2433	Wavell: Other Men's Flowers
13.3	M. E. News	Review (900) R [R = Rejected]	– –	2434	Laski: Faith, Reason, Civilisation
	Carried forward	11,200 + poem [11,800 [+ poem]	£82–15–0 [£82–13–0]		

Date	To whom	Particulars	Payment [£. s. d]	[Item]	[Notes]
	Carried forward	11,200 [+ poem] [11,800 + poem]	£82-15-0 [£82-13-0]		
20.3	Observer	Review (500)	5-5-0	2444	Leon: Tolstoy
22.3	M. Evening News	Review (900)	8-8-0	2439	Thomas: Way of a Countryman
22.3	J. Cape S. & W.	Book (30,000)	- - -	—	Animal Farm; see 2436
	Advance royalty not to be paid until end of 1944 (see bottom of next page)[3]				
3.4	Observer	Review (650)	7-7-0	2451	Hayek, Zilliacus
5.4	M. Evening News	Review (900)	8-8-0	2449	Collis; M. Mead: Coming of Age . . . .
15.4	"Nation" (N.Y.)	Review (700)	2-10-0	2468	Fischer: Empire
17.4	Observer	Review (800)	7-7-0	2458	Kingsmill: Poisoned Crown
17.4	Partisan Review	London Letter (2500)	2-10-0	2454	Pub. Summer 1944
19.4	M. E. News	Review (900)	8-8-0	2455	Blunden: Cricket Country
22.4	Gollancz & Warburg	Royalties	0-19-8	—	Not identified
28.4	Persuasion	Article (2250)	15-15-0	2523	Propaganda and Demotic Speech
2.5	Observer	Review (800)	7-7-0	2464	Brumwell; Huxley: re Changing World
3.5	M. E. News	Review (800)	8-8-0	2463	Hessenstein: De Gaulle
3.5	Warburg	Reading MS.	2-2-0	—	Not identified
16.5	Observer	Review (800)	7-7-0	2474	H. G. Wells: '42 to '44
17.5	M. Evening News	Review (800)	8-8-0	2470	Ervine: Parnell
22.5	Britain in Pictures★	Book (15,000)	- - -	2475	The English People; see 14.7.45

★Payment to be made later.

30.5	Observer	Article (800)	7–7–0	2484	Survey of 'Civvy Street'
30.5	M. Evening News	Review (800)	8–8–0	2482	Are Books Too Dear?
1.6	"Saturday Book"	Article (3000)	25–0–0	2481	Benefit of Clergy (*Cr. E.*, 1946)
7.6	Observer	Review (800)	7–7–0	2487	Seagrave; Alexander: Burma, India
13.6	M. Evening News	Review (800)	8–8–0	2489	Russell: *Robert Cain*
19.6	B.B.C. (European) [Latin American Dept]	Script (1400)	10–10–0	Lost	Political Theories and European Literature; see 2491, 2497
22.6	Observer	Review (800)	7–7–0	2495	Schucking: *Sociology of Lit. Taste*
28.6	M. Evening News	(Review)° (800)	8–8–0	2498	Martindale: *One Generation to Another*
7.7	Observer	Review (800)	7–7–0	2502	Gill: *In a Strange Land*
12.7	M. Evening News	Review (800)	8–8–0	2504	Johnson: *Art and Scientific Thought*
15.7	Observer	Article (650)	7–7–0	2510	Spanish Memories
Carried Forward		67,250 [+ poem]	290– 5–0		
		[81,550 + poem][4]	288–19–8		

Date	To whom	Particulars	Payment [£. s. d.]	[Item]	[Notes]
	Carried Forward	67,250 [+ poem] [81,550 + poem]	£290-5-0 [£288-19-8]		
20.7	Observer	Review (800)	7-7-0	2517	Barzun: *Romanticism*
24.7	Partisan Review	London Letter (2000)	2-0-0	2519	Pub. Fall 1944
27.7	M. E. News	Review (800)	8-8-0	2522	Aitken: *English Diaries*
2.8	Observer	Review (800)	10-0-0	2528	Ch'ien: *Dragon Beards . . . .*
9.8	M. E. News	Review (800)	8-8-0	2529	Church: *Porch and Stronghold*
11.8	Observer	Article (600)	8-0-0	2532	Paneth: *Branch Street*
17.8	Observer	Review (800)	10-0-0	2535	Saurat: *Milton*
23.8	M. E. News	Review (800)	8-8-0	2536	James: *South of the Congo*
28.8	Horizon	Article (4500)	13-0-0	2538	Raffles and Miss Blandish (Oct '44)
31.8	Observer	Review (800)	8-8-0	2542	*From Works of Winstanley*
6.9	M. E. News	Review (800)	8-8-0	2546	How Long is a Short Story?
11.9	"Focus"*	Article (4000)	- - -	2548	Arthur Koestler (and *Cr. E.*, 1946)
	[Item crossed through; Orwell noted:] *Payment to be made autumn 1945. See book for 1946				
15.9	Observer	Review (800)	10-0-0	2551	Brogan: *The American Problem*
29.9	Observer	Review (800)	10-0-0	2554	Books & pamphlets on Burma
4.10	M. E. News	Review (800)	8-0-0	2559	Eliot: *Four Quartets*
13.10	Observer	Article (600)	10-0-0	2564	Home Guard Lessons
18.10	M. E. News	Review (800)	8-0-0	2565	Murry: *Adam and Eve*
26.10	Observer	Review (800)	10-0-0	2570	Nichols: *Verdict on India*

Date	Publication	Type	Amount	No.	Description
25.10°	M. E. News	Review (800)	8–0–0	2572	Penguin books in English & French
8.11	M. E. News	Review (800)	8–0–0	2575	Playfair; Windstedt: on Malaya
10.11	Observer	Review (800)	10–0–0	2577	Gardner: *Hopkins*
14.11	M. E. News	Review (800)	8–0–0	2578	A. L. Rowse; Cassius (Michael Foot)
21.11	M. E. News	Review (800)	8–0–0	2580	J. A. Spender; Reg. Moore
24.11	Observer	Review (800)	10–0–0	2582	Grierson and Smith: *English Poetry*
28.11	M. E. News	Review (800)	8–0–0	2584	Controversy with Agate
1.12	Leader	Article (1500)	15–0–0	2585	Funny, But Not Vulgar (pub. 28.7.45)
6.12	M. E. News	Review (800)	8–0–0	2589	*Letters of Max Plowman*
22.12	Observer	Review (800)	10–0–0	2593	d'Ydewalle: *Interlude in Spain*
	[M. E. News	Review – not listed in Payments Book]		2594	See *n.* 5
29.12	Observer	Review (800)	10–0–0	2596	Morgan: *Flower of Evil*
(earlier)	Secker & Warburg	Royalty	45–0–0	—	*Animal Farm*; see 2539

	TOTAL	99,850 [+ poem]	586–4–0
	[inc. "Focus"]	113,150 [+ poem]	[£586–18–8]

Date	To whom	Particulars	Payment [£. s. d.]	[Item]	[Notes]
1945					
3.1	M. E. News	Review (800)	£8–0–0	2597	Heiden: Der Führer
10.1	M. E. News	Review (800)	8–0–0	2601	L. A. G. Strong: Authorship
11.1	Observer	Review (700)	10–0–0	2604	Palinurus (Connolly): Unquiet Grave
17.1	M. E. News	Review (800)	8–0–0	—	Not traced = 2594? See n. 5
24.1	M. E. News	Review (800)	8–0–0	2608	Massingham: The Natural Order
25.1	Observer	Review (800)	10–0–0	2610	Nevinson: Visions and Memories
31.1	M. E. News	Review (800)	8–0–0	2612	Farmer: Shanghai Harvest; Douglas
7.2	M. E. News	Review (800)	8–0–0	2615	Laxness: Independent People
1.2	S. & Warburg	Book (45,000)★	– –	2898	Critical Essays; pub. 14.2.46

★Not to be published till autumn 1945 or spring 1946.

26.2	Cont. Jewish Record	Article (3000)	30–0–0	2626	Anti-Semitism in Britain
20.2	Windmill	Article (5000)	10–0–0	2624	In Defence of P. G. Wodehouse

[The ink in which the two preceding items are written indicates that they were added in May 1945]

15.5	Polemic	Article (6000)	25–0–0	2668	Notes on Nationalism
25.5	Observer	Article (700)	10–3–4★	2671	Obstacles to Joint Rule in Germany

★Note. Income tax has been deducted at source on all these sums. It was decided that for the month of June the salary of £100 a month previously paid to me from Feb–May would be continued, & all contributions during June covered by it. Income tax was deducted at source, leaving a payment of £61 net. These six [asterisked] payments are therefore not included in the total at the bottom of the column.

1.6	Observer	Review Article (700)	10– 3–4★	2676	Maritain: *Christianity & Democracy*
4.6	B.B.C. (Schools)	Talk (2500)	12–12–0	2674	Butler: *Erewhon*
5.6	Partisan Review	London Letter (2000)	2–10–0	2672	Pub. Summer 1945
8.6	Observer	Article (700)	10– 3–4★	2675	Fate of Displaced Persons
6.6	M. E. News	Review (800)	8– 8–0	2673	Crozier, Baker: two historical novels
11.6	B.B.C. (Schools)	Talk (2500)	12–12–0	2679	Butler: *Way of All Flesh*
13.6	M. E. News	Review (800)	8– 8–0	2678	Sava, Grossman
20.6	M. E. News	Review (800)	8– 8–0	2681	Reddin; Baum: *Weeping Wood*
22.6	Observer	Review (700)	10– 3–4★	2683	Conrad
23.6	Observer	~~Article (800)~~	10– 3–4★	2684	Morrison & Bracken Face Stiff Fights
27.6	M. E. News	Review (800)	8– 8–0	2687	Conrad; *Poems . . . 1900–1942*
30.6	Observer	Article (700)	10– 3–4★	2692	Liberal Intervention Aids Labour
4.7	M. E. News	Article (800)	8– 8–0	2697	Authors Deserve a New Deal

Carried forward 35,600[1] £203–10–0

£195– 2–0

1 Does not include book of reprints mentioned [£202–14–0 is correct total; totals do not include on 1.2.45 [because written before 1945; asterisked amounts: see note after 25.5.45] Orwell omitted note reference after 35,600]

Carried forward 35,600 £203–10–0

~~£195– 2–0~~

[£202–14–0]

Date	To whom	Particulars	Payment £. s. d.	[Item]	[Notes]
6.7	Observer	Review (700)	10–0–0	2699	Balzac: Les Contes Drolatiques
9.7	Leader	Article (1250)	15–0–0	2705	Scientifiction
11.7	M. E. News	Review (800)	8–8–0	2701	Maillaud; Keenan; Th. Mann
14.7	Britain in P.	Advance*	20–0–0	2475	The English People (pub. 1947)
	*See 22.5.44.				
18.7	M. E. News	Review (800)	8–8–0	2704	Aguirre; Anthology of Exile
19.7	Observer	Review (800)	10–0–0	2706	Kahler: Man the Measure
24.7	Junior Digest	Article (2500)	13–2–6	2708	World Affairs 1945; see 2708, n. 1
25.7	M. E. News	Review (800)	8–8–0	—	Not published: see 2709
1.8	M. E. News	Review (800)	8–8–0	2713	Samuel: Memoirs; Isherwood; V. Woolf
2.8	Observer	Review (800)	10–0–0	2714	Sackville–West: The Rescue
8.8	M. E. News	Review (800)	8–8–0	2717	New Light on India
11.8	Partisan Review	London Letter (2500)	2–10–0	2719	Pub. Fall 1945
15.8	M. E. News	Review (800)	8–8–0	2720	C. S. Lewis; Nerina Shute
16.8	Observer	Review (700)	10–0–0	2726	James: Sewell of . . . Radley
17.8	B B C	Talk (2500)	15–15–0	2761	Jack London (8.10.45); see 2722
22.8	M. E. News	Review (800)	8–8–0	2729	Chukovsky: Chekov the Man
22.8	War Commentary*	Review (600)	– – –	2746	McCartney: French Cooks' Syndicate
	*Unpaid [War Commentary = Freedom—through Anarchism]				
29.8	M. E. News	Review (800)	8–8–0	2734	Anderson: Hammer or Anvil; Braunthal
30.8	Observer	Review (700)	10–0–0	2739	Pope-Hennessy: Charles Dickens

1.9	S. & Warburg	Royalty (see 22.3.44)	87–16–4	2721	Pub. 17.8.45
3.9	Tribune	Review (300)	1–1–0	2744	Sagittarius: *Quiver's Choice*
5.9	M. E. News	Review (800)	8–8–0	2742	Mass Obs.: *Britain and her Birth-Rate*
7.9	Observer	Article (800)	10–0–0	2765	Profile: Aneurin Bevan
9.9	M. E. News	Review (800)	8–8–0	2755	Merryman: *The Midnight Court*
29.9	L. P. Moore	Royalties	5–17–9	2756	French trans., *Burmese Days*
3.10	M. E. News	Review (800)	8–8–0	2757	Porteous; Kiacheli: *Bigva*
4.10	Observer	Review (700)	10–0–0	2760	Dostoevsky
5.10	Tribune	Article (1200)	5–0–0	2764	Ould, ed.: *Freedom of Expression*
	Carried Forward	61,550 [60,450]	530–0–7 [£531–4–7]		

Date	To whom	Particulars	Payment [£. s. d]	[Item]	[Notes]
	Carried forward	61,550 [60,450]	£530—0—7 [£531—4—7]		
6.10	Allen & Unwin ★On "Talking to India"	Royalties★	£16—0—0	2368	Pub. 18.11.43
10.10	M. E. News	Review (800)	8—8—0	2763	Vulliamy; Taylor; Inez Holden
11.10	Tribune	Article (1200)	3—3—0	2770	You and the Atom Bomb
17.10	M. E. News	Review (800)	8—8—0	2768	Rhys Davies: Selected Stories
18.10	Observer	Review (700) [entry crossed through]			
	[This might have been intended for the review (not entered) of O'Casey's Drums under the Windows, 2774]				
21.10	Common Wealth	Article (1400)	2—12—6	2778	Catastrophic Gradualism
24.10	M. E. News	Review (800)	8—8—0	2773	Mellanby: Human Guinea Pigs
18.10	Tribune	Article (1200)	3—3—0	2771	What is Science?
26.10	Tribune	Article (1200)	3—3—0	2780	Good Bad Books
31.10	M. E. News	Review (800)	8—8—0	2779	Clewes; Mazzini; Jones & Hulten
	[Article on General Election, Commentary (USA), November 1945, 3800 words, 2777, not logged]				
2.11	Tribune	Article (1200)	3—3—0	2786	Revenge Is Sour
5.11	Paul Elek	Introduction (2500)	21—0—0	2781	Jack London: Love of Life
7.11	M. E. News	Review (800)	8—8—0	2784	H. G. Wells: Mind at End of Its Tether
7.11	ditto	Article (1600)	12—12—0	3049A (see XX, App. 15)	The True Pattern of H. G. Wells

Date	Publication	Type	£-s-d	No.	Description
8.11	Observer	Review (700)	10-0-0	2790	Ch'ien: *Harp with Thousand Strings*
9.11	Tribune	Article (1200)	3-3-0	2796	Lawrence: *The Prussian Officer*
12.11	Polemic	Article (5000)	26-5-0	2792	The Prevention of Literature
13.11	S. & Warburg	Reader's report	- - -	—	Not identified (unpaid?)
14.11	M. E. News	Review (800)	8-8-0	2794	A. C. Doyle: *The True Conan Doyle*
15.11	Tribune	A Review [entry crossed through; 'A' began 'Article;' error for next entry?]			
15.11	Observer	Review Article (700)	10-0-0	2798	R. L. Stevenson: *Novels and Stories*
16.11	Tribune	Article (1200)	3-3-0	2801	Through a Glass, Rosily
21.11	M. E. News	Review (800)	8-8-0	2800	Hargest; Wrench; A. L. Lloyd
23.11	Tribune	Article (1200)	3-3-0	2808	Sartre; Ustinov; Koestler
28.11	M. E. News	Review Article (800)	8-8-0	2805	Collins: *London Belongs to Me*
29.11	Observer	Review (700)	10-0-0	2811	Connolly: *The Condemned Playground*
30.11	E. Standard	Article (900)	20-0-0	2809	Bare Christmas for the Children
30.11	Poetry Quarterly	Article (1500)	3-3-0	2807	Read: *A Coat of Many Colours*

Carried forward 93,250   745-18-1   [£752- 2-1]

[90,250]

[90,250 excludes 18.10.45 (700) and 2777 (3800)]

Date	To whom	Particulars	Payment [£. s. d.]	[Item]	[Notes]
	Carried forward	93,350 [90,250]	£745-18-1 [£752- 2-1]		
1.12	Royalties*		£77-1-10	2810	*American edition of "Critical Essays" & Portuguese rights of "Animal Farm"
3.12	Tribune	Article (1,200)	3-3-0	2813	Freedom of the Park
5.12	M. E. News	Review (800)	8-0-0°	2812	The Saturday Book
7.12	Tribune	Article (1,200)	3-3-0	2818	The Sporting Spirit
8.12	L. P. Moore	Second Rights*	14-15-5	2736	
	*World Digest abridgement of "Animal Farm."]				
16.12	E. Standard	Article (900)	20-0-0	2814	The Case for the Open Fire
11.12	Contact Horizon	Article (4,000)	- - -	2815	Politics and the English Language [For Contact, see 2815, n. 1]
[on facing verso] Payment will be entered in book for 1946. (See 18.4.46)					
12.12	M. E. News	Review (800)	8-8-0	2817	Weiskopf; Lord Dunsany.
13.12	Observer	Review (700)	10-0-0	2820	Honey: Science & Creative Arts
13.12	E. Standard	Article (900)	20-0-0	2819	In Defence of English Cooking
14.12	Tribune	Article (1,200)	3-3-0	2823	The Lear Omnibus
19.12	M. E. News	Review (800)	8-8-0[6]	2822	Russell: Cellar
20.12	E. Standard	Article (900)	20-0-0	2827	Banish This Uniform
20.12	Tribune	Article (1,200)	3-3-0	2829	Old George's Almanac
25.12	Observer	Review (700)	10-0-0	2843	Goldring: The Nineteen-Twenties
28.12	E. Standard	Article (900)			

[This article should have appeared on 29 December, on which date there is nothing by Orwell. His article published on 5 January 1946 ('Just Junk') was, presumably, entered in the next Payments Book. Perhaps the article submitted on 28 December was rejected. See *endnote* to 2894.]

Date	To whom	Particulars	Payment [£. s. d.]	[Item]	[Notes]
28.12	M.O.I.	Second Rights*	3-3-0	2828	Detective Story (2358)
	*Reprint of *Fontaine* article [probably Russian rights; see 2828]				
31.12	Tribune	Article (1,200)	3-3-0	2841	Freedom and Happiness
		109,850 [106,750]	£961-8-6 [£967-3-4]		

[106,750 excludes 18.10.45 (700), 2777 (3800), and 28.12.45 (900); total including these = 112,150]

[Register of Items Received, Censorship Department, Whitehall]
31 August 1940–6 September 1940

These tables, in Eileen's handwriting, occupy pages 40 verso and 41 recto of the notebook
used by Orwell to record payments received by him from 12 July 1943 to 31 December 1945.

DIPLOMATIC				STAMPS		
Day	Bags	Packets		Day	Censorable	Uncensorable
Saturday 31.8	71	16		Monday 2.9.40	3	62
Monday	341	35		Tuesday	5	65
Tuesday	122	19		Wednesday	4	65
Wednesday	228	28		Thursday	4	44
Thursday	81	24		Friday	3	53
Friday	349	29			19	289
	1192	151				

	FOREIGN		IRISH		TOTAL	
	Bags	Packets	Bags	Packets	Bags	Packets
Saturday	59	3352	28	1090	87	4442
Sunday	18	911	1	7	19	918
Monday	62	3038	45	1483	107	4521
Tuesday	77	3315	33	1274	110	4589
Wednesday	114	6870	42	1449	156	8319
Thursday	93	12294	35	1356	128	13650
Friday	78	4865	32	1284	110	6149
TOTAL	501	34645	216	7943	717	42588

Above 'Saturday' in last table Eileen wrote, and crossed through, 'Friday Aug. 31.'

1. The two *Partisan Review* entries for 15.9 and 'earlier' present an unresolved problem. They might seem to refer to the two London Letters published in 1943 (issues of March–April and July–August), but the date for the submission of copy, 15 September, cannot refer to either of these issues. An article sent on 15 September would normally be published in the November–December issue—the London Letter published in November–December 1942 is dated 29 August 1942—but there is no contribution from Orwell in November–December 1943. The next Letter appears in Spring 1944; entered by Orwell in his Payments Book on 15 January 1944. It looks as if, owing to editorial changes at *Partisan Review*, which included Dwight Macdonald's resignation, Orwell's Letter sent on 15 September was not published; hence Orwell's recording that he was not paid for that Letter. Payment was very small; Arthur Koestler described his being London correspondent of *Partisan Review* as 'a non-paying job bequeathed to me by George Orwell' (*Stranger on the Square*, edited by Harold Harris, 1984, 49).

2. If correctly described as a royalty, this could only apply to the Penguin edition of *Down and Out in Paris and London*, published 18 December 1940. However, it is improbable that a royalty would produce a round-figure sum: if Orwell's agent had taken 10% the sum paid by Penguin Books would have been £50, though there is evidence that Moore sometimes took 12½%. It is more likely that this is an advance against the publication by Penguin Books of *Burmese Days*, May 1944. The date, 6 December 1943, was probably that on which Orwell returned proofs. In 'As I Please,' 2, 10 December 1943, *2391*, Orwell refers to his 'going through the proofs of a reprinted book'; the context makes it clear that this is *Burmese Days*.

3. This annotation was written by Orwell on the facing verso. The 'bottom of the next page' refers to the last entry for 1944, the royalty of £45 from Secker & Warburg.

4. The total, 81,550, includes 30,000 for *Animal Farm* and 15,000 for *The English People*. Orwell's figure of 67,250 (if allowance is made for the 600 difference in the number brought down) ought to be 80,320 if both are included, but 50,320 if *Animal Farm* is omitted, 65,320 if *The English People* is omitted, and 35,320 if both are omitted. Despite the inexplicable nature of Orwell's calculation, it does seem that he intended to include *Animal Farm* and *The English People*.

5. Orwell's Payments Book shows, with great regularity, the completion of reviews and articles for *Tribune*, *The Observer*, and the *Manchester Evening News* a day or two before their appearance in print. There is no appropriate entry for the review which appeared in the *Manchester Evening News* on 28 December 1944 (*2594*). There is, however, an entry against 17 January 1945 for which no review has been traced. It is likely, therefore, that the entry at 17 January refers to the review published on 28 December.

6. When Julian Symons took over Orwell's column in 1946, though he was less well established than Orwell, the fee was increased to £9. (Julian Symons to the editor, 19 January 1993.)

INDEX

Volume XVII

This is an index of names of people, places, and institutions, and of titles of books, periodicals, broadcasts, and articles; it is not (with a very few exceptions) a topical index. However, topics discussed in his column 'As I Please', and the London Letters to *Partisan Review*, are listed alphabetically under these titles in the Cumulative Index in Volume XX. This index lists titles of books and articles in the text, headnotes and afternotes; incidental references to people and places are unindexed. In general, references to England and Britain are not indexed nor are the names of authors and books significant to an author being reviewed but not necessarily to Orwell. Inhabitants of countries are indexed under their countries (e.g., 'Germans' under 'Germany'). Numbered footnotes are indexed more selectively; for example, books listed by an author who is the subject of a footnote are not themselves indexed unless significant to Orwell. Payments entered by Orwell in his Payments Book (given at the end of reviews and articles to which they refer) are not individually indexed because they will all be found in the reproduction of the Payments Book in this volume (see item 2831).

Orwell's book titles are printed in CAPITALS; his poems, essays, articles, broadcasts, etc., are printed in upper and lower case roman within single quotation marks. Book titles by authors other than Orwell are in italic; if Orwell reviewed the book (in this volume), this is noted by 'Rev:' followed by the pagination and a semi-colon; other references follow. Both books and authors are individually listed unless a reference is insignificant. If Orwell does not give an author's name, when known this is added in parentheses after the title. Articles and broadcasts by authors other than Orwell are placed within double quotation marks. Page references are in roman except for those to numbered footnotes, which are in italic. The order of roman and italic is related to the order of references on the page. Editorial notes are printed in roman upper and lower without quotation marks. If an editorial note follows a title it is abbreviated to 'ed. note:' and the pagination follows. First and last page numbers are given of articles and these are placed before general references and followed by a semi-colon; specific pages are given for each book reviewed in a group. The initial page number is given for letters. Punctuation is placed outside quotation marks to help separate information. Salutations in letters to relatives and friends are not usually indexed.

Letters by Orwell, and those written on his behalf, are given under the addressee's name and the first letter is preceded by 'L:', which stands for letters, memoranda, letter-cards, and postcards; telegrams are distinguished by 'T:' to draw attention to their urgency. If secretaries sign letters on Orwell's behalf, they are not indexed. Letters from someone to Orwell follow the name of the sender and are indicated by 'L. to O:'. References to letters are given before other references, which are marked off by a semi-colon. Letters in response to Orwell's are indicated by (L) after the respondent's name and/or the page number; if they are summarised this is shown by 'sy'. Letters to *Tribune, Manchester Evening News*, or *The Observer* arising from Orwell's contributions to these serials are indexed immediately after the item to which they refer; the name of the correspondent (and first page of the letter) follow the indication 'corr:'. These letters are also indexed under the names of the correspondents and indicated by '(corr.)'. References to Orwell, except in correspondence following his contributions to these three serials, are listed under 'Orwell, refs to:'.

Items are listed alphabetically by the word or words up to the first comma or bracket, except that Mc and M' are regarded as Mac and precede words starting with 'M'. St and Sainte are regarded as Saint.

Three cautions. First, some names are known only by a surname and it cannot be certain that surnames with the same initials, refer to the same person. If there is doubt, both names are indexed. Secondly, the use of quotation marks in the index differs from that in the text in order to make Orwell's work listed here readily apparent. Thirdly, a few titles and names have been corrected silently and dates of those who have died in 1997 (after the page-proofs of the text were completed) are noted in the index.   P.D.; S.D.

Index

Bennett, Francis G. (corr) 459 (extract)
Béraud, Henri, 22–3
Berengaria, S. S., 24
Beresford, J. D., *A Candidate for Truth*, 348, 349; 350
Berlin, 51, 140, *147*, 237
Bers, Harold T. (corr) 322
Bertorelli's Restaurant, *431*
Bethnal Green Underground Station, *70*
Bevan, Aneurin, 'Aneurin Bevan, Profile', 310–13; 25, 48, 88, 264, *265, 313*
Beveridge Scheme, 247
Beveridge, Sir William, 162
Bevin, Ernest, 205, *234*, 341
Bibliothèque Nationale, 88
Bidault, Georges, 82
Bierut, President Boleslaw, *33*
Bing, Gladys (corr) 202
Binsted, A. T. E., 348
'Bird's Nest Soup? George Orwell Speaks Up For Our English Delicacies' (= 'In Defence of English Cooking'), 448
Birkett, Mr Justice, 135
Birmingham, George, 348
Biro (pen), 113, 116, *432*
Bishop, Reg, Rev of *The Yogi and the Commissar*, 344–5
Blackburn, Gladys M., 99, 101, 108, 110
Blackburn, Raymond, 95, 98, 99, *102*, 105
Blackshirts (Mosley's), 66, 151
Blaenau Ffestiniog, *409*
Blair, Avril, 108, *109*, 128
Blair, Eileen, L. to Orwell, 95, 107, 112, end note 113;
    L. to Mrs M. P. Cocking, 110; 110(L)(sy);
    L. to Cyril Connolly, 111;
    L. to Lettice Cooper, 104 (signed Emily, see *105*);
    L. to Leonard Moore, 81, 103, 112;
    Eileen's Will, 109–10
    15, 46, 63, *109*, 113, 118, 119, 120, *121*, 123, 124, 128, 138, 139, 227, 264, *273*, 273, 402, 463, 479
Blair, Richard, *39*, 81, 89, 95–102, 104, 108, 109, 110, *111*, 113, 118, 120, 123, 124, 128, 138, 139, 236
Blake, William, *Auguries of Innocence*, 397, *398*; 31, 34, 396–7
"Blessed Damozel, The", 350, 351, *351*
Blum, Léon, 23, 73, *73, 138*, 139, *141*
Blundell, Peter, *Mr Podd of Borneo*, 244; 348
Blunden, Edmund, 75, 208, *208*
BMA (British Medical Association), 312, *313*
Boccaccio, Giovanni, *Decameron*, 214; *213*, 214
Bodleian Library, 99

Boer War, 153, 382, 440
Bokhari, Prof. A. S., 186
Bone, Edith, 180
Book-of-the Month Club, 252, 457
'Books and the People: A New Year Message', 7–11; corr: Mrs O. Grant [9], 11(sy); A. Reid 11, 12 (references); Adelaide R. Poole 11(sy); Stephen Spender 11; John Atkins 11; M. E. Farmer 12
Booth, William, *In Darkest England*, 236
Boothby, Guy, *Dr Nikola*, 348
Boots the Chemists, 10, *12*
Bor-Komorowski, Gen. Tadeusz, *33*
Borsley, L. R. (corr) 322, 323
Boswell, Ronald, L: 199; 45, 110
Bozman, Mildred M. and Richard Church, *Poems of Our Time 1900–1942*, Rev: 197–8
Bracken, Brendan, 191, 193
Brady, Prof. Robert A., *The Spirit and Structure of German Fascism* (1937), 325
Bramah, Ernest, *Max Carrados*, 348
Brandt, R. A., 213
Braunthal, Julius, *In Search of the Millenium*, Rev: 272–3
Brehm, Eugen, 290, *290*
Brend, Dr W. A., *Foundations of Human Conflict: A Study in Group Psychology*, 444
Briffault, Robert Stephen (1876–1948), *Decline and Fall of the British Empire*, 396
Britain and Her Birth-Rate, Rev: 280–2; *282*
Britain: French attitude to, 93–4
Britain in Pictures, 114, 189, *189*, 207, 208, 450
British Council, 189, 309, 310, 371
'British General Election, The', 335–41
British League for European Freedom, 30, 31, 32
British Library, *115*
British Museum, 42, 115, *115*, 362
British Restaurants, 164, *166*
Brockway, Fenner, 357
Brooke, Rupert, "Grantchester", 385; 197
Brothers Karamazov, The, Rev: 296
Brown, Ivor, *Observer Profiles* (ed.), *313*; 96, 98, 100
Brown, Thos. Wm. (corr) 444
Browne, Laidman, 261, *261*
Browning, Robert, 214
Brunius, Jacques, B., L. to Orwell, ed. note: 280(sy); 286
Buchenwald Concentration Camp, 147, 163
Bulgaria, 323
Bulletin of the Freedom Defence Committee, ed. note: 207; *264*, 357, 419

Index

Index

Index

Index

Index